Guri Sohi

ISCA 2002

29TH ANNUAL INTERNATIONAL SYMPOSIUM ON COMPUTER ARCHITECTURE

Proceedings

29th Annual International Symposium on
Computer Architecture

25–29 May 2002

Anchorage, Alaska

Sponsored by

IEEE TCCA

ACM SIGARCH

Los Alamitos, California

Washington   •   Brussels   •   Tokyo

IEEE Computer Society Order Number PR01605
ACM Order Number 415024
ISBN 0-7695-1605-X
ISBN 0-7695-1606-8 (case)
ISBN 0-7695-1607-6 (microfiche)
ISSN 1063-6897

Additional copies may be ordered from:

IEEE Computer Society	IEEE Service Center	IEEE Computer Society
Customer Service Center	445 Hoes Lane	Asia/Pacific Office
10662 Los Vaqueros Circle	P.O. Box 1331	Watanabe Bldg., 1-4-2
P.O. Box 3014	Piscataway, NJ 08855-1331	Minami-Aoyama
Los Alamitos, CA 90720-1314	Tel: + 1 732 981 0060	Minato-ku, Tokyo 107-0062
Tel: + 1 714 821 8380	Fax: + 1 732 981 9667	JAPAN
Fax: + 1 714 821 4641	http://shop.ieee.org/store/	Tel: + 81 3 3408 3118
http://computer.org/	customer-service@ieee.org	Fax: + 81 3 3408 3553
csbooks@computer.org		tokyo.ofc@computer.org

ACM Order Department, P.O. Box 11405, New York, NY 10286-1405
Tel: +1-800-342-6626 (USA and Canada); Tel: +1-212-626-0500 (All other countries); Fax: +1-212-944-1318;
acmhelp@acm.org

Editorial production by Danielle C. Martin

Cover art production by Joe Daigle/Studio Productions

Printed in the United States of America by The Printing House

Table of Contents

29th Annual International Symposium on Computer Architecture (ISCA 2002)

Welcoming Remarks
Yale Patt, General Chair
Dirk Grunwald, Program Chair

Keynote Address
Burton J. Smith, Cray, Inc.

Session 1: Processor Pipelines

Session 2: Processor Scheduling

Keynote Address
Robert P. Colwell, R&E Colwell & Associates, Inc.

Session 3: Safety and Reliability

Session 4: Power Aware Architecture

Session 5: Memory Systems

Message from the General Chair

As General Chair of ISCA 2002, I have two very nice duties, to welcome you to this year's symposium, and to thank some of the people who have had major roles in making it happen.

It is not necessary to extol the importance of ISCA to the computer architecture research community. ISCA has been for some time our flagship symposium, and there is no reason to believe this won't continue to be the case. This year, Dirk Grunwald and his program committee culled 27 papers from an almost record number of submissions to put together the technical program. I hope you find some of these papers thought-provoking, inspiring, and useful to your needs.

We have continued the ISCA tradition, started in 1989 in Eilat by Doug DeGroot, of holding workshops (along with tutorials) the weekend before the symposium. Sanjay Patel, the Workshops/Tutorials Chair, has put together a collection of four workshops and four tutorials on particularly relevant topics. We have changed the registration procedure associated with workshops and tutorials this year to make it easier for attendees to sample all that is offered. I hope you can take advantage of them as well.

I am particularly pleased to welcome you to Anchorage. When we first suggested Alaska as the site for ISCA, some were skeptical. We politely listened to all the reasons why Alaska wouldn't work, and with the support of the many, we pushed forward. The result, I think you will find, is that our flagship symposium is being hosted in a flagship location. We will attempt to give you a taste of the majesty of Alaska during the conference, but we do not really have enough time to do it properly. I hope you are able to stay the weekend and continue where we leave off.

Several people have contributed in important ways to the organization of this conference this year, and it is a pleasure for me to acknowledge them. Dan Connors has handled publicity and Kevin Skadron has handled the proceedings thoroughly and efficiently. I worked with both of them last fall on Micro-34, and it was a particular pleasure for me to be able to count on them again. There is no substitute for working with people who you have worked with before and know that you can trust completely to do the job.

One fortuitous gift was an email from Kenrick Mock of the University of Alaska, Anchorage. I had been agonizing over the lack of a *local* Local Arrangements Chair, and had been unsuccessful in earlier attempts to locate someone at UAA. Kenrick saw a blurb on ISCA in Anchorage, and wrote asking if he could help. After checking him out (first via his Web site, and subsequently at UC Davis where he got his PhD — something he is learning only now as he reads this!), I willingly gave him the job. The result has been wonderful. He is enthusiastic, he is willing to help, he knows Alaska and has provided useful insights into many important non-technical aspects of the conference.

I also want to thank Amir Roth for handling Registration, the Anchorage Convention and Visitors Bureau for their enthusiastic soft-sell of Anchorage, and Jean-Luc Gaudiot and Alan Berenbaum, the chairs of our two co-sponsoring professional societies, IEEE_CS and ACM. Finally, April Blackmore, my assistant for more than a year now, who continues to be a major cause of my increased productivity that so many of you have noticed lately.

Most importantly, I thank you the attendees for showing up. ISCA is certainly about a strong technical program, but it is even more importantly about what each of you brings to the conference. I hope you enjoy the technical discourse you find in the sessions, and also the technical discourse that you find in the non-sessions. Please enjoy the full dimension of ISCA 2002.

Yale N. Patt

The University of Texas at Austin

General Chair, ISCA 2002

Message from the Program Chair

It is my pleasure to introduce this collection of papers selected for the 29th Annual International Symposium on Computer Architecture.

We received a total of 180 submissions for the conference, of which 27 were selected for the final program. The low acceptance rate (15%) reflects the growing number of submissions to ISCA, since the number of accepted papers was not significantly different than in the past. Each paper was reviewed by at least four reviewers, and at least two of those reviews were by program committee members. A total of 300 people helped review papers. All reviewing was double-blind. The review process was slightly different than in the past; authors were allowed to see and respond to reviews prior to the program committee meeting.

The actual program committee meeting was on January 25th, but the committee had already done a great deal of work. The author responses were made available to the program committee and despite the huge volume of additional work, the committee and program chair examined each rebuttal. Furthermore, papers that had any issues concerning reviews raised by authors were specifically discussed at the program committee meeting. Papers that involved program-committee member conflicts were handled using a "hot seat" method where the conflicting member was asked to leave the room. Equally important, authors were given the option to let reviewers see the outcome, other reviews and author responses for their papers. Our goal was to help authors educate reviewers; some reviewers had amazingly detailed reviews while others provided only cursory feedback.

Many people deserve thanks for their help. Foremost, I would like to thank the program-committee members for reviewing papers and finding high-quality external reviews. It was truly a pleasure to work with everyone on the committee, and several of them attended the meeting despite family and personal hardships. Having been on many program committees in the past, I have never seen a harder-working group. Dan Connors deserves special thanks for helping with the first version of the reviewing software. Soraya Ghiasi performed innumerable tasks and assisted during the review process. Shana Lourie helped with program-committee arrangements and made certain that PC members got their discounted ski tickets (a critical task). Most importantly, I would like to thank my family, who put up with my spending time on this meeting during the same week our house was ripped up for a remodel.

Dirk Grunwald

University of Colorado at Boulder

Program Chair, ISCA 2002

Organizing Committee

General Chair

Yale Patt, The University of Texas at Austin

Program Chair

Dirk Grunwald, University of Colorado at Boulder

Tutorial/Workshop Chair

Sanjay Patel, University of Illinois at Urbana-Champaign

Local Arrangements Chair

Kenrick Mock, University of Alaska - Anchorage

Publicity Chair

Dan Connors, University of Colorado at Boulder

Publications Chair

Kevin Skadron, University of Virginia

Registrations Chair

Amir Roth, University of Pennsylvania

Steering Committee

Alan Berenbaum, Lucent Technologies

Jean-Luc Gaudiot, University of California - Irvine

Allan Gottlieb, New York University and NEC Research

John Hennessy, Stanford University

Wen-mei Hwu, University of Illinois at Urbana-Champaign

Per Stenström, Chalmers University of Technology

Mateo Valero, Universitat Politècnica de Catalunya

Uri Weiser, Intel

Program Committee

Sarita Adve, University of Illinois at Urbana-Champaign

Saman Amarasinghe, Massachusetts Institute of Technology

Krste Asanovic, Massachusetts Institute of Technology

Luiz Barroso, Google

Doug Carmean, Intel DPG

Fred Chong, University of California – Davis

Dan Connors, University of Colorado at Boulder

Fredrik Dahlgren, Ericsson

Susan Eggers, University of Washington

Kourosh Gharachorloo, Compaq WRL

Seth Goldstein, Carnegie-Mellon University

Stephen Keckler, The University of Texas at Austin

Earl Killian, Tensilica

Artur Klauser, Intel VSSAD

Scott Mahlke, University of Michigan

Margaret Martonosi, Princeton University

Scott McFarling, Microsoft Research

David Nagle, Carnegie-Mellon University

Andreas Nowatzyk, Carnegie-Mellon University

Ashley Saulsbury, Sun Microsystems

André Seznec, IRISA

Steve Sheafor, Vitesse Semiconductors

Mateo Valero, Universitat Politècnica de Catalunya

David Wood, University of Wisconsin

Reviewers

Sarita Adve

Pritpal Ahuja

Hassan Al-Sukhni

Carlos Alvarez

Saman Amarasinghe

Jennifer Anderson

Boon S Ang

Krste Asanovic

Michel Auguin

David August

Todd Austin

Jean-Loup Baer

Iris Bahar

Aravindh Bakthavathsalu

Vas Bala

Luiz Barroso

Rajeev Barua

Allen Baum

Bradford Beckmann

John Bennett

Eric Borch

Pradip Bose

Ian Bratt

David Brooks

Mats Brorsson

Mary Brown

Randy Bryant

Mihai Budiu

Brad Budlong

Doug Burger

Jim Burr

Martin Burtscher

Jeffrey Butts

George Cai

Brad Calder

Timothy Callahan

Bryan Cantrill

Douglas Carmean

John Carter

Nick Carter

Jacqueline Chame

Chuan-Hua Chang

François Charot

Benjie Chen

Ding-Kai Chen

Trishul Chilimbi

Frederic T. Chong

Yuan Chou

Paul Chow

George Chrysos

Douglas Clark

Nathan Clark

Cristian Coarfa

Dennis Colarelli

Dan Connors

Robert Cooksey

Dean Copsey

Jesus Corbal

Sorin Cotofana

Darren Cronquist

Patrick Crowley

Josep-Llorenç Cruz

Fredrik Dahlgren

Jeff Dean

Nathalie Drach

Michel Dubois

Susan Eggers

Magnus Ekman

Joel Emer

Dan Ernst

Roger Espasa

Ayose Falcón

Babak Falsafi

Paolo Faraboschi

Alexandre Farcy

Keith Farkas

Matthew Farrens

Stephen Felix

Ed Felten

James A. Stuart Fiske

Alessandro Forin

Rob Fowler	CJ Hughes	Eric Larson
Matthew Frank	Huberth Hum	Corinna Lee
Hubertus Franke	Hillery Hunter	Charles Lefurgy
Chris Fraser	Sitaram Iyer	Calvin Lin
Steve Furber	Jonas Jalminger	Mikko Lipasti
Greg Ganger	Dhanendra Jani	Renaud Lottiaux
Lars Ganrot	Stephen Jenks	David Lowell
Kourosh Gharachorloo	Michael Ji	Geoff Lowney
Soraya Ghiasi	Daniel Jiménez	Chi-Keung Luk
Chris Gianos	Lucy John	Lars Lundberg
Seth Goldstein	Russ Joseph	Zhen Luo
Antonio Gonzalez	Norm Jouppi	Stephen Lyon
James Goodman	Stephan Jourdan	Scott Mahlke
David Goodwin	Toni Juan	Bill Mangione-Smith
Steven Gribble	David Kaeli	Srilatha Manne
Flavius Gruian	Magnus Karlsson	Pedro Marcuello
Dirk Grunwald	Stephen Keckler	Milo Martin
Erik Hagersten	Diana Keen	Jose F Martinez
Judith Hall	Rick Kessler	Margaret Martonosi
Erik Hallnor	Earl Killian	Joel McCormack
Per Hammarlund	Jason Kim	Scott McFarling
Lance Hammond	Artur Klauser	Matthew Merten
Seongmoo Heo	Allan Knies	Pierre Michaud
Mark Hill	Peter Kogge	Jason Miller
Sébastien Hily	Pavlos Konas	Miguel Miranda
James C. Hoe	Christos Kozyrakis	Jeffrey Mogul
Per Holmberg	Venkata Krishnan	Christine Morin
Garrett Holthaus	John Kubiatowicz	Andreas Moshovos
Mark Horowitz	Rajesh Kuman	Todd Mowry
Michael Huang	Partha Kundu	Trevor Mudge
Bill Huffman	Steve Kunkel	Shubu Mukherjee

Robert Muth	Kathy Richardson	Aaron Spink
Vijaykrishnan N.	Stephen Richardson	Eric Sprangle
David Nagle	Olivier Rochecouste	Jared Stark
Chris Newburn	Erven Rohou	J. Gregory Steffan
Jim Nilsson	Robert Rose	Per Stenstrom
Andreas Nowatzyk	Eric Rotenberg	Robert Stets
David Ofelt	Patrice Roussel	Volker Strumpen
Hidekazu Oki	Larry Rudolph	Arnaud Tisserand
Daniel Ortega	Pascal Sainrat	Steve Tjiang
Mark Oskin	Karthikeyan Sankaralingam	Josep Torrellas
Viktor Öwall	Barton Sano	Eric Toullec
Vijay Pai	Oliverio J. Santana	Dean Tullsen
Harish Patil	Ashley Saulsbury	Mateo Valero
David Penry	Jim Scott	Stephen Van Doren
Timothy Pink	Elizabeth Seamans	George Varghese
Andrew Pleszkun	Matthew Seidl	Girish Venkataramani
Massimo Poncino	Resit Sendag	Ben Verghese
Milos Prvulovic	Srinivasan Seshan	Stevan Vlaovic
Isabelle Puaut	Alex Settle	Steven Wallace
Ramu Pyreddy	Andre Seznec	Chris Wilkerson
Shaz Qadeer	Steve Sheafor	David Wood
Steven Raasch	Timothy Sherwood	Greg Wright
Ravi Rajwar	Kevin Skadron	Donald Yeung
Alex Ramirez	Jim Smith	Pen Yew
Parthasarathy Ranganathan	Mike Smith	Fancy Younglove
Ravishankar Rao	Avinash Sodani	Craig Zilles
Mosur Ravishankar	Gurindar Sohi	Ben Zorn
Matthew Reilly	Daniel Sorin	
Glenn Reinman	Randy Spaling	

Welcoming Remarks

Session 1: Processor Pipelines

The Optimum Pipeline Depth for a Microprocessor

A. Hartstein and Thomas R. Puzak
IBM - T. J. Watson Research Center
Yorktown Heights, NY 10598
hart@watson.ibm.com
trpuzak@us.ibm.com

Abstract

The impact of pipeline length on the performance of a microprocessor is explored both theoretically and by simulation. An analytical theory is presented that shows two opposing architectural parameters affect the optimal pipeline length: the degree of instruction level parallelism (superscalar) decreases the optimal pipeline length, while the lack of pipeline stalls increases the optimal pipeline length. This theory is tested by analyzing the optimal pipeline length for 35 applications representing three classes of workloads. Trace tapes are collected from SPEC95 and SPEC2000 applications, traditional (legacy) database and on-line transaction processing (OLTP) applications, and modern (e. g. web) applications primarily written in Java and C++. The results show that there is a clear and significant difference in the optimal pipeline length between the SPEC workloads and both the legacy and modern applications. The SPEC applications, written in C, optimize to a shorter pipeline length than the legacy applications, largely written in assembler language, with relatively little overlap in the two distributions. Additionally, the optimal pipeline length distribution for the C++ and Java workloads overlaps with the legacy applications, suggesting similar workload characteristics. These results are explored across a wide range of superscalar processors, both in-order and out-of-order.

1. Introduction

One of the fundamental decisions to be made in the design of a microprocessor is the choice of the structure of the pipeline. In this paper we explore the question as to whether or not there an optimum pipeline depth for a microprocessor that gives the best performance. The problem is treated both analytically and by simulation. We show that there is indeed an optimum pipeline depth and

determine the values of the parameters that yield this optimum performance. We also find that we can understand the results in an intuitive way. The optimum depth is found to depend on the detailed microarchitecture of the processor, details of the underlying technology used to build the processor, and certain characteristics of the workloads run on the processor. Essentially, there is a tradeoff between the greater throughput of a deeper pipeline and the larger penalty for hazards in the deeper pipeline. This tradeoff leads to an optimum design point.

These questions have been addressed previously, but not in the coherent theoretical framework that we employ here. Kunkel and Smith [1] considered the impact of pipeline depth, in the context of gate delay/segment, on the performance of a scalar processor, specifically addressing the effect of latch delays. Recently, Agarwal, et.al. [2] in analyzing microarchitecture scaling strategies, employed simulations, similar to ours, but considered combinations of pipeline and microarchitectural changes, which didn't allow them to elucidate the various dependencies observed. The most coherent previous treatment was given by Emma and Davidson [3]. They provide a theoretical treatment for an in-order scalar processor without the detailed simulations to test their theoretical predictions. Our theoretical treatment includes both out-of-order and superscalar processes, and we provide detailed simulations that confirm our predictions.

A simple intuitive way to see that performance will be optimal for a specific pipeline depth is to consider the changes in the CPI (Cycles / Instruction) and the cycle time of a processor as we change pipeline depth. In a qualitative way we can see that increasing the depth of the pipeline will increase the CPI as illustrated in Fig. 1 for a particular design. This is simply because each instruction must pass through more processor cycles for a deeper pipeline design. Our detailed simulations show that this increase is fairly linear, although this point is not necessary for our argument. At the same time the cycle time of the processor decreases

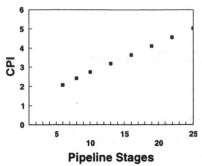

Fig. 1 shows the dependence of the CPI on the number of pipeline stages.

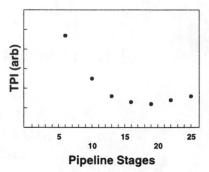

Fig. 3 shows TPI as a function of pipeline depth. The TPI scale is arbitrary.

as the pipeline depth is increased. This is an obvious result in that the amount of work does not increase with pipeline depth, so the total time needed to perform the logic functions of the processor stays the same, but the number of pipeline stages available to perform the work increases. This means that each stage can take less time. We will come back to this point later in a more formal way, but for now the result is shown qualitatively in Fig. 2.

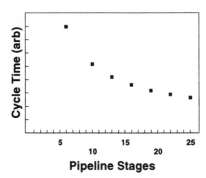

Fig. 2 depicts the dependence of the cycle time on the pipeline depth.

The true measure of performance in the processor is the average time it takes to execute an instruction. This is the Time / Instruction (TPI), which is just the inverse of the MIPs (Million Instructions per second) number, used to report the performance of some processors. The TPI is just the product of the cycle time and the CPI. This is shown qualitatively as a function of pipeline depth in Fig. 3. The optimum performance is then given as the minimum TPI point in the figure.

In the next section we present a formal theory of performance as a function of the pipeline depth. In Section 3 we introduce a methodology, which allows for the simulation of a variable pipeline depth microprocessor. In Section 4 this simulator model is used both to verify the formal theory and to quantify these results. Section 5 summarizes the differing results obtained for different workloads; and Section 6 contains further discussion.

2. Theory

In order to develop an expression for the optimum pipeline depth, we start by considering how a processor spends its time. The total time, T, is divided into the time that the execution unit is doing useful work, T_{BZ}, and the time that execution is stalled by any of a number of pipeline hazards, T_{NBZ}. This notation stands for the busy and not-busy times, which have been discussed previously [4, 5]. Typical pipeline stalls include branch prediction errors and both decode and execution data dependencies.

Let us first consider the busy time for the execution unit. The time that the e-unit is busy can be expressed in terms of the number of instructions, N_I, and the time for an instruction to pass each stage of the pipeline, t_S. The busy time is given by

$$T_{BZ} = N_I t_S \qquad (1)$$

for a scalar machine. Each pipeline stage delay can be expressed as

$$t_S = t_o + t_p/p, \qquad (2)$$

where t_p is the total logic delay of the processor, p is the number of pipeline stages in the design, and t_o is the latch overhead for the technology, being used. Eq. 2 says that the stage delay has two components, the portion of the total logic delay assigned to each pipeline stage and the latch overhead between pipeline stages. Substituting Eq. 2 into Eq. 1, we arrive at an expression for the e-unit busy time.

$$T_{BZ} = N_I(t_o + t_p/p), \qquad (3)$$

So far we have only considered a processor that executes instructions one at a time. For a superscalar processor multiple instructions may be executed at the same time. Therefore, less busy time is required to execute the instructions in a program. We model this by introducing a parameter, a, which is a measure of the average degree of superscalar processing whenever the e-unit is busy. Eq. 3 is then modified as follows.

$$T_{BZ} = \frac{N_I}{a}(t_o + t_p/p) \qquad (4)$$

It should be noted that a is not the superscalar issue width. Rather it is the actual degree of superscalar processing averaged over a particular piece of code. As such it varies with the workload running on the processor. a is obtained only when the e-unit is busy; the not busy times being caused by various hazards, to which we will now direct our attention.

Let us first consider the simple case in which each hazard causes a full pipeline stall. In this case the not busy time will be given in terms of the number of hazards, N_H, and the total pipeline delay, t_{pipe}.

$$T_{NBZ} = N_H t_{pipe} \qquad (5)$$

The total pipeline delay is just the product of each pipeline stage delay, t_S, and the number of pipeline stages in the processor. Combining this fact with Eqs. 2 and 5, we obtain the following expression for the not busy time.

$$T_{NBZ} = N_H(t_o p + t_p) \qquad (6)$$

In most processor designs this is too crude an approximation. Each particular pipeline hazard only stalls the pipeline for some fraction of the total delay. Execution dependencies will stall the pipeline less than decode (address generation) dependencies. Different types of branch misprediction hazards will stall the pipeline for different times. We can modify Eq. 6 to reflect this fact by allowing each hazard to have its own not busy time, t_{hazard}, which is a fraction, β_h, of the total pipeline delay. Then the expression for the not busy time must be summed over the not busy time for each individual hazard. Eq. 6 then becomes

$$T_{NBZ} = \sum^{N_H} t_{hazard} = N_H(t_o p + t_p)(\frac{1}{N_H}\sum^{N_H}\beta_h) \qquad (7)$$

Some comments are in order. The parameter, β_h, measures the fraction of the total pipeline delay encountered by each particular hazard. As such its value is constrained to the range 0 to 1. We have deliberately grouped the variables in Eq. 7 to form the last expression in parenthesis. This is a dimensionless parameter, which we will call $\gamma = \frac{1}{N_H}\sum\beta_h$. This parameter, γ, is the fraction of the total pipeline delay averaged over all hazards and contains all of the information about the hazards in a particular piece of

code as well as details of the microarchitecture of the processor. In practice γ is difficult to calculate, but like β_h, it is constrained to have a value between 0 and 1.

The final expression for the total time to process a program is simply given by adding Eqs. 4 and 7, the busy and not busy times. We then form our performance measure by dividing the total time by the number of instructions, N_I. The final result is then:

$$T/N_I = (\frac{t_o}{a} + \frac{\gamma N_H}{N_I}t_p) + \frac{t_p}{ap} + \frac{\gamma N_H t_o}{N_I}p. \qquad (8)$$

The first term in this expression is independent of the pipeline depth; the second term varies inversely with p; and the last term varies linearly with p. This result depends on numerous parameters. The ratio N_H/N_I is mainly dependent on the workload being executed, but is also dependent on the microarchitecture through, for instance, the branch prediction accuracy. a and γ are mainly microarchitecture dependent, but also depend on the workload. t_o is technology dependent, while t_p is dependent on both technology and the microarchitecture.

Eq. 8 has a minimum at a particular value of p, the pipeline depth. One can solve for this optimum performance point by differentiating Eq. 8 with respect to p, setting the resulting expression equal to 0, and solving for p_{opt}. The result is

$$p_{opt}^2 = \frac{N_I t_p}{a\gamma N_H t_o}. \qquad (9)$$

Some general observations about the optimum pipeline depth can be made from Eq. 9. The optimum pipeline depth increases for workloads with few hazards. As technology reduces the latch overhead, t_o, relative to the total logic path, t_p, the optimum pipeline depth increases. As the degree of superscalar processing, a, increases, the optimum pipeline depth decreases. And lastly, as the fraction of the pipeline that hazards stall, γ, decreases, the optimum pipeline depth increases. Intuitive explanations for these dependencies will be discussed in more detail in a later section.

The reader will note that in the derivation of this theory, no mention was made as to whether the instruction processing was in-order or out-of-order. That is because out-of-order processing does not change the analysis. However, it can effect the values of some of the parameters. In particular, the degree of superscalar processing will be altered with out-or-order processing. Also, the effective penalty incurred from various hazards will be reduced by allowing out-of-order processing of instructions to fill in some of the stall cycles.

It should be noted that an equivalent result was obtained by Emma and Davidson [3]. They confined their analysis to a one-at-a-time, in-order processor model. Most of their paper concerns the first principles determination of the parameter γ. The contributions of each type of hazard and the relative numbers of each type were estimated for a particular microarchitecture. We will not repeat that type of analysis here, but rather test various aspects of our theory with detailed modeling of a particular microarchitecture.

3. Simulation Methodology

In order to test the limits of our optimum pipeline depth theory and to explore additional ramifications of the theory, we have used a proprietary simulator. The simulator uses as input design parameters that describe the organization of the processor and a trace tape. It produces a very flexible cycle accurate model of the processor. With this tool we are able to model numerous pipeline designs, variable issue width superscalar designs, and either in-order or out-of-order execution processing. We also had the availability of 35 traces, encompassing traditional (legacy) workloads, "modern" workloads, SPEC95 and SPEC2000 workloads. The traditional workloads include both database and on-line transaction processing (OLTP) applications. These applications were originally written in S/360 assembler language over 30 years ago. They have continued to evolve and now run on S/390 (zSeries) processors. The modern workloads were written in either C++ or Java. These traces were carefully selected because they accurately reflect the instruction mix, module mix and branch prediction characteristics of the entire application, from which they were derived. This tool has mainly been used for work on S/390 processors.

In order to build a model to test the above theory we need to be able to expand the processor pipeline in a uniform manner. The theory assumes that the processor logic can be uniformly divided into p stages. In modeling, it is not practical to repartition the pipeline for each new design. Instead we have made use the pipeline shown in Fig. 4.

This is the pipeline model of a 4 issue superscalar, out-or-order execution machine. The model can handle S/390 code, so that register only instructions (RR), as well as register / memory access instructions (RX), must be executed efficiently. The pipeline has 2 major instruction flow paths. The RR instructions go sequentially through Decode - Register Rename - Execution Queue - Pipelined E-Unit - Completion - Retire. The RX instructions, including loads and stores, add to this pipeline the sequence: Address Queue - Pipelined Address Generation - Cache Access, between the register rename and execution queue stages.

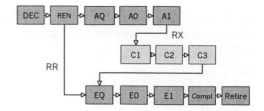

Fig. 4 shows the pipeline modeled in this study. The stages include: Decode, Rename, Agen Q, Agen, Cache Access, Execute Q, Execute, Completion and Retire.

This is the base pipeline we modeled. Address generation, cache access and execution are independently out-of-order processes. In testing the theory we utilize the flexibility of our simulator model. In particular we expand the pipeline depth by adding stages "uniformly". We insert extra stages in Decode, Cache Access and E-Unit pipe, simultaneously. For example, as the Cache Access pipe is increased (in Fig. 4) the Decode and E-Unit pipe stages are increased proportionally. This allows all hazards to see pipeline increases. Hazards, whose stalls cover a larger fraction of the pipeline, see larger increases due to the increased pipeline depth.

We have also utilized other aspects of our model flexibility in our studies. In one experiment the branch prediction accuracy was varied in order to alter the number of hazards encountered for a particular workload. In still another experiment we varied the superscalar issue width, to study the predicted dependence of the optimum pipeline depth on the average degree of superscalar processing. We have also run both in-order and out-of-order models to show that both show qualitatively the same results.

4. Simulator Results

Each particular workload was simulated in this way with pipeline depths ranging from 10 stages to 34 stages. We count the stages between decode and execution, rather than the entire pipeline. We determine the entire logic delay time in the same way. To compare with the theory, we use the detailed statistics obtained from each simulator run to determine the parameters in Eq. 8. Two of the parameters, N_I and N_H, are simply enumerated, but a and γ require more extensive analysis of the details of the pipeline and the particular distribution of instructions and hazards in each simulation run. The parameters, t_p and t_o, were chosen from a particular technology; but only the ratio $t_p/t_o = 55$ is important in determining the optimum pipeline depth.

Fig. 5 shows the results of the simulation, for a particular traditional workload, along with the corresponding theoretical curve. We plot TPI (Time per Instruction) as a function of the number of pipeline stages. The predicted minimum in the curve is clearly seen. It is fairly flat around the minimum, which leaves considerable latitude in choosing the best design point for a particular processor. The fact that the optimum pipeline depth is so large is due mainly to the small latch delay in our technology model.

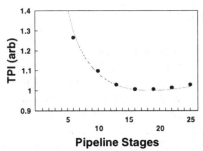

Fig. 5 is a direct comparison of the simulation (data points) and the theory (solid curve) for a particular workload. The TPI numbers are scaled to the minimum point.

As can be seen the agreement between theory and experiment is extraordinarily good. Because of the difficulty of determining the parameter, γ even from our detailed statistics, the fit between theory and experiment should be considered as a one parameter fit. We effectively chose a value of γ, consistent with our estimates from the statistics, which caused the theory and experiment to correspond at one point. This in no way diminishes the value of the comparison, which clearly shows that the theory adequately describes the functioning of the pipeline. This comparison could have been shown for any of the 35 workloads run, with equally good results, although some workloads show somewhat more scatter in the data.

Eq. 9 gives the minimum point in Fig. 5, and from the fit of theory and simulation, it clearly agrees with the simulation. To further explore the applicability of the theory one can construct experiments to test the various dependencies in Eq. 9. The first one we will test is the dependence on a, the degree of superscalar processing. In order to do this we first obtain the results for a particular workload (that has significant superscalar parallelism), and then obtain new results limiting the issue width to 1, i.e.. non-superscalar but still out-of-order processing. In this way the primary change in parameters will be to reduce a. Some secondary effect on γ may result, but will be small.

Fig. 6 shows these 2 simulation results for the IJPEG workload from the SPEC95 suite. The shift in the optimum pipeline depth point with decreased superscalar issue width is clearly evident. As expected, moving to a single issue E-Unit, decreases a, and shifts the optimum point to larger values of pipeline stages. Even the magnitude of the shift can be accurately accounted for by the theory. In passing

we should note that reducing the issue width, reduces the overall performance, as well.

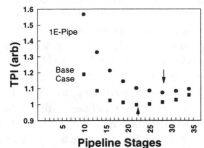

Fig. 6 shows the performance curves for 2 different superscalar issue widths: single and 4-issue for the IJPEG workload. The optimum performance positions are indicated by arrows.

We can test the dependence of Eq. 9 on γ by varying the branch prediction efficiency by reducing the size of the branch prediction table. If we reduce the branch prediction capability, we both increase the number of branch hazards contained in N_H; and since conditional branches cause pipeline stalls over the entire pipeline, we increase the value of γ. Both of these effects should shift the optimum pipeline point to lower values of p. Fig. 7 shows this effect for a particular modern workload. Also note that reducing branch prediction efficiency severely impacts the performance.

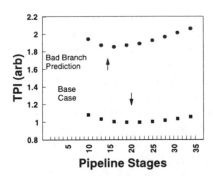

Fig. 7 shows the effect of changing branch prediction on the optimal pipeline depth.

5. Workload Specificity

No one doubts that there are significant differences between different types of workloads run on processors. Maynard, et. al. [6] have explored the workload differences between multi-user commercial workloads and technical workloads. Differences arise from branch prediction accuracy, the degree of operating system calls, I/O content and dispatch characteristics. Gee et.al. [7] and Charney et. al. [8] have addressed the cache performance of the SPEC

11

workloads compared to other workloads. The SPEC workloads tend to have small instruction footprints, and can achieve "good" performance, even for small caches. In this work we have employed both SPEC benchmark traces and workloads with much larger cache footprints. We have used both traditional S/390 legacy workloads and some modern workloads, written in Java and C++.

We have simulated all 35 of our workloads, obtained the TPI as a function of pipeline depth for each of them, and determined the optimum pipeline depth for each. In Fig. 8 we show the distribution of these optimum pipeline depths for different workloads. As one can see there is essentially a Gaussian distribution of the optimum pipeline depth over the workloads studied.

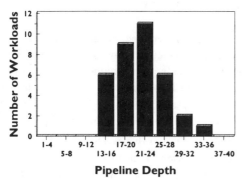

Fig. 8 shows the distribution of pipeline depth optima for all workloads.

It is perhaps more instructive to divide the distribution into the separate types of workloads. Fig. 9 shows this analysis, divided into SPEC workloads (programmed in C), traditional workloads (programmed largely in assembler), and "modern" workloads (programmed in C++ or Java). It is clear that there is a significant difference between the SPEC workloads and the other workloads in terms of the optimal pipeline depth. A pipeline optimized for real workloads, either traditional or modern, should be considerably deeper than a pipeline optimized for the SPEC workloads. This is true for both SPEC95 and SPEC2000

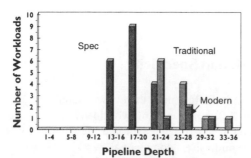

Fig. 9 shows the distribution of pipeline depth optima for different workload classes. Blue are the Spec (C) workloads, red are the traditional workloads, and green are the modern (C++ and Java) workloads.

workloads. Fortuitously, as we have seen, the dependence of the performance on the number of pipeline stages, leading to the optimum pipeline depth, is quite broad. Optimizing for the wrong type of workload will not incur too large a penalty.

6. Discussion

Now let us explore the consequences of this work in a more intuitive way. Looking back at Eq. 8, we see that this expression for the performance consists of four terms. The first two have no dependence on the pipeline depth. The first term is the constant performance degradation due to the latch overhead. The second term is an overhead from pipeline hazards. The next two terms are more interesting.

The third term is inversely proportional to the pipeline depth. This is the term that drives deeper pipelines to have better performance. Basically, what it says is that the total logic delay of the processor is divided up into separate parts for each pipeline stage. One then gets a larger throughput by "storing" instructions in the pipeline. The performance is given by the rate at which instructions finish the pipeline, not the time it takes an instruction in the pipeline. In fact if there were no hazards, as in Eq. 4, the only performance limitation would arise from the latch overhead.

The last term in Eq. 8 is linearly proportional to the pipeline depth. This term arises from the dependence of pipeline stalls on pipeline depth. Deeper pipelines suffer a larger penalty from hazards. The term is proportional to the fraction of the pipeline that each stall covers, as well as the number of hazards. It is also important to note that the term is proportional to the latch overhead; each additional hazard induced pipeline stall causes a performance degradation from that latch overhead. On the other hand the hazard related term which is proportional to the total logic depth, the second term, is independent of both pipeline depth and latch overhead.

There is a competition between greater pipeline throughput and pipeline hazards. If no hazards were present, the optimum performance would occur for an infinitely deep pipeline. One simply loads all of the instructions into the pipeline, and the performance, the rate at which the instructions complete, is optimized. On the other hand, hazards disrupt the pipeline flow by periodically draining the pipeline or a portion of the pipeline. This competition between increasing pipeline throughput, by "storing" instructions in the pipeline, and reducing pipeline hazard stalls, by minimizing pipeline depth, accounts for the observed behavior.

It is instructive to compute the portion of the cycle time allocated to latch overhead for the optimum pipeline depths. For the ratio of total logical delay of the processor to latch overhead, $t_p/t_o = 55$, latch overhead consumes 25% to

50% of the cycle time. Even though this may seem like a large portion of the cycle time, our results clearly show that this gives the optimal pipeline performance. It would be a difficult challenge to actually design a processor, which is so highly pipelined. Designing a processor, where latch overhead can account for ¼ to ½ of the time allocated to each cycle, offers significant new challenges in partitioning the logic and controlling the power.

Moving on to Eq. 9 we can understand the optimum pipeline depth dependencies in light of the above arguments. As the number of hazards per instruction increases, the optimum pipeline depth is pushed to lower values. As the fraction of the pipeline stalled by any one hazard increases, the optimum pipeline depth decreases. As the superscalar processing parallelism increases, the throughput increases without the need for a pipeline depth increase, and therefore the optimum pipeline depth decreases. As the latch overhead increases relative to the total logic delay, pipelining becomes more of a burden, and the optimum pipeline depth decreases.

The competing nature of these effects is inherent in Fig. 9. One might expect the SPEC workloads to have a longer optimal pipeline depth than the traditional legacy workloads, due to the fact that the SPEC applications have fewer pipeline stalls than the legacy applications. However, the opposing effect that the SPEC applications contain a higher degree of instruction level parallelism, that can be exploited by a superscalar processor, is even more important. The net result is that the SPEC workloads optimize for a shorter pipeline.

In all of the preceding, we have been implicitly considering an infinite cache model. We could have constructed a similar variable pipeline depth model, which included the multiple level cache access paths. As the pipeline depth increased, the latency of cache or memory accesses would have shown an increased number of cycles. However, the cache or memory access time would remain constant. Therefore, although the finite cache contribution to the CPI would increase, the finite cache contribution to TPI stays constant. The finite cache equivalent to Figs. 5-7 simply have a constant finite cache TPI adder. This in no way changes the optimum pipeline depth or any of the dependencies that have been discussed.

7. Summary

A theory has been presented of the optimum pipeline depth for a microprocessor. The theory has been tested by simulating a variable depth pipeline model, and the two are found to be in excellent agreement. It is found that the competition between "storing" instructions in a deeper pipeline to increase throughput, and limiting the number of pipeline stalls from various pipeline hazards, results in an optimum pipeline depth. That depth depends in a complex but understandable way on the detailed microarchitecture of the processor, details of the underlying technology used to build the processor, and certain characteristics of the workloads run on the processor. Our analysis clearly shows a difference between the optimum pipeline length for SPEC applications and the optimum pipeline length for both legacy applications and modern workloads. It would be instructive to gain a deeper understanding of the factors that produce similar optimal pipeline depths for the modern workloads and legacy applications.

8. Acknowledgments

The authors would like to thank P. G. Emma and E. S. Davidson for many stimulating discussions and helpful comments on this work.

9. References

[1] S. R. Kunkel and J. E. Smith. "Optimal pipelining in supercomputers", *Proc. of the 13th Annual International Symposium on Computer Architectures*, pp. 404 - 411, 1986.

[2] V. Agarwal, M. S. Hrishikesh, S. W. Keckler and D. Burger. "Clock Rate versus IPC: The End of the Road for Conventional Microarchitectures", *Proc. of the 27th Annual International Symposium on Computer Architectures*, pp. 248 - 259, 2000.

[3] P. G. Emma and E. S. Davidson. "Characterization of Branch and Data Dependencies in Programs for Evaluating Pipeline Performance", *IEEE Transactions on Computers* **C-36**, pp. 859 - 875, 1987.

[4] M. H. Macdougal. "Instruction-Level Program and Processor Modeling", *Computer*, pp. 14 - 24, 1984.

[5] P. Emma, J Knight, J Pomerene, T Puzak, R Rechschaffen. "Simulation and Analysis of a Pipeline Processor", *8th Winter Simulation Conference*, pp. 1047 - 1057, 1989.

[6] A. M. G. Maynard, C. M. Donnelly, and B. R. Olszewski. "Contrasting Characteristics and cache performance of technical and multi-user commercial workloads", *ASPLOS VI*, pp. 145 - 156, 1994.

[7] J. D. Gee, M. D. Hill, D. N Pnevmatikatos, and A. J. Smith. "Cache Performance of the SPEC Benchmark Suite", *Technical Report 1049, Computer Sciences Department, University of Wisconsin*, 1991.

[8] M. J. Charney and T. R. Puzak. "Prefetching and Memory System Behavior of the SPEC95 benchmark Suite" *IBM Journal of Research and Development* **41**, pp. 265 - 286, 1997.

The Optimal Logic Depth Per Pipeline Stage is 6 to 8 FO4 Inverter Delays

M.S. Hrishikesh*   Norman P. Jouppi+   Keith I. Farkas+
Doug Burger†   Stephen W. Keckler†   Premkishore Shivakumar†

*Department of Electrical and Computer Engineering
†Department of Computer Sciences
The University of Texas at Austin
http://www.cs.utexas.edu/users/cart

+Western Research Lab
Compaq Computer Corporation
http://research.compaq.com/wrl/

Abstract

Microprocessor clock frequency has improved by nearly 40% annually over the past decade. This improvement has been provided, in equal measure, by smaller technologies and deeper pipelines. From our study of the SPEC 2000 benchmarks, we find that for a high-performance architecture implemented in 100nm technology, the optimal clock period is approximately 8 fan-out-of-four (FO4) inverter delays for integer benchmarks, comprised of 6 FO4 of useful work and an overhead of about 2 FO4. The optimal clock period for floating-point benchmarks is 6FO4. We find these optimal points to be insensitive to latch and clock skew overheads. Our study indicates that further pipelining can at best improve performance of integer programs by a factor of 2 over current designs. At these high clock frequencies it will be difficult to design the instruction issue window to operate in a single cycle. Consequently, we propose and evaluate a high-frequency design called a segmented instruction window.

1   Introduction

Improvements in microprocessor performance have been sustained by increases in both instruction per cycle (IPC) and clock frequency. In recent years, increases in clock frequency have provided the bulk of the performance improvement. These increases have come from both technology scaling (faster gates) and deeper pipelining of designs (fewer gates per cycle). In this paper, we examine for how much further reducing the amount of logic per pipeline stage can improve performance. The results of this study have significant implications for performance scaling in the coming decade.

Figure 1 shows the clock periods of the Intel family of x86 processors on the y-axis. The x-axis shows the year of introduction and the feature size used to fabricate each processor. We computed the clock period by dividing the nominal frequency of the processor by the delay of one FO4 at the corresponding technology[1]. The graph shows that clock frequency has increased by approximately a factor of 60 over the past twelve years. During this period process technology

---

[1] We measure the amount of logic per pipeline stage in terms of fan-out-of-four (FO4) – the delay of one inverter driving four copies of itself. Delays measured in FO4 are technology independent. The data points in Figure 1 were computed assuming that 1 FO4 roughly corresponds to 360 picoseconds times the transistor's drawn gate length in microns [6].

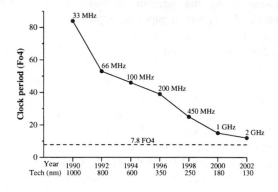

Figure 1: The year of introduction, clock frequency and fabrication technologies of the last seven generations of Intel processors. Logic levels are measured in fan-out-of-four delays (FO4). The broken line shows the optimal clock period for integer codes.

has been scaled from 1000nm to 130nm, contributing an 8-fold improvement in clock frequency. The amount of logic per pipeline stage decreased from 84 to 12 FO4, contributing to the increase in clock frequency by a factor of 7. So far, both technology scaling and reduction in logic per stage have contributed roughly equally to improvements in clock frequency.

However, decreasing the amount of logic per pipeline stage increases pipeline depth, which in turn reduces IPC due to increased branch misprediction penalties and functional unit latencies. In addition, reducing the amount of logic per pipeline stage reduces the amount of useful work per cycle while not affecting overheads associated with latches, clock skew and jitter. Therefore, shorter pipeline stages cause the overhead to become a greater fraction of the clock period, which reduces the effective frequency gains.

Processor designs must balance clock frequency and IPC to achieve ideal performance. Previously, Kunkel and Smith examined this trade-off [9] by investigating the pipelining of a CRAY 1-S supercomputer to determine the number of levels of logic per pipeline stage that provides maximum performance. They assumed the use of Earle latches between stages of the pipeline, which were representative of high-performance latches of that time. They concluded that, in the absence of latch and skew overheads, absolute performance increases as the pipeline is made deeper. But when the overhead is taken into account, performance increases up to a point beyond which increases in pipeline depth reduce performance. They found that maximum performance was obtained with 8

14

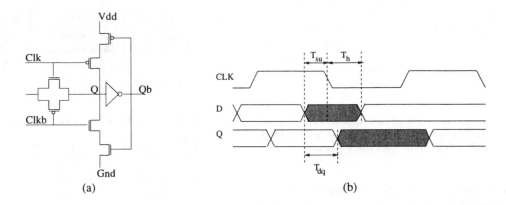

Figure 2: Circuit and timing diagrams of a basic pulse latch. The shaded area in Figure 2b indicates that the signal is valid.

gate levels per stage for scalar code and with 4 gate levels per stage for vector code, which, using the equivalence we develop in Appendix A, is approximately 10.9 and 5.4 FO4 respectively.

In the first part of this paper, we re-examine Kunkel and Smith's work in a modern context to determine the optimal clock frequency for current-generation processors. Our study investigates a superscalar pipeline designed using CMOS transistors and VLSI technology, and assumes low-overhead pulse latches between pipeline stages. We show that maximum performance for integer benchmarks is achieved when the logic depth per pipeline stage corresponds to 7.8 FO4—6 FO4 of useful work and 1.8 FO4 of overhead. The dashed line in Figure 1 represents this optimal clock period. Note that the clock periods of current-generation processors already approach the optimal clock period. In the second portion of this paper, we identify a microarchitectural structure that will limit the scalability of the clock and propose methods to pipeline it at high frequencies. We propose a new design for the instruction issue window that divides it into sections. We show that although this method reduces the IPC of integer benchmarks by 11% and that of floating-point benchmarks by 5%, it allows significantly higher clock frequencies.

The remainder of this paper is organized in the following fashion. To determine the ideal clock frequency we first quantify latch overhead and present a detailed description of this methodology in Section 2. Section 3 describes the methodology to find the ideal clock frequency, which entails experiments with varied pipeline depths. We present the results of this study in Section 4. We examine specific microarchitectural structures in Section 5 and propose new designs that can be clocked at high frequencies. Section 6 discusses related work, and Section 7 summarizes our results and presents the conclusions of this study.

2 Estimating Overhead

The clock period of the processor is determined by the following equation

$$\phi = \phi_{logic} + \phi_{latch} + \phi_{skew} + \phi_{jitter} \qquad (1)$$

where ϕ is the clock period, ϕ_{logic} is useful work performed by logic circuits, ϕ_{latch} is latch overhead, ϕ_{skew} is clock skew overhead and ϕ_{jitter} is clock jitter overhead. In this section, we describe our methodology for estimating the overhead components, and the resulting values.

A pipelined machine requires data and control signals at each stage to be saved at the end of every cycle. In the subsequent clock cycle this stored information is used by the following stage. Therefore, a portion of each clock period, called *latch overhead*, is required by latches to sample and hold values. Latches may be either edge triggered or level sensitive. Edge-triggered latches reduce the possibility of *race through*, enabling simple pipeline designs, but typically incur higher latch overheads. Conversely, level-sensitive latches allow for design optimizations such as "slack-passing" and "time borrowing" [2], techniques that allow a slow stage in the pipeline to meet cycle time requirements by borrowing unused time from a neighboring, faster stage. In this paper we model a level-sensitive pulse latch, since it has low overhead and power consumption [4]. We use SPICE circuit simulations to quantify the latch overhead.

Figure 2a shows the circuit for a pulse latch consisting of a transmission gate followed by an inverter and a feed-back path. Data values are sampled and held by the latch as follows. During the period that the clock pulse is high, the transmission gate of the latch is on, and the output of the latch (Q) takes the same value as the input (D). When the clock signal changes to low, the transmission gate is turned off. However, the transistors along one of the two feedback paths turn on, completing the feedback loop. The inverter and the feedback loop retain the sampled data value until the following clock cycle.

The operation of a latch is governed by three parameters—setup time (T_{su}), hold time (T_h), and propagation delay (T_{dq}), as shown in Figure 2b. To determine latch overhead, we measured its parameters using the test circuit shown in Figure 3. The test circuit consists of a pulse latch with its output driving another similar pulse latch whose transmission gate is turned on. On-chip data and clock signals may travel through a number of gates before they terminate at a latch. To simulate the same effect, we buffer the clock and data inputs to the latch by a series of six inverters. The clock signal has a 50% duty cycle while the data signal is a simple step function. We

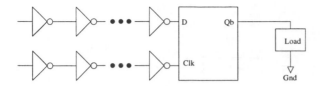

Figure 3: Simulation setup to find latch overhead. The clock and data signals are buffered by a series of six inverters and the output drives a similar latch with its transmission gate turned on.

Symbol	Definition	Overhead
ϕ_{latch}	Latch Overhead	1.0 FO4
ϕ_{skew}	Skew Overhead	0.3 FO4
ϕ_{jitter}	Jitter Overhead	0.5 FO4
$\phi_{overhead}$	Total	1.8 FO4

Table 1: Overheads due to latch, clock skew and jitter.

Integer	Vector FP	Non-vector FP
164.gzip	171.swim	177.mesa
175.vpr	172.mgrid	178.galgel
176.gcc	173.applu	179.art
181.mcf	183.equake	188.ammp
197.parser		189.lucas
252.eon		
253.perlbmk		
256.bzip2		
300.twolf		

Table 2: SPEC 2000 benchmarks used in all simulation experiments. The benchmarks are further classified into vector and non-vector benchmarks.

simulated transistors at 100nm technology and performed experiments similar to those by Stojanović *et al.* [14], using the same P-transistor to N-transistor ratios. In our experiments, we moved the data signal progressively closer to the falling edge of the clock signal. Eventually when D changes very close to the falling edge of the Clk signal the latch fails to hold the correct value of D. Latch overhead is the smallest of the D-Q delays before this point of failure [14]. We estimated latch overhead to be 36ps (1 FO4) at 100nm technology. Since this delay is determined by the switching speed of transistors, which is expected to scale linearly with technology, its value in FO4 will remain constant at all technologies. Note that throughout this paper transistor feature sizes refer to the drawn gate length as opposed to the effective gate length.

In addition to latch overhead, clock skew and jitter also add to the total overhead of a clock period. A recent study by Kurd *et al.* [10] showed that, by partitioning the chip into multiple clock domains, clock skew can be reduced to less than 20ps and jitter to 35ps. They performed their studies at 180nm, which translates into 0.3 FO4 due to skew and 0.5 FO4 due to jitter. Many components of clock skew and jitter are dependent on the speed of the components, and those that are dependent on the transistor components should scale with technology. However, other terms, such as delay due to process variation, may scale differently, hence affecting the overall scalability. For simplicity we assume that clock skew and jitter will scale linearly with technology and therefore their values in FO4 will remain constant. Table 1 shows the values of the different overheads that we use to determine the clock frequency in Section 4. The sum of latch, clock skew and jitter overhead is equal to 1.8 FO4. We refer to this sum in the rest of the paper as $\phi_{overhead}$.

3 Methodology

To study the effect of deeper pipelining on performance, we varied the pipeline depth of a modern superscalar architecture similar to the Alpha 21264. This section describes our simulation framework and the methodology we used to perform this study.

3.1 Simulation Framework

We used a simulator developed by Desikan *et al.* that models both the low-level features of the Alpha 21264 processor [3] and the execution core in detail. This simulator has been validated to be within an accuracy of 20% of a Compaq DS-10L workstation. For our experiments, the base latency and capacities of on-chip structures matched those of the Alpha 21264, and the level-2 cache was configured to be 2MB. The capacities of the integer and floating-point register files alone were increased to 512 each, so that the performance of deep pipelines was not unduly constrained due to unavailability of registers. We modified the execution core of the simulator to permit the addition of more stages to different parts of the pipeline. The modifications allowed us to vary the pipeline depth of different parts of the processor pipeline, including the execution stage, the register read stage, the issue stage, and the commit stage.

Table 2 lists the benchmarks that we simulated for our experiments, which include integer and floating-point benchmarks taken from the SPEC 2000 suite. Some of the floating-point (FP) benchmarks operate on large matrices and exhibit strong vector-like behavior; we classify these benchmarks as vector floating-point benchmarks. When presenting simulation results, we show individual results for integer, vector FP, and non-vector FP benchmarks separately. All experiments skip the first 500 million instructions of each benchmark and simulate the next 500 million instructions.

3.2 Microarchitectural Structures

We use Cacti 3.0 [12] to model on-chip microarchitectural structures and to estimate their access times. Cacti is an analytical tool originally developed by Jouppi and Wilton [7]. All major microarchitectural structures—data cache, register file, branch predictor, register rename table and instruction issue window—were modeled at 100nm technology and their capacities and configurations were chosen to match the corresponding structures in the Alpha 21264. We use the latencies of the structures obtained from Cacti to compute their access

ϕ_{logic} (FO4)	DL1	Branch Predictor	Rename Table	Issue Window	Register File	Integer		FLoating Point			
						Add	Mult	Add	Div	Sqrt	Mult
2	16	10	9	9	6	9	61	35	105	157	35
3	11	7	6	6	4	6	41	24	70	105	24
4	9	5	5	5	3	5	31	18	53	79	18
5	7	4	4	4	3	4	25	14	42	63	14
6	6	4	3	3	2	3	21	12	35	53	12
7	6	3	3	3	2	3	18	10	30	45	10
8	5	3	3	3	2	3	16	9	27	40	9
9	5	3	2	2	2	2	14	8	24	35	8
10	4	2	2	2	2	2	13	7	21	32	7
11	4	2	2	2	1	2	12	7	19	29	7
12	4	2	2	2	1	2	11	6	18	27	6
13	4	2	2	2	1	2	10	6	17	25	6
14	4	2	2	2	1	2	9	5	15	23	5
15	3	2	2	2	1	2	9	5	14	21	5
16	3	2	2	2	1	2	8	5	14	20	5
Alpha 21264 (17.4)	3	1	1	1	1	1	7	4	12	18	4

Table 3: Access latencies (clock cycles) of microarchitectural structures and integer and floating-point operations at 100nm technology (drawn gate length). The functional units are fully pipelined and new instructions can be assigned to them every cycle. The last row shows the latency of on-chip structures on the Alpha 21264 processor (180nm).

penalties (in cycles) at different clock frequencies.

3.3 Scaling Pipelines

We find the clock frequency that will provide maximum performance by simulating processor pipelines clocked at different frequencies. The clock period of the processor is determined by the following equation: $\phi = \phi_{logic} + \phi_{overhead}$. The overhead term is held constant at 1.8 FO4, as discussed in Section 2. We vary the clock frequency ($1/\phi$) by varying ϕ_{logic} from 2 FO4 to 16 FO4. The number of pipeline stages (clock cycles) required to access an on-chip structure, at each clock frequency, is determined by dividing the access time of the structure by the corresponding ϕ_{logic}. For example, if the access time of the level-1 cache at 100nm technology is 0.28ns (8 FO4), for a pipeline where ϕ_{logic} equals 2 FO4 (0.07ns), the cache can be accessed in 4 cycles.

Though we use a 100nm technology in this study, the access latencies at other technologies in terms of the FO4 metric will remain largely unchanged at each corresponding clock frequency, since delays measured in this metric are technology independent. Table 3 shows the access latencies of structures at each ϕ_{logic}. These access latencies were determined by dividing the structure latencies (in pico seconds) obtained from the cacti model by the corresponding clock period. Table 3 also shows the latencies for various integer and floating-point operations at different clocks. To compute these latencies we determined ϕ_{logic} for the Alpha 21264 processor (800MHz, 180nm) by attributing 10% of its clock period to latch overhead (approximately 1.8 FO4). Using this ϕ_{logic} and the functional unit execution times of the Alpha 21264 (in cycles) we computed the execution latencies at various clock frequencies. In all our simulations, we assumed that results produced by the functional units can be fully bypassed to any stage between Issue and Execute.

In general, the access latencies of the structures increase as ϕ_{logic} is decreased. In certain cases the access latency remains unchanged despite a change in ϕ_{logic}. For example, the access latency of the register file is 0.39ns at 100nm technology. If ϕ_{logic} was 10 FO4 the access latency of the register file would be approximately 1.1 cycles. Conversely, if ϕ_{logic} was reduced to 6 FO4, the access latency would be 1.8 clock cycles. In both cases the access latency is rounded to 2 cycles.

By varying the processor pipeline as described above, we determine how deeply a high-performance design can be pipelined before overheads, due to latch, clock skew and jitter, and reduction in IPC, due to increased on-chip structure access latencies, begin to reduce performance.

4 Pipelined Architectures

In this section, we first vary the pipeline depth of an in-order issue processor to determine its optimal clock frequency. This in-order pipeline is similar to the Alpha 21264 pipeline except that it issues instructions in-order. It has seven stages—fetch, decode, issue, register read, execute, write back and commit. The issue stage of the processor is capable of issuing up to four instructions in each cycle. The execution stage consists of four integer units and two floating-point units. All functional units are fully pipelined, so new instructions can be assigned to them at every clock cycle. We compare our results, from scaling the in-order issue processor, with the CRAY 1-S machine [9]. Our goal is to determine if either workloads or processor design technologies have changed the amount of useful logic per pipeline stage (ϕ_{logic}) that provides the best performance. We then perform similar experiments to find ϕ_{logic} that will provide maximum performance for a dynamically scheduled processor similar to the Alpha 21264. For our experiments in Section 4, we make the optimistic assumption that all microar-

17

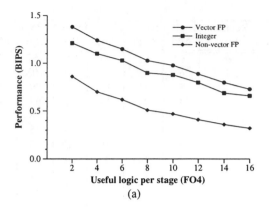
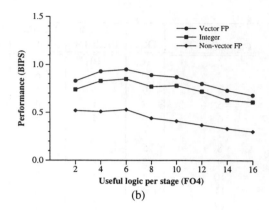

Figure 4: In-order pipeline performance with and without latch overhead. Figure 4a shows that when there is no latch overhead performance improves as pipeline depth is increased. When latch and clock overheads are considered, maximum performance is obtained with 6 FO4 useful logic per stage (ϕ_{logic}), as shown in Figure 4b.

chitectural components can be perfectly pipelined and be partitioned into an arbitrary number of stages.

4.1 In-order Issue Processors

Figure 4a shows the harmonic mean of the performance of SPEC 2000 benchmarks for an in-order pipeline, if there were no overheads associated with pipelining ($\phi_{overhead} = 0$) and performance was inhibited by only the data and control dependencies in the benchmark. The x-axis in Figure 4a represents ϕ_{logic} and the y-axis shows performance in billions of instructions per second (BIPS). Performance was computed as a product of IPC and the clock frequency—equal to $1/\phi_{logic}$. The integer benchmarks have a lower overall performance compared to the vector floating-point (FP) benchmarks. The vector FP benchmarks are representative of scientific code that operate on large matrices and have more ILP than the integer benchmarks. Therefore, even though the execution core has just two floating-point units, the vector benchmarks out perform the integer benchmarks. The non-vector FP benchmarks represent scientific workloads of a different nature, such as numerical analysis and molecular dynamics. They have less ILP than the vector benchmarks, and consequently their performance is lower than both the integer and floating-point benchmarks. For all three sets of benchmarks, doubling the clock frequency does not double the performance. When ϕ_{logic} is reduced from 8 to 4 FO4, the ideal improvement in performance is 100%. However, for the integer benchmarks the improvement is only 18%. As ϕ_{logic} is further decreased, the improvement in performance deviates further from the ideal value.

Figure 4b shows performance of the in-order pipeline with $\phi_{overhead}$ set to 1.8 FO4. Unlike in Figure 4a, in this graph the clock frequency is determined by $1/(\phi_{logic}+\phi_{overhead})$. For example, at the point in the graph where ϕ_{logic} is equal to 8 FO4, the clock frequency is $1/(10$ FO4$)$. Observe that maximum performance is obtained when ϕ_{logic} corresponds to 6 FO4. In this experiment, when ϕ_{logic} is reduced from 10 to 6 FO4 the improvement in performance is only about 9% compared to a clock frequency improvement of 50%.

4.2 Comparison with the CRAY-1S

Kunkel and Smith [9] observed for the Cray-1S that maximum performance can be achieved with 8 gate levels of useful logic per stage for scalar benchmarks and 4 gate levels for vector benchmarks. If the Cray-1S were to be designed in CMOS logic today, the equivalent latency of one logic level would be about 1.36 FO4, as derived in Appendix A. For the Cray-1S computer this equivalent would place the optimal ϕ_{logic} at 10.9 FO4 for scalar and 5.4 FO4 for vector benchmarks. The optimal ϕ_{logic} for vector benchmarks has remained more or less unchanged, largely because the vector benchmarks have ample ILP, which is exploited sufficiently well by both the in-order superscalar pipeline and the Cray-1S. The optimal ϕ_{logic} for integer benchmarks has more than halved since the time of the Cray-1S processor, which means that a processor designed using modern techniques can be clocked at more than twice the frequency.

One reason for the decrease in the optimal ϕ_{logic} of integer benchmarks is that in modern pipelines average memory access latencies are lower, due to on-chip caches. The Alpha 21264 has a two-level cache hierarchy comprising of a 3-cycle, level-1 data cache and an off-chip unified level-2 cache. In the Cray-1S all loads and stores directly accessed a 12-cycle memory. Integer benchmarks have a large number of dependencies, and any instruction dependent on loads would stall the pipeline for 12 cycles. With performance bottlenecks in the memory system, increasing clock frequency by pipelining more deeply does not improve performance. We examined the effect of scaling a superscalar, in-order pipeline with a memory system similar to the CRAY-1S (12 cycle access memory access, no caches) and found that the optimal ϕ_{logic} was 11 FO4 for integer benchmarks.

A second reason for the decrease in optimal ϕ_{logic} is the change in implementation technology. Kunkel and Smith assumed the processor was implemented using many chips at relatively small levels of integration, without binning of parts to reduce manufacturer's worst case delay variations. Consequently, they assumed overheads due to latches, data, and clock skew that were as much as 2.5 gate delays [9] (3.4 FO4).

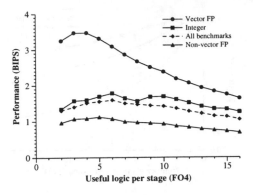

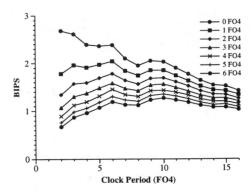

Figure 5: The harmonic mean of the performance of integer and floating point benchmarks, executing on an out-of-order pipeline, accounting for latch overhead, clock skew and jitter. For integer benchmarks best performance is obtained with 6 FO4 of useful logic per stage (ϕ_{logic}). For vector and non-vector floating-point benchmarks the optimal ϕ_{logic} is 4 FO4 and 5 FO4 respectively.

In contrast, modern VLSI microprocessors are comprised of circuits residing on the same die, so their process characteristics are more highly correlated than if they were from separate manufacturing runs fabricated perhaps months apart. Consequently, their speed variations and hence their relative skews are much smaller than in prior computer systems with lower levels of integration. Furthermore, the voltages and temperatures on one chip can be computed and taken into account at design time, also reducing the expected skews. These factors have reduced modern overhead to 1.8 FO4.

4.3 Dynamically Scheduled Processors

We performed similar experiments using a dynamically scheduled processor to find its optimal ϕ_{logic}. The processor configuration is similar to the Alpha 21264: 4-wide integer issue and 2-wide floating-point issue. We used a modified version of the simulator developed by Desikan *et al.* [3]. Figure 5 shows a plot of the performance of SPEC 2000 benchmarks when the pipeline depth of this processor is scaled. The performance shown in Figure 5 includes overheads represented by latch, clock skew and jitter ($\phi_{overhead}$). Figure 5 shows that overall performance of all three sets of benchmarks is significantly greater than for in-order pipelines. For a dynamically scheduled processor the optimal ϕ_{logic} for integer benchmarks is still 6 FO4. However, for vector and non-vector floating-point benchmarks the optimal ϕ_{logic} is 4 FO4 and 5 FO4 respectively. The dashed curve plots the harmonic mean of all three sets of benchmarks and shows the optimal ϕ_{logic} to be 6 FO4.

4.4 Sensitivity of ϕ_{logic} to $\phi_{overhead}$

Previous sections assumed that components of $\phi_{overhead}$, such as skew and jitter, would scale with technology and therefore overhead would remain constant. In this section, we examine performance sensitivity to $\phi_{overhead}$. Figure 6 shows a plot of the performance of integer SPEC 2000 benchmarks against ϕ_{logic} for different values of $\phi_{overhead}$. In general, if

Figure 6: The harmonic mean of the performance of integer benchmarks, executing on an out-of-order pipeline for various values of $\phi_{overhead}$.

the pipeline depth were held constant (i.e. constant ϕ_{logic}), reducing the value of $\phi_{overhead}$ yields better performance. However, since the overhead is a greater fraction of their clock period, deeper pipelines benefit more from reducing $\phi_{overhead}$ than do shallow pipelines.

Interestingly, the optimal value of ϕ_{logic} is fairly insensitive to $\phi_{overhead}$. In section 2 we estimated $\phi_{overhead}$ to be 1.8 FO4. Figure 6 shows that for $\phi_{overhead}$ values between 1 and 5 FO4 maximum performance is still obtained at a ϕ_{logic} of 6 FO4.

4.5 Sensitivity of ϕ_{logic} to Structure Capacity

In previous sections we found the optimal ϕ_{logic} by varying the pipeline depth of a superscalar processor with structure capacities configured to match those of the Alpha 21264. However, at future clock frequencies the Alpha 21264 structure capacities may not yield maximum performance. For example, the data cache in the Alpha 21264 processor is 64KB and has a 3-cycle access latency. When the processor pipeline is scaled to higher frequencies, the cache access latency (in cycles) will increase and may unduly limit performance. In such a situation, a smaller capacity cache with a correspondingly lower access latency could provide better performance.

The capacity and latency of on-chip microarchitectural structures have a great influence on processor performance. These structure parameters are not independent and are closely tied together by technology and clock frequency. To identify the best capacity and corresponding latency for various on-chip structures, at each of our projected clock frequencies, we determined the sensitivity of IPC to the size and delay of each individual structure. We performed experiments independent of technology and clock frequency by varying the latency of each structure individually, while keeping its capacity unchanged. We measured how IPC changed with different latencies for each structure. We performed similar experiments to find the sensitivity of IPC to the capacity of each structure. We then used these two IPC sensitivity curves to determine, at each clock frequency, the capacity (and therefore latency) of every structure that will provide maximum performance. With that "best" configuration we simulated structures that were

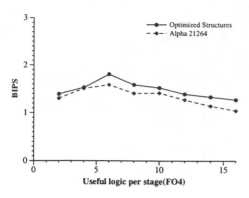

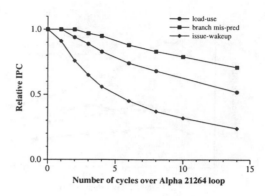

Figure 7: The harmonic mean of the performance of all SPEC 2000 benchmarks when optimal on-chip microarchitectural structure capacities are selected.

Figure 8: IPC sensitivity to critical loops in the data path. The x-axis of this graph shows the number of cycles the loop was extended over its length in the Alpha 21264 pipeline. The y-axis shows relative IPC.

slightly larger/slower and smaller/faster to verify that the configuration was indeed optimal for that clock rate. At a clock with ϕ_{logic} of 6 FO4, the major on-chip structures have the following configuration: a level-1 data cache of 64KB, and 6 cycle access latency; a level-2 cache with 512KB, and 12 cycle access latency and a 64 entry instruction window with a 3 cycle latency. We assumed all on-chip structures were pipelined.

Figure 7 shows the performance of a pipeline with optimally configured microarchitectural structures plotting performance against ϕ_{logic}. This graph shows the harmonic mean of the performance (accounting for $\phi_{overhead}$) of all the SPEC 2000 benchmarks. The solid curve is the performance of a Alpha 21264 pipeline when the best size and latency is chosen for each structure at each clock speed. The dashed curve in the graph is the performance of the Alpha 21264 pipeline, similar to Figure 5. When structure capacities are optimized at each clock frequency, on the average, performance increases by approximately 14%. However, maximum performance is still obtained when ϕ_{logic} is 6 FO4.

4.6 Effect of Pipelining on IPC

Thus far we have examined scaling of the entire processor pipeline. In general, increasing overall pipeline depth of a processor decreases IPC because of dependencies within *critical loops* in the pipeline [2] [13]. These critical loops include issuing an instruction and waking its dependent instructions (issue-wake up), issuing a load instruction and obtaining the correct value (DL1 access time), and predicting a branch and resolving the correct execution path. For high performance it is important that these loops execute in the fewest cycles possible. When the processor pipeline depth is increased, the lengths of these critical loops are also increased, causing a decrease in IPC. In this section we quantify the performance effects of each of the above critical loops and in Section 5 we propose a technique to design the instruction window so that in most cases the issue-delay loop is 1 cycle.

To examine the impact of the length of critical loops on IPC, we scaled the length of each loop independently, keeping the access latencies of other structures to be the same as those of the Alpha 21264. Figure 8 shows the IPC sensitivity

of the integer benchmarks to the branch misprediction penalty, the DL1 access time (load-use) and the issue-wake up loop. The x-axis of this graph shows the number of cycles the loop was extended over its length in the Alpha 21264 pipeline. The y-axis shows IPC relative to the baseline Alpha 21264 processor. IPC is most sensitive to the issue-wake up loop, followed by the load-use and branch misprediction penalty. The issue-wake up loop is most sensitive because it affects every instruction that is dependent on another instruction for its input values. The branch misprediction penalty is the least sensitive of the three critical loops because modern branch predictors have reasonably high accuracies and the misprediction penalty is paid infrequently. The floating-point benchmarks showed similar trends with regard to their sensitivity to critical loops. However, overall they were less sensitive to all three loops than integer benchmarks.

The results from Figure 8 show that the ability to execute dependent instructions back to back is essential to performance. Similar obsevations have been made in other studies [13] [1].

5 A Segmented Instruction Window Design

In modern superscalar pipelines, the instruction issue window is a critical component, and a naive pipelining strategy that prevents dependent instructions from being issued back to back would unduly limit performance. In this section we propose a method to pipeline the instruction issue window to enable clocking it at high frequencies.

To issue new instructions every cycle, the instructions in the instruction issue window are examined to determine which ones can be issued (wake up). The instruction selection logic then decides which of the woken instructions can be selected for issue. Stark *et al.* showed that pipelining the instruction window, but sacrificing the ability to execute dependent instructions in consecutive cycles, can degrade performance by up to 27% compared to an ideal machine [13].

Figure 9 shows a high-level representation of an instruction window. Every cycle that a result is produced, the tag associated with the result (*destination tag*) is broadcast to all entries

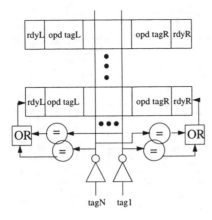

Figure 9: A high-level representation of the instruction window.

in the instruction window. Each instruction entry in the window compares the destination tag with the tags of its source operands (*source tags*). If the tags match, the corresponding source operand for the matching instruction entry is marked as ready. A separate logic block (not shown in the figure) selects instructions to issue from the pool of ready instructions. At every cycle, instructions in any location in the window can be woken up and selected for issue. In the following cycle, empty slots in the window, from instructions issued in the previous cycle, are reclaimed and up to four new instructions can be written into the window. In this section, we first describe and evaluate a method to pipeline instruction wake-up and then evaluate a technique to pipeline instruction selection logic.

5.1 Pipelining Instruction Wakeup

Palacharla *et al.* [11] argued that three components constitute the delay to wake up instructions: the delay to broadcast the tags, the delay to perform tag comparisons, and the delay to OR the individual match lines to produce the ready signal. Their studies show that the delay to broadcast the tags will be a significant component of the overall delay at feature sizes of 180nm and below. To reduce the tag broadcast latency, we propose organizing the instruction window into stages, as shown in Figure 10. Each stage consists of a fixed number of instruction entries and consecutive stages are separated by latches. A set of destination tags are broadcast to only one stage during a cycle. The latches between stages hold these tags so that they can be broadcast to the next stage in the following cycle. For example, if an issue window capable of holding 32 instructions is divided into two stages of 16 entries each, a set of tags are broadcast to the first stage in the first cycle. In the second cycle the same set of tags are broadcast to the next stage, while a new set of tags are broadcast to the first 16 entries. At every cycle, the entire instruction window can potentially be woken up by a different set of destination tags at each stage. Since each tag is broadcast across only a small part of the window every cycle, this instruction window can be clocked at high frequencies. However, the tags of results produced in a cycle can wake up instructions only in the first stage of the window during that cycle. Therefore, dependent instructions can be issued

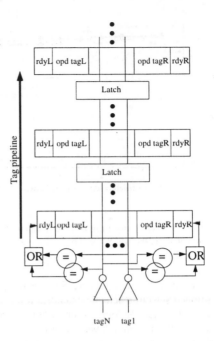

Figure 10: A segmented instruction window wherein the tags are broadcast to one stage of the instruction window at a time. We also assume that instructions can be selected from the entire window.

back to back only if they are in the first stage of the window.

We evaluated the effect of pipelining the instruction window on IPC by varying the pipeline depth of a 32-entry instruction window from 1 to 10 stages. Figure 11 shows the results from our experiments when the number of stages of the window is varied from 1 to 10. Note that the x-axis on this graph is the pipeline depth of the wake-up logic. The plot shows that IPC of integer and vector benchmarks remain unchanged until the window is pipelined to a depth of 4 stages. The overall decrease in IPC of the integer benchmarks when the pipeline depth of the window is increased from 1 to 10 stages is approximately 11%. The floating-point benchmarks show a decrease of 5% for the same increase in pipeline depth. Note that this decrease is small compared to that of naive pipelining, which prevents dependent instructions from issuing consecutively.

5.2 Pipelining Instruction Select

In addition to wake-up logic, the selection logic determines the latency of the instruction issue pipeline stage. In a conventional processor, the select logic examines the entire instruction window to select instructions for issue. We propose to decrease the latency of the selection logic by reducing its fan-in. As with the instruction wake-up, the instruction window is partitioned into stages as shown in Figure 12. The selection logic is partitioned into two operations: *preselection* and *selection*. A preselection logic block is associated with all stages of the instruction window (S2-S4) except the first one. Each of these logic blocks examines all instructions in its stage and picks one or more instructions to be considered for selection. A selection logic block (S1) selects instructions for issue from among all ready instructions in the first section

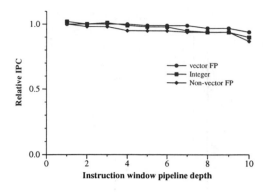

Figure 11: IPC sensitivity to instruction window pipeline depth, assuming all entries in the window can be considered for selection.

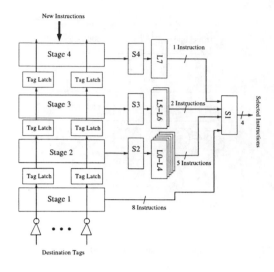

Figure 12: A 32-entry instruction window partitioned into four stages with a selection logic fan-in of 16 instructions

and the instructions selected by S2-S4. Each logic block in this partitioned selection scheme examines fewer instructions compared to the selection logic in conventional processors and can therefore operate with a lower latency.

Although several configurations of instruction window and selection logic are possible depending on the instruction window capacity, pipeline depth, and selection fan-in, in this study we evaluate the specific implementation shown in Figure 12. This instruction window consists of 32-entries partitioned into four stages and is configured so that the fan-in of S1 is 16. Since each stage in the window contains 8 instructions and all the instructions in Stage 1 are considered for selection by S1, up to 8 instructions may be pre-selected. Older instructions in the instruction window are considered to be more critical than younger ones. Therefore the preselection blocks are organized so that the stages that contain the older instructions have a greater share of the pre-selected instructions. The logic blocks S2, S3, and S4 pre-select instructions from the second, third, and fourth stage of the window respectively. Each select logic block can select from any instruction within its stage that is ready. However, S2 can pre-select a maximum of five instructions, S3 a maximum of 2 and S4 can pre-select only one instruction. The selection process works in the following manner. At every clock cycle, preselection logic blocks S2-S4 pick from ready instructions in their stage. The instructions pre-selected by these blocks are stored in latches L1-L7 at the end of the cycle. In the second cycle the select logic block S1 selects 4 instructions from among all the ready instructions in Stage 1 and those in L1-L7 to be issued to functional units.

With an instruction window and selection logic as described above, the IPC of integer benchmarks was reduced by only 4% compared to a processor with a single cycle, 32-entry, non-pipelined instruction window and select fan-in of 32. The IPC of floating-point benchmarks was reduced by only 1%. The rather small impact of pipelining the instruction window on IPC is not surprising. The floating-point benchmarks have fewer dependences in their instruction streams than integer codes, and therefore remain unaffected by the increased wake up penalties. For the integer benchmarks, most of the dependent instructions are fairly close to the instructions that produce their source values. Also, the instruction window adjusts its contents at the beginning of every cycle so that the

older instructions collect to one end of the window. This feature causes dependent instructions to eventually collect at the "bottom" of the window and thus enables them to be woken up with less delay. This segmented window design will be capable of operating at greater frequencies than conventional designs at the cost of minimal degradation in IPC.

6 Related Work

Aside from the work of Kunkel and Smith [9] discussed in Section 4, the most relevant related work explores alternate designs for improving instruction window latencies. Stark *et al.* [13] proposed a technique to pipeline instruction wake up and select logic. In their technique, instructions are woken up "speculatively" when their *grandparents* are issued. The rationale behind this technique is that if an instruction's grandparents' tags are broadcast during the current cycle its *parents* will probably be issued the same cycle. While speculatively woken instructions can be selected, they cannot be issued until their parents have been issued. Although this technique reduces the IPC of the processor compared to a conventional 1-cycle instruction window, it enables the instruction window to function at a higher clock frequency.

Brown *et al.* [1] proposed a method to move selection logic off the critical path. In this method, wake-up and select are partitioned into two separate stages. In the first stage (wake-up) instructions in the window are woken up by producer tags, similar to a regular instruction window. All instructions that wake up speculate they will be selected for issue in the following cycle and assert their "available" signals. In the next cycle, the result tags of these instructions are broadcast to the window, as though all of them have been issued. However, the selection logic selects only a limited number of instructions from those that asserted their "available" signal. Instructions that do not get selected (*collision victims*) and any dependents that are woken up before they can be issued (*pileup victims*) are detected and re-scheduled. The authors show that this technique has an IPC within 3% of a machine with single-cycle scheduling logic.

7 Conclusion

In this paper, we measured the effects of varying clock frequency on the performance of a superscalar pipeline. We determined the amount of useful logic per stage (ϕ_{logic}) that will provide the best performance is approximately 6 FO4 inverter delays for integer benchmarks. If ϕ_{logic} is reduced below 6 FO4 the improvement in clock frequency cannot compensate for the decrease in IPC. Conversely, if ϕ_{logic} is increased to more than 6 FO4 the improvement in IPC is not enough to counteract the loss in performance resulting from a lower clock frequency. For vector floating-point benchmarks the optimal ϕ_{logic} was at 4 FO4. The clock period (ϕ_{logic} + $\phi_{overhead}$) at the optimal point is 7.8 FO4 for integer benchmarks, corresponding to a frequency of 3.6GHz at 100nm technology. For vector floating-point benchmarks the optimal clock period is 5.8 FO4 which corresponds to 4.8GHz at 100nm technology.

These optimal clock frequencies can be achieved only if on-chip microarchitectural structures can be pipelined to operate at high frequencies. We identified the instruction issue window as a critical structure, which will be difficult to scale to those frequencies. We propose a segmented instruction window design that will allow it to be pipelined to four stages without significant decrease in IPC. Scaling the pipeline depth of the window to 10 stages only decreases the IPC of SPEC 2000 integer benchmarks by 11% and floating-point benchmarks by 5%.

Although this study uses the parameters of a 100nm technology, our use of the technology-independent FO4 metric will permit our results to be translated to other technologies. We assume that 1 FO4 corresponds to 360 picoseconds times the transistor's drawn gate length. But, for highly tuned processes, such as the Intel 0.13-μm process, the drawn gate length and effective gate length may differ substantially [16]. However, our estimate of the optimal pipeline depth remains unchanged regardless of the exact value assigned to a FO4 delay though the actual cycle time will depend on the operating conditions and process technology specifications.

While we did not consider the effects of slower wires, they should not affect this study, which uses a fixed microarchitecture. To first order, wire delays remain constant as a fixed design is scaled to smaller feature sizes [15]. Although wire resistance increases, wire lengths decrease, thus preserving the absolute wire delay across technologies. However, long wires that arise as design complexity increases can have a substantial impact on the pipelining of the microarchitecture. For example, the high clock rate target of the Intel Pentium IV forced the designers to dedicate two pipeline stages just for data transportation [5]. We will examine the effects of wire delays on our pipeline models and optimal clock rate selection in future work.

Microprocessor performance has improved at about 55% per year for the last three decades, with much of the gains resulting from higher clock frequencies, due to process technology and deeper pipelines. However, our results show that pipelining can contribute *at most* another factor of two to clock rate improvements. Subsequently, in the best case, clock rates will increase at the rate of feature size scaling, which is projected to be 12-20% per year. Any additional performance improvements must come from increases in concurrency, whether they be instruction-level parallelism, thread-level parallelism, or a combination of the two. If the goal is to maintain historical performance growth rates, concurrency must start increasing at 33% per year and sustain a total of 50 IPC within the next 15 years. While this goal presents tremendous challenges, particularly in the face of increasing on-chip communication delays, rich opportunities for novel architectures lie ahead.

Acknowledgments

We thank the anonymous referees for their comments and suggestions. Thanks also to Mary Brown and members of the CART research group for their valuable suggestions. This research is supported by the Defense Advanced Research Projects Agency under contract F33615-01-C-1892, NSF CAREER grants CCR-9985109 and CCR-9984336, two IBM University Partnership awards, and a grant from the Intel Research Council.

References

[1] Mary D Brown, Jared Stark, and Yale N. Patt. Select-free instruction scheduling logic. In *Proceedings of the 34rd International Symposium on Microarchitecture*, pages 204–213, December 2001.

[2] Anantha Chandrakasan, William J. Bowhill, and Frank Fox ,editors. *Design of High-Performance Microprocessor Circuits*. IEEE Press, Piscataway, NJ, 2001.

[3] Rajagopalan Desikan, Doug Burger, and Stephen W. Keckler. Measuring experimental error in microprocessor simulation. In *Proceedings of the 28th Annual International Symposium on Computer Architecture*, pages 266–277, July 2001.

[4] Seongmoo Heo, Ronny Krashinsky, and Krste Asanović. Activity-sensitive flip-flop and latch selection for reduced energy. In *Conference on Advanced Research in VLSI*, pages 59–74, March 2001.

[5] Glenn Hinton, Dave Sager, Mike Upton, Darrell Boggs, Doug Carmean, Alan Kyker, and Patrice Roussel. The microarchitecture of the pentium 4 processor. *Intel Technology Journal*, 1, February 2001.

[6] Ron Ho, Kenneth W. Mai, and Mark A. Horowitz. The future of wires. *Proceedings of the IEEE*, 89(4):490–504, April 2001.

[7] Norman P. Jouppi and Steven J. E. Wilton. An enhanced access and cycle time model for on-chip caches. Technical Report 93.5, Compaq Computer Corporation, July 1994.

[8] James S. Kolodzey. Cray-1 computer technology. *IEEE Transactions on Components, Hybrids, and Manufacturing Technology CHMT-4(2)*, 4(2):181–187, March 1981.

[9] Steven R. Kunkel and James E. Smith. Optimal pipelining in supercomputers. In *Proceedings of the 13th Annual International Symposium on Computer Architecture*, pages 404–411, June 1986.

[10] Nasser A. Kurd, Javed S. Barkatullah, Rommel O. Dizon, Thomas D. Fletcher, and Paul D. Madland. Multi-GHz clocking scheme for Intel Pentium 4 microprocessor. In *Proceedings of the International Solid-state Circuits Conference*, pages 404–405, February 2001.

[11] Subbarao Palacharla, Norman P. Jouppi, and J.E. Smith. Complexity-effective superscalar processors. In *Proceedings of the 24th Annual International Symposium on Computer Architecture*, pages 206–218, June 1997.

[12] Premkishore Shivakumar and Norman P. Jouppi. Cacti 3.0: An integrated cache timing, power and area model. Technical Report 2001/2, Compaq Computer Corporation, August 2001.

[13] Jared Stark, Mary D. Brown, and Yale N. Patt. On pipelining dynamic instruction scheduling logic. In *Proceedings of the 33rd International Symposium on Microarchitecture*, pages 57–66, December 2000.

[14] Vladimir Stojanović and Vojin G. Oklobdžija. Comparative analysis of master-slave latches and flip-flops for high-performance and low-power systems. *IEEE Journal of Solid-state Circuits*, 34(4):536–548, April 1999.

[15] Dennis Sylvester and Kurt Keutzer. Rethinking deep-submicron circuit design. *IEEE Computer*, 32(11):25–33, November 1999.

[16] S. Tyagi, M. Alavi, R. Bigwood, T. Bramblett, J. Brandenburg, W. Chen, B. Crew, M. Hussein, P. Jacob, C. Kenyon, C. Lo, B. Mcintyre, Z. Ma, P. Moon, P. Nguyen, L. Rumaner, R. Schweinfurth, S. Sivakumar, M. Stettler, S. Thompson, B. Tufts, J. Xu, S. Yang, and M. Bohr. A 130nm generation logic technology featuring 70nm transistors, dual vt transistors and 6 layers of cu interconnects. In *Proceedings of International Electronic Devices Meeting*, December 2000.

A ECL gate equivalent in FO4

The Cray-1S processor was designed in an ECL technology, using four and five input NAND gates [8] with eight gate levels at every pipeline stage. Because of its implementation from discrete ECL devices and the design of transmission lines for the wires connecting the chips, the latency of one wire and one gate delay were roughly equivalent. Furthermore, because of the transmission line effect of the wires, additional gate fanout loading can largely be ignored. The result is that the latency of a pipeline stage was approximately equal to the delay of 16 logic gates. Our CMOS equivalent of one Cray ECL gate circuit consists of a 4-input NAND driving a 5-input NAND, where the first accounts for gate delay and the second accounts for the wire delay. Figure 13 shows the test circuit we used to perform this measurement. SPICE simulations show that this one ECL gate equivalent has a latency equal to 1.36 FO4.

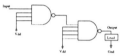

Figure 13: Circuit to measure the delay of CRAY-1S gates in terms of FO4.

Increasing Processor Performance by Implementing Deeper Pipelines

Eric Sprangle, Doug Carmean

Pentium® Processor Architecture Group, Intel Corporation

eric.sprangle@intel.com, douglas.m.carmean@intel.com

Abstract

One architectural method for increasing processor performance involves increasing the frequency by implementing deeper pipelines. This paper will explore the relationship between performance and pipeline depth using a Pentium® 4 processor like architecture as a baseline and will show that deeper pipelines can continue to increase performance.

This paper will show that the branch misprediction latency is the single largest contributor to performance degradation as pipelines are stretched, and therefore branch prediction and fast branch recovery will continue to increase in importance. We will also show that higher performance cores, implemented with longer pipelines for example, will put more pressure on the memory system, and therefore require larger on-chip caches. Finally, we will show that in the same process technology, designing deeper pipelines can increase the processor frequency by 100%, which, when combined with larger on-chip caches can yield performance improvements of 35% to 90% over a Pentium® 4 like processor.

1. Introduction

Determining the target frequency of the processor is one of the fundamental decisions facing a microprocessor architect. While historical debate of pushing frequency or IPC to improve performance continues, many argue that modern processors have pushed pipelines beyond their optimal depth. With the fundamental debate raging, most agree that the engineering complexity and effort increases substantially with deeper pipelines. Focusing on single stream performance, and using the Pentium® 4 processor as a baseline architecture, this paper will conclude that pipelines can be further lengthened beyond the Pentium® 4 processor's 20 stages to improve performance. We assert that architectural advances will enable even deeper pipelines, although engineering effort and other considerations may be the real limiter.

2. Overview

We will propose a model to predict performance as a function of pipeline depth and cache size. First, we will determine the sensitivity of IPC to the depth of important pipelines. Then, we will describe how a cycle can be thought of as the sum of "useful time" and "overhead time", and that the frequency can be increased by reducing the amount of "useful time" per cycle. We will then show that deeper pipelines can increase the frequency to more than offset the decrease in IPC. We will then describe how execution time can be thought of as the sum of "core time" and "memory time" and show how "memory time" can be reduced with larger caches. Finally, we will show how the combination of deeper pipelines and larger caches can increase performance significantly.

3. Fundamental processor loops

Performance can monotonically increase with increased pipeline depth as long as the latency associated with the pipeline is not exposed systematically. Unfortunately, due to the unpredictable nature of code and data streams, the pipeline cannot always be filled correctly and the flushing of the pipeline exposes the latency. These flushes are inevitable, and pipeline exposures decrease IPC as the pipeline depth increases. For example, a branch misprediction exposes the branch misprediction pipeline, and the exposure penalty increases as the pipeline depth increases. The L1 cache pipeline can also be exposed if there are not enough independent memory operations sent to the L1 cache to saturate the pipeline. Of course, some pipeline latencies are more important than others. We simulated the performance sensitivities to the various loops on a Pentium® 4 processor like architecture to understand which loops are the most performance sensitive.

4. Simulation methodology

We conducted our experiments using an execution driven simulator called "Skeleton", which is a high level simulator that is typically used for coarse level architectural trade-off analysis. The simulator is layered on top of a uOp-level, IA32 architectural simulator that executes "Long Instruction Trace (LIT)"s. A LIT is not, as the name implies, a trace, rather it is a snapshot of processor architectural state that includes the state of system memory. Included in the LIT is a list of "LIT injections" which are system interrupts that are needed to simulate system events such as DMA traffic. Since the LIT includes an entire snapshot of memory, this methodology can execute both user and kernel instructions, as well as wrong path effects. Our simulation methodology uses carefully chosen, 30 million instruction program snippets to model the characteristics of the overall application.

Our simulations are based on a Pentium® 4 like processor described in Table 1. The results will be limited to the suites listed in Table 2 for a total of 91 benchmarks that are comprised of 465 LITs.

Table 1: Simulated 2GHz Pentium® 4 like processor configuration.

Core
3-wide fetch/retire
2 ALUs (running at 2x frequency)
1 load and store / cycle
In-order allocation/de-allocation of buffers
512 rob entries, load buffers and store buffers
Memory System
64 kB/8-way I-cache
8 kB/4-way L1 D-cache, 2 cycle latency
256 kB/8-way unified L2 cache, 12 cycle latency
3.2 GB/sec memory system, 165ns average latency
Perfect memory disambiguation
16 kB Gshare branch predictor
Streaming based hardware prefetcher

Table 2: Simulated Benchmark Suites

Suite	Number of Benchmarks	Description
SPECint95	8	spec.org
Multimedia	22	speech recognition, mpeg, photoshop, ray tracing, rsa
Productivity	13	sysmark2k internet/business/ productivity, Premiere
SPECfp2k	10	spec.org
SPECint2k	12	spec.org
Workstation	14	CAD, rendering
Internet	12	webmark2k, specjbb

5. Efficiency vs. pipeline depth

Figure 1 shows the relative IPC as the branch misprediction penalty is increased from 20 to 30 cycles. We can determine the average branch misprediction latency sensitivity by calculating the average IPC degradation when increasing the branch misprediction latency by one cycle.

It is interesting to note that SPECint95 is much more sensitive to the branch misprediction latency than the other application classes. To a lesser extent SPECint2k also shows greater sensitivity to branch misprediction latency than the other application classes. In this sense, SPECint95 in particular is not representative of general desktop applications because of the higher branch misprediction rates.

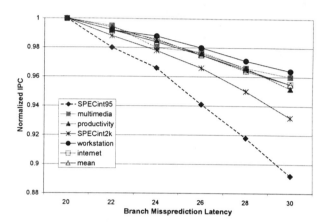

Figure 1: Normalized performance vs. branch misprediction latency.

To understand the sensitivity to the ALU loop latency, we started with a baseline processor that implements half clock cycle add operations, like the implementation in the Pentium® 4 processor. The Pentium® 4 processor pipelines the ALU operation into 3 "half" cycles: lower 16 bit ALU, upper 16 bit ALU, flag generation [2]. Figure 2 shows the effect of increasing the ALU latency from 1 half clock cycle to 3 full clock cycles while keeping the ALU throughput constant. Hence, for a workload that consists of independent ALU operations, we would expect to see no increase or degradation in performance, but for a stream of dependent ALU operations, execution time would increase linearly with the ALU latency.

In Table 3, we show the performance impact of adding an additional full cycle to a given loop. For example, the impact of increasing the ALU latency by a full clock cycle is 4.76%. As Table 3 shows, the ALU loop is, by far, the most performance sensitive loop on integer applications.

Table 3: Average percentage performance degradation when a loop is lengthened by 1 cycle.

Suite	ALU	L1 cache	L2 cache	Br Miss
SPECint95	5.64	0.72	0.32	1.08
Multimedia	3.84	2.08	0.54	0.40
Productivity	7.00	2.20	0.50	0.48
SPECfp2k	0.76	1.08	0.24	0.26
SPECint2k	4.96	2.56	0.90	0.68
workstation	3.16	2.64	0.82	0.36
internet	3.96	2.00	0.46	0.45
Average	4.76	2.04	0.54	0.45

It is important to note that the performance results are a strong function of algorithmic assumptions in the microarchitecture. For example, we would expect L2 cache sensitivity to be a function of the L1 cache size and branch misprediction latency sensitivity to be a function of the branch predictor.

We are also making the approximation that these sensitivities have a constant incremental impact on IPC for the pipeline length ranges we are interested in. For example, a path with a 10% sensitivity would drop performance to 90% on the first cycle and $(1-10\%)^2$ or to 81% on the second cycle.

Typically, a larger portion of the engineering effort allocated to a project is spent on the latency sensitive paths. The effort is spent developing aggressive architectural and circuit solutions to these paths, as well as careful analysis of the specific implementations. Solutions such as clustering[1] or slicing[2] are typically employed to limit performance degradation as pipeline frequency is increased.

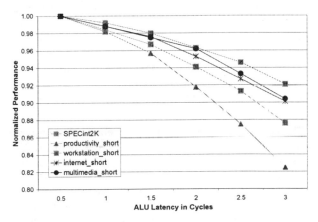

Figure 2: Performance vs. ALU latency.

6. Pipeline depth vs. frequency

Consider the branch misprediction pipeline in our Pentium® 4 like processor. The 20 stage misprediction pipeline includes the time required for a branch instruction to be issued, schedule, resolved and send a signal back to the front end to redirect the instruction stream.

A 2GHz Pentium® 4 processor has a 500ps cycle time, with a portion of the cycle used for skew, jitter, latching and other pipeline overheads. The cycle time that is not used for pipeline overhead is then dedicated for useful work. Assuming that the pipeline overhead per cycle is 90 ps, one can calculate the total "algorithmic work" associated with the branch misprediction pipeline as the number of stages * useful work/stage, or (20 stages* (500ps – 90ps) = 8200 ps of algorithmic work in branch miss loop).

In these calculations, we have included the communication time in the "useful work" component of the cycle time. The communication time includes the latency of wire delays, and therefore the "useful work" in a path is a function of the floorplan. This is particularly relevant in areas such as the branch misprediction loop, where the latency of driving the misprediction signal from the branch resolution unit to the front end becomes a key component of the overall loop latency

If we assume that the overhead per cycle is constant in a given circuit technology, in this case 90 ps, we can increase the processor frequency by reducing the "useful time" per cycle. As the useful time per cycle approaches zero, the total cycle time approaches the "overhead time". Because of the constant overhead, the frequency does not approach infinity but rather 1/90ps or 11.1GHz as shown in Figure 3. There are many other practical limits that would be reached before 11GHz, some of which will be discussed later.

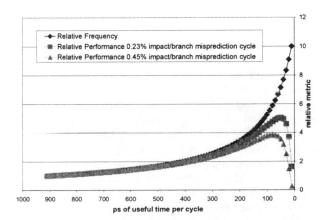

Figure 3: Frequency and relative performance vs. ps of useful time per cycle.

As we increase the pipeline depth, the staging overhead of the branch misprediction pipeline increases, which increases the branch misprediction latency, effectively lowering the overall IPC. If we assume IPC degrades by 0.45% per additional branch misprediction cycle (the average branch loop latency sensitivity from Table 3), we can calculate the overall performance as a function of "useful time" per cycle, as shown in Figure 3. (note that we are comprehending the efficiency impact of increasingly *only* the branch misprediction latency in this example).

As expected, the overall performance degrades when the decrease in IPC outweighs the increase in frequency. From Figure 3 we see that performance tracks closely with frequency until the useful time per cycle reaches about 90 ps, which equates to a cycle time of 180ps. As a point of comparison, the 180ps cycle time is roughly half the cycle time of a Pentium® 4 processor. If we assume that the sensitivity is cut in half, or 0.23% per additional branch misprediction cycle, we see that the potential overall performance increase is higher and the optimal point has a smaller useful time per cycle.

7. Off-chip memory latency

It is important to note that in the proceeding analysis, the percentage of time waiting for memory was held constant. This was a simplification that is technically incorrect, as the percentage of time waiting for memory increases as the core performance increases. This assumption does not change the optimal frequency, as minimizing the core time will minimize the overall program execution time. Further, we will show that the percentage of time that is spent waiting for memory can be reduced by increasing the size of the on-chip L2 cache. In subsequent discussions, we will show that the cache miss rate will decrease as the square root of the increase in L2 cache size.

8. Pipelining overhead

In the Pentium® 4 processor, the clock skew and jitter overhead is about 51ps [3]. In a conservative ASIC design, the overhead is the sum of the clock skew and jitter combined with the latch delay. In a standard 0.18um process, a typical flop equates to about 3 FO4 delays, with the FO4 delay being about 25ps [5]. Therefore in a 0.18um process, pipeline overhead would come out to about 75ps + 51ps = 125ps. In a custom design flow, most of the clock skew and jitter overhead can be hidden by using time borrowing circuit techniques. Time borrowing uses soft clock edges to reduce or eliminate the impact of clock skew and jitter [4] which would yield a 75ps pipeline overhead. In an extreme custom design style, the flop overhead could be reduced by using techniques like pulsed clocks and/or direct domino pipelines, yielding a sub-50ps pipelining overhead at the cost of a much larger design effort.

At the extreme edge of pipelining, here defined as a cycle time of less than 300ps in a 0.18um process, the design effort increases rapidly because of the minimum/maximum delay design windows that arises as the pipeline cycle is reduced. The minimum delay must always be larger than the sum of clock skew and jitter + latch hold time. If this constraint is not honored, then the output of combinational logic may be lost, through transitions, before it can be latched [4].

We will assume that most pipeline interfaces can be at least partially time borrowed and therefore use an average overhead of 90ps per cycle, which is the nominal overhead assumed on Pentium® 4 processor[5].

Note that, in the past, the global skew has been kept under control through better circuit techniques. For example, the Pentium® Pro processor global skew was 250ps [6] with an initial cycle time of 8000ps (3.1% cycle time) and the Pentium® 4 processor used a global skew of 20ps [3] with an initial cycle time of 667ps (3.0% of cycle time). However, this paper will assume overhead does not scale with frequency, and we will use 90ps as a baseline overhead time

9. The limits of pipelining

Implicit in our pipeline scaling analysis is that the pipeline depth can be arbitrarily increased. While this assumption is generally true, the complexity associated with increasing pipelines increases rapidly in some of the fundamental loops. Some of the pipelines in a processor include "loops" where a stage requires the result of the previous stage for execution. In these loops that require value bypassing between stages, any latency increase will directly reduce the processor's overall IPC. As we have shown, some of the loops are more critical than others (especially the ALU loop, L1 cache latency loop and branch misprediction loop). We will look at a case study to better understand the fundamental limits of pipelining.

9.1. Pipelining the RAT

The Pentium® 4 processor register renaming algorithm is similar to those implemented in other out-of-order processors, such as the Alpha 21264 [1]. The register renaming algorithm involves several steps where architectural registers are mapped to physical registers. The first step requires that the destination register in a given uOP is mapped to a physical register. Then, a mapping process renames all the register sources in the uop to the physical registers assigned to the previous uop that generated this particular register instance. A "Register Alias Table" (RAT) holds the mapping from architectural to physical register. Algorithmically, a uop reads the RAT to determine the physical register for each of its architectural source registers and then writes the RAT to record the physical location of its architectural destination. The next uop (in program order) reads and writes the RAT and so on. In this scheme, it is possible for a uop source to match the destination of the previous uop.

If we stretch the pipeline so that an update to a RAT entry followed by a read to the same entry takes 2 cycles, then a level of bypassing is needed to cover the write to read latency as seen in Figure 4, 2 stage pipeline. The multiplexer that is used to implement the bypassing increases the amount of useful work to cover the additional latency. If the pipeline is further stretched to 3 cycles, then an additional bypass stage is needed (Figure 4, 3 stage pipeline), but because the bypass is done in parallel with the RAT, the amount of useful work in the critical path does not increase. As we increase the depth of the pipeline in the RAT, the amount of useful work increases when going from 1 to 2 cycles, and then remains constant thereafter. This is because once we include a final bypass mux, we do not need to add additional bypass muxes in the rename path as the pipeline depth is increased.

What is the limit of pipelining for the RAT? Eventually the number of muxes needed to cover the write to read latency in the RAT causes the delay through the muxes to be larger than the delay through the RAT (Figure 4, 4 stage pipeline). When this happens, the amount of useful work as we go through the path is increased again. At this point we can continue to increase the depth of the pipeline, but at the expense of increased latency

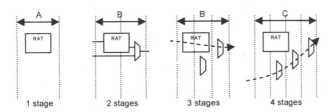

Figure 4: Pipelining the RAT

As we continue to increase the depth of the global pipeline, the next interesting challenge is posed by the register file. When the depth of the register file pipeline increases to the point where individual components of the array access need to be pipelined, it becomes convenient to add a latch immediately after the bit-line sense amplifiers. However, adding a latch in the word-line access or within the bit-line drive becomes very problematic. Rather than attempting to add a latch within a word or bit line, the preferred method is to partition the structure into one or more pieces. Our analysis implicitly

assumes we can overcome this problem through partitioning, or some other means, and that all of the pipelines that are scaled do not add useful work to the critical path.

9.2. Pipelining wires

There are plenty of places in the Pentium® 4 processor architecture where the wires were pipelined [9]. While it is straightforward to calculate the percentage of the processor that can be reached in a cycle, it is relatively uninteresting, as there is an existence proof that pipelining wires is an effective mechanism to overcome intrinsic wire latency.

10. Overall performance vs. pipeline depth

We can estimate overall performance vs. pipeline depth when using the same fundamental algorithms implemented in the Pentium® 4 processor architecture. We will assume we can pipeline the next fetch address generation loop (through architectural techniques, for example [7][8]) and the renaming loop without increasing the latency for back to back operations. However, the L1/L2 cache access time as well as the branch misprediction latency will increase. We will also assume that the ALUs in Pentium® 4 processor are running at the minimum possible latency, and that higher frequency designs will require additional latencies.

Based on these assumptions, we can build a model to estimate performance vs. pipeline depth. We will quote the branch missprediction pipeline depth, but we will scale all 4 of the critical loops. For example, we can calculate the frequency of a processor with a 50 stage branch misprediction loop by dividing the total useful time in the loop (assuming 90ps overhead per stage) as 20 stages * (500 ps − 90ps) = 8200ps. Dividing the total algorithmic time of 8200ps by 50 stages implies 164 ps useful time per stage. Adding back the 90ps overhead gives us a cycle time of 254ps for a frequency increase of 96%.

We can calculate the L1 cache latency in cycles by first calculating the algorithmic work as 2 stages * (500 ps − 90ps) = 820ps. Dividing this algorithmic work by the new "useful time" per cycle gives 820ps/164ps per stage or 5 stages. We can calculate the IPC impact of these loops by calculating all of the new loop latencies in cycles and calculating the degradation in IPC due to the increase of these individual loops. Taking the product of the individual components of IPC degradations gives the overall IPC degradation. Multiplying the new frequency by the new IPC gives the final performance curve vs pipeline depth as shown in Figure 5.

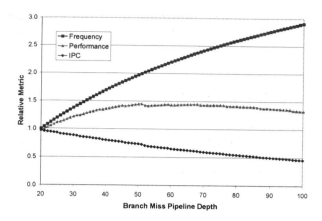

Figure 5: Frequency/IPC/Performance vs. branch misprediction pipeline depth.

Figure 5 shows that performance continues to increase as the pipeline is stretched up until the frequency is about doubled, which occurs when the branch misprediction pipeline reaches about 52 stages. The dips in the IPC and overall performance curves are due to the non-smooth nature of increasing pipeline depth – our analysis assumes that you can't add less then a full cycle to a pipeline.

Table 4 shows the individual loop lengths for a processor running at twice the frequency. Given these lengths, we can also calculate the individual IPC degradations due to each of the 4 loops, as well as the overall IPC degradation multiplier, as shown in Table 4. The relative IPC for each loop is calculated as $(1-\text{sensitivity})^{\text{increase in cycles}}$. The overall relative IPC is the product of the individual relative IPCs.

Even though the branch misprediction pipeline has the least per clock performance sensitivity, the absolute length of the branch misprediction pipeline makes it the loop with the single largest contribution to IPC loss. In a "from scratch" processor design, there is flexibility to change the fundamental algorithms that influence IPC. For example, there is opportunity to reduce IPC degradation by reducing the impact of branch misses through improved branch prediction.

Table 4: Pipeline lengths for a hypothetical Pentium® 4 like processor that runs at twice the frequency.

Loop	Pipeline Length	2x Freq Length	Sensitivity/ cycle	Relative IPC
ALU	0.5	1	4.76%	98%
L1 cache	2	4.5	2.04%	95%
L2 cache	12	32	0.54%	90%
Br Miss	20	52	0.45%	87%
Overall				72%

To validate the assumptions that the overall IPC degradation can be computed as the product of the individual degradations, we performed simulations at multiple effective frequencies, using the same methodology outlined above to generate the pipeline lengths.

Figure 6 shows the performance vs. pipeline depth as predicted by the analytical model and those produced by the performance simulator. As the data in the following chart shows, the simulated results align very closely with those produced by the analytical model for the pipeline depths of interest.

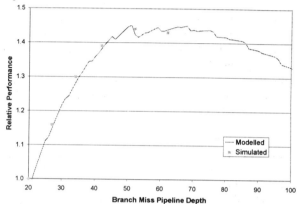

Figure 6: Simulated vs. modeled performance vs. branch misprediction pipeline depth.

11. Decreasing the impact of branch misses

There are many architectural and implementation methods for decreasing the branch misprediction penalty. Obviously, a more accurate branch predictor would decrease the IPC impact of additional cycles by reducing the number of times the branch misprediction loop is exposed. Alternatively, by implementing different architectural algorithms, a design can reduce the amount of useful work in the loop. For example, by more aggressively pre-decoding of instructions, perhaps by implementing a trace cache, a design can employ simpler, lower latency decoders, which reduces the algorithmic work in the branch misprediction loop.

In addition to reducing the algorithmic work, methods could try to reduce the "useless time" in the branch misprediction loop. For example, by implementing the front end to be twice as wide, and run at half the frequency, the amount of clock skew and jitter and latch delay associated with the loop is reduced while keeping the bandwidth the same (assuming the instruction fetch units that are twice as wide can really produce twice the number of uops per cycle). Another method that could reduce clock skew and jitter overhead involves using multiple clocks with smaller clock skew and jitter overheads within a clock domain, and larger overhead between clock domains.

Finally, designers can tune the speedpaths detected on silicon (by resizing transistors, and rearranging floorplans etc) which might exist because of the difficulties associated with identifying the speed paths pre-silicon. Determining speed paths beyond a given accuracy increases quickly because of complex interactions that determine speed path latencies. These interactions include in-die process variation, interconnect coupling, and the false path elimination problem (many of the speed paths that a tool may detect are "don't care" scenarios).

In our analytical model, we can estimate the upper bound potential of removing the branch misprediction penalty by eliminating the IPC degradation due to the longer branch misprediction penalty. Figure 7 shows the scaling benefits if the branch misprediction penalty could be completely removed, raising the performance increase potential from 45% to 90%. Deeper pipelines will increase the opportunity for new architectural techniques to improve performance.

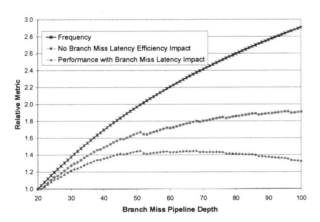

Figure 7: Freq/efficiency/performance vs. branch misprediction pipeline depth

Another way of improving the scaling of pipelines is to reduce the overhead due to pipelining (latch, clock skew, jitter, etc) through improvements in circuits and design methodologies. Moving from the 90ps overhead to a 50ps overhead, which is potentially achievable in an extreme custom design, the model predicts that the potential speedup improvement increases from about 45% to 65%, and as expected the optimal pipeline depth increases as the pipeline overhead is reduced, as shown in Figure 8.

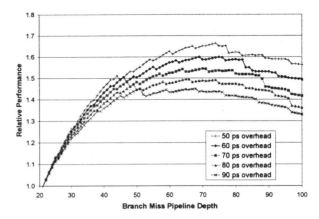

Figure 8: Performance vs. pipeline depth vs. pipeline overhead

12. Percentage time waiting for main memory

Program execution time can be broken into the "core time" (which scales with processor frequency) and "off-chip time" which is associated with off chip memory latencies. As we explained, our previous calculations have assumed that the percentage of time waiting for memory remains constant as the core performance is improved, which is wrong.

We can calculate the "core time" by running an application on two systems that differ only in processor frequency. We can get the performance of SPECint2k on multiple Pentium® 4 processors run between 1.5Ghz and 2GHz (we need to make sure the compiler does not change when quoting these numbers).

Figure 9 compares SPECint2k base (run on the Intel D850GB motherboard) for the Pentium® 4 processor vs. perfect scaling and shows that the Pentium® 4 processor converts about 65% of frequency increase into performance improvement. This degradation should be about the same for similar modern CPUs that use 256kB caches and have about the same performance (a quick analysis SPEC reported scores will confirm this). Therefore we can conclude that SPECint2k spends about 35% of its time waiting for main memory. This is important because it indicates the upper bound speedup achievable is 1/0.35 or 2.85x assuming we don't reduce the "off-chip time" (for example by improving the prefetching algorithms or increasing the size of the L2 cache).

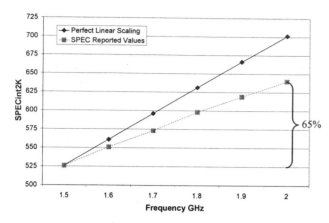

Figure 9: SPECint2K vs. frequency

We can calculate the percentage of time waiting for memory for each of our benchmark suites by varying the frequency of the simulated processor plus and minus 200 MHz, and running the LITs. Table 5 shows the percentage of time spent in core on the various benchmark suites on our base processor configuration. Notice that the percentage of core time generated by the simulator for SPECint2k matches closely the values reported to SPEC (65% calculated from SPEC numbers vs. 67% for the simulated results) which gives some confidence that the simulator is reasonably modeling the off chip memory system (bandwidth, latencies and prefetcher algorithms).

Table 5: Percentage of time spent in core calculated by simulating at 2 different frequencies.

Suite	% of core time
SPECint95	79
SPECint2k	67
Productivity	79
Workstation	76
Internet	70
Multimedia	74
SPECfp95	66
SPECfp2k	66
Average	72

13. Performance vs. cache size

To this point, all of the simulations have used the Pentium® 4 processor 256kB L2 cache configuration. As the frequency (performance) of the core is increased, the percentage of time spent waiting for memory increases. A common rule of thumb says that quadrupling the cache size will halve the miss rate of the cache. Figure 10 and

Figure 11 show that this rule of thumb is quite accurate for cache size ranges from 0.5 kB to 8 MB for SPECint2k and Sysmark2K. Since 30 million instruction traces might not be long enough to warm up an 8 MB cache, these simulations were done using much longer traces. While it is true that an individual benchmark can fit in a given cache size, the benchmark suites show that the rule of thumb holds for the average across all benchmarks in the suite.

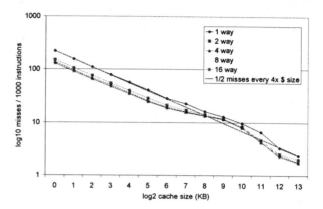

Figure 10: L2 cache misses/1000 instructions (SPECint2k average)

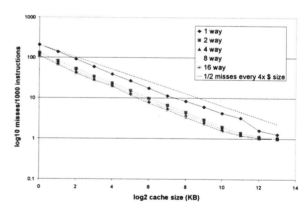

Figure 11: L2 cache misses / 1000 instructions (Sysmark2k average)

14. Increasing pipeline depth *and* L2 cache

Assuming that the miss rate decreases as 1/(sqrt (cache size)) as Figure 10 and Figure 11 suggest, then we can hold the percentage of time waiting for memory constant if we quadruple the size of the cache every time we double to core performance. We can apply this rule of thumb to our pipeline scaling model to estimate the speedups possible by both increasing pipeline depth and increasing L2 cache size as shown in Figure 12.

Assuming that 72% of the time scales with frequency with a 256kB cache, (the overall average for our benchmarks shown in Table 5), we can assume 28% of the time spent waiting for memory and will scale as 1/sqrt(cache size). The data shows that speedups of about 80% are possible when the pipeline is stretched to double frequency and L2 cache size is increased from 4MB to 8MB. Notice that the optimal pipeline depth is not a function of cache size, which makes sense because minimizing the core time is independent of minimizing the memory time.

In this analysis, we are not increasing the L2 cache latency as we increase the size, which is incorrect. Some portion of the L2 latency is a function of the L2 cache size.

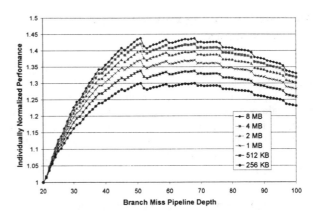

Figure 13: Performance vs. pipeline depth vs. L2$ size normalized.

15. Difficulties with deeper pipelines

Of course there are many issues associated with deeper pipelines that are beyond the scope of this paper. For example, *deeper pipelines* may imply more complex algorithms. On the other hand, *wider machines* may also imply more complex algorithms, so one might conclude that higher performance implies more complex algorithms. Given that we are attempting to build a higher performance processor, the fair question is "when is it easier to achieve higher performance through width vs. deeper pipelines?" The answer to this question may differ based on which part of the processor is being analyzed. For example, on the Pentium®4 processor, the answer in the fetch unit of the processor was presumably "wider is easier to achieve performance" since the fetch unit of the processor runs at half of the base frequency and achieves throughput by increasing width. This also makes sense in light of the relatively low branch misprediction latency sensitivity. The front end needs total bandwidth through whatever means possible and is less concerned with latency. On the other hand, the high sensitivity to latency in the execution core motivated running this piece of the processor at twice the base frequency.

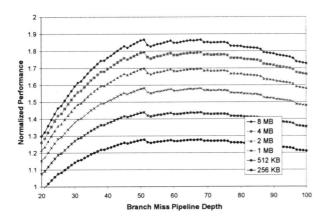

Figure 12: Performance vs. pipeline depth for different L2 cache sizes.

The next chart takes the same data and normalizes each of the cache size configurations so we can extract the performance improvement due only to the increase in pipeline depth. The data shows that increasing the pipeline depth can increase performance between about 30 and 45%, depending on how much of the speedup is watered down by waiting for the memory system.

There are many other problems associated with deeper pipelines. Deeper pipelines will put more pressure on accurate timing tools. New algorithms may need to be developed which will increase the number of interactions that need to be validated. More accurate architectural simulators will be needed to model those interactions to estimate performance and tune the architecture. Increasing performance through deeper pipelines will also increase power (although wider machines will also increase power).

16. Pipeline scaling and future process technologies

To a first order, increasing frequency by stretching the pipelines and increasing frequency by improving process are independent. Some components of skew and jitter will scale with process but some may not. Wires will not scale as fast as transistors [10], so wire dominated paths will need to be stretched even further (even an equivalent architecture, migrated to a future process, will require re-pipelining).

17. Conclusion and future directions

A simple model was discussed to predict processor performance as a function of pipeline depth and cache size. The model was shown to correlate to a simulator, and the simulator was shown to correlate to submitted SPEC results. Based on this model, we show that processor performance can in theory be improved relative to the Pentium® 4 processor by 35 to 90% by both increasing pipeline depth and cache size.

This paper argues that pipelines can be further optimized for performance given current architectural and circuit understanding. Better architectural algorithms and circuit techniques will increase the benefit of pipeline scaling. For example, SMT, which increases parallelism, should improve pipeline scaling. There are many exciting engineering challenges associated with deeper pipelines that will keep architects and designers entertained for years to come.

18. References

[1] R.E. Kessler. "The alpha 21264 microprocessor." IEEE Micro, 19(2):24-36, March/April 1999

[2] D. Sager et al., "A 0.18-um CMOS IA-32 microprocessor with a 4-GHz integer execution unit." In ISSCC Dig. Tech. Papers, February 2001, pp. 324-325

[3] N. Kurd et. al., "A Multigigahertz Clocking Scheme for the Pentium® 4 Microprocessor," in ISSCC Dig. Tech. Papers, February 2001, pp. 404-405.

[4] D. Harris, "Skew-Tolerant Circuit Design," Academic Press

[5] Personal communications with Rajesh Kumar, Pentium Processor Circuit Group, Intel

[6] R. P. Colwell and R. L. Steck. "A 0.6um BiCMOS processor with dynamic execution," International Solid State Circuits Conference (ISSCC) Digest of Technical Papers, pages 176-177, February 1995.

[7] Andre Seznec, Stephan Jourdan, Pascal Sainrat, and Pierre Michaud. Multiple-Block Ahead Branch Predictors. In Proceedings of the 7th Intl. Conf. on Architectural Support for Programming Languages and Operating Systems, pages 116--127, Cambridge, Massachusetts, October 1996.

[8] D. H. Friendly, S. J. Patel and Y. N. Patt. Alternative Fetch and Issue Policies for the Trace Cache Fetch Mechanism. Proceedings of the 30th Annual ACM/IEEE International Symposium on Microarchitecture, December, 1997.

[9] Personal communications with David Sager, Pentium Processor Architecture Group, Intel

[10] M. Horowitz, R. Ho, and K. Mai. "The future of wires." In Proceedings of the Semiconductor Research Corporation Workshop on Interconnects for Systems on a Chip, May 1999.

Session 2: Processor Scheduling

Efficient Dynamic Scheduling Through Tag Elimination

Dan Ernst and Todd Austin
Advanced Computer Architecture Laboratory
University of Michigan
Ann Arbor, MI 48109
{ernstd,austin}@eecs.umich.edu

Abstract

An increasingly large portion of scheduler latency is derived from the monolithic content addressable memory (CAM) arrays accessed during instruction wakeup. The performance of the scheduler can be improved by decreasing the number of tag comparisons necessary to schedule instructions. Using detailed simulation-based analyses, we find that most instructions enter the window with at least one of their input operands already available. By putting these instructions into specialized windows with fewer tag comparators, load capacitance on the scheduler critical path can be reduced, with only very small effects on program throughput. For instructions with multiple unavailable operands, we introduce a last-tag speculation mechanism that eliminates all remaining tag comparators except those for the last arriving input operand. By combining these two tag-reduction schemes, we are able to construct dynamic schedulers with approximately one quarter of the tag comparators found in conventional designs. Conservative circuit-level timing analyses indicate that the optimized designs are 20-45% faster and require 10-20% less power, depending on instruction window size.

1. Introduction

In an effort to secure higher levels of system performance, microprocessor designs often employ dynamic scheduling as a technique to extract instruction level parallelism (ILP) from serial instruction streams. Conventional dynamic scheduler designs house a "window" of candidate instructions from which ready instructions are sent to functional units in an out-of-order data flow fashion. The instruction window is implemented using large monolithic content addressable memories (CAMs) that track instructions and their input dependencies.

While more ILP can be extracted with a larger instruction window (and accordingly larger CAM structure), this increased parallelism will come at the expense of a slower scheduler clock speed. Recent circuit-level studies of dynamic scheduler logic have shown that the scheduler CAM logic will dominate the latency for the structure [12], and as such, window sizes cannot be increased without commensurate increases in scheduler operation latency. More recent studies [1] also suggest that increas-

ing wire latencies due to parasitic capacitance effects may make these trade-offs even more acute, with future designs seeing little benefit from smaller technologies. The optimal design is dependent on both the degree to which ILP can be harvested from the workload and the circuit characteristics of the technology used to implement the scheduler.

In addition to performance, power dissipation has become an increasing concern in the design of high-performance microprocessors. Increasing clock speeds and diminishing voltage margins have combined to produce designs that are increasingly difficult to cool. Additionally, embedded processors are more sensitive to energy usage as these designs are often powered by batteries. Empirical [9,7] and analytical [2,5] studies have shown that the scheduler logic consumes a large portion of a microprocessor's power and energy budgets, making the scheduler a prime target for power optimizations. For example, the scheduler components of the PentiumPro microarchitcture consume 16% of total chip power. A similar study for Compaq's Alpha 21264 microprocessor found that 18% of total chip power was consumed by the scheduler. Increasing window sizes and parasitic capacitances will continue to shift more of the power budget towards the scheduler.

Our techniques draw from the observation that most scheduler tag comparisons are superfluous to the correct operation of the instruction scheduler. Analyses reveal that most instructions placed into the instruction window do not require two source tag comparators because one or more operands are ready, or the operation doesn't require two register operands.

In this paper, we propose two scheduler tag reduction techniques that work together to improve the performance of dynamic scheduling while at the same time reducing power requirements. First, we propose a reduced-tag scheduler design that assigns instructions to reservation stations with two, one, or zero tag comparators, depending on the number of operands in flight. To reduce tag comparison requirements for instructions with multiple operands in flight, we introduce a last tag speculation technique. This approach predicts which input operand of an instruction will arrive last, and then schedules the execution of that instruction based solely on the arrival of this operand. Since the earlier arriving tags do not precipitate execution of the instruction, the scheduler can safely elim-

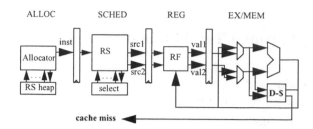

Figure 1: Conventional Dynamic Scheduler Pipeline

inate the comparator logic for all but the last arriving operand. A low cost and low latency misprediction recovery technique is presented.

The remainder of this paper is organized as follows. Section 2 gives background details into the design of a conventional high-performance scheduler, including the critical paths of the design and further motivation as to why removing comparators could improve its power and speed characteristics. Section 3 introduces our reduced-tag scheduler designs. Section 4 details our experimental evaluation of these new designs. Detailed cycle-accurate simulations and circuit-level timing and power analyses are combined to fully explore the benefits and costs of each approach. Section 5 details related prior work, and suggests how our approach could be combined with much of the previous work for further improvements in scheduler design. Section 6 gives conclusions and suggests future directions in the pursuit of high-performance schedulers. Appendix A includes a detailed description of our scheduler circuit design and analysis.

2. High-Performance Dynamic Scheduling

2.1. Scheduler Pipeline Overview

Figure 1 details the pipeline stages used to implement a high performance dynamic scheduler. The first stage, the allocator (ALLOC), is responsible for reserving all resources necessary to house an instruction in the processor instruction window. These resources include reservation stations, re-order buffer entries, and physical registers. Physical registers and re-order buffer entries typically use a FIFO allocation strategy in which the resources are allocated from a circular hardware queue.[1] This approach works well because resources are allocated in program order in ALLOC and held until instruction commit time, where the resources are released in program order. Reservation stations, while allocated in program order, may be released as soon as an instruction has begun execution (or as soon as an instruction has begun execution for the last time in a pipeline with replay/re-execution support). As such, a heap-style allocation strategy will

---

1. While it is conceivable that physical registers could delay allocation until writeback, *i.e.*, when the resource is needed to store the result, most designs avoid any type of out-of-order allocation because it introduces many deadlock scenarios. A good treatment on out-of-order register allocation and its potential hazards can be found in [6].

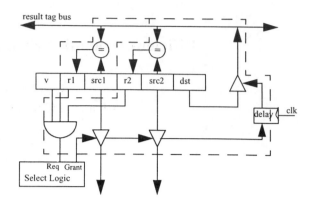

Figure 2: Reservation Station Datapaths and Control.
Critical path shown with dashed line.

result in more efficient use of reservation station resources than can be attained using a FIFO allocation policy.

The scheduler stage (SCHED) houses instructions in reservation stations until they are ready to execute. Reservation stations track the availability of instruction source operands. When all input operands are available, a request is made to the select logic for execution. The selection logic chooses the next instructions to execute from all ready instructions, based on the scheduler policy. The selected instructions receive a grant signal from the selection logic, at which point they will be sent forward to later stages in the pipeline.

Once granted execution, an instruction's source register tags are used to access the register file in the register read (REG) stage of the pipeline. In the following stage, operand values read from the register file are forwarded to the appropriate functional unit in the execute stage (EX/MEM) of the pipeline. If a dependent operation immediately follows an instruction, it will read a stale value from the physical register file. A bypass MUX is provided in the EX/MEM stage to will select between the incoming register operand, or a more recent value on the bypass bus. Dependent instructions that execute in subsequent cycles must communicate via the bypass bus. All other instructions communicate by way of the physical register file.

2.2. Reservation Stations

Figure 2 illustrates the datapaths and control logic contained in each reservation station. Each new instruction is placed into a reservation station by the allocator. If an instruction's input operand has already been computed (or if the operand is not used by the instruction), the ready bit for that operand is set as valid. If the operand has not yet been computed, a unique tag for the value is placed into the corresponding source operand tag field, either *src1* or *src2* depending on which instruction operand is being processed. Since all input operands are renamed to physical storage, the physical register index suffices as a unique *tag* for each value in flight within the instruction window. Unlike most textbook descriptions of Tomasulo's algorithm [14], most modern processors, such as the Alpha 21264 [8] and Pentium 4, use value-less reservation stations. Instead of storing instruction operand values and

38

opcodes in the CAM structure and making longer tag busses, these designs keep this data in the REG stage where it can be accessed on the way to execution.

When instructions are nearing the completion of their execution, they broadcast their result tag onto the result tag bus. Reservation stations snoop the result tag bus, waiting for a tag to appear that matches either of their source operand tags. If a match is found, the ready bit of the matching operand tag is set. When a valid reservation station has both operands marked ready, a request for execution is sent to the selection logic. The selection logic grants the execution request if the appropriate functional unit is available and the requesting instruction has the highest priority among instructions that are ready to execute. Policies for determining the highest priority instruction vary. Some proposed approaches include random [12], oldest-first [12], and highest-latency first [18]. However, more capable schedulers require more complex logic and thus run more slowly.

The selection logic sends an instruction to execution by driving its grant signal. The input operand tags are driven onto an output bus where they are latched for use by the REG stage in the following cycle. In addition, the grant signal is latched at the reservation station. In the following cycle, the instruction will drive its result tag on to the result tag bus. If the execution pipeline supports multi-cycle operations, the result tag broadcast must be delayed until the instruction result is produced. This can be implemented by inserting a small delay element into the grant latch, such as a small counter. If the execution time for an instruction is non-deterministic, such as for a memory operation, the scheduler can optimistically predict that the latency will be the most common case; *e.g.*, it predicts that all loads will hit in the data cache. If an instruction's latency is mispredicted, dependent instructions were scheduled too soon and must be rescheduled to execute after the operation completes. This rescheduling is sometimes called a scheduler replay [20].

The reservation station wakeup and select logic forms the control critical path in the dynamically scheduled pipeline [12]. This logic forms a critical speed path in most aggressive designs because it limits the rate at which instructions can begin execution. As shown by the dashed lines in Figure 2, the scheduler critical path includes the result tag driver, the result tag bus interconnect, the reservation station comparators, the selection logic, and the grant signal interconnect. It is possible that the operand tag output busses (src1 and src2) are on the critical path of the control loop, however, in aggressive designs this output can be pipelined or wave-pipelined [11] into subsequent scheduler cycles because the output bus value is not required to initiate the next scheduler loop iteration. As noted by Palacharla et al [12], the CAM structure formed by the result tag drivers, result tag bus, and comparators constitute the major portion of the control circuit latency, especially for large windows with many reservation stations.

3. Reduced-Tag Scheduler Designs

In this section, we present two reduced-tag scheduler designs. The first optimization, called window specialization, leverages the observation that many instruction input

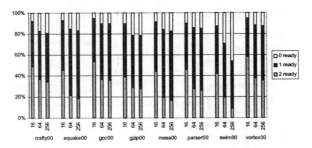

Figure 3: Runtime Distribution of Ready Input Operands for Varying Window Sizes

operands are available or unneeded when instructions are placed into a reservation station. As a result, these instructions can be scheduled with reservation stations containing fewer tag comparators. The second optimization uses a last-tag predictor to identify the operand of an instruction that will arrive last (and thus allow the instruction to commence execution). A design that can effectively make this prediction can eliminate the tag comparators of all other operands without impacting the dynamic instruction schedule.

3.1. Specialized Windows

When an instruction enters the instruction window, its input operand tag fields are loaded with the index of the physical register that will eventually hold the operand value. It may be the case that some of the operands will be ready at that time, either because the operand was computed in an earlier cycle or the operand is not required by the operation (e.g., one of the operands is an immediate value). Since these input operands are already available, their reservation station entries do not require tag comparators.

To quantify the degree to which tag comparators are not required by reservation stations, a typical 4-wide superscalar processor was simulated using the SimpleScalar toolset [3] with instruction window sizes of 16, 64, and 256 and an load/store queue size that was half the size of the instruction window. When instructions entered the scheduler, the number of ready input operands was counted. The results in Figure 3 show the dynamic distribution of the number of ready operands for all instructions. Results are shown for eight of the SPEC2000 benchmarks [17]. (More details on our experimental framework and baseline microarchitecture model can be found in Section 4.1.)

Clearly, a significant portion of all operands are marked ready when they enter reservation stations, for all instruction window sizes. Only about 10-20% of all dynamic instructions require a reservation station with two tag comparators, while the remaining instructions require either one or zero comparators. Much of this effect comes from the fact that very few instructions (20-35%) actually have two architectural operands (many are loads/stores or use immediates). As expected, larger window sizes result in fewer ready operands, because larger windows permit the front-end to get further ahead of instruction execution. Nonetheless, a window size of 256 instructions has a significant portion of instructions that do not require more than one tag comparator. In general, programs with poor

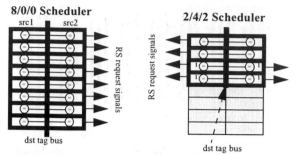

Figure 4: Conventional and Reduced-Tag Reservation Stations. The circles represent tag comparators. The bold tag entries include a comparator, the shaded tag entries are not necessary and so do not include comparators. One-tag entries are denoted with a "1".

branch prediction such as *GCC* and *Vortex* were less affected by the larger windows sizes, because branch mispredictions limit the degree to which the front-end can get ahead of instruction execution. In contrast, *SWIM* has nearly perfect branch predictor accuracy, which results in more slip between fetch and execute for large window sizes. Still, even in this extreme example, more than half of the instructions in a 256-entry instruction window require less than two tag comparators. Similar observations were made by Folegnani and Gonzalez [5]; they used this property to design low-power tag comparators.

It is possible to take advantage of ready input operands if the scheduler contains reservation stations with fewer than two tag comparators. Figure 4 illustrates a reservation station design that contains entries with two, one, and zero tag comparators. The design on the left side of the figure is a conventional scheduler configuration, where each reservation station contains two tag comparators. The optimized design, shown on the right side of the figure, eliminates tag comparators from some of the reservations stations. We label the configurations "x/y/z", where x, y, and z indicate the number of two, one and zero tag stations, respectively.

When the allocator encounters an instruction with one or more unavailable operands, the allocator will assign the instruction to a reservation station with a matching number of tag comparators. If both operands are ready, we can place the instruction into a reservation station without tag comparators that immediately requests execution. If there isn't an available reservation station with the same number of tag comparators, the allocator will assign the instruction to a reservation station with more tag comparators. For example, instructions waiting for one operand can be assigned to reservation stations with one or two tag comparators. Finally, if a reservation station with a sufficient number of tag comparators is not available, the allocator will stall the front-end pipeline until one is available.

This reduced-tag scheduler design has two primary advantages over a conventional design. First, the destination tag bus, which drives a physical register destination tag to all source tag comparators, need only run to the reservation stations with tag comparators. Since result tag drive latency is on the critical path of the control scheduler

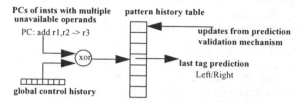

Figure 5: GSHARE-Style Last Tag Predictor

loop, the latency of this critical path will be reduced in proportion to the number of zero-tag reservation stations. The second advantage is that comparator circuits can be eliminated from the instruction window. With fewer comparators, load capacitance on the result tag bus is reduced, resulting in faster tag drive and lower power requirements. The downside of the reduced tag design is that additional allocator stalls may be introduced when there are insufficient reservation stations of a required class, potentially reducing extracted ILP and program performance.

3.2. Last Tag Speculation

While many instructions enter the instruction window with multiple unavailable operands, it is still possible to eliminate all but one of the tag comparators for these instructions. Since the arrival of the all but the last input operand tags will not initiate an execution request, these tag comparators can be safely removed. When the *last* input operand tag arrives, this sole event can be used to initiate instruction execution. We employ a last-tag predictor to predict the last arriving operand. As long as the last tag predictor is correct, the schedule will proceed as in the non-speculative case. A modified reservation station with one tag comparator monitors the arrival of the predicted last input operand.

We experimented with a number of last-tag predictors, including a predictor that predicts the last operand to arrive will be the same as in the previous execution, a bimodal-type last-tag predictor (similar to the grandparent predictor employed by Stark et al [19]), and a GSHARE-style last-tag predictor. The accuracy of these predictors was nearly identical to similarly configured branch predictors. For the sake of brevity we only present the GSHARE-style last-tag predictor as it consistently performed the best with only marginal additional cost over simpler predictors.

Figure 5 illustrates the GSHARE-style last-tag predictor. The predictor is indexed with the PC of an instruction (with multiple unavailable operands) hashed with global control history [10]. The control history is XOR'ed onto the least significant bits of the instruction PC and that result is used as an index into a table of two-bit saturating counters. The value of the upper counter bit indicates the prediction: one indicates the left operand will arrive last, zero indicates the right operand will arrive last. The predictors are updated when last tag predictions are validated. Figure 6 shows the prediction accuracy (for instructions with two operands in flight) for various sizes of the GSHARE-style last-tag predictors with 8 bits of control history and an instruction window size of 64. Most programs have good predictor performance for sizes larger than 1024 entries. We also implemented a confidence estimation technique for the predictor. The approach forced

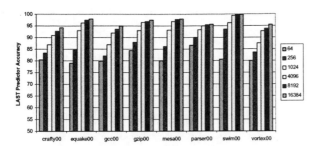

Figure 6: Accuracy of GSHARE-Style Last Tag Predictor for Various Predictor Sizes

hard to predict instructions to use two-tag entries, however, the results showed few gains.

As shown in the pipeline of Figure 7, the allocator accesses the last-tag predictor for instructions with multiple unavailable operands and inserts the instruction into a reservation station with a single tag comparator. The predictor will indicate whether the left or right operand for the instruction will complete last. If the last tag prediction is correct, the instruction will wake up at the exact same time it would have in a window without speculation. In the event that the prediction is incorrect, the instruction will wake up before all of its input operands are ready, and a misspeculation recovery sequence will have to be initiated.

Figure 8 illustrates the datapaths and control logic for a reservation station supporting last-tag speculation. The input operand tags are loaded into the reservation station with the tag predicted to arrive last placed under the comparator (*srcL*). The other input operand tag (*srcF*) and the result tag are also loaded into the reservation station. The reservation station operates in a manner similar to a conventional design. Instructions request execution once the predicted-last tag is matched on the result tag bus. When an instruction is granted permission to execute, the source operand register tags are driven out to the register stage of the pipeline. This drive operation requires a pair of muxes to sort the source operands into the original (left, right) instruction order, which is the format used by the register file and later functional units. In addition, the tag predicted to arrive first is forwarded to the register read stage (REG), where it is used to check the correctness of the last-tag prediction.

The last-tag prediction must be validated to ensure that the instruction does not commence execution before all of its operands are available. The prediction is valid if the operand predicted to arrive first (*srcF*) is available when the instruction enters the register read stage (REG) of the pipeline. In parallel with the register file access, the *srcF* tag is used to probe a small register scoreboard (*RDY*). The scoreboard contains one bit per physical register; bits are set if the register value is valid in the physical register file. This scoreboard is already available in the ALLOC stage of the pipeline, where it is used to determine if the valid bit should be set when operand tags are written into reservation stations. A number of ports equal to the issue width added to this scoreboard will suffice for validating last-tag predictions. Alternatively, an additional scoreboard could be maintained specifically for last-tag prediction validation.

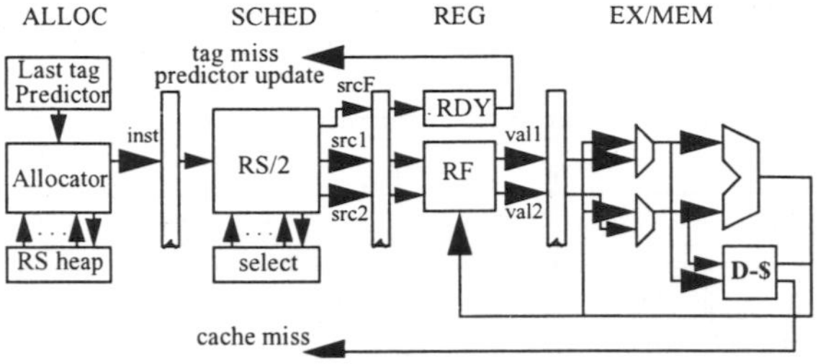

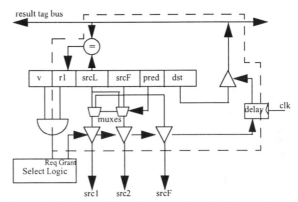

Figure 7: Scheduler Pipeline with Last Tag Speculation

Figure 8: Reduced-Tag Reservation Station with Last Tag Speculation

If the prediction is found to be correct, instructions may continue through the scheduler pipeline as the scheduler has made the correct scheduling decision. If the prediction is incorrect, the scheduler pipeline must be flushed and restarted, in a fashion identical to latency mispredictions. Unlike latency mispredictions, which are detected in MEM with a three cycle penalty, last-tag misspeculations can be detected before EX, and thus only cause a one cycle bubble in the scheduler pipeline.

The primary advantage of the last tag scheduler is that more than half of the comparator load on the result tag bus is eliminated, which can result in reduced scheduling latency and significant power reductions for large instruction windows. The drawback of this approach is, of course, the performance impacts that result when a last-tag prediction is incorrect. Fortunately, the accuracy of the last tag predictor, combined with the small penalty for mispredicting should make this approach an effective technique for improving scheduler speed and energy consumption.

4. Experimental Evaluation

4.1. Methodology

The architectural simulators used in this study are derived from the SimpleScalar/Alpha version 3.0 tool set [3], a suite of functional and timing simulation tools for the Alpha AXP ISA. The timing simulator executes only user-level instructions, performing a detailed timing simulation of an aggressive 4-way dynamically scheduled microprocessor with two levels of instruction and data

Table 1: Benchmarks and Baseline Statistics

Bench mark	Baseline IPC	Baseline IPns	Bench mark	Baseline IPC	Baseline IPns
crafty	2.018	4.330	mesa	2.695	5.783
equake	2.622	5.626	parser	1.736	3.725
gcc	1.675	3.593	swim	2.719	5.835
gzip	2.186	4.692	vortex	1.961	4.208

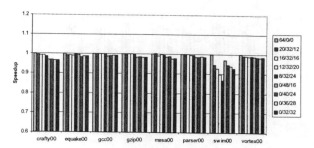

Figure 9: Normalized Instructions Per Cycle for Varying Configurations

cache memory. Simulation is execution-driven, including execution down any speculative path until the detection of a fault, TLB miss, or branch misprediction.

To perform our evaluation, we collected results from eight of the SPEC2000 benchmarks [17]. There are five integer programs and three floating point programs. All SPEC programs were compiled for a Compaq Alpha AXP-21264 processor using the Compaq C and Fortran compilers under the OSF/1 V4.0 operating system using full compiler optimization (-O4). The simulations were run for at least 250 million instructions using the SPEC reference inputs and all simulations were fast-forwarded through the first 100 million instructions to warm up the caches and predictors.

To get a full understanding of the effects of our optimizations, the circuit characteristics of scheduler structures must be examined. The circuit delays and power consumption statistics for scheduler windows used in this study were derived from an updated version of the SPICE models used in the work by Palacharla, Jouppi, and Smith [13]. All timing results are for the TSMC 0.18 μm process; a more detailed description of our circuit models can be found in Appendix A. In addition, we estimated the power consumed by the last tag prediction array using CACTI II [15]. Table 1 shows the benchmarks, their instructions per cycle (IPC) on the baseline microarchitectural model, and their maximum baseline scheduler performance in instructions per ns (IPns).

Our baseline simulation configuration models a current generation out-of-order processor microarchitecture. It can fetch and issue up to 4 instructions per cycle and it has a 64 entry dynamic scheduler window with a 32 entry load/store buffer. There is an 3 cycle minimum branch misprediction penalty. The processor has 4 integer ALU units, 2-load/store units, 4-FP adders, 4-integer MULT/DIV units, and 4-FP MULT/DIV units. The latencies vary depending on the operation, but all functional units, with the exception of the divide units, are fully pipelined allowing a new instruction to initiate execution each cycle.

The memory system consists of 32k 4-way set-associative L1 instruction and data caches. The data cache is dual-ported and pipelined to allow up to two new requests each cycle. There is also a 256k 4-way set-associative L2 cache with a 6 cycle hit latency. If there is a second-level cache miss it takes a total of 36 cycles to make the round trip access to main memory.

The model uses a GSHARE branch predictor with an 8-bit global history and an 8k entry BTB. The instruction fetch stage of the model has a 32 entry instruction queue and operates at twice the frequency as the rest of the pro-

cessor. While perhaps not realistic, this assures that the IPC results seen when changing scheduler configurations are not attenuated by bottlenecks in the front end. Since improvement in scheduler performance would have to be accompanied by commensurate improvement in fetch bandwidth, we feel that this configuration will accurately portray the benefits of our scheduler optimizations.

The dynamic scheduler distributed with SimpleScalar is overly simplistic compared to modern schedulers. A redesigned scheduler was added to sim-outorder to more accurately reflect the design presented in Section 2. Our new scheduler includes support for scheduler replay, more efficient scheduler resource management, decoupled ROB and RS resources, and support for our optimizations detailed in Section 3.

The last-tag predictor configuration simulated is a GSHARE-style predictor with an 8-bit global history and a 8192 entry pattern history table. The global history is updated when branch instructions complete in the same way that the branch predictor is updated. A last-tag mispredict causes a 1 cycle bubble in the scheduler pipeline.

4.2. Performance of Reduced-Tag Schedulers

When reduced-tag reservation stations are introduced, instructions have a new constraint on entering the instruction window. Not only must there be an empty reservation station, but the station must also have at least one tag comparator for each of the instruction's unavailable input operands. If the demand for any particular class of reservation stations is high, the reduced-tag designs may experience extra instruction stalls as the allocator waits for reservation stations to be freed.

These extra stalls reduce the effective number of reservation stations from which the scheduler can choose instructions to execute. The result, as shown in Figure 9, is a small IPC change for most configurations and benchmarks. We label the configurations "x/y/z", where x, y, and z indicate the number of two, one and zero tag stations, respectively. Only the configurations without two-tag stations employ last-tag speculation. The effects of the stalls show up most prominently in *SWIM*. This benchmark makes extremely efficient use of the machine because it has excellent branch predictor performance, very few stalls, and many tightly coupled dependent instructions. Consequently, many instructions require the full two tag comparators. The configurations using last-tag speculation perform very well, with slightly lower

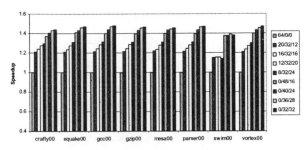

Figure 10: Normalized Instructions Per ns for Varying Configurations

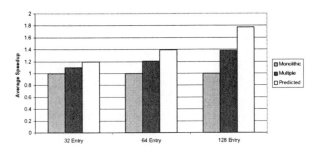

Figure 11: Impact of Tag-Reduction for Varying Window Sizes

Table 2: Energy and Power

Scheduler	Energy (nJ)	Power (W)	Scheduler	Energy (nJ)	Power (W)
64/0/0	0.468	1.550	0/48/16	0.255	1.548
20/32/12	0.314	1.435	0/40/24	0.222	1.416
16/32/16	0.289	1.375	0/36/28	0.207	1.372
12/32/20	0.263	1.322	0/32/32	0.191	1.281
8/32/24	0.239	1.250			

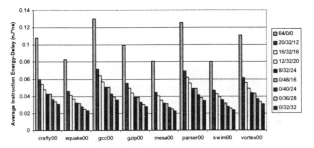

Figure 12: Energy-Delay Product for Varying Configurations

IPC's seen in benchmarks with poor branch predictor accuracy, such as *crafty* and *GCC*. In these programs, complex program control causes the register dependencies between instructions to change rapidly, making it more difficult to predict which operand will arrive last. The configurations without last-tag speculation slightly outperformed the configurations with speculation. Overall, the performance impacts amounted to only 1-3%.

The main benefit of removing tags from the scheduler critical path is the reduction in the load capacitance during instruction wakeup. Lower load capacitance allows for more aggressive clocking of scheduler circuitry. Based on our model of the wakeup and select circuitry, the specialized windows should allow for 25-45% faster clock rates, depending on configuration. Figure 10 shows the total performance (measured in instructions per ns and assuming no other critical path bottlenecks in the system) of each benchmark. With the exception of *SWIM*, the rate at which the scheduler can send instructions to execute measures between 20-45% higher, again depending on configuration[1].

To more accurately gauge the impact on modern superpipelined processors, we also simulated the scheduler with last-tag misprediction latencies of 2 and 4 cycles. In these cases, the IPC of the configurations using the predictor

were reduced an average of 0.7% and 2.4%, respectively. In every case, there was still a substantial speedup in instructions per ns.

4.3. Impact of Window Size

Figure 11 shows that reduced-tag scheduler optimizations continue to pay dividends for differing window sizes. The results given are the averages across all benchmarks for monolithic, multiple (5:8:3 ratio), and predicted (0:3:1 ratio) style windows. The gains become more prominent as total window size grows. The larger windows have fewer allocator stalls due to more reservation station resources. The large windows also bear more of the scheduler latency in result tag broadcasts (as opposed to the select logic), as a result, they show a larger percentage gain when tag comparators are eliminated. For a window with 128 entries, the optimized schedulers were 35-75% faster.

4.4. Energy and Power Characteristics

Often it is the case that to reduce power consumption, design changes must be made at the cost of lower performance. In our reduced-tag scheduler designs, lower load capacitance on the result tag bus provides both performance and power benefits. Table 2 shows the energy consumption for each configuration. The optimized designs use 30-60% less energy than the standard monolithic scheduler. Table 2 also shows the power used by each configuration if it were to be run at its maximum possible clock speed. The power reductions are not as pronounced as the energy improvements because the optimized designs run at a faster clock rate.

---

1. For the purposes of our study, we assume that the scheduler critical path is the limiting factor in determining the clock speed of the entire processor. This may or may not be true for actual full implementations. Alternatively, if another pipeline stage limits the clock speed gains that can be achieved, the performance headroom afforded by tag elimination can instead be used to make the scheduling window larger to provide more parallelism.

The power usage of the last-tag predictor was also calculated. It was found to consume less than 10% of the power used by the scheduler in all cases.

One way to quantify an architecture's ability to balance both power and performance is through the use of the energy-delay product [7]. This metric is the product of program run-time and total energy consumed to run the program. Figure 12 shows that the energy-delay product of the optimized scheduler is 50-75% lower than the baseline configurations. The 0/32/32 speculative configuration had the best return, with a 65-75% lower energy-delay across all experiments, including *SWIM*, which had the largest IPC impacts. The optimized designs show large gains because eliminating tag comparators and tag bus wiring lowers the result tag bus capacitance, which both reduces energy consumption and allows for higher clock speeds. The energy-delay products for 128 entry windows also showed a 70% gain for the optimized configurations, suggesting that these benefits continue with larger window sizes.

5. Related Work

There have been several other efforts to reduce the complexity of dynamic schedulers, many of which can be used in combination with tag elimination.

Some current designs bank their selection logic by having separate groups of reservation stations for each group of functional units. Each of these station groups has its own, smaller, selection network. While result tag broadcasts still need to be sent to all of the reservation stations, the latency for selecting instructions for execution can be reduced. As a consequence of this optimization, the latency of the wakeup path makes up a higher percentage of the total scheduler delay. Because of this, as Figure 13 shows, schedulers with banked selection logic reap a larger benefit from using tag elimination techniques.

Palacharla, Jouppi, and Smith studied the effects of process scaling on microprocessor design and proposed a complexity-effective superscalar processor [12,13]. Their design uses a set of FIFO queues for dynamic scheduling to reduce complexity and allow for very aggressive clocking. Instructions can only be issued from the front of the queues; instructions are steered into them using dependence information. This approach attempts to maximize the number of ready instructions at the issue boundary.

Stark, Brown, and Patt have proposed two methods for pipelining wakeup and selection logic, allowing for a faster clock. For their first method [19], each reservation station entry carries its own input tags along with its parent instructions' input tags in order to allow back-to-back dependent instructions to execute consecutively. They also propose speculating on which parent instruction will finish last, reducing the number of "grandparent" tags that must be stored.

Their second method, select-free logic [22], enables pipelining by allowing all instructions that wakeup to broadcast back into the window the following cycle, even though some of them may not be selected for execution. Combining tag elimination with either of these schemes could be very lucrative because the latency of the wakeup stage is fully exposed.

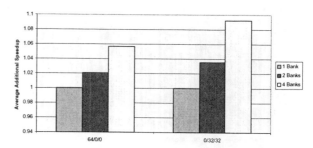

Figure 13: IPns Comparison of Banking Benefits

In their studies on energy-effective issue logic, Folegnani and Gonzalez [5] also made the observation that many comparators in the instruction window are unused and unnecessary. In their low-power scheduler design, tags that are marked ready do not precharge their match lines, resulting in lower comparator power consumption. This approach dynamically reduces the power consumption of the window, but it doesn't allow for a faster clock rate.

Gonzalez and Canal [23] also propose a way to reduce the overall complexity of scheduling logic by using N-Use issue scheme. Their optimization takes advantage of the observation that most instruction output values are ready only once.

Michaud and Seznec [21] proposed a method for reordering instructions as they enter the instruction window. By performing dependence analysis in a pre-schedule stage, they are able to place more usable instructions into the window, increasing its effective size.

Kucuk, *et al.* [24] propose an alternate comparator circuit to reduce energy dissipation in dynamic schedulers. Their optimization, like many of the others, could be used in combination with tag elimination for improved energy-efficiency.

6. Conclusions

The wakeup and select logic of dynamic schedulers has become one of the primary bottlenecks in high-performance microprocessor design. While architects have sought larger scheduling windows to allow for wider issue widths and higher IPCs, the circuit complexity of these devices forces any gains to be at the expense of clock speeds. Moreover, interconnect-intensive scheduling logic consumes a significant portion of processor design power budgets. Designers must be aware of all these factors when making scheduler design decisions because changes that improve one aspect of the design may adversely effect another.

We have introduced more efficient reduced-tag scheduler designs that improve both scheduler speed and power requirements. By employing more specialized window structures and last-tag speculation, a large percentage of tag comparisons were removed from the scheduler critical path. These optimizations reduced the load capacitance seen during tag broadcast while maintaining instruction throughputs that are close to those of inefficient monolithic scheduler designs. The optimized designs allow for more aggressive clocking and significantly reduce power consumption.

There are still many ideas to be explored in this area. There are potentially many improvements to be made in the last tag prediction mechanism. Specifically, in an effort to improve accuracy, factors that contribute to a change in issue order could be examined, such as branch mispredictions and instruction latency variations.

In addition, these techniques could be combined with many of the prior proposals detailed in the related work section to produce greater benefits. For example, tag elimination and last-tag prediction can be used to further reduce the complexity of banked-select scheduling logic or select-free logic. Similarly, the power-saving techniques introduced by Gonzalez could be combined with our scheduler for additional power savings or even for the purposes of allowing the logic to modify its own clock rate.

Acknowledgements

We would like to thank Chris Weaver and Matt Guthaus for their help with our CAD tools. We also thank all of the reviewers and our collegues for their insights and suggestions for strengthening our paper.

This work was supported by Contract No. 98-DT-660 to the Regents of the University of California from Microelectronic Advanced Research Corporation (MARCO) and by the National Science Foundation CADRE program, Grant No. EIA-9975286.

References

[1] V. Agarwal, M. Hrishikesh, S. Keckler, and D. Burger. "Clock Rate versus IPC: The End of the Road for Conventional Microarchitectures", *Proceedings of the 27th Annual International Symposium on Computer Architecture*, June 2000.

[2] D. Brooks, V. Tiwari, and M. Martonosi. "Wattch: A framework for architectural-level power analysis and optimizations", *In 27th Annual International Symposium on Computer Architecture*, June 2000.

[3] D. Burger and T. M. Austin. "The SimpleScalar tool set, version 2.0", Tech. Rep. CS-1342, University of Wisconsin-Madison, June 1997.

[4] Brian A Fields, Shai Rubin and Rastislav Bodik, "Focusing Processor Policies via Critical-Path Prediction", *28th Annual International Symposium on Computer Architecture*, June 2001.

[5] Daniele Folegnani and Antonio Gonzalez, "Energy-Effective Issue Logic", *In 28th Annual International Symposium on Computer Architecture*, June 2001.

[6] Antonio Gonzalez, Jose Gonzalez and Mateo Valero. "Virtual-Physical Registers", *Proc. 4th Intl. Symp. High-Performance Computer Architecture* (HPCA-4), Feb 1998.

[7] Ricardo Gonzalez and Mark Horowitz. "Energy Dissipation in General Purpose Microprocessors", *IEEE Journal of Solid-State Circuits*, 31(9):1277-1284, September 1996.

[8] Keller, J. 1996. "The 21264: a superscalar Alpha processor with out-of-order execution", Presented at the 9th Annual Microprocessor Forum, San Jose, CA.

[9] S. Manne, D. Grunwald, A. Klauser, "Pipeline Gating: Speculation Control for Energy Reduction", *25th Annual International Symposium on Computer Architechture*, June 1998.

[10] Scott McFarling. "Combining branch predictors", Technical Report TN-36, Digital Western Research Laboratory, June 1993.

[11] Kevin J. Nowka, "High-Performance CMOS System Design using Wave Pipelining", Stanford University Ph.D. Thesis, September 1995.

[12] Subbarao Palacharla, Norman P. Jouppi and J.E. Smith. "Complexity-Effective Superscalar Processors", *In 24th Annual International Symposium on Computer Architecture*, May 1997.

[13] Subbarao Palacharla, Norman P. Jouppi and J.E. Smith. "Quantifying the Complexity of Superscalar Processors", Tech. Rep. CS-1328, University of Wisconsin-Madison, May 1997.

[14] Patterson, D. A. and Hennessy, J. L. *Computer Architecture, A Quantitative Approach*. Morgan Kaufmann Publishers, Inc., San Francisco, CA, second edition, 1996.

[15] Glenn Reinman and Norm Jouppi, "An Integrated Cache Timing and Power Model", Compaq Technical Report, http://www.research.compaq.com/wrl/people/jouppi/cacti2.pdf.

[16] The MOSIS Service, http://www.mosis.com/Technical/ Processes/proc-tsmc-cmos018.html

[17] SPEC System Performance Evaluation Committee, www.spec.org.

[18] S. T. Srinivasan, A. R. Lebeck. "Load Latency Tolerance in Dynamically Scheduled Processors", *Proceedings of the 31st Annual ACM/IEEE International Symposium on Microarchitecture*, 148-159, 1998.

[19] J. Stark, M. Brown, and Y. Patt, "On Pipelining Dynamic Instruction Scheduling Logic", *Proceedings of the 33rd Annual ACM/IEEE International Symposium on Microarchitecture*, December 2000.

[20] Dean M. Tullsen, Susan J. Eggers, Joel S. Emer, Henry M. Levy, Jack L. Lo, and Rebecca L. Stamm. "Exploiting choice: Instruction fetch and issue on an implementable simultaneous multithreading processor", In *Proceedings of the 23rd Annual International Symposium on Computer Architecture*, pages 191-202, May 22-24, 1996.

[21] P. Michaud, A. Seznec. "Data Flow Prescheduling for Large Instruction Windows in Out-of-Order Processors", *HPCA-7*. January 2001.

[22] M. Brown, J. Stark, and Y. Patt, "Select-Free Instruction Scheduling Logic", To appear in *Proceedings of the 34th Annual ACM/IEEE International Symposium on Microarchitecture,* December 2-5, 2001.

[23] Ramon Canal and Antonio Gonzalez, "Reducing the Complexity of the Scheduling Logic", *ICS-01*, June 2001.

[24] G. Kucuk, K. Ghose, D. Ponomarev, and P. Kogge, "Energy-Efficient Instruction Dispatch Buffer Design for Superscalar Processors", *ISLPED '01*, August 2001.

Appendix A. Circuit Analysis Methodology

Our timing analyses are based on Palacharla's original wakeup and select circuit designs [12,13]. We ported Palacharla's physical design to Taiwan Semiconductor Corporation's (TSMC) 1.8V 0.18μm fabrication technology, using a physical design flow consisting of Cadence and Synopsis design tools. We first optimized Palacharla's original design using Synopsys's AMPS circuit optimization tool (version 5.5). AMPS attempts to optimize circuit latency, power, or area under a given set of constraints. We configured AMPS to optimize circuit latency, with the constraint that transistor area could not increase. AMPS provided the most benefit for the select circuit design, producing a re-sized design that is more than 25% faster, and with only 90% of the original area. AMPS improved wakeup latency nearly 5% with no reduction in area.

Once transistors were sized, timing analysis was performed on a SPICE representation of Palacharla's optimized scheduler design, augmented with parasitic wire delays. Wire parasitics were computed in the same fashion as Palacharla's earlier study, except wire resistance and capacitance was adjusted for the TSMC process. Finally, timing and power analysis was performed using Avant!'s HSPICE circuit tool (version 2001.2), using level 49 typical transistor parameters supplied by Taiwan Semiconductor Corporation for their TSMC 0.18μm 1.8V fabrication process. These parameters are available from MOSIS's secure website [16].

Palacharla's original analyses predate the existence of a functional 0.18μm fabrication technology. Because of this, the device parameters in that work were extrapolated from a Digital Equipment Corporation 0.8μm technology. The timing and power figures for our work were the result of porting Palacharla's original design to TSMC's 0.18μm production fabrication technology and performing timing optimizations using commercial tools configured for the implementation technology. Overall, the ported design is about 24% faster in the commercial technology. The primary factors leading to the faster design are roughly split between faster transistor speed (due to a lower threshold voltage and gate capacitance) and improved logic performance due to better transistor sizing.

Table 3 lists the circuit delay, power, and energy consumption for all analyzed scheduler configurations. For the table, all configurations assume a 4-wide machine capable of producing four results per cycle. In addition, the column labeled $f_{tagload}$ lists the relative tag broadcast bus capacitive load, compared to the same-sized two-tag baseline design. This value indicates the relative decrease in comparator diffusion capacitance, and the relative reduction in tag bus wire length due to elimination of 0-tag reservation stations and denser layout provided by the smaller 1-tag reservation stations.

Table 3: Characteristics of Studied Scheduler Configurations. Scheduler configuration are listed using the notation "x/y/z", where "x" represents the number of 2-tag reservation stations, "y" the number of 1-tag stations, and "z" the number of 0-tag stations. All schedulers are designed for use in a 4-wide microarchitecture and thus have 4 result buses.

Configuration	Total Delay (ps) (wakeup + select)	Total Power (W)	Total Energy (nJ)	$f_{tagload}$
64/0/0	466 (302 + 164)	1.550	0.468	1.0000
20/32/12	383 (219 + 164)	1.435	0.314	0.5625
16/32/16	374 (210 + 164)	1.375	0.289	0.5000
12/32/20	363 (199 + 164)	1.322	0.263	0.4375
8/32/24	355 (191 + 164)	1.250	0.239	0.3750
0/48/16	329 (165 + 164)	1.548	0.255	0.3750
0/40/24	321 (157 + 164)	1.416	0.222	0.3125
0/36/28	315 (151 + 164)	1.372	0.207	0.2813
0/32/32	313 (149 + 164)	1.281	0.191	0.2500
128/0/0	775 (573 + 202)	1.921	1.101	1.0000
40/64/24	552 (350 + 202)	2.064	0.722	0.5625
0/96/32	430 (228 + 202)	2.413	0.550	0.3750
32/0/0	349 (198 + 151)	1.068	0.211	1.0000
10/16/6	317 (166 + 151)	0.938	0.156	0.5625
0/24/8	290 (139 + 151)	0.968	0.135	0.3750

46

Slack: Maximizing Performance Under Technological Constraints

Brian Fields   Ràstislav Bodík   Mark D. Hill

Computer Sciences Department
University of Wisconsin–Madison
{fields,bodík,markhill}@cs.wisc.edu

Abstract

Many emerging processor microarchitectures seek to manage technological constraints (e.g., wire delay, power, and circuit complexity) by resorting to *non-uniform* designs that provide resources at multiple quality levels (e.g., fast/slow bypass paths, multi-speed functional units, and grid architectures). In such designs, the constraint problem becomes a control problem, and the challenge becomes designing a *control policy* that mitigates the performance penalty of the non-uniformity. Given the increasing importance of non-uniform control policies, we believe it is appropriate to examine them in their own right.

To this end, we develop *slack* for use in creating control policies that match program execution behavior to machine design. Intuitively, the slack of a dynamic instruction *i* is the number of cycles *i* can be delayed with *no effect on execution time*. This property makes slack a natural candidate for hiding non-uniform latencies.

We make three contributions in our exploration of slack. First, we formally define slack, distinguish three variants (*local*, *global* and *apportioned*), and perform a limit study to show that slack is prevalent in our SPEC2000 workload. Second, we show how to predict slack in hardware. Third, we illustrate how to create a control policy based on slack for steering instructions among fast (high power) and slow (lower power) pipelines.

1   Introduction

Recent years have witnessed a proliferation of technology *constraint-aware* design proposals. For example, physical clustering of functional units has attacked wire delays [7, 8], multi-frequency functional-units have addressed power consumption [13], and grid architectures have sought to reduce cycle time [11]. More importantly, it appears that wire, power, and circuit-complexity trends will make constraint-aware designs even more prevalent in the future.

A challenging feature of many constraint-aware designs is that they introduce *non-uniformity*, where one or more resources are available at multiple "quality" levels. For example, clustering introduce bypasses of multiple latencies, multi-speed functional units offer several execution latencies and effective issue bandwidths, and grid architectures come with a non-uniform L1-cache latency.

A key observation thus is that constraint-aware designs often turn the *constraint problem* into a *control problem*. Using a *control policy*, these designs hide non-uniformity by steering each dynamic instruction to an appropriate resource. For example, clustering comes with a register-dependence instruction-steering policy [8], multi-speed functional units come with a criticality-based steering policy [13], and grid-architecture come with a static hyperblock scheduler [11].

Common to these control policies is the goal of attempting to eliminate the performance impact of non-uniformity. The common underlying goal motivates this paper to treat the *non-uniform control* as a problem in its own right. Specifically, we ask: "Should control policies be guided by the same inputs?" and if so, "What might those unifying inputs be?" The answer to these questions may facilitate effective design of future control policies, especially in aggressively non-uniform designs where multiple control policies must coexist.

A common practice is to guide the policies with (ad hoc) design-specific inputs (such as register-dependence information that guides cluster steering). A natural and more general input is the *criticality* of a dynamic instruction. Motivated by the observation that the performance penalty is eliminated if low-quality resources never appear on an execution's critical path, one may use a criticality predictor [4, 13, 16] in an attempt to steer critical instructions to high-quality resources.

Unfortunately, criticality has several limitations. First, criticality does not tell us how many cycles a non-critical instruction can be delayed without impact. Second, criticality partitions instructions into only two classes (critical and non-critical), making it less suitable for multi-way control policies, which are needed when resources are available at more than two quality levels. Third, the relative sizes of the two classes may not match the balance desired by the control policy (typically, 95% of instructions are non-critical, which makes it difficult to obtain, for instance, a 1:1 ratio).

To address these deficiencies, we advocate guiding control policies with *slack*. Slack is a concept taken from network analysis [1] and recently applied to microarchitecture [3, 6, 12]. *Intuitively, the slack of a dynamic instruction i is the number of cycles i can be delayed with no effect on the execution.* Slack is inherently more powerful than criticality: since it reveals the "degree of criticality" of an instruction, it enables splitting instructions into more than two classes and tuning their sizes to match the needs of the various non-uniform resources.

Despite its simple definition, slack is a complex phenomenon. Even simply *exploring its potential* warrants closer examination of the definition. In particular, does "no effect on the execution" mean no effect on any dynamic instruction or no effect on the last dynamic instruction? Furthermore, how does one compute slack without having to delay the instruction and observing whether execution time increased? The task of *exploiting slack in practice* poses further challenges. In particular, how does one build a dynamic slack predictor and how should slack be used to guide a policy? This paper makes the following contributions in understanding and exploiting slack:

Modeling and characterizing microarchitectural slack. Section 2 makes three contributions. First, it defines slack formally, using a dependence-graph model that captures data dependences as well as microarchitectural resource constraints [4]. Second, it distinguishes three slack variants—*local*, *global*, and *apportioned*—that are appropriate to different control situations. Finally, a limit study reveals the existence of considerable slack. For example, 75% of dynamic instructions can be delayed by five or more cycles with no impact on program execution time. This result provides encouragement that future control policies may be able to use slack to hide the non-uniformities of emerging constraint-aware designs.

Slack prediction. To apply slack in practice, Section 3 contributes two algorithms for dynamic slack prediction. The first algorithm predicts *explicit* slack, i.e., the actual value of an instruction's slack. The second algorithm, for which we evaluate a hardware design, predicts *implicit* slack, i.e., whether an instruction can tolerate the delay of a particular slow (non-uniform) resource. The predictor effectively matches the slack available in the *microexecution* with the non-uniformity in the *machine design*, with the goal of hiding non-uniform delays. The predictor is relatively easy to implement, since it consists of only a simple state machine and the token-passing analyzer of Fields, et al. [4].

Application of slack in non-uniform control. In Section 4, we provide an example use of slack as a control mechanism. We show that slack can successfully guide a steering-and-scheduling policy on a non-uniform machine in which some pipelines (including the instruction window, register file, and functional units) run at half the frequency. Specifically, our slack-based policy improves performance on such a machine by up to 20% (10% on average) over the best existing policies, coming within 3% of a higher-power machine with all fast pipelines.

2 Characterizing Microarchitectural Slack

This section presents a study of microarchitectural slack. We explain its nature, measure its amount, and also discuss its implications on what non-uniform microarchitectures it encourages us to build.

The *slack* of an instruction i is the number of cycles i can be delayed without increasing the overall execution time. (Note that in this section, whenever we refer to an *instruction*, we mean a *dynamic instruction*.) Before conducting our experiments, we must carefully refine this seemingly simple definition and develop algorithms for its efficient computation. In the following subsections, we address four main issues:

Modeling microarchitectural slack (Section 2.1): In a complex processor, the impact of delaying an instruction i depends not only on program dependences but also on the resource constraints of the machine. What are the important machine resources to consider when computing slack, and how do we account for them?

Apportioning slack (Section 2.2): When an instruction has slack, that slack can be exploited either by the instruction itself, or by its dependent instructions. In general, the slack can be apportioned among multiple instructions that will be delayed simultaneously. What is a good way to report the amount and "apportioning flexibility" of slack?

Methodology (Section 2.3): To compute an optimal apportioning of slack across multiple instructions, it is necessary to examine large segments of the execution. How do we compute the apportioned slack efficiently?

Analysis (Section 2.4): The amount of slack affects microarchitectural decisions. What are the implications of our empirical observations on non-uniform control policies, and on the non-uniform machines that make sense to build in the future?

2.1 Modeling Slack

In order to experimentally determine *microarchitecturally accurate* slack, we must understand what impact delaying an instruction has on the complex mechanisms of an out-of-order processor—where resource constraints, as opposed to data dependences, sometimes dictate the amount of slack an instruction has. For example, if no instructions data dependent on i are fetched, we may be able to delay execution of i until just before it must be committed to avoid stalling the reorder buffer. We use the term *microexecution* to include all aspects of a given program execution on a given microarchitecture. Understanding microexecutions is important both for measuring slack via offline analysis (which we explore in this section) as well as predicting slack in hardware (discussed in Section 3).

A natural way to account for all microarchitectural effects on slack is to do so indirectly (but accurately), by employing a *delay-and-observe* approach: to determine the slack of an instruction, delay its execution by n cycles and observe if the *overall* execution time is increased. If it is not, the instruction has at least n cycles of slack. There are two serious complications with the practicality of this approach. First, to determine the precise value of slack, one needs to iterate over various values of n for a particular dynamic instruction, potentially restarting the simulation. Second, short of executing the whole program, it is not clear how to determine whether a given value of delay, n, actually slowed down the execution. These two problems make the delay-and-observe approach challenging for computing the slack of *every* dynamic instruction in the program.

Srinivasan, et al. [15] made the delay-and-observe approach feasible by sacrificing some accuracy. To avoid restarting the whole simulation, they equipped their simulator with a capability to roll back to the delayed instruction (which was always a load). To avoid rolling back from afar, they estimated early, using a set of heuristics, whether the delay actually slowed down the entire execution. The heuristics, such as whether the issue rate drops below a threshold, resulted in a measurement error of about 8%. While this methodology provided powerful (and reasonably efficient) analysis of load instructions, it may be difficult to extend its delay-and-observe approach to determining the slack when multiple non-load instructions are delayed (as opposed to a single load).

To avoid the problems with the delay-and-observe approach, our study uses an off-line method based on constructing a dependence-graph model of the execution. The graph is built by the simulator during the execution, with each edge corresponding to a dependence and annotated with the dependence's observed latency. After the execution, the slack is computed by determining how much latencies can be extended without growing the critical path of the graph (see Section 2.3).

Clearly, the graph composed of only *data* dependences will not provide much microarchitectural accuracy. The problem with a data dependence graph (DDG) is that it omits microarchitectural resource constraints, which can severely skew our slack measurements. Consider the extreme case of an instruction that writes a memory location that no other instruction in the program reads. According to the DDG, this instruction may have millions of cycles of slack. Its microarchitecturally accurate slack, however, is much shorter, as delaying the instruction by millions of cycles would stall the reorder buffer and cause a degradation in performance.

Casmira and Grunwald [3] avoid this problem by computing a "scheduling slack," which is the slack observed on a DDG constructed from instructions present in the instruction window each cycle. While this restriction adds a degree of resource sensitivity, it is still conservative in its estimation of slack. For instance, if there is only one instruction in the window, it will be determined to have a slack of zero (as it will be on the critical path), whereas this instruction may in fact have a great deal of slack (if none of its data-dependent instructions are going to be fetched for many cycles).

Fundamentally, a dependence graph is microarchitecturally accurate only when it models all dependences that govern the corresponding processor (or, equivalently, its simulator model). To obtain a microarchitecturally *sensitive* graph model, we use the model of Fields, et al. [4]. The model, summarized in Table 1 and Figure 1, accounts for in-order fetch (with edges from D_i to D_{i+1}), in-order commit (with edges from C_i to C_{i+1}), and out-of-order execution (by constraining pairs of E-nodes only with data-dependence edges). It also models fetch stalls due to the reorder buffer (with edges between C-nodes and D-nodes) and branch mispredictions (with edges between E-nodes and D-nodes, e.g., $E_7 \rightarrow D_8$). Finally, the graph also models functional-unit contention, by adding observed contention cycles into the execution latency (which is placed on EE and EC edges).

Once we have built the graph, we can identify the amount of slack an instruction has by determining how far it is from the critical path. In Figure 1, all instructions not on the critical path (marked in bold) have some amount of slack.

While this model omits some dependences, (for example, between loads that share a cache line), our validation described in Section 2.4 found that our slack calculation error is only about 1%.

2.2 Apportioning Slack

While the dependence-graph model solves the problem of how to accurately *identify* microarchitectural slack, it leaves open the question of how to *report* the slack available in the graph. The problem is that we want to distribute available slack among potentially many instructions (to be delayed simultaneously) but that distribution will vary depending on the non-uniformity to be hidden.

For example, to quantify the amount of slack available to a *set* of instructions that are to be delayed simultaneously, we define a notion of *apportioned* slack. Before we define apportioned slack, however, we will define *local* slack and *global* slack, which characterize the slack available to an *individual* instruction.

Local slack of a dynamic instruction i is the maximum number of cycles the execution of i can be delayed *without delaying **any** subsequent instructions*. From our measurements, approximately 20% of instructions have local slack greater than five cycles. Local slack is conservative because it prevents delaying any instruction in the program. To avoid impairing the overall execution, however, it suffices to ensure that the program completes in the original number of cycles. This more aggressive notion is captured by global slack.

Global slack of a dynamic instruction i is the maximum number of cycles the execution of i can be delayed *without delaying **the last** instruction in the program*. From our measurements, approximately 40% of instructions have global slack greater than 50 cycles. In other words, there is a particular set of 40% of all instructions of which *one* instruction can be picked and delayed by 50 cycles without increasing execution time. Global

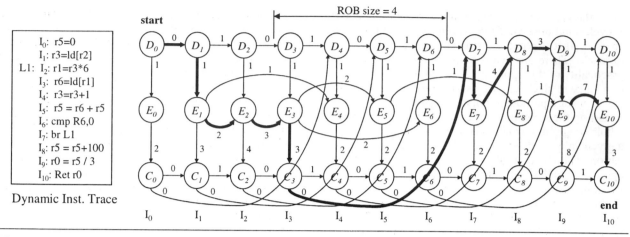

Figure 1: An instance of the critical-path model from Table 1. The dependence graph represents a sequence of dynamic instructions. Nodes are events in the lifetime of an instruction (the instruction being dispatched, executed, or committed); the edges are dependences between the occurrences of two events. A weight on an edge is the latency to resolve the corresponding dependence. The critical path is in bold.

name	constraint modeled	edge
DD	In-order dispatch	$D_{i-1} \rightarrow D_i$
CD	Finite re-order buffer	$C_{i-w} \rightarrow D_i{}^a$
ED	Control dependence	$E_{i-1} \rightarrow D_i{}^b$
DE	Execution follows dispatch	$D_i \rightarrow E_i$
EE	Data dependences	$E_j \rightarrow E_i{}^c$
EC	Commit follows execution	$E_i \rightarrow C_i$
CC	In-order commit	$C_{i-1} \rightarrow C_i$

[a] w = size of the re-order buffer
[b] inserted if $i - 1$ is a mispredicted branch
[c] inserted if instruction j produces an operand of i

Table 1: Dependences captured by the critical-path model, grouped by the target of the dependence.

slack thus reflects a policy that would seek to delay one instruction by many cycles. Global slack also serves as an upper bound on the amount of tolerable delay, since it is the maximum amount a particular instruction can be delayed without increasing execution time.

Apportioned slack captures slack available when we desire to delay *multiple instructions simultaneously*. Namely, we want to determine how many instructions can be delayed together by a certain amount of slack without impacting the execution. The desired amount of delay for each instruction depends on the apportioning strategy, which in turn depends on the particular non-uniformity whose latency we seek to hide. Thus, while global slack indicates how much *one instruction* can be delayed, apportioned slack indicates how much *a set of instructions* can be delayed simultaneously.

More formally, let S be an assignment of some amount of slack (possibly zero) to each instruction in such a way that **the last instruction is not delayed**. Given an assignment of slack S, the *apportioned slack* of instruction i is $S(i)$, i.e., the slack assigned to i. The assignment can be arbitrary (as long as it does not delay the last instruction) and is intentionally left up to the appor-

tioning strategy. Next, we define two such strategies we use later in our experiments.

Five-cycle apportioning. One way to apportion slack is to attempt to give each instruction, say, five cycles of slack. This strategy might be useful if we wanted to know how many instructions could tolerate a long (non-uniform) bypass. From our measurements (described in Section 2.4), approximately 75% of instructions have apportioned slack of five cycles. In other words, the execution contains a particular set of 75% of instructions that can be simultaneously delayed by five cycles. This surprising observation suggest tremendous optimization opportunities.

Latency-plus-one-cycle apportioning. Another apportioning strategy that we consider reflects a control policy for a constraint-aware processor that has a (power-efficient) ALU that runs at half the frequency of the other ALU. The goal of the control policy would be to maximize the number of instructions steered to the slow ALU, while maintaining the performance of a two-fast-ALUs machine. The corresponding apportioning strategy would be to maximize the number of instructions whose apportioned slack equals their original execution latency plus one cycle (so that they can tolerate the doubled latency of the slow unit plus some bypass overhead).

2.3 Algorithms for Calculating Slack

Next, we outline the algorithms for efficiently computing the three variants of slack on the dependence graph constructed during the simulation. For simplicity, we illustrate our algorithms using simple dependence graphs where *each node is a dynamic instruction*, but our experimental results use the graph of Section 2.1.

Local slack. The local slack of a *node* is determined by first computing the local slack of each *edge* in the graph. The local slack of an edge $e = u \rightarrow v$ is simply the number of cycles that the latency of e can be increased

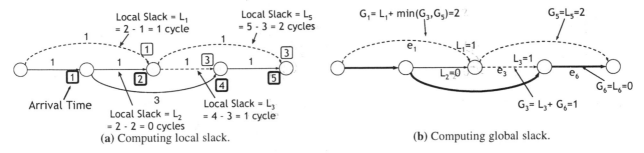

Figure 2: Computing local and global slack. Local slack is computed as the difference in arrival times of incoming edges. Global slack is computed via a reverse topological sort. Edges with nonzero local slack are dashed. In **(b)**, the critical path is in bold.

without delaying the target node v. The local slack of e is computed as the difference between the arrival time of the latest (*i.e.*, last-arriving) edge sinking on v and the arrival time of e (see Figure 2(a) for an example). The local slack of a node v is then the smallest local slack among the outgoing edges of v. Thus, the local slack of the middle node in the figure is $min(L_3, L_5) = 1$ cycle.

Global slack. As with local slack, we start by computing global slack of edges. The global slack of an edge e is the number of cycles that the latency of e can be increased without extending the graph's critical path. As with local slack, the global slack of a node v is the smallest global slack available among v's outgoing edges.

While local slack was computed by merely examining nodes and their edges, the computation of global slack involves backward propagation that accumulates local slack. Consider Figure 2(b) as an example. We start by knowing the value of local slack L_i of each edge e_i and end up computing, for each edge e_i, the value of global slack G_i for each edge.

In the example, G_3, the global slack of edge e_3, equals the sum of the local edge slacks L_3 and L_6. We can compute G_3 recursively, as the sum of L_3 and G_6. In general, the expression for computing the global slack of an edge e is $G_e = L_e + min(G_{out_1}, G_{out_2}, .., G_{out_n})$ where G_{out_1} to G_{out_n} are the global slacks of the outgoing edges of e's target node. This overall computation is a simple, linear time, reverse topological sort.

Apportioned slack. Having computed global slack, we are ready to compute apportioned slack. The goal of the algorithm is to apportion a certain amount of slack to *as many nodes as possible*, so that all nodes can be delayed (together) by the amount of slack apportioned to them without extending the critical path. The exact amount of slack we attempt to apportion to each node depends on the apportioning strategy.

The algorithm we use does not perform an optimal apportioning, but instead greedily apportions slack to the first nodes encountered during a forward pass. Due to space constraints, we only sketch the algorithm here, using the five-cycle apportioning strategy for illustration. Basically, the backward global-slack pass accumulates local slacks and deposits them on the earliest possible nodes, from where it is picked up by the forward apportioning pass. As the forward pass encounters each

node v, it is decided whether enough global slack exists to apportion v five cycles of slack. If enough exists, v is apportioned five cycles, and it is ensured that no other nodes further downstream are apportioned those five cycles. This process continues until the forward pass reaches the end of the program.

2.4 Experimental Characterization of Slack

This section presents experimental characterization of local, global and apportioned slack. Our results show that slack has a tremendous potential for hiding non-uniform latencies, in particular when large local slacks are apportioned to multiple instructions across dependence chains. This section also addresses the implications of slack: we discuss what types of design non-uniformities can be tolerated with slack and what cannot. Finally, we validate our methodology, demonstrating that our findings are very accurate.

First, we explore the *amount* of available slack, focusing on microexecutions of typical SPEC2000 programs on an unclustered version of the 6-wide processor described in Section 4.2. We compute slack using the graph of Section 2.1, and when we refer to the slack of an instruction, we mean the slack of that instruction's E node. Figures 3(a)-3(c) plot the local, global and apportioned slack found in *gcc*, *gzip*, and *perl*, respectively. These three benchmarks were chosen because they illustrate the two extreme results (*gcc* and *gzip*) and a typical result (*perl*) from the full set of measurements we performed.

Local and global slack. The slack measurements reported in the charts should be interpreted as follows: for each data point (**x**, **y**), **y**% of (dynamic) instructions have **x** *or more* cycles of slack. In *gcc*, for instance, approximately 36% of instructions have local slack of five or more cycles. In general, we observe that relatively few instructions contain local slack that is large enough to be exploitable: on average only about 20% of instructions have local slack of five or more cycles. At the same time, we notice that a small number of instructions contain extremely large local slack (in *gzip*, about 2% of instructions have more than 80 cycles of local slack). This large local slack is promising because a single instruction is unlikely to be able to exploit it all, allowing us to apportion it to instructions without enough local slack.

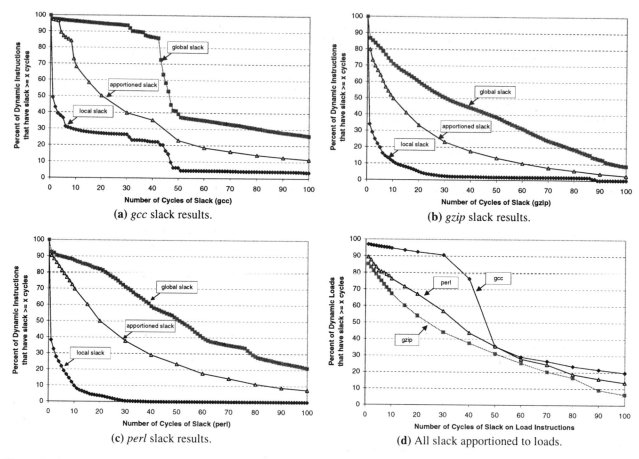

(a) *gcc* slack results.

(b) *gzip* slack results.

(c) *perl* slack results.

(d) All slack apportioned to loads.

Figure 3: **Across benchmarks, there is enormous potential for exploitation of slack.** (a)-(c) Measurements of local, apportioned, and global slack for SPEC2000 versions of *gcc*, *gzip*, and *perl*. *gcc* and *gzip* represent the two extremes in the amount of slack available in the full set of benchmarks we ran; *perl* is more typical. The measurements indicate that even in the least slackful benchmark, *gzip*, there is enormous potential for hiding delays introduced by nonuniform machines. (d) Measurements of apportioned slack when all available slack is apportioned to load instructions. These results show it may be possible to tolerate technologically-induced bottlenecks on load instructions if, for instance, wire delays cause some instructions to endure longer L1 data cache access times than others.

Note that, while the figures only show local slack for the *execution* of instructions (*E* nodes in our model), other micro-operations associated with an instruction may also exhibit local slack. For instance, we may be able to delay the *commit* of an instruction (represented by *C* nodes in our model) without delaying any other instructions. Since our dependence-graph model accounts for this commit micro-operation, we can also apportion this local slack to other instructions.

To determine to what extent large local slacks can be used by neighboring instructions, we examine global slack. Since the global slack of an instruction is the accumulation of all local slacks that could be "stolen" from other instructions, observing a lot of global slack on many instructions would speak well for the potential for exploitation, since this would mean that lots of local slack is "freely movable" across the microexecution. Indeed, this is the case: about 40% of instructions have more than 50 cycles of global slack. The key question now is what fraction of this global slack remains if we spread it out

across neighboring instructions. We answer this question using apportioned slack.

Apportioned slack. To calculate apportioned slack, we must first decide on the apportioning strategy. Let us first consider giving **x** cycles of slack to as many instructions as possible. The amount of such apportioned slack is shown along with local and global slack in Figures 3(a)-3(c) for a range of values of **x**.

Again, the experiments present good news: not only does the microexecution contain a lot of apportionable local slack (which we knew from global slack measurements), but this slack is also able to satisfy many instructions: on average, 75% of instructions can be apportioned slack of five cycles. Even in the least slackful benchmark, *gzip*, there are 64% of instructions that have 5 cycles of slack. This means, for instance, that most instructions can tolerate long-latency communication across a chip without hurting performance—as long as the delayed instructions are chosen wisely (*i.e*, with a good slack predictor and a good policy).

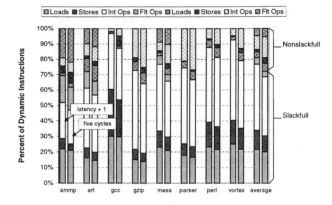

Figure 4: Limit studies. Measurements for two apportioning strategies are shown: *latency-plus-one-cycle* and *five-cycle* apportioning. These measurements provide an indication as to what types of non-uniform machine designs can be tolerated by a slack-based policy. For instance, latency-plus-one-cycle apportioning is relevant for the fast/slow pipeline microarchitecture studied in Section 4.

Of course, the above apportioning strategy does not reflect all non-uniformities that a control policy may have to tolerate. For instance, another interesting question is how many loads can tolerate a long latency to the L1 data cache, a concern of wire-constrained designs such as the Grid Architecture [11]. To maximize slack on loads, we modify the above apportioning strategy such that no slack is apportioned to non-load instructions. Figure 3(d) reports the results of such an apportioning. We see that a remarkable number of loads could tolerate a long-latency L1 data cache hit. Namely, there are more than 65% of load instructions with a slack of 12 cycles, enough to tolerate an L2 hit. Together, the data suggest an opportunity to build selective L1-cache bypasses.

Breakdown of slack per opcode. In Figure 4, we examine how much apportioned slack is available to instructions of various types. The figure computes the breakdown for the two apportioning strategies described in Section 2.2: five-cycles-per-instruction and latency-plus-one-cycle. The figure classifies instructions into four categories: loads, stores, integer operations, and floating-point operations. (Note that our simulator discards all NOP instructions after fetch, and, thus, they are not included in any of the slack measurements.)

Figure 4 leads to several conclusions about what types of non-uniformities can be tolerated with slack.

- Most instructions (on average, greater than 75%) have enough slack to tolerate doubling their latency. This means we can run most functional units at half-speed without losing performance, provided we are successful at predicting which instructions have slack. This result is good news for the fast/slow pipelines microarchitecture we study in Section 4.

- A large percentage of instructions of each type can have their latency doubled; this holds even for longer latency floating-point operations.

- There is no instruction type which nearly always has slack. Thus, a machine design that simply makes all functional units of a particular type slower is likely to degrade performance.

Validation. We need to validate our experiments since (as previously mentioned) the dependence-graph model we use to compute slack only includes the most significant microarchitectural dependences. Thus, the slack measurements have some error.

We confirm correctness of the slack measurements by the following two-step process: (1) we identify apportioned slack on the graph, as usual; and, then, (2) we re-run the simulation on which the graph was constructed, but in this new run, each dynamic instruction is delayed by its apportioned slack. Since we are delaying the instruction in the actual (simulated) execution, errors in the graph-computed slack will be manifested as increases in the execution time of the simulation.

We performed this validation with several different apportioning strategies: *latency-plus-one-cycle* and *five-cycle* apportioning from Figure 4 and *12-cycles to loads* from Figure 3(d). Space limitations prohibit detailed presentation of results, but the maximum error observed across all benchmarks and apportioning strategies was less than 3%, with an average error of about 1%, which is less than previous related efforts [15].

3 Predicting Slack

Our slack predictors follow the history-based approach used in most hardware predictors: the slack of a dynamic instruction, known after the instruction commits, trains a PC-indexed predictor, which is then used to predict the slack of future instances of the same static instruction. An alternative would be a context-based approach that would predict slack based on the current state of, say, the scheduling window [5]. The advantage of the history-based approach is that it allows predicting slack early in the pipeline.

Two conditions must be met to enable history-based slack prediction. First, there must be a locality of slack, in that dynamic instances of a given static instruction exhibit roughly the same slack. Second, we must design a hardware mechanism for measuring slack of a dynamic instruction. We meet the two conditions in the following two subsections. Then, equipped with a hardware slack *detector*, we develop two slack *predictors*. The predictors differ in what is stored in the predictor table: the *explicit-slack* predictor learns the actual value of slack of the static instruction; the *implicit-slack* predictor learns whether the static instruction can tolerate the delay of a particular non-uniform resource.

3.1 Locality of Slack

Since slack arises partly due to microarchitectural events, like reorder-buffer stalls caused by cache misses, one might expect that dynamic slack is distributed across the instruction stream more or less randomly, complicating

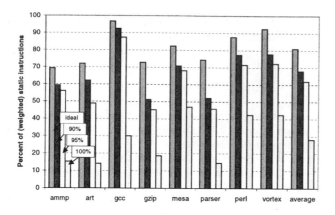

Figure 5: **Mapping dynamic slack behavior to static instructions.** Uses latency-plus-one-cycle apportioning. On the y-axis, the number of slackful static instructions is weighted by the number of each static instruction's dynamic instances.

predictability. Our experiments present good news: 68% of static instructions (dynamically weighted) *almost always* have enough slack to double their latency (precisely, they have enough slack on at least 90% of their dynamic instances; see Figure 5). More significantly, this slack represents about 80% of all apportioned slack (that is, 80% of slack exploitable by an oracle predictor that correctly predicts the slack of every dynamic instruction).

In more detail, our experiments used the following methodology. First, we computed the apportioned slack using the latency-plus-one strategy introduced in Section 2. Next, we identified *slackful* static instructions. A static instruction is slackful if $D\%$ of its dynamic instructions contained apportioned slack, where D was varied from 90 to 100. Figure 5 plots the amount of slackful static instructions. The chart also plots the total amount of apportioned slack (labeled *ideal*). This slack could be exploited with an oracle predictor that is correct on each dynamic instruction. Note that while relatively few static instructions are slackful all the time (28%, on average), allowing just 5% "misprediction rate" (*i.e.*, requiring them to be slackful 95% of the time) brings this amount to 62%, on average.

3.2   Measuring Slack in Hardware

In Section 2.1, we described the delay-and-observe approach, as a natural—but expensive approach—for accurately measuring slack in a processor *simulator*. In that approach, a dynamic instruction is delayed by n cycles, after which the execution is observed. If the overall execution is not slowed down, the instruction has at least n cycles of (global) slack.

In this section, we use the delay-and-observe paradigm to design *hardware* for measuring slack. We accomplish this goal by elegantly solving the two implementation challenges of the delay-and-observe approach. Specifically, the challenges are: **(1)** measuring slack of a dynamic instruction requires repeatedly delaying the instruction for various values of delay, which involves

rolling back the execution; and **(2)** determining (naively) whether the overall execution was affected by the delay requires comparing the original and the perturbed execution. To solve the first challenge, we sample each *dynamic* instruction at most once. Such sampling avoids the need for rollback yet is sufficient to determine the slack of a *static* instruction, since we exploit the locality of slack presented in Section 3.1.

To solve the second problem (determining whether the execution was affected by the delay), we exploit the following observation: *the overall execution is slowed down by the delay if and only if the delayed instruction appears on the critical path of the micro-execution.*[1] With this observation, we can reduce the problem of detecting slack to that of determining criticality, which can be easily performed using our token-passing criticality detector [4].

For the sake of completeness, we sketch here the algorithm behind the token-passing detector of criticality [4]. For simplicity, we will explain its operation on data dependences, but the detector actually operates on the graph model illustrated in Figure 1. The detector is based on the observation that a dynamic instruction i is not critical if either of two conditions hold: **(1)** the value v computed by i arrives at each consumer j before one of j's remaining operands arrives (*i.e.*, if v is not *last-arriving* and, hence, has non-zero local slack at j); or **(2)** if the consuming instruction j is not critical. Thus, we need to determine if the value v computed by i traverses a long chain of data dependences where consumers are always waiting for it (*i.e.*, where it was always last arriving). If this situation occurs, i is predicted critical—otherwise it is known to be non-critical.

This observation lends itself to an efficient hardware implementation: to determine if dynamic instruction i is critical, plant a token into i (the token can be thought of as an extra bit appended to the data computed by the instruction). The token is then propagated together with the data to all dependent instructions, except that it is killed whenever the data is not last-arriving at a consumer instruction. After a few hundred instructions, the detector examines the machine: if at least one copy of the token is alive, the dynamic instruction was critical (because there must have been at least one chain of data dependences on which the data was always last arriving.) With high probability, i is part of the critical path, since delaying i would delay all instructions on this long chain.

To put the pieces together, our slack detector works as follows. Given a dynamic instruction i and a value n, the slack detector answers the question "does i have at least n cycles of slack?" The slack detector is a simple delay-and-observe extension of the criticality detector [4]: it first delays the instruction by $n-1$ cycles (see footnote 1) and then observes, by planting a token into i, whether the delayed instruction i is critical. If i is critical, then it does not have n cycles of slack; otherwise it does.

---

[1]Strictly speaking, this observation makes a one-cycle mistake, because a delay may make the dynamic instruction critical without making the critical path any longer.

3.3 Explicit-Slack Predictor

The explicit slack predictor learns and predicts the *actual* number of cycles of slack available in each static instruction. The predictor is trained by sampling dynamic instructions—using the slack detector described above—under various values of slack n. The goal of sampling is to converge to the average value of slack for each static instruction, which can be achieved with a binary search (assuming the instruction has good slack locality).

It should be noted that training the predictor by delaying a dynamic instruction is not likely to noticeably slow down the program because (i) sampling is sparse (in our designs, the sampling rate is roughly 1 instruction per 100 instructions, and can be even sparser), and (ii) the inserted delay is typically just large enough to make the instruction critical, which means that the delay may extend the critical path by at most a few cycles.

Predicting explicit slack, however, produces some challenges. Most importantly, it is not clear how to avoid measurement perturbation due to non-uniform resources. For example, on a machine with both fast and slow functional units, an instruction will appear to have different slack, depending on which functional units it (and its dependents) were executing when its slack was sampled.

3.4 Implicit-Slack Predictor

We address the measurement perturbation problems with an *implicit-slack* predictor, which, instead of predicting *exactly* how much slack an instruction has, predicts whether it has *enough* slack to tolerate a particular non-uniform resource—for instance, whether its execution latency can be doubled without impact on performance.

The implicit-slack predictor works by dividing instructions into *slack bins*, according to the resources that these instructions can tolerate. The number of bins is determined by the number of decisions a control policy must make for each instruction. For an example, let us consider the non-uniform machine used in Section 4 for our experiments. The control policy for this machine must make two decisions for each instruction i: (1) should i be steered to the fast or slow pipeline? and (2) should i be scheduled with high priority or low priority within a pipeline? These two decisions lead to four slack bins:

1. steer to fast pipeline & schedule with high priority,

2. steer to fast pipeline & schedule with low priority,

3. steer to slow pipeline & schedule with high priority,

4. steer to slow pipeline & schedule with low priority.

These four bins can be viewed as corresponding to four *virtual* non-uniform resources, where each dynamic instruction is assigned to one resource. In general, if a control policy must make k decisions for each instruction, we have 2^k virtual resources, each corresponding to a slack bin.

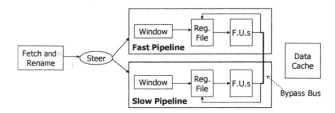

Figure 6: **The non-uniform microarchitecture used in our experiments.** The processor consists of one fast and one (or two) slow pipelines.

Measuring implicit slack has four important advantages. First, when sampling the slack, we don't need dedicated logic to artificially delay the instruction. Instead, the predictor can delay the instruction *naturally*, by steering it to the sampled non-uniform resource. Second, as desired, by measuring tolerance to non-uniform delays, we effectively remove the impact of perturbation on the measurement. Third, bin membership can be trained faster than the actual slack. Dealing with bins, rather than with the actual slack, can be much easier for the control policy.

Finally, it should be noted that while the four slack bins above are ordered in seemingly decreasing priority, it does not mean that the slack of instructions in bin 3 is greater than those in bin 2. In general, into which bin an instruction falls depends purely on which resource it can tolerate, which is the fourth advantage of the the implicit-slack approach.

4 Example Use of Slack in Non-Uniform Control

In this section, we evaluate the success of slack in guiding a non-uniform control policy. We define an aggressively non-uniform (power-aware) microarchitecture and design a slack-based control policy for hiding its non-uniformities. We compare the slack-based policy with several policies based on existing control techniques and discover that slack is remarkably more successful at hiding the performance penalties that arise due to non-uniform resources.

Specifically, we evaluate a slack-based control policy on the machine pictured in Figure 6. In this design, the microarchitecture is divided into two *pipelines*, with each pipeline consisting of half of the *instruction window, issue logic, and functional units*; and a copy of the register file. The design saves power by running one pipeline at half frequency, exploiting the (approximate) relationship $P \propto FV^2$ between power P, voltage V and frequency F. By halving the frequency, we can reduce voltage enough that the overall power consumption is reduced roughly to a fourth ($P \propto F^2$). (Note that reducing the frequency of such a large portion of the pipeline is a more aggressive power-aware design than one that only reduces the functional-unit speed.)

4.1 Control Policies

At a first glance, it may seem that reducing the frequency on one pipeline introduces only one kind of non-uniformity. The reality is that in our design we need to deal with three forms of non-uniformity:

1. The *execution latencies* of functional units in the slow pipeline will be twice as large as those in the fast pipeline.

2. The *bypass latency* between the two pipelines will be longer than the intra-pipeline bypass latency, due to physical distance and due to crossing voltage domains.

3. The *effective issue bandwidth* of the slow pipeline will be half of the bandwidth of the fast pipeline, because the slow pipeline issues instructions every other fast cycle. This reduction in issue bandwidth manifests itself as increased contention (which happens to be the hardest constraint to deal with).

The important consequence of the third point is that frequency reduction reduces the effective bandwidth of the *entire* machine. This observation is important because it sets the correct expectation on the control policy: when a workload is bandwidth-limited (i.e., exhibits high IPC rate), no control policy will be able to avoid the performance penalty.

To attack the above three non-uniformities, we design a slack-based policy that controls two machine aspects:

- *Instruction steering*, which determines into which pipeline a dynamic instruction is sent.

- *Instruction scheduling*, which determines which of the data-ready instructions in a pipeline are executed.

We assume that the steering decision is performed before any scheduling decisions are carried out.

Our slack-based policy employs four bins, as introduced and motivated in Section 3.4. These four bins control to which pipeline an instruction will be steered, and also how the instruction will be scheduled within the pipeline (see Table 3). Note that we also experimented with two-bin policies (which performed steering but no slack-based scheduling), but the four-bin scheme performed up to 5% better.

To assign a slack bin to each static instruction, our slack policy uses a 4K-entry array of 6-bit saturating counters, indexed by PC. The counter is decremented by one if the slack sampling (see Section 3.4) detects that the instruction can tolerate a given pipeline and a given scheduling policy (i.e., is slackful enough for the pipeline/scheduling combination). The instruction is moved to a lower-numbered bin when the counter reaches zero and to a higher-bin if it is detected that it does not have enough slack for the given level.

We compare our slack-based policy to several policies based on existing (non-slack-based) control techniques. While we experimented with many such policies, we only present three that performed best (see Table 2). The first is a simple register-dependence steering policy, while the other two "favor" the fast pipeline over the slow one in that instructions are steered to the fast pipeline until some condition is met. We also evaluate the use of the ALOLD criticality predictor from Tune, et al. [16], as a replacement for the token-passing criticality analyzer [4] in the slack detector (see Section 2.4). (We also experimented with the QOLD criticality predictor from the same work [13, 16], but the ALOLD predictor performed considerably better in our context.)

Name	Policy
Reg-Dependence	Perform load balancing if one pipeline is four times as full as another. Otherwise, steer instruction to pipeline that will produce one or more of its inputs. Steer to least-filled pipeline if all operands are ready
Fast-first Window	Send instructions to the fast pipeline until its window becomes half full, then apply register-dependence steering.
Fast-first Ready	Send instructions to fast pipeline until there were more ready instructions then issue slots over the last 5 cycles. Then, apply register-dependence steering.

Table 2: **Baseline policies for controlling fast/slow pipeline microarchitecture.**

4.2 Methodology

Our evaluation uses a typical dynamically-scheduled superscalar processor as a baseline whose configuration is detailed in Table 4. The simulator is built upon the SimpleScalar tool set [2]. Our benchmarks consist of a subset of the SPEC2000 benchmark suite; all are optimized Alpha binaries using reference inputs. Initialization phases were skipped and detailed simulation ran until 100 million instructions were committed.

4.3 Experimental Evaluation

We evaluate the set of control policies on a machine with one 3-wide fast pipeline and one 3-wide slow pipeline (*3f+3s*). The results, presented in Figure 7, yield two overall conclusions. First, our slack-based policy performs better than any non-slack policy, by 10% on average. Second, using slack reduces the performance degradation (with respect to the high-power *3f+3f* configuration) from an average of 16% to only 3%.

It is interesting to observe the effect of replacing the token-passing detector with the ALOLD predictor: while ALOLD performs better than the non-slack schemes, degrading performance by 10%, it appears that the token-passing detector is needed to accurately measure slack.

In an attempt to recoup the small performance loss of *3f+3s*, we experimented with other configurations where issue bandwidth is made equal to *3f+3f* through the ad-

Slack bin #	Policy decisions	Hysteresis counter
4	Fast pipeline, high priority schedule	Initialize to 0 upon entering level. Increase by 8 if detected not slackful.
3	Fast pipeline, low priority schedule	Initialize to 63 upon entering level. Immediately go to level 4 if detected not slackful.
2	Slow pipeline, high priority schedule	Initialize to 63 upon entering level. Immediately go to level 3 if detected not slackful.
1	Slow pipeline, low priority schedule	Initialize to 63 upon entering level. Immediately go to level 2 if detected not slackful.

Table 3: **Hysteresis implementing the four slack bins.** Note: if the slow instruction window contains four times as many instructions as the fast pipeline, the slack-based steering decision is overridden, and the incoming instruction is sent to the fast pipeline. Such load balancing never sends instructions to the slow pipeline.

Dynamically Scheduled Core	128-entry instruction window (64 entries in each of 2 pipelines) with critical-first scheduling, 256-entry re-order buffer, 6-way issue, 12-cycle pipeline, perfect memory disambiguation, fetch stops at second taken branch in a cycle, 1 cycle normal bypass latency plus one cycle extra delay if sending data from one clock domain to another.
Branch Prediction	Combined bimodal (8k entry)/gshare (8k entry) predictor with an 8k meta predictor, 4K entry 2-way associative BTB, 64-entry return address stack.
Memory System	64KB 2-way associative L1 instruction and data (2 cycle latency) caches, shared 1 MB 4-way associative 12 cycle latency L2 cache, 100 cycle memory latency, 128-entry DTLB; 64-entry ITLB, 30 cycle TLB miss handling latency.
Functional Units (latency)	In each of 2 pipelines: 3 Integer ALUs (1), 1 Integer MULT (3), 2 Floating ALU (2), 1 Floating MULT/DIV (4/12), 1 LD/ST ports (2).
Token-passing Slack Predictor	4K-entry array for storing predictions (2 bit bin, 6 bit hysteresis per entry), 768-byte training array—(8 tokens x 3 nodes x 256-entry ROB) bits

Table 4: **Configuration of simulated processor.**

dition of another slow pipeline. In these equi-bandwidth configurations, we found that our slack-based policy actually slightly improved performance over *3f+3f*, while the non-slack policies significantly degraded it, by 12–15% on average.

Specifically, the two additional configurations were *3f+3s+3s* and *Half_3f+3s+3s*, each with one 3-wide fast pipeline and two 3-wide slow pipelines; but, in *Half_3f+3s+3s*, the window size of each slow pipeline is halved (so that the effective window size is equal to that of *3f+3f*). The decrease in window size of *Half_3f+3s+3s* resulted in only a modest performance loss of 1–2% compared to *3f+3s+3s*,

To estimate the power savings obtained from the configurations, we can directly apply the relationship $P \propto F^2$. For the *3f+3s* configuration, we save 37.5% of the power of the *core* (including the instruction window, issue logic, register file, and functional units), and for the *3f+3s+3s* configuration, we save 25%. The latter result is interesting, since it suggests we can obtain significant power savings with some cost in area, but no loss in performance, by exploiting a control policy based on slack.

5 Related Work

As most related work has already been discussed in relevant sections, we will only summarize here. Srinivasan and Lebeck [15] and Rakvic, et al. [10] perform measurements of load latency tolerance in out-of-order processors. The concept of using dynamic scheduling slack

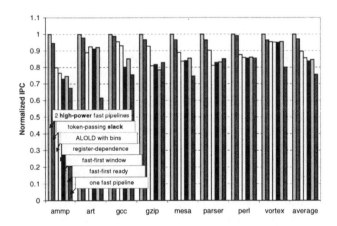

Figure 7: **Comparing control policies on fast/slow pipeline microarchitecture.** All measurements are normalized to the baseline of two fast 3-wide pipelines (*3f+3f*). Also, results are shown for a single fast 3-wide pipeline (*3f*) for reference. The rest of the measurements are different control policies for a *3f+3s* machine.

for controlling microarchitectures through clustered voltage scaling was proposed by Casmira and Grunwald [3]. In these works, no slack predictor design was studied.

Much research has explored using critical-path predictions in control policies for various optimizations, including power optimizations [9, 13], cluster steering [4, 16], dynamic instruction scheduling [4], value prediction [4,16], and cache optimizations [5,14]. In our work, we characterize and exploit the more powerful property of *slack* and show how to predict it. We show how to exploit prior research into criticality predictors when designing an efficient slack predictor, principally by "binning" instructions based on the latency they can tolerate.

Semeraro, et al. [12] use a dependence-graph model similar to ours for doing an offline slack analysis to determine when different parts of the machine can be executed at a slower rate, for power efficiency. Our work characterizes slack more fully and provides an online predictor. Grunwald [6] describes a hardware predictor based on measuring how much an instruction's execution can be delayed without delaying subsequent instructions. This hardware appears to predict what we call local slack in our work. As shown in Section 2, local slack is only a small part of all the slack that is available.

The model and token-passing criticality detector we used came from our previous work on critical-path prediction [4]. We have extended this research to measure and predict slack, as opposed to simple criticality, and showed how slack can be exploited to hide the latencies of nonuniform machine designs.

6 Conclusion

We have developed slack as a useful input for guiding control policies in modern processors. We defined three variants of slack (having in mind various applications of slack) and presented a novel methodology for accurately measuring the amount of slack available in programs. We have shown there is a surprisingly large amount of exploitable slack and that most of it can be predicted easily with a token-passing criticality analyzer.

Finally, we showed how to design a slack-based control policy for a power-efficient microarchitecture with fast and slow pipelines. Our experiments showed that the slack-based policy eliminates most of the penalty due to the non-uniformities, such that the fast/slow pipeline microarchitecture performs nearly as well as a uniform machine with only fast pipelines. This experiment has significant implications for future machine designs: we may be able to mitigate technological constraints (e.g., wire delay, power, and circuit complexity) by building non-uniform machines and then controlling them with a slack-based policy.

Acknowledgements. We thank Alvy Lebeck, Sanjay Patel, Nilofer Motiwala, Paramjit Oberoi, Shai Rubin, Craig Zilles, and the anonymous reviewers for comments on drafts of the paper. We also thank Konrad Lai, C.J. Newburn, Jared Stark, Srikanth Srinivasan, Chris Wilkerson, and the Wisconsin Architecture Industrial affiliates for discussions on slack and its exploitation. This work was supported in part by an IBM Faculty Partnership Award, National Science Foundation grants (EIA-0103670, EIA-9971256, CDA-9623632, and CCR-0105721), an NSF CAREER award (CCR-0093275), a Wisconsin Romnes Fellowship, and donations from Intel, Microsoft, and Sun Microsystems. Brian Fields was partially supported by an NSF Graduate Research Fellowship.

References

[1] A. Battersby. *Network Analysis for Planning and Scheduling, 3rd. ed.* John Wiley and Sons, Inc., 1970.

[2] D. C. Burger and T. M. Austin. The simplescalar tool set, version 2.0. Technical Report CS-TR-1997-1342, University of Wisconsin, Madison, Jun 1997.

[3] J. Casmira and D. Grunwald. Dynamic instruction scheduling slack. In *Kool Chips Workshop in conjunction with MICRO 33*, Dec 2000.

[4] B. Fields, S. Rubin, and R. Bodík. Focusing processor policies via critical-path prediction. In *Proceedings of the 28th Annual International Symposium on Computer Architecture*, Jun–Jul 2001.

[5] B. R. Fisk and R. I. Bahar. The non-critical buffer: Using load latency tolerance to improve data cache efficiency. In *IEEE International Conference on Computer Design*, Oct 1999.

[6] D. Grunwald. Chapter 4: Micro-architecture design and control speculation for energy reduction. *To Appear in Power-Aware Computing*, edited by R. Graybill and R. Melhem, Kluwer Academic Publishers.

[7] L. Gwennap. Digital 21264 sets new standard. *Microprocessor Report*, 10:9–15, Oct 1996.

[8] S. Palacharla, N. P. Jouppi, and J. E. Smith. Complexity-effective superscalar processors. In *24th Annual International Symposium on Computer Architecture*, Jun 1997.

[9] R. Pyreddy and G. Tyson. Evaluating design tradeoffs in dual speed pipelines. In *Workshop on Complexity-Effective Design in conjunction with ISCA 2001*, Jun 2001.

[10] R. Rakvic, D. Limaye, and J. P. Shen. Non-vital loads. Technical Report CMuART-2000-02, Carnegie Mellon University, 2000.

[11] K. Sankaralingam, R. Nagarajan, D.C. Burger, and S.W. Keckler. A design space evaluation of grid processor architectures. In *Proceedings of the 34th Annual International Symposium on Microarchitecture*, Dec 2001.

[12] G. Semeraro, G. Magklis, R. Balasubramonian, D.H. Albonesi, S. Dwarkadas, and M.L. Scott. Energy-efficient processor design using multiple clock domains with dynamic voltage and frequency scaling. In *Proceedings of the 8th International Symposium on High-Performance Computer Architecture*, Feb 2002.

[13] John S. Seng, Eric S. Tune, and Dean M. Tullsen. Reducing power with dynamic critical path information. In *Proceedings of the 34th Annual International Symposium on Microarchitecture*, Dec 2001.

[14] S. T. Srinivasan, R. Dz ching Ju, A. R. Lebeck, and C. Wilkerson. Locality vs. criticality. In *Proceedings of the 28th Annual International Symposium on Computer Architecture*, Jun 2001.

[15] S. T. Srinivasan and A. R. Lebeck. Load latency tolerance in dynamically scheduled processors. In *Proceedings of the 31st Annual International Symposium on Microarchitecture*, Nov–Dec 1998.

[16] E. Tune, D. Liang, D. M. Tullsen, and B. Calder. Dynamic prediction of critical path instructions. In *Proceedings of the Seventh International Symposium on High-Performance Computer Architecture*, Jan 2001.

A Large, Fast Instruction Window for Tolerating Cache Misses

Alvin R. Lebeck[†]   Jinson Koppanalil[‡]   Tong Li[†]   Jaidev Patwardhan[†]   Eric Rotenberg[‡]

[†] Department of Computer Science
Duke University
Durham, NC 27708-90129 USA
{alvy,tongli,jaidev}@cs.duke.edu

[‡] Department of Electrical and Computer
Engineering
North Carolina State University
Raleigh, NC 27695-7914 USA
{jjkoppan,ericro}@ece.ncsu.edu

Abstract

Instruction window size is an important design parameter for many modern processors. Large instruction windows offer the potential advantage of exposing large amounts of instruction level parallelism. Unfortunately, naively scaling conventional window designs can significantly degrade clock cycle time, undermining the benefits of increased parallelism.

This paper presents a new instruction window design targeted at achieving the latency tolerance of large windows with the clock cycle time of small windows. The key observation is that instructions dependent on a long latency operation (e.g., cache miss) cannot execute until that source operation completes. These instructions are moved out of the conventional, small, issue queue to a much larger waiting instruction buffer *(WIB). When the long latency operation completes, the instructions are reinserted into the issue queue. In this paper, we focus specifically on load cache misses and their dependent instructions. Simulations reveal that, for an 8-way processor, a 2K-entry WIB with a 32-entry issue queue can achieve speedups of 20%, 84%, and 50% over a conventional 32-entry issue queue for a subset of the SPEC CINT2000, SPEC CFP2000, and Olden benchmarks, respectively.*

1 Introduction

Many of today's microprocessors achieve high performance by combining high clock rates with the ability to dynamically process multiple instructions per cycle. Unfortunately, these two important components of performance are often at odds with one another. For example, small hardware structures are usually required to achieve short clock cycle times, while larger structures are often necessary to identify and exploit instruction level parallelism (ILP).

A particularly important structure is the issue window, which is examined each cycle to choose ready instructions for execution. A larger window can often expose a larger number of independent instructions that can execute out-of-order. Unfortunately, the size of the issue window is limited due to strict cycle time constraints. This conflict between cycle time and dynamically exploiting parallelism is exacerbated by long latency operations such as data cache misses or even cross-chip communication [1, 22]. The challenge is to develop microarchitectures that permit both short cycle times and large instruction windows.

This paper introduces a new microarchitecture that reconciles the competing goals of short cycle times and large instruction windows. We observe that instructions dependent on long latency operations cannot execute until the long latency operation completes. This allows us to separate instructions into those that will execute in the near future and those that will execute in the distant future. The key to our design is that the entire chain of instructions dependent on a long latency operation is removed from the issue window, placed in a *waiting instruction buffer* (WIB), and reinserted after the long latency operation completes. Furthermore, since all instructions in the dependence chain are candidates for reinsertion into the issue window, we only need to implement select logic rather than the full wakeup-select required by a conventional issue window. Tracking true dependencies (as done by the wakeup logic) is handled by the issue window when the instructions are reinserted.

In this paper we focus on tolerating data cache misses, however we believe our technique could be extended to other operations where latency is difficult to determine at compile time. Specifically, our goal is to explore the design of a microarchitecture with a large enough "effective" window to tolerate DRAM accesses. We leverage existing techniques to provide a large register file [13, 34] and assume that a large active list[1] is possible since it is not on the critical path [4] and techniques exist for keeping the active list

---

[1]By active list, we refer to the hardware unit that maintains the state of in-flight instructions, often called the reorder buffer.

large while using relatively small hardware structures [31].

We explore several aspects of WIB design, including: detecting instructions dependent on long latency operations, inserting instructions into the WIB, banked vs. non-banked organization, policies for selecting among eligible instructions to reinsert into the issue window, and total capacity. For an 8-way processor, we compare the committed instructions per cycle (IPC) of a WIB-based design that has a 32-entry issue window, a 2048-entry banked WIB, and two-level register files (128 L1/2048 L2) to a conventional 32-entry issue window with single-level register files (128 registers). These simulations show WIB speedups over the conventional design of 20% for SPEC CINT2000, 84% for SPEC CFP2000, and 50% for Olden. These speedups are a significant fraction of those achieved with a 2048-entry conventional issue window (35%, 140%, and 103%), even ignoring clock cycle time effects.

The remainder of this paper is organized as follows. Section 2 provides background and motivation for this work. Our design is presented in Section 3 and we evalute its performance in Section 4. Section 5 discusses related work and Section 6 summarizes this work and presents future directions.

2 Background and Motivation

2.1 Background

Superscalar processors maximize serial program performance by issuing multiple instructions per cycle. One of the most important aspects of these systems is identifying independent instructions that can execute in parallel. To identify and exploit instruction level parallelism (ILP), most of today's processors employ dynamic scheduling, branch prediction, and speculative execution. Dynamic scheduling is an all hardware technique for identifying and issuing multiple independent instructions in a single cycle [32]. The hardware looks ahead by fetching instructions into a buffer—*called a window*—from which it selects instructions to issue to the functional units. Instructions are issued only when all their operands are available, and independent instructions can execute out-of-order. Results of instructions executed out-of-order are committed to the architectural state in program order. In other words, although instructions within the window execute out-of-order, the window entries are managed as a FIFO where instructions enter and depart in program order.

The above simplified design assumes that all instructions in the window can be examined and selected for execution. We note that it is possible to separate the FIFO management (active list or reorder buffer) from the independent instruction identification (issue queue) as described below. Regardless, there is a conflict between increasing the window (issue queue) size to expose more ILP and keeping clock cycle time low by using small structures [1, 22]. Historically, smaller windows have dominated designs resulting in higher clock rates. Unfortunately, a small window can quickly fill up when there is a long latency operation.

In particular, consider a long latency cache miss serviced from main memory. This latency can be so large, that by the time the load reaches the head of the window, the data still has not arrived from memory. Unfortunately, this significantly degrades performance since the window does not contain any executing instructions: instructions in the load's dependence chain are stalled, and instructions independent of the load are finished, waiting to commit in program order. The only way to make progress is to bring new instructions into the window. This can be accomplished by using a larger window.

2.2 Limit Study

The remainder of this section evaluates the effect of window size on program performance, ignoring clock cycle time effects. The goal is to determine the potential performance improvement that could be achieved by large instruction windows. We begin with a description of our processor model. This is followed by a short discussion of its performance for various instruction window sizes.

2.2.1 Methodology

For this study, we use a modified version of SimpleScalar (version 3.0b) [8] with the SPEC CPU2000 [17] and Olden [11] benchmark suites. Our SPEC CPU2000 benchmarks are pre-compiled binaries obtained from the SimpleScalar developers [33] that were generated with compiler flags as suggested at www.spec.org and the Olden binaries were generated with the Alpha compiler (cc) using optimization flag -O2. The SPEC benchmarks operate on their reference data sets and for the subset of the Olden benchmarks we use, the inputs are: em3d 20,000 nodes, arity 10; mst 1024 nodes; perimeter 4Kx4K image; treeadd 20 levels. We omit several benchmarks either because the L1 data cache miss ratios are below 1% or their IPCs are unreasonably low (health and ammp are both less than 0.1) for our base configuration.

Our processor design is loosely based on the Alpha 21264 microarchitecture [12, 14, 19]. We use the same seven stage pipeline, including speculative load execution and load-store wait prediction. We do not model the clustered design of the 21264. Instead, we assume a single integer issue queue that can issue up to 8 instructions per cycle and a single floating point issue queue that can issue up to 4 instructions per cycle. Table 1 lists the various parameters for our base machine. Note that both integer and floating

Active List	128, 128 Int Regs, 128 FP Regs
Load/Store Queue	64 Load, 64 Store
Issue Queue	32 Integer, 32 Floating Point
Issue Width	12 (8 Integer, 4 Floating Point)
Decode Width	8
Commit Width	8
Instruction Fetch Queue	8
Functional Units	8 integer ALUs (1-cycle), 2 integer multipliers (7-cycle), 4 FP adders (4-cycle), 2 FP multipliers (4-cycle), 2 FP dividers (nonpipelined, 12-cycle), 2 FP square root units (nonpipelined, 24-cycle)
Branch Prediction	Bimodal & two-level adaptive combined, with speculative update, 2-cycle penalty for direct jumps missed in BTB, 9-cycle for others
Store-Wait Table	2048 entries, bits cleared every 32768 cycles
L1 Data Cache	32 KB, 4 Way
L1 Inst Cache	32 KB, 4 Way
L1 Latency	2 Cycles
L2 Unified Cache	256 KB, 4 Way
L2 Latency	10 Cycles
Memory Latency	250 Cycles
TLB	128-entry, 4-way associative, 4 KB page size, 30-cycle penalty

Table 1. Base Configuration

point register files are as large as the active list. For the remainder of this paper we state a single value for the active list/register file size, this value applies to both the integer and floating point register files.

The simulator was modified to support speculative update of branch history with history-based fixup and return-address-stack repair with the pointer-and-data fixup mechanism [26, 27]. We also modified the simulator to warm up the instruction and data caches during an initial fast forward phase. For the SPEC benchmarks we skip the first four hundred million instructions, and then execute the next one hundred million instructions with the detailed performance simulator. The Olden benchmarks execute for 400M instructions or until completion. This approach is used throughout this paper. We note that our results are qualitatively similar when using a different instruction execution window [24].

2.2.2 Varying Window Size

We performed simulations varying the issue queue size, from 32 (the base) in powers of 2, up to 4096. For issue queue sizes of 32, 64, and 128 we keep the active list fixed at 128 entries. For the remaining configurations, the ac-

tive list, register files and issue queue are all equal size. The load and store queues are always set to one half the active list size, and are the only limit on the number of outstanding requests unless otherwise stated. Figure 1 shows the committed instructions per cycle (IPC) of various window sizes normalized to the base 32-entry configuration ($Speedup = IPC_{new}/IPC_{old}$) for the SPEC integer, floating point, and Olden benchmarks. Absolute IPC values for the base machine are provided in Section 4, the goal here is to examine the relative effects of larger instruction windows.

These simulations show there is an initial boost in the IPC as window size increases, up to 2K, for all three sets of benchmarks. With the exception of mst, the effect plateaus beyond 2K entries, with IPC increasing only slightly. This matches our intuition since during a 250 cycle memory latency 2000 instructions can be fetched in our 8-way processor. Larger instruction windows beyond 2K provide only minimal benefits. Many floating point benchmarks achieve speedups over 2, with art achieving a speedup over 5 for the 2K window. This speedup is because the larger window can unroll loops many times, allowing overlap of many cache misses. A similar phenomenon occurs for mst.

The above results motivate the desire to create large instruction windows. The challenge for architects is to accomplish this without significant impact on clock cycle time. The next section presents our proposed solution.

3 A Large Window Design

This section presents our technique for providing a large instruction window while maintaining the advantages of small structures on the critical path. We begin with an overview to convey the intuition behind the design. This is followed by a detailed description of our particular design. We conclude this section with a discussion of various design issues and alternative implementations.

3.1 Overview

In our base microarchitecture, only those instructions in the issue queue are examined for potential execution. The active list has a larger number of entries than the issue queue (128 vs. 32), allowing completed but not yet committed instructions to release their issue queue entries. Since the active list is not on the critical path [4], we assume that we can increase its size without affecting clock cycle time. Nonetheless, in the face of long latency operations, the issue queue could fill with instructions waiting for their operands and stall further execution.

We make the observation that instructions dependent on long latency operations cannot execute until the long latency operation completes and thus do not need to be exam-

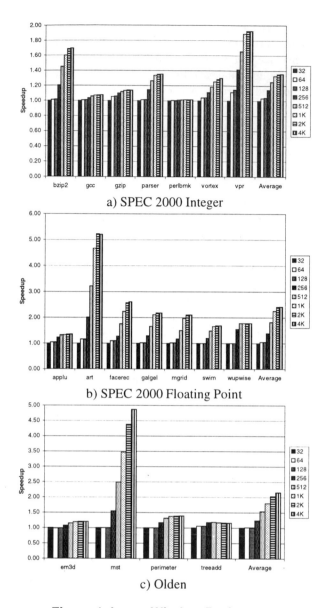

a) SPEC 2000 Integer

b) SPEC 2000 Floating Point

c) Olden

Figure 1. Large Window Performance

ined by the wakeup-select logic on the critical path. We note this same observation is exploited by Palacharla, et. al [22] and their technique of examining only the head of the issue queues. However, the goal of our design is to remove these waiting instructions from the issue queue and place them in a *waiting instruction buffer* (WIB). When the long latency operation completes, the instructions are moved back into the issue queue for execution. In this design, instructions remain in the issue queue for a very short time. They either execute properly or they are removed due to dependence on a long latency operation.

For this paper we focus specifically on instructions in the dependence chain of `load` cache misses. However, we believe our technique could be extended to other types of long latency operations. Figure 2 shows the pipeline for a WIB-based microarchitecture, based on the 21264 with two-level register files (described later).

The fetch stage includes the I-cache, branch prediction and the instruction fetch queue. The slot stage directs instructions to the integer or floating point pipeline based on their type. The instructions then go through register rename before entering the issue queue. Instructions are selected from the issue queue either to proceed with the register read, execution and memory/writeback stages or to move into the WIB during the register read stage. Once in the WIB, instructions wait for the specific cache miss they depend on to complete. When this occurs, the instructions are reinserted into the issue queue and repeat the wakeup-select process, possibly moving back into the WIB if they are dependent on another cache miss. The remainder of this section provides details on WIB operation and organization.

3.2 Detecting Dependent Instructions

An important component of our design is the ability to identify all instructions in the dependence chain of a load cache miss. To achieve this we leverage the existing issue queue wakeup-select logic. Under normal execution, the wakeup-select logic determines if an instruction is ready for execution (i.e., has all its operands available) and selects a subset of the ready instructions according to the issue constraints (e.g., structural hazards or age of instructions).

To leverage this logic we add an additional signal—called the *wait bit*—that indicates the particular source operand (i.e., input register value) is "pretend ready". This signal is very similar to the ready bit used to synchronize true dependencies. It differs only in that it is used to indicate the particular source operand will not be available for an extended period of time. An instruction is considered pretend ready if one or more of its operands are pretend ready and all the other operands are truly ready. Pretend ready instructions participate in the normal issue request as if they were truly ready. When it is issued, instead of being sent to the functional unit, the pretend ready instruction is placed in the WIB and its issue queue entry is subsequently freed by the issue logic as though it actually executed. We note that a potential optimization to our scheme would consider an instruction pretend ready as soon as one of its operands is pretend ready. This would allow instructions to be moved to the WIB earlier, thus further reducing pressure on the issue queue resources.

In our implementation, the wait bit of a physical register is initially set by a load cache miss. Dependent instructions observe this wait bit, are removed from the issue queue, and set the wait bit of their destination registers. This causes their dependent instructions to be removed from the issue queue and set the corresponding wait bits of their result

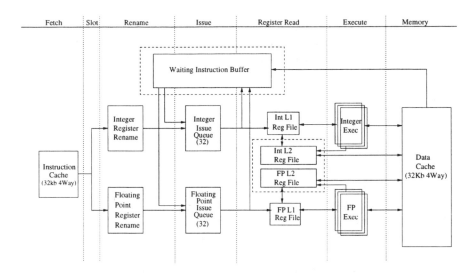

Figure 2. WIB-based Microarchitecture

registers. Therefore, all instructions directly or indirectly dependent on the load are identified and removed from the issue queue. The load miss signal is already generated in the Alpha 21264 since load instructions are speculatively assumed to hit in the cache allowing the load and dependent instructions to execute in consecutive cycles. In the case of a cache miss in the Alpha, the dependent instructions are retained in the issue queue until the load completes. In our case, these instructions move to the WIB.

An instruction might enter the issue queue after the instructions producing its operands have exited the issue queue. The producer instructions could have either executed properly and the source operand is available or they could be in the WIB and this instruction should eventually be moved to the WIB. Therefore, wait bits must be available wherever conventional ready bits are available. In this case, during register rename. Note that it may be possible to steer instructions to the WIB after the rename stage and before the issue stage, we plan to investigate this as future work. Our current design does not implement this, instead each instruction enters the issue queue and then is moved to the WIB if necessary.

3.3 The Waiting Instruction Buffer

The WIB contains all instructions directly or indirectly dependent on a load cache miss. The WIB must be designed to satisfy several important criteria. First, it must contain and differentiate between the dependent instructions of individual outstanding loads. Second, it must allow individual instructions to be dependent on multiple outstanding loads. Finally, it must permit fast "squashing" when a branch mispredict or exception occurs.

To satisfy these requirements, we designed the WIB to operate in conjunction with the active list. Every instruction in the active list is allocated an entry in the WIB. Although this may allocate entries in the WIB that are never dependent on a load miss, it simplifies squashing on mispredicts. Whenever active list entries are added or removed, the corresponding operations are performed on the WIB. This means WIB entries are allocated in program order.

To link WIB entries to load misses we use a bit-vector to indicate which WIB locations are dependent on a specific load. When an instruction is moved to the WIB, the appropriate bit is set. The bit-vectors are arranged in a two dimensional array. Each column is the bit-vector for a load cache miss. Bit-vectors are allocated when a load miss is detected, therefore for each outstanding load miss we store a pointer to its corresponding bit-vector. Note that the number of bit-vectors is bounded by the number of outstanding load misses. However, it is possible to have fewer bit-vectors than outstanding misses.

To link instructions with a specific load, we augment the operand wait bits with an index into the bit-vector table corresponding to the load cache miss this instruction is dependent on. In the case where an instruction is dependent on multiple outstanding loads, we use a simple fixed ordering policy to examine the source operand wait bits and store the instruction in the WIB with the first outstanding load encountered. This requires propagating the bit-vector index with the wait bits as described above. It is possible to store the bit-vector index in the physical register, since that space is available. However, this requires instructions that are moved into the WIB to consume register ports. To reduce register pressure we assume the bit-vector index is stored in a separate structure with the wait bits.

63

Instructions in the WIB are reinserted in the issue queue when the corresponding load miss is resolved. Reinsertion shares the same bandwidth (in our case, 8 instructions per cycle) with those newly arrived instructions that are decoded and dispatched to the issue queue. The dispatch logic is modified to give priority to the instructions reinserted from the WIB to ensure forward progress.

Note that some of the instructions reinserted in the issue queue by the completion of one load may be dependent on another outstanding load. The issue queue logic detects that one of the instruction's remaining operands is unavailable, due to a load miss, in the same way it detected the first load dependence. The instruction then sets the appropriate bit in the new load's bit-vector, and is removed from the issue queue. This is a fundamental difference between the WIB and simply scaling the issue queue to larger entries. The larger queue issues instructions only once, when all their operands are available. In contrast, our technique could move an instruction between the issue queue and WIB many times. In the worst case, all active instructions are dependent on a single outstanding load. This requires each bit-vector to cover the entire active list.

The number of entries in the WIB is determined by the size of the active list. The analysis in Section 2 indicates that 2048 entries is a good window size to achieve significant speedups. Therefore, initially we assume a 2K-entry active list and 1K-entry load and store queues. Assuming each WIB entry is 8 bytes then the total WIB capacity is 16KB. The bit-vectors can also consume a great deal of storage, but it is limited by the number of outstanding requests supported. Section 4 explores the impact of limiting the number of bit-vectors below the load queue size.

3.3.1 WIB Organization

We assume a banked WIB organization and that one instruction can be extracted from each bank every two cycles. These two cycles include determining the appropriate instruction and reading the appropriate WIB entry. There is a fixed instruction width between the WIB and the issue queue. We set the number of banks equal to twice this width. Therefore, we can sustain reinsertion at full bandwidth by reading instructions from the WIB's even banks in one cycle and from odd banks in the next cycle, if enough instructions are eligible in each set of banks.

Recall, WIB entries are allocated in program order in conjunction with active list entries. We perform this allocation using round-robin across the banks, interleaving at the individual instruction granularity. Therefore, entries in each bank are also allocated and released in program order, and we can partition each load's bit-vector according to which bank the bits map to. In our case, a 2K entry WIB with a dispatch width to the issue queue of 8 would

have 16 banks with 128 entries each. Each bank also stores its local head and tail pointers to reflect program order of instructions within the bank. Figure 3 shows the internal organization of the WIB.

During a read access each bank in a set (even or odd) operates independently to select an instruction to reinsert to the issue queue by examining the appropriate 128 bits from each completed load. For each bank we create a single bit-vector that is the logical OR of the bit-vectors for all completed loads. The resulting bit-vector is examined to select the oldest active instruction in program order. There are many possible policies for selecting instructions. We examine a few simple policies later in this paper, but leave investigation of more sophisticated policies (e.g., data flow graph order or critical path [15]) as future work. Regardless of selection policy, the result is that one bit out of the 128 is set, which can then directly enable the output of the corresponding WIB entry without the need to encode then decode the WIB index. The process is repeated with an updated bit-vector that clears the WIB entry for the access just completed and may include new eligible instructions if another load miss completed during the access.

The above policies are similar to the select policies implemented by the issue queue logic. This highlights an important difference between the WIB and a conventional issue queue. A conventional issue queue requires wakeup logic that broadcasts a register specifier to each entry. The WIB eliminates this broadcast by using the completed loads' bit-vectors to establish the candidate instructions for selection. The issue queue requires the register specifier broadcast to maintain true dependencies. In contrast, the WIB-based architecture leverages the much smaller issue queue for this task and the WIB can select instructions for reinsertion in any order.

It is possible that there are not enough issue queue entries available to consume all instructions extracted from the WIB. In this case, one or more banks will stall for this access and wait for the next access (two cycles later) to attempt reinserting its instruction. To avoid potential livelock, on each access we change the starting bank for allocating the available issue queue slots. Furthermore, a bank remains at the highest priority if it has an instruction to reinsert but was not able to. A bank is assigned the lowest priority if it inserts an instruction or does not have an instruction to reinsert. Livelock could occur in a fixed priority scheme since the instructions in the highest priority bank could be dependent on the instructions in the lower priority bank. This could produce a continuous stream of instructions moving from the WIB to the issue queue then back to the WIB since their producing instructions are not yet complete. The producing instructions will never complete since they are in the lower priority bank. Although this scenario seems unlikely it did occur in some of our benchmarks and thus we use

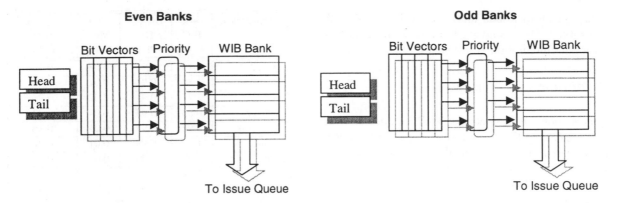

Figure 3. WIB Organization

round-robin priority.

3.3.2 Squashing WIB Entries

Squashing instructions requires clearing the appropriate bits in each bit-vector and resetting each banks' local tail pointer. The two-dimensional bit-vector organization simplifies the bit-vector clear operation since it is applied to the same bits for every bit-vector. Recall, each column corresponds to an outstanding load miss, thus we can clear the bits in the rows associated with the squashed instructions.

3.4 Register File Considerations

To support many in-flight instructions, the number of rename registers must scale proportionally. There are several alternative designs for large register files, including multi-cycle access, multi-level [13, 34], multiple banks [5, 13], or queue-based designs [6]. In this paper, we use a two-level register file [13, 34] that operates on principles similar to the cache hierarchy. Simulations of a multi-banked register file show similar results. Further details on the register file designs and performance are available elsewhere [20].

3.5 Alternative WIB Designs

The above WIB organization is one of several alternatives. One alternative we considered is a large non-banked multicycle WIB. Although it may be possible to pipeline the WIB access, it would not produce a fully pipelined access and our simulations (see Section 4) indicate pipelining may not be necessary.

Another alternative we considered is a pool-of-blocks structure for implementing the WIB. In this organziation, when a load misses in the cache it obtains a free block to buffer dependent instructions. A pointer to this block is stored with the load in the load queue (LQ) and is used to deposit dependent instructions in the WIB. When the load completes, all the instructions in the block are reinserted into the issue queue. Each block contains a fixed number of instruction slots and each slot holds information equivalent to issue queue entries.

An important difference in this approach compared to the technique we use is that instructions are stored in dependence chain order, and blocks may need to be linked together to handle loads with long dependence chains. This complicates squashing since there is no program order associated with the WIB entries. Although we could maintain information on program order, the list management of each load's dependence chain becomes too complex and time consuming during a squash. Although the bit-vector approach requires more space, it simplifies this management. The pool-of-blocks approach has the potential of deadlock if there are not enough WIB entries. We are continuing to investigate techniques to reduce the list management overhead and handle deadlock.

3.6 Summary

The WIB architecture effectively enlarges the instruction window by removing instructions dependent on load cache misses from the issue queue, and retaining them in the WIB while the misses are serviced. In achieving this, we leverage the existing processor issue logic without affecting the processor cycle time and circuit complexity. In the WIB architecture, instructions stay in the issue queue only for a short period of time, therefore new instructions can be brought into the instruction window much more rapidly than in the conventional architectures. The fundamental difference between a WIB design and a design that simply scales up the issue queue is that scaling up the issue queue significantly complicates the wakeup logic, which in turn affects the processor cycle time [1, 22]. However, a WIB requires a very simple form of wakeup logic as all the instructions in the dependence chain of a load miss are awakened when the miss is resolved. There is no need to broadcast and have all the instructions monitor the result buses.

4 Evaluation

In this section we evaluate the WIB architecture. We begin by presenting the overall performance of our WIB design compared to a conventional architecture. Next, we explore the impact of various design choices on WIB performance. This includes limiting the number of available bit-vectors, limited WIB capacity, policies for selecting instructions for reinsertion into the issue queue, and multicycle non-banked WIB.

These simulations reveal that WIB-based architectures can increase performance, in terms of IPC, for our set of benchmarks by an average of 20%, 84%, and 50% for SPEC INT, SPEC FP, and Olden, respectively. We also find that limiting the number of outstanding loads to 64 produces similar improvements for the SPEC INT and Olden benchmarks, but reduces the average improvement for the SPEC FP to 45%. A WIB capacity as low as 256 entries with a maximum of 64 outstanding loads still produces average speedups of 9%, 26%, and 14% for the respective benchmark sets.

4.1 Overall Performance

We begin by presenting the overall performance improvement in IPC relative to a processor with a 32-entry issue queue and single cycle access to 128 registers, hence a 128-entry active list (32-IQ/128). Figure 4 shows the speedups (IPC_{new}/IPC_{old}) for various microarchitectures. Although we present results for an 8-issue processor, the overall results are qualitatively similar for a 4-issue processor. The WIB bar corresponds to a 32-entry issue queue with our banked WIB organization, a 2K-entry active list, and 2K registers, using a two-level register file with 128 registers in the first level, 4 read ports and 4 write ports to the pipelined second level that has a 4-cycle latency. Assuming the 32-entry issue queue and 128 level one registers set the clock cycle time, the WIB-based design is approximately clock cycle equivalent to the base architecture. For these experiments the number of outstanding loads (thus bit-vectors) is not limited, we explore this parameter below. Table 2 shows the absolute IPC values for the base configuration and our banked WIB design, along with the branch direction prediction rates, L1 data cache miss rates, and L2 unified cache local miss rates for the base configuration.

For comparison we also include two scaled versions of a conventional microarchitecture. Both configurations use a 2K-entry active list and single cycle access to 2K registers. One retains the 32-entry issue queue (32-IQ/2K) while

Benchmark	Base IPC	Branch Dir Pred	DL1 Miss Ratio	UL2 Local Miss Ratio	WIB IPC
bzip2	1.19	0.94	0.03	0.47	1.59
gcc	1.34	0.94	0.01	0.09	1.38
gzip	2.25	0.91	0.02	0.04	2.25
parser	0.83	0.95	0.04	0.22	0.95
perlbmk	0.96	0.99	0.01	0.28	0.95
vortex	1.52	0.99	0.01	0.06	1.68
vpr	0.49	0.90	0.04	0.41	0.86
HM	1.00	-	-	-	1.24
applu	4.17	0.98	0.10	0.26	4.28
art	0.42	0.96	0.35	0.73	1.64
facrec	1.47	0.99	0.05	0.48	3.02
galgel	1.92	0.98	0.07	0.26	3.97
mgrid	2.58	0.97	0.06	0.42	2.57
swim	2.41	1.00	0.21	0.27	3.98
wupwise	3.38	1.00	0.03	0.25	3.99
HM	1.42	-	-	-	3.02
em3d	2.28	0.99	0.02	0.16	2.27
mst	0.96	1.00	0.07	0.49	2.51
perimeter	1.00	0.93	0.04	0.38	1.16
treeadd	1.05	0.95	0.03	0.33	1.28
HM	1.17	-	-	-	1.61

Table 2. Benchmark Performance Statistics

the other scales the issue queue to 2K entries (2K-IQ/2K). These configurations help isolate the issue queue from the active list and to provide an approximate upper bound on our expected performance.

From the results shown in Figure 4, we make the following observations. First, the WIB design produces speedups over 10% for 12 of the 18 benchmarks. The average speedup is 20%, 84%, and 50% for SPEC INT, SPEC FP, and Olden, respectively. The harmonic mean of IPCs (shown in Table 2) increases from 1.0 to 1.24 for SPEC INT, from 1.42 to 3.02 for SPEC FP, and from 1.17 to 1.61 for Olden.

For most programs with large speedups from the large 2K issue queue, the WIB design is able to capture a significant fraction of the available speedup. However, for a few programs the 2K issue queue produces large speedups when the WIB does not. mgrid is the most striking example where the WIB does not produce any speedup while the 2K issue queue yields a speedup of over two. This phenomenon is a result of the WIB recycling instructions through the issue queue. This consumes issue bandwidth that the 2K issue queue uses only for instructions ready to execute. As evidence of this we track the number of times an instruction is inserted into the WIB. In the banked implementation the average number of times an instruction is inserted into the

66

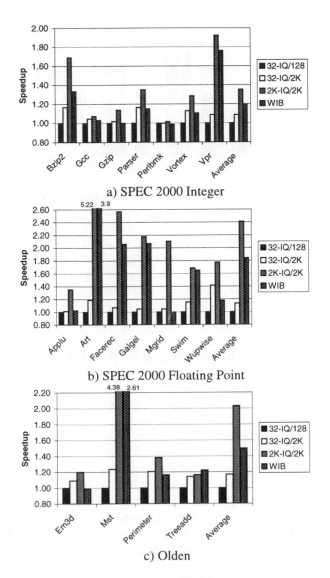

a) SPEC 2000 Integer

b) SPEC 2000 Floating Point

c) Olden

Figure 4. WIB Performance

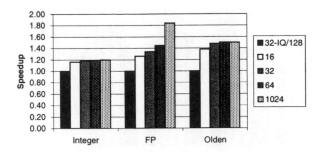

Figure 5. Performance of Limited Bit-Vectors

the WIB may be a better use of this space. We explore this tradeoff more later in this section.

We also performed two sensitivity studies by reducing the memory latency from 250 cycles to 100 cycles and by increasing the unified L2 cache to 1MB. The results match our expectations. The shorter memory latency reduces WIB speedups to averages of 5%, 30%, and 17% for the SPEC INT, SPEC FP, and Olden benchmarks, respectively. The larger L2 cache has a smaller impact on the speedups achieved with a WIB. The average speedups were 5%, 61%, and 38% for the SPEC INT, SPEC FP, and Olden benchmarks, respectively. The larger cache has the most impact on the integer benchmarks, which show a dramatically reduced local L2 miss ratio (from an average of 22% to 6%). Caches exploit locality in the program's reference stream and can sometimes be sufficiently large to capture the program's entire working set. In contrast, the WIB can expose parallelism for tolerating latency in programs with very large working sets or that lack locality.

For the remainder of this paper we present only the average results for each benchmark suite. Detailed results for each benchmark are available elsewhere [20].

4.2 Limited Bit-Vectors

The number of bit-vectors is important since each bit-vector must map the entire WIB and the area required can become excessive. To explore the effect of limited bit-vectors (outstanding loads), we simulated a 2K-entry WIB with 16, 32, and 64 bit-vectors. Figure 5 shows the average speedups over the base machine, including the 1024 bit-vector configuration from above. These results show that even with only 16 bit-vectors the WIB can achieve average speedups of 16% for SPEC INT, 26% for SPEC FP, and 38% for the Olden benchmarks. The SPEC FP programs (particularly art) are affected the most by the limited bit-vectors since they benefit from memory level parallelism. With 64 bit-vectors (16KB) the WIB can achieve speedups of 19%, 45%, and 50% for the three sets of benchmarks, respectively.

WIB is four with a maximum of 280. Investigations of other insertion policies (see below) reduces these values to an average insertion count of one and a maximum of 9, producing a speedup of 17%.

We also note that for several benchmarks just increasing the active list produces noticable speedups, in some cases even outperforming the WIB. This indicates the issue queue is not the bottleneck for these benchmarks. However, overall the WIB significantly outperforms an increased active list.

Due to the size of the WIB and larger register file, we also evaluated an alternative use of that space by doubling the data cache size in the base configuration to 64KB. Simulation results reveal less than 2% improvements in performance for all benchmarks, except vortex that shows a 9% improvement, over the 32KB data cache, indicating

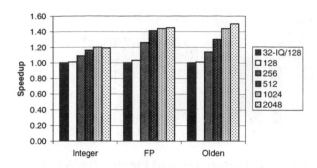

Figure 6. WIB Capacity Effects

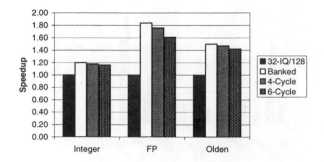

Figure 7. Non-Banked WIB Performance

4.3 Limited WIB Capacity

Reducing WIB area by limiting the number of bit-vectors is certainly a useful optimization. However, further decreases in required area can be achieved by using a smaller capacity WIB. This section explores the performance impact of reducing the capacity of the WIB, active list and register file.

Figure 6 shows the average speedups for WIB sizes ranging from 128 to 2048 with bit-vectors limited to 64. These results show that the 1024-entry WIB can achieve average speedups of 20% for the SPEC INT, 44% for SPEC FP, and 44% for Olden. This configuration requires only 32KB extra space (8KB for WIB entries, 8KB for bit-vectors, and 8KB for each 1024-entry register file). This is roughly area equivalent to doubling the cache size to 64KB. As stated above, the 64KB L1 data cache did not produce noticable speedups for our benchmarks, and the WIB is a better use of the area.

4.4 WIB to Issue Queue Instruction Selection

Our WIB design implements a specific policy for selecting from eligible instructions to reinsert into the issue queue. The current policy chooses instructions from each bank in program order. Since the banks operate independently and on alternate cycles, they do not extract instructions in true program order. To evaluate the impact of instruction selection policy we use an idealized WIB that has single cycle access time to the entire structure. Within this design we evaluate the following instruction selection policies: (1) the current banked scheme, (2) full program order from among eligible instructions, (3) round robin across completed loads with each load's instructions in program order, and (4) all instructions from the oldest completed load.

Most programs show very little change in performance across selection policies. mgrid is the only one to show significant improvements. As mentioned above, mgrid shows speedups over the banked WIB of 17%, 17%, and

13% for each of the three new policies, respectively. These speedups are due to better scheduling of the actual dependence graph. However, in some cases the schedule can be worse. Three programs show slowdowns compared to the banked WIB for the oldest load policy (4): bzip 11%, parser 15%, and facerec 5%.

4.5 Non-Banked Multicycle WIB Access

We now explore the benefits of the banked organization versus a multicycle non-banked WIB organization. Figure 7 shows the average speedups for the banked and non-banked organizations over the base architecture. Except the different WIB access latencies, the 4-cycle and 6-cycle bars both assume a non-banked WIB with instruction extraction in full program order. These results show that the longer WIB access delay produces only slight reductions in performance compared to the banked scheme. This indicates that we may be able to implement more sophisticated selection policies and that pipelining WIB access is not necessary.

5 Related Work

Our limit study is similar to that performed by Skadron et al. [28]. Their results show that branch mispredictions limit the benefits of larger instruction windows, that better branch prediction and better instruction cache behavior have synergistic effects, and that the benefits of larger instruction windows and larger data caches trade off and have overlapping effects. Their simulation assumes a very large 8MB L2 cache and models a register update unit (RUU) [29], which is a unified active list, issue queue, and rename register file. In their study, only instruction window sizes up to 256 are examined.

There has been extensive research on architecture designs for supporting large instruction windows. In the multiscalar [30] and trace processors [23], one large centralized instruction window is distributed into smaller windows among multiple parallel processing elements. Dynamic multithreading processors [2] deal with the complexity of a large window by employing a hierarchy of instruction windows. Clustering provides another approach, where a collection of small windows with associated functional units is used to approximate a wider and deeper instruction window [22].

Recent research [7, 18] investigates issue logic designs that attemp to support large instruction windows without impeding improvements on clock rates. Michaud and Seznec [21] exploit the observation that instructions dependent on long latency operations unnecessarily occupy issue queue space for a long time, and address this problem by prescheduling instructions based on data dependencies. Other dependence-based issue queue designs are studied in [9, 10, 22]. Zilles et al. [35] and Balasubramonian et al. [4] attack the problem caused by long latency operations by utilizing a future thread that can use a portion of the issue queue slots and physical registers to conduct precomputation. As power consumption has become an important consideration in processor design, researchers have also studied low power instruction window design [3, 16].

6   Conclusion

Two important components of overall execution time are the clock cycle time and the number of instructions committed per cycle (IPC). High clock rates can be achieved by using a small instruction window, but this can limit IPC by reducing the ability to identify independent instructions. This tension between large instruction windows and short clock cycle times is an important aspect in modern processor design.

This paper presents a new technique for achieving the latency tolerance of large windows while maintaining the high clock rates of small window designs. We accomplish this by removing instructions from the conventional issue queue if they are directly or indirectly dependent on a long latency operation. These instructions are placed into a waiting instruction buffer (WIB) and reinserted into the issue queue for execution when the long latency operation completes. By moving these instructions out of the critical path, their previously occupied issue queue entries can be further utilized by the processor to look deep into the program for more ILP. An important difference between the WIB and scaled-up conventional issue queues is that the WIB implements a simplified form of wakeup-select. This is achieved by allowing all instructions in the dependence chain to be considered for reinsertion into the issue window. Compared to the full wakeup-select in conventional issue queues, the WIB only requires select logic for instruction reinsertion.

Simulations of an 8-way processor with a 32-entry issue queue reveal that adding a 2K-entry WIB can produce speedups of 20%, 84%, and 50% for a subset of the SPEC CINT2000, SPEC CFP2000, and Olden benchmarks, re-spectively. We also explore several WIB design parameters and show that allocating chip area for the WIB produces signifcantly higher speedups than using the same area to increase the level one data cache capacity from 32KB to 64KB.

Our future work includes investigating the potential for executing the instructions from the WIB on a separate execution core, either a conventional core or perhaps a grid processor [25]. The policy space for selecting instructions is an area of current research. Finally, register file design and management (e.g., virtual-physical, multi-banked, multi-cycle, prefetching in a two-level organization) require further investigation.

Acknowledgements

This work was supported in part by NSF CAREER Awards MIP-97-02547 and CCR-0092832, NSF Grants CDA-97-2637 and EIA-99-72879, Duke University, and donations from Intel, IBM, Compaq, Microsoft, and Ericsson. We thank the anonymous reviewers for comments and suggestions on this work.

References

[1] V. Agarwal, M. S. Hrishikesh, S. W. Keckler, and D. Burger. Clock Rate Versus IPC: The End of the Road for Conventional Microarchitectures. In *Proceedings of the 27th Annual International Symposium on Computer Architecture*, pages 248–259, June 2000.

[2] H. Akkary and M. A. Driscoll. A Dynamic Multithreading Processor. In *Proceedings of the 31st Annual International Symposium on Microarchitecture*, pages 226–236, December 1998.

[3] R. I. Bahar and S. Manne. Power and Energy Reduction via Pipeline Balancing. In *Proceedings of the 28th Annual International Symposium on Computer Architecture*, pages 218–229, July 2001.

[4] R. Balasubramonian, S. Dwarkadas, and D. Albonesi. Dynamically Allocating Processor Resources Between Nearby and Distant ILP. In *Proceedings of the 28th Annual International Symposium on Computer Architecture*, pages 26–37, July 2001.

[5] R. Balasubramonian, S. Dwarkadas, and D. Albonesi. Reducing the Complexity of the Register File in Dynamic Superscalar Processors. In *Proceedings of the 34th International Symposium on Microarchitecture*, December 2001. To appear.

[6] B. Black and J. Shen. Scalable Register Renaming via the Quack Register File. Technical Report CMuArt 00-1, Carnegie Mellon University, April 2000.

[7] M. D. Brown, J. Stark, and Y. N. Patt. Select-Free Instruction Scheduling Logic. In *Proceedings of the 34th Annual International Symposium on Microarchitecture*, December 2001. To appear.

[8] D. C. Burger, T. M. Austin, and S. Bennett. Evaluating Future Microprocessors-the SimpleScalar Tool Set. Technical Report 1308, University of Wisconsin–Madison Computer Sciences Department, July 1996.

[9] R. Canal and A. González. A Low-Complexity Issue Logic. In *Proceedings of the 2000 International Conference on Supercomputing*, pages 327–335, May 2001.

[10] R. Canal and A. González. Reducing the Complexity of the Issue Logic. In *Proceedings of the 2001 International Conference on Supercomputing*, pages 312–320, June 2001.

[11] M. C. Carlisle, A. Rogers, J. H. Reppy, and L. J. Hendren. Early Experiences with Olden. In *Proceedings of the 6th International Workship on Languages and Compilers for Parallel Computing*, pages 1–20, August 1993.

[12] Compaq Computer Corporation. *Alpha 21264 Microprocessor Hardware Reference Manual*, July 1999.

[13] J.-L. Cruz, A. González, M. Valero, and N. P. Topham. Multiple-Banked Register File Architectures. In *Proceedings of the 27th Annual International Symposium on Computer Architecture*, pages 316–325, June 2000.

[14] J. A. Farrell and T. C. Fischer. Issue Logic for a 600-MHz Out-of-Order Execution Microprocessor. *IEEE Journal of Solid-State Circuits*, 33(5):707–712, May 1998.

[15] B. A. Fields, S. Rubin, and R. Bodik. Focusing Processor Policies via Critical-Path Prediction. In *Proceedings of the 28th Annual International Symposium on Computer Architecture*, pages 74–85, July 2001.

[16] D. Folegnani and A. González. Energy-Effective Issue Logic. In *Proceedings of the 28th Annual International Symposium on Computer Architecture*, pages 230–239, July 2001.

[17] J. L. Henning. SPEC CPU2000: Measuring CPU Performance in the New Millennium. *IEEE Computer*, 33(7):28–35, July 2000.

[18] D. S. Henry, B. C. Kuszmaul, G. H. Loh, and R. Sami. Circuits for Wide-Window Superscalar Processors. In *Proceedings of the 27th Annual International Symposium on Computer Architecture*, pages 236–247, June 2000.

[19] R. E. Kessler. The Alpha 21264 Microprocessor. *IEEE Micro*, 19(2):24–36, March 1999.

[20] T. Li, J. Koppanalil, A. R. Lebeck, J. Patwardhan, and E. Rotenberg. A Large, Fast Instruction Window for Tolerating Cache Misses. Technical Report CS-2002-03, Department of Computer Science, Duke University, March 2002.

[21] P. Michaud and A. Seznec. Data-flow Prescheduling for Large Instruction Windows in Out-of-Order Processors. In *Proceedings of the Seventh International Symposium on High-Performance Computer Architecture*, pages 27–36, January 2001.

[22] S. Palacharla, N. P. Jouppi, and J. E. Smith. Complexity-Effective Superscalar Processors. In *Proceedings of the 24th Annual International Symposium on Computer Architecture*, pages 206–218, June 1997.

[23] E. Rotenberg, Q. Jacobson, Y. Sazeides, and J. Smith. Trace Processors. In *Proceedings of the 30th Annual International Symposium on Microarchitecture*, pages 138–148, December 1997.

[24] S. Sair and M. Charney. Memory Behavior of the SPEC2000 Benchmark Suite. Technical Report RC-21852, IBM T.J. Watson, October 2000.

[25] K. Sankaralingam, R. Nagarajan, D. Burger, and S. W. Keckler. A Design Space Evaluation of Grid Processor Architectures. In *Proceedings of the 34th Annual International Symposium on Microarchitecture*, December 2001. To appear.

[26] K. Skadron. *Characterizing and Removing Branch Mispredictions*. PhD thesis, Department of Computer Science, Princeton University, June 1999.

[27] K. Skadron, P. S. Ahuja, M. Martonosi, and D. W. Clark. Improving Prediction for Procedure Returns with Return-Address-Stack Repair Mechanisms. In *Proceedings of the 31st Annual International Symposium on Microarchitecture*, pages 259–271, December 1998.

[28] K. Skadron, P. S. Ahuja, M. Martonosi, and D. W. Clark. Branch Prediction, Instruction-Window Size, and Cache Size: Performance Tradeoffs and Simulation Techniques. *IEEE Transactions on Computers*, 48(11):1260–1281, November 1999.

[29] G. S. Sohi. Instruction Issue Logic for High-Performance, Interruptable, Multiple Functional Unit, Pipelined Processors. *IEEE Transactions on Computers*, 39(3):349–359, March 1990.

[30] G. S. Sohi, S. E. Breach, and T. N. Vijaykumar. Multiscalar Processors. In *Proceedings of the 22nd Annual International Symposium on Computer Architecture*, pages 414–425, June 1995.

[31] J. M. Tendler, S. Dodson, S. Fields, H. Le, and B. Sinharoy. POWER4 System Microarchitecture. White Paper, IBM, October 2001.

[32] R. M. Tomasulo. An Efficient Algorithm for Exploiting Multiple Arithmetic Units. *IBM Journal*, pages 25–33, January 1967.

[33] C. T. Weaver. Pre-compiled SPEC2000 Alpha Binaries. Available: http://www.simplescalar.org.

[34] J. Zalamea, J. Llosa, E. Ayguadé, and M. Valero. Two-Level Hierarchical Register File Organization For VLIW Processors. In *Proceedings of the 33rd Annual International Symposium on Microarchitecture*, pages 137–146, December 2000.

[35] C. B. Zilles and G. S. Sohi. Understanding the Backward Slices of Performance Degrading Instructions. In *Proceedings of the 27th Annual International Symposium on Computer Architecture*, pages 172–181, June 2000.

An Instruction Set and Microarchitecture for Instruction Level Distributed Processing

Ho-Seop Kim and James E. Smith
Department of Electrical and Computer Engineering
University of Wisconsin—Madison
{hskim,jes}@ece.wisc.edu

Abstract

An instruction set architecture (ISA) suitable for future microprocessor design constraints is proposed. The ISA has hierarchical register files with a small number of accumulators at the top. The instruction stream is divided into chains of dependent instructions (strands) where intra-strand dependences are passed through the accumulator. The general-purpose register file is used for communication between strands and for holding global values that have many consumers.

A microarchitecture to support the proposed ISA is proposed and evaluated. The microarchitecture consists of multiple, distributed processing elements. Each PE contains an instruction issue FIFO, a local register (accumulator) and local copy of register file. The overall simplicity, hierarchical value communication, and distributed implementation will provide a very high clock speed and a relatively short pipeline while maintaining a form of superscalar out-of-order execution.

Detailed timing simulations using translated program traces show the proposed microarchitecture is tolerant of global wire latencies. Ignoring the significant clock frequency advantages, a microarchitecture that supports a 4-wide fetch/decode pipeline, 8 serial PEs, and a two-cycle inter-PE communication latency performs as well as a conventional 4-way out-of-order superscalar processor.

1 Introduction

During the past two decades, researchers and processor developers have achieved significant performance gains by finding and exploiting instruction level parallelism (ILP). Today, however, trends in technology, pipeline design principles, and applications all point toward architectures that rely less on increasing ILP and more on simpler, modular designs with distributed processing at the instruction level, i.e. *instruction level distributed processing* (ILDP) [25]. Technology trends point to increasing emphasis on on-chip interconnects and better power efficiency. Microarchitects are pushing toward pipelined designs with fewer logic levels per clock cycle (exacerbat-

ing interconnect delay problems and reducing sizes of single-cycle RAM) [1, 15]. Finally, design complexity has become a critical issue. In the RISC heyday of the mid-80s, the objective was a new processor design every two years; now it takes from four to six.

To study the full potential of future ILDP architectures, we are considering new instruction sets that are suitable for highly distributed microarchitectures. The goal is to avoid the encumbrances of instruction sets designed in a different era and with different constraints. This will enable us to study, in their simplest form, microarchitectures that are highly tolerant of interconnect delays, use a relatively small number of fast (high power) transistors, and support both very high clock frequencies and short pipelines. The resulting fast, lightweight processors will be ideal for chip multiprocessors supporting high throughput server applications [3] and for general-purpose processor cores that can drive highly integrated systems supporting various consumer applications.

The overall microarchitecture we propose consists of pipelined instruction fetch, decode, and rename stages of modest width that feed a number of distributed processing elements, each of which performs sequential in-order instruction processing. The instruction set exposes instruction dependences and local value communication patterns to the microarchitecture, which uses this information to steer chains of dependent instructions (*strands*) to the sequential processing elements. Dependent instructions executed within the same processing element have minimum communication delay as the results of one instruction are passed to the next through an accumulator. Taken collectively, the multiple sequential processing elements implement multi-issue out-of-order execution.

For applications where binary compatibility may not be a major issue (e.g. in some embedded systems), a new instruction set may be used directly in its native form. However, for general-purpose applications, a requirement of binary compatibility is a practical reality that must be dealt with. For general purpose applications there are two possibilities, both involve binary translation. One method is to perform on-the-fly hardware translation similar to the methods used today by Intel and AMD when they convert x86 binaries to micro-operations. Such a translation re-

71

quires somewhat higher-level analysis than simple instruction mapping, however. Hence, the second method relies on virtual machine software, co-designed with the hardware and hidden from conventional software. This software can map existing binaries to the new ILDP instruction set in a manner similar in concept to the method used by the Transmeta Crusoe processor [19] and the IBM DAISY project [10]. A very important difference is that here the binary translation does not require the complex optimizations and scheduling that are used for VLIW implementations. Rather, the hardware we propose will be capable of dynamic instruction scheduling, so translation will involve a straightforward mapping of instructions. Consequently, the emphasis during translation is on identifying instruction inter-dependences and on making register assignments that reduce intra-processor communication. Binary translation can be performed either by a special co-processor [6] or by the main processor, itself.

2 Instruction Set and Microarchitecture

We begin with a brief description of the ILDP instruction set we propose. Following that is a description of the proposed microarchitecture. Then we discuss the specific features of both.

2.1 Instruction set overview

The proposed ISA uses a hierarchical register file. It has 64 general-purpose registers (GPRs) and 8 accumulators. We refer to the GPRs as registers R0-R63, and the accumulators as A0-A7. We focus here on the integer instruction set. Floating point instructions would likely use additional floating point accumulators, but would share the GPRs.

In any instruction, a GPR is either the source or destination, but not both; this is intended to simplify the renaming process. In addition, when an accumulator is used for the last time, i.e. becomes dead, this is specified in the instruction's opcode (possibly via a reserved opcode bit).

The instruction formats are given in Fig. 1. Instructions may be either 16 bits (one parcel) or 32 bits (two parcels).

2.1.1 Load/Store instructions

The memory access instructions load or store an accumulator value from/to memory. These instructions may only specify one GPR and one accumulator (as with all instructions). All load/store instructions are one parcel and do not perform an effective address addition.

```
Ai <- mem(Ai)
Ai <- mem(Rj)
mem(Ai) <- Rj
mem(Rj) <- Ai
```

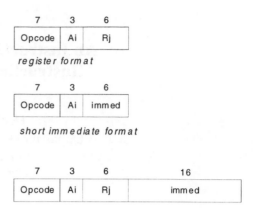

Figure 1. Instruction formats. Instructions are either 1 parcel (2 bytes) or 2 parcels (4 bytes).

2.1.2 Register instructions

The register instructions typically perform an operation on the accumulator and either a GPR or an immediate value, and the result is placed back in the accumulator. However, some instructions place the result into a GPR. Typical register instructions follow.

```
Ai <- Ai op Rj
Ai <- Ai op immed
Ai <- Rj op immed
Rj <- Ai
Rj <- Ai op immed
```

2.1.3 Branch/Jump instructions

The conditional branch instructions compare the accumulator with zero or the contents of a GPR. All the usual predicates (>, <, >=, <=, ==, !=) can be used. Branch targets are program counter (P) relative. The indirect jump is through either the accumulator or a GPR. For jump and link, the return address is always stored to a GPR.

```
P <- P + immed; Ai pred Rj
P <- P + immed; Ai pred 0
P <- Ai
P <- Rj
P <- Ai; Rj <- P++
```

2.1.4 Example

Figure 2 is a sequence of code from SPEC benchmark *164.gzip*, as compiled for the Alpha ISA. It is one of the more frequently executed parts of the program. Some Alpha instructions map to multiple ILDP instructions. However, the total number of bytes for instructions is slightly reduced. The Alpha version requires 40 bytes, and the ILDP version requires 36 bytes.

```
        if (n) do {
                c = crc_32_tab[((int)c ^ (*s++)) & 0xff] ^ (c >> 8);
        } while (--n);
```

a) C source code

Alpha assembly code	**Equivalent register transfer notation**	**ILDP code**
L1: ldbu t2, 0(a0)	L1: R2 <- mem(R0)	L1: A0 <- mem(R0)
subl a1, 1, a1	R1 <- R1 - 1	A1 <- R1 - 1
		R1 <- A1
lda a0, 1(a0)	R0 <- R0 + 1	A2 <- R0 + 1
		R0 <- A2
xor t0, t2, t2	R2 <- R2 xor R8	A0 <- A0 xor R8
srl t0, 8, t0	R8 <- R8 << 8	A3 <- R8 << 8
		R8 <- A3
and t2, 0xff, t2	R2 <- R2 and 0xff	A0 <- A0 and 0xff
s8addq t2, v0, t2	R2 <- 8*R2 + R9	A0 <- 8*A0 + R9
ldq t2, 0(t2)	R2 <- mem(R2)	A0 <- mem(A0)
xor t2, t0, t0	R8 <- R2 xor R8	A0 <- A0 xor R8
		R8 <- A0
bne a1, L1	P <- L1, if (R1 != 0)	P <- L1, if (A1 != 0)

b) Alpha assembly code, equivalent register transfer notation, and corresponding ILDP code

Figure 2. Example program segment from benchmark *164.gzip*

2.2 Microarchitecture

The concept behind the instruction set is that the dynamic program dependence graph can be decomposed into strands – chains of dependent instructions. Instructions in each strand are linked via an accumulator. The strands communicate with each other through the GPRs.

The strand per accumulator concept is reflected in the microarchitecture. Referring to Fig. 3a, instructions are fetched, parceled, renamed, and steered to one of eight processing elements. Instructions will be *fetched* four words (16 bytes) at a time. However, in most cases these four words contain more than 4 instructions. After I-fetch, the remainder of the instruction decode/rename pipeline is four instructions wide. *Parceling* is the process of identifying instruction boundaries and breaking instruction words into individual instructions. One simplification we are considering is to have instructions start and end on a cache line (at least 8 words) boundary. This will avoid instruction words spanning cache line (and page) boundaries – an unnecessary complication. The *renaming* stage renames only GPRs. The accumulators are not renamed at this stage; they undergo a simpler type of renaming as a byproduct of steering to the sequential processing elements.

The *steering* logic directs strands of renamed instructions to one of eight issue FIFOs, depending on the accumulator to be used. Each FIFO feeds a sequential processing element with its own internal physical accumulator (Fig. 3b). Any instruction that has an accumulator as an output, but not as an input, is steered to the first empty FIFO; consequently, the logical accumulator is renamed to the physical accumulator. Any later instruction that uses the same accumulator as an input is steered to the same FIFO. Whenever all the FIFOs are non-empty and a new accumulator is called for, the steering process either stalls, or uses a heuristic to choose a FIFO to use next. If a FIFO has a "dead" accumulator instruction at its tail, then instructions from a new strand can be steered into the FIFO. A good heuristic is to use the first such FIFO likely to go empty (e.g. the one with the fewest instructions).

The instructions in a FIFO form a dependence chain, and therefore will issue and execute sequentially. The instruction at the head of the FIFO passes through the GPR pipeline stage, reads its GPR value (if available), and moves into the issue register (IR). If the GPR value is not available, the instruction waits in the IR until the value becomes available. Hence, the IR is like a single reservation station with a single data value entry. When its GPR value is available, the instruction issues and begins execution. Fig. 3b shows an ALU and an L1 cache as functional units; in practice there will also be a shifter, and some other units. There is no contention/arbitration for any of the replicated functional units. A sequential control unit drives the processing element. Note that the functional units can be single or multi-cycle, but do not require pipelining. Because accumulator values stay within the same processing element, they can be bypassed without additional delay. However, GPR values produced in one PE must be communicated to the others. This will take additional clock cycles. The network for communicating GPR values can be a bus, a ring, or point-to-point. As will be shown, the bandwidth requirements are very modest and performance is relatively insensitive to this latency. The PE in the figure has two write ports to the GPR file; this will avoid contention between the accumu-

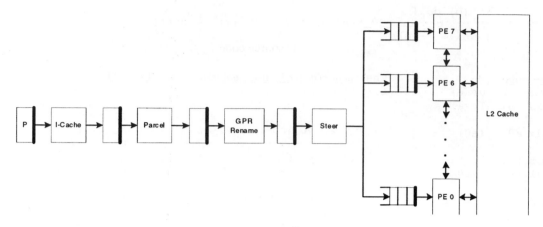

a) Block diagram of ILDP processor

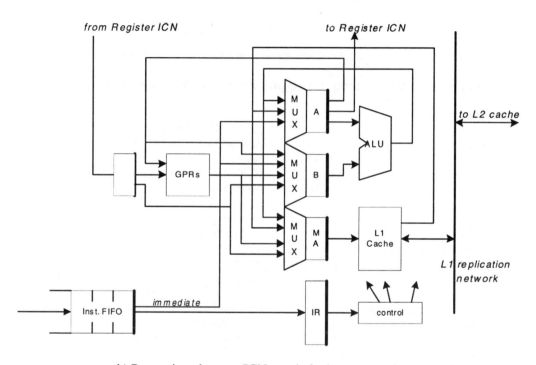

b) Processing element (ICN stands for interconnection network)

Figure 3. The distributed processor and detail of processing element

lator path and the GPR interconnection network. However, an alternate design could arbitrate the two and have a single write port. Simulation results in Section 4.3 will explore GPR write bandwidth requirements and the importance of inter-PE latency for communicating GPR values.

We plan to replicate the (small) low-latency L1 data cache and use a replication network to keep the contents of all the L1 caches equal (within a 2 clock period window as values are communicated). The L1 cache is fed directly from the issue stage of the PE because the memory instructions do not perform effective address addi-

tions. Because the PEs are sequential, issue bandwidth within a PE is not a critical resource as it is in a conventional superscalar processor, so issuing two instructions (in two cycles) for those load/stores that require address additions does not pose a performance problem. However, it does provide a performance *advantage* for those loads where an effective address addition is not needed (statistics are given in Section 4). Having the memory address available at issue time has other advantages; for example, store address queue checking can be done as part of the issue function, in much the same way as the Cray-1 does memory bank conflict checking at issue time [7]. Block-

	ILDP microarchitecture	4-way out-of-order superscalar
Parcel stage	Yes (if 2 inst. Lengths are used)	No
Decode bandwidth	4 instructions per cycle	4 instructions per cycle
Rename bandwidth	Total 4 read or write ports to map table	Total 12 read or write ports to map table
Steering logic	Simple, based on accumulator number	Complex dependence-based heuristic (if clustered)
Issue logic	Sequential in-order issue	4-way out-of-order issue from 128-entry RUU
Register file	2 write ports, 1 read port	4 write ports, 8 read ports
Bypasses	N x 2; for N functional units in a PE	M x 8; for M total functional units (M > N)

Table 1. Complexity comparison: ILDP processor vs. conventional out-of-order superscalar processor

ing on an L1 cache miss can also be done by blocking issue of the next instruction.

Each PE has a copy of the store address queue for memory disambiguation (not shown in the figure). Every load instruction consults the queue for possible conflicts with preceding store instructions. If all previous store addresses are known and do not conflict with the load, the load instruction is allowed to issue. Store address queue entries are allocated prior to the steering stage. As store addresses are computed, the address bits (or, for simplicity, a subset of 8-16 bits) are communicated to the replicated store queues.

Both GPRs and accumulators need to be rolled back when there is an exception or a branch misprediction. A conventional reorder buffer-based recovery mechanism can be used for GPRs; the GPR rename map is restored to the exception/misprediction point. To recover accumulators, produced accumulator values are buffered by a FIFO inside a PE. In effect, this is a small history buffer. When an instruction retires, the previous older value of the instruction's accumulator is also retired from the accumulator value FIFO. Should there be an exception, the oldest entries in the accumulator value FIFOs (or architectural accumulators) are rolled back. Similar to the GPR rename map recovery, steering information is also rolled back from the reorder buffer. Recovery from a mispredicted branch is done similarly. Here accumulator steering information can be recovered either from branch checkpoints or by sequential roll back from the saved information in the reorder buffer entries.

2.3 Discussion

As stated earlier, we are targeting a microarchitecture that will be simple and provide very high performance through a combination of a very fast clock and modest ILP. Because the clock cycle of an aggressive design depends on the details of every pipeline stage, we prefer not to use a few gross aspects of the design (e.g. bypasses, issue logic) to verify a quantitative clock cycle estimate. We prefer to let the simplicity stand as self-evident and defer clock cycle estimates until we have done some detailed, gate-level design. Table 1 compares complexity of several of the key functions with a baseline superscalar processor (similar to the one we use in Section 4 for per-

formance comparisons). The ILDP microarchitecture complexities are given on a per PE basis, because that is the complexity that will ultimately determine the clock cycle.

Variable length instructions are aimed at reducing the instruction footprint to permit better I-cache performance, especially if a small single-cycle L1 I-cache is used. Although it may seem un-RISC-like, variable length instructions were a hallmark of the original RISCs at Control Data and Cray Research. That a RISC should have single-length instructions has intuitive appeal, but to some extent it was a 1980s reaction to the very complex multi-length instruction decoding required by the VAX. There is little real evidence that having only one instruction size is significantly better than having a small number of easily decoded sizes. It is entirely possible that the advantages of a denser instruction encoding and more efficient I-fetch bandwidth may outweigh the disadvantage of having to parcel a simple variable-width instruction stream [12]. This is *not* a key part of our research, however, but we feel it is worth exploring, and if it appears that a single instruction size is the better approach, we can go back to all 32-bit instructions with relatively little effort.

3 Strand Formation

The most important aspect of strand formation is assignment of values to GPRs and accumulators, because, in effect, these assignments drive strand formation itself. To understand the basic idea of accumulator-oriented register assignment it is helpful to consider important register usage patterns, see Fig. 4.

We are interested in separating register values that have a relatively long lifetime and are used many times from those that are used only once or a small number of times in close proximity [13]. In general, the former values should be placed in GPRs and the latter in accumulators. A useful heuristic is to find register values that are consumed multiple times by the same static instruction. These are defined to be *static global* register values and will be assigned to GPRs (Ri in the figure). All the other register values will be considered *local* and will be assigned to accumulators, Ak and An in the figure. If a local value is used only once, then it will never be placed in a GPR. However, if one of these local values is used by

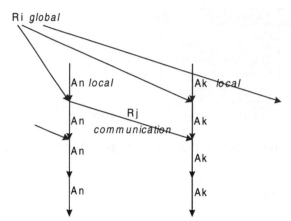

Figure 4. Types of values and associated registers. *Static global* and *communication global* values are held in GPRs, and *local* values are held in accumulators.

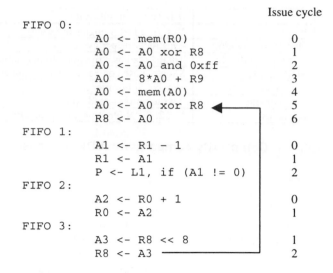

Figure 5. Issue timing of the example code

more than one consuming instruction, then a copy will be made to a GPR thereby communicating the value to other strands. These are referred to as *communication globals*.

If binary compatibility is not required, a static compiler can be used to generate programs in the native ILDP ISA. The compiler will allocate temporary register values to accumulators while keeping the rest in the GPRs. The compiler performs this non-conventional register allocation based on register usage and lifetime analysis.

In our research, dynamic binary translation is used to form strands. Currently we are using Alpha instruction binaries as the source ISA for translation. For our initial studies, we are analyzing simulator-generated instruction traces, but in the future we plan to use the basic method in [10, 16, 19], where interpretation is first used to produce profile data that is fed to a translator.

Given a code sequence and the above profile information that identifies static global values, strand formation is implemented via a single-pass linear scan of instructions to be translated; currently we do not perform code re-ordering during translation. For this discussion, we assume the source instruction set is RISC-like (Alpha in particular), with two source registers and one destination register, and simple addressing modes. At any given point in the scan, some register values are held in accumulators and others are held in GPRs.

When the scan reaches an instruction that has no input value currently assigned to an accumulator, it begins a new strand. If an instruction has a single input value assigned to an accumulator, then the same accumulator is used as the instruction's input, and the instruction is added to the producer's strand. If there are two input values assigned to accumulators, then two strands are intersecting. At this point, one of the strands is terminated by copying its accumulator into a GPR (to be communicated to the other strand). The other strand continues with the already-assigned accumulator and the just-assigned GPR

as inputs. To decide which strand to terminate, a good heuristic is to follow the strand that is longer, up to that point, to avoid introducing the communication latency into the already longer strand.

If an instruction has its output assigned to a static global register (or has no output value) the strand is terminated. If the new strand requires an accumulator when all the accumulators are live, then one of the live strands is terminated by copying its accumulator into a GPR. We choose the longest active strand as the victim. This tends to balance the lengths of the strands in the FIFOs.

Example

We complete this section with a continuation of the code example given in Section 2.1.4. Four accumulators are used (A0 through A3), so the instructions are steered to four different processing elements (FIFOs) as shown in Fig. 5. The strands are relatively independent, except where two strands converge to form inputs to the second *xor*. For this short code sequence, 14 instructions are issued in six clock cycles.

4 Evaluation

This section contains experimental evaluation of the instruction set properties and microarchitecture design decisions made in the previous sections.

4.1 Simulation methodology

To evaluate the proposed ILDP instruction set and microarchitecture, we first developed a functional simulator, which will be referred to as the *profiler* to distinguish it from the timing simulator. The profiler runs Alpha 21264 programs and profiles the dynamic register value usage. If a load/store instruction uses a non-zero immediate field

76

Bench-mark	Alpha instruction count	% of instructions w/ zero or one input register operand	% of loads w/o immediate	% of stores w/o immediate
164.gzip	3.50 bil.	55.09	43.6	50.6
175.vpr	1.54 bil.	51.16	34.9	29.1
176.gcc	1.89 bil.	62.38	34.8	15.8
181.mcf	260 mil.	57.74	30.4	11.9
186.crafty	4.18 bil.	54.34	27.0	13.4
197.parser	4.07 bil.	57.68	44.8	22.2
252.eon	95 mil.	55.83	15.7	15.4
254.gap	1.20 bil.	61.60	44.9	27.1
300.twolf	253 mil.	50.48	41.5	31.2

Table 2 Benchmark program properties

(i.e. requires an address add), then the instruction is split into two instructions for address calculation and memory access. Alpha conditional move instructions require three source operands and are also split into two instructions. Note that the Alpha 21264 processor similarly splits conditional moves into two microinstructions [18]. Static global registers are first identified using the heuristic of selecting all registers that are consumed multiple times by the same static instruction. Strands are then identified and accumulators and communication globals are assigned using the method described in the previous section.

Simulation tools were built on top of the SimpleScalar toolset 3.0B [4]. The profiler maps the strand-identified Alpha traces into ILDP traces and feeds the timing simulator. The timing simulator models the proposed microarchitecture and executes translated traces of ILDP instructions.

We selected nine programs from the SPEC 2000 integer benchmarks compiled at the base optimization level (-arch ev6 -non_shared -fast). The compiler flags are same as those reported for Compaq AlphaServer ES40 SPEC 2000 benchmark results. DEC C++ V.6.1-027 (for *252.eon*) and C V.5.9-005 (for the rest) compilers were used on Digital UNIX 4.0-1229. The test input set was used and all programs were run to completion.

4.2 Strand Characteristics

Table 2 contains some general statistics from the Alpha traces. More than half of the dynamic instructions have zero or one input register operand. Loads, conditional branches, and integer instructions with an immediate operand belong to this category. This statistic implies the data dependence graphs are rather "thin", with relatively little inter-strand communication. We also note there are substantial numbers of load and store instructions that do not require address calculation. With the proposed ILDP instruction set, these instructions can bypass the address addition and be sent to the data cache directly.

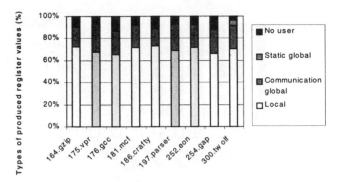

Figure 6. Types of register values

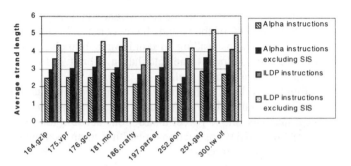

Figure 7. Average strand lengths

We also collected data regarding types of register values: static global, communication global, and local. Fig. 6 shows the fraction of values for each of the three classes (and those that have no consumers). Most values produced are locals (about 70%). Since these values are used only once, they do not have to leave their processing element and do not consume GPR bandwidth. Only about 20% of the values have to be placed in global registers (which suggests relatively low global register write bandwidth). Finally, 10% of produced values are never used. Some of these come from high-level program semantics; for example, a function's return value or some of its input arguments might not be used, depending on the program control flow. Also aggressive compiler optimizations, e.g. hoisting instructions above branches, sometimes result in unused values.

Fig. 7 shows the lengths of strands measured in both Alpha and ILDP instructions. Average strand size is 3.85 in ILDP instructions or 2.54 Alpha instructions. There are many single-instruction strands (SIS in the figure) that do not contribute much to the total number of instructions but affect the average strand size significantly. These single-instruction strands include unconditional branch and jump instructions, and instructions whose produced value is not used. An important characteristic of the single-instruction strands is that they can be steered to any FIFO; no other instruction depends on them. If the single-instruction strands are ignored, the average size of strands is 4.62 in ILDP instructions and 3.04 in Alpha instructions.

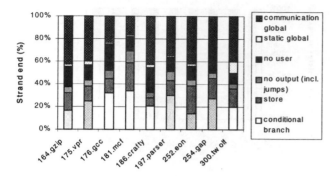

Figure 8. Strand end

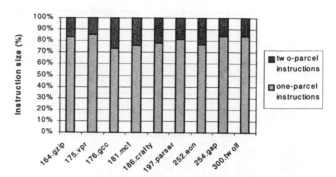

Figure 9. Instruction size

It is also interesting to see how strands end (Figure 8). About 35 to 70% of the strands have a "natural" ending – dependence chains leading to conditional branch resolution and store address/value calculation. About 20 to 45% produce communicated globals.

Finally we look at the impact of using two instruction sizes in translated ILDP ISA traces. Fig. 9 shows that on a dynamic basis, single parcel instructions account for 73 to 85% of total ILDP instructions, resulting in an average of 2.39 bytes per instruction.

4.3 Performance Results

Timing simulations are trace-driven. Because of different instruction sizes, it was easiest to simply assume an ideal I-cache for both the baseline superscalar and the ILDP microarchitecture. (All nine Alpha benchmark programs with the `test` input set have an L1 I-cache miss rate less than 0.7% with a 2-way set-associative, 32KB, 64-byte line size I-cache; less than 3.8% for an 8KB I-cache). We also believe the performance results from the

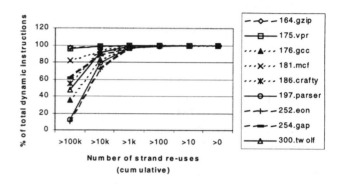

Figure 10. Cumulative strand re-use

trace-driven simulations will closely track those of a true dynamically translated system because program execution is dominated by small number of repeating strands in most cases. Fig. 10 shows more than 95% of total executed instructions belong to the strands that repeat more than 1000 times.

Simulator configurations are summarized in Table 3.

	ILDP microarchitecture	Out-of-order superscalar processor
Branch prediction	16K entry, 12-bit global history Gshare predictor 3-cycle fetch redirection latencies for both misfetch and misprediction	
I-cache, I-TLB	Ideal	
D-cache, D-TLB	L1: 2-way set-assoc., 8KB size, 64-byte line size, 1-cycle latency, random replacement	L1: 4-way set-assoc., 32KB size, 64-byte line size, 2-cycle latency, random replacement
	L2: 2-way set-assoc., 256KB size, 128-byte lines, 8-cycle latency, random replacement TLB: 4-way set-associative, 32-entry, 4KB page size, LRU replacement	
Memory	72-cycle latency, 64-bit wide, 4-cycle burst	
Reorder buffer size	128 ILDP instructions	128 Alpha instructions
Fetch/decode/retire bandwidth	4 ILDP instructions	4 Alpha instructions
Issue window size	8 (FIFO heads)	128 (same as the ROB)
Issue bandwidth	8	4 or 8
Execution resources	8 fully symmetric functional units	4 or 8 fully symmetric functional units
Misc.	2 or 0 cycle global communication latency	No communication latency, oldest-first issue

Table 3. Simulator configurations

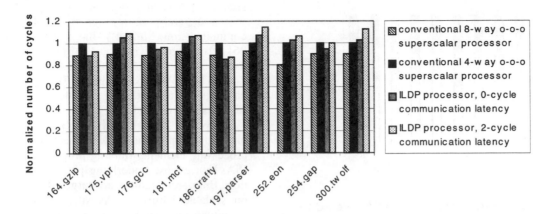

Figure 11. Normalized number of cycles with the 4-way with superscalar processor as the baseline

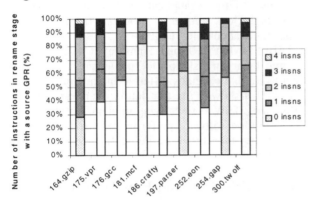

Figure 12. Global register rename map read bandwidth

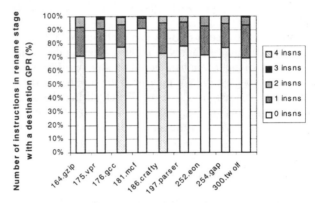

Figure 13. Global register rename map write bandwidth

Note that in keeping with the philosophy of smaller/faster memory structures, the L1 caches in the proposed microarchitecture are one quarter the size of the superscalar counterpart. The latency difference of one cycle results from the ILDP microarchitecture not having an address addition in the load path (as described previously); for those loads that require an add, the latencies are effectively the same.

Because the two microarchitectures being simulated have different ISAs, Instructions Per Cycle (IPC) is not a good metric for comparing performance. Instead the total number of cycles is used.

The results show that the proposed microarchitecture performs approximately as well as a conventional 4-way out-of-order superscalar processor *ignoring any clock frequency advantage*, which, based on Table 1 and the smaller data cache should be considerable.

More importantly, the proposed microarchitecture is tolerant of global communication latency. There is only a 2 to 7 percent performance degradation as communication latency increases from 0-cycles to 2-cycles. In most cases global communication latency is not imposed on the critical path by the dependence-based strand formation algorithm.

For *164.gzip* and *186.crafty*, the proposed microarchitecture with 0-cycle communication latency outperforms an 8-way out-of-order superscalar processor despite the reduced issue freedom of the proposed microarchitecture. This comes primarily from the reduced load latency for as many as 43.6% of loads where there is no need for an effective address addition.

To further understand implementation complexity issues, we collected statistics related to rename, steering, and global register bandwidths. Fig. 12, 13 show the global register rename bandwidths per cycle. With a four-wide pipeline, over 95% of the time three or fewer global register mappings are read, and over 90% of the time only zero or one register mapping is updated. This suggests that three read ports and one write port in the mapping table will likely be sufficient *if* we want to add the complexity of adding stall logic.

A significant complexity issue is the number of write ports to the GPR file. Using accumulators for local values greatly reduces the required GPR bandwidth. Collected GPR write bandwidth statistic closely follows Fig. 13; it shows one register write port is enough more than 95% of time. Hence, if we are willing to add arbitration for a single write port, then the GPR can be reduced to a single

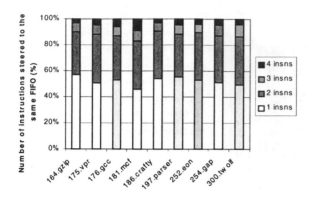

Figure 14. Number of instructions steered to the same FIFO at the same cycle

read port and a single write port with little performance impact.

Although the steering logic is simplified by only considering accumulator names in making steering decisions, the number of instructions steered to any one FIFO can also affect complexity. We measured the number of ILDP instructions steered to the same FIFO during the same cycle. The results in Fig. 14 show that two or fewer instructions are steered to the same FIFO over 82% of the time.

5 Related Work

The instruction set is very much inspired by the S. Cray scalar ISAs (just as the 1980s microprocessor RISCs were). However, in a sense, we follow the Cray ISAs more closely than the microprocessor-based RISCs. In particular, we use hierarchical register files with a very small file at the top of the hierarchy, variable length instructions, and in-order instruction issue (albeit within individual processing elements). Even though the technology was quite different when Cray's designs were undertaken, the issues of interconnect delays, power consumption, and design complexity were of critical importance, just as they are today, and will be in the future. In effect, the proposed ILDP ISA is a cross product of two Cray-2 designs. One is an abandoned Cray-2 design [8] that had a single re-named accumulator and a general register file of 512 elements. The completed Cray-2 design [9] had 8 integer registers, 64 lower level registers, and used conventional 3 operand instructions.

The ZS-1 [24] was an early superscalar design with instructions issuing simultaneously from two FIFOs, motivated by issue logic simplicity. The RS/6000 [2] used a similar design. In [22] a dependence-based microarchitecture that issues instructions from multiple FIFOs was proposed. That work, and others [5, 11] proposed clustered microarchitectures to localize register communication. Trace processors [23, 27] are another form of distributed microarchitecture, with each processing element being a simple superscalar processor. Trace processors also support a hierarchy of register files for local and global communication. Similarly, the multiscalar paradigm [14, 26] was designed with a goal of processor scalability and used a number of innovative distributed processing features. The PEWS mechanism [17] also uses dependence-based instruction steering but uses versioning for both registers and memory.

RAW architecture [20] and Grid Processor Architecture [21] propose network-connected tiles of distributed processing elements running programs compiled for new ISAs that expose underlying parallel hardware organization. Both architectures are targeted to achieve high ILP on scalable hardware. As such, both are sensitive to communication latency and depend heavily on the compiler. In contrast, our aim is to achieve high performance in general purpose applications with a combination of a very high clock frequency, moderate ILP and a relatively conventional compiler target.

IBM DAISY [10] and Transmeta Crusoe [19] use dynamic binary translation to run legacy software on the hardware that executes different instruction set. Ebcioglu et al. [10] showed the translation overhead is negligible. Both use VLIW as underlying implementation; as a result, the run-time software performs extensive instruction rescheduling to achieve desirable ILP on in-order VLIW implementation.

6 Conclusions and Future Research

For future processors, we propose an instruction set that exposes inter-instruction *communication* and is targeted at a distributed microarchitecture with both short pipelines and high frequency clocks. A primary goal is high performance by using a small number of logic transistors. This is counter to the conventional trend that uses instruction sets that expose instruction *independence*; use very long (deep) pipelines, and high logic transistor counts. The major challenge is not to think of enhancements that consume transistors and yield small incremental performance gains, but to develop an overall paradigm that achieves high performance through simplicity.

The overall microarchitecture we propose consists of a number of distributed processing elements, each of which is a simple in-order pipeline. By using an accumulator-based instruction set, the hardware implementation can steer chains of dependent instructions, "strands", to the simple in-order issue processing elements. In aggregate, the multiple in-order processing elements enable superscalar out-of-order execution as each of the processing elements adapts to the delays it encounters.

In this paper we have demonstrated that a distributed microarchitecture is capable of IPC performance levels that are roughly equivalent to a homogeneous 4-to-8-way superscalar processor. Most of the processing stages – renaming, register access, issuing, bypassing, data cache –

are much simpler than in a conventional superscalar processor, however, and the prospects for a much faster clock frequency are very good.

The distributed microarchitecture has other advantages that have not been discussed thus far. First, it will be amenable to multiple clock domains, which may be asynchronous with respect to one another. This is a very important feature for an aggressively clocked implementation where clock skew is critical. Second, it is also amenable to microarchitecture-level clock- and power-gating. Some of the processing elements can be gated off when not needed to save power.

In the future we plan to explore the proposed ISA and microarchitecture greater detail. First, we plan to perform a gate level design of the integer proportion of the proposed processor. This will validate claims of simplicity. Second, we plan to implement a binary translation infrastructure to allow on-the-fly translation of existing program binaries. Then, we will be able to provide accurate overall performance estimates that will demonstrate the feasibility of this overall approach.

7 Acknowledgements

We would like to thank Timothy H. Heil and Martin J. Licht for discussions and S. Subramanya Sastry for help on the initial version of the profiling simulator. This work is being supported by SRC grants 2000-HJ-782 and 2001-HJ-902, NSF grants EIA-0071924 and CCR-9900610, Intel and IBM.

8 References

[1] V. Agrawal et al., "Clock Rate vs. IPC: The End of the Road for Conventional Microarchitectures", *27th Int. Symp. on Computer Architecture*, pp. 248-259, Jun 2000.

[2] H. Bakoglu et al., "The IBM RISC System/6000 Processor: Hardware Overview", *IBM Journal of Research and Development*, pp. 12-23, Jan 1990.

[3] L. Barroso et al., "Piranha: A Scalable Architecture Based on Single-Chip Multiprocessing", 27th Int. Symp. on Computer Architecture, pp. 282-293, Jun 2000.

[4] D. Burger et al., "Evaluating Future Microprocessors: The SimpleScalar Toolset", *Tech. Report CS-TR-96-1308*, Univ. of Wisconsin—Madison, 1996.

[5] R. Canal et al., "A Cost-Effective Clustered Architecture", *Int. Conf. On Parallel Architectures and Compilation Techniques (PACT99)*, pp. 160-168, Oct 1999.

[6] Yuan Chou and J. Shen, "Instruction Path Coprocessors", *27th Int. Symp. on Computer Architecture*, pp. 270-279, Jun 2000.

[7] CRAY-1 S Series, Hardware Reference Manual, Cray Research, Inc., *Publication HR-808*, Chippewa Falls, WI, 1980.

[8] CRAY-2 Central Processor, *unpublished document*, circa 1979. http://www.ece.wisc.edu/~jes/papers/cray2a.pdf.

[9] CRAY-2 Hardware Reference Manual, Cray Research, Inc., *Publication HR-2000*, Mendota Heights, MN, 1985.

[10] K. Ebcioglu et al., "Dynamic Binary Translation and Optimization", *IEEE Trans. on Computers*, Vol. 50, No. 6, pp. 529-548, Jun 2001.

[11] K. Farkas et al., "The Multicluster Architecture: Reducing Cycle Time Through Partitioning", *30th Int. Symp. on Microarchitecture*, pp. 149-159, Dec 1997.

[12] M. Flynn, *Computer Architecture: Pipelined and Parallel Processor Design*, Jones and Bartlett Publishers, pp. 109-132, 1995.

[13] M. Franklin and G. Sohi, "Register Traffic Analysis for Streamlining Inter-Operation Communication in Fine-Grain Parallel Processors", *25th Int. Symp. on Microarchitecture*, pp. 236-245, Dec 1992.

[14] M. Franklin and G. Sohi, "The Expandable Split Window Paradigm for Exploiting Fine-Grain Parallelism", *19th Int. Symp. on Computer Architecture*, pp. 58-67, Dec 1992.

[15] R. Ho et al., "The Future of Wires", *Proceedings of the IEEE*, Vol. 89, No. 4, pp. 490-504, Apr 2001.

[16] R. Hookway and M. Herdeg, "DIGITAL FX!32: Combining Emulation and Binary Translation", *Digital Technical Journal*, Vol. 9, No. 1, pp. 3-12, 1997.

[17] G. Kemp and M. Franklin, "PEWs: A Decentralized Dynamic Scheduler for ILP Processing", *Int. Conf. On Parallel Processing*, pp. 239-246, Aug 1996.

[18] R. E. Kessler, "The Alpha 21264 Microprocessor", *IEEE Micro*, Vol. 19, No. 2, pp. 24-36, Mar/Apr 1999.

[19] A. Klaiber, "The Technology Behind Crusoe Processors," *Transmeta Technical Brief*, 2000.

[20] W. Lee et al., "Space-Time Scheduling of Instruction-Level Parallelism on a Raw Machine", *8th Int. Conf. Architectural Support for Programming Languages and Operating Systems*, pp. 46-57, Oct 1998.

[21] R. Nagarajan et al., "A Design Space Evaluation of Grid Processor Architectures", *34th Int. Symp. on Microarchitecture*, pp. 40-51, Dec 2001.

[22] S. Palacharla et al., "Complexity-Effective Superscalar Processors," *24th Int. Symp. on Computer Architecture*, pp. 206-218, Jun 1997.

[23] E. Rotenberg, et al., "Trace Processors", *30th Int. Symp. on Microarchitecture*, pp. 138-148, Dec 1997.

[24] J. E. Smith et al., "Astronautics ZS-1 Processor", *2nd Int. Conf. Architectural Support for Programming Languages and Operating Systems*, pp. 199-204, Oct 1987.

[25] J. E. Smith, "Instruction-Level Distributed Processing", *IEEE Computer*, Vol. 34, No. 4, pp. 59-65, Apr 2001.

[26] G. Sohi et al., "Multiscalar Processors", *22nd Int. Symp. on Computer Architecture*, pp. 414-415, Jun 1995.

[27] S. Vajapeyam and T. Mitra, "Improving Superscalar Instruction Dispatch and Issue by Exploiting Dynamic Code Sequences", *24th Int. Symp. on Computer Architecture*, pp. 1-12, Jun 1997.

Keynote Address

Session 3: Safety and Reliability

Transient-Fault Recovery Using Simultaneous Multithreading

T. N. Vijaykumar, Irith Pomeranz, and Karl Cheng

School of Electrical and Computer Engineering, Purdue University, W. Lafayette, IN 47907

{vijay, pomeranz, kkcheng}@ecn.purdue.edu

Abstract

We propose a scheme for transient-fault recovery called **Simultaneously and Redundantly Threaded processors with Recovery (SRTR)** *that enhances a previously proposed scheme for transient-fault detection, called Simultaneously and Redundantly Threaded (SRT) processors. SRT replicates an application into two communicating threads, one executing ahead of the other. The trailing thread repeats the computation performed by the leading thread, and the values produced by the two threads are compared. In SRT, a leading instruction may commit* **before** *the check for faults occurs, relying on the trailing thread to trigger detection. In contrast, SRTR must* **not** *allow* **any** *leading instruction to commit before checking occurs, since a faulty instruction cannot be undone once the instruction commits.*

To avoid stalling leading instructions at commit while waiting for their trailing counterparts, SRTR exploits the time between the completion and commit of leading instructions. SRTR compares the leading and trailing values as soon as the trailing instruction completes, typically before the leading instruction reaches the commit point. To avoid increasing the bandwidth demand on the register file for checking register values, SRTR uses the **register value queue (RVQ)** *to hold register values for checking. To reduce the bandwidth pressure on the RVQ itself, SRTR employs* **dependence-based checking elision (DBCE)**. *By reasoning that faults propagate through dependent instructions, DBCE exploits register (true) dependence chains so that only the last instruction in a chain uses the RVQ, and has the leading and trailing values checked. SRTR performs within 1% and 7% of SRT for SPEC95 integer and floating-point programs, respectively. While SRTR without DBCE incurs about 18% performance loss when the number of RVQ ports is reduced from four (which is performance-equivalent to an unlimited number) to two ports, with DBCE, a two-ported RVQ performs within 2% of a four-ported RVQ.*

1 Introduction

The downscaling of feature sizes in CMOS technologies is resulting in faster transistors and lower supply voltages. While this trend contributes to improving the overall performance and reducing per-transistor power, it also implies that microprocessors are increasingly more susceptible to transient faults of various types. For instance, cosmic alpha particles may charge or discharge internal nodes of logic or SRAM cells; and lower supply voltages result in reduced noise margins allowing high-frequency crosstalk to flip bit values. The result is degraded reliability even in commodity microprocessors for which reliability has not been a concern until recently.

To address reliability issues, Simultaneously and Redundantly Threaded (SRT) processors are proposed in [10] based on the Simultaneous Multithreaded architecture (SMT) [17]. SRT detects transient faults by replicating an application into two communicating threads, one (called the leading thread) executing ahead of the other (called the trailing thread). The trailing thread repeats the computation performed by the leading thread, and the values produced by the two threads are compared.

Although SRT does not support recovery from faults, the following features introduced by SRT for fault detection [10] are important for recovery as well: (1) Replicating cached loads is problematic because memory locations may be modified by an external agent (e.g., another processor during multiprocessor synchronization) between the time the leading thread loads a value and the time the trailing thread tries to load the same value. The two threads may diverge if the loads return different data. SRT allows only the leading thread to access the cache, and uses the Load Value Queue (LVQ) to hold the leading load values. The trailing thread loads from the LVQ instead of repeating the load from the cache. (2) The leading thread runs ahead of the trailing thread by a long *slack* (e.g., 256 instructions), and provides the leading branch outcomes to the trailing thread through the Branch Outcome Queue (BOQ). The slack and the use of branch outcomes hide the leading thread's memory latencies and branch mispredictions from the trailing thread, since by the time the trailing thread needs a load value or a branch outcome, the leading thread has already produced it. (3) By replicating register values but not memory values, SRT compares *only* stores and uncached loads, but not register values, of the two threads. Because an incorrect value caused by a fault propagates through computations and is eventually consumed by a store, checking *only* stores suffices.

We propose *Simultaneously and Redundantly Threaded processors with Recovery (SRTR)* to extend SRT to include recovery. Although systems using software recovery often employ hardware detection [3,13], software checkpointing incurs considerable performance cost even when there are no faults. Therefore, hardware recovery at a modest performance cost over detection is an attractive option, especially because hardware recovery permits the use of off-the-shelf software. We identify, for the first time, the following key issues:

- **Problem:** A fundamental implication of the SRT detection scheme is that a leading non-store instruction may commit *before* the check for faults occurs, relying on the trailing thread to trigger detection. SRTR, on the other hand, must *not* allow *any* leading instruction to commit before checking occurs, since a faulty instruction cannot be undone once the instruction commits. Unless care is taken, leading instructions will stall at commit waiting for their trailing counterparts to complete and undergo checking. This stalling will create pressure on the instruction window and physical registers, and degrade performance.

- **Solution:** To avoid stalling leading instructions, SRTR exploits the time between the completion and commit of leading instructions. SRTR checks the results of a leading and the corresponding trailing instruction as soon as the trailing instruction completes, well before the leading instruction reaches the commit point. For the SPEC95 benchmarks, complete to commit times average at 29 cycles. This gap provides sufficient time for a trailing instruction to complete before the leading instruction reaches the commit point. To exploit the complete to commit time, the slack between the leading and trailing threads in SRTR must be short. At the same time, a slack that is too short would cause the trailing thread to stall due to unavailable branch outcomes and load values from the leading thread. To support an appropriately short slack, SRTR's leading thread provides the trailing thread with branch predictions instead of outcomes. Because the leading thread's branch predictions are available much earlier than the branch outcomes, and because a short slack is sufficient for hiding on-chip cache hit latencies, SRTR avoids trailing thread stalls *even* with a short slack. We show that high prediction accuracies and low off-chip miss rates in the underlying SMT enable SRTR, using a slack of 32, to perform within 5% of SRT, using a slack of 256 (as in [10]), when the recovery mechanisms of SRTR are disabled so that both schemes target only detection.

- **Problem:** By the time a leading instruction reaches the commit point, its register value often has been written back to the physical register file. Because *all* instructions are checked in recovery, accessing the register file in order to perform the check will add substantial bandwidth pressure.

- **Solution:** SRTR uses a separate structure, the *register value queue (RVQ)*, to store register values and other information necessary for checking of instructions, avoiding bandwidth pressure on the register file.

- **Problem:** There is bandwidth pressure on the RVQ.

- **Solution:** We propose *dependence-based checking elision (DBCE)* to reduce the number of checks, and thereby, the RVQ bandwidth demand. By reasoning that faults propagate through dependent instructions, DBCE exploits register (true) dependence chains so that *only* the last instruction in a chain uses the RVQ and has leading and trailing values checked. The chain's earlier instructions in *both* threads completely elide the RVQ. SRT can be viewed as taking such elision to the extreme by observing that stores are the last instructions in any register dependence chain, and that only stores need to be checked. However, SRT's chains are too long for SRTR because the leading thread cannot commit until the last instruction in the long chain is checked. DBCE forms short chains by exploiting the abundant register dependencies in near-by instructions. Because of the short slack and short chains, the trailing chain's

last instruction completes only a few cycles behind the leading chain's earlier instructions. Consequently, checking of the last instruction is usually done between the time the earliest leading instruction completes and the time it reaches the commit point. DBCE redundantly builds chains in both threads and checks its own functionality for faults. DBCE elides 35% of checks for the benchmarks we consider. SRTR performs within 1% and 7% of SRT for SPEC95 integer and floating-point programs, respectively. SRTR without DBCE incurs about 18% performance loss when the number of RVQ ports is reduced from four (which is performance-equivalent to an unlimited number) to two ports. With DBCE, a 2-ported RVQ performs within 2% of a 4-ported RVQ.

SRTR is guaranteed to provide recovery from single transient faults except those that affect the register file and that fail to propagate through dependence chains, in which case SRTR guarantees detection.

We review SRT in Section 2. We describe the SRTR scheme in Section 3 and DBCE in Section 4. In Section 5, we present experimental results. In Section 6, we discuss related work, and conclude in Section 7.

2 Transient-fault detection: background

SRT uses SMT's multithreaded execution to replicate an application into two communicating threads, one executing ahead of the other. Comparing the results of two redundant executions is the underlying scheme to detect transient faults in SRT. Because detection is based on replication, the extent to which the application is replicated is important. SRT formalizes this notion by defining the *sphere of replication (SoR)* [10], pointing out that (1) all computation and data within this sphere are replicated such that each thread uses its own copy, (2) data entering the SoR is independently read by the two threads using *input replication*, (3) data exiting the SoR from the two threads are compared using *output comparison*, and only one copy of the checked data is stored outside the SoR. Note that the input replicator and output comparator are outside the SoR. The input replicator and output comparator must be self-checked and are typically implemented using dual-rail logic. Because data outside the SoR is not replicated, other forms of protection such as ECC are needed outside the SoR.

Two possible SoRs defined in [10] are: processor and registers inside the SoR, with the cache hierarchy outside; and only the processor inside the SoR, with the registers and cache hierarchy outside. In the first SoR, leading and trailing thread values need to be compared only for stores and uncached loads, while other instructions can commit without comparing values. SRT uses a store buffer (StB) in which the leading thread places its committed store values and addresses. The trailing thread's store values and addresses are compared against the StB entries to determine whether a fault has occurred. In the second SoR, all register values need to be checked. Checking registers requires large buffers with high bandwidth to avoid performance degradation.

As explained in Section 1, to handle cached loads, SRT uses the ECC-protected Load Value Queue (LVQ) in which the

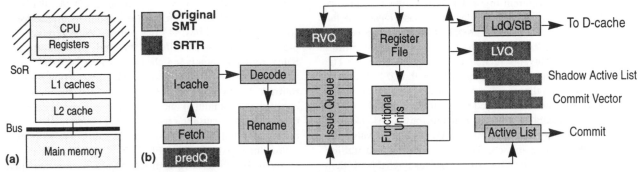

FIGURE 1: (a) SRTR's Sphere of Replication. (b) SRTR's additions to SMT.

leading thread deposits its committed load values and addresses. The trailing thread obtains the load value from the LVQ, instead of repeating the load from the memory hierarchy. The Active Load Address Buffer proposed in [10] is an alternative for the LVQ that also addresses this problem. We use the LVQ because it is simpler.

A key optimization in SRT is that the leading thread runs ahead of the trailing thread by an amount called the *slack* (e.g., the slack may be 256 instructions). In addition, the leading thread provides its branch outcomes via the branch outcome queue (BOQ) to the trailing thread. The slack and the communication of branch outcomes hide the leading thread's memory latencies and avoids branch mispredictions from the trailing thread. Due to the slack, by the time the trailing thread needs a load value or branch outcome, the leading thread has already produced it.

SRT assumes that uncached accesses are performed non-speculatively. SRT synchronizes uncached accesses from the leading and trailing threads, compares the addresses, and replicates the load data. SRT assumes that code does not modify itself, although self-modifying code in regular SMTs already requires thread synchronization and cache coherence which can be extended to keep the leading and trailing threads consistent. For input replication of external interrupts, SRT suggests forcing the threads to the same execution point and then delivering the interrupt synchronously to both threads.

3 Transient-fault recovery

We propose *Simultaneously and Redundantly Threaded processors with Recovery (SRTR)* that enhances SRT to include transient-fault recovery. A natural way to extend SRT to achieve recovery is to use the rollback ability of modern pipelines, which is provided to support precise interrupts and speculative execution [9]. Because transient faults do not persist, rolling back to the offending instruction and re-executing guarantees forward progress.

In SRT, a leading non-store instruction may commit *before* the check for faults occurs. SRTR, on the other hand, must *not* allow *any* instruction to commit before it is checked for faults. Trailing instructions must complete and results must be compared as much before the leading instructions reach the commit point as possible, so that leading instructions do not stall at commit. Therefore, the slack between the threads cannot be

long. At the same time, a near-zero slack would cause the trailing thread to stall due to unavailable branch outcomes and load values from the leading thread. To support a short slack, SRTR's leading thread provides the trailing thread with branch predictions. In contrast, SRT's leading thread provides branch outcomes. Accordingly, SRTR counts slack in terms of fetched (speculative) instructions, while SRT counts slack in terms of committed instructions.

SRT uses committed values for branch outcomes, load addresses and values, and store addresses and values. Consequently, the StB, LVQ, and BOQ are simple queues that are not affected by mispredictions. Because SRTR compares speculative values of the leading and trailing threads, SRTR needs to handle the effects of mispredictions on these structures.

SRTR uses the SoR that includes the register file. Like SRT, SRTR uses an out-of-order, SMT pipeline [16]. The pipeline places instructions from all threads in a single *issue queue*. Instructions wait in this queue until source operands become available, enabling out-of-order issue. Apart from the issue queue, each thread's instructions are also held in the thread's private *active list (AL)*. When an instruction is issued and removed from the issue queue, the instruction stays in its AL. Instructions commit from the AL in program order, enabling precise interrupts. We illustrate SRTR's SoR and SRTR's additions to SMT in Figure 1.

3.1 Synchronizing leading and trailing threads

For every branch prediction, the leading thread places the predicted PC value in the *prediction queue (predQ)*. This queue is similar to the BOQ except that it holds predictions instead of outcomes. The predQ is emptied in queue-order by the trailing thread. Using the predQ, the two threads fetch essentially the same instructions without diverging.

Because the ALs hold the instructions in predicted program order and because the two threads communicate via the predQ, corresponding leading and trailing instructions occupy the same positions in their respective ALs. Thus, they can be easily located for checking. Note that corresponding leading and trailing instructions may enter their ALs at different times, and become ready to commit at different times. However, we use the fact that the instructions occupy the same position in their ALs to keep the implementation simple.

Due to the slack, the leading and trailing threads resolve

their branches at different times. Upon detecting a misprediction in the leading thread, the leading thread cleans up the predQ, preventing the trailing thread from using mispredicted entries placed earlier in the predQ. There are two possibilities for the timing of events related to a misprediction: (1) The leading branch resolves after the trailing thread has already used the corresponding predQ entry, or (2) the leading branch resolves before the entry is used by the trailing thread.

The first possibility implies that the trailing AL position which mirrors the leading branch's AL position is valid and contains the trailing branch. There are mispredicted trailing instructions in the trailing AL. The leading thread then squashes the mispredicted instructions in the trailing AL, and the existing predQ entries which contain fetch PCs from the incorrect path. Because the leading and trailing ALs are identical, the leading branch can use its own AL pointer to squash the trailing AL. The second possibility implies that the trailing AL position which mirrors the leading branch's AL position is beyond the tail of the trailing AL. In this case, the leading branch squashes all predQ entries later than its own predQ entry, and places the branch outcome in the predQ to be used by the trailing thread later. To prevent faults from causing incorrect squashing, AL pointers are protected by ECC.

Although the leading thread rolls back the predQ and the ALs of both threads upon a misprediction, the leading branch's outcome is still checked against the trailing branch's outcome. The rollback is an optimistic action to reduce the number of mispredicted trailing instructions, assuming that the leading thread is fault-free. If the leading thread's misprediction is incorrectly flagged due to a fault, the trailing branch's check triggers a rollback. We discuss the details of checking in Section 3.3.

3.2 Modifying LVQ

SRT uses a strict queue-ordering for the LVQ, i.e., the leading thread inserts committed load values and addresses at the tail, and the trailing thread empties the load values and addresses from the head of the queue. SRTR modifies SRT's LVQ to operate on speculative cached loads, and therefore, cannot maintain the strict queue order of SRT. To keep the LVQ as compact as possible, we use a table, called the *shadow active list (SAL)*, to hold pointers to LVQ entries (Figure 1(b)). The SAL mirrors the AL in length but is much narrower than the LVQ, and instructions can use the AL pointer to access their information in the SAL. The SAL is also helpful in checking register values as explained in Section 3.3.

A leading load allocates an LVQ entry when the load enters the AL, and places a pointer to the entry in the SAL. Because loads enter the AL in (speculative) program order, LVQ entries are allocated in the same order, simplifying misprediction handling, as explained at the end of the section. Upon issue, the leading load obtains its LVQ pointer from the SAL and places its load value and address in the LVQ. The trailing load also obtains the LVQ pointer from the SAL, and the trailing load's address and the leading load address stored in the LVQ are compared, as done in SRT. On a match, the trailing load

obtains the leading load value from the LVQ. A mismatch of the addresses flags a rollback (as explained in Section 3.3) with three possibilities: (1) the address value produced by a previous instruction is faulty and the faulty instruction will initiate a rollback upon being checked; (2) the address computation of the load is faulty and the load instruction will cause rollback to be initiated; (3) the previous instruction was checked and committed and the address register has been corrupted since. Because the register file is inside the SoR, SRTR flags a fault but cannot recover in the third case without protecting the register file with ECC.

Even though leading instructions are fetched and placed ahead of the corresponding trailing instructions in the issue queue, it is possible that a trailing load is issued before the leading load. A possible solution is to place the premature trailing load's address in the empty LVQ entry. When the leading load arrives at the LVQ, the addresses are compared and the pending trailing load is satisfied. This solution naturally extends to the case where a trailing load issues after the leading load, but finds the LVQ entry empty due to the leading load missing in the cache. Note that the LVQ is ECC-protected and so values stored in it are not vulnerable to faults.

An LVQ entry is relinquished in queue order after the trailing instruction reads the entry. Upon a leading branch misprediction, the SAL is rolled back in parallel with the clean-up of the AL. To facilitate the rollback of the LVQ, branches place the LVQ tail pointer in the SAL at the time they enter the AL. Because the LVQ is in (speculative) program order, the LVQ tail pointer points to the LVQ entry to which the LVQ needs to be rolled back, if the branch mispredicts. A mispredicted branch's AL pointer locates the LVQ tail pointer in the SAL, and the LVQ is rolled back to the pointer. Like the predQ's rollback, the LVQ's rollback is also an optimistic action and the leading branch is checked to confirm the misprediction.

3.3 Checking leading and trailing instructions

SRTR checks the leading and trailing instructions as soon as the trailing instruction completes. Register values often have been written back to the physical register file by the time the check is performed. To address this issue, SRTR uses a separate structure, the *register value queue (RVQ)* to store register values for checking, avoiding bandwidth pressure on the register file (Figure 1(b)). In this section, we assume that all the instructions including branches, but excluding loads and stores use the RVQ to be checked. We assume that the RVQ can provide the required bandwidth. We address the bandwidth pressure on the RVQ in Section 4.

Because the trailing instructions need to locate the leading counterpart's value in the RVQ, the leading instruction allocates an RVQ entry at the time of entering the AL, and places a pointer to the entry in the SAL for the trailing instruction. After the leading instruction writes its result back, it enters the *fault-check* stage, as shown in Figure 2. In the fault-check stage, the leading instruction puts its value (for branches, the next PC, the prediction and the outcome are all part of the value) in the RVQ using the pointer from the SAL. The

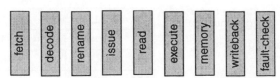

FIGURE 2: SRTR pipeline with fault-check stage.

instruction then waits in the AL to commit or squash due to faults or mispredictions. Because the fault-check stage is *after* writeback, the stage does not affect branch misprediction penalty, or the number of bypass paths.

The trailing instructions also use the SAL to obtain their RVQ pointers and find their leading counterparts' values. While it is likely that the leading instruction reaches the fault-check stage before the trailing instruction, out-of-order pipelines may reverse the order. To handle such reversals, if the trailing instruction finds the RVQ entry of its leading counterpart to be empty, it places its own value. When the leading instruction reaches the fault-check stage, it finds the value and the check is performed. A full/empty bit in the RVQ is used to indicate whether or not the RVQ entry contains leading or trailing values. The full/empty bits need to be ECC-protected to prevent corrupted full/empty bits from causing leading and trailing instruction pairs to wait forever. An RVQ entry is relinquished in queue order after the checking is done. Branch misprediction clean-up of the RVQ uses the SAL in the same way as the clean-up of the LVQ.

SRTR places completed leading store values and addresses in the StB. When a trailing store completes, its value and address are compared to the leading store's value and address in the StB, similar to the checking of load addresses in the LVQ.

Register values, store addresses and values, and load addresses are checked in the RVQ, StB, and LVQ, respectively. If a check succeeds, the *commit vector (CV)* entries corresponding to the leading and trailing instructions are set to the *checked-ok* state. Indexed by AL pointers, the CVs are parallel to the ALs (Figure 1(b)). As instructions are placed in the AL, their CV entries are set to the *not-checked-yet* state. A leading instruction commits only if its CV entry and its trailing counterpart's CV entry are in the checked-ok state. If the state is not-checked-yet, the instruction is stalled at commit until it is checked. Due to the slack, leading instructions may commit ahead of their trailing counterparts.

If a check fails, the CV entries of the leading and trailing instructions are set to the *failed-check* state. When a failed-check entry reaches the head of the leading AL, all later instructions are squashed. The leading thread waits until the trailing thread's corresponding entry reaches the head of the trailing AL before restarting both threads at the offending instruction. Because there is a time gap between the setting and the reading of the CV and between the committing of leading and trailing counterparts, the CV is protected by ECC to prevent faults from corrupting it in the time gap.

There are faults from which SRTR cannot recover: After a register value is written back and the instruction producing the value has committed, if a fault corrupts the register, then the fact that leading and trailing instructions use different physical registers will allow us to detect the fault on the next use of the register value. However, SRTR cannot recover from this fault. To avoid this loss of recovery, one solution is to provide ECC on the register file.

4 Reducing bandwidth demand on RVQ

The RVQ needs to allow as many writes or reads of register values per cycle as the number of leading and trailing non-memory instructions completing in one cycle. Because the RVQ has as many entries as in-flight leading instructions (around 120 64-bit values, totaling to 1KB), providing multiple ports to support high bandwidth (e.g., four 64-bit values per cycle) may be hard.

We propose *dependence-based checking elision (DBCE)* to reduce the number of instructions accessing the RVQ. To keep the implementation simple, we use only simple dependence chains such that each instruction in a chain has at most one parent and one child (instead of maintaining the full dependence graph). By reasoning that faults propagate through dependent instructions, DBCE exploits register (true) dependence chains so that *only* the last instruction in a chain uses the RVQ, and has the leading and trailing values checked. We show an example of a five-instruction sequence in Figure 3(a). The chain's earlier instructions in *both* threads completely elide the RVQ. If the last instruction check succeeds, it signals the previous instructions in the chain that they may commit; if the check fails, all the instructions in the chain are marked as having failed and the earliest instruction in the chain triggers a rollback. A key feature of DBCE is that both leading and trailing instructions redundantly go through the same dependence chain formation and checking-elision decisions, allowing DBCE to check its own functionality for faults.

If the last instruction of a chain is further in the instruction stream and completes much later than the other instructions, the chain's earlier instructions will stall at commit. To avoid this situation, DBCE forms short dependence chains (e.g., 3-4 instructions) by exploiting the abundant register dependencies in near-by instructions. If DBCE's chains are m instructions long, DBCE checks only one out of m instructions, reducing the bandwidth by a factor of m. Because of short slack and short chains, the trailing chain's last instruction completes just a few cycles behind the leading chain's earlier instructions. Consequently, checking of the last instructions is usually done between the time the earliest leading instruction completes and the time it reaches the commit point.

Because leading loads deposit their values in the LVQ for the trailing loads, there is no notion of eliding of checking for load values, and hence loads are not included in the chains. Stores are checked in the StB and do not use the RVQ. Therefore, stores are not included in the chains as well. Because branches do not produce register values, branches cannot be in the middle of a chain. A branch may be at the end of a chain and in that case it itself cannot elide checking but it helps elide checking for the instructions preceding it in its chain. If chains are allowed to cross branches, mispredictions will require

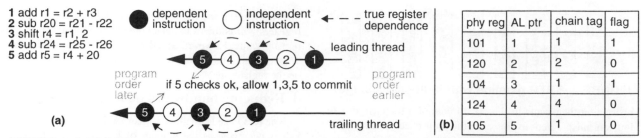

FIGURE 3: (a) DBCE concept. (b) DCQ entries showing only leading instructions.

clean-up of chains whose later instructions have been squashed due to an intervening branch misprediction. To avoid such clean-ups, DBCE disallows chains from crossing branches.

Care must be taken in forming chains with instructions that mask a subset of bits (e.g., r2 := r1 & 0xff00), or that compare two values (e.g., r1 := (r2 < r3)). If a masking (or comparing) instruction is in a chain, then the instruction may mask a fault in its source operands. Such masking violates the key assumption behind DBCE, that faults are propagated by dependences, and a later instruction included in the masking instruction's chain cannot detect the masked fault. For instance, in a chain containing r1 := r2 + r3, r2 := r1 & 0xff00, and r4 := r2 + r3, the check done on the value of r4 does not cover all the bits of r1. If the first instruction produces a faulty value for r1, and r1 is used by instructions other than the one shown above, recovery will not be possible. This issue can be resolved by disallowing masking instructions in the middle of a chain. A masking instruction may, however, start a chain because the instruction's source operands will be checked in previous chains, without allowing any faults to be masked. If an instruction masks some bits for specific inputs (e.g., multiply masks all the bits if one of its source operands is zero), a pessimistic approach would be to disallow the instruction in the middle of a chain. Since the likelihood of such input-specific masking is low, it may be acceptable to ignore the masking and treat the instruction as a non-masking instruction.

Exploiting dependence chains consists of (1) forming dependence chains in the leading thread and the corresponding chains in the trailing thread, and tagging each chain with a unique tag, (2) identifying the instructions in the leading and trailing threads requiring the check, (3) preventing the rest of the instructions (leading and trailing) in the chains from accessing the RVQ and from checking, and (4) notifying the non-checking instructions in the chains after the check is performed.

4.1 Forming dependence chains

To form dependence chains, DBCE uses the dependence chain queue (DCQ), which holds information about renamed instructions that were fetched in the last few cycles (e.g., 1-2 cycles). The instructions are kept in the instruction fetch order. Each DCQ entry holds the destination physical register and the AL pointer of an instruction, a tag which identifies the chain to which the instruction belongs, and a flag to indicate if the instruction already has a dependent instruction in its depen-

dence chain. The AL pointer of the first instruction in a chain is used as the chain's tag. Figure 3(b) shows the DCQ entries for only the leading instructions in the example of Figure 3(a), assuming that logical register x maps to physical register 100 + x.

Upon entering the DCQ, an instruction associatively searches the DCQ using its source physical register numbers, matching them against destination physical register numbers of instructions in the DCQ. If there is no match on any source register, or if all the matching instructions already have their flags set indicating that those instructions already have children, there is no live chain to which the current instruction can belong; then the instruction uses its own AL pointer as its tag, and clears its own flag to start a new chain. Branches cannot start a chain, and are removed from the DCQ if they cannot join a live chain. If there is a matching entry with a clear flag, the current instruction adds itself to the matching entry's chain by setting the matching entry's flag and obtaining the matching entry's AL pointer and tag. It clears its flag to allow additional instructions to join the chain. If two sources of an instruction match entries with clear flags, the current instruction adds itself to the chain corresponding to the first source.

Leading and trailing instructions form chains independently. Because there are no dependencies between the two threads, the DCQ can hold the two threads simultaneously. However, because fetching of leading and trailing instructions is interleaved, care must be taken to ensure that the DCQ will form identical dependence chains in the leading and trailing threads. The chains formed may be different if fetch brings a number of leading instructions, switches and brings a smaller number of trailing instructions before switching back to the leading thread. The larger number of leading instructions may cause longer chains to be formed than the fewer trailing instructions.

A simple solution is to have the leading and trailing threads each occupy half the DCQ, as shown in Figure 4(a). Every cycle either leading or trailing thread instructions reach the DCQ. The DCQ evicts the oldest entries of the same thread to make room for the new instructions. Upon evicting the oldest entries, the DCQ terminates the chains originating at the entries, ensuring that the chains stay short and span at most as many cycles as the DCQ depth. The instructions in the terminated chains are recorded in the *check table* for later use. The AL pointer of each of the oldest entries is used to search the DCQ tags, and the matching entries are all the instructions in the chain originating at the oldest entry. Although the number

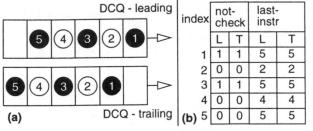

index	not-check		last-instr	
	L	T	L	T
1	1	1	5	5
2	0	0	2	2
3	1	1	5	5
4	0	0	4	4
5	0	0	5	5

FIGURE 4: (a) DCQ. (b) Check Table.

of oldest entries may be as large as the fetch width requiring as many parallel searches of the DCQ, the DCQ's small size keeps this parallel search manageable (e.g., 8-way search of 16 entries).

The matching DCQ entry that has a clear flag is the last instruction in the oldest entry's chain. The chain's non-last instructions use their AL pointers to index into the check table. In the table, the non-last instructions set the *not-check* bits to indicate that they elide checking, and they update their *last-instruction* fields with the last instruction's AL pointer. The chain's last instruction keeps its not-check bit clear and updates its last-instruction field with its own AL pointer. Figure 4(b) shows the fields for the example in Figure 3(a), using "L" to denote leading instructions and "T" to denote trailing instructions. Thus, the check table records the chain, identifying the chain's last instruction as needing to check and the rest of the instructions as eliding checking. The check table also associates the eliding instructions with the last instruction whose check covers them.

Operating on renamed instructions guarantees that matching source registers with previous destinations without checking for multiple matches in the DCQ is correct. Also, the DCQ implements a subset of the functionality of renaming and bypass. While it may be possible to use the existing renaming and bypass logic, we describe the DCQ separately for clarity, avoiding implementation details of rename and bypass.

4.2 Using dependence chains

When a leading or trailing instruction reaches writeback, the instruction uses its AL pointer to index into the check table and obtain the AL pointer of the last instruction in its chain. Then the leading and trailing not-check bits in the check table entry are compared. If the bits do not match (indicating a mismatch between the leading and trailing chains caused by a fault), the CV entries of the last instructions in both chains are set to failed-check. Otherwise, if the not-check bit is set, the instruction elides checking and waits in the AL to commit, holding its last instruction AL pointer. If the not-check bit is clear, the leading instruction places its value in the RVQ for later checking. Note that the AL pointers carried by the instructions are ECC-protected. This allows the leading and trailing instructions to access the check table independently without checking against each other's AL pointers.

Later, the trailing instruction indexes into the check table and the not-check bits are compared as above. If both the lead-

ing and trailing not-check bits are clear, the leading instruction's value is obtained from the RVQ. The leading and trailing instructions' values are then compared. If the check succeeds, the trailing AL pointer is used to mark the CV entries of both leading and trailing instructions as checked-ok. If the check fails, the CV entries are marked as failed-check. In a chain, only the last-instruction's CV entries are marked, and the rest of the instructions' CV entries remain in the not-checked-yet state. If the trailing instructions reach the RVQ first, then the role of the leading and trailing instructions reverse in the above.

When a leading instruction reaches the head of the AL, its last-instruction's AL pointer is compared to that of its trailing counterpart. On a match, the leading instruction uses its last-instruction's AL pointer to probe the leading and trailing CV entries. Depending on the CV entries, the instruction waits (if the CV entries are not-checked-yet), commits (if the CV entries are checked-ok), or squashes (if the CV entries are failed-check); squashing also occurs on a mismatch. When a trailing instruction reaches the head of its AL, if the leading thread has already committed, the CV entry of the trailing thread is guaranteed to be checked-ok and the trailing instruction will commit.

Upon instruction commit, the check table entry corresponding to the committing instruction's AL pointer are cleared. On an instruction squash, the check table entries corresponding to the squashed AL pointers are invalidated. Because the DCQ holds later instructions down the stream from the squashing instruction, all the DCQ entries from the squashing thread are discarded on a squash.

DBCE needs to guarantee that a dependence chain is fully formed before any of the instructions in the chain enter the writeback stage. Otherwise, when earlier instructions need to know the identity of the last instruction to update the CV and AL, the last instruction will not yet have been identified. We avoid this situation by ensuring that the number of cycles the DCQ spans (1-2 cycles) is smaller than the number of pipeline stages between issue and writeback (usually more than two).

If an interrupt/exception occurs in the middle of a chain, the exception delivery (which is the same as in SRT, as described at the end of Section 2) places the exception at the same execution point in both threads. The excepting instruction and all the previous instructions in the chain wait in the active list for the last instruction in the chain to complete and be checked. Even though the last instruction may be after the excepting instruction in program order, it is acceptable to allow the last instruction to complete but not commit. Only after the checking occurs, is the excepting instruction (and all the previous instructions in the chain) deemed ready to commit. Under this condition, when the excepting instruction reaches the commit point in both threads, an exception is flagged. The rest of the instructions in both threads are now squashed. After the interrupt is handled, execution restarts at the same point for both threads, and new chains are formed afresh. Thus, instructions are committed one by one, exactly as in conventional SMT.

Table 1: Hardware parameters for base system.

Component	Description
Processor	8-way out-of-order issue,128-entry issue queue
Branch prediction	hybrid 8K-entry bimodal, 8K-entry gshare, 8K 2-bit selector 16-entry RAS, 4-way1K BTB (10-cycle misprediction penalty)
L1 I- and D-cache	64KB, 32-byte blocks, 4-way, 2-cycle hit, lock-up free
L2 unified cache	1 Mbyte,64-byte blocks, 4-way, 12-cycle hit, pipelined
Main memory	Infinite capacity, 100 cycle latency

Table 2: Benchmarks and inputs.

Benchmark	Input	#instrs x 10^6	single thread IPC
go	train	600	1.17
lisp	test	1000	1.63
gcc	test	1000	1.28
perl	jumble	1000	1.90
ijpeg	vigo	1000	2.58
vortex	train	1000	2.12
m88ksim	test	500	2.89
compress	train	40	2.16
swim	test	780	2.53
applu	train	680	2.93
fpppp	train	510	0.59
su2cor	test	1000	2.18
hydro2d	test	1000	1.94
tomcatv	test	1000	2.69

To allow several accesses every cycle, the DCQ has to provide high bandwidth. Because the DCQ holds a small number of instructions, it can be implemented to support high bandwidth (e.g., 8-16 instructions each requiring one 8-bit destination register number, three 8-bit AL pointers, and a few bits for a flag, totaling to about 80 bytes). Building a high-bandwidth RVQ, which is kilobytes in size, is harder, for the same reason that rename tables are widely multiported but D-caches are only dual-ported. The check table is also a high-bandwidth structure because every leading and trailing instruction accesses it. Because the check table holds only two AL pointers and two flags per entry, multi-porting it is easier than multi-porting the much-larger RVQ.

5 Experimental results

We modify the Simplescalar out-of-order simulator [2] to model SMT and SRT. Table 1 shows the base system configuration parameters used throughout the experiments. The front-end of our base pipeline is long to account for SMT and deep pipelines corresponding to high clock speeds. Like SRT, we approximate a high-bandwidth trace cache by fetching past three branches, and at most eight instructions, per cycle [10]. Table 2 presents the SPEC95 benchmarks and their inputs used in this study. In the interest of space, we show results for a subset of the SPEC95 applications, which are representative of our results over the entire SPEC95 suite. We run the benchmarks to completion, or stop at 1 billion instructions in the interest of simulation time.

We present results in the absence of faults in order to study the performance cost of SRTR over SRT. In the presence of faults, SRTR can recover but SRT will stop as soon as it detects a fault. Therefore, a comparison of performance is not possible when faults occur. In addition, faults are expected to be rare enough that the overall performance will be determined by fault-free behavior.

Because the basic scheme used in SRTR for detection is different from that used in SRT, we start by comparing the SRTR detection scheme (without recovery) against SRT. We refer to the detection scheme implemented in SRTR as *SRTRd*. SRTRd uses a short slack and it communicates branch predictions between the leading and trailing threads, while SRT uses a long slack and communicates branch outcomes. In the same experiment, we also show the performance impact of near-zero

slack. Then, we report the average time gap between complete to commit, and average memory latencies in the base SMT. These parameters determine the constraints on SRTR's slack which needs to be shorter than the average complete to commit times to avoid leading thread stalls at commit, but long enough to avoid trailing thread stalls due to empty LVQ. We then compare SRTR (providing recovery) using a high-bandwidth RVQ, to SRTRd and SRT. This comparison gives the performance cost of recovery over detection. We show the impact of the RVQ size on SRTR's performance. Finally, we show the bandwidth reduction achieved by DBCE while maintaining the same performance as the high-bandwidth RVQ.

5.1 SRT versus SRTRd

In Figure 5, we compare SRTRd and SRT. We show the performance normalized to the base SMT executing only the standard program. We use a slack of 256 and a 256-entry BOQ, 256-entry LVQ and 256-entry StB for SRT, exceeding the sizes for the best performance reported by SRT [10]. For SRTRd, we use predQ/LVQ/StB sizes of 128/128/128 for a slack of 128, 80/96/80 for a slack of 64, 48/96/48 for a slack of 32, and 18/96/18 for a slack of 2. The purpose of this experiment is to compare using a short slack and communicating branch predictions between the leading and trailing threads, against using a long slack and communicating branch outcomes. We do not want the queues to fill up and interfere with this comparison. Therefore, we keep the sizes of SRTRd's queues appropriately large for each slack value. It is important to note that SRTR needs a short slack to avoid leading instructions stalling at commit while waiting for trailing instructions to complete and be checked. This effect does not exist in SRTRd, which performs well with higher values of slack.

From Figure 5, the performance of SRT is between 2% to 45% worse than the base SMT. These numbers are in line with SRT [10]. On average, SRT is 21% worse than SMT for the integer programs (*go* through *compress*), and 27% worse than SMT for the floating point (FP) programs (*swim* through *tomcatv*). In general, programs which exhibit enough ILP to saturate the processor resources in the base SMT incur higher

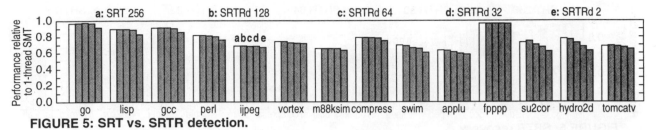

FIGURE 5: SRT vs. SRTR detection.

performance loss due to replication in SRT (and SRTRd).

While a short slack of 64 or 32 performs close to a slack of 256, a near-zero slack of 2 incurs greater performance loss for many programs. For the integer programs, SRTRd on average performs as well as SRT for slacks of 128 and 64, and within 1% of SRT for a slack of 32, showing that communicating branch predictions works as well as outcomes. For a slack of 2, STRTd performs about 5%, on average, worse than SRT, with *lisp* incurring a 10% performance loss. This loss is mainly due to unavailable load values in the LVQ (explained in Section 5.2). For the FP programs, SRTRd performs as well as SRT for a slack of 128, and within 3% and 5% of SRT for a slack of 64 and 32, respectively. For a slack of 2, SRTRd performs about 8%, on average, worse than SRT, with *hydro2d* incurring a 26% performance loss.

In a few cases such as *go*, *tomcatv*, and *su2cor*, SRTRd performs slightly better than SRT due to the interaction between branch mispredictions and slack. Branch mispredictions cause the actual slack to reduce temporarily. In SRT, this reduction results in the trailing thread stalling for branch outcomes, whereas SRTRd is not affected by this reduction because SRTRd's trailing thread uses branch predictions which are available earlier than branch outcomes. Long delays in branch resolution in *tomcatv* and *su2cor*, and *go*'s frequent mispredictions make these programs vulnerable to this effect.

5.2 Constraints on SRTR's slack

While SRTRd performs well with a large slack, recovery will require a shorter slack as discussed earlier. In this section, we explain why a short slack suffices, and how short the slack

Table 3: Slack constraints.

Benchmark	Ave. memory latency	#Ave. complete to commit time
go	2.02	15.5
lisp	2.0	22.8
gcc	2.15	20.5
perl	2.22	27.3
ijpeg	2.15	27.4
vortex	2.15	39.4
m88ksim	2.01	25.4
compress	2.89	26.5
swim	3.36	39.5
applu	3.64	34.3
fpppp	2.0	20.6
su2cor	3.83	40.1
hydro2d	5.80	45.4
tomcatv	2.01	31.3

may be and still not impact performance. For SRT, SRTRd, and SRTR (providing recovery), the slack needs to be long enough to hide the leading thread's average memory latency from the trailing thread. However, SRTR's slack needs to be short enough so that trailing instructions can complete and be checked before the leading counterparts reach the commit point. Hence, SRTR's slack needs to be longer than the memory latency but shorter than the complete to commit time.

In Table 3, we tabulate the average number of cycles between complete and commit and the average memory latency for the base SMT. We compute the average memory latency as L1 hit time + L1 miss rate * L1 miss penalty + L2 miss rate * L2 miss penalty. This latency is the impact of the leading thread's load latency on the trailing thread assuming the worst case where the latency is completely exposed in the trailing thread. We see that due to good cache performance, the average memory latency is close to the hit time suggesting that the slack primarily needs to hide on-chip cache hit latencies. In general, the FP programs (*swim* through *tomcatv*) have a higher memory latency explaining their worse performance with shorter slacks. For instance, *hydro2d* has a long average memory latency, and performs poorly with a slack of 2.

For all the programs, the gap between the average complete to commit time and the average memory latency is large enough to allow a slack longer than the average memory latency but shorter than the average complete to commit time. Even for memory-intensive applications which may have higher miss rates than our benchmarks, the gap is likely to be large enough to allow a reasonable slack. Note that slack is counted in number of instructions by which the leading thread is ahead, and the numbers in Table 3 are numbers of cycles. Because fetch can obtain up to 8 instructions per cycle, a slack of 32 is equivalent to 4 cycles.

5.3 SRTR recovery

The average complete to commit times in Table 3 suggest a range for appropriate slack values. To select an acceptable value for the slack, it is important to note that the complete to commit time of individual instructions vary quite widely. For instance, *lisp, compress* and *tomcatv* have 40%, 50%, and 40%, respectively, instructions whose complete to commit times are fewer than 10 cycles. Therefore, a long slack may cause many leading instructions to stall at commit waiting for their trailing counterparts to complete and be checked. It is thus important to select a slack value which accommodates the majority of the instructions.

In Figure 6, we compare SRT using a slack of 256 to SRTR

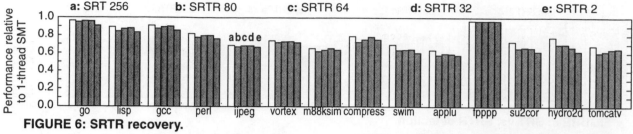

FIGURE 6: SRTR recovery.

(providing recovery) varying the slack for SRTR as 80, 64, 32, and 2. Because SRTRd using a slack of 128 performs as well as SRT, we do not show SRTRd in this graph. To isolate the effect of the slack, we use a bandwidth-unlimited (i.e., 8 ports), 128-entry RVQ (we vary the RVQ size later). We use a 256-entry BOQ, 256-entry LVQ and 256-entry StB for SRT. For SRTR, we use predQ/LVQ/StB sizes of 128/128/128 for a slack of 80, 80/96/80 for a slack of 64, 48/96/48 for a slack of 32, and 18/96/18 for a slack of 2. As in Section 5.1, we show performance normalized to the base SMT executing only the standard program.

It can be seen that SRTR's average performance peaks at a slack of 32. For the integer programs (*go* through *compress*), SRTR using a slack of 64 and 32 on average performs 3% and 1% worse than SRT. For the FP programs (*swim* through *tomcatv*), SRTR on average performs 7% worse than SRT for both a slack of 64 and 32. As expected, decreasing the slack to 2 causes performance degradation. Increasing the slack to 80 also causes performance degradation. SRTR using a slack of 80 on average performs 5% and 9% worse than SRT for the integer and FP programs, respectively. A slack of 80 makes the leading thread stall at commit, putting pressure on the instruction window. Thus, using a slack of 32 seems to be the best choice for these benchmarks.

5.4 RVQ size

In this experiment, we measure the impact of varying the RVQ size on the performance of SRTR. RVQ entries are allocated as leading instructions enter the AL and freed in queue-order as the trailing counterparts obtain the RVQ values. Hence, the RVQ size depends on the issue queue size and the slack. In Figure 7, we compare SRT using a slack of 256 to SRTR using a slack of 32 (which was identified as the best value in the last section) and predQ/LVQ/StB sizes of 48/96/48, but varying the RVQ size as 128, 96, 80, and 64 entries. As before, we show performance normalized to the base SMT executing only the standard program.

It can be seen that an RVQ size of 80 entries works as well as 128 entries for all the programs. With 64 entries, while most programs experience no degradation, a few programs like *gcc*, *compress* and *su2cor* incur a small performance loss while *ijpeg*, *applu*, *hydr2d* and *tomcatv* slow down considerably. For these benchmarks, an RVQ size of 80 entries seems appropriate and achieves the same performance as a 128-entry RVQ.

5.5 DBCE

In this section, we show the effectiveness of DBCE in reducing the bandwidth demand on the RVQ. We measure the impact of RVQ bandwidth on SRTR without and with DBCE. Loads and stores do not use the RVQ and hence the RVQ bandwidth demand comes solely from the ALU/FPU and branch instructions. Both with and without DBCE, SRTR uses a slack of 32, predQ/LVQ/StB sizes of 48/96/48 entries, and an 80-entry RVQ (which was identified as the best size in the last section). We use a DCQ size of 16 (8 for each thread). We varied the DCQ size but did not find much difference mainly because the chains are broken at branches, and branch frequency impacts the chain length more than the DCQ size. Because four RVQ ports are as good as five or more for SRTR without DBCE, we vary the number of RVQ ports as 2, 3, and 4. We use SRT with a slack of 256 as the reference, and show performance normalized to the base SMT executing only the standard program.

We show the results in Figure 8. In our implementation, we assume that faults propagate through all instructions, including those that may mask faults. Because the percentage of masking instructions is usually low [10], this assumption will not affect our results significantly.

In Table 4, we show the number of RVQ accesses elided by DBCE as a percentage of all RVQ accesses made without DBCE. On average, DBCE elides 35.3% of all RVQ accesses in both leading and trailing threads. For most programs, the percentage of elided instructions is high using a DCQ of just 16 entries because the programs have an abundance of register

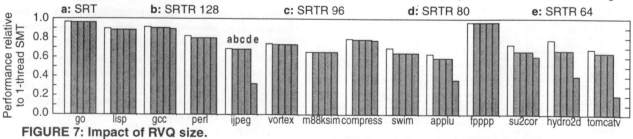

FIGURE 7: Impact of RVQ size.

Table 4: Percent RVQ accesses elided.

Benchmark	Percent elided	Benchmark	Percent elided
go	53.1	swim	43.7
lisp	24.7	applu	50.1
gcc	41.3	fpppp	18.4
perl	33.5	su2cor	40.8
ijpeg	49.4	hydro2d	39.5
vortex	15.7	tomcatv	35.1
m88ksim	38.4	AVERAGE	35.3
compress	38.5		

dependences in nearby instructions. The exceptions are *vortex* and *fpppp*; both programs have a high fraction (52.8% and 53.2%, respectively) of memory instructions. Because loads and stores are not included in the DBCE chains, the programs cannot elide as many instructions as the others.

Let us first analyze SRTR performance without DBCE. From Figure 8, we see that for all the programs, a 4-ported RVQ (third bar) performs as well as an 8-ported RVQ (second bar). As the number of RVQ ports decreases from 3 to 2, most programs incur significant performance loss. For the integer programs (*go* thorough *compress*), performance drops by 2% and 18%, on average, with 3 and 2 RVQ ports, respectively, compared to 4 RVQ ports. For the FP programs (*swim* through *tomcatv*), performance degrades by 1% and 20%, on average, with 3 and 2 RVQ ports, respectively. *vortex* and *fpppp* are the two exceptions that perform as well with 2 RVQ ports as with 4 RVQ ports, because more than half of the instructions are loads and stores, and do not access the RVQ.

On the other hand, SRTR with DBCE incurs little performance loss even with two RVQ ports. Comparing four ports to two ports, performance degrades by 1% and 2% for the integer and FP programs, respectively. Note that in the case of 4 ports where DBCE is not needed, using DBCE does not degrade performance. This point implies that by exploiting complete to commit time, DBCE avoids stalling the early instructions in the chains waiting for the last instruction in the chain to complete. Looking at SRTR using 2 RVQ ports with and without DBCE, DBCE boosts SRTR's performance by 17% and 18% for the integer and FP programs, respectively.

6 Related work

Watchdog processors are the key concept behind many fault tolerance schemes [5]. The AR-SMT processor is the first to use SMT to execute two copies of the same program [12]. AR-SMT also proposes using speculation techniques to allow communication of data values and branch outcomes between the leading and trailing threads to accelerate execution. A later paper applies the concepts from AR-SMT to CMPs [15]. SRT improves on AR-SMT via the two optimizations of slack fetch and checking only stores for an SoR that includes the register file [10]. A recent paper explores design options for fault detection via multithreading [6].

The AR-SMT paper mentions recovery stating that the state of the R-stream (which corresponds to our trailing thread) is the checkpointed state and can be used for recovery. SRTR and AR-SMT are fundamentally different ways of performing recovery, with different costs. SRTR disallows the leading thread from committing until the trailing thread completes and is checked, and uses instruction squash to rollback to a committed state before the fault. AR-SMT allows the leading thread to commit potentially faulty state, and let the trailing thread be checked upon completion of each instruction; upon detecting a fault, AR-SMT uses the trailing thread's committed state (up to but not including the fault) to restore the leading thread's state for recovery. SRTR delays the leading thread from committing and our paper shows the performance impact of this choice. AR-SMT doubles the bandwidth pressure on the data cache by requiring both threads to access the cache, while SRTR (and SRT) uses the LVQ for the trailing thread accesses. Furthermore, AR-SMT requires memory to be doubled (two copies of memory, one for each thread) because committing faulty state of the leading thread will corrupts memory. Doubling the memory size may stress the memory hierarchy and degrade performance. Because faults are not allowed to reach memory in SRTR, there is only one copy of memory in SRTR (and SRT).

DIVA is another fault-tolerant superscalar processor that uses a simple, in-order checker processor to check the execution of the complex out-of-order processor [1]. DIVA can recover from permanent faults and design errors in the aggressive processor but assumes that no transient faults occur in the checker processor itself. Other works on fault tolerance focus on functional units [11, 7, 4, 14].

A recent paper [9] proposes hardware recovery using superscalar hardware without any SMT support. The paper advocates the natural way to achieve recovery by using superscalar's rollback ability. The paper does not use the LVQ, does not address the issues related to cached loads, and claims that there is no need for any slack.

The Compaq NonStop Himalaya [3] and IBM z900 (formerly S/390) [13] employ redundant hardware to achieve fault

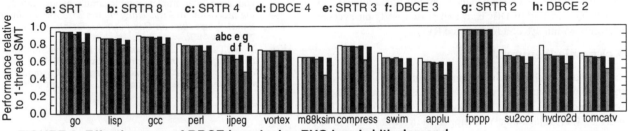

a: SRT b: SRTR 8 c: SRTR 4 d: DBCE 4 e: SRTR 3 f: DBCE 3 g: SRTR 2 h: DBCE 2

FIGURE 8: Effectiveness of DBCE in reducing RVQ bandwidth demand.

tolerance. The z900 uses the G5 microprocessor which includes replicated, lock-stepped pipelines. The NonStop Himalaya uses off-the-shelf, lock-stepped microprocessors and compares the external pins on every cycle. In both systems, when the lock-stepped components disagree, the components are stopped to prevent propagation of faults. The z900 uses special microcode to restore program state from a hardware checkpoint module. The NonStop Himalaya does not provide hardware support for recovery. SRT has shown that avoiding lock-stepping achieves better performance.

7 Conclusions

We proposed *Simultaneously and Redundantly Threaded processors with Recovery (SRTR)* that enhances SRT to include transient-fault recovery. In SRT, a leading instruction may commit *before* the check for faults occurs, relying on the trailing thread to trigger detection. SRTR, on the other hand, must *not* allow *any* leading instruction to commit before checking occurs, since a faulty instruction cannot be undone once the instruction commits. To avoid leading instructions stalling at commit waiting for their trailing counterparts, SRTR exploits the time between completion and commit of a leading instruction. SRTR checks as soon as the trailing instruction completes, well before the leading instruction reaches commit. To avoid increasing the bandwidth demand on the register file, SRTR uses the *register value queue (RVQ)* to hold register values for checking. To reduce the bandwidth pressure on the RVQ itself, SRTR employs *dependence-based checking elision (DBCE)*. By reasoning that faults propagate through dependent instructions, DBCE exploits register (true) dependence chains so that *only* the last instruction in a chain uses the RVQ, and has the leading and trailing values checked. DBCE redundantly builds chains in both the leading and trailing threads and checks its own functionality for faults.

We evaluated SRTR using the SPEC95 benchmarks. SRTR on average performs within 1% and 7% of SRT for integer and floating-point programs, respectively. We showed that high prediction accuracies and low off-chip miss rates in the underlying SMT enable SRTR detection using a slack of 32 to perform on average within 5% of SRT using a slack of 256. For our benchmarks, the gap between the average complete to commit time and average memory latency is large enough to allow a slack longer than the average memory latency but shorter than the average complete to commit time. DBCE elides about 35% of RVQ accesses. SRTR without DBCE on average incurs 18% performance loss on reducing from four (which is performance-equivalent to an unlimited number) to two RVQ ports. With DBCE, a two-ported RVQ on average performs within 2% of a four-ported RVQ.

Acknowledgements

We thank Shubu Mukherjee and the anonymous reviewers for their comments. The work of I. Pomeranz and K. Cheng was supported in part by NSF Grant No. CCR-0049081. The work of T. N. Vijaykumar was supported in part by NSF Grant No. CCR-9875960.

References

[1] T. M. Austin. DIVA: A reliable substrate for deep-submicron microarchitecture design. In *Proceedings of the 32nd Annual International Symposium on Microarchitecture*, pages 196–207, Nov. 1999.

[2] D. Burger, T. M. Austin, and S. Bennett. Evaluating future microprocessors: the simplescalar tool set. Technical Report CS TR-1308, University of Wisconsin, Madison, July 1996.

[3] Compaq Computer Corporation. *Data integrity for Compaq Non-Stop Himalaya servers.* http://nonstop.compaq.com, 1999.

[4] J. G. Holm and P. Banerjee. Low cost concurrent error detection in a VLIW architecture using replicated instructions. In *Proceedings of the International Conference on Parallel Processing*, 1992.

[5] A. Mahmood and E. J. McCluskey. Concurrent error detection using watchdog processors–A survey. *IEEE Trans. on Computers*, 37(2):160–174, Feb. 1988.

[6] S. S. Mukherjee, M. Kontz, and S. K. Reinhardt. Detailed design and evaluation of redundant multithreading alternatives. In *Proceedings of the 29th Annual International Symposium on Computer Architecture*, May 2002.

[7] J. H. Patel and L. Y. Fung. Concurrent error detection on ALU's by recomputing with shifted operands. *IEEE Trans. on Computers*, 31(7):589–595, July 1982.

[8] D. A. Patterson and J. L. Hennessy. *Computer Architecture: A Quantitative Approach.* Morgan Kaufmann Publishers, 1998.

[9] J. Ray, J. C. Hoe, and B. Falsafi. Dual use of superscalar datapath for transient-fault detection and recovery. In *Proceedings of the 34th annual IEEE/ACM international symposium o n Microarchitecture*, Dec. 2001.

[10] S. K. Reinhardt and S. S. Mukherjee. Transient-fault detection via simultaneous multithreading. In *Proceedings of the 27th Annual International Symposium on Computer Architecture*, pages 25–36, June 2000.

[11] D. A. Reynolds and G. Metze. Fault detection capabilities of alternating logic. *IEEE Trans. on Computers*, 27(12):1093–1098, Dec. 1978.

[12] E. Rotenberg. AR-SMT: A microarchitectural approach to fault tolerance in microprocessors. In *Proceedings of Fault-Tolerant Computing Systems*, 1999.

[13] T. J. Slegel, et al. IBM's S/390 G5 microprocessor design. *IEEE Micro*, 19(2):12–23, 1999.

[14] G. S. Sohi, M. Franklin, and K. K. Saluja. A study of time-redundant fault tolerance techniques for high-performance, pipelined computers. In *Digest of papers, 19th International Symposium on Fault-Tolerant Computing*, pages 436–443, 1989.

[15] K. Sundaramoorthy, Z. Purser, and E. Rotenberg. Slipstream processors: Improving both performance and fault-tolerance. In *Proceedings of the Ninth International Symposium on Architectural Support for Programming Languages and Operating Systems*, pages 257–268. Association for Computing Machinery, Nov. 2000.

[16] D. M. Tullsen, S. J. Eggers, J. S. Emer, H. M. Levy, J. L. Lo, and R. L. Stamm. Exploiting choice: Instruction fetch and issue on an implementable simultaneous multithreading processor. In *Proceedings of the 23rd Annual International Symposium on Computer Architecture*, pages 191–202, May 1996.

[17] D. M. Tullsen, S. J. Eggers, and H. M. Levy. Simultaneous multithreading: maximizing on-chip parallelism. In *Proceedings of the 22th Annual International Symposium on Computer Architecture*, pages 392–403, June 1995.

Detailed Design and Evaluation of Redundant Multithreading Alternatives*

Shubhendu S. Mukherjee
VSSAD
Massachusetts Microprocessor Design Center
Intel Corporation
334 South Street, SHR1-T25
Shrewsbury, MA 01545
Shubu.Mukherjee@intel.com

Michael Kontz
Colorado VLSI Lab
Systems & VLSI Technology Operations
Hewlett-Packard Company
3404 East Harmony Road, ms 55
Fort Collins, CO 80525
michael_kontz@hp.com

Steven K. Reinhardt
EECS Department
University of Michigan, Ann Arbor
1301 Beal Avenue
Ann Arbor, MI 48109-2122
stever@eecs.umich.edu

ABSTRACT

Exponential growth in the number of on-chip transistors, coupled with reductions in voltage levels, makes each generation of microprocessors increasingly vulnerable to transient faults. In a multithreaded environment, we can detect these faults by running two copies of the same program as separate threads, feeding them identical inputs, and comparing their outputs, a technique we call Redundant Multithreading (RMT).

This paper studies RMT techniques in the context of both single- and dual-processor simultaneous multithreaded (SMT) single-chip devices. Using a detailed, commercial-grade, SMT processor design we uncover subtle RMT implementation complexities, and find that RMT can be a more significant burden for single-processor devices than prior studies indicate. However, a novel application of RMT techniques in a dual-processor device, which we term chip-level redundant threading (CRT), shows higher performance than lockstepping the two cores, especially on multithreaded workloads.

1. INTRODUCTION

Modern microprocessors are vulnerable to transient hardware faults caused by alpha particle and cosmic ray strikes. Strikes by cosmic ray particles, such as neutrons, are particularly critical because of the absence of any practical way to protect microprocessor chips from such strikes. As transistors shrink in size with succeeding technology generations, they become individually less vulnerable to cosmic ray strikes. However, decreasing voltage levels and exponentially increasing transistor counts cause overall chip susceptibility to increase rapidly. To compound the problem, achieving a particular failure rate for a large multiprocessor server requires an even lower failure rate for the individual microprocessors that comprise it. Due to these trends, we expect fault detection and recovery techniques, currently used only for mission-critical systems, to become common in all but the least expensive microprocessor devices.

One fault-detection approach for microprocessor cores, which we term *redundant multithreading* (RMT), runs two identical copies of the same program as independent threads and compares their outputs. On a mismatch, the checker flags an error and initiates a hardware or software recovery sequence. RMT has been proposed as a technique for implementing fault detection efficiently on top of a simultaneous multithreaded (SMT) processor (e.g., [18], [17], [15]). This paper makes contributions in two areas of RMT. First, we describe our application of RMT techniques to a processor that resembles a commercial-grade SMT processor design. The resulting design and its evaluation are significantly more detailed than previous RMT studies. Second, we examine the role of RMT

techniques in forthcoming dual-processor single-chip devices.

Our implementation of the single-processor RMT device is based on the previously published simultaneous and redundantly threaded (SRT) processor design [15] (Figure 1a). However, unlike previous evaluations, we start with an extremely detailed performance model of an aggressive, commercial-grade SMT microprocessor resembling the Compaq Alpha Araña (a.k.a. 21464 or EV8) [12]. We call this our base processor. We found several subtle issues involved in adding SRT features to such a base SMT design. For example, adapting the SRT branch outcome queue, which uses branch outcomes from one thread (the "leading" thread) to eliminate branch mispredictions for its redundant copy (the "trailing" thread), to our base processor's line-prediction-driven fetch architecture proved to be a particularly difficult task. We also describe and analyze a simple extension to the proposed SRT design, called *preferential space redundancy*, which significantly improves coverage of permanent faults.

We then compare the performance of our SRT implementation with the baseline processor using the same detailed performance model. Our results indicate that the performance degradation of RMT (running redundant copies of a thread) compared to our baseline processor (running a single copy of the same thread) is 32% on average, greater than the 21% indicated by our previous work [15]. We also find that store queue size has a major impact on SRT performance. Our SRT implementation lengthens the average lifetime of a leading-thread store by roughly 39 cycles, requiring a significantly greater number of store queue entries to avoid stalls. We propose the use of per-thread store queues to increase the number of store queue entries without severely impacting cycle time. This optimization reduces average performance degradation from 32% to 30%, with significant benefits on several individual benchmarks.

We also expand our performance study beyond that of previous work by examining the impact of SRT on multithreaded workloads. We run two logical application threads as two redundant thread pairs, consuming four hardware thread contexts on a single processor. We find our SRT processor's performance degradation for such a configuration is about 40%. However, the use of per-thread store queues can reduce the degradation to about 32%.

Our second area of contribution involves the role of RMT techniques in dual-processor single-chip devices. Initial examples of these two-way chip multiprocessors (CMPs) are shipping (e.g., the IBM Power4 [7] and the HP Mako [8]). We expect this configuration to proliferate as transistor counts continue to grow exponentially and wire delays, rather than die area, constrain the size of a single processor core.

A two-way CMP enables on-chip fault detection using *lockstepping*, where the same computation is performed on both processors on a cycle-by-cycle basis, that is, in "lockstep" (Figure 1b). Lockstepping has several advantages over SRT-style redundancy. Lockstepping is a well-understood technique, as it has long been

* This work was performed at Compaq Computer Corporation, where Shubhendu S. Mukherjee was a full-time employee, Michael Kontz was an intern, and Steven K. Reinhardt was a contractor.

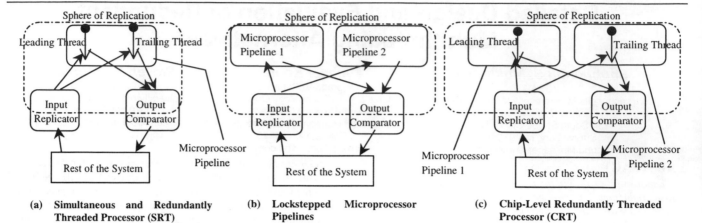

Figure 1. Fault Detection Using SRT, Lockstepped Microprocessors, and CRT. Specifically, in our implementations, the microprocessor pipelines, input replicators, and output comparators are on the same chip. The "rest of the system" is split into on-chip components (L2 cache, memory controllers, on-chip router) and off-chip components (memory, disks, other I/O devices).

used across separate chips on commercial fault-tolerant systems (e.g., Compaq Himalaya systems [30]), and is used on-chip in some fault-tolerant processors (e.g., the IBM G5 [21]). Lockstepping also provides more complete fault coverage than SRT, particularly for permanent faults, as redundant computations are executed on physically separate hardware. However, lockstepping uses hardware resources less efficiently than SRT, as both copies of a computation are forced to waste resources—in lockstep—on misspeculation and cache misses. Lockstepping also requires all signals from both processors to be routed to a central checker module before being forwarded to the rest of the system, increasing cache-miss latencies.

To combine the fault coverage of lockstepping with the efficiency of SRT, we propose a new technique—*chip-level redundant threading (CRT)*—that extends SRT techniques to a CMP environment (Figure 1c). As in SRT, CRT uses loosely synchronized redundant threads, enabling lower checker overhead and eliminating cache miss and misspeculation penalties on the trailing thread copy. As in lockstepping, the two redundant thread copies execute on separate processor cores; they are not multiplexed as different thread contexts on a single core as in SRT.

On single-thread workloads, CRT performs similarly to lockstepping, because the behavior of CRT's leading thread is similar to that of the individual threads in the lockstepped processors. However, with multithreaded workloads, CRT "cross-couples" the cores for greater efficiency. For example, with two application threads, each core runs the leading thread for one application and the trailing thread for the other. The resources freed up by CRT on each core from optimizing one application's trailing thread are then applied to the more resource-intensive leading thread of a different application. On these multithreaded workloads, CRT outperforms lockstepping by 13% on average, with a maximum improvement of 22%.

The rest of the paper is organized as follows. The next two sections discuss background material: Section 3 describes the specifics of the previously proposed SRT scheme and Section 4 briefly describes our baseline processor architecture. Section 5 begins our contributions, describing our adaptation of SRT concepts to our baseline processor model. Section 6 covers our new chip-level redundant threading (CRT) technique for two-way CMP devices. We describe our evaluation methodology in Section 7 and present results in Section 8. We conclude in Section 9.

2. BASIC SRT CONCEPTS

An SRT processor detects faults by running two identical copies of the same program as independent threads on an SMT processor [15]. For several reasons, it is useful to maintain one thread slightly further along in its execution than the other, creating a distinct *leading* thread and *trailing* thread within the pair. Adding SRT support to an SMT processor involves two key mechanisms: *input replication* and *output comparison*. Input replication guarantees that both threads see identical input values; otherwise, they may follow different execution paths even in the absence of faults. Output comparison verifies that the results produced by the two threads are identical before they are forwarded to the rest of the system, signaling a fault and possibly initiating a system-dependent recovery process if they are not identical.

A key concept introduced in the SRT work is the *sphere of replication*, the logical boundary of redundant execution within a system. Components within the sphere enjoy fault coverage due to the redundant execution; components outside the sphere do not, and therefore, must be protected via other means, such as information redundancy. Values entering the sphere of replication are inputs that must be replicated; values leaving the sphere of replication are outputs that must be compared.

For this paper, we chose the larger of the spheres of replication described in the SRT paper, including the processor pipeline and register files, but excluding the L1 data and instruction caches. Sections 2.1 and 2.2, respectively, review the required input replication and output comparison mechanisms for this sphere. Section 2.3 reviews two SRT performance optimization techniques: *slack fetch* and the *branch outcome queue*.

2.1 Input Replication

Because our sphere of replication excludes the L1 data and instruction caches, we must perform input replication on values coming from these structures, i.e., the results of cacheable loads and instruction fetches. For cached load value replication, SRT proposes a first-in first-out *load value queue*. As each leading-thread load retires, it writes its address and load value to the load value queue. The trailing thread's loads read the load value queue in program order, verifying the load address and retrieving the data. Because the data is not read redundantly out of the cache, the load value queue contents must be protected by some other means, e.g., ECC. The load value queue prevents external updates to shared

Table 1. Base Processor Parameters

IBOX	Fetch Width	2 8-instruction chunks (from same thread) per cycle
	Line Predictor	Predicts two chunks per cycle. The two chunks can be non-sequential Total number of entries = 28K
	L1 Instruction Cache	64 Kbytes, 2-way set associative with way prediction, 64 byte blocks
	Branch Predictor	208 Kbits
	Memory Dependence Predictor	Store Sets, 4K entries [2]
	Rate Matching Buffer	Collapses 2 8-instruction chunks (from same thread) to create one map chunk with up to 8 instructions
PBOX	Map Width	One 8-instruction chunk (from same thread) per cycle
QBOX	Instruction Queue	128 entries window
	Issue Width	8 instructions per cycle
RBOX	Register File	512 physical registers, 256 architectural registers (64 registers per thread)
EBOX & FBOX	Functional Units (includes a register cache)	8 operations per cycle 8 integer units, 8 logic units, 4 memory units, 4 floating point units
MBOX	L1 Data Cache	64 Kbytes, 2-way set associative, 64 byte blocks, 3 load ports, one write port
	Load Queue	64 entries
	Store Queue	64 entries
	Coalescing Merge Buffer	16 64-byte blocks
System Interface	L2 Cache	3 Megabytes, 8-way set-associative, 64 byte cache blocks
	Memory Interface	2 Rambus controllers, 10 Rambus channels
	Network Router & Interface	On-chip two-dimensional mesh router, similar to the Alpha 21364 [10]

memory locations—e.g., from other processors or I/O devices—from causing the threads to diverge.

As in the original SRT work, we assume that the instruction space is read-only. Thus, as long as both threads generate the same sequence of program counter values (which they will in the absence of faults), they will receive the same instruction values from the memory system. Most modern systems already require special synchronization operations to modify the instruction space safely; these can be extended if necessary to provide proper replication of instruction values.

Techniques for replicating less frequent inputs, such as uncached load values and interrupt inputs, are also described in the original SRT paper. We leave detailed implementation of these replication mechanisms for future work.

2.2 Output Comparison

Cacheable stores are the primary form of output from our sphere of replication. SRT proposes an enhanced store queue for output comparison of cacheable stores. Leading-thread store addresses and data are held in the store queue until they are verified by comparing the address and data values generated by the corresponding store in the trailing thread. Once a store has been matched and verified, a single store operation is forwarded outside the sphere. Again, we defer implementation of other required, but less frequent, output comparisons identified in the SRT paper, such as uncached stores and uncached load addresses, to future work.

I	P	Q	R	E	M

Figure 2. Base Processor's Integer Pipeline. I = IBOX consisting of the thread chooser, line prediction, instruction cache access, and the rate matching buffer. P = PBOX consisting of wire delays and register rename, Q = QBOX consisting of instruction queue operations, R = RBOX consisting of register read stages, E = EBOX consisting of functional units, and M = MBOX consisting of data caches, load queue, and store queue. In our evaluation, we assumed the following latencies: I = 4, P = 2, Q = 4, R = 4, E =1, and M = 2 cycles.

2.3 Performance Optimizations

An SRT processor lends itself to a few significant performance optimizations. The key insight is that the trailing thread can use information from the leading thread's execution to make its own execution more efficient.

One such situation occurs when the leading thread encounters an instruction cache miss. If the trailing thread is sufficiently delayed, then its corresponding fetch may not occur until the block has been loaded into the instruction cache, avoiding a stall. A similar benefit can be obtained on data cache misses; even though the trailing thread reads load values out of the load value queue, a sufficient lag between the threads will guarantee that the load value queue data will be present when the trailing thread's load executes, even if the corresponding leading-thread access was a cache miss. The original SRT work proposed a *slack fetch* mechanism to achieve this benefit. In slack fetch, instruction fetch of the trailing thread is delayed until some number of instructions from the leading thread has retired, forcing a "slack" between the threads to absorb these cache delays. Our earlier work [15] showed that slack fetch could achieve about a 10% boost in performance on average.

A second optimization uses the result of leading-thread branches to eliminate control-flow mispredictions in the trailing thread. To achieve this effect, SRT proposes a *branch outcome queue*, a simple FIFO that forwards branch and other control flow targets from the leading thread's commit stage to the trailing thread's fetch stage.

3. BASE PIPELINE

Our base processor is an eight-way superscalar SMT machine with four hardware thread contexts. Table 1 lists some of the architectural parameters of our base processor used in this paper.

Figure 2 shows the base processor's pipeline. The pipeline is divided into the following segments: IBOX (instruction fetch), PBOX (instruction rename), QBOX (instruction queue), RBOX (register read), EBOX & FBOX (integer and floating point functional units), and MBOX (memory system). There are additional cycles incurred to retire instructions beyond the MBOX. Below we describe our base processor architecture's specific portions and boxes, which we modified to create an SRT architecture.

3.1 IBOX

The IBOX fetches instructions in 8-instruction "chunks" and forwards them to the instruction rename unit or PBOX. In each cycle, the IBOX fetches up to 16 instructions (two chunks) from a single thread.

In our evaluation, we assume a four-stage IBOX. The first stage chooses the thread for which instructions will be fetched in each cycle. We pick the thread with the minimum number of instructions in its rate-matching buffer, giving an approximation of the ICOUNT fetch policy described by Tullsen, et al [28]. The second stage uses the line predictor to predict two chunk addresses per

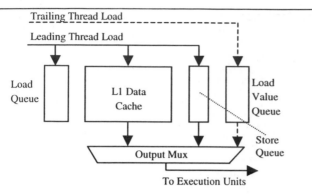

Figure 3. The load value queue integrated in the MBOX.

cycle. As in the Alpha 21264, our base processor's line predictor generates a sequence of predicted instruction-cache line (set and way) indices to drive instruction fetch. The third stage uses these addresses to fetch two potentially non-contiguous chunks of eight instructions each from the instruction cache. In the fourth stage, the processor writes these instructions to the per-thread rate matching buffers. Control-flow predictions from the branch predictor, jump target predictor, and return address stack become available in this stage. If these predictions disagree with the line prediction, the line predictor is retrained and the fetch is re-initiated.

In our base processor, the line predictor is indexed by the predicted line index from the previous cycle. Thus the line predictor must be "primed" with a line prediction from an external source to begin predicting down a different instruction stream, e.g., when the thread chooser decides to switch to a different thread. The thread chooser stores the line predictor's last predictions for each thread and reissues those predictions whenever fetching for a thread is suspended and restarted. The task of selecting either the line predictor's output or the thread chooser's stored prediction to use as the instruction cache index falls on the instruction cache address driver, which is located in the second IBOX stage after the line predictor. There exists a complex interaction between the thread chooser, line predictor, and address driver to facilitate instruction fetch. Section 4.4 discusses how we overcame this complexity to mimic the functionality of SRT's branch outcome queue in this line-prediction-oriented fetch scheme.

3.2 PBOX

The PBOX performs initial processing on instructions fetched by the IBOX, including register renaming and partial decoding. The PBOX also maintains checkpoints of various mapping tables to facilitate fast recovery from branch mispredictions and other exceptional conditions. In our evaluation, we assume that the PBOX occupies two pipeline stages.

3.3 QBOX

The QBOX receives instructions in program order from the PBOX and issues them out of order to the EBOX, FBOX or MBOX when their operands become ready. The QBOX also retires instructions, committing their results to architectural state in program order. The QBOX contains three main structures: the instruction queue, which schedules and issues instructions from the PBOX; the in-flight table, which tracks instructions from issue until they complete execution; and the completion unit, which tracks them up to retirement.

The instruction queue is the most complex part of the QBOX. It holds 128 instructions, and accepts and issues up to eight instruc-

tions per cycle. The queue is divided into upper and lower halves, each with 64 entries. Both halves have the same capabilities (in terms of functional units) and each can issue up to four instructions per cycle. An instruction is assigned to a particular queue half based on its position in the chunk created by the rate-matching buffer.

3.4 MBOX

The MBOX processes memory instructions, such as loads, stores, and memory barriers. The QBOX can issue a maximum of four memory operations per cycle, with a maximum of two stores and three loads.

Loads entering the MBOX record themselves in the load queue, probe the data cache and store queue simultaneously, and return their result to the load queue in a single cycle. On a data cache or store queue hit, the data is forwarded in the next cycle to the execution units for bypassing to dependent instructions.

Similarly, stores entering the MBOX record themselves in the store queue and probe the load queue to check for store-load order violation. Store data arrives at the store queue two cycles after the store address. When a store retires, its address and data are forwarded to a coalescing merge buffer, which eventually updates the data cache.

For multithreaded runs, we divide up the 64-entry load and store queues statically among the different threads. Thus, when this base processor runs two threads, we allocate 32 entries to each thread. For multithreaded runs with four threads, we allocate 16 entries to each thread.

4. SRT ON OUR BASE PROCESSOR

One of the major goals of this work is to understand the feasibility and performance impact of implementing SRT extensions on a realistic, commercial-grade SMT processor. As discussed in Section 2, the key SRT mechanisms are input replication and output comparison; we discuss our implementation of these mechanisms on our base processor in Sections 4.1 and 4.2. Section 4.3 describes additional changes required to avoid deadlock situations. One of the greatest challenges in our effort was to map SRT's branch outcome queue to our base processor's line-predictor driven fetch architecture; the specific problems and our solutions are detailed in Section 4.4. Finally, Section 4.5 describes our implementation of *preferential space redundancy*, an enhancement to the original SRT proposal for improved fault coverage.

4.1 Input Replication

We use a variant of SRT's load value queue (LVQ), described in Section 2.1, to forward cached load values from the leading to the trailing thread. Figure 3 shows the relationship of the LVQ to the rest of the MBOX.

Leading-thread loads entering the MBOX probe the load queue, data cache, and store queue, as in the base design. The QBOX completion unit writes the address and data values generated by these loads to the LVQ as the loads retire. Trailing-thread loads bypass all three structures and directly access the LVQ. The LVQ forwards load values to the MBOX output mux, which now has one additional input. Because the QBOX can issue up to three loads per cycle, the LVQ must support three concurrent accesses.

The original SRT design assumes that the trailing thread issues its loads in program order, preserving the FIFO structure of the LVQ. Although we could easily add this constraint to the QBOX scheduler by creating dependences between loads, this approach would limit the trailing thread to issuing at most one load per cycle. Rather than modifying the scheduler to allow three "dependent"

102

loads to issue to the LVQ in a single cycle, we modified the LVQ to allow out-of-order load issue from the trailing thread. Each leading-thread load is assigned a small load correlation tag value by the PBOX, which is written to the LVQ entry along with the load's address and data. Using the line prediction queue, described in Section 4.4, we can easily associate the same tag with the corresponding load from the trailing thread. When the trailing thread issues, it uses this tag to perform an associative lookup in the LVQ to read out the appropriate address and data values. Then, the LVQ entry is deallocated.

This LVQ probe is similar to the lookup done on each load address in the store queue; in fact, it is slightly simpler, since the LVQ need not worry about multiple address matches, partial forwarding cases, or relative ages of entries. Thus, an associative LVQ equal in size to the store queue should be able to support three simultaneous accesses per cycle without adding to the critical path.

The LVQ provides a small additional performance benefit because it keeps the trailing thread's loads out of the load queue, thereby freeing up entries for the leading thread's loads. Thus, when one application program runs in SRT mode with two redundant threads, the leading thread gets all 64 load-queue entries. Similarly, when two application programs run in SRT mode, each with two redundant threads, each leading thread gets 32 load queue entries.

4.2 Output Comparison

As described in Section 2.2, the original SRT proposal included an enhanced store queue to perform output comparison on cacheable stores. We implemented a separate structure, the *store comparator*, which sits next to the store queue and monitors its inputs. When a trailing-thread store instruction and its data enter the store queue, the store comparator searches itself for a matching entry from the leading thread. If a matching entry exists, the store comparator performs the store comparison and signals the store queue that the specific store is ready to be retired to the data cache.

Forcing every leading-thread store to wait in the store queue until the corresponding trailing-thread store is executed increases store-queue utilization significantly, causing additional pipeline stalls when the store queue becomes full. Section 7 shows that these stalls degrade SRT performance noticeably relative to the base architecture. However, because the data cache is outside our sphere of replication, the cache cannot be updated until this output comparison is performed. Meanwhile, subsequent leading-thread loads must compare against these waiting stores to obtain the latest memory values, just as they compare against speculative stores in the base architecture. Thus we see no practical alternative to leaving these stores in the store queue until they are checked.

Unfortunately, the store queue CAM is a critical path in our base architecture; increasing its size beyond 64 entries would force the CAM to be pipelined across multiple cycles, increasing the load-to-use delay and adversely affecting performance. Instead, we propose addressing this problem by creating separate per-thread store queues of 64 entries each. Although this proposal does not increase the size of any individual store queue CAM, the physical implementation may still be challenging because of the additional wires and multiplexors introduced in the path of the load probe. Nevertheless, our results in Section 7 do show that per-thread store queues can provide a significant boost in performance.

4.3 Avoiding Deadlocks

An SMT machine is vulnerable to deadlock if one thread is allowed to consume all of a particular resource (e.g., instruction queue slots) while stalled waiting for another thread to free a

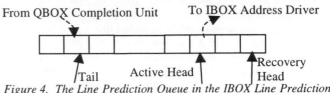

Figure 4. *The Line Prediction Queue in the IBOX Line Prediction Unit.*

different resource or post a synchronization event. Our base design assumes that such inter-thread dependencies do not exist. While this assumption is valid for conventional multithreaded workloads, dependencies between leading and trailing threads in an SRT machine significantly increase the possibility of deadlock. In particular, the leading thread's dependence on seeing a corresponding store from the trailing thread before freeing a store-queue entry can lead to frequent deadlocks.

For example, the leading thread can easily fill the QBOX instruction queue, backing up into the PBOX pipeline itself. In this case, the trailing thread is unable to move instructions from its IBOX rate-matching buffer into the PBOX. If the leading thread is stalled waiting for a matching trailing-thread store, deadlock results. To avoid this situation, we made all PBOX storage structures per thread, and reserved space for one chunk per thread in the QBOX queue. Because the IBOX already contained per-thread rate matching buffers, no changes were needed there.

A second class of deadlocks induced by our line prediction queue is covered in Section 4.4.2.

4.4 Implementing the Branch Outcome Queue

The original SRT design proposed a simple FIFO called the branch outcome queue, which forwards leading-thread branch targets to the trailing thread's fetch stage. Ideally, since this queue represents a perfect stream of target predictions (in the absence of faults), the trailing thread should never fetch a misspeculated instruction. Unfortunately, our base processor uses a line predictor to access the instruction cache; the branch and other control-flow predictors serve only to verify these line predictions. Because the line predictor's misprediction rate is significant (between 14% and 28% for our benchmarks), using the branch outcome queue in place of the branch target prediction structures, as originally proposed, would still allow a noticeable amount of misfetching on the trailing thread.

A simple alternative is to share the line predictor between the two redundant threads, in the hope that the leading thread would train the line predictor, improving prediction accuracy for the trailing thread. Unfortunately, this scheme does not work well due to excessive aliasing in the line prediction table.

Instead, we adapt the concept of the branch outcome queue to fit the base design, and use a *line prediction queue* to forward correct line predictions from the leading to the trailing thread. The line prediction queue provides perfect line predictions to the trailing thread in the absence of faults, thereby completely eliminating misfetches.

The implementation of the line prediction queue was quite challenging, and required careful consideration to maintain perfect line prediction accuracy and avoid deadlocks. We organize the design issues into two parts: those involved with reading predictions from the line prediction queue on the IBOX end and those regarding writing predictions to the line prediction queue on the QBOX end. Although the details of our design are specific to our base architecture, we believe many of the challenges we encountered are inherent to most modern microarchitectures, which are not designed to generate or operate on a precise sequence of fetch addresses. We were certainly surprised that a seemingly straightforward feature, added easily to our earlier SimpleScalar-based simulator, induced such complexities in this more realistic design.

After incorporating the line prediction queue into our design, we found that the "slack fetch" mechanism of the original SRT design, described in Section 2.3, was not necessary. The inherent delay introduced by waiting for leading-thread retirement before initiating the corresponding trailing-thread fetch was more than adequate to provide the benefits of slack fetch. In fact, given the store-queue pressure discussed in Section 7.1, we found that the best performance was achieved by giving the trailing thread priority, and fetching based on the line prediction queue whenever a prediction was available.

4.4.1 Reading from the Line Prediction Queue

One set of line prediction queue challenges came about because the IBOX was not designed to expect a precise stream of line predictions. Specifically, as described in Section 3.1, the line predictor sends predictions to the address driver mux, but does not know whether the prediction is selected by the address driver or not. Even if the address driver selects the line predictor's output, the access may be a cache miss, requiring the prediction to be re-sent after the needed block is filled from the L2 cache.

A conventional line predictor is happy to repeatedly predict the same next line, given the same input (e.g. from the thread chooser's stored prediction latch). However, the line prediction queue stores a precise sequence of chunk addresses; if a prediction is read from the line prediction queue but not used, a gap will appear in the trailing thread's instruction stream.

We addressed this problem in two steps. First, we enhanced the protocol between the address driver and line predictor to include an acknowledgment signal. On a successful acceptance of a line prediction, the address driver acks the line predictor, which advances the head of the line prediction queue. Otherwise, the line prediction queue does not adjust the head, and resends the same line prediction on the subsequent cycle.

Instruction cache misses require additional sophistication; in these cases, the address driver does accept a line prediction from the line prediction queue, but must reissue the same fetch after the miss is handled. To deal with this and similar situations, we provided the line prediction queue with two head pointers (Figure 4). The *active head* is advanced by acks from the address driver, and indicates the next prediction to send. A second *recovery head* is advanced only when the corresponding instructions have been successfully fetched from the cache. Under certain circumstances, including cache misses, the IBOX control logic can request the line prediction queue to roll the active head back to the recovery head, and reissue a sequence of predictions.

4.4.2 Writing to the Line Prediction Queue

The tail end of the line prediction queue, where leading-thread instructions retiring from the QBOX generate predictions for the trailing thread, also presented some challenges. Each line prediction queue entry corresponds to a single fetch chunk, i.e., a contiguous group of up to eight instructions. To achieve reasonable fetch efficiency, the logic at the QBOX end of the line prediction queue must aggregate multiple retired instructions into a single chunk prediction. The key decision made by this logic is when to terminate a trailing-thread fetch chunk and actually record a prediction in the line prediction queue.

Some chunk-termination situations are clear, such as when two retiring instructions have non-contiguous addresses, or when the eight-instruction chunk limit has been reached. However, other necessary criteria were more subtle, and resulted in deadlocks when they were ignored. For example, a memory barrier instruction is not eligible to retire until all preceding stores have flushed from the store queue. If a store precedes a memory barrier in the same leading-thread fetch chunk, the store will not flush until the corresponding trailing-thread store executes. However, this trailing-thread store will not be fetched until the chunk is terminated and its address is forwarded via the line prediction queue. Under normal circumstances (in non-SRT mode), we will not terminate the chunk until the memory barrier retires, as it is a contiguous instruction and can be added to the current chunk. To avoid this deadlock situation, however, we must force termination of the trailing-thread fetch chunk whenever the oldest leading-thread instruction is a memory barrier.

A similar situation arises due to base processor's handling of partial data forwarding. For example, if a word load is preceded by a byte store to the same location, our base processor flushes the store from the store queue so that the load can pick up the full word from the data cache. If the store and load are in the same leading-thread fetch chunk, we must terminate the chunk at the store to allow the trailing-thread's store to be fetched. Then the store will be verified and exit the store queue, enabling the load to execute.

Interestingly, the line prediction queue logic can occasionally create trailing-thread fetch chunks that are larger than those of the leading thread. For example, a predicted taken branch in the middle of a leading-thread fetch chunk will cause the chunk to be terminated. If the branch was mispredicted, and actually fell through, we can add the fall-through instructions to the trailing thread's fetch chunk.

4.5 Improving Fault Coverage

The original SRT proposal focuses on detection of *transient* faults, which only temporarily disrupt processor operation. For example, a cosmic ray may strike a latch and change its stored value; this fault will last only until the latch is next written, at which time it will again have a correct state. However, microprocessors are also vulnerable to *permanent* faults, which can arise due to manufacturing defects or electromigration. A transient fault in a rarely written latch value (e.g., a mode bit written only at boot time) may also behave like a permanent fault. This section describes how we extended our SRT design to provide improved coverage of permanent faults with negligible performance impact.

The original SRT design's vulnerability to permanent faults is due to the combination of space redundancy (where redundant instructions use physically distinct hardware resources) and time redundancy (where redundant instructions use the same hardware resource at different times). Note that the same pair of instructions can be covered by space redundancy in some portions of the pipeline and time redundancy in others. Time redundancy provides effective coverage for transient and some timing-dependent faults, but is not effective for detecting permanent hardware faults.

We introduce a new technique, called *preferential space redundancy*, which simply biases an SRT processor to provide space redundancy rather than only time redundancy whenever the option exists. As a concrete example, we implemented preferential space redundancy for the QBOX instruction queue, providing extremely high coverage of permanent faults in this critical structure. We leverage our base processor's partitioning of the queue into upper and lower halves. When a leading-thread instruction executes, it records which half of the queue it traversed. We add the up-

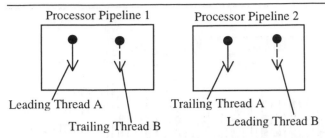

Figure 5. CRT processor configuration. The arrows represent threads in the processors. A and B are logically distinct programs. Each program runs a redundant copy: a leading copy and a trailing copy in the physically distinct processor pipelines. Note that the leading thread of A is coupled with the trailing thread of B and vice versa in the two processors.

per/lower selection bits for all instructions in a fetch chunk to each line prediction queue entry as it is forwarded to the trailing thread's fetch stage. These bits are carried along to the QBOX, which then assigns the corresponding trailing-thread instructions to the *opposite* half of the queue relative to their leading-thread counterparts. We thus guarantee that corresponding instructions are handled by distinct IQ entries. Section 7.1.1 will show that this technique virtually eliminates all time redundancy in the instruction queue and function units without any loss in performance.

Preferential space redundancy applies only to situations in which there are multiple identical structures to provide space redundancy, such as queue entries or function units. Fortunately, the remaining structures that provide only time redundancy are primarily transmission lines, which can be protected from single permanent faults by the addition of parity bits. We therefore believe that an SRT processor can be designed to detect most, if not all, single permanent faults, in addition to the transient faults for which it was originally designed.

5. CHIP-LEVEL REDUNDANT THREADING

In this section, we extend SRT techniques to the emerging class of chip multiprocessors (CMPs) to create a *chip-level redundantly threaded (CRT)* processor, achieving lockstepping's permanent fault coverage while maintaining SRT's low-overhead output comparison and efficiency optimizations. The basic idea of CRT is to generate logically redundant threads, as in SRT, but to run the leading and trailing threads on separate processor cores, as shown in Figure 5.

The trailing threads' load value queues and line prediction queues now receive inputs from leading threads on the other processor. Similarly, the store comparator, which compares store instructions from redundant threads, receives retired stores from the leading thread on one processor and trailing thread on another processor. Clearly, to forward inputs to the load value queue, line prediction queue, and the store comparator, we need moderately wide datapaths between the processors. We believe that the processor cores can be laid out on the die such that such datapaths do not traverse long distances. These datapaths will be outside the sphere of replication and must be protected with some form of information redundancy, such as parity.

CRT processors provide two advantages over lockstepped microprocessors. First, in lockstepped processors, all processor output signals must be compared for mismatch, including miss requests from the data and instruction caches. This comparison is in the critical path of the cache miss, and often adversely affects performance. More generally, the checker must interpose on every logical signal from the two processors, check for mismatch, and

then forward the signal outside the sphere of replication. Of course, a CRT processor incurs latency to forward data to the line prediction queue, load value queue, or store comparator, but these queues serve to decouple the execution of the redundant threads and are not generally in the critical path of data accesses.

Second, CRT processors can run multiple independent threads more efficiently than lockstepped processors. By pairing leading and trailing threads of different programs on the same processor, we maximize overall throughput. A trailing thread never misspeculates, freeing resources for the other application's leading thread. Additionally, in our implementation, trailing threads do not use the data cache or the load queue, freeing up additional resources for leading threads.

Our evaluation, detailed in Section 7.2, shows that our CRT processor performs similarly to lockstepping for single-program runs, but outperforms lockstepping by 13% on average (with a maximum improvement of 22%) for multithreaded program runs.

6. METHODOLOGY

This section describes the performance model, benchmarks, target architecture parameters, and evaluation metric that we used for our evaluation.

6.1 Asim: The Performance Model Framework

Asim [4] is a performance model framework, which was used to build an extremely detailed performance model of a modern, aggressive, dynamically scheduled, eight-wide SMT processor resembling the Alpha Araña processor. This model provides cycle-by-cycle simulation of most of the components in this base processor. We modified this detailed base processor model written in Asim to create the SRT and the CRT processor models.

6.2 Benchmarks

For our evaluation with single programs, we used all the 18 SPEC CPU95 benchmarks (http://www.spec.org). To get to the interesting portions of the benchmarks, we skipped between 250 million and 2 billion instructions. Then, we warmed up the processor structures for one million instructions and executed 15 million committed instructions for each program.

For our evaluation with multiple programs, we combined a subset of the SPEC CPU95 programs. For runs with two programs, we combined two of *gcc*, *go*, *fpppp*, and *swim*. The four benchmarks generate a total of six pairs. Similarly, for our four-program runs, we combined four of *gcc*, *go*, *ijpeg*, *fpppp*, and *swim* to generate a total of 15 combinations. We ran 15 million committed instructions for each program. Thus, our CRT processor running four logical threads executed a total of 120 million instructions (15 million instructions per program × 4 programs × 2 redundant threads per program).

We did not use the SPEC CPU2000 suite partly due to limitations in our simulation environment, and partly to allow us to compare our single-program SRT results with our earlier evaluation [15], which also used SPEC CPU95.

6.3 Target Architecture & Parameters

We simulate four target architectures: the base processor, lockstepping, SRT, and CRT. We listed the basic processor's parameters in Table 1.

For the lockstepped processor, we chose two configurations. The first one—Lock0—has an ideal (but unrealistic) checker that executes in zero cycles. The second one—Lock8—is a more realistic checker that incurs an eight-cycle penalty to do the lockstep checking. We believe 8 cycles is realistic because of dense wiring to the centralized checker, wire delays, latency within

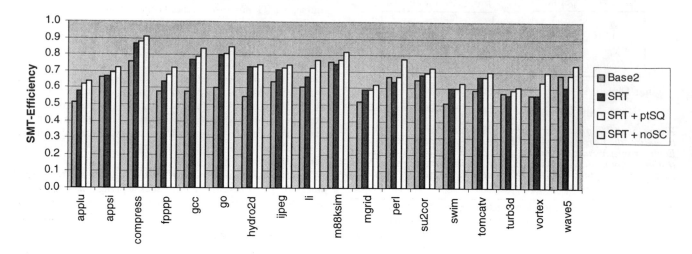

Figure 6. *SMT-Efficiencies for one logical thread for four single-processor configurations. Base2 = base processor running one logical thread with two redundant copies, but no input replication or output comparison. SRT + ptSQ = SRT with per-thread store queue (with each store queue having 64 entries). SRT + noSC = SRT with no Store Comparison. "1.0" on the vertical axis represents the SMT-Efficiency of the base processor for one logical thread (running the same program) with no redundant copies.*

the checker itself to do the comparisons, and the logic required to tolerate minor synchronization errors between processors. Many checkers allow processors to go out of lockstep briefly to tolerate non-deterministic timing, as can occur when one processor requires an extra cycle to address a correctable ECC fault in an internal structure such as the TLB.

For the SRT architecture, we conservatively assumed 4 cycles to forward line predictions from the QBOX to IBOX and 2 cycles to forward load values from the QBOX to the MBOX. For the CRT architecture, we assumed an additional 4-cycle penalty to forward data from one processor to the other processor's line prediction queue, load value queue, and store comparator.

6.4 Evaluation Metric

Instructions per cycle (IPC) is not a useful metric to compare SMT architectures, even though it has proven to be quite useful for single-threaded machines [22][19]. An SMT architecture may improve its overall IPC by favoring a more efficient thread (perhaps one with fewer cache misses and branch mispredictions), simply avoiding the challenging part of the workload.

Instead, we use *SMT-Efficiency* as a metric to evaluate the performance of our SRT, lockstepped, and CRT architectures. We compute SMT-Efficiency of an individual thread as the IPC of the thread in SMT mode (and running with other threads) divided by the IPC of the thread when it would run in single-thread mode through the same SMT machine. Then, we compute the SMT-Efficiency for all threads, as the arithmetic mean of the SMT-Efficiencies of individual threads. This arithmetic mean is the same as Snavely and Tullsen's weighted speedup metric [22].

7. RESULTS

This section evaluates the performance of the SRT, lockstepping, and CRT techniques using one or more independent logical threads. A logical thread runs an independent program, such as gcc. Normally, without any fault detection, a logical thread maps to a single hardware thread. However, in redundant mode, a logical thread is further decomposed into two hardware threads, each running a redundant copy of the program. Section 7.1 examines the performance of our SRT design using one and two logical threads.

This section also shows how preferential space redundancy can improve SRT's fault coverage. Section 7.2 compares the performance of lockstepped and CRT processors using one, two, and four logical threads.

7.1 SRT

This section begins by analyzing the impact of preferential space redundancy, then evaluates the performance of our SRT design for one and two logical threads in detail.

7.1.1 Preferential Space Redundancy

This section examines the preferential space redundancy technique described in Section 4.5. We changed the scheduling policy of the SRT processor to direct corresponding instructions from the redundant threads to different halves of the QBOX, thereby improving fault coverage.

Figure 7 shows that, on average, without preferential space redundancy 65% of instructions go to the same functional unit. The fraction of corresponding instructions entering the same functional unit is higher than 50% because instructions are directed to a specific half of the queue based on their positions in the chunk forwarded to the QBOX. It is likely that instructions in both the leading and trailing threads will have instructions in similar positions of their chunks, which force them to go to the same half of the queue and, eventually, to the same functional unit. However, enabling preferential space redundancy reduces such instructions to 0.06%, thereby dramatically improving the fault coverage of the processor. The number is non-zero because if a different half is not available for the trailing thread, then the scheduler is forced to issue it in the same half. This technique, however, provides no performance degradation (not shown here), and in a few cases, such as hydro2d, improves performance because of better load balancing on the QBOX halves. Our remaining results in this section use preferential space redundancy.

7.1.2 One Logical Thread

Figure 6 shows the performance of the SRT processor for one logical thread. SRT, on average, degrades performance over running just the single thread (without any redundant copies) by 32%. However, SRT techniques improve performance over

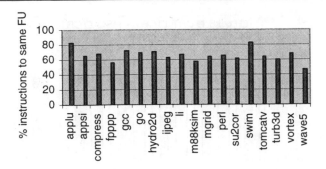

Figure 7. Percentage of corresponding instructions from redundant threads in the SRT processor entering the same functional unit (for one logical thread) in the absence of preferential space redundancy. With preferential space redundancy (not shown), the fraction of corresponding instructions entering the same functional unit is almost zero.

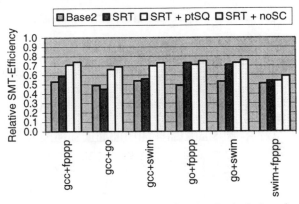

Figure 8. Relative SMT-Efficiencies for two logical threads for four single-processor configurations. The numbers are relative to SMT-Efficiencies for two logical threads running through our base processor without any redundancy. Base 2 = base processor running two logical threads, each with two redundant copies, but no input replication or output comparison. SRT + ptSQ = SRT with per-thread store queue (with each store queue having 64 entries). SRT + noSC = SRT with no store comparator.

running two redundant copies of the same program (without any input replication or output comparison)—base2 in the figure—by 11%. This improvement is due to the positive effects of the load value queue and line prediction queue in the SRT processor. The load value queue reduces data-cache misses in two ways: the trailing thread cannot miss, as it never directly accesses the cache, and the leading thread thrashes less in "hot" cache sets because it does not compete with the trailing thread. We find that the SRT processor, on average, has 68% fewer data cache misses compared to the base processor running redundant copies of two threads.

The store comparator is one of the key bottlenecks in the SRT design. As explained in Section 4.2, the store comparator increases the lifetime of a leading thread's stores, which must now wait for the corresponding stores from the trailing thread to show up before they can retire. On average, for one logical thread, the store comparator increases the lifetime of a leading thread's store by 39 cycles. Eighteen of these cycles represent the minimum latency for the trailing-thread store to fetch and execute; the extra 21 cycles come from queuing delays in the line prediction queue and processor pipeline.

Consequently, increasing the size of the store queue has significant impact on performance because this allows other stores from the leading thread to make progress. Using a per-thread store queue (with 64 entries per thread) improves the SMT-Efficiency by 4%, bringing the degradation to only roughly 30%. Completely eliminating the impact of the store comparator (SRT + noSC in the figure), perhaps with an even bigger store queue, would improve performance by another 5% and reduce the performance degradation to 26%.

Our 30% performance degradation for an SRT processor (with the per-thread store queue) is higher than our prior work [15], which reported only 21% degradation. We believe this discrepancy arises because our base processor's structures are optimized primarily for uniprocessor performance, making its multithreaded performance relatively worse than that reported by our Simplescalar/SMT model.

7.1.3 Two Logical Threads

Interestingly, the per-thread store queue provides significantly greater benefits for two logical threads. Figure 8 shows results for the SRT processor variants for two logical threads. The overall degradation of the base SRT processor is 40% on average, about 8% higher than experienced by one logical thread, due to the

greater resource pressures caused by the additional threads. However, adding a per-thread store queue significantly boosts the performance (by 15%) and reduces the degradation to only 32%, which is comparable to the 30% degradation experienced by one logical thread. The performance boost from the per-thread store queue is higher because the average lifetime of a leading thread's store goes up to 44 cycles with two logical threads (compared to 39 cycles for one logical thread). Eliminating the store comparator entirely would provide only another 5% boost in performance, indicating that other resources are now the primary bottleneck.

The per-thread store queue provides significantly greater improvement in SMT-Efficiencies for gcc+fpppp, gcc+go, and gcc+swim compared to go+fpppp, go+swim, and swim+fpppp. Nevertheless, the overall IPC improvements of the SMT machines are comparable across all six benchmark configurations. The IPC improvements are 23%, 18%, 11%, 26%, 13%, and 9%, respectively for the six configurations. This suggests that the absence of the per-thread store queue penalizes the threads with low IPCs more than it penalizes threads with high IPCs, thereby decreasing the overall SMT-Efficiency.

7.2 CRT

This section compares the performance of our CRT processor with lockstepping for one, two, and four logical threads. We examine two versions of lockstepping—Lock0 and Lock8. Lock0 is an unrealistic implementation with a zero-cycle penalty for the checker. Lock8 is a more realistic implementation with an eight-cycle penalty for the checker.

7.2.1 One Logical Thread

Figure 9 compares the performance of CRT variants with lockstepping for one logical thread. For a single logical thread, a CRT processor performs similarly to Lock8 (about 2% better on average). This result is expected, because the CRT processor's leading thread, which behaves similarly to the threads in the lockstepped processor, dominates its performance. The slight improvement in performance arises because all L2 cache misses incur higher penalty in Lock8 due to the presence of the checker. The absence of the checker (as in Lock0, the base case for the figure) would improve Lock8's performance by about 5%.

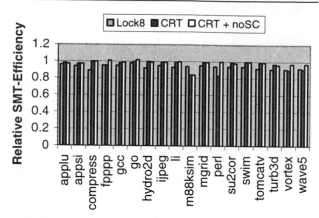

Figure 9. Comparison of Relative SMT-Efficiencies of Lockstepped and CRT processors for one logical thread. The numbers are relative to lockstepped processor with zero-cycle penalty for the checker. Lock8 is the lockstepped processor with an eight-cycle penalty for the checker. CRT is the Chip-Level Redundantly Threaded processor. CRT + noSC is the CRT processor with no store comparator (SC).

7.2.2 Two logical threads

Figure 10 compares CRT variants with lockstepping for two logical threads. On average, CRT outperforms Lock8 by 10% and Lock0 by about 2%. This performance improvement arises due to the cache and misspeculation effects of CRT. First, the presence of multiple threads creates cache contention in the lockstepped processors (where both threads contend in both caches) but not in the CRT processors (where the trailing threads get their data solely via the load value queue, leaving each leading thread with exclusive use of one cache). As a result, the CRT processor incurs 61% fewer data cache misses. In addition, the larger number of misses in the lockstepped configuration increases the performance impact of the checker penalty.

Second, CRT trailing threads do practically no misspeculation, unlike the lockstepped processors on which both threads misspeculate equally. The CRT processor has 24% fewer squashed instructions compared to a lockstepped processor. The percentage is lower than 50% because the CRT leading thread does more misspeculation than a lockstepped processor thread. Relative to a lockstepped thread, the CRT trailing thread uses reduced resources, allowing the CRT leading thread to run faster and, thereby, misspeculate more.

Adding the per-thread store queue to the CRT processor further improves the performance by 6%, making the CRT processor 13% better in performance than Lock8 on average, with a maximum improvement of 22%. The average lifetime of a store in a CRT processor goes up to 69 cycles (compared to 39 cycles for SRT and 49 cycles for CRT with one logical thread), so clearly a bigger store queue helps. Eliminating the store comparator completely, as in the CRT + noSC configuration, would give it another boost of 6%.

7.2.3 Four Logical Threads

Figure 11 compares the performance of CRT variants with lockstepping for four logical threads. Interestingly, unlike for two logical threads, CRT with a shared store queue performs similarly to Lock8. This result occurs because of the smaller number of entries per thread in the store queue. Thus, adding the per-thread store queue makes the CRT processor 13% better than Lock8 in performance on average, with a maximum improvement of 22%, which is similar to the improvements for two logical threads.

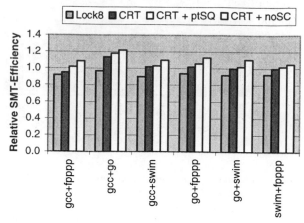

Figure 10. Comparison of Relative SMT-Efficiencies of Lockstepped and CRT processors for two logical threads. The numbers are relative to lockstepped processor with zero-cycle penalty for the checker. Lock8 is the lockstepped processor with 8 cycle penalty for the checker. CRT is the Chip-Level Redundantly Threaded processor. CRT + ptSQ =CRT with per-thread store queue. CRT + noSC is the CRT processor with no store comparator (SC).

Eliminating the store comparator, however, would only improve performance by another 2%.

8. RELATED WORK

Section 8.1 and 8.2 discuss related work in detecting faults in a single processor and dual processor systems, respectively. Section 8.3 discusses how our work relates to recent proposals for fault recovery.

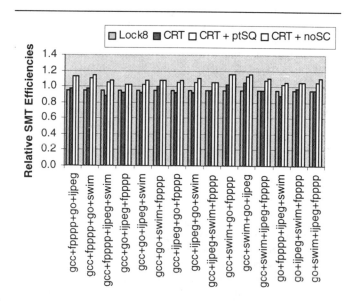

Figure 11. Comparison of Relative SMT-Efficiencies of Lockstepped and CRT processors for four logical threads. The numbers are relative to lockstepped processor with zero-cycle penalty for the checker. Lock8 is the lockstepped processor with 8 cycle penalty for the checker. CRT is the Chip-Level Redundantly Threaded processor. CRT + ptSQ =CRT with per-thread store queue. CRT + noSC is the CRT processor with no store comparator (SC).

8.1 Fault Detection using a Single Processor

Several researchers have proposed the use of RMT techniques in single-processor SMT devices to detect transient faults. Saxena and McCluskey [18] were the first to propose the use of SMT processors for transient fault detection. Subsequently, Rotenberg's AR-SMT [17] and our SRT design [15] expanded this idea and proposed mechanisms to efficiently implement RMT techniques on a single-processor SMT device. We improve upon this body of prior work in four ways. First, we uncovered subtle implementation complexities by attempting to design a single-processor RMT processor based on a pre-existing SMT core resembling a commercial-grade microprocessor. For example, we had to replace the branch outcome queue—used both by AR-SMT and SRT—with a line prediction queue to help replicate the instruction stream in the redundant threads. Similarly, we found subtleties in the implementations of the load value replicator and store instruction comparator.

Second, we found that RMT techniques can incur a higher performance penalty for single-processor devices than previous studies on AR-SMT and SRT processors have demonstrated. Specifically, we find that the size of the store queue for the leading thread has a significant impact on the performance of single-processor RMT devices. This result led us to propose the use of per-thread store queues to enhance performance.

Third, we provide the first characterization of the performance of RMT devices with multithreaded workloads. We found that, with multithreaded workloads, the store queue size has a significantly higher impact on the performance of single-processor RMT devices. Nevertheless, with the use of per-thread store queues, the performance penalty of multithreaded workloads is similar to that of single-threaded workloads.

Finally, we demonstrated that even single-processor RMT devices could be modified effectively (e.g., with the use of preferential space redundancy) to significantly improve coverage of permanent faults, unlike prior work that only focused on transient fault detection for these devices.

Several researchers (e.g., [3,4,6,7,9,11]) have proposed a host of other non-multithreaded techniques for fault detection for uniprocessors.

8.2 Fault Detection using Two Processors

Lockstepped dual processors—both on a single die and different dies—have long been used for fault detection. Commercial fault-tolerant computers used for mission-critical applications have typically employed two processors with cycle-by-cycle lockstepping, such as the IBM S/390 with the G5 processor [21] and the Compaq Himalaya system [30].

Recently, Mahmood and McCluskey [9], Austin [1], and Sundaramoorthy, et al. [26] proposed the use of RMT techniques on dual-processor CMP cores. Mahmood and McCluskey's design uses a main processor core and a watchdog processor that compares its outputs with the outputs of the main processor. Austin's DIVA processor employs two processor cores—an aggressive high-performance processor, resembling a leading thread, and a low-performance checker processor, resembling a trailing thread. Because the processor cores are different, Austin's DIVA processor can potentially detect design faults, in addition to transient and permanent faults. Sundaramoorthy, et al.'s Slipstream processor uses a variant of AR-SMT on CMP processors. Although a Slipstream processor improves fault coverage, it cannot detect all single transient or permanent faults because it does not replicate all instructions from the instruction stream.

We improve upon this body of work on fault detection using dual processor cores in two ways. First, we show that the efficiency techniques of SRT can be extended to dual-processor CMPs. Second, we compared the performance of these CRT processors with on-chip lockstepping, using both single-threaded and multithreaded workloads. We demonstrated that CRT processors provide little advantage for single-threaded workloads, but perform significantly better than lockstepped processors for multithreaded workloads.

8.3 Fault Recovery

Recently, Vijaykumar et al. [29] proposed an architecture called SRTR, which extends SRT techniques to support transparent hardware recovery. SRTR compares instructions for faults before they retire and relies on the processor's intrinsic checkpointed state for recovery. Unlike SRTR, the RMT techniques in this paper assume that instructions are compared for faults after the instructions retire and rely on explicit software checkpoints (e.g., as in Tandem systems [30]) or hardware checkpoints (e.g., [25], [13]) for recovery.

9. CONCLUSIONS

Exponential growth in the number of on-chip transistors, coupled with reductions in voltage levels, has made microprocessors extremely vulnerable to transient faults. In a multithreaded environment, we can detect these faults by running two copies of the same program as separate threads, feeding them identical inputs, and comparing their outputs, a technique we call Redundant Multithreading (RMT).

This paper studied RMT techniques in the context of both single- and dual-processor simultaneous multithreaded (SMT) single-chip devices. Using a detailed, commercial-grade, SMT processor design we uncovered subtle RMT implementation complexities in the implementation of the load value queue, line prediction queue, and store comparator—structures that were necessary for efficient implementation of a single-processor RMT device.

We found that RMT techniques may have a more significant performance impact on single-processor devices than prior studies indicated. RMT degraded performance on single-threaded and multithreaded workloads on a single processor on average by 30% and 32%, respectively, noticeably higher than prior studies indicated. We also found that the store queue size could have a significant impact on performance. Because simply increasing the store queue size is likely to impact the processor cycle time, we proposed the use of per-thread store queues to allow greater number of store queue entries per thread.

We also demonstrated that a single-processor RMT device could not only cover transient faults, but could also significantly improve its permanent fault coverage by using a technique called preferential space redundancy. Preferential space redundancy directs a processor to choose space over time redundancy, given a choice between the two.

Although RMT techniques could be a significant performance burden for single-processor SMT devices, we found that a novel application of RMT techniques in a dual-processor device, which we term chip-level redundant threading (CRT), showed higher performance than lockstepping, especially on multithreaded workloads. We demonstrated that a CRT dual processor outperforms a pair of lockstepped CPUs by 13% on average (with a maximum improvement of 22%) on multithreaded workloads. This makes CRT a viable alternative for fault detection in upcoming dual-processor devices.

Acknowledgments

We thank Bob Jardine and Alan Wood for inspiring many of the ideas in this paper. We thank George Chrysos, Joel Emer, Stephen Felix, Tryggve Fossum, Chris Gianos, Matthew Mattina, Partha Kundu, and Peter Soderquist for helping us understand the intricacies of the Alpha 21464 processor architecture. We also thank Eric Borch, Joel Emer, Artur Klauser, and Bobbie Manne for helping us with the Asim modeling environment. Finally, we thank Joel Emer and Geoff Lowney for providing helpful comments on initial drafts of this paper.

References

[1] Todd M. Austin, "DIVA: A Reliable Substrate for Deep Submicron Microarchitecture Design," *Proc. 32nd Annual Int'l Symp. on Microarchitecture*, pp. 196-207, Nov. 1999.

[2] George Chrysos and Joel Emer, "Memory Dependence Prediction using Store Sets," *Proc. 25th Int'l Symp. on Computer Architecture*, pp. 142-153, Jun. 1998.

[3] Joel S. Emer, "Simultaneous Multithreading: Multiplying Alpha Performance," *Microprocessor Forum*, Oct. 1999.

[4] Joel Emer, Pritpal Ahuja, Nathan Binkert, Eric Borch, Roger Espasa, Toni Juan, Artur Klauser, Chi-Keung Luk, Srilatha Manne, Shubhendu S. Mukherjee, Harish Patil, and Steven Wallace, "Asim: A Performance Model Framework", *IEEE Computer*, 35(2):68-76, Feb. 2002.

[5] Manoj Franklin, "Incorporating Fault Tolerance in Superscalar Processors," *Proc. 3rd Int'l Conf. on High Performance Computing*, pp. 301-306, Dec. 1996.

[6] John G. Holm and Prithviraj Banerjee, "Low Cost Concurrent Error Detection in a VLIW Architecture Using Replicated Instructions," *Proc. Int'l Conf. on Parallel Processing*, Vol. I, pp. 192-195, Aug. 1992.

[7] IBM, "Power4 System Microarchitecture," http://www1.ibm.com/servers/eserver/pseries/hardware/whitepapers/power4.html.

[8] David J.C. Johnson, "HP's Mako Processor," Fort Collins Microprocessor Lab, Oct. 16, 2001. http://cpus.hp.com/technical_references/mpf_2001.pdf.

[9] A. Mahmood and E. J. McCluskey, "Concurrent Error Detection Using Watchdog Processors—A Survey," *IEEE Trans. on Computers*, 37(2):160–174, Feb. 1988.

[10] Shubhendu S. Mukherjee, Peter Bannon, Steven Lang, Aaron Spink, and David Webb, "The 21364 Network Architecture," *IEEE Micro*, 22(1):26-35, Jan/Feb 2002.

[11] Janak H. Patel and Leona Y. Fung, "Concurrent Error Detection in ALU's by Recomputing with Shifted Operands," *IEEE Trans. on Computers*, 31(7):589–595, Jul. 1982.

[12] R. Preston, et al., "Design of an 8-Wide Superscalar RISC Microprocessor with Simultaneous Multithreading," *Digest of Technical Papers, 2002 IEEE International Solid State Circuits Conference*, pp. 334-335, San Francisco, CA.

[13] Milos Prvulovic, Zheng Zhang, and Josep Torrellas, "Cost-Effective Architectural Support for Rollback Recovery in Shared-Memory Multiprocessors," *Proc. 29th Annual Int'l Symp. on Computer Architecture*, May 2002.

[14] Joydeep Ray, James Hoe, and Babak Falsafi, "Dual Use of Superscalar Datapath for Transient-Fault Detection and Recovery," *Proc. 34th Int'l Symp. on Microarchitecture*, pp. 214-224, Dec. 2001.

[15] Steven K. Reinhardt and Shubhendu S. Mukherjee, "Transient Fault Detection via Simultaneous Multithreading," *Proc. 27th Int'l Symp. on Computer Architecture*, Jun. 2000.

[16] Dennis A. Reynolds and Gernot Metze, "Fault Detection Capabilities of Alternating Logic," *IEEE Trans. on Computers*, 27(12):1093–1098, Dec. 1978.

[17] Eric Rotenberg, "AR-SMT: A Microarchitectural Approach to Fault Tolerance in Microprocessor," *Proc. of Fault-Tolerant Computing Systems*, pp. 84-91, Jun. 1999.

[18] N. R. Saxena and E. J. McCluskey, "Dependable Adaptive Computing Systems," *Proc. IEEE Systems, Man, and Cybernetics Conf.*, pp. 2172-2177, Oct. 11-14, 1998.

[19] Yiannakis Sazeides and Toni Juan, "How to Compare the Performance of Two SMT Architectures," *Proc. 2001 Int'l Symp. on Performance Analysis of Systems and Software*, Nov. 2001.

[20] Daniel P. Siewiorek and Robert S. Swarz, *Reliable Computer Systems: Design and Evaluation*, A.K. Peters Ltd, Oct. 1998.

[21] T. J. Slegel, et al., "IBM's S/390 G5 Microprocessor Design," *IEEE Micro*, 19(2):12–23, Mar/Apr 1999.

[22] Allan Snavely and Dean Tullsen, "Symbiotic Job scheduling for a Simultaneous Multithreading Processor," *Proc. Ninth Int'l Conf. on Architectural Support for Programming Languages and Operating Systems*, pp. 234–244, Nov. 2000.

[23] G. S. Sohi, M. Franklin, and K. K. Saluja, "A Study of Time-Redundant Fault Tolerance Techniques for High-Performance Pipelined Computers," *Digest of Papers, 19th Int'l Symp. on Fault-Tolerant Computing*, pp. 436–443, 1989.

[24] G. S. Sohi, "Instruction Issue Logic for High-Performance, Interruptible, Multiple Functional Unit, Pipelined Computers," *IEEE Trans. on Computers*, 39(3):349–359, March 1990.

[25] Daniel J. Sorin, Milo M. K. Martin, Mark D. Hill, and David A. Wood, "SafetyNet: Improving the Availability of Shared Memory Multiprocessors with Global Checkpoint/Recovery," *Proc. 29th Annual Int'l Symp. on Computer Architecture*, May 2002.

[26] Karthik Sundaramoorthy, Zach Purser, and Eric Rotenberg, "Slipstream Processors: Improving both Performance and Fault Tolerance," *Proc. Ninth Int'l Conf. on Architectural Support for Programming Languages and Operating Systems*, pp. 257–268, Nov. 20001.

[27] Dean M. Tullsen, Susan J. Eggers, and Henry M. Levy, "Simultaneous Multithreading: Maximizing On-Chip Parallelism," *Proc. 22nd Annual Int'l Symp. on Computer Architecture*, pp. 392-403, Jun. 1995.

[28] Dean M. Tullsen, Susan J. Eggers, Joel S. Emer, Henry M. Levy, Jack L. Lo, and Rebecca L. Stamm, "Exploiting Choice: Instruction Fetch and Issue on an Implementable Simultaneous Multithreading Processor," *Proc. 23rd Annual Int'l Symp. on Computer Architecture*, pp. 191-202, May 1996.

[29] T. N. Vijaykumar, Irith Pomeranz, and Karl Cheng, "Transient Fault Recovery using Simultaneous Multithreading," *Proc. 29th Annual Int'l Symp. on Computer Architecture*, May 2002.

[30] Alan Wood, "Data Integrity Concepts, Features, and Technology," White paper, Tandem Division, Compaq Computer Corporation.

[31] Wayne Yamamoto and Mario Nemirovsky, "Increasing Superscalar Performance Through Multistreaming," *Proc. 1995 Annual Int'l Conf. on Parallel Architectures and Compilation Techniques*, pp. 49–58, June 1995.

ReVive: Cost-Effective Architectural Support for Rollback Recovery in Shared-Memory Multiprocessors *

Milos Prvulovic, Zheng Zhang[‡†], Josep Torrellas
University of Illinois at Urbana-Champaign
[‡]Hewlett-Packard Laboratories
http://iacoma.cs.uiuc.edu

Abstract

This paper presents ReVive, a novel general-purpose rollback recovery mechanism for shared-memory multiprocessors. ReVive carefully balances the conflicting requirements of availability, performance, and hardware cost. ReVive performs checkpointing, logging, and distributed parity protection, all memory-based. It enables recovery from a wide class of errors, including the permanent loss of an entire node. To maintain high performance, ReVive includes specialized hardware that performs frequent operations in the background, such as log and parity updates. To keep the cost low, more complex checkpointing and recovery functions are performed in software, while the hardware modifications are limited to the directory controllers of the machine. Our simulation results on a 16-processor system indicate that the average error-free execution time overhead of using ReVive is only 6.3%, while the achieved availability is better than 99.999% even when the errors occur as often as once per day.

1 Introduction

Cache-coherent shared-memory multiprocessors are seeing widespread use in commercial, technical, and scientific applications. In recent years, fault-tolerance has become an increasingly important feature of such systems. In some commercial applications, high *availability* is needed, as business transactions are being processed by the system. Some applications execute for a long time and require a highly *reliable* execution environment. Examples of such applications are those that mine large data sets and many simulations. Unfortunately, both availability and reliability are difficult to achieve in modern large systems. Improvements in silicon technology result in smaller feature sizes, while power dissipation constraints result in lower operating voltages. Both of these make modern integrated circuits prone to transient and permanent faults. In large systems the problem is worse, as those systems contain many interacting components that must all operate correctly.

To deal with these problems, much work has been done in error recovery. Typically, error recovery mechanisms are categorized into Forward and Backward Error Recovery (FER and BER). With FER, hardware redundancy is added to the system, which makes it possible to determine the correct outcome of an operation, even

if one (or more) of the participating devices fails. It is possible to design cost-effective FER that targets only a single device, such as the processor core [3, 28, 30]. However, general-purpose FER is not cheap. The most popular such method is triple-modular redundancy (TMR), in which each operation is performed by three identical devices and a majority vote decides the correct result. For most systems, the cost of TMR is prohibitively high. BER, also called *rollback recovery* or *checkpointing*, can be used in such systems. With rollback recovery, the system stores information about its past state. When an error is detected, this information allows the system to be restored into a previous error-free state. The main advantage of BER is that no hardware replication is required. However, it has three disadvantages: the performance overhead during error-free execution, storage overhead, and the higher recovery latency.

In this paper, we present ReVive, a novel, cost-effective scheme for rollback recovery in shared-memory multiprocessors with distributed memory. ReVive is compatible with off-the-shelf processors, caches, and memory modules. It only requires modifications to the directory controllers of the machine, to perform memory-based distributed parity protection and logging in the background. Both hardware and storage requirements are very modest.

ReVive has both good error-free performance and quick recovery from a wide class of errors, including permanent loss of an entire node. Our experiments with 12 applications on a simulated 16-processor system show that the average overhead of error-free execution is only 6.3%. When an error occurs, the system is unavailable for less than half a second on average, including the correct work lost due to the rollback. The resulting availability is better than 99.999%, even when errors occur as often as once per day.

This paper is organized as follows: Section 2 presents a novel taxonomy of BER schemes for multiprocessors; Section 3 presents the design of ReVive; Section 4 explains some implementation issues in ReVive; Section 5 presents our evaluation setup; Section 6 contains the evaluation; Section 7 describes related work; finally, Section 8 concludes.

2 BER in Multiprocessors: A Taxonomy

To understand the design space of BER schemes, we have designed a taxonomy that classifies the schemes according to three axes: how checkpoint *consistency* is achieved, how the *separation* between the checkpoint and the working data is done, and how checkpoint *storage* is protected from errors. Figure 1 shows the resulting design space. We now consider each axis in turn.

---
*This work was supported in part by the National Science Foundation under grants CCR-9970488, EIA-0081307, EIA-0072102, and CHE-0121357; by DARPA under grant F30602-01-C-0078; and by gifts from IBM, Intel, and Hewlett-Packard.

[†]Currently at Microsoft Research Asia: zzhang@microsoft.com.

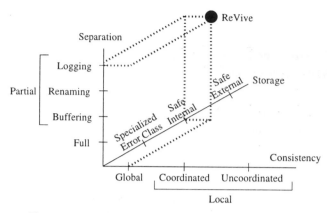

Figure 1. Design space of multiprocessor BER schemes.

2.1 Checkpoint Consistency

Since threads executing on different processors interact with each other, they may create *recovery dependences*: when one processor is rolled back, it may be necessary to also roll back other processors. To maintain checkpoint consistency, three approaches are used:

Global. All processors periodically synchronize to create a single, global checkpoint [8, 13, 14, 15, 20, 21]. This is the simplest approach.

Coordinated Local. Each processor periodically creates a local checkpoint of its own state. If the processor has been interacting with some other processors, then those other processors are forced to create their own checkpoints at the same time [1, 4, 5, 25, 32]. The advantage is that independent computations do not synchronize for checkpointing, while a disadvantage is that interactions must be recorded.

Uncoordinated Local. Each processor periodically creates local checkpoints. Interactions between processors are recorded but do not affect checkpoint creation. At recovery time, however, local checkpoints and interactions are used to find a consistent recovery line. This approach allows synchronization-free checkpointing, but runs the risk of the *domino effect* [22]. Uncoordinated checkpointing is mostly used in loosely-coupled systems, where communication is infrequent and synchronization expensive [6, 7, 26]. However, it has also been used in tightly-coupled systems [27].

2.2 Checkpoint Separation

We group schemes into four classes based on how checkpoint data is separated from working data.

Full Separation. Checkpoint data is completely separate from working data [4, 6, 26]. A naive way to establish a checkpoint is to copy the entire state of the machine to another area. A better way is to realize that much of the machine state does not change between checkpoints. Thus, establishing a new checkpoint consists of merely updating the old one, by copying into it the state that has changed since the old checkpoint was established. There are other optimizations to reduce copying, such as *memory exclusion* [18].

Partial Separation with Buffering. With partial separation, checkpoint data and working data are one and the same, except for those elements that have been modified since the last checkpoint. Consequently, less storage is needed [21]. With buffering, the modified elements are accumulated in a buffer, typically a cache or a write buffer [1, 5, 32]. When a new checkpoint is created, the main state of the machine is typically updated by flushing the buffer into main memory. While checkpoint generation may be regularly scheduled, it may also be asynchronously triggered by buffer overflow.

Partial Separation with Renaming. When a checkpoint is established, all state is marked as read-only. An update to a page causes the page to be copied to a new location, which is marked as writable and mapped into the working state in place of the original page. The original page is no longer part of the working state but remains in the checkpoint state. When a new checkpoint is established, all such pages are garbage-collected [8, 15, 20]. In COMA machines, this approach can be used at the granularity of memory lines [14, 15].

Partial Separation with Logging. Logging does the opposite of renaming: the old, checkpoint value, is copied to a *log*, while the original location is modified and remains part of the working state [13, 25, 27, 32]. As a result, logging does not require support to map and unmap pages or memory lines into and out of the working state. This makes logging more suitable to fine grain copying, which minimizes fragmentation. Typically, the log is a contiguous structure which contains data that is needed only for rollback recovery to a previous checkpoint. Once a new checkpoint is established, the log space can be easily reclaimed without requiring garbage collection mechanisms.

Different separation mechanisms may be used for different parts of a machine's state. For example, both buffering and logging are used in [32].

2.3 Checkpoint Storage Protection

Finally, we group schemes into three classes based on how the checkpoint storage is protected from errors:

Safe External Storage. The checkpoint is stored in external storage that is assumed to be safe [6, 26]. Typically, such storage is a disk array. Since RAID can be used to protect disks against most common errors [17], the assumption of safety is reasonable.

Safe Internal Storage. The checkpoint is stored in main memory or other internal storage and made safe through redundancy across the nodes. Checkpoint state can be restored even if storage on a limited number of nodes (typically one) is damaged. In some systems, safe internal storage is provided by duplication of checkpoint data in main memory [5, 8, 14, 15]. Alternatively, it can be provided using $N + 1$ parity. In this case, lost checkpoint data in a node can be recovered by examining the memories of the other N nodes [20, 21]. Checkpointing to main memory is much faster than checkpointing to external storage [21].

Specialized Fault Class. The checkpoint storage is not protected with redundancy across nodes. However, the system is not expected to recover from faults that can damage that storage [1, 4, 13, 25, 27, 32]. For example, a design for recovery from processor errors can keep the checkpoint in caches or memory without redundancy, while a system designed for recovery from cache errors can keep the checkpoint in main memory.

Overall, designs using safe external storage can recover from even the most general fault, namely loss of the entire machine. The designs using safe internal storage cannot recover if more than a certain number (typically, one) of internal storage components are faulty. Finally, the designs with a specialized fault class cannot recover from even a single error that makes any checkpoint storage component unavailable.

3   ReVive Design

This section presents our cost-effective design for rollback recovery. We first discuss the choice of design point (Section 3.1), then describe the mechanisms supported (Section 3.2), and finally explain our choice of parameters for the design (Section 3.3).

3.1   Choice of Design Point

Our goal is a cost-effective general-purpose rollback recovery mechanism for high-availability and high-performance shared-memory multiprocessors. Cost-effectiveness implies that only a modest amount of extra hardware can be added. General-purpose implies recovery from a wide class of errors, including permanent loss of an entire node. High availability requires that system downtime due to an error be short. Finally, high performance mandates low overhead during error-free operation.

ReVive is compatible with off-the-shelf processors, caches, and memory modules used in modern multiprocessors. For example, the SGI Origin 2000 [11] uses off-the-shelf processor chips, which include caches and cache controllers, and can use off-the-shelf DRAM modules. The major custom-designed components are the directory controller, the network interface and the memory controller. We keep our hardware modifications limited to the directory controller (Figure 2).

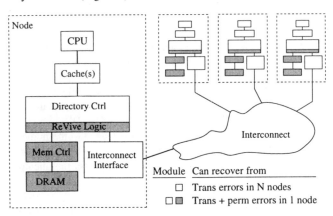

Figure 2. Scalable shared-memory multiprocessor with ReVive.

Our design choice is influenced by the availability requirements. The error frequency we expect is from once a day to once a month [19]. To achieve reliability of 99.999%, our target system's unavailable time due to an error should be no more than 864 milliseconds for the high error frequency range and no more than 24 seconds for the low error frequency range.

In the rest of this section, we discuss which design point in our taxonomy of Section 2 is most conducive to our goal, give an overview of our solution, and then explain the types of errors from which our scheme can recover.

Checkpoint Consistency: Global. Global schemes are the simplest because they do not need to record interactions between processors. Furthermore, they are suited to shared-memory machines, where processor communication and synchronization are efficiently supported. For example, in the Origin 2000, 16 processors can synchronize at a barrier in 10 μs [10].

Checkpoint Separation: Partial Separation with Logging. Partial Separation schemes have low storage overhead and, because they restore only a fraction of the working state, recover quickly. Among these schemes, Logging is the most flexible. With Logging, we can choose the checkpoint frequency; with Buffering, buffer overflows trigger checkpoint generation. With Logging, we perform fine-grain copying, which has low overhead and minimizes memory fragmentation; with Renaming, the copying can only be easily done in software at the page granularity. Finally, the simplicity of logging allows an efficient hardware-assisted implementation through simple extensions to the directory controller.

Checkpoint Storage: Safe Internal Storage with Distributed Parity. Given the low speed of disks, using external storage for checkpoints typically induces a high recovery time. Furthermore, it dictates a low checkpoint frequency to maintain tolerable overhead under error-free conditions [21]. For this reason, we store the checkpoint data in memory. However, since we target a broad range of errors, we must assume that the contents of main memory can be damaged and even a node can be lost. Consequently, we protect memory with parity distributed across memory modules. This scheme uses much less memory than mirroring. Additionally, instead of having dedicated parity node(s) as in [20], we distribute the parity pages evenly across the system. This approach allows all nodes to be used for computation and avoids possible bottlenecks in the parity node(s). Finally, instead of updating the parity in software at checkpoint creation time, we extend the directory controller hardware to automatically update the distributed parity whenever a memory write occurs. This approach reduces the overhead of creating a checkpoint.

3.1.1   Overview of Solution

During error-free execution, all processors are periodically interrupted to establish a global checkpoint. Establishing a checkpoint involves flushing the caches to memory and performing a two-phase commit operation [23]. After that, main memory contains the checkpoint state. Between checkpoints, the memory content is being modified by program execution. When a line of checkpoint data in main memory is about to be overwritten, the home directory controller logs its content to save its checkpoint state. After the next checkpoint is established, the logs can be freed and their space reused. In practice, sufficient logs are kept to enable recovery across as many checkpoints as the worst-case error detection latency requires.

When an error is detected, the logs are used to restore the memory state at the time of the last checkpoint that precedes the error. The caches are invalidated to eliminate any data modified since the checkpoint and the execution can proceed.

To enable recovery from errors that result in lost memory content, pages from different nodes are organized into parity groups. Each main memory write is intercepted by the home directory controller, which triggers an update of the corresponding parity located in a page on another node. The parity information will be used when the system detects an error that caused the loss of memory content in one node (e.g., if a memory module fails or the node is disconnected). Then, the parity and data from the remaining nodes are used to reconstruct the lost memory content, which includes both the logs and the program state. Logs are recovered first. Then the regular rollback described above can proceed. After that, normal execution can continue, while the remaining lost memory is reconstructed in the background.

3.1.2 Types of Errors Supported

Error Detection Assumptions. In our system, we assume error detection support that provides fail-stop behavior [23] for the ReVive hardware in the directory controller (Figure 2). This can be done with careful design and judicious use of replication in that module. In addition, parity update messages and their acknowledgments have to be protected by error detection codes. Finally, the data paths in the memory controllers and memory modules also have to use error detection codes. All of this is needed to detect garbled parity or log updates before they damage the checkpoint state. We do not make any additional fail-stop assumptions. Of course, error detection latency must have an upper bound of no more than a few checkpoint intervals, to keep the space requirements in the logs reasonably modest. Further discussion of error detection mechanisms is beyond the scope of this paper.

Recovery from Multi-Node Errors. ReVive can recover from multiple transient errors that occur in the white areas of Figure 2 in multiple nodes simultaneously. For example, consider a glitch that causes a reset of all the processors in the system and the loss of all cached data. This leaves the checkpoint and the logs in memory intact, and so ReVive can recover. Another example when ReVive recovery is possible is an interconnect glitch that damages several in-transit messages in different parts of the network or network interfaces. However, ReVive cannot recover from multiple errors that occur in the gray areas of Figure 2 in multiple nodes simultaneously. For example, two malfunctioning memory modules on different nodes may damage a parity group beyond ReVive's ability to repair.

Recovery from One-Node Errors. ReVive can recover from multiple permanent or transient errors that occur in a single node. This includes complete loss of an entire node. For example, this occurs when a node's network interface permanently fails. In this case, ReVive performs recovery of the lost memory and a rollback. Another example of a one-node error is a single faulty processor that erroneously modifies memories in several nodes. After this error is detected, a rollback to a past checkpoint restores the system.

3.2 Mechanisms in ReVive

The new mechanisms are hardware-based distributed parity protection in memory and hardware-based logging. This section describes these mechanisms plus how to perform a global checkpoint and a rollback.

3.2.1 Distributed Parity Protection in Memory

In Section 3.1, we explained our decision to protect the checkpoint data in main memory by using distributed parity. Technically, parity protection is needed only for checkpoint data, as recovery would overwrite non-checkpoint data with checkpoint contents. However, in error-free execution non-checkpoint data later *becomes* the new checkpoint data. We speed up the creation of a

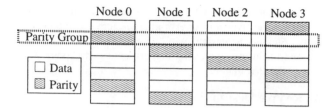

Figure 3. Distributed parity organization (3+1 parity).

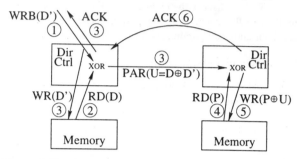

Figure 4. Distributed parity update on a write-back. Messages are numbered in the chronological order.

new checkpoint by protecting the *entire* main memory with distributed parity that is updated whenever the memory is updated. In this way, the distributed parity is already up-to-date when a new checkpoint is to be created.

Figure 3 shows how memory pages are organized into parity groups (3 + 1 parity is shown). Figure 4 shows the actions performed when a memory line is written-back to main memory. The home directory controller intercepts the write-back request D'. It first reads the current contents D of the line from memory. Then the new contents D' are written. At this time, the write-back can be acknowledged to the requester, if such an acknowledgment is required, but the directory entry for the line stays busy. The *parity update* $U = D \; XOR \; D'$ is computed and sent to the home of the parity. When it arrives there, the directory controller of the parity's home node reads the previous parity P, computes the updated parity $P' = P \; XOR \; U = P \; XOR \; (D \; XOR \; D')$, and stores it back. Then, the parity update is acknowledged to the home of the data. At such time, the directory entry for the memory line is marked as no longer busy and other transactions for that memory line can be processed.

Note that the same hardware can be used to support *distributed memory mirroring* (maintaining an exact copy of each page on another node). Mirroring is just a degenerate case of our parity protection mechanism, when one parity page is used to protect only one data page. In that case, the two memory reads and and the XOR operations in Figure 4 can be omitted.

Finally, we note that updating parity (or even mirroring) whenever data is written to memory would be prohibitively expensive if performed in software. However, with our hardware implementation, these updates are performed in the background while the processors continue program execution uninterrupted.

3.2.2 Logging

After a checkpoint is established, the checkpoint state consists of all the data in main memory. Subsequent program execution modifies this data. To prevent the loss of part of the checkpoint

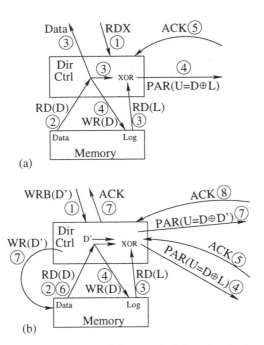

(a)

(b)

Figure 5. Logging and parity updates for (a) read-exclusive and (b) write-back access to a line that has not already been logged since the last checkpoint. Only the home node of both the data and the log is shown.

state, we use logging. Before a line in memory is written for the first time after a checkpoint, the previous content of the line is logged. In this way, all checkpoint data that has been overwritten can still be found in the log. Like the parity updates in Section 3.2.1, the logging is performed by our enhanced directory controller.

Main memory is modified by write-backs of dirty lines. When a write-back arrives at the home node of the data, we check whether this is the first modification of the line since the last checkpoint. If it is, the previous content of the line is read from memory and saved in the log before the new content of the line is written to memory. Note that the log and the data are in the main memory of the same node, and that both are protected by distributed parity. The log *and its parity* must be fully updated before the data line can be written.

Fortunately, most often we know that the block will be modified before the write-back is received by the home. Requests like *read-exclusive* or *upgrade*, which result from write misses in the cache or write hits on shared lines, signal an intent to modify the block. Figure 5(a) shows the operations performed by the hardware when a read-exclusive (RDX) message is received by the memory for a line that has not yet been logged since the last checkpoint. From Figure 5(a) we see that the data can be supplied to the requester as soon as it is read from memory. Alternatively, if an upgrade permission is all that is needed, it can be granted immediately. The logging is performed in the background by the directory controller. The directory entry for the block stays busy until the acknowledgment is received for the parity update. This ensures that no new operation is started for this block until its log entry has been fully created. When the write-back arrives, the line has already been logged and the write-back proceeds as shown in Figure 4.

In some cases, the directory controller may not receive a read-exclusive or upgrade message before it receives the write-back for a line. For example, this occurs in uncached writes and when the processor writes to lines in shared-exclusive state. In this case, the operations on the log and the data are performed as part of the same transaction. This case is shown in Figure 5(b). Note that the second read to the line D in memory could be eliminated if the contents read by the first read are cached by the directory controller. In our evaluation we do not assume such support, as it would require a small data cache in the directory controller.

A modified line only needs to be logged *once* between a pair of checkpoints. To this end, the directory controller is extended with one additional state bit for each memory line, which we call the *Logged (L)* bit. This bit is used to detect whether a particular line has already been logged. The L bits of all lines are gang-cleared after each new checkpoint is established. The L bit of a line is set when the line is logged, to prevent future logging of that line.

Table 1 summarizes the events that trigger parity updates and logging, the actions performed, whether the actions are on the critical path of the processor's execution, the number of additional memory accesses performed, the number of additional memory lines accessed and the number of additional inter-node messages required. As we can see, none of the actions directly affect the processor's execution, although the most complicated and, fortunately, least frequent case does result in delaying the acknowledgment of a writeback. We also see that, although the new operations require 3 to 8 additional memory accesses, they access only 1 to 3 additional memory lines. The remaining additional accesses are re-accessing already accessed memory locations. Furthermore, the log is accessed in a sequential manner, and so is its parity. Repeated accesses to the same memory line and accesses to consecutive lines can be performed very efficiently in modern DRAMs.

3.2.3 Establishing a Global Checkpoint

Parity updates and logging allow the machine to recover to a previous checkpoint state. Establishing a new checkpoint essentially commits the work done since the previous checkpoint. Because the main memory contains the checkpoint state, to create a new checkpoint we must first ensure that the entire current state of the machine is in the main memory. This is done by storing the execution context of each processor to memory and writing-back all dirty cached data to memory. Each processor waits until all its outstanding operations are complete. Then, we atomically commit the global checkpoint on all processors, which we do using a two-phase commit protocol [23]: all processors synchronize, mark the state as tentatively committed, synchronize again and fully commit. After the new checkpoint is established, we can free the space used by logs needed to recover to an old checkpoint that is no longer needed. If the maximum detection latency is small, we keep only two most recent checkpoints. This is needed because an error can occur just before establishing the newest checkpoint, but be detected after it is already established. In that case we recover to the second most recent checkpoint. For larger error detection latencies we can keep sufficient logs to recover to as many past checkpoints as needed. Support for that can be easily provided without additional hardware modifications.

Figure 6 shows the time-line of establishing a global checkpoint. The timing parameters are discussed in Section 3.3.

Event	Actions	Critical Path?	# of Extra Memory Accesses	# of Extra Lines Accessed	# of Extra Network Messages
Write-back to memory, already logged (L=1). Figure 4.	Update data parity	No, done after ack to CPU	3	1	2
Read-exclusive or upgrade, not yet logged (L=0). Figure 5(a).	Copy data to log	No, done after reply to CPU	1	1	0
	Update log parity	No, done after reply to CPU	3	1	2
Write-back to memory, not yet logged (L=0). Figure 5(b).	Copy data to log	No, but ack to CPU delayed	2	1	0
	Update log parity	No, but ack to CPU delayed	3	1	2
	Update data parity	No, done after ack to CPU	3	1	2

Table 1. Events that trigger parity updates and logging.

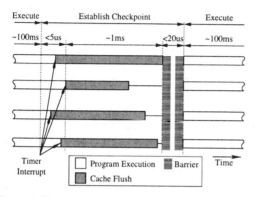

Figure 6. Time-line of establishing a global checkpoint.

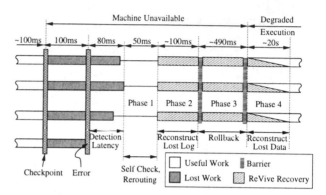

Figure 7. Time-line of recovering from node loss.

3.2.4 Rollback

Finally, we examine the operations performed when an error is detected and our rollback mechanism is activated. Figure 7 shows a time-line of recovery in the worst scenario, in which a node is permanently lost just before a new checkpoint is created[1]. When the error is detected, the Phase 1 of recovery involves testing the hardware and re-initializing it. This includes resetting the processors, invalidating the caches and directory entries and, in case of permanent errors, routing around the failed component. These steps are outside the scope of this paper. Phase 2 involves using the distributed parity to rebuild the contents of the lost node's log. This is needed only if the main memory contents of a node have been damaged or lost. Phase 3 involves using the logs to restore the main memory into a checkpoint state (rollback). Pages to which checkpoint data is restored are rebuilt on demand, using the distributed parity. At the end of Phase 3, parity groups affected by losing a node are marked as inaccessible and the program execution can continue. Figure 7 also shows barriers at the end of phases 2 and 3.

Recovery is not complete when the program execution continues. Because memory content has been lost, unavailable parity groups must be repaired. This is done by background processes, as Phase 4 of the recovery. The processes rebuild the missing pages of inaccessible parity groups. In addition, if program execution attempts to access an inaccessible page, the resulting page fault is handled by immediately rebuilding the group's missing page.

If an entire node has been lost, a large amount of memory can be inaccessible. Specifically, with $N + 1$ parity and M megabytes

per node, $M \times N$ megabytes of data and M megabytes of parity are inaccessible[2] due to either being lost or belonging to a parity group where another page has been lost. This means that the performance of the machine after the recovery can be degraded for two reasons: the machine has one less processor and the remaining processors are devoting some of their time to rebuilding the damaged parity groups. However, the machine is available during this time, performing useful computation and responding to external events, although with reduced computational capabilities.

The times shown in Figure 7 are worst-case unavailable times for the application that required the longest recovery time in our evaluation (Section 6.3). The unavailable time due to a node loss in the average case (error half-way into a checkpoint interval) and on average across the applications we study is only about 350 ms. We also note that there are many transient and even permanent errors that do not result in the loss of a node's memory. For example, errors in the processor core or caches of a node may leave the memory of that node fully operational and accessible. In such cases, no reconstruction of any lost pages is needed. Consequently, Phases 2 and 4 in Figure 7 are completely eliminated and Phase 3 is significantly faster. In such cases, the unavailable time in the average case and on average across the applications is only about 250 ms, using the same parameters as in Figure 7.

3.3 Overheads

3.3.1 Error-Free Execution

Logging and Parity Maintenance. These operations overlap with useful computation on the processors. They cause performance overhead only through increased contention for memory and the

---

[1] In reality, this particular error will be detected when the missing node fails to arrive to the barrier when establishing the checkpoint. To conservatively determine the worst-case timing, we ignore this and allow the remaining processors to establish a faulty checkpoint and continue.

[2] Minus those pages already rebuilt because they contained the logs or the data accessed during the rollback phase.

116

network. In general, the overhead of logging is proportional to the number of lines written between two checkpoints, while the overhead of parity maintenance is proportional to the number of dirty lines displaced from the caches. Consequently, the parity maintenance overhead depends on whether or not the working set of the application fits in the L2 cache: if it does not fit, the resulting frequent write-backs can cause a high overhead of parity maintenance. Finally, note that logging and parity maintenance are performed by the directory controllers and do not significantly affect scalability of the system: adding more nodes to the system results in more logging and parity maintenance, but also adds more directory controllers to perform these operations.

Establishing Global Checkpoints. When it is time to create a new checkpoint, a cross-processor interrupt is delivered to all the processors. This interrupt can be delivered in under 5 μs [24]. Saving the processor's execution context takes little time. Most of the overhead in establishing a new checkpoint comes from writing the dirty cached data back to memory[3]. The time this takes depends on the cache size. Our simulation experiments show this to be on the order of 100 μs for small (128 Kbyte) caches, and 1 ms for larger (2 Mbyte) caches. In Figure 6 we assume 2 Mbyte caches. In the two-phase commit, most of the overhead comes from two global barrier synchronizations, which take up to 10 μs each [10]. Reclaiming the log space only involves moving the log head pointer and a few bookkeeping operations locally performed by each processor, which have negligible overheads. To keep checkpointing overheads small (about 1% of the execution time), the checkpoints in Figure 6 are created once every 100 ms.

Table 2 summarizes the overheads in the error-free execution.

Characteristics of the application's working set	High Checkpoint Frequency	Low Checkpoint Frequency
Does not fit in L2	High Overhead	High Overhead
Fits in L2, mostly dirty	High Overhead	Low Overhead
Fits in L2, mostly clean	Medium Overhead	Low Overhead

Table 2. Effect of application behavior and checkpoint frequency on error-free performance.

3.3.2 Recovery

Recovery. The first phase of recovery is to check the system components to determine what happened and, in case of permanent faults, route around the faulty component. While the implementation of this phase is outside the scope of this paper, its duration has to be taken into account. It has been reported in [29] that the hardware recovery time for Hive/FLASH are about 50 ms for a 16-processor system. This time includes diagnosis, reconfiguration and a reset of the coherence protocol. We assume that a similar hardware recovery can be performed in our system in 50 ms. Phase 2, rebuilding the log pages of the failed node, takes the time proportional to the size of the log, but can be done in parallel by the remaining processors. Our experimental results indicate that in the scenario of Figure 7 this phase takes up to 100 ms, assuming checkpoint frequency of once every 100 ms. In Phase 3 each processor uses the local log to roll back the memory content of its own

---

[3]Note that these operations trigger the parity updates and possibly even logging.

node. If the log entry is to be restored into a page that is unavailable, that page's parity group is rebuilt first. The time to perform the rollback is proportional to the size of the logs, but also depends on how many lost data pages have to be rebuilt while rolling back. Rebuilding the parity groups of these pages, if it is needed, takes more time than the actual copying of data from the log into these pages. Our experiments indicate that this phase takes up to 490 ms in the scenario presented in Figure 7.

Redoing the Work. When an error occurs, rollback recovery restores the system to the checkpoint state that precedes the error. All work performed between that checkpoint and the activation of the rollback has to be re-done. On the average, the lost work performed before the error occurs is half of the checkpoint interval's. Also lost is the work performed until the error is actually detected. If we assume a checkpointing frequency of once every 100 ms and error detection latency of 80 ms, the resulting lost work is 130 ms. The worst case is if the error occurs just before the system establishes a new checkpoint, in which case 180 ms of work is lost.

Overall, assuming the parameters explained above, the machine is unavailable for about 820ms in the worst case. The availability of the machine is $A = (T_E - T_U)/T_E$, where T_E is mean time between errors and T_U is the mean time the machine is not available due to an error. Even assuming $T_E = 1$ day, the resulting availability with ReVive is $A = 99.999\%$. If most errors do not result in losing memory contents, the average unavailable time is only 250 ms, which results in $A = 99.9997\%$ availability.

Rebuilding Lost Memory Pages. Our experiments indicate that, if the lost node had 2GB of memory and $7 + 1$ parity was used, a 16-processor machine requires about 20 seconds to fully rebuild all affected parity groups, if it devotes half of its computation to rebuilding the damaged parity groups and the other half to useful computation. Note that this step is not needed if the error does not result in losing memory contents.

4 ReVive Implementation Issues

ReVive does not require processor or cache modifications. All hardware modifications are confined to the directory controller. Now we discuss these modifications, as well as the possible races.

4.1 Extensions to the Directory Controller

The additional supports required by ReVive are protocol extensions and, optionally, the L bit for each directory entry as described in Section 3.2.2.

4.1.1 Protocol Extensions

ReVive requires protocol extensions to perform the parity and log operations described in Sections 3.2.1 and 3.2.2, respectively. These extensions need new transient states in the directory controller entries and new types of messages. The new transient states implement the protocols in Figures 4 and Figure 5. The new messages are the *parity update* message and its acknowledgment. Only the directory controller is affected by these changes – the new messages are communicated between directory controllers and need not be observed by the caches.

4.1.2 Hardware Modifications

Recall that the L bit indicates if the line has already been logged in this checkpoint interval. Using this bit improves performance, but is not needed for the correctness of ReVive. Indeed, without it we simply have to log the previous content of a memory line every time it the line is written back. However, recovery is still possible by restoring the log entries back into memory lines in the reverse order of their insertion into the log.

Since the L bits are optional, we can design the controller so that they are supported inexpensively. For example, if the system has a directory cache, then only the entries in that cache need to have the L bit. When the entry of a line is displaced from the directory cache, its L bit is lost. As a new entry is allocated, the L bit is reset to zero. With this approach, a memory line is occasionally logged multiple times between two checkpoints, but the correctness of ReVive is unaffected.

During the operations on the parity and the log for a line, the line remains in a new transient state in the directory. Once the operations are complete, the line reverts to one of the normal coherence states. Overall, this support requires only some additional storage (at most a few additional bits per directory entry) and does not interfere with the overall design of the directory controller.

4.2 Race Conditions

Most race conditions in our extended protocol can be handled in the same way other similar race conditions are handled in the baseline protocol without ReVive – by serializing accesses to the same memory line and sending negative acknowledgments to avoid deadlocks and livelocks. However, some race conditions are related to error recovery and need to be carefully considered. We identify five classes of race conditions. Four are specific to our protocol, while the fifth one is common to all checkpointing protocols. In the following we assume that D is the checkpoint content of a data line and that D' is the modified content of that data line. Before D is overwritten with D', it is logged into a log entry L'. Creation of L' overwrites some previous memory content L. The parities of D, D', L, and L' are D_p, D'_p, L_p, and L'_p, respectively. Note that if D is lost but D_p is still in memory, memory rebuilding using parity groups will restore D, and vice versa. A similar property holds for D' and D'_p, L and L_p, and L' and L'_p.

Log-Data Update Race. We do not allow any update to data (or its parity) before the log (and its parity) are fully updated. In this way, if an error occurs before L' and L'_p are safely stored, D and D_p are still in memory. If, on the other hand, an error occurs while D' or D'_p are written to memory, L' and L'_p are safely stored and can be used to roll back to D and D_p.

Atomic Log Update Race. Consider an error that results in a partial update of a log entry. It would be a mistake to use such an entry to "restore" the data content. Thus, the log entry is created in the following manner: the log entry is written, followed by a Marker that validates it. Incomplete entries have no valid Markers and are not used for recovery. Similarly, the parity update for the log entry is written before the parity update for the Marker. This prevents an incomplete parity update from being used in a recovery.

Log-Parity Update Race. Consider an error that occurs after log entry L' has been written, but before its parity L'_p is updated. If

the L' becomes inaccessible, then the memory where it was written will be rebuilt using L_p into the L state. Because L does not contain a valid Marker for the current checkpoint, it will not be used for recovery. The original checkpoint data D is still unmodified in memory, so no recovery is needed to restore it. Similarly, if the node where L_p is stored becomes inaccessible, L' will be used to restore its memory to the L'_p state. Then the log entry L' will be used to restore D. This operation is unnecessary because the data memory still contains the checkpoint data D. However, it is correct.

Data-Parity Update Race. An error that occurs after the log and its parity have been correctly updated does not compromise recovery, even if the write of D', D'_p, or both is incomplete or not performed at all. This is because the checkpoint content D is found in the log and restored into data memory.

Checkpoint Commit Race. To make sure that checkpoint data from different checkpoints is cleanly separated, we use a variant of the two-phase commit protocol [23]. It is implemented with two barrier synchronizations. Passing the first barrier indicates that all processors have flushed their caches and all resulting memory updates are complete. After the first barrier, each processor marks in the local log that the new checkpoint is established. Then, passing the second barrier means that *all* processors have marked the checkpoint as established. Without the second barrier, it would be possible for a processor X to continue executing before processor Y has marked its checkpoint as established. As a result, data stored in Y's local memory and modified by X would be logged as part of the old checkpoint instead of the new one. After creating the new checkpoint, the log space that is no longer needed can be reclaimed. For example, assume that the error detection latency is such that two checkpoints must be kept. After creating checkpoint N, checkpoint $N-2$ is no longer needed. Therefore, log entries created between checkpoints $N-2$ and $N-1$ can be reclaimed.

5 Evaluation Environment

Architecture. To evaluate ReVive, we use execution-driven simulation. Our simulator is based on an extension to MINT that can model dynamic superscalar processors in detail [9]. The architecture modeled is a CC-NUMA multiprocessor with 16 nodes. Each node contains a processor, two levels of cache, a directory controller, a network interface, and a portion of the main memory of the system (Figure 2). The processor is a 6-issue dynamic superscalar. The caches are non-blocking and write-back. The system uses a full-map directory and a cache coherence protocol similar to that used in DASH [12]. The directory controller is extended to support logging and distributed parity needed for ReVive, as described in Section 3.2. Contention is accurately modeled in the entire system, including the busses, the network and the main memory. Table 3 lists the main characteristics of the architecture.

Applications. We evaluate our scheme using all 12 applications from the Splash-2 suite [31]. These applications are representative of parallel scientific workloads and exhibit a wide variety of sharing and memory access patterns. Table 4 shows the application names and the input sets we used. The data are allocated on the nodes of the machine according to the first-touch policy. This results in local allocation of private data, while shared data are allocated in the memory of the first node that accesses them. Cache sizes of 16kB for L1 and 128kB for L2 are chosen following [31],

Processor	
6-issue dynamic 1GHz	Int,fp,ld/st FU: 5,3,2
Inst. window: 96	Pending ld,st: 16,16

Memory System
L1: 16KB, 2ns hit, 4-way assoc, 64-B line, write back
L2: 128KB, 12ns hit, 4-way assoc, 64-B line, write back
Bus: 100MHz 64-bit quad-data-rate (Like Pentium 4 system bus)
Memory: 100MHz 16-bank DDR, 128 bits wide, 60ns row miss
(Essentially, two PC1600 DDR SDRAM modules in parallel)
Dir controller latency: 21ns (pipelined at 333MHz)
Network: 2-D torus, virtual cut-through routing
Message transfer time 30ns + 8ns * # hops
No-contention latency (ns):
2 (L1 hit), 14 (L2 hit), 105 (Local Mem), 191 (Neighbor Mem)

Table 3. Architectural characteristics of the system we model.

to produce representative behavior given the relatively small input sets of Splash-2. The working sets of most Splash-2 applications fit even in relatively small caches [31]. The only exception is Radix, where about 256kB are needed to accommodate the first working set. Only FFT, Ocean, and Radix have important second working sets large enough to overflow our L2 caches. In Radix, we use 4 million keys instead of the default 256 thousand. In FFT, we use 1 million complex numbers instead of the default 64 thousand. These inputs are needed to get a long enough running time, but result in larger working sets for these applications. Because both the first and the second working sets of Radix are larger than our L2 cache, we expect ReVive to exhibit close to worst-case performance on this application.

Application	Problem Size	Total # of Instructions	Global L2 Miss Rate
Barnes	16K particles	1230M	0.05%
Cholesky	tk29.0	1224M	0.26%
FFT	1M points	468M	1.78%
FMM	16K particles	1002M	0.24%
LU	512x512 matrix, 16x16 block	336M	0.07%
Ocean	258x258 grid	270M	2.02%
Radiosity	-test	744M	0.15%
Radix	4M keys, radix 1024	186M	2.51%
Raytrace	car	612M	0.26%
Volrend	head	984M	0.29%
Water-N2	1000 molecules	1074M	0.02%
Water-Sp	1728 molecules	870M	0.02%

Table 4. Characteristics of the applications.

Overheads in Error-Free Execution. The applications simulated have smaller problem sizes and run for shorter periods than real-life workloads. We need to consider how these issues affect the way we model ReVive error-free overheads, namely maintaining logs and parities, and establishing checkpoints.

The overhead of keeping logs and parities is dominated by parity updates, which are both more expensive and more frequent. Parity overhead depends on the rate of write-backs which, to a large extent, is proportional to the cache miss rate. In our simulations with the small problem sizes of Splash-2, we reduced the cache sizes to preserve the cache miss rates. Therefore, the logging and parity overheads that we measure in the simulations should match those that would be observed in a real system.

As for the overhead of establishing checkpoints, most of it is due to writing back all the dirty lines in the caches. This overhead is largely proportional to the size of the L2 cache. Since we use small caches, we can model the overhead in a real system by checkpointing proportionally more often. In Section 3.3.2, we estimated that a real system needs to checkpoint once every 100ms to achieve 99.999% availability when error frequency is once a day. This estimate assumes 2MB L2 caches. According to Section 3.3.1, the time to establish a checkpoint in a system with 128KB L2 caches is an order of magnitude smaller than with 2MB L2 caches. Consequently, our simulated system checkpoints one order of magnitude more frequently – once every 10ms.

To help isolate the overheads of parity updates and log maintenance, we also perform simulations with an infinite checkpoint interval.

Comparison to Commercial Workloads. While ReVive targets commercial, technical, and scientific workloads, the evaluation in this paper does not include commercial loads. We have focused on recovering the computational part of the state of an application. Further work is required to fully flesh out the details when ReVive has to recover in the presence of external network communication and disk activity. These issues have to be addressed to present a fair evaluation of ReVive on commercial workloads. We leave these issues for future work.

Another characteristic of commercial workloads is that they tend to have high miss rates. As a result, ReVive could induce high overheads in error-free execution. In practice, the set of applications used in our evaluation covers a range of miss rates that includes those typically found in commercial workloads. Specifically, the number of L2 misses per 1,000 instructions in our applications ranges from 0.06 in Water-Sp to 6.4 in Ocean and 9.3 in Radix. This range covers typical miss rates in OLTP and other commercial applications. As one example, several web server and OLTP applications have been reported to have around 3 misses per 1,000 instructions [2]. Consequently, ReVive overheads with commercial workloads should not be higher than those we report here.

6 Evaluation

To evaluate ReVive, we examine three issues: overhead in error-free execution, storage requirements, and recovery overhead.

6.1 Overhead in Error-Free Execution

To evaluate the impact of ReVive on error-free execution, we compare ReVive to a baseline system that includes no recovery support. As explained in Section 3.3.1, the sources of performance overhead in error-free execution with ReVive are parity and log updates, and checkpoint generation. For given cache sizes and other machine parameters, the overhead of parity and log updates mainly depends on the characteristics of the application being executed. The overhead of checkpoint generation depends on the frequency of checkpointing. To better understand these overheads, Figure 8 shows the performance overhead of our mechanism using 7 + 1 parity and with checkpoints performed every 10ms (Cp10ms) and with an infinite checkpoint interval (CpInf). For comparison, we also show the results of our scheme when mirroring is used instead of parity (as described in Section 3.2.1), for the same checkpoint

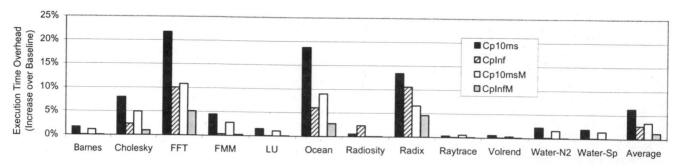

Figure 8. Performance overhead of ReVive in error-free execution.

frequencies: once every 10ms (`Cp10msM`) and with an infinite checkpoint interval (`CpInfM`). The CpInf and CpInfM bars reveal the overheads of logging and parity maintenance with 7+1 parity and mirroring, respectively. The difference between Cp10ms and CpInf, and between Cp10msM and CpInfM, represents the overhead of establishing checkpoints every 10ms, using 7 + 1 parity and mirroring, respectively.

The average overhead of logging and parity maintenance is low, 2.7% for 7+1 parity (CpInf) and 1% for mirroring (CpInfM). In applications with important working sets that do not fit in the L2 cache (FFT, Ocean, and Radix), this overhead can be high. It reaches 11% in Radix.

The overhead of establishing checkpoints every 10ms is usually small, but it can be relatively high, as in FFT and Ocean. When the checkpoint is established in these applications, almost all lines in their caches are dirty, so the checkpoint takes close to worst case time. In FFT, this effect combines with the high logging and parity maintenance overheads for an overall overhead of 22%, the highest overhead we observe in any of the twelve applications. It is important to note that a checkpoint interval of 10ms is the least favorable end of the spectrum for our scheme. Increasing the checkpoint interval or simply using mirroring instead of parity can reduce the overhead to 10% in FFT. When mirroring is used and the checkpoints are infrequent, the overhead is reduced to 5% on FFT and 1% on the average.

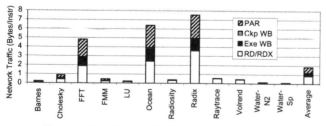

Figure 9. Breakdown of network traffic in Cp10ms.

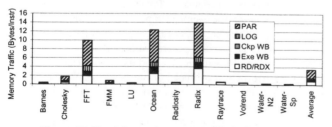

Figure 10. Breakdown of memory traffic in Cp10ms.

ReVive can be designed to be configured at boot time to support parity or mirroring. If the machine is mostly going to run applications that exhibit good caching behavior, the performance overheads are small and parity should be used to reduce the memory space overhead (Section 6.2). For applications with poorer caching behavior, a tradeoff exists between memory space overheads and performance: mirroring is faster but uses more memory. In reality, parity and mirroring need not be used in a mutually exclusive fashion. For example, a small part of the memory can be protected by mirroring, while the rest is protected by parity. Careful allocation of frequently used pages into the mirrored region should result in low overheads, as most of the memory modifications result in mirroring updates, while reducing the memory space overheads, as most of the memory space is uses the efficient parity approach.

To help understand the overheads observed, Figures 9 and 10 show the network and memory traffic in the machine with the `Cp10ms` configuration. The breakdown of the traffic is as follows: RD/RDX represents the traffic due to supplying the data on cache misses; Exe WB is the traffic due to writing back dirty lines to memory in regular execution; Ckp WB is the traffic due to writing back dirty lines when checkpoints are established; LOG is the traffic of writing data to the logs; PAR is the traffic due to parity updates (for both data and logs). Traffic shown as RD/RDX and Exe WB is the same as in the baseline system. Traffic shown as Ckp WB, LOG, and PAR is caused by ReVive. If mirroring was used instead of parity, the network traffic would stay the same as in Figure 9; the memory traffic would change only in that PAR would shrink to one third of its size.

Figures 9 and 10 show that, for most of the applications, both the network and the memory traffic are low, without or with ReVive. The exceptions are FFT, Ocean, and Radix, where traffic is already high in the baseline system. For these three applications, the additional traffic, mostly resulting from parity maintenance, further degrades the already poor performance.

6.2 Storage Requirements

ReVive requires additional memory space to store distributed parity and logs.

Parity Storage Requirements. To keep the hardware simple, the number of nodes should be a multiple of the parity group size. In addition, the latter should be a power of two, so that to determine which node has the parity page for a given group, we can use a trivial implementation of the *mod* operation. With 7 + 1 parity, 88% of the main memory is used for data, while 12% is used for parity. We can reduce this requirement by employing larger parity groups. However, doing so slows down recovery and increases the risk of contention in the home of a parity page belonging to a particularly popular parity group. If mirroring is used instead of parity, the overhead is 50% of the memory.

Log storage requirements. Figure 11 shows the maximum log size for different applications for the Cp10ms configuration, assuming that logs for two most recent checkpoints are kept. As we can see, the largest log is about 2.5MB. With the conservative assumption of a log growing proportionally to the checkpoint interval, that yields 25MB for a checkpoint interval of 100ms. In reality, we expect the actual size to be significantly less, as longer intervals allow more filtering out of redundant log entries (Section 3.2.2).

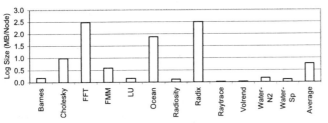

Figure 11. Maximum log size in the Cp10ms configuration.

Overall, if we assume 2GB of DRAM memory per node and a checkpoint interval of 100ms, each node needs 256MB for parity and 25MB for logs, bringing the total memory overhead of ReVive to 14%. Increasing the checkpoint interval to one second would result in up to 25% memory overhead. In comparison, using mirroring instead of parity could result in as much as 62% of memory overhead.

6.3 Recovery Overhead

To estimate the unavailability due to an error, we trigger the error recovery mechanism in each benchmark 8 ms after the second checkpoint in *Cp10ms* is committed. With a checkpoint interval of 100 ms this corresponds to an error that occurs just before the second checkpoint is established, and is detected 80 ms later. As discussed in Section 3.3.2, this results in maximum lost work and maximum ReVive recovery time. Figure 12 shows the resulting ReVive recovery time during which the machine is unavailable (Phases 2 and 3 in Figure 7). The longest such time is 59ms (in Radix), while the average is 17ms. This corresponds to 590ms and 170ms with a 100ms checkpoint interval. After adding 180 ms for lost work and 50 ms for hardware recovery, the resulting unavailable time is 820 ms for Radix and 400 ms on average. If errors occur one per day and all are worst-case node losses, this results in 99.999% availability for Radix and 99.9995% on average.

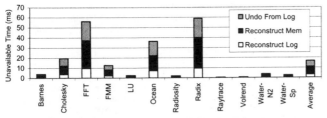

Figure 12. Breakdown of the unavailable time due to an error in the Cp10ms configuration.

7 Related Work

The work most related to our distributed parity mechanism is [20], which implements a software-only checkpointing mechanism where special nodes store parity information. Our work differs from [20] in several important aspects. First, we use hardware to maintain the parity, which significantly reduces the performance overhead. Second, we overlap parity maintenance with useful execution, while [20] performs all parity maintenance while establishing a checkpoint. As a result, the time needed to establish a checkpoint in [20] is a few seconds, instead of a few milliseconds with ReVive. Third, we distribute our parity across the system, rather than keeping it on a few dedicated nodes that can become potential bottlenecks in [20]. Fourth, our parity is updated at a memory line granularity, as opposed to the page granularity used in [20]. Finally, we protect the entire main memory with our parity, rather than just the checkpoint data as in [20]. Protecting the entire memory could make it easier to prevent loss of information about recent external I/O operations when an error occurs.

The work most related to our log-based rollback mechanism is [13], where a snooping device is attached to the bus to intercept write-back and write-miss operations and log previous values of modified memory lines. Our mechanism differs from the one proposed in [13] in several important ways. First, ReVive allows recovery from errors that occur anywhere in the system, while the design in [13] recovers from errors in the processor and cache, as well as from some operating system errors. Second, we use main memory to store the logs, whereas the logs in [13] are stored on their dedicated bus-snooping device. Our approach results in higher flexibility in choosing how much memory is dedicated to logging, while allowing us to store the logs in the cost-effective high-capacity memory modules together with other data. Finally, using hardware-maintained distributed parity with a logging device like that in [13] would be difficult.

Concurrently to our work, a system called SafetyNet that targets some classes of system-wide transient faults has been proposed in [25]. While both ReVive and SafetyNet use log-based rollback mechanisms, Revive differs from SafetyNet in several important ways. First, ReVive enables recovery from permanent faults such as losing a node, in addition to the transient faults that can be tolerated by SafetyNet. Second, ReVive does not require any changes to the processor's caches. In SafetNet, each line in the cache is augmented with a checkpoint number, which is then checked whenever the line is modified by the processor. Furthermore, SafetyNet adds a 256-512KB checkpoint log buffer to the cache. Third, the error detection latency that SafetyNet can tolerate is largely determined by the size of the checkpoint log buffers. In contrast, ReVive uses the main memory to store its logs and, as a result, can tolerate longer detection latencies. Finally, because of ReVive's more general fault model, ReVive causes more network and memory traffic, which may result in larger performance overheads than with SafetyNet.

While we target errors whose effect modifies the system-wide state, other work has targeted errors that can be contained within a single device such as a processor [3, 16, 28, 30]. Our scheme is fully compatible with such mechanisms. The lightweight recovery of a device-specific mechanism would be used for such device-specific errors. Errors whose effect escapes the device and errors not covered by device-specific mechanisms would be recovered using ReVive.

8 Conclusions

This paper presented ReVive, a new cost-effective rollback recovery mechanism for shared-memory multiprocessors. ReVive performs memory-based checkpointing, logging, and distributed parity maintenance without requiring any hardware modification to the processors or caches. ReVive enables recovery from a wide range of system-level errors, including total loss of a node. ReVive's average execution time overhead is only 6.3%, even when establishing checkpoints as often as once every 100ms. Assuming an error detection latency of 80 ms, an error results in up to 820ms unavailable time, including lost work. The resulting availability is better than 99.999% even if errors occur as frequently as once per day. Finally, the main memory space overhead is only 14% of the main memory, and external storage is not used.

The work is being extended in three ways. First, we are examining mirroring support for the most frequently accessed pages and N+1 parity for all other pages in memory, as suggested in Section 6.1. Second, we are evaluating ReVive with commercial workloads and with longer run times to use realistic checkpointing frequencies. Third, we are further developing details of ReVive to support recovery in the presence of I/O activity such as network or disk access. In general, our distributed parity mechanism is a powerful building block that can be used to protect the I/O buffers. In the long term, we plan to combine ReVive with error detection schemes to fully evaluate error recovery.

Acknowledgments

This work is partially based on the ideas from [33]. The authors would like to thank Manohar Prabhu for proposing log updates on read-exclusive and upgrade requests.

References

[1] R. E. Ahmed, R. C. Frazier, and P. N. Marinos. Cache-Aided Rollback Error Recovery (CARER) Algorithms for Shared-Memory Multiprocessor Systems. In *Proc. 20th Intl. Symp. on Fault-Tolerant Computing Systems*, pages 82–88, June 1990.

[2] A. R. Alameldeen et al. Evaluating Non-deterministic Multithreaded Commercial Workloads. In *5th Workshop on computer Architecture Evaluation using Commercial Workloads*, pages 30–38, Feb. 2002.

[3] T. M. Austin. DIVA: A Reliable Substrate for Deep Submicron Microarchitecture Design. In *Proc. 32nd Annual Intl. Symp. on Microarchitecture*, pages 196–207, Nov. 1999.

[4] M. Banatre et al. An Architecture for Tolerating Processor Failures in Shared-Memory Multiprocessors. *IEEE Trans. Computers*, 45(10):1101–1115, Oct. 1996.

[5] M. Banatre and P. Joubert. Cache Management in a Tightly Coupled Fault Tolerant Multiprocessor. In *Proc. 20th Intl. Symp. on Fault-Tolerant Computing*, pages 89–96, June 1990.

[6] E. N. Elnozahy and W. Zwaenepoel. Manetho: Transparent Rollback-Recovery with Low Overhead, Limited Rollback, and Fast Output Commit. *IEEE Trans. Computers*, 41(5):526–531, May 1992.

[7] M. Elnozahy, L. Alvisi, Y.-M. Wang, and D. B. Johnson. A Survey of Rollback-Recovery Protocols in Message-Passing Systems. Tech. Rep. CMU-CS-99-148, Carnegie Mellon University, June 1999.

[8] A.-M. Kermarrec et al. A Recoverable Distributed Shared Memory Integrating Coherence and Recoverability. In *Proc. 25th Intl. Symp. on Fault-Tolerant Computing*, pages 289–298, June 1995.

[9] V. Krishnan and J. Torrellas. An Execution-Driven Framework for Fast and Accurate Simulation of Superscalar Processors. In *Proc. 1998 Intl. Conf. on Parallel Architectures and Compilation Techniques*, pages 286–293, Oct. 1998.

[10] R. Kufrin. Barrier Synchronization on the Origin 2000. http://www.ncsa.uiuc.edu/~rkufrin/projects/CompSci/Barriers/, July 1999.

[11] J. Laudon and D. Lenoski. The SGI Origin: A ccNUMA Highly Scalable Server. In *Proc. 24th Intl. Symp. on Computer Architecture*, pages 241–251, June 1997.

[12] D. Lenoski et al. The Stanford Dash Multiprocessor. *IEEE Computer*, pages 63–79, Mar. 1992. It is Dash, not DASH.

[13] Y. Masubuchi et al. Fault Recovery Mechanism for Multiprocessor Servers. In *Proc. 27th Intl. Symp. on Fault-Tolerant Computing*, pages 184–193, June 1997.

[14] C. Morin, A. Gefflaut, M. Banatre, and A.-M. Kermarrec. COMA: an Opportunity for Building Fault-tolerant Scalable Shared Memory Multiprocessors. In *Proc. 23rd Intl. Symp. on Computer Architecture*, pages 56–65, May 1996.

[15] C. Morin, A.-M. Kermarrec, M. Banatre, and A. Gefflaut. An Efficient and Scalable Approach for Implementing Fault-Tolerant DSM Architectures. *IEEE Trans. Computers*, 49(5):414–430, May 2000.

[16] S. S. Mukherjee, M. Kontz, and S. K. Reinhardt. Detailed Design and Evaluation of Redundant Multithreading Alternatives. In *Proc. 29th Intl. Symp. on Computer Architecture*, May 2002.

[17] D. A. Patterson, G. Gibson, and R. H. Katz. A Case for Redundant Arrays of Inexpensive Disks (RAID). In *Proc. ACM SIGMOD Intl. Conf. on the Management of Data*, pages 109–116, June 1988.

[18] J. S. Plank et al. Memory Exclusion: Optimizing the Performance of Checkpointing Systems. *Software – Practice and Experience*, 29(2):125–142, Feb. 1999.

[19] J. S. Plank and W. R. Elwasif. Experimental Assessment of Workstation Failures and Their Impact on Checkpointing Systems. In *Proc. 28th Intl. Symp. on Fault-Tolerant Computing*, pages 48–57, June 1998.

[20] J. S. Plank and K. Li. Faster Checkpointing with N + 1 Parity. In *Proc. 24th Intl. Symp. on Fault-Tolerant Computing*, pages 288–297, June 1994.

[21] J. S. Plank, K. Li, and M. A. Puening. Diskless Checkpointing. *IEEE Trans. Parallel and Distributed Systems*, 9(10):972–986, Oct. 1998.

[22] B. Randell. System Structure for Software Fault Tolerance. *IEEE Trans. Soft. Eng.*, SE-1(2):220–232, June 1975.

[23] A. Silberschatz, H. F. Korth, and S. Sudarshan. *Database System Concepts, 3rd edition*. McGraw-Hill, 1999.

[24] Silicon Graphics, Inc. REACT™ in IRIX™ 6.4 Technical Report. http://www.sgi.com/software/react/react_tr.pdf, 1997.

[25] D. J. Sorin, M. M. K. Martin, M. D. Hill, and D. A. Wood. SafetyNet: Improving the Availability of Shared Memory Multiprocessors with Global Checkpoint/Recovery. In *Proc. 29th Intl. Symp. on Computer Architecture*, May 2002.

[26] F. Sultan, T. D. Nguyen, and L. Iftode. Scalable Fault-Tolerant Distributed Shared Memory. In *Proc. Supercomputing 2000*, Nov. 2000.

[27] D. Sunada, D. Glasco, and M. Flynn. Multiprocessor Architecture Using an Audit Trail for Fault Tolerance. In *Proc. 29th Intl. Symp. on Fault-Tolerant Computing*, pages 40–47, June 1999.

[28] K. Sundaramoorthy, Z. Purser, and E. Rotenberg. Slipstream Processors: Improving both Performance and Fault Tolerance. In *Proc. 9th Intl. Conf. on Arch. Support for Prog. Lang. and OS*, Nov. 2000.

[29] D. Teodosiu et al. Hardware Fault Containment in Scalable Shared-Memory Multiprocessors. In *Proc. 24th Intl. Symp. on Computer Architecture*, pages 73–84, June 1997.

[30] T. N. Vijaykumar, I. Pomeranz, and K. Cheng. Transient-Fault Recovery Using Simultaneous Multithreading. In *Proc. 29th Intl. Symp. on Computer Architecture*, May 2002.

[31] S. C. Woo et al. The SPLASH-2 Programs: Characterization and Methodological Considerations. In *Proc. 22nd Intl. Symp. on Computer Architecture*, pages 24–38, June 1995.

[32] K.-L. Wu, W. K. Fuchs, and J. H. Patel. Error Recovery in Shared Memory Multiprocessors Using Private Caches. *IEEE Trans. Parallel and Distributed Systems*, 1(2):231–240, Apr. 1990.

[33] Z. Zhang. Single system high-availability solutions. Tech. Rep. HPL-2001-81, Hewlett-Packard Laboratories, Apr. 2001.

SafetyNet: Improving the Availability of Shared Memory Multiprocessors with Global Checkpoint/Recovery

Daniel J. Sorin, Milo M. K. Martin, Mark D. Hill, David A. Wood

Computer Sciences Department

University of Wisconsin—Madison

{sorin, milo, markhill, david}@cs.wisc.edu

http://www.cs.wisc.edu/multifacet/

Abstract

We develop an availability solution, called SafetyNet, *that uses a unified, lightweight checkpoint/recovery mechanism to support multiple long-latency fault detection schemes. At an abstract level,* SafetyNet *logically maintains multiple, globally consistent checkpoints of the state of a shared memory multiprocessor (i.e., processors, memory, and coherence permissions), and it recovers to a pre-fault checkpoint of the system and re-executes if a fault is detected.* SafetyNet *efficiently coordinates checkpoints across the system in logical time and uses "logically atomic" coherence transactions to free checkpoints of transient coherence state.* SafetyNet *minimizes performance overhead by pipelining checkpoint validation with subsequent parallel execution.*

We illustrate SafetyNet *avoiding system crashes due to either dropped coherence messages or the loss of an interconnection network switch (and its buffered messages). Using full-system simulation of a 16-way multiprocessor running commercial workloads, we find that* SafetyNet *(a) adds statistically insignificant runtime overhead in the common-case of fault-free execution, and (b) avoids a crash when tolerated faults occur.*

1 Introduction

Availability has become increasingly important as internet services are integrated more tightly into society's infrastructure. Availability is particularly crucial for the shared-memory multiprocessor servers that run the application services and database management systems that must robustly manage business data. However, unless architectural steps are taken, availability will decrease over time as implementations use larger numbers of increasingly unreliable components in search of higher performance [21, 43]. The high clock frequencies and small circuit dimensions of future systems will increase their susceptibility to both transient and permanent faults. For example, higher frequencies exacerbate crosstalk [3, 8] and supply voltage noise [39], and smaller devices and wires suffer more from electromigration and alpha particle disruptions [36, 49].

Decades of research in fault-tolerant systems suggest a path toward addressing this problem. Mission-critical systems routinely employ redundant processors, memories, and interconnects (e.g., triple-modular redundancy [26] or pair-and-spare [45]) to tolerate a broad class of faults. However, for many applications, the highly competitive commercial market will seek lower overhead solutions. For example, RAID level 5 [31] has been deployed widely because its overhead is 1/Nth (for N data disks) rather than the 100% overhead for mirroring. In contrast to mission-critical systems, commercial servers aim for high availability but will accept occasional crashes to improve cost/performance. Software-visible techniques—including database logging and clustering—help preserve data integrity and service availability in these cases.

Current servers employ a range of hardware mechanisms to improve availability. RAID, error correcting codes (ECC), interconnection network link-level retry [18], and duplicate ALUs with processor retry [40] target specific, localized faults such as transient bit flips at memory, links, or ALUs. Computer architects seeking system-wide coverage currently must integrate a patchwork of localized detection and recovery schemes.

In this paper, we seek a unified, lightweight mechanism that provides end-to-end recovery from a broad class of transient and permanent faults. This recovery mechanism can be combined with a wide range of fault detection mechanisms, including strong error detection codes (e.g., CRCs), redundant processors and ALUs [18, 40], redundant threads [37], and system-level state checkers [9]. By decoupling recovery from detection, our approach allows a range of implementations with varying cost-performance.

We develop a lightweight global checkpoint/recovery scheme called *SafetyNet*, and we illustrate its abstraction in Figure 1. *SafetyNet* periodically creates a system-wide (logical) checkpoint. *SafetyNet* checkpoints can span thousands or even millions of execution cycles, permitting

This work is supported in part by the National Science Foundation, with grants EIA-9971256, CDA-9623632, and CCR-0105721, Intel Graduate Fellowship (Sorin), IBM Graduate Fellowship (Martin), two Wisconsin Romnes Fellowships (Hill and Wood), and donations from Compaq Computer Corporation, Intel Corporation, IBM, and Sun Microsystems.

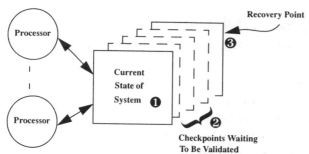

Figure 1. *SafetyNet* **Abstraction. In SafetyNet, ❶ processors operate on the current state of the system, ❷ the system recovers to the recovery point if a fault is detected, and ❸ some number of non-current checkpoints can be pending validation.**

powerful detection mechanisms with long latencies. After detecting a fault, all processors, caches, and memories revert to and resume execution from a consistent system-wide state, the *recovery point*. *SafetyNet* is a hardware scheme that requires no changes to any software or the instruction set. Moreover, *SafetyNet* has limited impact on the processor, coherence protocol, and I/O subsystem.

SafetyNet's basic approach is to log all changes to the architected state. This presents three main challenges for a lightweight recovery scheme. First, naively saving previous values before every register update, cache write, and coherence response would require a prohibitive amount of storage. Second, all processors, caches, and memories in a shared-memory multiprocessor must recover to a consistent point. For example, recovery must ensure that all nodes agree on the coherence ownership and data values of each memory block. Third, *SafetyNet* must determine when it is safe to advance the recovery point (i.e., validate a new checkpoint), without degrading performance to wait for slow fault detection mechanisms.

SafetyNet efficiently meets these three challenges, as described in Section 2. First, logging is reduced by check-pointing at a coarse granularity (e.g., 100,000 cycles). Only the first change to a piece of architectural state—register, memory block, or coherence permission—within a checkpoint interval requires a log entry, reducing the log over-head by one or two orders of magnitude. Second, *SafetyNet* efficiently coordinates checkpoint creation using *global logical time* and *logically atomic coherence transactions*, ensuring a consistent recovery point. Third, checkpoint validation is pipelined and overlapped with normal execution. Pipelining validation allows *SafetyNet* to tolerate long latency detection mechanisms while continuing execution.

In Section 3, we develop a *SafetyNet* implementation that minimizes runtime overheads for actions in the common case of fault-free execution, including memory operations and coherence transactions. Figure 2 depicts the structures

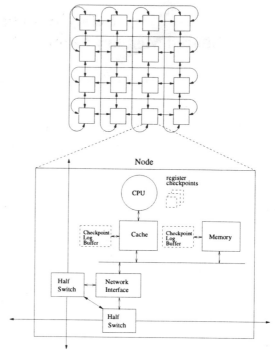

Figure 2. Example *SafetyNet* System

necessary to maintain checkpoint state—register check-point buffers and Checkpoint Log Buffers (CLBs)—added to processor-memory nodes of an example system implementation. Register checkpoints, CLBs, caches, and memories are deemed "stable storage" and must be protected by ECC, because *SafetyNet* cannot recover from uncorrectable errors to these structures. Addressing this class of faults, including processor-cache chip kills, is future work.

SafetyNet is a recovery mechanism that is largely decoupled from any specific fault detection mechanisms. However, to make the exposition more concrete, we use two system-level faults as running examples. We focus on the two faults presented below, and we describe their causes and detection mechanisms in more detail in Table 1.

(1) **Dropped Message**: A transient fault causes the loss of a coherence message in the interconnect.

(2) **Failed Switch**: A hard fault kills a switch element, irretrievably losing all buffered messages.

In Section 4, full system simulations with commercial workloads show that, in the common case of fault-free execution, *SafetyNet* does not increase execution time (relative to an unprotected system) by a statistically significant amount. Moreover, *SafetyNet* continues to run after the injection of the two example faults. Recovery time is reduced from a system crash/reboot to a performance "speed bump" of less than one millisecond. We also show that 512 kbyte CLBs are large enough, for our commercial

Table 1. Two Example Faults

Dropped Message: This example fault assumes a lost or misrouted coherence message due to a transient environmental condition (e.g., alpha particle [28, 36, 49]). The fault may corrupt the message while it is stored in a switch buffer or by disrupting a switch's internal logic. The fault might be detected using an error detection code (e.g., CRC), by an endpoint receiving an illegal message, or by a request timing out. The detection latency may be large in the case of request timeout or if longer error detection codes are used (longer codes are inherently stronger).
Failed Switch: This example fault assumes the permanent loss of an interconnect switch element (e.g., due to electromigration), causing the loss of all buffered messages. We consider a 2D torus topology that prevents a single point-of-failure by splitting each switch into two half-switches. As illustrated in Figure 2, nodes have separate paths to the north-south and east-west half-switches, providing redundancy in case one half-switch fails. We use the same mechanisms discussed above to detect the fault. Execution may resume after reconfiguring the interconnect to route around the lost switch [14], but with some loss of bandwidth.

workloads, to tolerate fault detection mechanisms with over 100,000 cycles of latency.

Section 5 expands upon the wide variety of faults and detection mechanisms compatible with *SafetyNet*. Like most prior work, we focus on tolerating all single faults, plus coverage for many double faults.

2 *SafetyNet* Overview

This section presents a high-level overview of *SafetyNet*, while Section 3 describes one specific implementation.

2.1 High-Level View

SafetyNet periodically checkpoints the system state, to allow the system to recover its state to a consistent previous checkpoint. If a fault is detected, *SafetyNet* recovers the state to the *recovery point*, the old checkpoint most recently validated fault-free. Checkpoints between the recovery point and the active system state are pending validation. A system-wide checkpoint includes the state of the processor registers, memory values, and coherence permissions. *SafetyNet* has a small impact on the underlying cache coherence protocol. We assume a sequentially consistent memory model, and *SafetyNet* does not affect its implementation.

SafetyNet addresses the three challenges for logging schemes described in Section 1. First, *SafetyNet* exploits a coarse checkpoint granularity to reduce the amount of logging (Section 2.2). Second, *SafetyNet* creates consistent global checkpoints (Section 2.3) such that all processors and memories recover to a consistent recovery point upon fault detection. Third, *SafetyNet* pipelines checkpoint validation off the critical path and hides the latencies of fault detection mechanisms (Section 2.4).

2.2 Checkpointing Via Logging

Logically, *SafetyNet* checkpoints contain a complete copy of the system's architectural state. For efficiency, *SafetyNet* explicitly checkpoints registers and incrementally checkpoints memory state by logging previous values and coherence permissions. Conceptually, processors and memory controllers log every change to the memory/coherence state (i.e., save the *old* copy of the block) whenever an action (i.e., a store or a transfer of ownership) might have to be undone. To reduce storage and bandwidth requirements, *SafetyNet* only logs the block on the first such action per checkpoint interval. By using coarse checkpoint intervals (e.g., 100,000 cycles), *SafetyNet* significantly reduces logging overhead (evaluated in Section 4.3). Checkpointing of processor register state can be done in many ways, including shadow copies or writing the registers into the cache.

2.3 Creating Consistent Checkpoints

All of the components (caches and memory controllers) coordinate their local checkpoints, so that the collection of local checkpoints represents a consistent global recovery point. Coordinated system-wide checkpointing avoids both cascading rollbacks [15] and an output commit problem [16] for inter-node communication. Checkpoints are coordinated across the system in *logical time* to avoid a potentially costly exchange of synchronization messages.

To ensure that checkpoints reflect consistent system states, the logical time base must ensure that all components can independently determine the checkpoint interval in which any coherence transaction occurs (not just its request). We exploit the key insight that, in retrospect, a coherence transaction appears logically atomic once it completes. A transaction's *point of atomicity* occurs when the previous owner of the requested block processes the request. To inform the requestor, the response includes the checkpoint number of the point of atomicity. Figure 3 illustrates how *SafetyNet* determines this point. Note that the requestor does not learn the location of the atomicity point until it receives the response that completes the transaction. To ensure that the system never recovers to the "middle" of a transaction, the requestor does not agree to advance the recovery point until all of its outstanding transactions complete successfully. After completion, the transaction appears atomic, so there is no "middle." Furthermore, by waiting for outstanding transactions to complete, *SafetyNet* avoids checkpointing transient coherence states and in-flight messages.

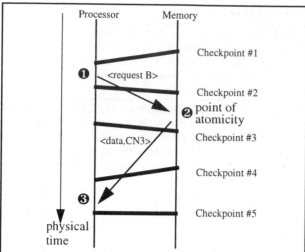

Figure 3. Example of Checkpoint Coordination

In this example, physical time flows downwards, and checkpoint lines in logical time are not necessarily horizontal, since logical time is not equal to physical time. Logical time respects causality, so a message cannot be sent in one checkpoint interval and arrive in an earlier interval. At **❶**, the processor requests ownership of block B from the memory, which is currently the owner of the block. The memory processes the request at **❷** and defines the transaction's point of atomicity, sending checkpoint number (CN) 3 along with the data. In retrospect, the transaction appears to have occurred atomically at this point. A recovery to CN 2 or before would restore ownership to the memory. A recovery to CN 3 or later would maintain ownership at the processor. A recovery to CN 2-5 (the duration of the transaction) is not possible until after the transaction, since the processor would not validate any of these checkpoints until the transaction completed successfully at **❸**.

Many bases of logical time exist. A simple example in a broadcast snooping system is for each component to count the number of coherence requests it has processed and use that as its logical time. If components create checkpoints every K logical cycles, it is trivial for all components to agree on the interval in which a transaction's request occurred. In this paper, we focus on systems with directory protocols, and thus we need a different logical time base. If we could distribute a perfectly synchronous physical clock, we would have a viable logical time base in which logical and physical time are the same. In Section 3, we relax this requirement by deriving a logical time base from a loosely synchronized *checkpoint clock*.

2.4 Validating Checkpoints

Checkpoint validation is the process of determining which checkpoint is the recovery point. Processors and memories coordinate checkpoint validation so that all components recover to the same checkpoint number on a recovery.

Coordination can be pipelined and performed in the background. For example, checkpoint number k can be validated only if every component agrees that it could be the recovery point, i.e, all execution prior to checkpoint number k was fault-free. For a checkpoint interval to be fault-free, every transfer of ownership in that interval must complete successfully, by which we mean that the data was transferred fault-free to the requestor. Once every component has independently declared that it has received fault-free data in response to all of its requests in the interval before the checkpoint, the recovery point can be advanced. At this point, all transactions prior to this checkpoint have had their points of atomicity determined. After validation, state for the prior recovery point can be deallocated lazily.

Validation latency depends on fault detection latency, since a checkpoint cannot be validated until it has been verified fault free. For our fault examples, the detection latency is as long as the requestor's timeout latency. Timeout latency can be many traversals of the interconnect, plus some slack built in for contention delays. Adding to validation latency, validation cannot occur until all nodes have coordinated their validations, and this involves an exchange of messages. Since validation latency is long, *SafetyNet* performs validation in the background and off the critical path.

Checkpoint validation also determines when the system can interact with the outside world of I/O devices. The *output commit problem* [16] requires that only validated, fault-free data can be communicated outside of the sphere of recovery. For example, the system cannot communicate unvalidated data with the disks if the effects of this communication cannot be undone through recovery. A standard solution is to delay all output events generated within a checkpoint until that checkpoint is validated. A standard solution for the *input commit problem* [16] is to log incoming messages so that they can be replayed after recovery.

2.5 Recovering to a Consistent Global State

If a fault is detected, *SafetyNet* restores the globally consistent recovery point. The recovery point represents the consistent state of the system at the *logical time* that this checkpoint was taken. Recovery itself requires that the processors restore their register checkpoints and that the caches and memories unroll their local logs to recover the system to the consistent global state at the pre-fault recovery point. All state associated with transactions in progress at the time of recovery is discarded, since this state is (by definition) unvalidated state that occurs logically after the recovery point. After recovery, the system reconfigures, if necessary, and resumes execution from the recovery point. For the lost switch example, reconfiguration involves routing around the faulty switch.

126

3 A *SafetyNet* Implementation

In this section, we discuss one implementation of the *SafetyNet* abstraction. Our goal is to incur low overhead in the common case of fault-free execution, while not allocating resources towards optimizing the rare case of recovery.

3.1 System Model

Figure 2 illustrates a single node, containing a processor, a cache, and a portion of the system's shared memory. A *Checkpoint Log Buffer (CLB)*, associated with each cache hierarchy and each memory controller, stores logged state. Processor register checkpoints are maintained in shadow registers. Nodes communicate through a 2D torus interconnection network. The cache coherence protocol is based on a typical MOSI directory protocol[1], and *SafetyNet* has only a slight impact on it. The system also includes redundant system service controllers (which exist in many servers, such as the UltraEnterprise E10000's service processors [10]), that help coordinate advancement of the recovery point as well as system restart after recovery.

3.2 Logical Time Base

As discussed in Section 2, checkpoints are coordinated across the system in logical time. For our system with directory-based coherence, we use a loosely synchronous (in physical time) *checkpoint clock* that is distributed redundantly to ensure no single point of failure. On each edge of this clock, each component creates a checkpoint and increments its *current checkpoint number (CCN)*. While it might be difficult to distribute a synchronous clock across a system with near-zero skew, it is not nearly so difficult to distribute one with the same frequency and some amount of skew between nodes. As long as the skew between any two nodes is less than the minimum communication time between these nodes, the checkpoint clock is a valid base of logical time, since no message can travel backwards in logical time.[2]

We use logical time to address the primary challenge in coordinating checkpoints across a system, which is keeping checkpoints consistent with respect to memory and coherence state. All components must agree, for every coherence transaction, on the checkpoint interval in which that transaction occurred. Assigning a transaction to a checkpoint interval is protocol-dependent, and it is the only significant difference in implementing *SafetyNet* on top of different classes of protocols (i.e., directory vs. snooping). In a directory protocol, the point of atomicity occurs when the block's owner processes the request.

3.3 Logging

SafetyNet uses *Checkpoint Log Buffers (CLBs)* to incrementally checkpoint memory and coherence state. Logically, *SafetyNet* writes a memory block to a CLB whenever an *update-action* (i.e., store or transfer of ownership) might have to be undone in the case of a recovery. Since processors perform stores into caches and both caches and memories can transfer ownership of blocks, both caches and memories have CLBs. Except during recovery, CLBs are write-only and off the critical path.

SafetyNet only logs a block on the first update-action per checkpoint interval. To detect this case, *SafetyNet* adds a *checkpoint number (CN)* to each block in the cache, denoting to which checkpoint it belongs. On each update-action, *SafetyNet* (1) compares the component's current checkpoint number (CCN) with the block's CN, (2) logs the block if CCN ≥ CN, (3) updates the block's CN to CCN+1, and (4) performs the update-action. For example, a store by a processor with CCN=3 to a block with CN=4 need not be logged. Blocks with null CNs have not been written or transferred lately, and they implicitly belong to the recovery point as well as all subsequent checkpoints. Having CNs on blocks is an optimization that enables logic to determine whether logging an update-action is redundant. Figure 4 illustrates an example of logging at a cache.

When giving up ownership of a block, a component performs logging (as described above) and then sends a response with the block *and the updated CN* to the requestor. This policy follows from a key insight from Wu et al. [48]: a transfer of ownership is just like a write, in that we cannot be sure that it will not be undone by a recovery. Consider the case where ownership is transferred with its CN set to 3 (i.e., the sender's CCN is 2) and the receiver wishes to then perform a store to it while its CCN is still 2. Logging is unnecessary, since the receiver was not the owner at checkpoint 2. This case is the same as an owner of a block with CN=3 overwriting it while its CCN is still 2.

The CLBs can be sized for performance and not correctness, since *SafetyNet* can avoid situations in which the CLB fills up. Even when it appears that an entry must be logged in the CLB, logging can be avoided at the cost of some performance. In the case of store overwrites, we can throttle requests from the CPU. For coherence ownership transfers, we can negatively acknowledge (nack) coherence requests, although this may require changing the protocol. Note that

---

1. In this paper, we assume a directory protocol and a 2D torus, but we have also implemented *SafetyNet* on a system with a broadcast snooping protocol and a totally ordered interconnect.

2. Otherwise, the following inconsistency could arise. Consider the case where processor P1 has a CCN of 3 and sends a request to the owner, P2, while P2's CCN is still 2. Thus, checkpoint 3 would include the reception of the request but not its sending!

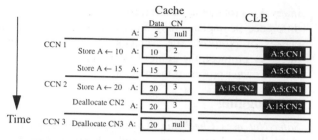

Figure 4. Logging at the Cache

a stall due to a full CLB will not cause deadlock, since the CLB will eventually either deallocate state from a checkpoint that validates or recovery occurs if validation fails.

3.4 Checkpoint Creation

Checkpoint creation must be lightweight, since it is a common-case event that occurs on each edge of the checkpoint clock. A processor checkpoints its non-memory architectural state (i.e., registers) and increments its CCN.[3] A memory controller simply increments its CCN. Checkpointing of memory and coherence state is achieved through logging, so no checkpointing of that state is necessary at checkpoint creation.

Checkpoint creation policy is simply choosing a suitable checkpoint clock frequency, f_c. As f_c decreases (given a constant number of outstanding checkpoints), *SafetyNet* can tolerate longer fault detection latencies. For example, we allow four outstanding checkpoints and choose f_c equal to 10 kHz (i.e., the checkpoint interval is 100,000 processor cycles at a processor clock of 1 GHz) to enable 400,000 cycles (0.4 msec) of detection latency tolerance. The cost of increasing tolerable detection latency is larger CLBs and longer output commit delays. While decreasing f_c allows for more optimized logging, since we log only the first update-action on a block in an interval, total CLB storage is a function both of logging frequency and interval length. The value of f_c has little effect on performance, since we show in Section 4 that *SafetyNet* adds little overhead.

3.5 Checkpoint Validation

Checkpoint validation requires that all components agree that execution up until that checkpoint was fault-free. A cache controller only agrees to validate a checkpoint once every transaction it initiated in the interval before that checkpoint completed successfully. A directory controller only agrees to validate after every transaction for which it

---

3. Since CNs are encoded in a finite number of bits, an implementation should not re-use a CN until its previous incarnation has been discarded. We ensure this by setting the request timeout latency to be less than the minimum wraparound time.

forwarded a request to a processor owner (i.e., 3-hop transaction) completed successfully. Thus, the requestor must send an acknowledgment to the directory after its request has been satisfied, so that the directory can deallocate its buffer entry for the transaction. Any lost message will prevent recovery point advancement. If the recovery point cannot be advanced after a given amount of time, the system assumes an error has occurred (such as a lost message) and triggers a system recovery. *SafetyNet* can maintain a recovery point as long as necessary, in the worst case, by stalling execution. However, fault-free performance is best if, in the average case, fault detection mechanisms validate checkpoints fault-free in one or a few checkpoint intervals (e.g, in 100,000 cycles or 0.1 milliseconds).

We coordinate validation with a 2-phase scheme. Once every component has informed the service controllers that it is ready to advance the recovery point, the service controllers broadcast the new *recovery point checkpoint number (RPCN)*. Similar to a fuzzy barrier [22], execution does not slow while checkpoints validate in the background.

Components deallocate a checkpoint by discarding their now unneeded architectural checkpoints. A processor discards its register checkpoint. In the caches, a checkpoint is deallocated by clearing the CN of all blocks that had CN set to the newly deallocated checkpoint. Logged data at the CLBs from this checkpoint is discarded.

3.6 System Recovery and Restart

If a component detects a fault, it triggers a recovery. The recovery message, which includes the RPCN, is broadcast by the service controllers, and all nodes then recover to the recovery point. The process of recovery involves several steps, and it leverages the insight that any transactions in progress, by definition, belong to unvalidated checkpoints. First, the interconnection network is drained, and all state related to coherence transactions that were in progress at the time of the recovery is discarded. Second, processors, caches, and memories recover the RPCN checkpoints. Memories sequentially undo the actions in their CLBs. Processors restore their register checkpoints. Caches invalidate all blocks written or sent in an unvalidated checkpoint interval (i.e., blocks with non-null CNs) and undo the logged actions in their CLBs.

After recovery and reconfiguration (if needed), the service controllers broadcast a restart message to instruct the nodes to resume operation. The restart cannot begin until every node has finished its recovery. As with coordination to validate checkpoints, we implement a 2-phase coordination where every node informs the system service controllers once it is ready to restart and then the service controllers broadcast the restart message.

3.7 Summary of Implementation

We have developed an implementation of the *SafetyNet* abstraction that addresses the three challenges that were raised for logging schemes. First, we exploit checkpoint granularity to reduce the amount of logging necessary. Second, we efficiently coordinate checkpoints across the system in a logical time base that is loosely tied to physical time. Third, we enable checkpoint validation to be performed in the background, thus hiding the potentially lengthy latency of fault detection. To achieve these features, we made limited changes to the processor and the coherence protocol.

This implementation required three changes to the processor and L1 cache. First, the processor must be able to checkpoint its register state. This is not performance-critical, since it is infrequent, and copying out registers is straightforward if it does not need to be fast (we will assume 100 cycles in later results). Second, we must be able to copy old versions of blocks out of the cache before overwriting or transferring them. This increases cache bandwidth, but we will show in Section 4.3 that the increase is a small fraction. Third, we add CNs to L1 cache blocks, to enable optimized logging.

This implementation also required three changes to the underlying directory coherence protocol. First, we add checkpoint numbers on data response messages, so that the requestor knows the transaction's point of atomicity. Second, we allow both directories and processors to nack coherence requests, in order to avoid filling a CLB. Third, a three-hop transaction requires a final acknowledgment from the requestor to the directory (to inform the directory of the transaction's point of atomicity).

4 Evaluation

In this section, we evaluate *SafetyNet*. We begin in Section 4.1 by describing our methodology. Then, in Section 4.2, we quantitatively determine *SafetyNet* performance by running three experiments in which we compare the performance of *SafetyNet* versus that of an unprotected system. We seek to determine the impact of *SafetyNet* on fault-free performance and to determine how *SafetyNet* behaves in the presence of hard and soft faults. Lastly, in Section 4.3, we perform sensitivity analyses on the amount of cache bandwidth and CLB storage that *SafetyNet* uses.

4.1 Methodology

We simulate a 16-processor target system with the Simics full-system, multiprocessor, functional simulator [29], and we extend Simics with a memory hierarchy simulator to compute execution times. We evaluate *SafetyNet* with four commercial workloads and one scientific workload.

Table 2. Target System Parameters

L1 Cache (I and D)	128 KB, 4-way set associative
L2 Cache	4 MB, 4-way set-associative
Memory	2 GB, 64 byte blocks
Miss From Memory	180 ns (uncontended, 2-hop)
Checkpoint Log Buffer	512 kbytes total, 72 byte entries
Interconnection Network	2D torus, link b/w = 6.4 GB/sec
Checkpoint Interval	100,000 cycles = 100 μsec

Simics. Simics is a system-level architectural simulator developed by Virtutech AB. We use Simics/sun4u, which simulates Sun Microsystems's SPARC V9 platform architecture (e.g., used for Sun E6000s) in sufficient detail to boot unmodified Solaris 8. Simics is a functional simulator only, and it assumes that each instruction takes one cycle to execute (although I/O may take longer), but it provides an interface to support detailed memory hierarchy simulation.

Processor Model. We use Simics to model a processor core that, given a perfect memory system, would execute four billion instructions per second and generate blocking requests to the cache hierarchy and beyond. We use this simple processor model to enable tractable simulation times for full-system simulation of commercial workloads. While an out-of-order processor model might have an impact on the absolute values of the results, it would not qualitatively change them (e.g., whether a crash is avoided). For evaluating overhead for checkpointing register state, we model a conservative latency of 100 cycles. We conservatively charge eight cycles for logging store overwrites (8 bytes/cycle for 64 byte cache blocks), but these are only about 0.1% of instructions.

Memory Model. We have implemented a memory hierarchy simulator that supports a MOSI directory protocol, similar to that of the SGI Origin, with and without *Safety-Net* support. The simulator captures all state transitions (including transient states) of our coherence protocols in the cache and memory controllers. We model a 2D torus interconnection and the contention within this interconnect, including contention due to validation coordination messages. In Table 2, we present the design parameters of our target memory system. With a checkpoint interval of 100,000 cycles and four outstanding checkpoints, *Safety-Net* can tolerate fault detection latencies up to 400,000 cycles (0.4 msec at 1GHz). To exercise the protocol implementation, we drove it for billions of cycles with a random tester that injected faults and stressed corner cases by exploiting false sharing and reordering messages [47]. Using a methodology described by Alameldeen et al. [2], we simulate each design point multiple times with small, pseudo-random perturbations of memory latencies to cause

Table 3. Workloads

OLTP: Our OLTP workload is based on the TPC-C v3.0 benchmark using IBM's DB2 v7.2 EEE database management system. We use a 1 GB 10-warehouse database stored on five raw disks and an additional dedicated database log disk. There are 8 simulated users per processor. We warm up for 10,000 transactions, and we run for 500 transactions.

Java Server: SPECjbb2000 is a server-side java benchmark that models a 3-tier system with driver threads. We used Sun's HotSpot 1.4.0 Server JVM. Our experiments use 24 threads and 24 warehouses (~500 MB of data). We warm up for 100,000 transactions, and we run for 50,000 transactions.

Static Web Server: We use Apache 1.3.19 (www.apache.org) for SPARC/Solaris 8, configured to use pthread locks and minimal logging as the web server. We use SURGE [6] to generate web requests. We use a repository of 2,000 files (totalling ~50 MB). There are 10 simulated users per processor. We warm up for ~80,000 requests, and we run for 5000 requests.

Dynamic Web Server: Slashcode is based on a dynamic web message posting system used by slashdot.com. We use Slashcode 2.0, Apache 1.3.20, and Apache's mod_perl 1.25 module for the web server. MySQL 3.23.39 is the database engine. The database is a snapshot of slashcode.com, and it contains ~3,000 messages. A multithreaded driver simulates browsing and posting behavior for 3 users per processor. We warm up for 240 transactions, and we run for 50 transactions.

Scientific Application: We use *barnes-hut* from the SPLASH-2 suite [46], with the 16K body input set. We measure from the start of the parallel phase to avoid measuring thread forking.

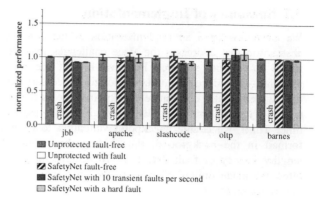

Figure 5. Performance Evaluation of *SafetyNet*

alternative scheduling paths. Error bars in our results represent one standard deviation in each direction.

Workloads. Commercial applications are an important workload for high availability systems. As such, we evaluate *SafetyNet* with four commercial applications and one scientific application, described briefly in Table 3 and in more detail by Alameldeen et al. [2].

4.2 Experiments

We perform three experiments to evaluate *SafetyNet* performance and show the results in Figure 5. For each workload, we plot five bars: two bars for systems unprotected by *SafetyNet* and three bars for systems with *SafetyNet*.

Experiment 1: Fault-Free Performance. In this experiment, we run two systems, *SafetyNet* and a similar system that is unprotected by *SafetyNet*, in a fault-free environment. In Figure 5, the first and the third bars (from the left) for each workload reflect the normalized performances of the unprotected system and *SafetyNet*, respectively. We observe that the two systems perform statistically similarly for all workloads. Intuitively, *SafetyNet* does not impact common case actions, such as loads and stores that do not

require logging. Overheads due to register checkpointing (every 100,000 cycles) and stores that require logging (0.1% of all instructions) are negligible, and back pressure due to filling up the CLBs is rarely needed. We present sensitivity analysis of CLB sizing in Section 4.3.

Experiment 2: Dropped Messages. In this experiment, we periodically inject transient faults into the system by dropping a message every 100 million cycles (i.e., ten times per second). The requestor times out on its request and triggers recovery. The second "bar" reflects the unprotected system performance (crash). The fourth bar from the right represents *SafetyNet* behavior, and we see that it is statistically similar to the fault-free scenario.[4]

The exact recovery latency is not critical, since *SafetyNet*'s recovery latency is orders of magnitude shorter than the latency of crashing and rebooting (and also preserves data integrity). Recovery latency consists of discarding unvalidated checkpoint state, restoring the state from the recovery point, re-configuring if necessary (e.g., changing the routing to avoid a dead switch), and re-executing the work that was lost between the recovery point and the fault. Re-executing lost work is the dominant factor, since the recovery point can be hundreds of thousands of cycles in the past. *SafetyNet* can tolerate longer fault detection latencies with less frequent (i.e., larger) checkpoints, at the cost of more potential lost work. Nevertheless, even a one million cycle recovery latency is still only one millisecond (i.e., much shorter than a crash).

Experiment 3: Lost Switch. In this experiment, we inject a hard fault into an interconnection network switch after one million cycles, killing the half-switch and dropping its buffered messages. The second "bar" reflects the crash of

---

4. The variability for the static web server and OLTP workloads is high enough to erroneously suggest, if one considers only mean values, that *SafetyNet* performs better when faults are injected.

the unprotected system. The fifth bar reflects *SafetyNet* performance, and we observe that, most importantly, *SafetyNet* avoids a crash. Performance suffers, with respect to the fault-free case, due to restricted post-fault bandwidth.

4.3 Sensitivity Analyses

To explore *SafetyNet*'s sensitivity to implementation parameters, we present analyses of *SafetyNet*'s usage of cache bandwidth and the impact of CLB sizing.

Cache Bandwidth. *SafetyNet*'s additional consumption of cache bandwidth depends on the frequencies of stores that require logging. These stores consume additional cache bandwidth for reading out the old copy of the block. Logging due to transferring cache ownership, however, does not incur additional bandwidth, since the cache line must be read anyway. In Figure 6, for the static web server workload[5], we plot this frequency as a function of the checkpoint interval. Both axes use log scales. Distinguishing between all stores and only those stores that require logging, we notice the drop-off in the latter as the checkpoint interval increases. These trends are the same for the other workloads, and the intuition is that spatial and temporal locality reduce the number of distinct blocks touched per interval. For an interval of 100,000 cycles, only 2-3% of stores (less than 0.1% of all instructions) require logging. In Figure 7, for the static web server workload, we plot the percentage of cache bandwidth used by cache hits, cache fills, responding to coherence requests, and logging due to store overwrites. The additional cache bandwidth used by *SafetyNet* ranges from 0.3% for million cycle intervals up to 4% for short 5,000 cycle intervals.

Storage Cost. An implementation of *SafetyNet* seeks to size the CLBs to avoid performance degradation due to full CLBs. Total CLB storage is proportional to the number of allowable checkpoints and the number of entries per checkpoint. We allow for four checkpoints and a CLB entry is 72 bytes (8-byte address and 64-byte data block). The number of entries per checkpoint corresponds to logging frequency which is, in turn, a function of the frequencies of stores and coherence requests. Figure 6 shows that, on average, only about 100-150 CLB entries are created per 100,000 instructions (although the variance in this rate requires more storage). In Figure 8, we plot the performance of *SafetyNet* as a function of CLB size. While 512 kbyte and 1 Mbyte CLBs produce statistically equivalent performances across the workloads, 256 kbyte CLBs degrade the performances of *jbb* and *apache*, and 128 kbyte CLBs degrade the performances of all of our workloads.

---

5. We only present the results for the static web server, but these results are qualitatively the same for all of our other workloads.

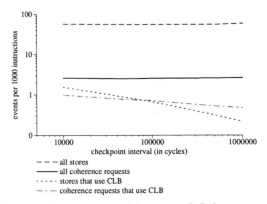

Figure 6. Frequencies of Stores and Coherence Requests (Static Web Server Workload)

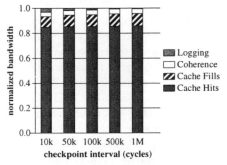

Figure 7. Bandwidth vs. Checkpoint Interval (Static Web Server Workload)

We do not claim that 512 kbyte CLBs are sufficient for all workloads or all design points. These workloads are necessarily scaled to enable tractable simulation times, and larger workloads may place more pressure on the CLBs. However, the primary determinants of CLB usage are the checkpoint interval length and the program behavior, and not the cache sizes. This is because logging occurs the first time a block is overwritten or transferred outside of the node during an interval, but not for transfers between caches within a given node.

5 Discussion

To this point, this paper has explained how *SafetyNet* can enable a recovery after the detection of a lost message or failed switch fault. Most generally, *SafetyNet* can enable recovery for any fault that does not corrupt ECC architectural state, provided that:

- a system can be augmented with a mechanism to detect the fault (or sign off on its absence),
- and faults are detected while *SafetyNet* still maintains a fault-free recovery point.

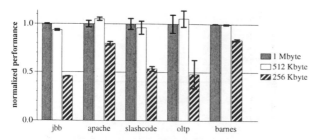

Figure 8. Performance vs. CLB Size

We now discuss other faults, including those that *SafetyNet* can tolerate, those for which other schemes are sufficient, and faults in the *SafetyNet* hardware itself.

5.1 Tolerating Other Faults with *SafetyNet*

This section considers additional faults, in the interconnection network and coherence protocol, that *SafetyNet* could tolerate. A typical interconnection network fault model focuses on link errors, trying to detect single, double, or burst errors. Link errors are normally detected with error detecting codes, such as parity, SECDED, or cyclic redundancy check (CRC) [14, 33]. Current systems, such as the SGI Origin's Spider router [18], use short codes (e.g., on 8 or 16 bytes), since the code must be checked before data is forwarded or used. *SafetyNet* permits longer, and inherently stronger, codes because of its ability to tolerate long detection latencies. *SafetyNet* is also compatible with other fault models, such as lost and misrouted messages (detected with timeouts), corrupted internal switch state (detected with error detecting codes), and switch controller malfunction (detected with internal consistency checks).

There are numerous soft faults in the protocol engine that can be tolerated with global checkpoint/recovery. This class of faults includes sending the wrong message or sending duplicate messages, as well as faults in the reception of messages. *SafetyNet* also could be used to recover from design faults in the protocol, if they could be detected reliably [9, 17] and would not keep recurring after recovery (leading to livelock).

5.2 Faults Tolerated with Existing Schemes

Processor faults can be detected with numerous schemes, including parity, redundant ALUs, and redundant threads [35, 37, 42]. Localized recovery schemes, including DIVA [4], can tolerate processor faults, but *SafetyNet* combined with processor fault detection provides a unified mechanism to tolerate these and other faults.

Fault tolerance schemes for memory, both SRAM and DRAM, are already well-established, and we present the fault model and prior detection techniques for complete-

ness. Detecting faults in storage cells can be accomplished with error detecting codes. A system with *SafetyNet* has to protect the cache hierarchy and memory with ECC, since they contain memory blocks that could potentially be the only valid copies in the system, so an uncorrectable fault could be unrecoverable. Memory chip kills can be tolerated by using a RAID-like scheme for DRAM [13].

5.3 *SafetyNet* Hardware Faults

The *SafetyNet* hardware itself is also susceptible to faults, and we target single fault instances. We ensure that the service controller is not a single point of failure by using redundant controllers. The other possible single point of failure is in the communication of validation messages, but a dropped or corrupted validation message will lead to a timeout and recovery. Most other faults in the *SafetyNet* hardware only manifest themselves during a recovery, which implies a double fault situation.

6 Related Work

Related research exists in fault tolerance, as well as in logging for speculation and versioning of data. Prior work in fault tolerance can be classified into two broad categories: backward error recovery (BER) and forward error recovery (FER). Among other differences, the evaluation of *SafetyNet* also advances previous work in fault tolerance by using full-system simulation of commercial workloads.

Hardware Backward Error Recovery. In BER schemes, the state of the system is checkpointed periodically (or differences are logged), and a fault is tolerated by recovering to a pre-fault checkpoint. IBM mainframes [23, 40] use register checkpoint hardware and store-through caches to recover from processor and memory system errors, respectively. The CARER scheme [24] for uniprocessors uses a normal cache with a writeback update policy to assist rapid rollback recovery. Checkpointed system state is maintained in main memory, and checkpoints are established whenever a modified cache block needs to be replaced. Ahmed et al. [1] extend CARER for multiprocessors by synchronizing the processors whenever one needs to take a checkpoint. Wu et al.'s [48] multiprocessor extension of CARER allows a processor to write into its cache between checkpoints. Checkpointing, which flushes all modified blocks, is performed when ownership of a block modified since the last checkpoint changes. *SafetyNet* is more efficient, since it does not checkpoint before every ownership transfer. The Sequoia system [7] uses caches to hold state between checkpoints, and flushes dirty cache blocks to memory at every checkpoint. Banâtre et al. [5] describe a Recoverable Shared Memory module that requires a shadow copy of the entire memory and a mechanism for maintaining the interprocessor dependence graph.

Software Backward Error Recovery. Software checkpointing has also been used, but at radically different engineering costs. In Tandem NonStop machines, every process periodically checkpoints its state on another processor [38]. Work by Plank [32] and Wang and Hwang [44] uses software to periodically checkpoint applications to aid fault tolerance. These schemes differ in the degree of support required from the programmer, libraries, and operating system. At the link level, SCI [25] supports software retry of dropped or corrupted messages. *SafetyNet* differs from these works in that it is a hardware solution.

(Hardware) Forward Error Recovery. FER schemes use redundant hardware to mask faults. For example, redundant processors [4, 26, 27, 45] or redundant threads within a processor [42] can be used to mask processor faults. Redundant paths through adaptive networks allow packets to be routed around faults [12, 14]. The Intel 432 [27] uses replication of commodity parts to achieve a range of fault tolerance needs. The Stratus [45] computer system uses pair-and-spare processors, and the Tandem S2 [26] uses triply modular redundant (TMR) processors, for masking faults. Slipstream [42] is a lighter-weight processor scheme that uses redundant threads within a processor to mask faults. DIVA [4] uses a checker processor to implement FER on the processor (but not on the system).

Speculation and Versioning of Data. Prior research for supporting speculation has logged changes in state that is local to a node [19, 34]. *SafetyNet*'s logging is similar, although it must also log transfers of coherence ownership in our global scheme. Speculative multithreading schemes use versioning to implement sequential program semantics [11, 20, 30, 41]. Our goal differs in that we superimpose checkpoints on system execution with *parallel semantics*, to support availability. We use globally consistent checkpoints rather than local checkpoints at different places in a sequential execution.

7 Conclusions

In this paper, we develop a scheme, called *SafetyNet*, that improves the availability of shared memory multiprocessors. We describe an implementation of *SafetyNet*, and we demonstrate that it adds little performance overhead and has reasonable storage costs. In developing *SafetyNet*, this paper makes three contributions which allow *SafetyNet* to be efficient in the common case of fault free execution.

- *SafetyNet* adds no latency to the common case of 99.9% of all instructions.

- *SafetyNet* hides the latency of fault detection by pipelining the validation of checkpoints. The system can continue to execute while it determines if old checkpoints can be validated.

- *SafetyNet* efficiently coordinates checkpoint creation in logical time, without having to either quiesce the system or exchange synchronization messages.

We see interesting avenues for future work. First, one could use *SafetyNet* to tolerate many of the faults discussed in Section 5 by developing suitable detection mechanisms. Since *SafetyNet* provides recovery for long-latency detection mechanisms, we can focus on stronger, high-latency codes and signatures. Second, one could use *SafetyNet* to tolerate harder faults, such as the loss of architectural state in a processor-cache chip kill. However, this alternative design will achieve this higher level of fault-tolerance for increased overheads in time, space, and/or cost.

Acknowledgments

We would like to thank the Wisconsin Multifacet group, Virtutech AB, the Wisconsin Condor group, Jim Goodman, Peter Hsu, Alain Kägi, Mikko Lipasti, Mark Oskin, Ravi Rajwar, Kewal Saluja, Bob Zak, and Craig Zilles.

References

[1] R. E. Ahmed, R. C. Frazier, and P. N. Marinos. Cache-Aided Rollback Error Recovery (CARER) Algorithms for Shared-Memory Multiprocessor Systems. In *Proceedings of the 20th International Symposium on Fault-Tolerant Computing Systems*, pages 82–88, June 1990.

[2] A. R. Alameldeen, C. J. Mauer, M. Xu, P. J. Harper, M. M. Martin, D. J. Sorin, M. D. Hill, and D. A. Wood. Evaluating Non-deterministic Multi-threaded Commercial Workloads. In *Proceedings of the Fifth Workshop on Computer Architecture Evaluation Using Commercial Workloads*, pages 30–38, Feb. 2002.

[3] R. Anglada and A. Rubio. An Approach to Crosstalk Effect Analyses and Avoidance Techniques in Digital CMOS VLSI Circuits. *International Journal of Electronics*, 6(5):9–17, 1988.

[4] T. M. Austin. DIVA: A Reliable Substrate for Deep Submicron Microarchitecture Design. In *Proceedings of the 32nd Annual IEEE/ACM International Symposium on Microarchitecture*, pages 196–207, Nov. 1999.

[5] M. Banâtre, A. Gefflaut, P. Joubert, P. Lee, and C. Morin. An Architecture for Tolerating Processor Failures in Shared-Memory Multiprocessors. *IEEE Transactions on Computers*, 45(10):1101–1115, Oct. 1996.

[6] P. Barford and M. Crovella. Generating Representative Web Workloads for Network and Server Performance Evaluation. In *Proceedings of the 1998 ACM Sigmetrics Conference on Measurement and Modeling of Computer Systems*, pages 151–160, June 1998.

[7] P. Bernstein. Sequoia: A Fault-Tolerant Tightly Coupled Multiprocessor for Transaction Processing. *IEEE Computer*, 21(2), Feb. 1988.

[8] M. Bohr. Interconnect Scaling - The Real Limiter to High Performance. In *Proceedings of the International Electron Devices Meeting*, pages 241–244, Dec. 1995.

[9] J. F. Cantin, M. H. Lipasti, and J. E. Smith. Dynamic Verification of Cache Coherence Protocols. In *Workshop on Memory Performance Issues*, June 2001. In conjunction with ISCA.

[10] A. Charlesworth. Starfire: Extending the SMP Envelope. *IEEE Micro*, 18(1):39–49, Jan/Feb 1998.

[11] M. Cintra, J. Martinez, and J. Torrellas. Architectural Support for Scalable Speculative Parallelization in Shared-Memory Systems. In *Proceedings of the 27th Annual International Symposium on Computer Architecture*, June 2000.

[12] W. J. Dally, L. R. Dennison, D. Harris, K. Kan, and T. Xanthopoulos. Architecture and Implementation of the Reliable Router. In *Proceedings of 2nd Hot Interconnects Symposium*, Aug. 1994.

[13] T. J. Dell. A White Paper on the Benefits of Chipkill-Correct ECC for PC Server Main Memory. IBM Microelectronics Division Whitepaper, Nov. 1997.

[14] J. Duato, S. Yalamanchili, and L. Ni. *Interconnection Networks*. IEEE Computer Society Press, 1997.

[15] E. Elnozahy, D. Johnson, and Y. Wang. A Survey of Rollback-Recovery Protocols in Message-Passing Systems. Technical Report CMU-CS-96-181, Department of Computer Science, Carnegie Mellon University, Sept. 1996.

[16] E. Elnozahy and W. Zwaenepoel. Manetho: Transparent Rollback-Recovery with Low Overhead, Limited Rollback, and Fast Output Commit. *IEEE Transactions on Computers*, 41(5):526–531, May 1992.

[17] S. J. Frank. Tightly Coupled Multiprocessor System Speeds Memory-access Times. *Electronics*, 57(1):164–169, Jan. 1984.

[18] M. Galles. Spider: A High-Speed Network Interconnect. *IEEE Micro*, 17(1):34–39, Jan/Feb 1997.

[19] C. Gniady, B. Falsafi, and T. Vijaykumar. Is SC + ILP = RC? In *Proceedings of the 26th Annual International Symposium on Computer Architecture*, pages 162–171, May 1999.

[20] S. Gopal, T. Vijaykumar, J. E. Smith, and G. S. Sohi. Speculative Versioning Cache. In *Proceedings of the Fourth IEEE Symposium on High-Performance Computer Architecture*, pages 195–205, Feb. 1998.

[21] G. Grohoski. Reining in Complexity. *IEEE Computer*, pages 41–42, Jan. 1998.

[22] R. Gupta. The Fuzzy Barrier: A Mechanism for High Speed Synchronization of Processors. In *Proceedings of the Third International Conference on Architectural Support for Programming Languages and Operating Systems*, pages 54–63, Apr. 1989.

[23] R. Gustafson and F. Sparacio. IBM 3081 Processor Unit: Design Considerations and Design Process. *IBM Journal of Research and Development*, 26:12–21, Jan. 1982.

[24] D. Hunt and P. Marinos. A General Purpose Cache-Aided Rollback Error Recovery (CARER) Technique. In *Proceedings of the 17th International Symposium on Fault-Tolerant Computing Systems*, pages 170–175, 1987.

[25] IEEE Computer Society. *IEEE Standard for Scalable Coherent Interface (SCI)*, Aug. 1993.

[26] D. Jewett. Integrity S2: A Fault-Tolerant UNIX Platform. In *Proceedings of the 21st International Symposium on Fault-Tolerant Computing Systems*, pages 512–519, June 1991.

[27] D. Johnson. The Intel 432: A VLSI Architecture for Fault-Tolerant Computing. *IEEE Computer*, pages 40–48, Aug. 1984.

[28] T. Juhnke and H. Klar. Calculation of the Soft Error Rate of Submicron CMOS Logic Circuits. *IEEE Journal of Solid-State Circuits*, 30(7):830–834, July 1995.

[29] P. S. Magnusson et al. Simics: A Full System Simulation Platform. *IEEE Computer*, 35(2):50–58, Feb. 2002.

[30] J. Oplinger, D. Heine, S.-W. Liao, B. A. Nayfeh, M. S. Lam, and K. Olukotun. Software and Hardware for Exploiting Speculative Parallelism with a Multiprocessor. Technical Report CSL-TR-97-715, Stanford University, May 1997.

[31] D. A. Patterson, G. Gibson, and R. H. Katz. A Case for Redundant Arrays of Inexpensive Disks (RAID). In *Proceedings of 1988 ACM SIGMOD Conference*, June 1988.

[32] J. S. Plank, K. Li, and M. A. Puening. Diskless Checkpointing. *IEEE Transactions on Parallel and Distributed Systems*, 9(10):972–986, Oct. 1998.

[33] D. K. Pradhan. *Fault-Tolerant Computer System Design*. Prentice-Hall, Inc., 1996.

[34] P. Ranganathan, V. S. Pai, and S. V. Adve. Using Speculative Retirement and Larger Instruction Windows to Narrow the Performance Gap between Memory Consistency Models. In *Proceedings of the Ninth ACM Symposium on Parallel Algorithms and Architectures*, pages 199–210, June 1997.

[35] S. K. Reinhardt and S. S. Mukherjee. Transient Fault Detection via Simultaneous Multithreading. In *Proceedings of the 27th Annual International Symposium on Computer Architecture*, pages 25–36, June 2000.

[36] J. Robertson. Alpha Particles Worry IC Makers as Device Features Keep Shrinking. *Semiconductor Business News*, October 21, 1998.

[37] E. Rotenberg. AR-SMT: A Microarchitectural Approach to Fault Tolerance in Microprocessors. In *Proceedings of the 29th International Symposium on Fault-Tolerant Computing Systems*, pages 84–91, June 1999.

[38] O. Serlin. Fault-Tolerant Systems in Commercial Applications. *IEEE Computer*, pages 19–30, Aug. 1984.

[39] K. Seshan, T. Maloney, and K. Wu. The Quality and Reliability of Intel's Quarter Micron Process. *Intel Technology Journal*, Sept. 1998.

[40] L. Spainhower and T. A. Gregg. IBM S/390 Parallel Enterprise Server G5 Fault Tolerance: A Historical Perspective. *IBM Journal of Research and Development*, 43(5/6), September/November 1999.

[41] J. G. Steffan and T. C. Mowry. The Potential for Using Thread-Level Data Speculation to Facilitate Automatic Parallelization. In *Proceedings of the Fourth IEEE Symposium on High-Performance Computer Architecture*, Feb. 1998.

[42] K. Sundaramoorthy, Z. Purser, and E. Rotenberg. Slipstream Processors: Improving both Performance and Fault Tolerance. In *Proceedings of the Ninth International Conference on Architectural Support for Programming Languages and Operating Systems*, Nov. 2000.

[43] M. Tremblay. Increasing Work, Pushing the Clock. *IEEE Computer*, pages 40–41, Jan. 1998.

[44] Y.-M. Wang, Y. Huang, K.-P. Vo, P.-Y. Chung, and C. Kintala. Checkpointing and Its Applications. In *Proceedings of the 25th International Symposium on Fault-Tolerant Computing Systems*, pages 22–31, June 1995.

[45] D. Wilson. The Stratus Computer System. In *Resilient Computer Systems*, pages 208–231, 1985.

[46] S. C. Woo et al. The SPLASH-2 Programs: Characterization and Methodological Considerations. In *Proceedings of the 22nd Annual International Symposium on Computer Architecture*, pages 24–37, June 1995.

[47] D. A. Wood, G. A. Gibson, and R. H. Katz. Verifying a Multiprocessor Cache Controller Using Random Test Generation. *IEEE Design and Test of Computers*, Aug. 1990.

[48] K. Wu, W. K. Fuchs, and J. H. Patel. Error Recovery in Shared Memory Multiprocessors Using Private Caches. *IEEE Transactions on Parallel and Distributed Systems*, 1(2):231–240, Apr. 1990.

[49] J. Ziegler et al. IBM Experiments in Soft Fails in Computer Electronics. *IBM Journal of Research and Development*, 40(1):3–18, Jan. 1996.

Session 4: Power Aware Architecture

Dynamic Fine-Grain Leakage Reduction Using Leakage-Biased Bitlines

Seongmoo Heo, Kenneth Barr, Mark Hampton, and Krste Asanović

MIT Laboratory for Computer Science
200 Technology Square, Cambridge, MA 02139
E-mail: {heomoo,kbarr,mhampton,krste}@lcs.mit.edu

Abstract

Leakage power is dominated by critical paths, and hence dynamic deactivation of fast transistors can yield large savings. We introduce metrics for comparing fine-grain dynamic deactivation techniques that include the effects of deactivation energy and startup latencies, as well as long-term leakage current. We present a new circuit-level technique for leakage current reduction, leakage-biased bitlines, that has low deactivation energy and fast wakeup times. We show how this technique can be applied at a fine grain within an active microprocessor, and how microarchitectural scheduling policies can improve its performance. Using leakage-biased bitlines to deactivate SRAM read paths within I-cache memories saves over 24% of leakage energy and 22% of total I-cache energy when using a 70 nm process. In the register file, fine-grained read port deactivation saves nearly 50% of leakage energy and 22% of total energy. Independently, turning off idle register file subbanks saves over 67% of leakage energy (57% total register file energy) with no loss in performance.

1. Introduction

Energy dissipation has emerged as a primary design constraint for all microprocessors, from those in portable devices to those in high-performance servers and mainframes. Until recently, the primary source of energy dissipation in digital CMOS circuits has been the dynamic switching of load capacitances. The continuing reduction in feature size reduces capacitance and the accompanying reductions in supply voltage help to further reduce the dynamic switching energy per operation. To maintain performance scaling, threshold voltages must also be scaled along with supply voltage. But lowering threshold voltage increases leakage current exponentially, and within a few process generations it is predicted energy dissipation from static leakage current could be comparable to dynamic switching energy [4, 5]. The trend toward ever more complex microprocessors fur-

ther exacerbates the situation, as large numbers of transistors are added for relatively small improvements in performance. These additional transistors may dissipate considerable leakage power even when not actively switching.

We can divide previous approaches to reducing leakage power into two categories. Techniques that trade increased circuit delay for reduced leakage current include: conventional transistor sizing, lower Vdd [32, 30], stacked gates [25, 35, 9], longer channels [23], higher threshold voltages [19, 34, 21, 13, 1], and thicker T_{ox}; we collectively refer to these as statically-selected slow transistors (SSSTs). Techniques for dynamic run-time deactivation of fast transistors include body biasing [24, 17, 18, 20, 15], sleep transistors [24, 29, 13, 11, 16], and sleep vectors [35, 9]; we collectively refer to these as dynamically-deactivated fast transistors (DDFTs). SSSTs and DDFTs are complementary approaches: SSSTs reduce leakage on non-critical paths and DDFTs reduce leakage on critical paths. Both can be simultaneously applied to yield larger overall savings [12].

Although many leakage-reduction techniques are implemented at the circuit or device level, architects have considerable scope to influence processor leakage power [3]. One approach is to increase the use of SSSTs by finding additional parallelism, so that a given throughput can be achieved with a larger parallel array of units built with slower, less-leaky transistors, rather than with a smaller number of lower-latency units built with faster but leaky transistors. Unfortunately, available parallelism is limited in single-threaded general-purpose applications, and much of the complexity of modern microprocessors is due to the difficulties of finding such parallelism.

Alternatively, architects can focus on finding opportunities to exploit DDFTs, whereby fast, leaky circuits are deactivated when not required. This approach can potentially maintain the lowest latency for applications with little parallelism, while reducing leakage power to acceptable levels. The difficulty with this approach is that most existing circuit techniques for DDFTs are only effective at reducing leakage energy if a circuit block will be inactive for a long time. This limits the scope for applying DDFTs within an active processor, where some blocks may only be inactive for a small number of cycles.

In this paper, we introduce a new DDFT circuit technique for reducing leakage power in memory arrays, *leakage-biased bitlines* (LBB). LBB uses leakage currents themselves to bias the bitlines of unused memory subbanks into a low-leakage state. LBB need have no performance impact and has very low transition energy overheads, and can convert even short idle times into leakage energy savings.

We apply LBB to the instruction cache and register file of an out-of-order superscalar microprocessor using predicted process parameters from 180 nm to 70 nm technology generations. For the instruction cache in 70 nm technology, we save 24% of leakage energy, or 22% of total energy, with a maximum performance penalty of 2.5%. For register files, we exploit idleness in two spatial dimensions: we deactivate subbanks when their registers are unused saving over 57% of register file energy. We also deactivate unused read ports when there is not enough parallelism to keep them busy. We save nearly 50% of leakage energy, or around 20% of total register file energy in this fashion, with no loss in performance and minimal area overhead.

This paper is organized as follows. Sections 2 and 3 review previous work in SSFT and DDFT techniques respectively. Section 4 presents the metrics we use to compare DDFT techniques. We show how some existing DDFT techniques require long idle times to be effective because of the large energy overhead of transitioning into a low-leakage state. Section 5 describes how we estimated the process parameters for future process technologies. Section 6 introduces leakage-biased bitlines and describes how we apply it to an instruction cache. Section 7 describes how we apply LBB to multiport register files. Section 8 discusses the results from our evaluation, and Section 9 concludes the paper.

2. Statically-Selected Slow Transistors

SSST techniques replace fast transistors with slow transistors on non-critical paths. This has been common design practice for many decades, where traditional transistor sizing reduces transistor gate width on non-critical paths to reduce parasitic load on critical nodes and to save switching power. Leakage is proportional to gate width, and so these narrower transistors also have lower leakage. Non-critical paths also use slower, more complex gate topologies to reduce area. These more complex gates have deeper transistor stacks, which also reduces leakage.

As leakage power increases, further techniques are being considered for non-critical paths. Leakage decreases superlinearly with gate length and a small increase in transistor length away from minimum can give a significant reduction in leakage current with a small impact on delay. Accord-

ingly, the designers of the StrongARM-1 slightly lengthened cache and pad transistors to reduce leakage in standby mode, yielding a five-fold reduction in leakage with only a small performance penalty [23]. The Alpha 21164 used this approach to control the effects of leakage on dynamic gates [8]. Lengthening gates is only effective for a small increment in channel length, and has the disadvantage of increasing active power because of increased gate capacitance.

At the expense of additional mask processing steps, it is possible to manufacture transistors with several different threshold voltages on the same die. By using slower, high-threshold transistors on non-critical paths it is possible to reduce leakage current without impacting performance [34]. Even though most transistors are non-critical, the achievable leakage reduction is limited, because the non-critical transistors have already been reduced in width and stacked into complex gates and hence have low leakage.

3. Dynamically-Deactivated Fast Transistors

After application of SSST techniques to non-critical paths, leakage is even more highly concentrated in the critical path transistors. One example is a recent embedded PowerPC 750, which employs three threshold voltages: high, standard, and low. The low threshold transistors account for only 5% of the total transistor width, but around 50% of the total leakage [7]. Several techniques have been developed to reduce leakage current from transistors on the critical path. Unlike SSST techniques, where non-critical path transistors are made permanently slower to reduce leakage, DDFT techniques attempt to dynamically switch critical path transistors between fast, leaky, active operation and inactive low-leakage states.

One DDFT technique, popular in low-power processors for portable devices, is a dynamically varying body bias to modulate transistor threshold voltages [24, 29, 13, 11, 16]. Reverse body biasing, by setting the p-well voltage higher than Vdd and the n-well voltage lower than GND, increases V_T because of the body effect, thereby reducing leakage current. This technique requires twin or triple well processes and therefore increases manufacturing costs. A variation on the body biasing approach is to fabricate high-V_T transistors then actively *forward* bias the wells during normal operation to lower V_T [22]. In the idle state, the forward bias is removed returning the transistors to their natural high-V_T state. Other advantages of this technique are that it has less threshold variation than using low-V_T devices directly, and hence can allow higher speed operation for a given leakage current budget [22]. Because of the large capacitance and distributed resistance of the wells, charging or discharging the well has a relatively high time constant and dissipates considerable energy. To allow the latency and

138

energy costs of transitioning into the low leakage state to be amortized, these schemes are used when the processor enters a sleep state where it will be idle for at least $0.1-100\,\mu s$ [28, 17, 30].

An alternative DDFT approach is power gating [24, 29, 13, 11, 16]. The power supply to circuits can be cut off by inserting a high V_T *sleep transistor* between Vdd and virtual Vdd (or GND and virtual GND). When turned off, the sleep transistor adds an extra high-V_T transistor in series with the logic transistors, dramatically reducing leakage current. Some of the disadvantages of sleep transistors are that they add additional impedance in the power supply network which reduces circuit speed, they require additional area and routing resources for the virtual power supply nets, and they may consume considerable deactivation energy to switch between active and inactive states. By sizing the sleep transistor [13], boosting the gate voltage for the sleep transistor [11], or forward-biasing the sleep transistor [16], the delay penalty can be reduced in exchange for greater sleep leakage currents and increased deactivation energy.

Another interesting DDFT technique exploits the fact that the leakage current of a block depends on the input pattern and internal state [35, 9]. A *sleep vector* is a combination of input patterns and internal state which minimizes the leakage current, and is applied by forcing internal latches into the correct state and forcing inputs to the correct polarity. However, the application of the sleep vector can require additional circuitry, which reduces performance, and can cause spurious circuit switching, which results in significant deactivation energy.

All DDFT circuits require a policy to decide when to switch to a low-leakage mode. Current microprocessors use a simple policy, usually implemented by the operating system, whereby the entire processor is deactivated when it enters a sleep mode. This coarse-grain policy cannot reduce active mode leakage power.

A few researchers have proposed more fine-grained deactivation techniques that place portions of an active processor into low-leakage states. The dynamically-resized instruction cache [26] uses a virtual-GND power gate to supply power to just enough RAM subbanks to hold the active working set of the current application. An adaptive hardware algorithm is used to determine an adequate cache capacity by monitoring miss rates as the active partition size is varied. This scheme is more complex than using leakage-biased bitlines, and is limited to a direct-mapped instruction cache, but reduces leakage further as both storage cell and access port leakage is cut off. Cache decay [14] dynamically predicts which cache blocks are unlikely to be accessed in the near future, marks them invalid, then powers them down using a power gate. Both of these techniques have long deactivation times of thousands of cy-

cles. Hamzaoglu et al. briefly describe a "precharge-as-needed" scheme [10], apparently similar to our leakage-biased bitlines, but do not describe the dynamic transient effects of the leakage reduction or the use of this technique within a microprocessor. Zhang et al. [36] explored the use of compiler-controlled dynamic leakage reduction mechanisms in a VLIW processor using sleep vectors and sleep transistors.

For more general application of DDFT techniques within an active microprocessor, it is necessary to have circuit techniques that make it worthwhile to deactivate a circuit block for short periods of time, and microarchitectural mechanisms that can detect, or force, a block into an idle state.

4. Comparing DDFT Techniques

The goal of applying a fine-grain DDFT technique is to reduce total processor energy. When attempting to deactivate a block for a short period of time, the performance and energy impacts of entering and leaving the low-leakage state must be considered. Figure 1 introduces the different parameters we use to compare DDFT techniques.

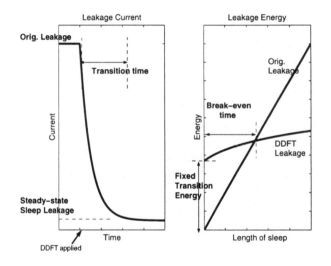

Figure 1. Transition time, steady-state leakage current, and break-even time of DDFT leakage-reduction techniques.

The left-hand side of Figure 1 shows the evolution of leakage current over time on entering the deactivated state. Once deactivated, a block requires some time to reach the lowest leakage state. For example, a substrate biasing scheme will require time to bias the wells, and a virtual-GND scheme requires time for leakage currents to charge up the virtual-GND node. During the transition, leakage current can be substantially higher than in the steady state. For clarity, this graph only shows the leakage current. When switching into and out of the low-leakage state there can be substantial switching current spikes.

Switching between active and deactivated modes requires additional transition energy, for example, to switch the gates of power-gating transistors or to charge and discharge well capacitances. The right-hand side of Figure 1 illustrates how we compare the overall energy consumed over time when idling in a normal, high-leakage state versus transitioning into a low-leakage state. The original idle leakage energy is shown by the straight line which rises at a constant rate dependent on the leakage current. On the same graph, we show an example curve for a DDFT technique. The fixed energy costs of first moving to the low-leakage state, then moving back to the active state, are summed to give the fixed transition energy cost. In addition to the fixed transition energy, there may be additional variable transition energy costs proportional to the time that the block is deactivated. For example, in a virtual GND scheme, the virtual GND node is slowly charged over the transition time. The amount of energy dissipated when the block wakes up and discharges the virtual GND depends on the idle time. These variable transition energy costs are factored into the energy curve. The curve rises more steeply initially during the transition time, where variable transition energy costs are being incurred and as leakage current drops to its steady state value. After the transition time, the energy curve rises more slowly, as only the steady-state leakage current is being dissipated.

We define the break-even time as the time at which the two curves cross, i.e., when the leakage energy of remaining in an active idle state matches the energy consumed when switching to the DDFT low-leakage state. The circuit must be idle for considerably longer than the break-even time to save significant energy.

Another important factor in comparing DDFT techniques is the wakeup latency (not shown). The wakeup latency is the time for a block to become usable after being in an inactive state. Faster wakeup time is usually preferable to faster transition time because it reduces any performance penalty. Wakeup latency can sometimes be traded for transition energy, for example, using a wider transistor to accelerate discharge of a biased well increases the transition energy to switch the transistor.

Although DDFT techniques do not use slower transistors to reduce leakage power, some DDFT techniques affect the delay and power of the active state. For example, the NMOS sleep transistor technique causes virtual GND to be a slightly higher potential than GND and so the circuit is somewhat slower.

5. Process Technologies

To evaluate our DDFT techniques, we used models of four dual-V_T processes, including 180 nm, 130 nm, 100 nm, and 70 nm process generations. The 180 nm high-V_T and low-V_T transistors were modeled after 0.18 μm TSMC low-leakage and medium-V_T processes respectively. The parameters of the 180 nm process were scaled to future technologies using the SIA roadmap [6]. For example, the SIA roadmap predicts that I_{on} remains the same, but I_{off} jumps twice for each technology generation. Because of the difficulty in predicting future leakage numbers, we bracket our results using our own pessimistic and optimistic estimates of how leakage currents will scale. The pessimistic estimates assume 4× leakage increase per generation while the optimistic estimates assume 2× leakage increase per generation. Important parameters of the processes are summarized in Table 1. We only considered subthreshold leakage in our estimates; although gate leakage might become significant at some point in these technology generations, it is also likely that new gate dielectrics will make gate leakage insignificant again. We believe future leakage currents might be considerably higher that even our pessimistic numbers indicate, as these are based on a low-leakage, moderate-performance base case.

Table 1. Process parameters.

Parameter (nm)	180	130	100	70
Vdd (V)	1.8	1.5	1.2	0.9
Temp (Celsius)	100	100	100	100
FO4 delay (ps)	61.1	47.4	36.7	24.0
16 FO4 freq. (GHz)	1.0	1.3	1.7	2.6
LVT I_{on} (μA/μm)	732	732	732	732
LVT I_{off} (nA/μm) (optimistic)	21.8	43.6	87.2	174
LVT I_{off} (nA/μm) (pessimistic)	21.8	87.2	349	1395
HVT I_{on} (μA/μm)	554	554	554	554
HVT I_{off} (nA/μm) (optimistic)	0.35	0.71	1.42	2.83
HVT I_{off} (nA/μm) (pessimistic)	0.35	1.42	5.68	22.6

Based on the table, we estimated the scaling of active and leakage power for circuits. The results are shown in Figure 2, where numbers are normalized to the 180 nm process. It is important to note that leakage power per transistor increases significantly although Vdd and the total area of the circuit decreases. The active power is decreasing quadratically as expected from constant field scaling. If the leakage power was 10% of the total power at the 180 nm process, it will increase to 47-87% for the 70 nm process if the circuit is scaled unchanged. In practice, devices, circuits, and microarchitectures will be redesigned to limit leakage to a manageable fraction of total power. The techniques in this paper can be used to help keep leakage current within this budget without sacrificing performance.

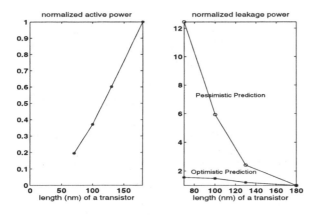

Figure 2. Normalized active and leakage power for different processes.

6. Leakage-Biased Bitlines for Caches

The L1 caches of microprocessor can cause significant leakage current, as they contain a large number of transistors which must be high-speed to avoid impacting processor performance. Figure 3 shows the structure of an L1 cache SRAM cell together with the two primary leakage current paths when the word line is off. One leakage path, L_1, is from the precharged bit-line, through the access transistor, and across the turned-on n-type pull-down. The other leakage path, L_2, is from the enabled p-type pullup to the turned-off n-type in the cross-coupled inverters. The pullup transistors have been made high-V_T so that there is negligible leakage current across the turned-off p-type ($L_3 \simeq 0$), and the access and pulldown transistors have been made low-V_T to maintain circuit speed. The current through the leakage path, L_4, is insignificant since the path has two turned-off transistors and the V_{DS} of the access transistor is zero.

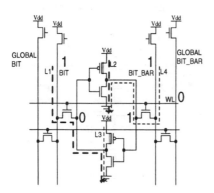

Figure 3. A dual-V_T SRAM cell. High V_T transistors are shaded.

With technology scaling, the leakage currents from non-accessed bits will reduce the effective signal from the accessed bit, requiring that SRAMs have fewer cells connected to each bitline segment to obtain sufficient noise margin. We assume that only 32 bit cells are attached to each local bitline within a subbank, and that these local bitlines are connected through pass-transistor switches to a global bitline which in turn connects to the senseamp.

A key observation is that the leakage current, L_1, from each bitline into the cell depends on the stored value on that side of the cell; there is effectively no leakage if the bitline is at the same value as that stored in the cell (L_4). We might consider using a sleep vector on the bitlines to force the SRAM subbank into a low leakage state. For example, it is known that there are usually more zeros than ones stored in a cache [33], so if we force the true bitline to a zero value while keeping the complement bitline precharged, we could statistically reduce the bitline leakage of an inactive cache subbank. There are two disadvantages to this approach. First, if the percentage of zero bits is under 50%, the sleep vector technique *increases* leakage energy. Second, this technique requires additional transition energy to force the bitlines into and out of the sleep vector state.

We have developed a simple circuit technique, *leakage-biased bitlines* (LBB), that reduces bitline leakage current due to the access transistors of these structures with minimal transition energy and wakeup time. Rather than force zero sleep values onto the read bit lines of inactive subbanks, this technique just lets the bitlines float by turning off the high-V_T NMOS precharging transistors. The leakage currents from the bit cells *automatically* bias the bitline to a mid-rail voltage that minimizes the bitline leakage current. If all the cells store a zero, the leakage currents will fully discharge the non-inverted bitline ("BIT" in Figure 3) while the inverted bitline ("BITBAR") will be held high. If all the cells store a one, the non-inverted bitline will be held high and the inverted bitline will discharge. For a mix of ones and zeros, the leakage currents bias the bitline at an appropriate midrail voltage to minimize leakage. Although the bitline floats to mid-rail, it is disconnected from the senseamp by the local-global bitline switch, so there is no static current draw. This technique has little additional transition energy because the precharge transistor switches exactly the same number of times as in a conventional SRAM—we only delay the precharge until the subbank needs to be accessed. The wakeup latency is just that of the precharge phase.

Figure 4 compares the steady-state leakage power of the leakage-biased bitline and the forced-zero/forced-one sleep vector techniques with the original leakage power for a 32-row×16B SRAM subarray with varying numbers of stored ones and zeros. It is clear that the leakage-biased bitline technique has the lowest leakage power independent of stored bit values.

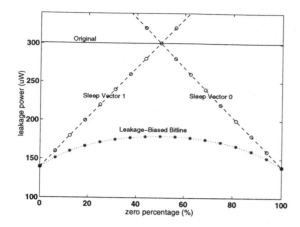

Figure 4. The leakage power of 32-row×16B SRAM subbank for forced-zero and forced-one sleep vectors and leakage-biased bitlines versus percentage of stored zero bits.

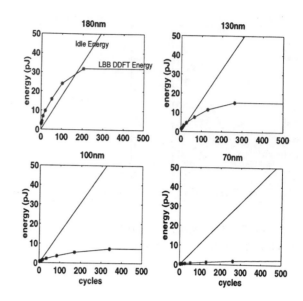

Figure 5. Idle energy and LBB DDFT energy of 32-row×32B SRAM subbank for different processes (optimistic leakage current was used).

Figure 5 compares the cumulative idle energy and the LBB DDFT energy consumption for different processes. The LBB DDFT technique must replace the lost charge on the bitline before the attached memory cells can be used. The break-even time, is around 200 cycles in a 180 nm process. However, since active energy scales down faster than leakage energy, the break-even time decreases with feature size. In a 70 nm process, the break-even time is less than one cycle.

Each subbank must be precharged before use, which will add latency to the cache access if the subbank is not known in time. We focus in this paper on the application of LBB DFFT technique to the processor instruction cache, because of its predictable access pattern. For an N-way set-associative cache structure, each way consists of some number of subbanks and we access N subbanks in parallel, where each subbank returns a fetch group of instructions. In the most optimistic case, we can assume that the simple subbank decode happens sufficiently before the more complex word-line decode to allow precharge to complete before word-line drive; in this case, there would be no performance penalty. In the most pessimistic case, we can assume that the additional precharge latency adds an additional cycle to the fetch pipeline, and hence increases the branch misprediction penalty by one cycle.

7. LBB for Multiport Register Files

Multiport register files can also consume considerable leakage power. For example, in the proposed Alpha 21464 design, the multiported register file was several times larger than the 64 KB primary caches [27]. Figure 6 shows an

8-read port, 4-write port, register file cell. Because there are many leakage paths in a multiport register file cell, we chose a baseline design that was already optimized for leakage power. The cell has a high-V_T storage cell connected to multiple low-V_T single-ended read ports. The write ports are not as latency critical and so these access transistors are high-V_T. To reduce active and leakage energy further, we make the cell asymmetrical, with all read ports arranged so that if the cell stores a zero, the single-ended bitline is not discharged [31]. Our experiments showed that around 75% of the bits read from the register file are zero.

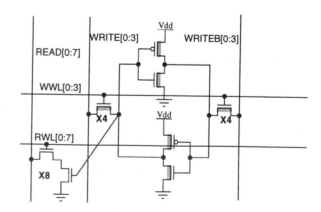

Figure 6. An embedded dual V_T unbalanced 8-read, 4-write register file cell. High V_T transistors are shaded.

As with the cache SRAM, the register file array is divided into subbanks with local bitlines connected to global bitlines to save switching energy and to increase speed and noise margin. The LBB technique can be applied to the single-ended read port bitlines. By turning off the precharger on an idle subbank read port, leakage currents will discharge the bitlines towards ground if any bits are holding a one, reducing bit line leakage current significantly. If the dead time is long enough, the energy overhead to precharge the bitline before an access becomes relatively small compared to the leakage energy saved. Note that this technique does not corrupt the state stored in the register file. Figure 7 shows the hierarchical bitlines and a modified column cell for the LBB multiported register file.

We deactivate read ports using two orthogonal techniques. The first deactivates dead registers whose contents are not needed. We exploit the fact that in a superscalar machine with register renaming, the contents of a physical register are not needed from the time the register enters the free list until the time it is next written. If all the registers in a subbank are dead, then all subbank read ports can be turned off. Because the register is allocated in the decode stage of the pipeline and written to several cycles later (and before any read access), there is ample time to precharge the floating bitline with no performance impact.

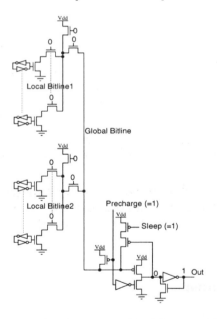

Figure 7. Leakage-biased bitline scheme for multiported register file. Each local bitline can be left unprecharged, biased by local leakage currents.

As a comparison, we considered an alternative DDFT approach to turn off dead registers using a virtual-GND sleep transistor (Figure 8). This approach has the advantage that registers can be turned off individually, rather than a subbank at a time, but has the disadvantage that the read access time increases due to the sleep transistor in the pull-down path. The delay penalty can be reduced by increasing the size of the sleep transistor, but this also increases the steady-state leakage current and the transition energy. We sized the sleep transistor to give an overall 5% slowdown.

The second technique deactivates idle read ports. In a superscalar machine, when fewer than the maximum number of instructions issue, some register file read ports will be idle. There is no performance impact when the port is reactivated because it is known whether a read port is needed before it is known which register will be accessed in the pipeline. The port precharge time can be overlapped with register file address decode.

Table 2 shows the energy consumption when reading/writing 32-bit zeros or ones from the 32×32-bit register file with the unbalanced embedded dual V_T cells. All read/write energy numbers are per single read/write port. The energy consumption for 180 nm was measured using Hspice simulation and those for other processes were scaled using Figure 2. The average read and write energy numbers were calculated assuming 75% of values stored in the register files and write data are zero and that the values are statistically independent. The total active energy consumption is simply the sum of total read energy and total write energy.

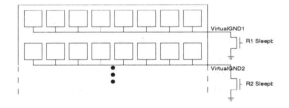

Figure 8. Idle register deactivation scheme using NMOS high V_T sleep transistors.

Table 3 shows the steady-state leakage power when different leakage techniques are applied to the register file and the idle leakage power of the original circuit for different processes. We again assumed 75% of the bits in the register file are zeros when measuring the leakage power. We also include numbers for the sleep vector fixed-zeros technique. All three techniques, sleep vector (SV), leakage-biased bitline (LBB), and NMOS sleep transistor (NST) reduce the leakage power to less than 1.5% of the original idle power when in the steady state.

Figure 9 shows the sleep-time dependent energy consumption of the register file DDFT techniques across the set of process technologies. We can see that all of the DDFT techniques become applicable at shorter time scales as transistors scale down. This is partly because leakage current

Table 2. The active read and write energy consumption of 32×32b multiported register file subbank for different processes.

tr. length(nm)	180	130	100	70
zero read E(pJ)	6.0	2.9	1.4	0.5
one read E(pJ)	17.3	8.2	4.0	1.4
avg. read E(pJ) (E_r)	8.8	4.2	2.0	0.7
0-to-0 write E(pJ)	0.7	0.4	0.2	0.1
0-to-1 write E(pJ)	16.5	7.9	3.8	1.3
1-to-0 write E(pJ)	2.2	1.0	0.5	0.2
1-to-1 write E(pJ)	13.0	6.2	3.0	1.0
avg. write E(pJ) (E_w)	4.7	2.3	1.1	0.4

Table 3. The leakage power of 32×32-b multiported register file subbank (optimistic leakage current was used).

Process Tech. (nm)	180	130	100	70
Original (uW)	177.9	214.1	263.6	276.7
SV steady-state (uW)	2.0	2.4	3.0	3.1
LBB steady-state (uW)	2.0	2.4	3.0	3.1
NST steady-state (uW)	1.8	2.2	2.7	2.9

grows as a fraction of active power, but also partly because most of the transition energy cost scales with active power and so the relative overhead of switching is reduced. Figure 10 is an expanded view of the graph for the 70 nm process technology.

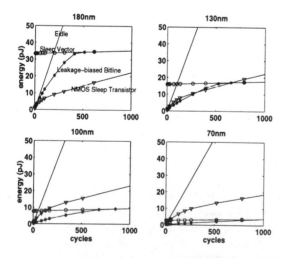

Figure 9. Sleep-time-dependent cumulative leakage energy of different register file DDFT techniques for different processes (optimistic leakage current was used).

We see that for the sleep vector technique, the break-even time is around 200 cycles at the 180 nm process, but shrinks to only 24 cycles in the 70 nm process. The sleep vector technique has high fixed transition energy costs, and so below the break-even time, the energy consumption is much higher than the original leakage energy.

For the leakage-biased bitline, the break-even time in the 180 nm process is only around 10 cycles. Moreover, the cumulative energy rises slowly from the initial deactivation time, and is not much larger than the original leakage before the break-even time. With technology scaling, the break-even time becomes less than a cycle and this technique can therefore give useful leakage energy savings even for a few cycles of dead time.

The NMOS sleep-transistor performs better than the leakage-biased bitlines in the coarser feature sizes, but suffers from a long transition time in the finer-pitch process technologies. The time taken to charge the virtual GND node leaves this scheme with higher cumulative leakage energy for small numbers of cycles in the 70 nm technology, though at large numbers of cycles the cumulative energy drops below that of the leakage-biased bitline scheme.

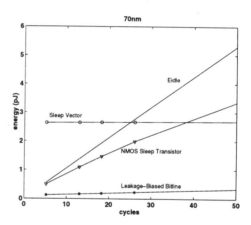

Figure 10. Expanded view of cumulative leakage energy in 70 nm process technology (optimistic leakage current was used).

8. Evaluation

In this section, we use detailed simulation of an out-of-order processor to estimate the energy savings that can be achieved by using DDFT techniques on instruction cache subbanks and a multiported register file.

8.1. Simulation Methodology

We instrumented SimpleScalar 3.0b [2], an out-of-order, superscalar processor simulator, to track the activity of the

144

Table 4. Simulated Processor Configuration

Issue Width	4
RUUs	64
Integer Physical Registers	100
Integer ALUs (Mult/Div)	4 (1)
FP ALUs (Mult/Div)	1 (1)
Load/Store Units	2
Load/Store Queue Depth	32
Instruction length	4 Bytes
I-Cache/D-Cache	16KB/4-Way/32B Block
Unified L2-Cache	256KB/4-Way/64B Block 6 cycle latency
Memory Latency	First access: 50 cycs. Subsequently: 2 cycs.

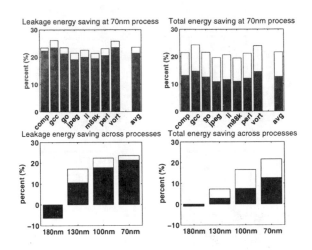

Figure 11. I-cache energy savings for sub-bank deactivation.

instruction cache and the physical register file. We obtained results for a four-wide issue machine with the configuration shown in Table 4. We also simulated a four-wide issue machine with 128 RUUs and performed cache simulation on an eight-wide issue machine with 256 RUUs, but the results were similar and thus we omit them for brevity. We used the SPECint95 benchmark suite and the benchmarks were run on their reference data sets until 100 million instructions had committed. In the figures that follow, black bars denote the optimistic assumptions of future leakage as described in Section 5. White bars denote the pessimistic view of the future (greater leakage).

8.2. Cache Subbank Deactivation Results

Figure 11 shows the energy savings achieved for the instruction cache subbank deactivation scheme. For the 180 nm generation, there is a net energy increase, but for all other process technologies there is a net energy savings. In the 70 nm generation, over 20% of total instruction cache energy is saved.

As discussed in Section 6 there can be a performance penalty from the additional precharge latency if the subbank precharge cannot be overlapped with the rest of the bank address decode. We modeled the effect of lengthening the fetch pipeline by one cycle to allow for subbank precharge, which increases branch misprediction latency from 3 to 4 cycles. Our results show that this decreases IPC by around 2.5% on average across all benchmarks. We note that this estimate of performance impact is highly pessimistic, as the precharge latency is much less than one cycle and the extended pipeline could be used to support a much larger instruction cache.

8.3. Dead Register Deactivation Results

To quantify energy saved by deactivating dead registers, we modified SimpleScalar to model a machine with a separate unified physical register file pool holding both committed architectural registers and renamed registers. We maintain a set of physical register tags which move between a free list and the register update units. We restricted our study to the integer register file. The number of physical registers is determined by the number of writable architected registers (fixed by the ISA at 33) plus the number of values that can be produced by in-flight instructions.

Figure 12 presents results for the dead register deactivation techniques. For reference, we present two variants of the NMOS sleep transistor (NST) technique. The two variants of NST are FIFO and LIFO free list policies. A FIFO policy (or circular queue) is the conventional free list policy, but a LIFO policy (stack) has the advantage of keeping some registers dead for very long times. Experiments with the 70 nm process reveal that LIFO gives an additional 2.4 to 10.0% savings over FIFO in terms of total register file energy saved. The figure also shows the benefits of LIFO increasing as feature size decreases.

We also show results for LBBs used in a subbanked register file, where a subbank's read ports are deactivated when all registers in the subbank are dead. The allocation policy is a stack of subbanks, where registers are allocated from a new bank only when the previous bank is empty. As shown in Figure 12, despite the increased granularity of deactivation, LBB is competitive with NST in terms of energy savings. Because the cumulative sleep energy of LBB circuits is less than that of NST circuits for the majority of sleep times encountered in practice, LBB outperforms NST by 31.5% for the worst case leakage. In addition, LBB has no

145

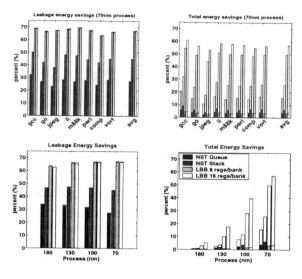

Figure 12. Register file energy savings by dead register deactivation.

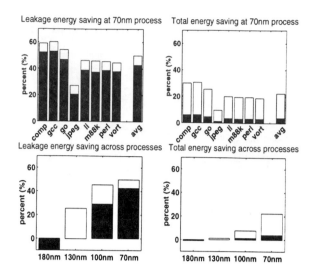

Figure 13. Register file energy savings by global read port deactivation.

performance penalty, whereas NST has a 5% performance slowdown. The figure also shows that having fewer registers per bank (eight rather than sixteen) allows deactivation at a finer granularity which translates to greater savings.

8.4. Regfile Global Read Port Deactivation Results

Figure 13 shows the energy savings achieved by deactivating the read ports. As with cache subbank deactivation, there is a net energy increase for the 180 nm generation, but for the remaining process technologies, there is a net energy savings. In the 70 nm generation, nearly half of the leakage energy is removed, resulting in a total register file energy savings of over 20% with no performance penalty.

As the processor's issue width increases, the peak number of read ports increases. However, IPC does not scale linearly with issue width, so in general a greater percentage of read ports will be idle. Thus, we expect the energy savings to be greater for wider-issue processors.

The savings from global read port deactivation can be combined with those from dead subbank deactivation, giving greater total energy savings while still avoiding any performance penalty.

9. Conclusion

Most leakage current is dissipated on critical paths, especially after slower, low-leakage transistors are used on non-critical paths. To reduce leakage energy further without impacting performance, it is desirable to dynamically deactivate the fast transistors on the critical path. This paper has shown that fine-grain leakage reduction techniques,

whereby a small piece of a processor is placed in a low-leakage state for a short amount of time, can yield significant energy savings in future process technologies. To attain savings, the circuit-level leakage reduction technique must have low transition energy and rapid wakeup times. We present leakage-biased bitlines, a circuit technique that has these properties. To exploit a DDFT technique, the microarchitecture must be designed to force blocks to be idle for multiple cycles and preferably to give early notice when the blocks are to be reawakened.

We have presented three applications of leakage-biased bitlines that apply these principles and have shown how they enable leakage current reductions in the context of a wide superscalar processor. SRAM read path deactivation saves over 22% of leakage energy and nearly 24% of total I-cache energy when using a 70 nm process. Dynamically deactivating idle registers reduces register file leakage energy by up to 67.1% and total register file energy by 57.1%. Dynamically deactivating read ports within a multiported register file saves 42.7-49.8% of leakage energy and 3.9-22.3% of total energy depending on the prediction of the future process. We are investigating further circuit techniques of this type for other components of a superscalar microprocessor.

10. Acknowledgments

We'd like to thank Christopher Batten, Ronny Krashinsky, Rajesh Kumar, and the anonymous reviewers for comments on earlier drafts. This work was funded by DARPA PAC/C award F30602-00-2-0562, NSF CAREER award CCR-0093354, and a donation from Infineon Technologies.

References

[1] M. Allarm, M. H. Anis, and M. I. Elmasry. High-speed dynamic logic styles for scaled-down CMOS and MTCMOS technologies. In *ISLPED*, pages 155–160, 2000.

[2] D. Burger and T. Austin. The SimpleScalar tool set, version 2.0. Technical Report CS-TR-97-1342, University of Wisconsin, Madison, June 1997.

[3] J. A. Butts and G. S. Sohi. A static power model for architects. In *MICRO-33*, pages 191–201, December 2000.

[4] A. Chandrakasan, W. J. Bowhill, and F. Fox. *Design of High Performance Microprocessor Circuits*. IEEE Press, 2000.

[5] V. De and S. Borkar. Technology and design challenges for low power and high performance. In *ISLPED*, pages 163–168, 1999.

[6] I. T. R. for Semiconductors. 2000 update, process integration, devices, and structures. Technical report, ITRS, 2000.

[7] S. Geissler et al. A low-power RISC microprocessor using dual PLLs in a 0.13 μm SOI technology with copper interconnect and low-k BEOL dielectric. In *ISSCC Digest*, February 2002.

[8] P. E. Gronowski et al. A 433-MHz 64-b quad-issue RISC microprocessor. *IEEE JSSC*, 31(11):1687–1696, November 1996.

[9] J. P. Halter and F. Najm. A gate-level leakage power reduction method for ultra-low-power CMOS circuis. In *Custom Integrated Circuits Conf.*, pages 457–478, 1997.

[10] F. Hamzaoglu et al. Dual-vt SRAM cells with full-swing single-ended bit line sensing for high-performance on-chip cache in 0.13 μm technology generation. In *ISLPED*, pages 15 – 19, 2000.

[11] T. Inukai. Boosted-gate MOS (BGMOS): Device/circuit co-operation scheme to achieve leakage-free giga-scale integration. In *Custom Integrated Circuits Conf.*, pages 409–412, 2000.

[12] M. C. Johnson, D. Somasekhar, L.-Y. Chiou, and K. Roy. Leakage control with efficient use of transistor stacks in single threshold cmos. In *IEEE Transactions on VLSI Systems*, February 2002.

[13] J. T. Kao and A. P. Chandrakasan. Dual-threshold voltage techniques for low-power digital circuits. *IEEE JSSC*, 35(7):1009–1018, July 2000.

[14] S. Kaxiras, Z. Hu, and M. Martonosi. Cache decay: exploiting generational behavior to reduce cache leakage power. In *ISCA 28*, pages 240–251, May 2001.

[15] A. Keshavarzi et al. Effectiveness of reverse body bias for leakage control in scaled dual Vt CMOS ICs. In *ISLPED*, pages 207–212, 2001.

[16] S. V. Kosonocky et al. Enhanced multi-threshold (MTC-MOS) circuits using variable well bias. In *ISLPED*, pages 165–169, 2001.

[17] T. Kuroda et al. A 0.9-V, 150-MHz, 10-mW, 4 mm^2, 2-D discrete cosine transform core processor with variable threshold-voltage (VT) scheme. *IEEE JSSC*, 31(11):1770–1779, November 1996.

[18] T. Kuroda et al. Variable supply-voltage scheme for low-power high-speed CMOS digital design. *IEEE JSSC*, 33(3):454–462, March 1998.

[19] W. Lee et al. A 1-V programmable DSP for wireless communications. *IEEE JSSC*, 32(11):1766–1776, November 1997.

[20] H. Makino et al. An auto-backgate-controlled MT-CMOS circuit. In *Symp. on VLSI Circuits*, pages 42–43, 1998.

[21] T. McPherson et al. 760MHz G6 S/390 microprocessor exploiting multiple Vt and copper interconnects. In *ISSCC Digest*, pages 96–97, 2000.

[22] M. Miyazaki et al. A 1000-MIPS/W microprocessor using speed-adaptive threshold-voltage CMOS with forward bias. In *ISSCC Digest*, pages 420–421, 2000.

[23] J. Montanaro et al. A 160-MHz, 32-b, 0.5-W CMOS RISC microprocessor. *IEEE JSSC*, 31(11):1703–1714, November 1996.

[24] S. Mutoh et al. 1-V power supply high-speed digital circuit technology with multithreshold-voltage CMOS. *IEEE JSSC*, 30(8):847–854, August 1995.

[25] S. Narendra et al. Scaling of stack effect and its application for leakage reduction. In *ISLPED*, pages 195–200, 2001.

[26] M. Powell et al. Gated Vdd: A circuit technique to reduce leakage in deep-submicron cache memories. In *ISLPED*, 2000.

[27] R. P. Preston et al. Design of an 8-wide superscalar RISC microprocessor with simultaneous multithreading. In *ISSCC Digest and Visuals Supplement*, February 2002.

[28] K. Seta et al. 50% active-power saving without speed degradation using standby power reduction (SPR) circuit. In *ISSCC Digest*, pages 318–319, 1995.

[29] S. Shigemasu et al. A 1-V high-speed MTCMOS circuit scheme for power-down application circuits. *IEEE JSSC*, 32(6):861–869, June 1997.

[30] M. Takahasi et al. A 60-mw MPEG4 video codec using clustered voltage scaling with variable supply-voltage scheme. *IEEE JSSC*, 33(11):1772–1778, November 1998.

[31] J. Tseng and K. Asanović. Energy-efficient register access. In *Proc. of the 13th Symposium on Integrated Circuits and Systems Design*, Manaus, Brazil, September 2000.

[32] K. Usami et al. Automated low-power technique exploiting multiple supply voltages applied to a media processor. *IEEE JSSC*, 33(3):463–471, March 1998.

[33] L. Villa, M. Zhang, and K. Asanović. Dynamic zero compression for cache energy reduction. In *MICRO-33*, 2000.

[34] L. Wei et al. Design and optimization of low voltage high performance dual threshold CMOS circuits. In *DAC*, pages 489–494, 1998.

[35] Y. Ye, S. Borkar, and V. De. A technique for standby leakage reduction in high-performance circuits. In *Symp. on VLSI Circuits*, pages 40–41, 1998.

[36] W. Zhang et al. Exploiting VLIW schedule slacks for dynamic and leakage energy reduction. In *MICRO-34*, December 2001.

Drowsy Caches: Simple Techniques for Reducing Leakage Power

Krisztián Flautner, Nam Sung Kim, Steve Martin, David Blaauw, Trevor Mudge

krisztian.flautner@arm.com
ARM Ltd
110 Fulbourn Road
Cambridge, UK CB1 9NJ

{kimns, stevenmm, blaauw, tnm}@eecs.umich.edu
Advanced Computer Architecture Lab
The University of Michigan
1301 Beal Ave. Ann Arbor, MI 48109-2122

Abstract

On-chip caches represent a sizable fraction of the total power consumption of microprocessors. Although large caches can significantly improve performance, they have the potential to increase power consumption. As feature sizes shrink, the dominant component of this power loss will be leakage. However, during a fixed period of time the activity in a cache is only centered on a small subset of the lines. This behavior can be exploited to cut the leakage power of large caches by putting the cold cache lines into a state preserving, low-power drowsy mode. Moving lines into and out of drowsy state incurs a slight performance loss. In this paper we investigate policies and circuit techniques for implementing drowsy caches. We show that with simple architectural techniques, about 80%-90% of the cache lines can be maintained in a drowsy state without affecting performance by more than 1%. According to our projections, in a 0.07um CMOS process, drowsy caches will be able to reduce the total energy (static and dynamic) consumed in the caches by 50%-75%. We also argue that the use of drowsy caches can simplify the design and control of low-leakage caches, and avoid the need to completely turn off selected cache lines and lose their state.

1. Introduction

Historically one of the advantages of CMOS over competing technologies (e.g. ECL) has been its lower power consumption. When not switching, CMOS transistors have, in the past, consumed negligible amounts of power. However, as the speed of these devices has increased along with density, so has their leakage (static) power consumption. We now estimate that it currently accounts for about 15%-20% of the total power on chips implemented in high-speed processes. Moreover, as processor technology moves below 0.1 micron, static power consumption is set to increase exponentially, setting static power consumption on the path to dominating the total power used by the CPU (see Figure 1).

Various circuit techniques have been proposed to deal with the leakage problem. These techniques either completely turn off circuits by creating a high-impedance path to ground (gating) or trade off increased execution time for reduced static power consumption. In some cases, these techniques can be implemented entirely at the circuit level

without any changes to the architecture or may involve only simple architectural modifications. The on-chip caches are one of the main candidates for leakage reduction since they contain a significant fraction of the processor's transistors.

Approaches for reducing static power consumption of caches by turning off cache lines using the gated-V_{DD} technique [1] have been described in [2][3]. These approaches reduce leakage power by selectively turning off cache lines that contain data that is not likely to be reused. The drawback of this approach is that the state of the cache line is lost when it is turned off and reloading it from the level 2 cache has the potential to negate any energy savings and have a significant impact on performance. To avoid these pitfalls, it is necessary to use complex adaptive algorithms and be conservative about which lines are turned off.

Turning off cache lines is not the only way that leakage energy can be reduced. Significant leakage reduction can also be achieved by putting a cache line into a low-power drowsy mode. When in drowsy mode, the information in the cache line is preserved; however, the line must be reinstated to a high-power mode before its contents can be accessed. One circuit technique for implementing drowsy caches is

FIGURE 1. Normalized leakage power through an inverter

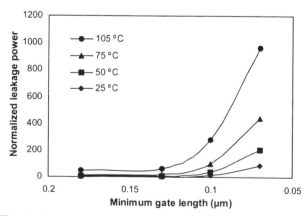

The circuit simulation parameters including threshold voltage were obtained from the Berkeley Predictive Spice Models [4]. The leakage power numbers were obtained by HSPICE simulations.

FIGURE 2. Implementation of the drowsy cache line

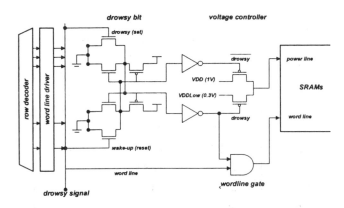

Note that, for simplicity, the word line, bit lines, and two pass transistors in the drowsy bit are not shown in this picture.

adaptive body-biasing with multi-threshold CMOS (ABB-MTCMOS) [5], where the threshold voltage of a cache line is increased dynamically to yield reduction in leakage energy. We propose a simpler and more effective circuit technique for implementing drowsy caches, where one can choose between two different supply voltages in each cache line. Such a dynamic voltage scaling or selection (DVS) technique has been used in the past to trade off dynamic power consumption and performance [6][7][8]. In this case, however, we exploit voltage scaling to reduce *static power* consumption. Due to short-channel effects in deep-submicron processes, leakage current reduces significantly with voltage scaling [9]. The combined effect of reduced leakage current and voltage yields a dramatic reduction in leakage power.

On a per-bit basis, drowsy caches do not reduce leakage energy as much as those that rely on gated-V_{DD}. However, we show that for the total power consumption of the cache, drowsy caches can get close to the theoretical minimum. This is because the fraction of total energy consumed by the drowsy cache in low power mode (after applying our algorithms) tends to be only about 25%. Reducing this fraction further may be possible but the pay-off is not great (Amdahl's Law). Moreover, since the penalty for waking up a drowsy line is relatively small (it requires little energy and only 1 or 2 cycles, depending on circuit parameters), cache lines can be put into drowsy mode more aggressively, thus saving more power.

Figure 2 shows the changes necessary for implementing a cache line that supports a drowsy mode. There are very few additions required to a standard cache line. The main additions are a drowsy bit, a mechanism for controlling the voltage to the memory cells, and a word line gating circuit. In order to support the drowsy mode, the cache line circuit includes two more transistors than the traditional memory circuit. The operating voltage of an array of memory cells in the cache line is determined by the voltage controller, which switches the array voltage between the high (active) and low (drowsy) supply voltages depending on the state of the drowsy bit. If a drowsy cache line is accessed, the drowsy bit is cleared, and consequently the supply voltage is switched to high V_{DD}. The wordline gating circuit is used to prevent accesses when in drowsy mode, since the supply voltage of the drowsy cache line is lower than the bit line precharge voltage; unchecked accesses to a drowsy line could destroy the memory's contents.

Whenever a cache line is accessed, the cache controller monitors the condition of the voltage of the cache line by reading the drowsy bit. If the accessed line is in normal mode, we can read the contents of the cache line without losing any performance. No performance penalty is incurred, because the power mode of the line can be checked by reading the drowsy bit concurrently with the read and comparison of the tag. However, if the memory array is in drowsy mode, we need to prevent the discharge of the bit lines of the memory array because it may read out incorrect data. The line is woken up automatically during the next cycle, and the data can be accessed during consecutive cycles.

In this paper we focus on the policy implications of using L1 drowsy data caches. Since, compared to the L1 cache, the impact of an extra cycle of wake-up on the L2 access latencies is small, all lines in an L2 cache can be kept in drowsy mode without significant impact on performance. This intuition is confirmed by the data presented in [10]. In Section 2 and Section 3 we evaluate the design trade-offs between simple drowsy policies. We argue that the simplest policy of periodically putting the entire cache into drowsy mode does about as well as a policy that tracks accesses to cache lines. Section 4 provides details about various circuit techniques for reducing leakage power and Section 5 evaluates the impact of drowsy caches on energy consumption.

2. Policies

The key difference between drowsy caches and caches that use gated-V_{DD} is that in drowsy caches the cost of being wrong—putting a line into drowsy mode that is accessed soon thereafter—is relatively small. The only penalty one must contend with is an additional delay and energy cost for having to wake up a drowsy line. One of the simplest policies that one might consider is one where, periodically, all lines in the cache—regardless of access patterns—are put into drowsy mode and a line is woken up only when it is accessed again. This policy requires only a single global counter and no per-line statistics. Table 1 shows the working set characteristics of some of our workloads using a 2000 cycle update window, meaning that all cache lines are put into drowsy mode every 2000 cycles. Observations of cache activity are made over this same period. Based on this information we can estimate how effective this simpleminded policy could be.

The results show that on most of the benchmarks the working set—the fraction of unique cache lines accessed during an update window—is relatively small. On most benchmarks more than 90% of the lines can be in drowsy mode at any one time. This has the potential to significantly reduce the static power consumption of the cache. The downside of the approach is that the wake-up cost has to be amortized over a relatively small number of accesses: between 7 and 21, depending on the benchmark.

TABLE 1. Working set and reuse characteristics

	Level 1 data cache 32K, 4-way, 32byte line, window size = 2000 cycles						
	Working set	Number of accesses	Accesses per line	Accesses per cycle	Fraction of accesses same as in the nth previous window		
					n=1	n=8	n=32
crafty	17.6%	1250.56	6.95	0.63	65.2%	54.9%	49.3%
vortex	10.8%	1209.07	10.89	0.60	54.3%	29.0%	31.0%
bzip	5.9%	1055.84	17.35	0.53	32.5%	19.7%	17.2%
vpr	9.2%	1438.69	15.27	0.72	62.2%	46.9%	45.6%
mcf	8.9%	1831.68	20.05	0.92	61.0%	60.8%	60.4%
parser	8.7%	971.73	10.85	0.49	46.9%	34.6%	28.4%
gcc	8.1%	809.69	9.78	0.40	36.9%	24.9%	21.1%
facerec	10.4%	970.04	9.15	0.49	37.4%	27.5%	33.6%
equake	7.0%	1513.27	21.09	0.76	92.8%	91.4%	90.7%
mesa	8.0%	1537.09	18.69	0.77	83.8%	76.8%	74.5%

$$ExecFactor = \frac{accs\left(\frac{wakelatency \times memimpact}{accsperline}\right) + (wsize - accs)}{wsize} \quad (EQ\ 1)$$

Equation 1 shows the formula for computing the expected worst-case execution time increase for the baseline algorithm. All variables except *memimpact* are directly from Table 1. The variable *accs* specifies the number of accesses, *wakelatency* the wakeup latency, *accsperline* the number of accesses per line, and *wsize* specifies the window size. Memimpact can be used to describe how much impact a single memory access has on overall performance. The simplifying assumption is that any increase in cache access latency translates directly into increased execution time, in which case memimpact is set to 1. Using this formula and assuming a 1 cycle wake-up latency, we get a maximum of 9% performance degradation for crafty and under 4% for equake. One can further refine the model by coming up with a more accurate value for memimpact. Its value is a function of both the microarchitecture and the workload:

- The workload determines the ratio of the number of memory accesses to instructions.
- The microarchitecture determines what fraction of wake-up transitions can be hidden, i.e., not translated into global performance degradation.
- The microarchitecture also has a significant bearing on IPC which in turn determines the number of memory accesses per cycle.

Assuming that half of the wake-up transition latencies can be hidden by the microarchitecture, and based on a ratio of 0.63 of memory accesses per cycle, the prediction for worst-case performance impact for the crafty benchmark reduces to 2.8%. Similarly, using the figure of 0.76 memory accesses per cycle and the same fraction of hidden wake-up transitions, we get a performance impact of about 1.4%. The actual impact of the baseline technique is likely to be significantly lower than the results from the analytical model, but

nonetheless, these results show that there is no need to look for prediction techniques to control the drowsy cache; as long as the drowsy cache can transition between drowsy and awake modes relatively quickly, simple algorithms should suffice.

The right side of Table 1 contains information about how quickly the working set of the workloads are changing. The results in the table specify what fraction of references in a window are to lines that had been accessed 1, 8, or 32 windows before. This information can be used to gauge the applicability of control policies that predict the working set of applications based on past accesses. As can be seen, on many benchmarks (e.g. bzip, gcc), a significant fraction of lines are not accessed again in a successive drowsy window, which implies that past accesses are not always a good indication of future use. Aside from the equake and mesa benchmarks, where past accesses do correlate well with

TABLE 2. Latencies of accessing lines in the drowsy cache

		Awake	Drowsy
Awake Tags	Hit	1 cycle	1 cycle - wake up line 1 cycle - read/write line
	Miss	1 cycle - find line to replace memory latency	1 cycle - find line to replace memory latency Overlapped with memory latency: wake up line.

		Awake	Drowsy
Drowsy Tags	Hit	1 cycle	1 cycle - time for possible awake hit 1 cycle - wake up drowsy lines in set 1 cycle - read/write line Off-path: put unneeded lines in set back to drowsy mode
		All lines in set are awake	Not all lines in set are awake
	Miss	1cycle - find line to replace memory latency Off-path: put unneeded lines in set back to drowsy mode	1cycle - time for possible awake hit 1cycle - wake up drowsy lines in set 1cycle - find line to replace memory latency Off-path: put unneeded lines in set back to drowsy mode

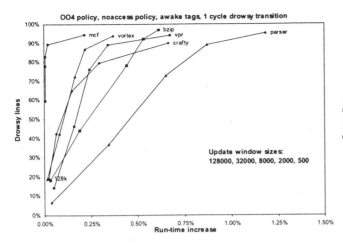

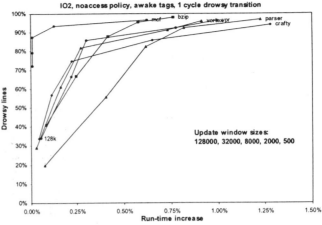

future accesses, most benchmarks only reaccess 40%-60% of the lines between windows. The implications of this observation are twofold: If an algorithm keeps track of which cache lines are accessed in a window, and only puts the ones into drowsy mode that have not been accessed in a certain number of past windows, then the number of awake to drowsy transitions per window can be reduced by about 50%. This in turn decreases the number of later wakeups, which reduces the impact on execution time. However, the impact on energy savings is negative since a larger fraction of lines are kept in full power mode, and in fact many of those lines will not be accessed for the next several windows, if at all.

Another important consideration is whether the tags are put into drowsy mode along with the data or whether they are always on. Table 2 shows the latencies associated with the different modes of operation. In both cases, no extra latencies are involved when an awake line is accessed. If tags are always on, then the cost of accessing a drowsy line is an additional cycle for waking it up first. Hits and misses are determined the same way as in normal caches. However, if tags—along with the data—can be drowsy, then the situation gets more complicated. Access hits to an awake cache line take a single cycle just as in the first case, however access hits to a drowsy line take a cycle longer. The reason for the extra delay is that during the first access cycle the cache is indexed, awake lines are read out and their tags are compared. If none of the awake tags match after the first read, then the controller wakes up all the drowsy lines in the indexed set and only then, an additional cycle later, can it read and compare the data. Thus, a drowsy access takes at least three cycles to complete. Another issue is that when drowsy lines are woken up in a set just so that their tags can be compared, they should be put back to sleep soon thereafter. It is not likely that these lines will be accessed soon, since in that case they would have been awake already. The controller can easily put these lines back into drowsy mode without having to wait for the sleep transition to complete.

Note that in direct-mapped caches there is no performance advantage to keeping the tags awake. There is only one possible line for each index, thus if that line is drowsy, it needs to be woken up immediately to be accessed.

3. Policy evaluation

In this section we evaluate the different policy configurations with respect to how they impact performance and the fraction of cache lines that are in drowsy mode during the execution of our benchmarks. All our algorithms work by periodically evaluating the contents of the cache and selectively putting lines into drowsy mode. The following parameters can be varied:

- *Update window size*: specifies in cycles how frequently decisions are made about which lines to put into drowsy mode.
- *Simple or Noaccess policy*: The policy that uses no per-line access history is referred to as the *simple* policy. In this case, all lines in the cache are put into drowsy mode periodically (the period is the window size). The *noaccess* policy means that only lines that have not been accessed in a window are put into drowsy mode.
- *Awake or drowsy tag*: specifies whether tags in the cache may be drowsy or not.
- *Transition time*: the number of cycles for waking up or putting to sleep cache lines. We only consider 1 or 2 cycle transition times, since our circuit simulations indicate that these are reasonable assumptions.

We use various benchmarks from the SPEC2000 suite on SimpleScalar using the Alpha instruction set to illustrate our points. Most of the results are shown using the out-of-order core in SimpleScalar. However, when appropriate we also show results for a simpler in-order core. The simulator configuration parameters are summarized below:

- *OO4*: 4-wide superscalar pipeline, 32K direct-mapped L1 icache, 32 byte line size - 1 cycle hit latency, 32K 4-way set associative L1 dcache, 32 byte line size - 1 cycle hit latency, 8 cycle L2 cache latency.
- *IO2*: 2-wide in-order pipeline, cache parameters same as for OO4.

All simulations were run for 1 billion instructions.

Figure 3 shows how window size impacts performance and the fraction of drowsy lines. For clarity, we are showing only a subset of the benchmarks. On an out-of-order core,

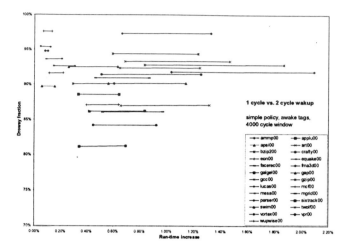

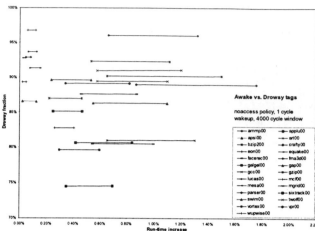

the sweetspot—where the energy-delay product is maximized—is around 2000 cycles. The same spot moves to between a window size of 4000 and 8000 cycles on the in-order core. The reason for this is that since the IPCs of the benchmarks using the IO2 model tend to be a little less than half as much as in the OO4 model, fewer memory accesses are made within the same amount of clock cycles. Since both the drowsy cache's run-time overhead and its effectiveness are correlated with the number of cache accesses within a window, comparable power-performance trade-off points are found at about twice the window size on the IO2 model as on OO4. Aside from the data for small window sizes, the two graphs look very similar.

The reason for the relatively small impact of the drowsy wake-up penalty on the in-order processor's performance is due to the non-blocking memory system, which can handle a number of outstanding loads and stores while continuing execution of independent instructions. Moreover, the drowsy wake-up penalty is usually only incurred with load instructions, since stores are put into a write buffer, which—if not full—allows execution to continue without having to wait for the completion of the store instruction.

The impact of increased transition latencies is shown in Figure 4. The top graph in the figure shows the impact of doubled wakeup latency using the *simple* policy, while the bottom graph shows the impact on the *noaccess* policy due to the use of drowsy tags. In both graphs, the two end points of a line represent the two different configurations of each benchmark. Both of the different types of overhead have similar impact on the given policy: the fraction of drowsy lines is unchanged, while the impact on run-time increases (the lines connecting the two points are horizontal and the points corresponding to the two cycle wakeup or the drowsy tags are always on the right). The run-time impact on the *simple* policy is larger compared to the *noaccess* policy, since a larger fraction of the cache is drowsy at any one time. Also note that for a given policy, the run-time overhead of using drowsy tags should be very similar to increasing the transition latency to two cycles. This is because both models increase the most common type of drowsy access—the drowsy hit—by the same amount.

Figure 5 contrasts the *noaccess* and the *simple* policies. The main question that we are trying to answer is whether there is a point to keeping any per-line statistics to guide drowsy decisions or if the indiscriminate approach is good enough. We show three different configurations for each benchmark on the graph: the *noaccess* policy with a 2000 cycle window and two configurations of the *simple* policy (4000 cycle and 2000 cycle windows). In all cases, the policy configurations follow each other from bottom to top in the aforementioned order. This means that in all cases, the *noaccess* policy has the smallest fraction of drowsy lines, which is to be expected, since it is conservative about which lines are put into drowsy mode. In all configurations, the performance impact is never more than 1.2% and the fraction of drowsy lines is never under 74%.

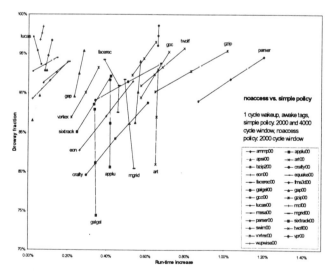

The bottom marker on each line corresponds to the *noaccess* policy with 2000 cycle window, the markers above it represent the *simple* policy with 4000 and 2000 cycle windows respectively

The benchmarks on the graph can be partitioned into two groups: ones on lines whose slopes are close to the vertical, and ones on lines that are more horizontal and thus have a smaller positive slope. All the benchmarks that are close to the vertical are floating point benchmarks and their orientation implies that there is very little or no performance benefit to using the *noaccess* policy or larger window sizes. In fact, the mgrid, galgel, applu, facerec, and lucas benchmarks have a slight negative slope, implying that not only would the simpler policy win on power savings, it would also win on performance. However, in all cases the performance difference is negligible and the potential power improvement is under 5%. The reason for this behavior is the very bad reuse characteristics of data accesses in these benchmarks. Thus keeping lines awake (i.e. *noaccess* policy, or larger window sizes) is unnecessary and even counterproductive.

This anomalous behavior is not replicated on the integer benchmarks, where in all cases the *noaccess* policy wins on performance but saves the least amount of power. Does this statement imply that if performance degradation is an issue then one should go with the more sophisticated *noaccess* policy? It does not. The slope between the upper two points on each line is almost always the same as the slope between the bottom two points, which implies that the rates of change between the datapoints of a benchmark are the same; the data point for the *noaccess* policy should be able to be matched by a different configuration of the *simple* policy. We ran experiments to verify this hypothesis and found that a window size of 8000 of the *simple* policy comes very close to the coordinates for the *noaccess* policy with a window size of 2000.

We find that the *simple* policy with a window size of 4000 cycles reaches a reasonable compromise between simplicity of implementation, power savings, and performance. The impact of this policy on leakage energy is evaluated in Section 5.

4. Circuit issues

Traditionally, two circuit techniques have been used to reduce leakage power in CMOS circuits: V_{DD}-gating and ABB-MTCMOS. Recently, both of these methods were applied to cache design as well [2][3][10]. In this paper, we instead propose the use of dynamic voltage scaling (DVS) for leakage control. While voltage scaling has seen extensive use for dynamic power reduction, short-channel effects also make it very effective for leakage reduction. Below, we discuss the traditional V_{DD}-gating and ABB-MTCMOS techniques for cache leakage reduction, as well as our proposed method using dynamic voltage scaling and a comparison between the different methods.

4.1 Gated-V_{DD}

The gated-V_{DD} structure was introduced in [1]. This technique reduces the leakage power by using a high threshold (high-V_t) transistor to turn off the power to the memory cell when the cell is set to low-power mode. This high-V_t device drastically reduces the leakage of the circuit because of the exponential dependence of leakage on V_t. While this method is very effective at reducing leakage, its main disadvantage lies in that it loses any information stored in the cell when switched into low-leakage mode. This means that a

significant performance penalty is incurred when data in the cell is accessed and more complex and conservative cache policies must be employed.

4.2 ABB-MTCMOS

The ABB-MTCMOS scheme was presented in [5]. In this method, the threshold voltages of the transistors in the cell are dynamically increased when the cell is set to drowsy mode by raising the source to body voltage of the transistors in the circuit. Consequently, this higher V_t reduces the leakage current while allowing the memory cell to maintain its state even in drowsy mode. However, to avoid the need for a twin-well process, the dynamic V_t scaling is accomplished by increasing the source of the NMOS devices and by increasing the body voltage of the wells of the PMOS devices significantly when the circuit is in drowsy mode. While the leakage current through the memory cell is reduced significantly in this scheme, the supply voltage of the circuit is increased, thereby offsetting some of the gain in total leakage power.

Also, this leakage reduction technique requires that the voltage of the N-well and of the power and ground supply lines are changed each time the circuit enters or exits drowsy mode. Since the N-well capacitance of the PMOS devices is quite significant, this increases the energy required to switch the cache cell to high-power mode and can also significantly increase the time needed to transition to/from drowsy mode. Similarly to the gated-V_{DD} technique, ABB-MTCMOS also requires special high-V_t devices for the control logic.

4.3 Dynamic V_{DD} Scaling (DVS)

The method proposed in this paper utilizes dynamic voltage scaling (DVS) to reduce the leakage power of cache cells. By scaling the voltage of the cell to approximately 1.5 times V_t, the state of the memory cell can be maintained. For a typical 0.07um process, this drowsy voltage is conservatively set to 0.3V. Due to the short-channel effects in high-performance processes, the leakage current will reduce dramatically with voltage scaling. Since both voltage and current are reduced in DVS, a dramatic reduction in leakage power can be obtained. Since the capacitance of the power rail is significantly less than the capacitance of the N-wells, the transition between the two power states occurs more

FIGURE 6. Schematic of the drowsy memory circuit

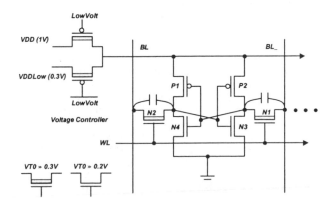

FIGURE 7. Leakage power reduction and performance

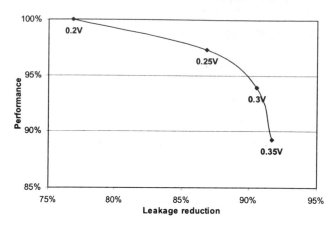

The figure shows various V_t numbers (next to the data points) and how these values impact performance and leakage reduction.

FIGURE 8. Cross-talk stability of the drowsy memory cell

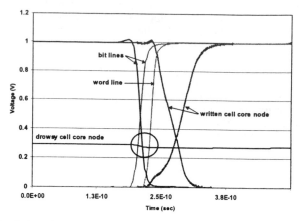

Simulation of a write operation to the normal mode (awake) memory cell adjacent to a drowsy memory cell.

quickly in the DVS scheme than the ABB-MTCMOS scheme.

Figure 6 illustrates the circuit schematic of memory cells connected to the voltage-scaling controller. High-V_t devices are used as the pass transistors that connect the memory's internal inverters to the read/write lines (N1 and N2). This is necessary because the read/write lines are maintained in high-power mode and the leakage through the pass transistors would be too large otherwise. One PMOS pass gate switch supplies the normal supply voltage and the other supplies the low supply voltage for the drowsy cache line. Each pass gate is a high-V_t device to prevent leakage current from the normal supply to the low supply through the two PMOS pass gate transistors. A separate voltage controller is needed for each cache line.

In determining the high-V_t value for the access transistors of the memory cell (N1 and N2) we must consider the leakage power reduction as well as the performance impact of using a high-V_t device. Figure 7 shows leakage power reduction versus performance impact for various V_t values. Our HSPICE simulations using access transistors with 0.2V V_t show that the portion of leakage power caused by the pass transistors is 16.78% and 71.77% for normal and low supply voltage modes respectively. These values are quite significant. As we increase V_t of the access transistors towards 0.35V, the leakage power decreases exponentially and it approaches the maximum reduction ratio (92.15%) that can be achieved by eliminating leakage current entirely through the access transistor.

To estimate the performance degradation from increasing V_t, we measured the delay from the word line assertion to the point where there is a 50mV voltage difference between two complementary bit lines using a netlist with extract capacitances. This voltage difference is the threshold for sense-amp activation. The value of 50mV was obtained by conservatively scaling the value used in the former memory design technology [11]. Clearly the delay is increased as the V_t is increased as shown in Figure 7, but the fraction of the delay from the word line activation to the sense-amp activation is only about 22% among other delay factors that

contribute to the total access time of the memory system, according to our CACTI calculations. We chose 0.3V for the high-V_t value because it results in a sensible trade-off point between performance loss (6.05%) and leakage reduction (91.98%). However, we can compensate for the performance loss by carefully tuning the size of the access and cross-coupled inverter transistors. We have not done so in this study because it may increase the dynamic power dissipation as a result of the increase in switching capacitance of the bit lines.

A possible disadvantage of the circuit in Figure 6 is that it has increased susceptibility to noise and the variation of V_t across process corners. The first problem may be corrected with careful layout because the capacitive coupling of the lines is small. To examine the stability of a memory cell in the low power mode, we simulated a write operation to an adjacent memory cell that shares the same bit lines but whose supply voltage was normal. The coupling capacitance and the large voltage swing across the bit lines would make the bit in the drowsy memory cell vulnerable to flipping if this circuit had a stability problem. However, our experiments show (Figure 8) that the state of the drowsy memory cell is stable. There is just a slight fluctuation in the core node voltage caused by the signal cross-talk between the bit lines and the memory internal nodes. In addition, there is no cross-talk noise between the word line and the internal node voltage, because word line gating prevents accesses to drowsy mode memory cells. Of course, this voltage scaling technique has less immunity against a single event upset (SEU) from alpha particles [12], but this problem can be relieved by process techniques such as silicon on insulator (SOI). Other static memory structures also suffer from this problem. The second problem, variation of V_t, may be handled by choosing a conservative VDD value, as we have done in our design.

The memory cell layout was done in TSMC 0.18um technology, which is the smallest feature size available to the academic community. The dimensions of our memory cell is 1.84um by 3.66um, and those for the voltage controller are 6.18um by 3.66um. We estimate the area overhead of the voltage controller is equivalent to 3.35 memory cells for

TABLE 3. Comparison of various low-leakage circuit techniques

	Advantages	Disadvantages	Leakage power in low power mode
DVS	• Retains cell information in low-power mode. • Fast switching between power modes. • Easy implementation. • More power reduction than ABB-MTCMOS.	• Process variation dependent. • More SEU noise susceptible.	6.24nW
ABB-MTCMOS	• Retains cell information in low-power mode.	• Higher leakage power. • Slower switching between power modes.	13.20nW
Gated-V_{DD}	• Largest power reduction. • Fast switching between power modes. • Easy implementation.	• Loses cell information in low-power mode.	0.02nW

a 64 x Leff (effective gate length) voltage controller. This relatively low area overhead can be achieved because the routing in the voltage controller is simple compared to the memory cell. In addition, we assumed the following (conservative) area overhead factors: 1) 1.5 equivalent memory cells for the drowsy bit (the 0.5 factor arises from the two additional transistors for set and reset); 2) 1 equivalent memory cell for the control signal driver (two inverters); and 3) 1.5 equivalent memory cells for the wordline gating circuit (a nand gate). The total overhead is thus equivalent to 7.35 memory cells per cache line. The total area overhead is less than 3% for the entire cache line. To examine the effects of circuit issues like stability and leakage power reduction, we applied a linear scaling technique to all the extracted capacitances.

In Table 3, we list the advantages and disadvantages for the two traditional circuit techniques for leakage reduction as well as for DVS, and we show the power consumption for the three schemes in both normal and low power mode. The leakage power in the gated-V_{DD} method is very small compared to the other schemes, however, this technique does not preserve the state of the cache cell. Comparing the DVS and ABB-MTCMOS techniques, the DVS method reduces leakage power by a factor of 12.5, while the ABB-MTCMOS method reduces leakage by only a factor of 5.9.

Detailed power values for drowsy mode and normal-power mode for the proposed method are shown in Table 4. In order to determine the time required to switch a cache line from drowsy mode to normal power mode, we measured the delay time of the supply lines with HSPICE and the Berkeley Predictive Model [4] for a 0.07um process. To measure the transition delay, we connected a 32KB memory cell array to the supply voltage controllers and then estimated the capacitances of the supply voltage metal line and bit lines. The transition delay varies depending on the transistor width of the pass gate switch in the voltage controller.

A 16 x Leff PMOS pass-transistor is needed for a two cycle transition delay. A single cycle transition delay can be obtained by increasing the width of this transistor to 64 x Leff. The cycle time of the cache was estimated using the CACTI model with the supported process scaling. We found that the access time of the cache is 0.57ns and that the transition time to and from drowsy mode is 0.28ns with a 64 x Leff width PMOS pass-transistor in the normal mode voltage supplier.

5. Energy consumption

Table 5 compares the energy savings due to the *simple* policy with a window size of 4000 cycles and with and without the use of drowsy tags. Normalized total energy is the ratio of total energy used in the drowsy cache divided by the total energy consumed in a regular cache. Similarly, normalized leakage energy is the ratio of leakage energy in the drowsy cache to leakage energy in a normal cache. The data in the DVS columns correspond to the energy savings resulting from the scaled-V_{DD} (DVS) circuit technique while the theoretical minimum column assumes that leakage in low-power mode can be reduced to zero (without losing state). The theoretical minimum column estimates the energy savings given the best possible hypothetical circuit technique. For all the results in the table, we conservatively assume that there are only 19 tag bits (corresponding to 32 bit addressing) per line, which translates into 6.9% of the bits on a cache line.

The table shows that our implementation of a drowsy cache can reduce the total energy consumed in the data cache by more than 50% without significantly impacting performance. Total leakage energy is reduced by an average of 71% when tags are always awake and by an average of 76% using the drowsy tag scheme. Leakage energy could potentially be cut in half if the efficiency of the drowsy cir-

TABLE 4. Energy parameters and drowsy transition time for 32-KB 4-way set associative cache with 32Wmin for voltage controller switch size

Dynamic energy per access	Leakage energy per bit	Drowsy leakage energy per bit	Transition energy (W=64Leff)	Drowsy transition latency
2.94E-10J	1.63E-15J	2.59E-16J	2.56E-11J	1 cycle

TABLE 5. Normalized energy results and run-time increase for the OO4 core, *simple* policy, 1 cycle drowsy transition, 4000 cycle window for both awake and drowsy tags

	Awake tags					Drowsy tags				
	Normalized total energy		Normalized leakage energy		Run-time increase	Normalized total energy		Normalized leakage energy		Run-time increase
	DVS	Theoretical min.	DVS	Theoretical min.		DVS	Theoretical min.	DVS	Theoretical min.	
ammp	0.25	0.11	0.24	0.09	0.66%	0.20	0.05	0.18	0.03	1.33%
applu	0.47	0.36	0.33	0.20	0.42%	0.43	0.32	0.28	0.14	0.84%
apsi	0.46	0.36	0.30	0.17	0.06%	0.43	0.32	0.25	0.11	0.22%
art	0.39	0.27	0.32	0.19	0.66%	0.35	0.22	0.27	0.13	1.32%
bzip2	0.45	0.34	0.26	0.12	0.59%	0.41	0.30	0.21	0.06	1.23%
crafty	0.53	0.44	0.34	0.22	0.45%	0.50	0.41	0.29	0.16	0.92%
eon	0.55	0.47	0.32	0.19	0.40%	0.52	0.43	0.27	0.13	0.64%
equake	0.50	0.41	0.27	0.13	0.08%	0.47	0.37	0.21	0.06	0.20%
facerec	0.46	0.36	0.29	0.15	0.46%	0.42	0.31	0.24	0.09	0.87%
fma3d	0.41	0.30	0.26	0.12	0.10%	0.37	0.25	0.20	0.05	0.08%
galgel	0.52	0.42	0.37	0.25	0.34%	0.49	0.39	0.32	0.19	0.69%
gap	0.52	0.43	0.28	0.14	0.26%	0.49	0.40	0.22	0.08	0.63%
gcc	0.43	0.32	0.28	0.14	0.65%	0.39	0.27	0.23	0.08	1.25%
gzip	0.46	0.36	0.28	0.14	0.83%	0.43	0.32	0.22	0.07	1.87%
lucas	0.43	0.32	0.25	0.11	0.04%	0.39	0.27	0.20	0.05	0.12%
mcf	0.55	0.46	0.28	0.15	0.11%	0.52	0.42	0.23	0.08	0.22%
mesa	0.51	0.42	0.27	0.14	0.14%	0.48	0.38	0.22	0.07	0.30%
mgrid	0.47	0.36	0.33	0.20	0.52%	0.43	0.32	0.28	0.14	0.97%
parser	0.46	0.35	0.28	0.15	1.03%	0.42	0.31	0.23	0.08	2.09%
sixtrack	0.48	0.38	0.31	0.18	0.33%	0.44	0.34	0.26	0.11	0.65%
swim	0.40	0.28	0.30	0.16	0.56%	0.36	0.24	0.24	0.10	1.14%
twolf	0.40	0.28	0.27	0.13	0.69%	0.35	0.23	0.22	0.07	1.48%
vortex	0.49	0.39	0.30	0.16	0.29%	0.46	0.35	0.24	0.10	0.60%
vpr	0.51	0.42	0.29	0.15	0.51%	0.48	0.38	0.23	0.09	1.25%
wupwise	0.36	0.24	0.24	0.09	0.07%	0.31	0.18	0.18	0.02	0.13%
Average	0.46	0.35	0.29	0.15	0.41%	0.42	0.31	0.24	0.09	0.84%

cuit techniques are improved (see the theoretical minimum column). However, the benefits of any further reduction of leakage in drowsy mode are tempered by the fact that lines must still spend time in full-power mode when being accessed, and consequently their leakage power consumption is at least an order of magnitude higher. Thus, the impact of more efficient drowsy circuits on total energy savings is reduced. Nonetheless, if there are circuits that are more efficient without significantly increasing the transition time, the *simple* policy can take advantage of it.

An important question is whether it is worth using the more complex drowsy tag scheme. The energy-delay product of the benchmarks when using drowsy tags are always lower than without. So the decision about whether to use drowsy tags or not comes down to acceptable engineering trade-offs. Also note that in direct-mapped caches, tags can be put into drowsy mode without undue performance impact or implementation complexity (see Section 2). However, using a direct mapped data cache instead of the 4-way associative one has its own costs: miss rates on our benchmarks are approximately tripled, which—aside from the performance penalty—can significantly impact the total energy consumption of the processor.

6. Conclusions and future work

During our investigations of drowsy caches we found that our simplest policy—where cachelines are periodically put into a low-power mode without regard to their access histories—can reduce the cache's static power consumption by more than 80%. The fact that we do not propose a more sophisticated policy with better characteristics should not be taken as proof that such policy does not exist. However, we believe that our combination of a simple circuit technique with a simple microarchitectural mechanism provides sufficient static power savings at a modest performance impact, that it makes sophistication a poor trade-off. The *simple* policy is not a solution to all caches in the processor. In particular, the L1 instruction cache does not do as well with the simple algorithm and only slightly better with the *noaccess* policy. We are investigating the use of instruction prefetch algorithms combined with the drowsy circuit technique for reducing leakage power in the instruction caches. Our ongoing work also includes the extension of our techniques to other memory structures, such as branch predictors.

An open question remains as to the role of adaptivity in determining the window size. We found that for a given machine configuration, a single static window size (2000 to 8000 cycles, depending on configuration) performs adequately on all of our benchmarks. However, the optimum varies slightly for each workload, thus making the window size adaptive would allow a finer power-performance trade-off. One way of accomplishing this is by monitoring the microarchitecture and counting the number of stall cycles that can be attributed to the drowsy wakeup latency, and only putting the cachelines into drowsy mode again after their previous wakeup overheads have been amortized (i.e. the performance impact falls under a given threshold). The user's preference for trading-off performance and power savings could be controlled by the setting of the threshold value.

While our dynamic voltage scaling circuit does not offer the lowest leakage per bit, the fact that it maintains its stored value, allows for an aggressive algorithm when deciding which cache lines to put into drowsy mode. Using our policy and circuit technique, the total energy consumed in the cache can be reduced by an average of 54%. This compares well with the theoretical maximum reduction of 65% corresponding to a hypothetical circuit that consumes no leakage energy in drowsy mode. Since the amount of leakage energy consumed in drowsy mode is only an average of 24% of total, further reductions of this fraction will yield only diminished returns.

Moreover, as the fraction of leakage energy is reduced from an average of 76% in projected conventional caches to an average of 50% in the drowsy cache, dynamic energy once again becomes a prime candidate for reduction.

7. Acknowledgements

This work was supported by DARPA/AFRL F33615-00-C-1678, DARPA MDA972-33-1-0010, MACO 98-DF-660, and SRC-2001-HJ-904.

References

[1] M. Powell, et. al. Gated-Vdd: A circuit technique to reduce leakage in deep-submicron cache memories. *Proc. of Int. Symp. Low Power Electronics and Design*, 2000, pp. 90-95.

[2] S. Kaxiras, Z. Hu, and M. Martonosi. Cache decay: Exploiting generational behavior to reduce cache leakage power. *Proc. of Int. Symp. Computer Architecture*, 2001, pp. 240-251.

[3] H. Zhou, et. al. Adaptive mode-control: A static-power-efficient cache design. *Proc. of Int. Conf. on Parallel Architectures and Compilation Techniques*, 2001, pp. 61-70.

[4] http://www-device.eecs.berkeley.edu

[5] K. Nii, et. al. A low power SRAM using auto-backgate-controlled MT-CMOS. *Proc. of Int. Symp. Low Power Electronics and Design*, 1998, pp. 293-298.

[6] M. Weiser, et. al. Scheduling for reduced CPU energy. *Proc. of the First Symp. of Operating Systems Design and Implementation*. November 1994

[7] T. Pering, T. Burd, and R. Brodersen. The Simulation and Evaluation of Dynamic Voltage Scaling Algorithms. *Proceedings of International Symposium on Low Power Electronics and Design*, June, 1998, pp. 76-81.

[8] K. Flautner, S. Reinhardt, and T. Mudge. Automatic performance-setting for dynamic voltage scaling. *Proc. of Int. Conf. on Mobile Computing and Networking (MOBICOM-7)*, July 2001, pp. 260-271.

[9] S. Wolf. Silicon processing for the VLSI era Volume 3 - The submicron MOSFET. *Lattice Press*, 1995, pp. 213-222.

[10] H. Hanson, et al. Static energy reduction techniques for microprocessor caches. *Proc. of the Int. Conf. Computer Design*, 2001.

[11] K. Itoh. VLSI memory chip design. *Springer Publisher*, 2001, pp. 413-423.

[12] T. May and M. Woods. Alpha-particled-induced soft errors in dynamic memories. *IEEE Trans. on Electron Devices*, Vol. ED-26, No. 1, Jan. 1979.

Power and Performance Evaluation of Globally Asynchronous Locally Synchronous Processors *

Anoop Iyer   Diana Marculescu

Electrical and Computer Engineering Department
Carnegie Mellon University, Pittsburgh, PA 15213
Email: {aiyer, dianam}@ece.cmu.edu

Abstract

Due to shrinking technologies and increasing design sizes, it is becoming more difficult and expensive to distribute a global clock signal with low skew throughout a processor die. Asynchronous processor designs do not suffer from this problem since they do not have a global clock. However, a paradigm shift from synchronous to asynchronous is unlikely to happen in the processor industry in the near future. Hence the study of Globally Asynchronous Locally Synchronous (or GALS) systems is relevant. In this paper we use a cycle-accurate simulation environment to study the impact of asynchrony in a superscalar processor architecture. Our results show that as expected, going from a synchronous to a GALS design causes a drop in performance, but elimination of the global clock does not lead to drastic power reductions. From a power perspective, GALS designs are inherently less efficient when compared to synchronous architectures. However, the flexibility offered by the independently controllable local clocks enables the effective use of other energy conservation techniques like dynamic voltage scaling. Our results show that for a 5-clock domain GALS processor, the drop in performance ranges between 5-15%, while power consumption is reduced by 10% on the average. Fine-grained voltage scaling reduces the gap between fully synchronous and GALS implementations, allowing for better power efficiency.

1 Introduction

Most conventional microprocessor designs are synchronous in their construction; that is, they have a global clock signal which provides a common timing reference for the operation of all the circuitry on the chip. On the other hand, fully asynchronous designs built using self-timed circuits do not have any global timing reference; examples of this design style are given in Sutherland's work on *Micropipelines* [1]. Globally Asynchronous Locally Synchronous systems (which we refer to as GALS systems in this paper) are an intermediate style of design between these two. GALS systems contain several independent synchronous blocks which operate with their own local clocks and communicate asynchronously with each other. The main feature of these systems is the absence of a global timing reference and the use of several distinct local clocks (or clock domains), possibly running at different frequencies.

1.1 Motivation

The idea of GALS system design is in itself not new [2]. Interest in GALS design is now growing due to the following reasons:

- **Global clock distribution:** Trends of increasing die sizes and rising transistor counts may soon lead to a situation in which distributing a high-frequency global clock signal with low skew throughout a large die is prohibitively expensive in terms of design effort, die area, and power dissipation. GALS systems eliminate the need for careful design and fine-tuning of a global clock distribution network.

- **Design reuse:** Designers are now seriously exploring opportunities for reusing IP cores, and system-on-chip design is gaining popularity. Integrating several cores on one chip may not always be possible with a single clock system; different cores may have different clock requirements and operating frequencies. GALS systems with standardized asynchronous interfaces will facilitate design reuse.

- **Inertia:** While a fully asynchronous design style promises to solve both the above problems, a complete migration from synchronous to asynchronous systems is

*This work was supported in part by IBM Corp. SUR Grant No. 4901B10170 and by SRC Grant No. 2001-HJ-898.

not likely to happen in the immediate future; CAD tools for asynchronous design are mature, but not commercially strong yet.

In the microprocessor industry, global clock distribution issues (further discussed in section 2) are perhaps the best motivating factor for the study of GALS systems. However since products in this arena are highly performance-driven, we need to evaluate the impact of asynchronous communication on performance and power. We describe in this paper the development of a modeling and simulation framework and the results of some experiments with a hypothetical superscalar GALS processor design. We have attempted to address the following issues:

- If we design a microprocessor in a GALS style with multiple clock domains, how much performance overhead will it incur over a fully synchronous processor?

- Will the elimination of the global clock network help in reducing power in a microprocessor, as other works have claimed?

- How can we exploit the extra flexibility offered by independent clock domains in a GALS processor?

In this work, we show that GALS processors are *not* necessarily more power efficient than fully synchronous designs, as it has been previously claimed, but they *may* become so if clock speed and supply voltage are tuned for each synchronous block. Eventually, fine adaptation can be extended to support application-driven, multiple-domain dynamic clock/voltage scaling.

1.2 Related Work

Sutherland's paper on *Micropipelines* [1] contains a good introduction to asynchronous design. Asynchronous processor cores have been in development for over a decade now; for example, the Amulet processor core developed at Manchester, which implements the ARM instruction set, is in its third generation and is commercially viable and competitive [3]. GALS systems were studied in detail by Chapiro in his 1984 PhD thesis [2]. His work covers metastability issues in GALS systems and outlines a stretchable clocking strategy which provides a mechanism for asynchronous communication. Chelcea and Nowick propose in [4, 5] the use of FIFOs as a low-latency asynchronous communication mechanism between synchronous blocks. Hemani *et al.* estimated in [6] the clock power savings in GALS designs compared to synchronous designs. However, their work targets a regular ASIC design flow with simpler clocking strategies rather than the aggressive clock distribution networks used in microprocessors. Muttersbach *et al.* have implemented asynchronous wrappers around synchronous blocks [7]; they have

used these wrappers along with asynchronous memory blocks to implement an ASIC and have thus proved the feasibility of GALS design in silicon. However they have not provided any direct performance comparisons between GALS systems and synchronous systems. A similar system has been proposed by Moore *et al.* in [8]; pausible clocking for GALS systems has been described by Yun and Dooply in [9]. The work of Semeraro *et al.* [10] is the closest to our GALS study. They show the effect of voltage scaling by using off-line profiling of the application.

1.3 Organization of this Paper

The rest of this paper is organized as follows:

- In section 2 we discuss global clock distribution methods and the challenges it poses, and thus motivate the study of GALS systems.

- In section 3 we describe some of the issues involved in GALS processor design.

- In section 4 we outline an architecture for a hypothetical GALS processor and describe the simulation and modeling setup which we used to study power and performance trends in this processor.

- In section 5 we show some results on power and performance trends.

- Finally in section 6 we summarize our contributions and conclude with some future directions for research on GALS processors.

2 Clock Distribution

2.1 Design Practices

Generating a high frequency clock signal and distributing it across a large die with low skew is a challenging task demanding a lot of design effort, die area and power. Restle *et al.* [11] and Bailey and Benschneider [12] give a good overview of clocking system design for high-performance processors.

In most processors, a phase lock loop (PLL) generates a high frequency clock signal from a slower external clock. A combination of a metal grid and a tree of buffers is used to distribute the clock throughout the chip. Trees have low latency, dissipate less power and use less wiring; but they need to be rerouted whenever the logic is modified even slightly, and in a custom-designed processor, this requires a lot of effort. Trees work well if the clock loading is uniform across the chip area; unfortunately, most microprocessors have widely varying clock loads. Metal grids provide a regular structure to facilitate the early design and characterization of the clock network. They also minimize local skew by providing more direct interconnections between clock pins.

Moreover, clocking in most processors today is hierarchical. Figure 1 shows an example of a hierarchical distribution network; several major clocks are derived from a global clock grid, and local clocks are in turn derived from the major clocks. This approach serves to modularize the overall design and to minimize the local skew inside a block. It also has the advantage that clock drivers for each functional block can be customized to the skew and drive requirements of that block; thus the drive on the global clock grid need not be designed for the worst-case clock loading.

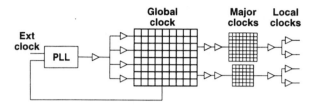

Figure 1. An example of a hierarchical clock distribution network

2.2 Case Study

Restle *et al.* have argued in [11] that clock skew arises mainly due to process variations in the tree of buffers driving the clock. Since device geometries will continue to shrink and clock frequencies and die sizes will continue to increase, global clock skew induced by such process variations can only get worse. Hence we argue that we will reach a point where skew will thus eat up a significant proportion of the cycle time and thus will directly affect performance.

This point may already have been reached. Table 1 shows a case study of a few processor designs spanning four major CMOS technology generations which entered the market during the last decade. The numbers in the table clearly show that technology scaling has led to a dramatic increase in design size and speed. However, since interconnects do not scale as well as transistor gate lengths do, these numbers indicate that the complexity of the clock distribution task has increased even more dramatically; we now have to clock many more registers with much smaller skew budgets than before.

Designers have handled this increased design complexity using complicated hierarchical distribution systems like the one shown in Figure 1. However, even a complex system of multiple grids and H-trees is not sufficient for today's Gigahertz clocks. For instance, the 800-MHz prototype of the Itanium chip has a projected skew of 110 ps using a hierarchical distribution scheme with multiple grids and trees. This skew is almost 10% of the total cycle time. The Itanium designers have added a network of 32 active deskewing circuits [13]

which connect multiple local clock grids together and help in bringing down the overall skew to 28 ps.

While techniques like active deskewing help to push the envelope for clocked systems further, they come at a significant cost in terms of die area and power dissipation. At some point, pushing the limits of clock distribution networks will lead to diminishing marginal returns. At that stage, GALS design techniques will come in useful.

3 Globally Asynchronous Locally Synchronous Processor Design

In this section we discuss some architectural issues involved in the design of a globally asynchronous locally synchronous processor, with focus on performance and power evaluation. Since our primary focus is at the architecture level, we choose to omit several lower-level issues in our study. Some areas which have been dealt with in detail elsewhere are:

- **Metastability resolution:** The problem of metastable signals and techniques for metastability resolution using synchronizers and arbiters are discussed in [14]. Our approach uses asynchronous FIFOs [4, 5] between clock domains and this in turn relies on synchronizers.

- **Local clock generation:** Each clock domain in a GALS system needs its own local clock generator; ring oscillators have been proposed as a viable clock generation scheme [2, 7]. We assume that we can use ring oscillators in each synchronous block in the GALS processor.

- **Failure modeling:** A system with multiple clock domains is prone to synchronization failures; we do not attempt to model these since their probabilities are miniscule (but non-zero) [14] and our work does not target mission-critical systems.

3.1 Defining Synchronous Blocks

Hemani *et al.* have described an automated strategy for defining locally synchronous blocks in a GALS design [6]. Starting from a hierarchical RTL description of the system, their method uses iterative refinement to get an optimal partitioning of the system into a number of synchronous blocks, using clock power as an objective function for optimization. In a custom-designed system like a microprocessor, performance requirements justify manual intervention in the partitioning phase. Since the primary motivation behind GALS design is to avoid distributing a common clock signal over large areas, the strategy for partitioning the design into synchronous blocks will largely be dictated by physical design aspects. However, since asynchrony can lead to higher latencies, it is crucial to take architecture issues into account when partitioning the design.

160

Design	Technology	Device count	Cycle time	Skew	Remarks
Alpha 21064	0.8 μm (1992)	1.6M	5 ns	200 ps	Single line of drivers for clock grid
Alpha 21164	0.5 μm (1995)	9.3M	3.3 ns	80 ps	Two lines of drivers for clock grid
Alpha 21264	0.35 μm (1998)	15.2M	1.7 ns	65 ps	16 distributed lines of drivers
Itanium (with active deskewing)	0.18 μm (2001)	25.4M	1.25 ns	28 ps	32 active deskewing circuits
Itanium (without active deskewing)	0.18 μm (2001)	25.4M	1.25 ns	110 ps	Projected skew without deskewing

Table 1. Trends in global clock skew for microprocessor designs across process generations

In the traditional superscalar out-of-order processor model the *instruction flow* consists of fetching instructions from the instruction cache, using the branch predictor for successive fetch addresses. The *register dataflow* consists of issuing instructions out of the instruction window and forwarding results to dependent instructions. The *memory dataflow* consists of issuing loads to the data cache and forwarding data to dependent instructions. Introducing high latencies in any of these three crucial flows will have an impact on the processor's performance.

The level 1 instruction cache and the branch predictor taken together are a good candidate for one synchronous block corresponding to the front-end of the pipeline. In some architectures, notably in CISC architectures like Intel's IA-32, the decode logic occupies a large area and consists of several pipe stages; in such cases, decode would be a good candidate for another synchronous block.

Inside the out-of-order execution core, it is difficult to make generalizations and say which parts of the core may be decoupled without much overhead and which may not; such decisions are very specific to the microarchitecture and the instruction set of the processor. Area and clock distribution considerations obviously suggest this partitioning to some extent. For instance in the 21264 Alpha the 'major clocks' (tapped from the global clock and distributed locally) are defined this way, based mostly on the top-level hierarchy of the design; they suggest a partitioning system for that specific implementation. The 21264 has the following major clocks [12]: (1) instruction fetch and branch predict (2) bus interface unit (3) integer issue and execution units (4) floating point issue and execution units (5) load/store unit (6) pad ring. We shall revisit this implementation in section 4 where we describe our proposed GALS architecture.

3.2 Asynchronous Communication Mechanisms

Many methods have been proposed for clocking GALS systems with *stretchable clocks* [2, 7, 8]. Such clocking systems manage asynchronous communication between two clock domains by stretching one phase of both the clocks while the handshaking and data transfer takes place. This is typically done using an arbiter element inside the loop of a ring oscillator. While this mechanism provides an elegant and fail-safe method of communication, it also stalls both the synchronous blocks during the transaction. In a proces-

sor pipeline, transactions occur practically during every cycle. Stretching the clock every cycle would lead to a situation where the effective clock frequency is determined not by the clock generator but by the rate of communication with other synchronous modules.[1] This is not desirable, especially in systems where the frequencies of the different clocks have been chosen to meet performance and power requirements.

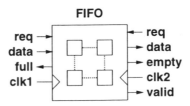

Figure 2. Asynchronous FIFO for interfacing two clock domains

Chelcea and Nowick have presented in [4, 5] a design for a low-latency token-ring based FIFO which can be used for asynchronous communication between synchronous blocks. The interfaces to the FIFO are shown in Figure 2. Their design uses *full* and *empty* signals to indicate the occupancy of the FIFO. The *empty* signal is controlled by the producer of data into the FIFO and is synchronized to the consumer's clock; similarly, the *full* signal is controlled by the consumer and is synchronized to the producer's clock. A few modifications are made to the circuit to account for latencies in synchronization and to prevent deadlock. In addition to providing high throughput in the steady state, the design has low latency when compared to other methods we tested. Since the focus of our work is at a higher level of abstraction, we shall not go into further details; a complete description of the operation of the circuit is given in [4, 5]. We shall refer back to this FIFO structure when describing our experiments with GALS design.

3.3 Multiple Supply Voltages

An interesting possibility with the use of multiple local clocks with potentially different speeds is the use of multiple

---

[1]To an extent, this behavior is rather like the timing behavior of Sutherland's *Micropipelines*, where the rate of forward communication in the pipeline makes the system *self-timed*.

local supply voltages in a dynamic or application-dependent manner. Since applications vary in their usage of processor resources, intelligent selection of clock frequencies can give us significant power savings with minimal impact on performance. The simplest example of this is slowing down or shutting off the floating-point units while running integer applications. Selectively slowing down certain regions of the processor is more easily achieved in a GALS design than in a synchronous design because different subsystems run on different clocks and these clocks can be independently controlled.

If some parts of the core are slowed down, they can be operated at a lower supply voltage too. In such a system, the asynchronous communication interfaces between synchronous blocks will need to have level-conversion circuits. The amount by which we can reduce the voltage depends on the slowdown of the clock. Since energy consumption is dependent on the *square* of the supply voltage, reducing the supply voltage will lead to significant energy benefits.

The relationship between logic delay D and supply voltage V_{dd} is given by the following equation [15]:

$$D \propto \frac{V_{dd}}{(V_{dd} - V_t)^\alpha} \qquad (1)$$

where V_t is the threshold voltage of the transistor and α is a technology-dependent factor. For a 0.35 μm technology, α is 2; for smaller technologies, the value of α is between 1 and 2. This implies that savings arising out of dynamic voltage scaling for a given delay value are higher for smaller technology generations.

4 A GALS Architecture

We have studied a superscalar processor model and have attempted to build a GALS model which duplicates its pipeline structure for the most part, so that we can compare GALS processors with synchronous processors in terms of power and performance. The architecture that we chose for our study is a hypothetical processor resembling the 21264 Alpha in some ways.

4.1 The Architecture

After a detailed look at the architecture, we chose to have five clock domains in the GALS version of the design. Figure 3 shows the pipeline structure of both the synchronous (base) processor and the GALS processor we designed. The boundaries between clock domains in the GALS processor are indicated by dotted lines. In the base (synchronous) model, all the logic runs off the same clock. In the GALS model, various regions are clocked using different clock signals independent of each other. The first stage of the pipeline consists of an instruction cache and branch prediction unit (clock domain 1). The next stages are instruction decode and register rename (clock domain 2). There are three issue queues in the

Stage	Operation	Domains
1	Fetch from I-cache	1
2	Decode	2
3	Register rename, Regfile read	2
4	Dispatch into issue queue	2, 3/4/5
5	Issue to functional unit	3/4/5
6	Execute	3/4/5
7	Wakeup, Writeback	3/4/5
8	Regfile write, Commit	3/4/5, 2

Table 2. Pipeline stages in our processor models

Fetch and decode rate	4 inst/cycle
Integer issue queue size	20
FP issue queue size	16
Memory issue queue size	16
Integer registers	72
FP registers	72
L1 data cache	16KB 4-way
	1 cycle latency
L1 instruction cache	16KB direct-mapped
	1 cycle latency
L2 unified cache	256KB 4-way
	6 cycles latency
ALUs	4 integer, 4 FP

Table 3. Microarchitecture details of our processor models

design: one for integer instructions (clock domain 3), one for floating-point instructions (clock domain 4) and one for loads and stores (clock domain 5). In the GALS processor, the integer ALUs and the integer issue queue are in the same clocking region. This ensures that dependent instructions within the integer issue queue can be issued back-to-back as soon as operands are available. Similarly, floating-point ALUs and the floating-point issue queue share one clock, and the data-cache, the level-2 cache and memory issue queue share one clock.

In the synchronous version, communication between successive logic blocks is done using regular pipe stages. In the present version of the GALS model, asynchronous FIFOs described in section 3.2 have been used.

Table 2 gives a summary of the pipeline stages in the processor models we developed for our experiments, along with a listing of the clock domains of the GALS processor which are involved in each pipe stage. Table 3 describes the microarchitecture in some detail.

4.2 A GALS Simulation Framework

Building a cycle-accurate simulator for a single-clock pipelined system is simple; in C, we only need to call various pipe-stage functions in the reverse order of their occurrence in the pipeline. However, to simulate a multiple-clock

162

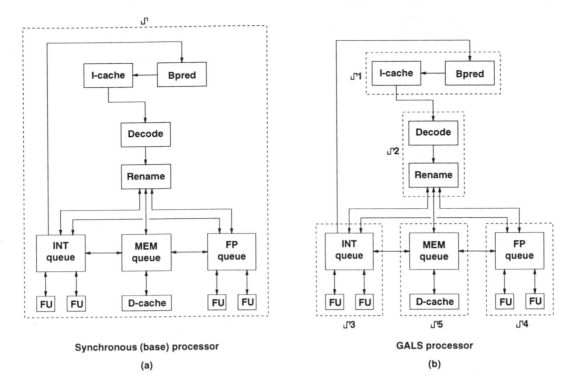

Figure 3. Pipeline of the simulated architecture

system where the different clocks have entirely independent frequency and phase, we need a more detailed simulation infrastructure.

We have written a general-purpose event-driven simulation engine which can be used to simulate any asynchronous system, synchronous (clocked) system, or a system which contains both asynchronous and synchronous components. The guts of this event-driven simulation engine consist of an event queue and a global timer. The event queue is implemented as a singly linked list in C. Each node of the queue contains the following fields:

- a function to call at each occurrence of the event;

- a parameter to call the function with;

- a time at which the event is scheduled to occur;

- a priority number to determine the order of execution of events which are scheduled occur at the same time instant;

- for periodic events, a time period of repetition (for simulation of clocked systems), and

- a pointer to the next queue item.

To set the system in motion, we need to insert one or more starting events into the event queue. The queue contains events sorted in increasing order of their scheduled times.

Hence, processing the event queue for running the simulation is easy; we only need to read successive events from the head of the queue and execute them by calling the appropriate execution functions. To simulate clocked systems, we need to insert one event for each clock domain; for each such event, we need to specify a time period. When the execution engine processes such a periodic event, it schedules another instance of the same event into the queue, thus representing the next cycle of execution of the clocked system.

Figure 4 (a) shows an example of a system with three clock domains, each of which has a different clock frequency. To simulate this system, we need to add three starting events into the event queue, all of which are periodic, to represent the three clock domains. Figure 4 (b) shows the C code which models the system.

4.3 Performance and Power Models

To evaluate the above architecture, we wrote models of both the synchronous and the GALS processors using the Simplescalar toolset [16]. Simplescalar provides a comprehensive infrastructure for modeling and simulation of microarchitecture features. To simulate the GALS processor, we made use of the event-driven simulation engine described earlier in section 4.2. We have set up five clock domains in our simulator and in the first set of experiments, had all the clocks running at the same speed. The starting phase of each clock was set to a random value at runtime.

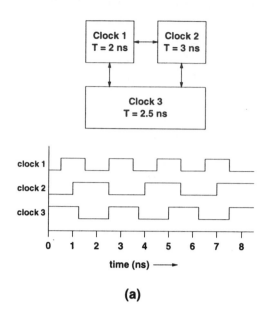

(a)

```
init_event_queue ();
add_event (/* start time */ 0.5,
           /* function */ &clock1_logic,
           /* param */ NULL,
           /* period */ 2.0);
add_event (/* start time */ 1.0,
           /* function */ &clock2_logic,
           /* param */ NULL,
           /* period */ 3.0);
add_event (/* start time */ 0.0,
           /* function */ &clock3_logic,
           /* param */ NULL,
           /* period */ 2.5);
process_event_queue ();
```

(b)

Figure 4. Event-driven GALS system simulation. (a) An example system. (b) C code for simulating this system.

We used the Wattch framework [17] to add power models to our processor simulation. Wattch provides switching capacitance modeling for structures like ALUs, caches, arrays and buses in a processor. These are integrated into our base and GALS simulators to provide energy statistics. To account for overheads arising from clock-gating and leakage currents, we modeled unused modules as consuming 10% of their full power. We also modeled power consumed by the FIFOs used for communication between domains.

In addition to modeling the switching capacitance of memories and buses inside the processor, we have also modeled the switching capacitance of clock grids. For the synchronous

base processor model, we assumed a clock distribution hierarchy resembling that of the 21264 Alpha processor. We modeled one global clock grid and five local clock grids corresponding to the five clock domains discussed in section 3.1. The areas and metal densities of each clock grid were approximated by the numbers published for the 21264 processor. For the GALS processor, since there is no global clock, we eliminated the switching capacitance of the global clock grid and retained the five major clock grids, corresponding to the distribution networks for each of the synchronous blocks.

5 Experimental Results

To assess the performance and power of our proposed GALS processor design, we tested the base and the GALS simulators with a set of benchmarks taken from the Spec95 [18] and the Mediabench [19] benchmark suites. We have performed two sets of experiments:

1. Base versus GALS performance and power analysis with all synchronous blocks running at the same clock frequency and supply voltage.

2. Base versus a multiple-clock, multiple-voltage GALS design.

5.1 Power and Performance Analysis

Performance

Not surprisingly, the GALS processor is slowed down by asynchronous communication and does not perform as well as the synchronous processor. Figure 5 shows the relative slowdown of various benchmarks running on the GALS processor when compared to the synchronous processor. On an average, the benchmarks we ran on GALS were slower by 10% when compared to base. As expected, the *fpppp* benchmark had the lowest performance hit. This is due to the application's exceptionally small proportion of branch instructions; on an average only one in every 67 instructions is a branch in this benchmark, while most other applications have one branch for every five to six instructions. This indicates that the asynchronous FIFO models used in our design have good throughput in the steady state when there are no branch mispredictions. This also suggests that branch mispredictions will prove more expensive in the GALS model due to its longer recovery pipeline.

We have also observed that the performance of the GALS processor varies with the relative phase of the various clocks, especially in the case where all the clocks are of the same frequency. This variation is of the order of 0.5%.

Instruction Latencies

On close examination of other statistics in the processor pipeline, we can see that the introduction of asynchronous

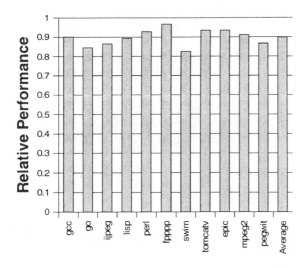

Figure 5. Performance of the GALS model relative to the base model

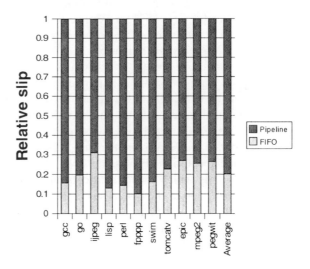

Figure 7. Relative Slip

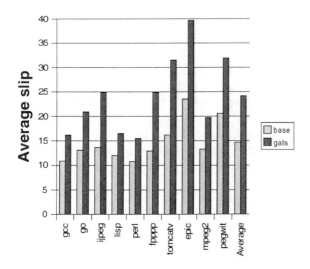

Figure 6. Average slip of an instruction in the base and GALS designs

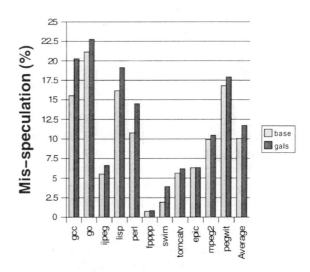

Figure 8. Percentage of mis-speculated instructions in the base and GALS processors

communication latencies inside the design has led to various other overheads which in some cases offset the power gains due to the absence of global clock. For instance, the *slip* (the average time taken by each instruction from the fetch to the commit stage) increases by 65% on average for all benchmarks in the GALS processor, as seen in Figure 6. This is because the addition of asynchronous communication channels leads to an increase in the effective length of the pipeline. Figure 7 shows the proportion of this slip time which is spent in the FIFOs (marked "FIFO" in the graph) versus the proportion of time spent in execution units, issue queues, etc. (marked "pipeline" in the graph). As we expect, the difference in slip between the GALS and the base versions is due in part to the time spent in the FIFOs. However, there is still an increase in the slip which cannot be accounted for by the time spent in FIFOs alone; this is caused by the latency in forwarding results from one queue to another through FIFOs. Note that this delay is caused by the FIFO latency of forwarding results and not by the latency in the instruction flow.

Speculation

This increase in pipeline length in the GALS processor also leads to higher speculative execution, as shown in Figure 8. This is most marked for the integer applications we tested, where the percentage of mis-speculated instructions goes up from 13.8 percent in the base processor to 16.7 percent in the GALS processor. Increase in speculation is less for applications containing many long-latency instructions. Similarly, we have observed that the average number of in-flight instructions in the pipeline is higher in the GALS model; so is the average occupancy of the register allocation tables and issue queues. For instance the integer register allocation table occupancy went up from 15 in base to 24 in GALS for the *ijpeg* benchmark.

Power

Figure 9 shows the relative total energy and average power consumption of the GALS processor, normalized to the respective measures of the base processor. In most benchmarks, the elimination of the global clock has resulted in some savings in the per-cycle power dissipation. But due to the extra switching activity inside the core, higher occupancies of the issue queues and register allocation tables, increased speculation and higher execution times, the total energy needed for execution is not necessarily lower, but is higher for the GALS processor in some cases. For the benchmarks we tested, this increase in energy is 1% on average.

Figure 10 shows the breakdown of the base and GALS model power consumption into various macro blocks. From the figure, we can see that power gains arising from elimination of the global clock are offset by the increased power consumption of other blocks.

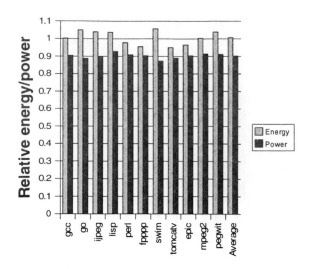

Figure 9. Energy and power consumption of the GALS processor normalized to those of the base processor

5.2 Multiple-Clock, Multiple-Voltage Processors

In a second set of experiments, we tried to determine which parts of the processor could be slowed down in an application-dependent manner without affecting performance. The technique of multiple supply voltages described in section 3.3 was used to determine an optimal supply voltage for lowest operating power, using equation 1 with a value of $\alpha = 1.6$ which is appropriate for today's 0.13 μm devices. The voltage thus determined is of course the ideal case; in practice, there will be an overhead due to DC-DC level conversion circuits.

Figure 11 shows the results of slowing down some clock domains in a generic fashion; the fetch clock and memory clock were slowed down by 10% and the floating point clock was slowed by 50%. The energy and power benefits are decent but performance losses are substantial (about 18%). From this graph, we see that we can apply clock slowdown only on a selective basis, after studying the application's characteristics.

- **perl:** Since there are virtually no floating-point instructions in this integer benchmark, we slowed down the FP clock by a factor of 3. The performance drop was 9% over the base version; the total energy was reduced by 10.8% and the average power by 18%.

- **ijpeg:** In this case, we have considered simultaneous slowing down the fetch, floating point and memory clocks (domains 1, 4 and 5 in Figure 3 (b)). We chose to study the impact of slowing down the memory clock on the power and performance of *ijpeg* since this benchmark has a very low proportion of memory accesses. In

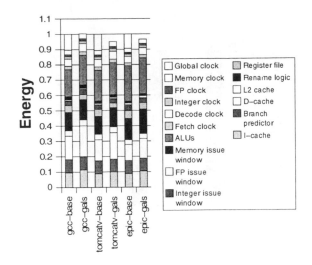

Figure 10. Breakdown of energy into various macro blocks

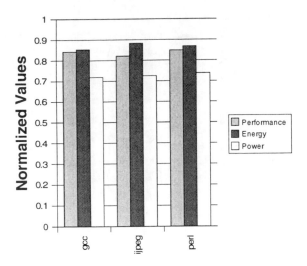

Figure 11. Results from selective slowdown applied on three benchmarks

all cases reported in Figure 12, the fetch clock has been slowed down by 10% and the FP clock by 20%, while for the memory clock we have considered four cases: no slowdown (gals-00), slowdown of 10% (gals-10), 20% (gals-20) and 50% (gals-50). Figure 12 shows that we can trade off performance for energy savings for this benchmark. Energy savings vary between 4 and 13% with a performance drop between 15 and 25% when compared to the fully synchronous processor.

- **gcc:** We chose this integer benchmark to apply a slower clock to the floating-point queue and units. Since the instruction bandwidth of this benchmark is also low, we slowed down the fetch unit by 10%. Figure 13 shows the results for performance, power and energy, normalized to the base case. The numbers marked "gals-1" are from the case where the floating-point clock is slower by 50% and the numbers marked "gals-2" are from the case where it slower by a factor of 3. The graph shows that *gcc* can afford to have a slower floating point unit without too much performance hit. Given scaleable voltage supplies, this technique also provides energy savings of 11% and power savings of 21% with a performance loss of 13% when compared to the fully synchronous processor.

To compare the capability of the GALS processor to trade off power for performance, we have also provided the normalized energy of the base (synchronous) processor when run at a slower clock (and lower voltage) that would exhibit an equivalent performance penalty (the column labeled "ideal" in Figures 12 and 13). It can be seen that by slowing down the floating-point clock domain, the GALS processor is able

to trade off performance for energy in case of the *gcc* benchmark. Figure 12 shows that slowing down the memory clock does not lead to a good performance-energy tradeoff for the *ijpeg* benchmark. Hence the extent of the tradeoff we can achieve by slowing down various clock domains is dictated by the nature of the application.

Overall, our experimental evidence shows that naive GALS implementations (with all clocks running at the same frequency) may not necessarily be very energy efficient as claimed previously. Instead, the increased flexibility of running local clocks at different speeds (and thus different voltages) offers a viable solution for energy aware computing under the increasing pressure of handling clock skew and distribution issues.

6 Conclusion

Our modeling and simulation setup has given direct comparisons of power and performance of GALS systems against those of synchronous systems. Our experimental evidence shows that the overhead associated with GALS processors renders them inefficient; hence eliminating the global clock is not in itself a solution for low power. However, combined with intelligent fine-tuning of clock frequency and supply voltage, GALS systems can provide some power benefits. Clocking smaller areas will mean smaller skew values and hence faster clocks; we have not modeled such effects in this work because skew estimates require extensive physical design. Besides, having independent clock domains eliminates the need for balanced pipelines and could provide more avenues for fine-tuning performance.

Since clock distribution issues may necessitate the prac-

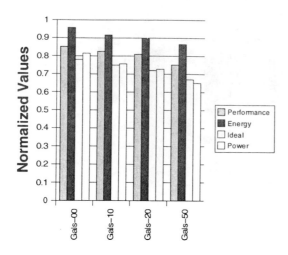

Figure 12. Impact of selective fetch, memory, and FP clock slowdown (ijpeg benchmark)

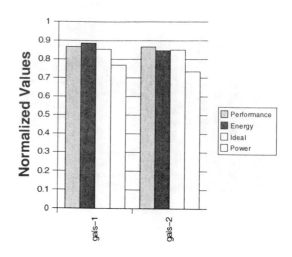

Figure 13. Impact of selective fetch and FP clock slowdown (gcc benchmark)

tice of GALS design in the future, studies on performance enhancement in GALS systems are worthwhile. Further studies in this direction could involve latency-hiding techniques like multithreaded execution in hardware.

References

[1] I. E. Sutherland, "Micropipelines," *Communications of the ACM*, June 1989.

[2] D. M. Chapiro, *Globally Asynchronous Locally Synchronous Systems*. PhD thesis, Stanford University, 1984.

[3] S. B. Furber, D. A. Edwards, and J. D. Garside, "AMULET3: A 100 MIPS Asynchronous Embedded Processor," in *Proc. Intl. Conference on Computer Design (ICCD)*, 2000.

[4] T. Chelcea and S. M. Nowick, "A Low-Latency FIFO for Mixed-Clock Systems," in *Proc. IEEE Computer Society Workshop on VLSI*, 2000.

[5] T. Chelcea and S. M. Nowick, "Robust Interfaces for Mixed-Timing Systems with Application to Latency-Insensitive Protocols," in *Proc. Design Automation Conference (DAC)*, 2001.

[6] A. Hemani, T. Meincke, S. Kumar, A. Postula, T. Olsson, P. Nilsson, J. Oberg, P. Ellervee, and D. Lundqvist, "Lower Power Consumption in Clock By Using Globally Asynchronous Locally Synchronous Design Style," in *Proc. Design Automation Conference (DAC)*, 1999.

[7] J. Muttersbach, T. Villiger, and W. Fitchner, "Practical Design of Globally Asynchronous Locally Synchronous Systems," in *Proc. Intl. Symposium on Advanced Research in Asynchronous Circuits and Systems (ASYNC)*, 2000.

[8] S. W. Moore, G. S. Taylor, P. A. Cunningham, R. D. Mullins, and P. Robinson, "Self Calibrating Clocks for Globally Asynchronous Locally Synchronous Circuits," in *Proc. Intl. Conference on Computer Design (ICCD)*, 2000.

[9] K. Y. Yun and A. E. Dooply, "Pausible Clocking-Based Heterogeneous Systems," *IEEE Transactions on VLSI Systems*, December 1999.

[10] G. Semeraro, G. Magklis, R. Balasubramonian, D. H. Albonesi, S. Dwarakadas, and M. L. Scott, "Energy-Efficient Processor Design Using Multiple Clock Domains with Dynamic Voltage and Frequency Scaling," in *Proc. Intl. Symp. on High Performance Computer Architecture (HPCA)*, 2002.

[11] P. J. Restle *et al.*, "A Clock Distribution Network for Microprocessors," *IEEE Journal of Solid State Circuits (JSSC)*, May 2001.

[12] D. W. Bailey and B. J. Benschneider, "Clocking Design and Analysis for a 600-MHz Alpha Microprocessor," *IEEE Journal of Solid State Circuits (JSSC)*, Nov 1998.

[13] S. Tam, S. Rusu, U. N. Desai, R. Kim, J. Zhang, and I. Young, "Clock Generation and Distribution for the First IA-64 Microprocessor," *IEEE Journal of Solid State Circuits (JSSC)*, November 2000.

[14] J. M. Rabaey, *Digital Integrated Circuits: A Design Perspective*. Prentice Hall, 1996.

[15] K. Chen and C. Hu, "Performance and Vdd Scaling in Deep Submicrometer CMOS," *IEEE Journal of Solid State Circuits (JSSC)*, October 1998.

[16] D. Burger and T. M. Austin, "The SimpleScalar Tool Set, version 2.0," Tech. Rep. 1342, University of Wisconsin-Madison, CS Department, June 1997.

[17] D. Brooks, V. Tiwari, and M. Martonosi, "Wattch: A Framework for Architectural-level Power Analysis and Optimizations," in *Proc. Intl Symp on Computer Architecture (ISCA)*, 2000.

[18] "Spec95 Benchmarks." http://www.spec.org.

[19] C. Lee, M. Potkonjak, and W. H. Mangione-Smith, "Mediabench: a Tool for Evaluating and Synthesizing Multimedia and Communications Systems," in *International Symposium on Microarchitecture (MICRO)*, 1997.

Session 5: Memory Systems

Using a User-Level Memory Thread for Correlation Prefetching*

Yan Solihin [†]   **Jaejin Lee** [‡]   **Josep Torrellas** [†]

[†] University of Illinois at Urbana-Champaign
[‡] Michigan State University
http://iacoma.cs.uiuc.edu
http://www.cse.msu.edu/~jlee

Abstract

This paper introduces the idea of using a User-Level Memory Thread (ULMT) for correlation prefetching. In this approach, a user thread runs on a general-purpose processor in main memory, either in the memory controller chip or in a DRAM chip. The thread performs correlation prefetching in software, sending the prefetched data into the L2 cache of the main processor. This approach requires minimal hardware beyond the memory processor: the correlation table is a software data structure that resides in main memory, while the main processor only needs a few modifications to its L2 cache so that it can accept incoming prefetches. In addition, the approach has wide usability, as it can effectively prefetch even for irregular applications. Finally, it is very flexible, as the prefetching algorithm can be customized by the user on an application basis. Our simulation results show that, through a new design of the correlation table and prefetching algorithm, our scheme delivers good results. Specifically, nine mostly-irregular applications show an average speedup of 1.32. Furthermore, our scheme works well in combination with a conventional processor-side sequential prefetcher, in which case the average speedup increases to 1.46. Finally, by exploiting the customization of the prefetching algorithm, we increase the average speedup to 1.53.

1. Introduction

Data prefetching is a popular technique to tolerate long memory access latencies. Most of the past work on data prefetching has focused on processor-side prefetching [6, 7, 8, 12, 13, 14, 15, 19, 20, 23, 25, 26, 28, 29]. In this approach, the processor or an engine in its cache hierarchy issues the prefetch requests. An interesting alternative is memory-side prefetching, where the engine that prefetches data for the processor is in the main memory system [1, 4, 9, 11, 22, 28].

Memory-side prefetching is attractive for several reasons. First, it eliminates the overheads and state bookkeeping that prefetch requests introduce in the paths between the main processor and its caches. Second, it can be supported with a few modifications to the controller of the L2 cache and no modification to the main processor. Third, the prefetcher can exploit its proximity to the memory to its advantage, for example by storing its state in memory. Finally, memory-side prefetching has the additional attraction of riding the technology trend of increased chip integration. Indeed, popular platforms like PCs are being equipped with graphics engines in the memory system [27]. Some chipsets like NVIDIA's nForce even integrate a powerful processor in the North Bridge chip [22]. Simpler

engines can be provided for prefetching, or existing graphics processors can be augmented with prefetching capabilities. Moreover, there are proposals to integrate processing logic in DRAM chips, such as IRAM [16].

Unfortunately, existing proposals for memory-side prefetching engines have a narrow scope [1, 9, 11, 22, 28]. Indeed, some designs are hardware controllers that perform simple and specific operations [1, 9, 22]. Other designs are specialized engines that are custom-designed to prefetch linked data structures [11, 28]. Instead, we would like an engine that is usable in a wide variety of workloads and that offers flexibility of use to the programmer.

While memory-side prefetching can support a variety of prefetching algorithms, one type that is particularly suited to it is Correlation prefetching [1, 6, 12, 18, 26]. Correlation prefetching uses past sequences of reference or miss addresses to predict and prefetch future misses. Since no program knowledge is needed, correlation prefetching can be easily moved to the memory side.

In the past, correlation prefetching has been supported by hardware controllers that typically require a large hardware table to keep the correlations [1, 6, 12, 18]. In all cases but one, these controllers are placed between the L1 and L2 caches, or between the processor and the L1. While effective, this approach has a high hardware cost. Furthermore, it is often unable to prefetch far ahead enough and deliver good prefetch coverage.

In this paper, we present a new scheme where correlation prefetching is performed by a User-Level Memory Thread (ULMT) running on a simple general-purpose processor in memory. Such a processor is either in the memory controller chip or in a DRAM chip, and prefetches lines to the L2 cache of the main processor. The scheme requires minimal hardware support beyond the memory processor: the correlation table is a software data structure that resides in main memory, while the main processor only needs a few modifications to its L2 cache controller so that it can accept incoming prefetches. Moreover, our scheme has wide usability, as it can effectively prefetch even for irregular applications. Finally, it is very flexible, as the prefetching algorithm executed by the ULMT can be customized by the programmer on an application basis.

Using a new design of the correlation table and correlation prefetching algorithm, our scheme delivers an average speedup of 1.32 for nine mostly-irregular applications. Furthermore, our scheme works well in combination with a conventional processor-side sequential prefetcher, in which case the average speedup increases to 1.46. Finally, by exploiting the customization of the prefetching algorithm, we increase the average speedup to 1.53.

This paper is organized as follows: Section 2 discusses memory-side and correlation prefetching; Section 3 presents ULMT for correla-

---
*This work was supported in part by the National Science Foundation under grants CCR-9970488, EIA-0081307, EIA-0072102, and CHE-0121357; by DARPA under grant F30602-01-C-0078; by Michigan State University; and by gifts from IBM, Intel, and Hewlett-Packard.

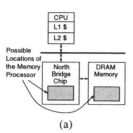
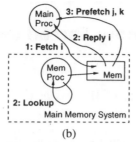
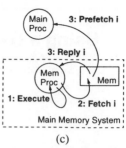

Figure 1. Memory-side prefetching: some locations where the memory processor can be placed (a), and actions under push passive (b) and push active (c) prefetching.

tion prefetching; Section 4 discusses our evaluation setup; Section 5 evaluates our design; Section 6 discusses related work; and Section 7 concludes.

2. Memory-Side and Correlation Prefetching

2.1. Memory-Side Prefetching

Memory-Side prefetching occurs when prefetching is initiated by an engine that resides either close to the main memory (beyond any memory bus) or inside of it [1, 4, 9, 11, 22, 28]. Some manufacturers have built such engines. Typically, they are simple hardwired controllers that probably recognize only simple stride-based sequences and prefetch data into local buffers. Some examples are NVIDIA's DASP engine in the North Bridge chip [22] and Intel's prefetch cache in the i860 chipset.

In this paper, we propose to support memory-side prefetching with a user-level thread running on a general-purpose core. The core can be very simple and does not need to support floating point. For illustration purposes, Figure 1-(a) shows the memory system of a PC. The core can be placed in different places, such as in the North Bridge (memory controller) chip or in the DRAM chips. Placing it in the North Bridge simplifies the design because the DRAM is not modified. Moreover, some existing systems already include a core in the North Bridge for graphics processing [22], which could potentially be reused for prefetching. Placing the core in a DRAM chip complicates the design, but the resulting highly-integrated system has lower memory access latency and higher memory bandwidth. In this paper, we examine the performance potential of both designs.

Memory- and processor-side prefetching are not the same as *Push* and *Pull* (or *On-Demand*) prefetching [28], respectively. Push prefetching occurs when prefetched data is sent to a cache or processor that has not requested it, while pull prefetching is the opposite. Clearly, a memory prefetcher can act as a pull prefetcher by simply buffering the prefetched data locally and supplying it to the processor on demand [1, 22]. In general, however, memory-side prefetching is most interesting when it performs push prefetching to the caches of the processor because it can hide a larger fraction of the memory access latency.

Memory-side prefetching can also be classified into *Passive* and *Active*. In passive prefetching, the memory processor observes the requests from the main processor that reach main memory. Based on them, and after examining some internal state, the memory processor prefetches other data for the main processor that it expects the latter to need in the future (Figure 1-(b)).

In active prefetching, the memory processor runs an abridged version of the code that is running on the main processor. The execution of the code induces the memory processor to fetch data that the main

processor will need later. The data fetched by these requests is also sent to the main processor (Figure 1-(c)).

In this paper, we concentrate on passive push memory-side prefetching into the L2 cache of the main processor. The memory processor aims to eliminate only L2 cache misses, since they are the only ones that it sees. Typically, L2 cache miss time is an important contributor to the processor stall due to memory accesses, and is usually the hardest to hide with out-of-order execution.

This approach to prefetching is inexpensive to support. The main processor core does not need to be modified at all. Its L2 cache needs to have the following supports. First, as in other systems [11, 15, 28], the L2 cache has to accept lines from the memory that it has not requested. To do so, the L2 uses free Miss Status Handling Registers (MSHRs) in such events. Secondly, if the L2 has a pending request and a prefetched line with the same address arrives, the prefetch simply steals the MSHR and updates the cache as if it were the reply. Finally, a prefetched line arriving at L2 is dropped in the following cases: the L2 cache already has a copy of the line, the write-back queue has a copy of the line because the L2 cache is trying to write it back to memory, all MSHRs are busy, or all the lines in the set where the prefetched line wants to go are in transaction-pending state.

2.2. Correlation Prefetching

Correlation Prefetching uses past sequences of reference or miss addresses to predict and prefetch future misses [1, 6, 12, 18, 26]. Two popular correlation schemes are *Stride-Based* and *Pair-Based* schemes. Stride-based schemes find stride patterns in the address sequences and prefetch all the addresses that will be accessed if the patterns continue in the future. Pair-based schemes identify a correlation between pairs or groups of addresses, for example between a miss and a sequence of successor misses. A typical implementation of pair-based schemes uses a *Correlation Table* to record the addresses that are correlated. Later, when a miss is observed, all the addresses that are correlated with its address are prefetched.

Pair-based schemes are attractive because they have general applicability: they work for any miss patterns as long as miss address sequences repeat. Such behavior is common in both regular and irregular applications, including those with sparse matrices or linked data structures. Furthermore, pair-based schemes, like all correlation schemes, need neither compiler support nor changes in the application binary.

Pair-based correlation prefetching has only been studied using hardware-based implementations [1, 6, 12, 18, 26], typically by placing a custom prefetch engine and a hardware correlation table between the processor and L1 cache, or between the L1 and L2 caches. The typical correlation table, as used in [6, 12, 26], is organized as follows. Each row stores the tag of an address that missed, and the addresses of a set of *immediate* successor misses. These are misses that have been seen to *immediately* follow the first one at different points in the application. The parameters of the table are the maximum number of immediate successors per miss (*NumSucc*), the maximum number of misses that the table can store predictions for (*NumRows*), and the associativity of the table (*Assoc*). According to [12], for best performance, the entries in a row should replace each other with a LRU policy.

Figure 4-(a) illustrates how the algorithm works. We call the algorithm *Base*. The figure shows two snapshots of the table at different points in the miss stream ((i) and (ii)). Within a row, successors are listed in MRU order from left to right. At any time, the hardware keeps a pointer to the row of the last miss observed. When a miss occurs, the table learns by placing the miss address as one of the immediate successors of the last miss, and a new row is allocated for the new miss unless it already exists. When the table is used to prefetch ((iii)), it reacts to an observed miss by finding the corresponding row and prefetching all *NumSucc* successors, starting from the MRU one.

The designs in [1, 18] work slightly differently. They are discussed in Section 6.

Overall, past work has demonstrated the applicability of pair-based correlation prefetching for many applications. However, it has also revealed the shortcomings of the approach. One critical problem is that, to be effective, this approach needs a large table. Proposed schemes typically need a 1-2 Mbyte on-chip SRAM table [12, 18], while some applications with large footprints even need a 7.6 Mbyte off-chip SRAM table [18].

Furthermore, the popular schemes that prefetch several potential *immediate* successors for each miss [6, 12, 26] have two limitations: they do not prefetch very far ahead and, intuitively, they need to observe one miss to eliminate another miss (its immediate successor). As a result, they tend to have low coverage. *Coverage* is the number of useful prefetches over the original number of misses [12].

3. ULMT for Correlation Prefetching

We propose to use a ULMT to eliminate the shortcomings of pair-based correlation prefetching while enhancing its advantages. In the following, we discuss the main concept (Section 3.1), the architecture of the system (Section 3.2), modified correlation prefetching algorithms (Section 3.3), and related operating system issues (Section 3.4).

3.1. Main Concept

A ULMT running on a general-purpose core in memory performs two conceptually distinct operations: *learning* and *prefetching*. Learning involves observing the misses on the main processor's L2 cache and recording them in a correlation table one miss at a time. The prefetching operation involves reacting to one such miss by looking up the correlation table and triggering the prefetching of several memory lines for the L2 cache of the main processor. No action is taken on a write-back to memory.

In practice, in agreement with past work [12], we find that combining both learning and prefetching works best: the correlation table continuously learns new patterns, while uninterrupted prefetching delivers higher performance. Consequently, the ULMT executes the infinite loop shown in Figure 2. Initially, the thread waits for a miss to be observed. When it observes one, it looks up the table and generates the addresses of the lines to prefetch (*Prefetching Step*). Then,

it updates the table with the address of the observed miss (*Learning Step*). It then resumes waiting.

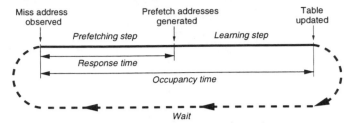

Figure 2. Infinite loop executed by the ULMT.

Any prefetch algorithm executed by the ULMT is characterized by its *Response* and *Occupancy* times. The response time is the time from when the ULMT observes a miss address until it generates the addresses to prefetch. For best performance, the response time should be as small as possible. This is why we always execute the Prefetching step before the Learning one. Moreover, we shift as much computation as possible from the Prefetching to the Learning step, retaining only the most critical operations in the Prefetching step.

The occupancy time is the time when the ULMT is busy processing a single observed miss. For the ULMT implementation of the prefetcher to be viable, the occupancy time has to be smaller than the time between two consecutive L2 misses most of the times.

The correlation table that the ULMT reads and writes is simply a *software* data structure in memory. Consequently, our scheme eliminates the costly hardware table required by current implementations of correlation prefetching [12, 18]. Moreover, accesses to the software table are inexpensive because the memory processor transparently caches the table in its cache. Finally, our new scheme enables the redesign of the correlation table and prefetching algorithms (Section 3.3) to address the low-coverage and short-distance prefetching limitations of current implementations.

3.2. Architecture of the System

Figures 3-(a) and (b) show the architecture of a system that integrates the memory processor in the North Bridge chip or in a DRAM chip, respectively. The first design requires no modification to the DRAM or its interface, and is largely compatible with conventional memory systems. The second design needs changes to the DRAM chips and their interface, and needs special support to work in typical memory systems, which have multiple DRAM chips. However, since our goal is to examine the performance potential of the two designs, we abstract away some of the implementation complexity of the second design by assuming a single-chip main memory. In the following, we outline how the systems work. In our discussion, we only consider memory accesses resulting from misses; we ignore write-backs for simplicity and because they do not affect our algorithms.

In Figure 3-(a), the key communication occurs through queues *1*, *2*, and *3*. Miss requests from the main processor are deposited in queues *1* and *2* simultaneously. The ULMT uses the entries in queue *2* to build its table and, based on it, generate the addresses to prefetch. The latter are deposited in queue *3*. Queues *1* and *3* compete to access memory, although queue *3* has a lower priority than *1*.

When the address of a line to prefetch is deposited in queue *3*, the hardware compares it against all the entries in queue *2*. If a match for address address *X* is detected, *X* is removed from both queues. We remove *X* from queue *3* because it is redundant: a higher-priority

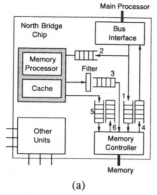
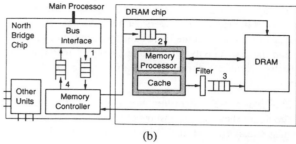

(a)   (b)

Figure 3. Architecture of a system that integrates the memory processor in the North Bridge chip (a) or in a DRAM chip (b).

request for X is already in queue *1*. X is removed from queue *2* to save computation in the ULMT. Note that it is unclear whether we lost the opportunity to prefetch X's successors by not processing X. The reason is that our algorithms prefetch several levels of successor misses (Section 3.3) and, as a result, some of X's successors may already be in queue *3*. Processing X may help improve the state in the correlation table. However, minimizing the total occupancy of the ULMT is crucial in our scheme.

Similarly, when a main-processor miss is about to be deposited in queues *1* and *2*, the hardware compares its address against those in queue *3*. If there is a match, the request is put only in queue *1* and the matching entry in queue *3* is removed.

It is possible that requests from the main processor arrive too fast for the ULMT to consume them and queue *2* overflows. In this case, the memory processor simply drops these requests.

Figure 3-(a) also shows the *Filter* module associated with queue *3*. This module improves the performance of correlation prefetching, which may sometimes try to prefetch the same address several times in a short time. The Filter module drops prefetch requests directed to any address that has been recently issued another prefetch requests. The module is a fixed-sized FIFO list that records the addresses of all the recently-issued requests. Before a request is issued to queue *3*, the hardware checks the Filter list. If it finds its address, the request is dropped and the list is left unmodified. Otherwise, the address is added to the tail of the list. With this support, some unnecessary prefetch requests are eliminated.

For completeness, the figure shows other queues. Replies from memory to the main processor go through queue *4*. In addition, the ULMT needs to access the software correlation table in main memory. Recall that the table is transparently cached by the memory processor. Logical queues *5* and *6* provide the necessary paths for the memory processor to access main memory. In practice, queues *5* and *6* are merged with the others.

If the memory processor is in the DRAM chip (Figure 3-(b)), the system works slightly differently. Miss requests from the main processor are deposited first in queue *1* and then in queue *2*. The ULMT in the memory processor accesses the correlation table from its cache and, on a miss, directly from the DRAM. The addresses to prefetch are passed through the Filter module and placed in queue *3*. As in Figure 3-(a), entries in queues *2* and *3* are checked against each other, and the common entries are dropped. The replies to both prefetches and main-processor requests are returned to the memory controller. As they reach the memory controller, their addresses are compared to the processor miss requests in queue *1*. If a memory-prefetched line matches a miss request from the main processor, the former is

considered to be the reply of the latter, and the latter is not sent to the memory chip.

Finally, in machines that include a form of processor-side prefetching, we envision our architecture to operate in two modes: *Verbose* and *Non-Verbose*. In Verbose mode, queue *2* in Figures 3-(a) and (b) receives both main-processor misses and main-processor prefetch requests. In Non-Verbose mode, queue *2* only receives main-processor misses. This mode assumes that main-processor prefetch requests are distinguishable from other requests, for example with a tag as in the MIPS R10000 [21].

The Non-Verbose mode is useful to reduce the total occupancy of the ULMT. In this case, the processor-side prefetcher can focus on the easy-to-predict sequential or regular miss patterns, while the ULMT can focus on the hard-to-predict irregular ones. The Verbose mode is also useful: the ULMT can implement a prefetch algorithm that enhances the effectiveness of the processor-side prefetcher. We present an example of this case in Section 5.2.

3.3. Correlation Prefetching Algorithms

Simply taking the current pair-based correlation table and algorithm and implementing them in software is not good enough. Indeed, as indicated in Section 2.2, the *Base* algorithm has two limitations: it does not prefetch very far ahead and, intuitively, it needs to observe one miss to eliminate another miss (its immediate successor). As a result, it tends to have low coverage.

To increase coverage, three things need to occur. First, we need to eliminate these two limitations by storing in the table (and prefetching) *several levels* of successor misses per miss: immediate successors, successors of immediate successors, and so on for several levels. Second, these prefetches have to be highly accurate. Finally, the prefetcher has to take decisions early enough so that the prefetched lines reach the main processor before they are needed.

These conditions are easier to support and ensure when the correlation algorithm is implemented as a ULMT. There are two reasons for it. The first one is that storage is now cheap and, therefore, the correlation table can be inexpensively expanded to hold multiple levels of successor misses per miss, even if that means replicating information. The second reason is the *Customizability* provided by a software implementation of the prefetching algorithm.

In the rest of this section, we describe how a ULMT implementation of correlation prefetching can deliver high coverage. We describe three approaches: using a conventional table organization, using a table re-organized for ULMT, and exploiting customizability.

174

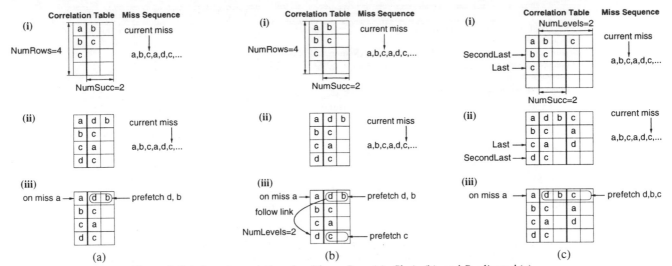

Figure 4. Pair-based correlation algorithms: *Base* (a), *Chain* (b), and *Replicated* (c).

3.3.1. Using a Conventional Table Organization

As a first step, we attempt to improve coverage without specifically exploiting the low-cost storage or customizability advantages of ULMT. We simply take the conventional table organization of Section 2.2 and force the ULMT to prefetch multiple levels of successors for every miss. The resulting algorithm we call *Chain*. *Chain* takes the same parameters as *Base* plus *NumLevels*, which is the number of levels of successors prefetched. The algorithm is illustrated in Figure 4-(b).

Chain updates the table like *Base* ((i) and (ii)) but prefetches differently ((iii)). Specifically, after prefetching the row of immediate successors, it takes the MRU one among them and accesses the correlation table again with its address. If the entry is found, it prefetches all *NumSucc* successors there. Then, it takes the MRU successor in that row and repeats the process. This is done *NumLevels*-1 times. As an example, suppose that a miss on *a* occurs ((iii)). The ULMT first prefetches *d* and *b*. Then, it takes the MRU entry *d*, looks-up the table, and prefetches *d*'s successor, *c*.

Chain addresses the two limitations of *Base*, namely not prefetching very far ahead, and needing one miss to eliminate a second one. However, *Chain* may not deliver high coverage for two reasons: the prefetches may not be highly accurate and the ULMT may have a high response time to issue all the prefetches.

The prefetches may be inaccurate because *Chain* does not prefetch the *true MRU* successors in each level of successors. Instead, it only prefetches successors found along the MRU path. For example, consider a sequence of misses that alternates between *a,b,c* and *b,e,b,f*: *a,b,c,...,b,e,b,f,...,a,b,c,....* When miss *a* is encountered, *Chain* prefetches its immediate successors (*b*), and then accesses the entry for *b* to prefetch *e* and *f*. Note that *c* is not prefetched.

The high response time of *Chain* to a miss comes from having to make *NumLevels* accesses to different rows in the table. Each access involves an associative search because the table is associative and, potentially, one or more cache misses.

3.3.2. Using a Table Re-Organized for ULMT

We now attempt to improve coverage by exploiting the low cost of storage in ULMT solutions. Specifically, we expand the table to allow replicated information. Each row of the table stores the tag of the miss address, and *NumLevels* levels of successors. Each level

contains *NumSucc* addresses that use LRU for replacement. Using this table, we propose an algorithm called *Replicated* (Figure 4-(c)). *Replicated* takes the same parameters as *Chain*.

As shown in Figure 4-(c), *Replicated* keeps *NumLevels* pointers to the table. These pointers point to the entries for the address of the last miss, second last, and so on, and are used for efficient table access. When a miss occurs, these pointers are used to access the entries of the last few misses, and insert the new address as the MRU successor of the correct level ((i) and (ii)). In the figure, the *NumSucc* entries at each level are MRU ordered. Finally, prefetching in *Replicated* is simple: when a miss is seen, all the entries in the corresponding row are prefetched ((iii)).

Note that *Replicated* eliminates the two problems of *Chain*. First, prefetches are accurate because they contain the *true MRU* successors at each level. This is the result of grouping together all the successors from a given level, irrespective of the path taken. In the sequence shown above *a,b,c,...,b,e,b,f,...,a,b,c,...*, on a miss on *a*, *Replicated* prefetches *b* and *c*.

Second, the response time of *Replicated* is much smaller than *Chain*. Indeed, *Replicated* prefetches several levels of successors with a single row access, and maybe even with a single cache miss. *Replicated* effectively shifts some computation from the Prefetching step to the Learning one: prefetching needs a single table access, while learning a miss needs multiple table updates. This is a good trade-off because the Prefetching step is the critical one. Furthermore, these multiple learning updates are inexpensive: the use of the pointers eliminates the need to do any associative searches on the table, and the rows to be updated are most likely still in the cache of the memory processor (since they were updated most recently).

3.3.3. Exploiting the Customizability of ULMT

We can also improve coverage by exploiting the second advantage of ULMT solutions: customizability. The programmer or system can choose to run a different algorithm in the ULMT for each application. The chosen algorithm can be highly customized to the application's needs.

One approach to customization is to use the table organizations and prefetching algorithms described above but to tune their parameters on an application basis. For example, in applications where the miss sequences are highly predictable, we can set the number of levels of successors to prefetch (*NumLevels*) to a high value. As a result,

Characteristics	Base	Chain	Replicated
Levels of successors prefetched	1	NumLevels	NumLevels
True MRU ordering for each level?	Yes	No	Yes
Number of row accesses in the Prefetching step (Requires SEARCH)	1	NumLevels	1
Number of row accesses in the Learning step (Requires NO SEARCH)	1	1	NumLevels
Response time	Low	High	Low
Space requirement (for constant number of prefetches)	x	x	$NumLevels \times x$

Table 1. Comparing different pair-based correlation prefetching algorithms running on a ULMT.

we will prefetch more levels of successors with high accuracy. In applications with unpredictable sequences, we can do the opposite. We can also tune the number of rows in the table (*NumRows*). In applications that have large footprints, we can set *NumRows* to a high value to hold more information in the table. In small applications, we can do the opposite to save space.

A second approach to customization is to use a different prefetching algorithm. For example, we can add support for sequential prefetching to all the algorithms described above. The resulting algorithms will have low response time for sequential miss patterns.

Another approach is to adaptively decide the algorithm on-the-fly, as the application executes. In fact, this approach can also be used to execute different algorithms in different parts of one application. Such intra-application customizability may be useful in complex applications.

Finally, the ULMT can also be used for profiling purposes. It can monitor the misses of an application and infer higher-level information such as cache performance, application access patterns, or page conflicts.

3.3.4. Comparing the Algorithms

Table 1 compares the *Base*, *Chain*, and *Replicated* algorithms executing on a ULMT. *Replicated* has the highest potential for high coverage: it supports far-ahead prefetching by prefetching several levels of successors, its prefetches have high accuracy because they prefetch the true MRU successors at each level, and it has a low response time, in part because it only needs to access a single table row in the Prefetching step. Accessing a single row minimizes the associative searches and the cache misses. The only shortcoming of *Replicated* is the larger space that it requires for the correlation table. However, this is a minor issue since the table is a software structure allocated in main memory. Note that all these algorithms can also be implemented in hardware. However, *Replicated* is more suitable for an ULMT implementation because providing the larger space required in hardware is expensive.

3.4. Operating System Issues

There are some operating system issues that are related to ULMT operation. We outline them here.

Protection. The ULMT has its own separate address space with its instructions, the correlation table, and a few other data structures. The ULMT shares neither instructions nor data with any application. The ULMT can observe the physical addresses of the application misses. It can also issue prefetches for these addresses on behalf of the main processor. However, it can neither read from nor write to these addresses. Therefore, protection is guaranteed.

Multiprogrammed Environment. It is a poor approach to have all the applications share a single table: the table is likely to suffer a lot of interference. A better approach is to associate a different ULMT, with its own table, to each application. This eliminates interference in the tables. In addition, it enables the customization of each ULMT

to its own application. If we conservatively assume a 4-Mbyte table on average per application, 8 applications require 32 Mbytes, which is only a modest fraction of today's typical main memory. If this requirement is excessive, we can save space by dynamically sizing the tables. In this case, if an application does not use the space, its table shrinks.

Scheduling. The scheduler knows the ULMT associated with each application. Consequently, the scheduler schedules and preempts both application and ULMT as a group. Furthermore, the operating system provides an interface for the application to control its ULMT.

Page Re-mapping. Sometimes, a page gets re-mapped. Since ULMTs operate on physical addresses, such events can cause some table entries to become stale. We can choose to take no action and let the table update itself automatically through learning. Alternatively, the operating system can inform the corresponding ULMT when a re-mapping occurs, passing the old and new physical page number. Then, the ULMT indexes its table for each line of the old page. If the entry is found, the ULMT relocates it and updates both the tag and any applicable successors in the row. Given current page sizes, we estimate the table update to take a few microseconds. Such overhead may be overlapped with the execution of the operating system page mapping handler in the main processor. Note that some other entries in the table may still keep stale successor information. Such information may cause a few useless prefetches, but the table will quickly update itself automatically.

4. Evaluation Environment

Applications. To evaluate the ULMT approach, we use nine mostly-irregular, memory-intensive applications. Irregular applications are hardly amenable to compiler-based prefetching. Consequently, they are the obvious target for ULMT correlation prefetching. The exception is CG, which is a regular application. Table 2 describes the applications. The last four columns of the table will be explained later.

Simulation Environment. The evaluation is done using an execution-driven simulation environment that supports a dynamic superscalar processor model [17]. We model a PC architecture with a simple memory processor that is integrated in either the North Bridge chip or in a DRAM chip, following the micro-architecture of Figure 3. Table 3 shows the parameters used for each component of the architecture. All cycles are 1.6 GHz cycles. The architecture is modeled cycle by cycle.

We model only a uni-programmed environment with a single application and a single ULMT that execute concurrently. We model all the contention in the system, including the contention of the application thread and the ULMT on shared resources such as the memory controller, DRAM channels, and DRAM banks.

Processor-Side Prefetching. The main processor optionally includes a hardware prefetcher that can prefetch multiple streams of stride 1 or -1 into the L1 cache. The prefetcher monitors L1 cache misses and can identify and prefetch up to *NumSeq* sequen-

176

Appl	Suite	Problem	Input	Correlation Table			
				NumRows (K)	Size (Mbytes)		
					Base	Chain	Repl
CG	NAS	Conjugate gradient	Class S	64	1.3	0.8	1.8
Equake	SpecFP2000	Seismic wave propagation simulation	Test	128	2.5	1.5	3.5
FT	NAS	3D Fourier transform	Class S	256	5.0	3.0	7.0
Gap	SpecInt2000	Group theory solver	Rako (subset of test)	128	2.5	1.5	3.5
Mcf	SpecInt2000	Combinatorial optimization	Test	32	0.6	0.4	0.9
MST	Olden	Finding minimum spanning tree	1024 nodes	256	5.0	3.0	7.0
Parser	SpecInt2000	Word processing	Subset of train	128	2.5	1.5	3.5
Sparse	SparseBench[10]	GMRES with compressed row storage	32^3	256	5.0	3.0	7.0
Tree	Univ. of Hawaii[3]	Barnes-Hut N-body problem	2048 bodies	8	0.2	0.1	0.2
Average	—	—	—	140	2.7	1.6	3.8

Table 2. Applications used.

PROCESSOR

Main Processor:
  6-issue dynamic. 1.6 GHz. Int, fp, ld/st FUs: 4, 4, 2
  Pending ld, st: 8, 16. Branch penalty: 12 cycles
Memory Processor:
  2-issue dynamic. 800 MHz. Int, fp, ld/st FUs: 2, 0, 1
  Pending ld, st: 4, 4. Branch penalty: 6 cycles

MEMORY

Main Processor's Memory Hierarchy:
  L1 data: write-back, 16 KB, 2 way, 32-B line, 3-cycle hit RT
  L2 data: write-back, 512 KB, 4 way, 64-B line, 19-cycle hit RT
  RT memory latency: 243 cycles (row miss), 208 cycles (row hit)
  Memory bus: split-transaction, 8 B, 400 MHz, 3.2 GB/sec peak
Memory Processor's Memory Hierarchy:
  L1 data: write-back, 32 KB, 2 way, 32-B line, 4-cycle hit RT
  In North Bridge: RT mem latency: 100 cycles (row miss),
                                           65 cycles (row hit)
  Latency of a prefetch request to reach DRAM: 25 cycles
  In DRAM: RT mem latency: 56 cycles (row miss),
                                 21 cycles (row hit)
  Internal DRAM data bus: 32-B wide, 800 MHz, 25.6 GB/sec peak
DRAM Parameters (applicable to all procs):
  Dual channel. Each channel: 2 B, 800 MHz. Total: 3.2 GB/sec peak
  Random access time (tRAC): 45 ns
  Time from memory controller (tSystem): 60 ns

OTHER

  Depth of queues 1 through 6: 16
  Filter module: 32 entries, FIFO

Table 3. Parameters of the simulated architecture. Latencies correspond to contention-free conditions. *RT* stands for round-trip *from the processor*. All cycles are 1.6 GHz cycles.

tial streams concurrently. It works as follows. When the third miss in a sequence is observed, the prefetcher recognizes a stream. Then, it prefetches the next *NumPref* lines in the stream into the L1 cache. Furthermore, it stores the stride and the next address expected in the stream in a special register. If the processor later misses on the address in the register, the prefetcher prefetches the next *NumPref* lines in the stream and updates the register. The prefetcher contains *NumSeq* such registers. As we can see, while this scheme works somewhat like stream buffers [13], the prefetched lines go to L1. We choose this approach to minimize hardware complexity. A shortcoming is that the L1 cache may get polluted. For completeness, we resimulated the system with the prefetches going into separate buffers rather than into L1. We found that the performance changes very little, in part because checking the buffers on L1 misses introduces delay.

Algorithm Parameters. Table 4 lists the prefetching algorithms that we evaluate and the default parameters that we use. The sequential prefetching supported in hardware by the main processor is called *Conven4* for conventional. It can also be implemented in software

by a ULMT. We evaluate two such software implementations (*Seq1* and *Seq4*). In this case, the prefetcher in memory observes L2 misses rather than L1.

Unless otherwise indicated, the processor-side prefetcher is off and, if it is on, the ULMT algorithms operate in Non-Verbose mode (Section 3.2). For the *Base* algorithm, we choose the parameter values used by Joseph and Grunwald [12] so that we can compare the work. The last four columns of Table 2 give a conservative value for the size of the correlation table for each application. The table is two-way set-associative. We have sized the number of rows in the table (*NumRows*) to be the lowest power of two such that, with a trivial hashing function that simply takes the lower bits of the line address, less than 5% of the insertions replace an existing entry. This is a very generous allocation. A more sophisticated hash function can reduce *NumRows* significantly without increasing conflicts much. In any case, knowing that each row in *Base*, *Chain*, and *Repl* takes 20, 12, and 28 bytes, respectively, in a 32-bit machine, we can compute the total table size. Overall, while some applications need more space than others, the average value is tolerable: 2.7, 1.6, and 3.8 Mbytes for *Base*, *Chain*, and *Repl*, respectively.

ULMT Implementation. We wrote all ULMTs in C and hand-optimized them for minimal response and occupancy time. One major performance bottleneck of the implementation is frequent branches. We remove branches by unrolling loops and hardwiring all algorithm parameters. We also perform optimizations to increase the spatial locality and to reduce instruction count. None of the algorithms uses floating-point operations.

5. Evaluation

5.1. Characterizing Application Behavior

Predictability of the Miss Sequences. We start by characterizing how well our ULMT algorithms can predict the miss sequences of the applications. For that, we run each ULMT algorithm simply observing all L2 cache miss addresses without performing prefetching. We record the fraction of L2 cache misses that are correctly predicted. For a sequential prefetcher, this means that the upcoming miss address matches the next address predicted by one of the streams identified; for a pair-based prefetcher, the upcoming address matches one of the successors predicted for that level.

Figure 5 shows the results of prediction for up to three levels of successors. Given a miss, the *Level 1* chart shows the predictability of the immediate successor, while *Level 2* shows the predictability of the next successor, and *Level 3* the successor after that one. The experiments for the pair-base schemes use large tables to ensure that practically no prediction is missed due to conflicts in the table: *NumRows* is 256 K, *Assoc* is 4, and *NumSucc* is 4. Under these condi-

Prefetching Algorithm	Implementation	Name	Parameter Values
Base		*Base*	*NumSucc = 4, Assoc = 4*
Chain		*Chain*	*NumSucc = 2, Assoc = 2, NumLevels = 3*
Replicated	Software in memory as ULMT	*Repl*	*NumSucc = 2, Assoc = 2, NumLevels = 3*
Sequential 1-Stream		*Seq1*	*NumSeq = 1, NumPref = 6*
Sequential 4-Streams		*Seq4*	*NumSeq = 4, NumPref = 6*
Sequential 4-Streams	Hardware in L1 of main processor	*Conven4*	*NumSeq = 4, NumPref = 6*

Table 4. Parameter values used for the different algorithms.

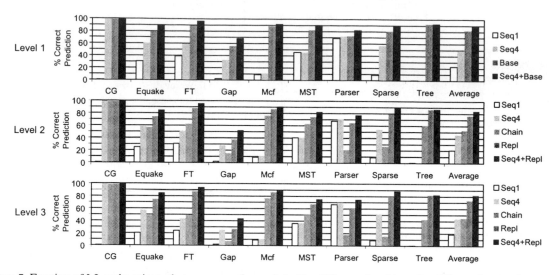

Figure 5. Fraction of L2 cache misses that are correctly predicted by different algorithms for different levels of successors.

tions, for level 1, *Chain* and *Repl* are equivalent to *Base*. For levels 2 and 3, *Base* is not applicable. The figure also shows the effect of combining algorithms.

Figure 5 shows that our ULMT algorithms can effectively predict the miss streams of the applications. For example, at level 1, *Seq4* and *Base* correctly predict on average 49% and 82% of the misses, respectively. Moreover, the best algorithms keep predicting correctly across several levels of successors. For example, *Repl* correctly predicts on average 77% and 73% of the misses for levels 2 and 3, respectively. Therefore, these algorithms have good potential.

The figure also shows that different applications have different miss behavior. For instance, applications such as Mcf and Tree do not have sequential patterns and, therefore, only pair-based algorithms can predict misses. In other applications such as CG, instead, sequential patterns dominate. As a result, sequential prefetching can predict practically all L2 misses. Most applications have a mix of both patterns.

Among pair-based algorithms, *Repl* almost always outperforms *Chain* by a wide margin. This is because *Chain* does not maintain the true MRU successors at each level. However, while *Repl* is effective under all patterns, it is better when combined with multi-stream sequential prefetching (*Seq4+Repl*).

Time Between L2 Misses. Another important issue is the time between L2 misses. Figure 6 classifies L2 misses according to the number of cycles between two consecutive misses arriving at the memory. The misses are grouped in bins corresponding to [0,80) cycles, [80,200) cycles, etc. The unit is 1.6 GHz processor cycles.

The most significant bin is [200,280), which contributes with 60% of all miss distances on average. These misses are critical beyond their numbers because their latencies are hard to hide with out-of-order execution. Indeed, since the round-trip latency to memory is 208-243 cycles, dependent misses are likely to fall in this bin. They contribute

more to processor stall than the figure suggests because dependent misses cannot be overlapped with each other. Consequently, we want the ULMT to prefetch them. To make sure that the ULMT is fast enough to learn these misses, its occupancy should be less than 200 cycles.

The misses in the other bins are fewer and less critical. Those in [280,∞) are too far apart to put pressure on the ULMT's timing. Those in [0,80) may not give enough time to the ULMT to respond. Fortunately, these misses are more likely to be overlapped with each other and with computation.

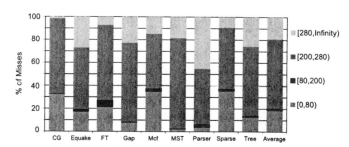

Figure 6. Characterizing the time between L2 misses.

5.2. Comparing the Different Algorithms

Figure 7 compares the execution time of the applications under different cases: no prefetching (*NoPref*), processor-side prefetching as listed in Table 4 (*Conven4*), different ULMT schemes listed in Table 4 (*Base, Chain,* and *Repl*), the combination of *Conven4* and *Repl* (*Conven4+Repl*), and some customized algorithms (*Custom*). The results are for the case where the memory processor is integrated in the DRAM. For each application and the average, the bars are normalized to *NoPref*. The bars show the memory-induced processor stall time that is caused by requests between the processor and the L2 cache (*UptoL2*), and by requests beyond the L2 cache (*Be-*

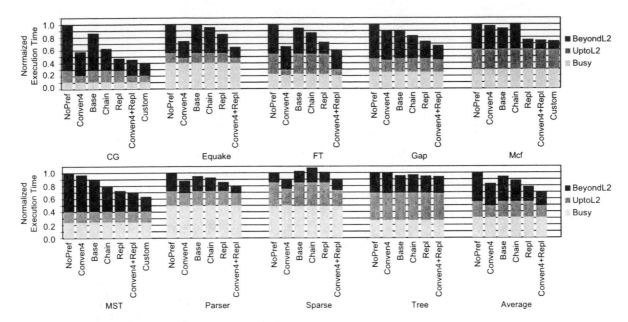

Figure 7. Execution time of the applications with different prefetching algorithms.

yondL2). The remaining time (*Busy*) includes processor computation plus other pipeline stalls. A system with a perfect L2 cache would only have the *Busy* and *UptoL2* times.

On average, *BeyondL2* is the most significant component of the execution time under *NoPref*. It accounts for 44% of the time. Thus, although our ULMT schemes only target L2 cache misses, they target the main contributor to the execution time.

Conven4 performs very well on CG because sequential patterns dominate. However, it is ineffective in applications such as Mcf and Tree that have purely irregular patterns. On average, *Conven4* reduces the execution time by 17%.

The pair-based schemes show mixed performance. *Base* shows limited speedups, mostly because it does not prefetch far enough. On average, it reduces *NoPref*'s execution time by 6%. *Chain* performs a little better, but it is limited by inaccuracy (Figure 5) and high response time (Section 3.3.1). On average, it reduces *NoPref*'s execution time by 12%.

Repl is able to reduce the execution time significantly. It performs well in almost all applications. It outperforms both *Base* and *Chain* in all cases. Its impact comes from the nice properties of the *Replicated* algorithm, as discussed in Section 3.3.4. The average of the application speedups of *Repl* over *NoPref* is 1.32.

Finally, *Conven4+Repl* performs the best. On average, it removes over half of the *BeyondL2* stall time, and delivers an average application speedup of 1.46 over *NoPref*. If we compare the impact of processor-side prefetching only (*Conven4*) and memory-side prefetching only (*Repl*), we see that they have a constructive effect in *Conven4+Repl*. The reason is that the two schemes help each other. Specifically, the processor-side prefetcher prefetches and eliminates the sequential misses. The memory-side prefetcher works in Non-Verbose mode (Section 3.2) and, therefore, does not see the prefetch requests. Therefore, it can fully focus on the irregular miss patterns. With the resulting reduced load, the ULMT is more effective.

Algorithm Customization. In this first paper on ULMT prefetching, we have attempted only very simple customization for a few applications. Table 5 shows the changes. For CG, we run *Seq1+Repl* in

Verbose mode. For MST and Mcf, we run *Repl* with a higher *NumLevels*. In all cases, *Conven4* is on. The results are shown in Figure 7 as the *Custom* bar in the three applications.

Application	Customized ULMT Algorithm
CG	*Seq1+Repl* in Verbose mode
MST, Mcf	*Repl* with *NumLevels = 4*

Table 5. Customizations performed. *Conven4* is also on.

The customization in CG tries to further exploit positive interaction between processor- and memory-side prefetching. While CG only has sequential miss patterns (Figure 5), its multiple streams overwhelm the conventional prefetcher. Indeed, although processor-side prefetches are very accurate (99.8% of the prefetched lines are referenced), they are not timely enough (only 64% are timely) because some of them miss in the L2 cache. In our customization, we turn on the Verbose mode so that processor-side prefetch requests are seen by the ULMT. Furthermore, the ULMT is extended with a single-stream sequential prefetch algorithm (*Seq1*) before executing *Repl*. In this environment, the positive interaction between the two prefetchers increases. Specifically, while the application references the different streams in an interleaved manner, the processor-side prefetcher "unscrambles" the miss sequence into chunks of same-stream prefetch requests. The *Seq1* prefetcher in the ULMT then easily identifies each stream and, very efficiently, prefetches ahead. As a result, 81% of the processor-side prefetches arrive in a timely manner. With this customization, the speedup of CG improves from 2.19 (with *Conven4+Repl*) to 2.59. This case demonstrates that even regular applications that are amenable to sequential processor-side prefetching can benefit from ULMT prefetching.

The customization in MST and Mcf tries to exploit predictability beyond the third level of successor misses by setting *NumLevels* to 4 in *Repl*. As shown in Figure 7, this approach is successful for MST, but it produces marginal gains in Mcf.

Overall, this initial attempt at customization shows promising results. After applying customization on three applications, the average execution speedup of the nine applications relative to *NoPref* becomes 1.53.

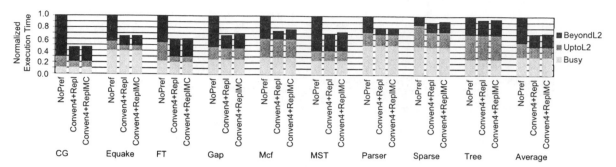

Figure 8. Execution time for different locations of the memory processor.

Location of Memory Processor. Figure 8 examines the impact of where we place the memory processor (Figure 3). The first two bars for each application are taken from Figure 7: *NoPref* and *Conven4+Repl*. The last bar for each application corresponds to the *Conven4+Repl* algorithm with the memory processor placed in the memory controller (North Bridge) chip (*Conven4+ReplMC*). With the processor in the North Bridge chip, we have twice the memory access latency (100 cycles vs. 56 cycles), eight times lower memory bandwidth (3.2 GB/sec vs. 25.6 GB/sec), and an additional 25-cycle delay seen by the prefetch requests before they reach the DRAM[1]. However, Figure 8 shows that the impact on the execution time is very small. It results in a small decrease in average speedups from 1.46 to 1.41. The impact is small thanks to the ability of *Repl* to accurately prefetch far ahead. Only the timeliness of the immediate successor prefetches is affected, while the prefetching of further levels of successors is still timely. Overall, given these results and the hardware cost of the two designs, we conclude that putting the memory processor in the North Bridge chip is the most cost-effective design of the two.

Prefetching Effectiveness. To gain further insight into these prefetching schemes, Figure 9 examines the effectiveness of the lines prefetched into the L2 cache by the ULMT. These lines are called *prefetches*. The figure shows data for Sparse, Tree, and the average of the other seven applications. The figure combines both L2 misses and prefetches, and breaks them down into 5 categories: prefetches that eliminate an L2 miss (*Hits*), prefetches that eliminate part of the latency of an L2 miss because they arrive a bit late (*DelayedHits*), L2 misses that pay the full latency (*NonPrefMisses*), and useless prefetches. Useless prefetches are further broken down into prefetches that are brought into the L2 but that are not referenced by the time they are replaced (*Replaced*), and prefetches that are dropped on arrival to L2 because the same line is already in the cache (*Redundant*). Since *Coverage* is the fraction of the original L2 misses that are fully or partially eliminated, it is represented by the sum of *Hits* and *DelayedHits* as shown in Figure 9. *NonPrefMisses* in Figure 9 is the number of L2 misses left after prefetching, relative to the original number of L2 misses. Note that *NonPrefMisses* can be higher than 1.0 for some algorithms. $1.0 - NonPrefMisses$ is the number of L2 misses eliminated relative to the original number of L2 misses. *NonPrefMisses* can be broken down into two groups: those misses below the 1.0 line in Figure 9 ($1.0 - Hits - DelayedHits$) come from the original misses, while those above the 1.0 line ($Hits + DelayedHits + NonPrefMisses - 1.0$) are the new L2 conflict misses caused by prefetches.

Looking at the average of the seven applications, we see why *Base* and *Chain* are not effective: their coverage is small. *Base* is hurt

---

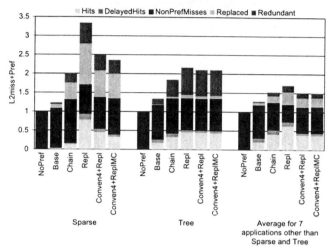

Figure 9. Breakdown of the L2 misses and lines prefetched by the ULMT (prefetches). The original misses are normalized to 1.

by its inability to prefetch far ahead, while *Chain* is hampered by its high response time and limited accuracy. The figure also shows that *Repl* has a high coverage (0.74). However, this comes at the cost of useless prefetches (*Replaced* plus *Redundant* are equivalent to 50% of the original misses) and additional misses due to conflicts with prefetches (20% of the original misses). We can see, therefore, that advanced pair-based schemes need additional bandwidth.

Conven4+Repl seems to have low coverage, despite its high performance in Figure 7. The reason is that the prefetch requests issued by the processor-side prefetcher, while effective in eliminating L2 misses, are lumped into the *NonPrefMisses* category in the figure if they reach memory. Since the ULMT prefetcher is in Non-Verbose mode, it does not see these requests. Consequently, the ULMT prefetcher only focuses on the irregular miss patterns. ULMT prefetches that eliminate irregular misses appear as *Hits+DelayedHits*.

Finally, Figure 9 also shows why *Sparse* and *Tree* showed limited speedups in Figure 7. They have too many conflicts in the cache, which results in many remaining *NonPrefMisses*. Furthermore, their prefetches are not very accurate, which results in large *Replaced* and *Redundant* categories.

Work Load of the ULMT. Figure 10 shows the average response time and occupancy time (Section 3.1) for each of the ULMT algorithms, averaged over all applications. The times are measured in 1.6 GHz cycles. Each bar is broken down into computation time (*Busy*) and memory stall time (*Mem*). The numbers on top of each bar show the average IPC of the ULMT. The IPC is calculated as the number

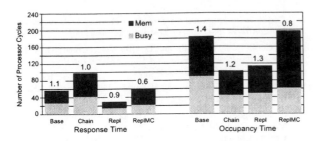

Figure 10. Average response and occupancy time of different ULMT algorithms in main-processor cycles.

of instructions divided by the number of *memory processor* cycles.

The figure shows that, in all the algorithms, the occupancy time is less than 200 cycles. Consequently, the ULMT is fast enough to process most of the L2 misses (Figure 6). Memory stall time is roughly half of the ULMT execution time when the processor is in the DRAM, and more when the processor is in the North Bridge chip (*ReplMC*). *Chain* and *Repl* have the lowest occupancy time. Note that *Repl*'s occupancy is not much higher than *Chain*'s, despite the higher number of table updates performed by *Repl*. The reasons are the fewer associative searches and the better cache line reuse in *Repl*.

The response time is most important for prefetching effectiveness. The figure shows that *Repl* has the lowest response time, at around 30 cycles. The response time of *ReplMC* is about twice as much. Fortunately, the *Replicated* algorithm is able to prefetch far ahead accurately and, therefore, the effectiveness of prefetching is not very sensitive to a modest increase in the response time.

Main Memory Bus Utilization. Finally, Figure 11 shows the utilization of the main memory bus for various algorithms, averaged over all applications. The increase in bus utilization induced by the advanced algorithms is divided into two parts: increase caused naturally by the reduced execution time, and additional increase caused by the prefetching traffic. Overall, the figure shows that the increase in bus utilization is tolerable. The utilization increases from the original 20% to only 36% in the worst case (*Conven4+Repl*). Moreover, most of the increase comes from the faster execution; only a 6% utilization is directly attributable to the prefetches. In general, the fact that memory-side prefetching only adds one-way traffic to the main memory bus, limits its bandwidth needs.

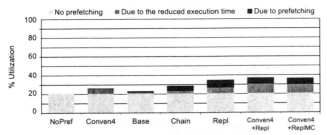

Figure 11. Main memory bus utilization.

6. Related Work

Memory-Side Prefetching. Some memory-side prefetchers are simple hardware controllers. For example, the NVIDIA chipset includes the DASP controller in the North Bridge chip [22]. It seems that it is mostly targeted to stride recognition and buffers data locally. The i860 chipset from Intel is reported to have a prefetch cache, which may indicate the presence of a similar engine. Cooksey *et al.* [9] propose the Content-Based prefetcher, which is a hardware

controller that monitors the data coming from memory. If an item appears to be an address, the engine prefetches it. Alexander and Kedem [1] propose a hardware controller that monitors requests at the main memory. If it observes repeatable patterns, it prefetches rows of data from the DRAM to an SRAM buffer inside the memory chip. Overall, our scheme is different in that we use a general-purpose processor running a prefetching algorithm as a user-level thread.

Other studies propose specialized programmable engines. For example, Hughes [11] and Yang and Lebeck [28] propose adding a specialized engine to prefetch linked data structures. While Hughes focuses on a multiprocessor processing-in-memory system, Yang and Lebeck focus on a uniprocessor and put the engine at every level of the cache hierarchy. The main processor downloads information on these engines about the linked structures and what prefetches to perform. Our scheme is different in that it has general applicability.

Another related system is Impulse, an intelligent memory controller capable of remapping physical addresses to improve the performance of irregular applications [4]. Impulse could prefetch data, but only implements next-line prefetching. Furthermore, it buffers data in the memory controller, rather than sending it to the processor.

Correlation Prefetching. Early work on correlation prefetching can be found in [2, 24]. More recently, several authors have made further contributions. Charney and Reeves study correlation prefetching and suggest combining a stride prefetcher with a general correlation prefetcher [6]. Joseph and Grunwald propose the basic correlation table organization and algorithm that we evaluate [12]. Alexander and Kedem use correlation prefetching slightly differently [1], as we indicate above. Sherwood *et al.* use it to help stream buffers prefetch irregular patterns [26]. Finally, Lai *et al.* design a slightly different correlation prefetcher [18]. Specifically, a prefetch is not triggered by a miss; instead, it is triggered by a dead-line predictor indicating that a line in the cache will not be used again and, therefore, a new line should be prefetched in. This scheme improves prefetching timeliness at the expense of tighter integration of the prefetcher with the processor, since the prefetcher needs to observe not only miss addresses, but also reference addresses and program counters.

We differ from the recent works in important ways. First, they propose hardware-only engines, which often require expensive hardware tables; we use a flexible user-level thread on a general-purpose core that stores the table as a software structure in memory. Second, except for Alexander and Kedem [1], they place their engines between the L1 and L2 caches, or between the processor and the L1; we place the prefetcher in memory and focus on L2 misses. Time intervals between L2 misses are large enough for a ULMT to be viable and effective. Finally, we propose a new table organization and prefetching algorithm that, by exploiting inexpensive memory space, increases far-ahead prefetching and prefetch coverage.

Prefetching Regular Structures. Several schemes have been proposed to prefetch sequential or strided patterns. They include the Reference Prediction table of Chen and Baer [7], and the Stream buffers of Jouppi [13], Palacharla and Kessler [23], and Sherwood *et al.* [26]. We base our processor-side prefetcher on these schemes.

Processor-Side Prefetching. There are many more proposals for processor-side prefetching, often for irregular applications. A tiny, non-exhaustive list includes Choi *et al.* [8], Karlsson *et al.* [14], Lipasti *et al.* [19], Luk and Mowry [20], Roth *et al.* [25], and Zhang and Torrellas [29]. Most of these schemes specifically target linked data structures. They tend to rely on program information that is available to the processor, like the addresses and sizes of data structures. Often, they need compiler support. Our scheme needs neither program information nor compiler support.

Other Related Work. Chappell *et al.* [5] use a subordinate thread in a multithreaded processor to improve branch prediction. They suggest using such a thread for prefetching and cache management. Finally, our work is also related to data forwarding in multiprocessors, where a processor pushes data into the cache hierarchy of another processor [15].

7. Conclusions

This paper introduced memory-side correlation prefetching using a User-Level Memory Thread (ULMT) running on a simple general-purpose processor in main memory. This scheme solves many of the problems in conventional correlation prefetching and provides several important additional features. Specifically, the scheme needs minimal hardware modifications beyond the memory processor, uses main memory to store the correlation table inexpensively, can exploit a new table organization to increase far-ahead prefetching and coverage, can effectively prefetch for applications with largely any miss pattern as long as it repeats, and supports customization of the prefetching algorithm by the programmer for individual applications. Our results showed that the scheme delivers an average speedup of 1.32 for nine mostly-irregular applications. Furthermore, our scheme works well in combination with a conventional processor-side sequential prefetcher, in which case the average speedup increases to 1.46. Finally, by exploiting the customization of the prefetching algorithm, we increased the average speedup to 1.53.

This work is being extended by designing effective techniques for ULMT customization. In particular, we are customizing for linked data structure prefetching, cache conflict detection and elimination, and general application profiling. Customization for cache conflict elimination should improve Sparse and Tree, the applications with the smallest speedups.

Acknowledgments

The authors thank the anonymous reviewers, Hidetaka Magoshi, Jose Martinez, Milos Prvulovic, Marc Snir, and James Tuck.

References

[1] T. Alexander and G. Kedem. Distributed Predictive Cache Design for High Performance Memory Systems. In *the Second International Symposium on High-Performance Computer Architecture*, pages 254–263, February 1996.

[2] J. L. Baer. Dynamic Improvements of Locality in Virtual Memory Systems. *IEEE Transactions on Software Engineering*, 2:54–62, March 1976.

[3] J. E. Barnes. Treecode. Institute for Astronomy, University of Hawaii. 1994. *ftp://hubble.ifa.hawaii.edu/pub/barnes/treecode*.

[4] J. B. Carter et al. Impulse: Building a Smarter Memory Controller. In *the 5th International Symposium on High-Performance Computer Architecture*, pages 70–79, January 1999.

[5] R. S. Chappell, J. Stark, S. Kim, S. K. Reinhardt, and Y. N. Patt. Simultaneous Subordinate Microthreading (SSMT). In *the 26th International Symposium on Computer Architecture*, pages 186–195, May 1999.

[6] M. J. Charney and A. P. Reeves. Generalized Correlation Based Hardware Prefetching. *Technical Report EE-CEG-95-1, Cornell University*, February 1995.

[7] T. F. Chen and J. L.Baer. Reducing Memory Latency via Non-Blocking and Prefetching Cache. In *the 5th International Conference on Architectural Support for Programming Languages and Operating Systems*, pages 51–61, October 1992.

[8] S. Choi, D. Kim, and D. Yeung. Multi-Chain Prefetching: Effective Exploitation of Inter-Chain Memory Parallelism for Pointer-Chasing Codes. In *International Conference on Parallel Architectures and Compilation Techniques*, pages 51–61, September 2001.

[9] R. Cooksey, D. Colarelli, and D. Grunwald. Content-Based Prefetching: Initial Results. In *the 2nd Workshop on Intelligent Memory Systems*, pages 33–55, November 2000.

[10] J. Dongarra, V. Eijkhout, and H. van der Vorst. SparseBench: A Sparse Iterative Benchmark. *http://www.netlib.org/benchmark/sparsebench*.

[11] C. J. Hughes. Prefetching Linked Data Structures in Systems with Merged DRAM-Logic. Master's thesis, University of Illinois at Urbana-Champaign, May 2000. Technical Report UIUCDCS-R-2001-2221.

[12] D. Joseph and D. Grunwald. Prefetching Using Markov Predictors. In *the 24th International Symposium on Computer Architecture*, pages 252–263, June 1997.

[13] N. Jouppi. Improving Direct-Mapped Cache Performance by the Addition of a Small Fully-Associative Cache and Prefetch Buffers. In *the 17th International Symposium on Computer Architecture*, pages 364–373, May 1990.

[14] M. Karlsson, F. Dahlgren, and P. Stenstrom. A Prefetching Technique for Irregular Accesses to Linked Data Structures. In *the 6th International Symposium on High-Performance Computer Architecture*, pages 206–217, January 2000.

[15] D. Koufaty and J. Torrellas. Comparing Data Forwarding and Prefetching for Communication-Induced Misses in Shared-Memory MPs. In *International Conference on Supercomputing*, pages 53–60, July 1998.

[16] C. Kozyrakis et al. Scalable Processors in the Billion-Transistor Era: IRAM. *IEEE Computer*, pages 75–78, September 1997.

[17] V. Krishnan and J. Torrellas. A Direct-Execution Framework for Fast and Accurate Simulation of Superscalar Processors. In *International Conference on Parallel Architectures and Compilation Techniques*, pages 286–293, October 1998.

[18] A. Lai, C. Fide, and B. Falsafi. Dead-Block Prediction and Dead-Block Correlating Prefetchers. In *the 28th International Symposium on Computer Architecture*, pages 144–154, June 2001.

[19] M. H. Lipasti, W. J. Schmidt, S. R. Kunkel, and R. R. Roediger. Spaid: Software Prefetching in Pointer and Call Intensive Environments. In *the 28th International Symposium on Microarchitecture*, pages 231–236, November 1995.

[20] C. Luk and T. C. Mowry. Compiler-Based Prefetching for Recursive Data Structures. In *the 7th International Conference on Architectural Support for Programming Languages and Operating Systems*, pages 222–233, October 1996.

[21] MIPS. MIPS R10000 Microprocessor User's Manual. *Version 2.0*, January 1997.

[22] NVIDIA. Technical Brief: NVIDIA nForce Integrated Graphics Processor (IGP) and Dynamic Adaptive Speculative Pre-Processor (DASP). *http://www.nvidia.com/*.

[23] S. Palacharla and R. Kessler. Evaluating Stream Buffers as a Secondary Cache Replacement. In *the 21st International Symposium on Computer Architecture*, pages 24–33, April 1994.

[24] J. Pomerene, T. Puzak, R. Rechtschaffen, and F. Sparacio. Prefetching System for a Cache Having a Second Directory for Sequentially Accessed Blocks. *U.S. Patent 4,807,110*, February 1989.

[25] A. Roth, A. Moshovos, and G. Sohi. Dependence Based Prefetching for Linked Data Structures. In *the 8th International Conference on Architectural Support for Programming Languages and Operating Systems*, pages 115–126, October 1998.

[26] T. Sherwood, S. Sair, and B. Calder. Predictor-Directed Stream Buffers. In *the 33rd International Symposium on Microarchitecture*, pages 42–53, December 2000.

[27] Sony Computer Entertainment Inc. *http://www.sony.com*.

[28] C.-L. Yang and A. R. Lebeck. Push vs. Pull: Data Movement for Linked Data Structures. In *International Conference on Supercomputing*, pages 176–186, May 2000.

[29] Z. Zhang and J. Torrellas. Speeding up Irregular Applications in Shared-Memory Multiprocessors: Memory Binding and Group Prefetching. In *the 22nd International Symposium on Computer Architecture*, pages 188–199, June 1995.

Avoiding Initialization Misses to the Heap

Jarrod A. Lewis[†], Bryan Black[‡], and Mikko H. Lipasti[†]

[†]*Electrical and Computer Engineering*
University of Wisconsin-Madison
{lewisj, mikko}@ece.wisc.edu

[‡]*Intel Labs*
Intel Corporation
bryan.black@intel.com

Abstract

This paper investigates a class of main memory accesses (invalid memory traffic) that can be eliminated altogether. Invalid memory traffic is real data traffic that transfers invalid data. By tracking the initialization of dynamic memory allocations, it is possible to identify store instructions that miss the cache and would fetch uninitialized heap data. The data transfers associated with these initialization misses can be avoided without losing correctness. The memory system property crucial for achieving good performance under heap allocation is cache installation *- the ability to allocate and initialize a new object into the cache without a penalty. Tracking heap initialization at a cache block granularity enables cache installation mechanisms to provide zero-latency prefetching into the cache. We propose a hardware mechanism, the* Allocation Range Cache, *that can efficiently identify initializing store misses to the heap and trigger cache installations to avoid invalid memory traffic.*

Results: *For a 2MB cache 23% of cache misses (35% of compulsory misses) to memory are initializing the heap in the SPEC CINT2000 benchmarks. By using a simple base-bounds range sweeping scheme to track the initialization of the 64 most recent dynamic memory allocations, nearly 100% of all initializing store misses can be identified and installed in cache without accessing memory. Smashing invalid memory traffic via cache installation at a cache block granularity removes 23% of all miss traffic and can provide up to 41% performance improvement.*

1. Introduction

Microprocessor performance has become extremely sensitive to memory latency as the gap between processor and main memory speed widens [17]. Consequently, main memory bus access has become a dominating performance penalty and machines will soon be penalized thousands of processor cycles for each data fetch. Substantial research has been devoted to reducing or burying these large memory access latencies. Latency hiding techniques include lockup-free caches, hardware and software prefetching, and multithreading. However, many of these techniques used to tolerate growing memory latency do so at the expense of increased bandwidth requirements [3]. It is apparent in our quest for performance that memory bandwidth will be a critical resource in future microprocessors.

This work investigates the reduction of bandwidth requirements by avoiding initialization misses to dynamically-allocated memory. The use of dynamic storage allocation in application programs has increased dramatically, largely due to the use of object-oriented programming [18]. Traditional caching techniques are generally ineffective at capturing reference locality in the heap due to its extremely large data footprint [7][18]. Dynamic memory allocation through the heap can cause invalid, uninitialized memory to be transferred from main memory to on-chip caches. *Invalid memory traffic* is real data traffic that transfers invalid data. This traffic can be avoided without affecting program correctness. We observe that a significant percentage of bus accesses transfer invalid data from main memory in the SPEC CINT2000 benchmarks. For a 2MB cache, 23% of all misses (35% of all compulsory misses) that access memory are transferring invalid heap data.

First, this paper discusses the program semantics that lead to invalid memory traffic in Section 2, then it quantifies its contribution to compulsory misses and total cache misses in Section 5. In Section 6, we propose an allocation range base-and-bounds tracking scheme for dynamically tracking and eliminating excess invalid memory traffic. Finally, we propose an implementation scheme and quantify potential performance gains in Section 7.

2. Invalid Memory Traffic

Invalid memory traffic is the transfer of data between caches and main memory that has either not been initialized by the program, or has been released by the program. Invalid memory traffic can only occur in the dynamically-allocated structures of the heap and stack, because instruction and static memory are always valid to the application. Hardware will transfer data, based on demand, regardless of memory state, but the operating system must maintain a strict distinction and track valid and invalid data in order to maintain program correctness. During program execution, all stack and heap memory is invalid until allocated and initialized for use. Figure 1 illustrates the memory states and transitions for dynamic heap space. Until heap space is allocated, it remains unallocated-invalid. After allocation the new memory location transitions from unallocated-invalid to allocated-invalid. Memory transferred in allocated-invalid state is considered *invalid memory traffic*. It remains allocated-invalid until it is initialized by a write to that memory location. It will then transition to allocated-valid. Once a memory location is allocated-valid it is ready for program use. The application program can read and write this location numerous times until it is no longer needed. When the application is finished with the memory, it returns the memory back to the heap, and the memory location's state transitions back into unallocated-invalid. There are three memory states in Figure 1, of which only the allocated-valid state contains valid data. All memory transfers in the remaining two states transfer invalid data. There are two causes of invalid memory traffic: 1) An initializing store miss to allocated-invalid memory; 2) A writeback of allocated-invalid or unallocated-invalid memory. It is also possible to load from allocated-invalid memory, but reading uninitialized data is an undefined operation.

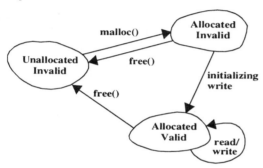

Figure 1. Dynamic memory states and transitions

Initializing stores may occur each time a program allocates new memory. A data writeback occurs when a dirty/modified cache line is evicted from a cache that is not write-through. If the evicted line was deallocated by the program before eviction, the writeback becomes invalid memory traffic. If an invalid writeback occurs or an initializing store misses all on-chip caches, an unnecessary and avoidable bus transfer of invalid data is created to access main memory.

This study focuses on invalid memory traffic that arises from initializing stores to the heap. All dynamic memory allocation activity is tracked in the SPEC CINT2000 benchmarks via the `malloc()` memory allocation routine. Using the memory states of Figure 1 (unallocated-invalid, allocated-invalid, and allocated-valid) heap data traffic can be tracked and identified as either valid or invalid memory traffic. Note that this discussion is specific to the semantics of C/C++ dynamic memory allocation; other languages have differing semantics and must be treated accordingly.

3. Related Work

Diwan et.al. [7] observe that heap allocation can have a significant memory system cost if new objects cannot be directly allocated into cache. They discover that by varying caching policies (sub-blocking) and increasing capacity, the allocation space of programs can be captured in cache, thus reducing initializing write misses. Similarly, in Jouppi's [12] investigation of cache write policies, he introduces the "write-validate" policy, which performs word-level sub-blocking [6]. With write-validate, the line containing the write is not fetched. The data is written into a cache line with valid bits turned off for all but the data that is being written. A write validate policy would effectively eliminate 100% of initializing write misses; however, the implementation overhead of this scheme is significant.

Wulf and McKee [20] explore the exponential advancement disparity between processor and memory system speeds. They conclude that system speed will be dominated by memory performance in future-generation microprocessors. To hurdle the imminent memory wall [20][7], they propose the idea of reducing compulsory misses, arising from dynamic memory initialization, by possibly having the compiler add a "first write" instruction that would bypass cache miss stalls. Such instructions now exist, for example `dcbz` in PowerPC [11]. These instructions allocate entries directly into cache and initialize them without incurring a miss penalty (cache installation). These installation instructions can be an extremely effective method for eliminating initializing write misses.

The compiler is statically limited to using cache installation immediately after new memory is allocated because it can not track memory use beyond the initial allocation. The operating system, on the contrary, could potentially make effective use of an installation instruction. Our work proposes eliminating initializing write misses at a cache block granularity, in contrast to the sub-blocking of write-validate and the software-controlled page-granular cache installation of uninitialized memory by an operating system. In Section 7 we show that both cache block- and page-granular cache installation can improve performance dramatically. Moreover we will demonstrate instances where block-granular installation performs significantly better than page-granular installation by avoiding cache pollution effects.

4. Methodology

This section outlines the full-system simulation environment used to gather all data for this study.

4.1. Simulation Environment

This work utilizes the PharmSim simulator, developed at the University of Wisconsin-Madison. PharmSim incorporates a version of SimOS adapted for the 64-bit Power-PC ISA that boots AIX 4.3.1. SimOS is the full-system simulator originally developed at Stanford University [15][16]. SimOS is a unique simulation environment that simulates both application and operating system code, and enables more accurate workload simulations by accounting for the interaction between the operating system and applications. PharmSim incorporates with SimOS a detailed, execution-driven out-of-order processor and memory subsystem model that precisely simulates all of the semantics of the entire PowerPC instruction set. This includes speculative execution of supervisor-mode instructions, memory barrier semantics, all aspects of address translation, including hardware page table walks, page faults, external interrupts, and so on. We have found that accurate modeling of all of these effects is vitally important, even when studying SPEC benchmarks. For example, we found that the AIX page fault handler already performs page-granular cache installation for newly-mapped uninitialized memory using the dcbz instruction. Had we employed a user-mode-only simulation environment like Simplescalar, this effect would have been hidden, and the performance results presented in Section 7 would have been overstated.

For the characterization data in Section 5 and Section 6, all memory references are fed through a one-level data cache model. Cache sizes of 512KB, 1MB, and 2MB are simulated for block sizes of 64, 128, and 256 bytes. To reduce the design space, a fixed associativity of 4 was chosen for each configuration. It is assumed that this single cache will represent total on-die cache capacity, thus all cache misses result in bus accesses. For the detailed timing simulations presented in Section 7, the baseline machine is configured as an 8-wide, 6-stage pipeline with an 8K combining predictor, 128 RUU entries, 64 LSQ entries, 64 write buffers, 256KB 4-way associative L1D cache, 64KB 2-way associative L1I, and a 2MB 4-way associative L2 unified cache. All cache blocks are 64 bytes. L2 latency is 10 cycles; memory latency is fixed at 70 cycles. We purposely chose an aggressive baseline machine to devaluate the impact of store misses.

The SPEC CINT2000 integer benchmark suite is used for all results presented in this paper. All benchmarks were compiled with the IBM xlc compiler, except for the C++ eon code which was compiled using g++ version 2.95.2. The first one billion instructions of each benchmark were simulated under PharmSim for all characterization and performance data. It is necessary to simulate from the very beginning of these applications in order to capture all dy-namic memory allocation and initialization. The input set, memory instruction percentage, and miss rates for a 1MB 4-way set-associative cache with 64 byte blocks are summarized for all benchmarks in Table 4-1.

Table 4-1. Characteristics of benchmark programs

SPEC CINT2000	Input Sets	Memory Instr%	Misses per 1000 Instr
bzip2	lgred.graphic	37.9%	0.683
crafty	oneboard.in	39.3%	0.053
eon	cook	55.9%	0.015
gap	test.in	46.1%	0.335
gcc	lgred.cp-decl.i	42.7%	0.159
gzip	lgred.graphic	41.0%	0.156
mcf	lgred.in	37.2%	7.533
parser	lgred.in	39.5%	0.982
perlbmk	lgred.makerand	55.1%	0.346
twolf	lgred.in	42.8%	0.022
vortex	lgred.raw	48.1%	0.164
vpr	lgred.raw	34.2%	0.015

4.2. Dynamic Memory Allocation Tracking

In order to study initialization cache misses to the heap all dynamic memory allocation and initialization must be tracked. Tracking dynamic memory behavior allows the simulator to identify initializing stores that cause invalid memory traffic. Dynamic memory behavior is easily identified through the C standard library memory allocation function malloc(). The operating system maintains a free list of available heap memory. During memory allocation, the free list is searched for sufficient memory to handle the current request. If there is insufficient memory the heap space is extended. When available memory is found, a portion of the heap is removed from the free list and an allocation block is created. By identifying the calls to malloc() during simulation, the dynamic memory allocation activity can be precisely quantified and analyzed.

5. Heap Initialization Analysis

Before any memory traffic activity results are presented it is important to discuss dynamic memory allocation patterns. As discussed in Section 2, dynamic memory allocation is the source of the invalid memory traffic this work seeks to eliminate.

5.1. Dynamic Memory Allocation

All dynamic memory activity to the heap is tracked by monitoring both user- and kernel-level invocations of the malloc() memory allocation routine. Figure 2 itemizes the raw number of dynamic procedure calls to malloc() according to different allocation sizes. For example twolf

Dynamic memory allocation instances

	<64 B	<2 KB	<256 KB	<16 MB	≥16 MB
bzip2	320	47	9	9	0
crafty	319	78	12	2	0
eon	1,948	145	28	0	0
gap	325	46	11	0	1
gcc	665	258	1,594	4	0
gzip	2,492	636	95	3	0
mcf	354	52	16	0	1
pars	390	46	59	0	1
perl	804	87	12	2	0
twolf	28,438	841	38	0	0
vortex	319	29,279	1,006	0	0
vpr	1865	93	22	0	0

Total dynamic memory allocated (in KB)

	<64 B	<2 KB	<256 KB	<16 MB	≥16 MB
bzip2	6.3	19.1	295.8	13,198	0
crafty	6.4	22.1	631.8	512	0
eon	35.6	41.3	371.8	0	0
gap	6.3	18.1	362.8	0	100MB
gcc	13.9	63.7	7,199.8	1,654	0
gzip	65.9	212.4	640.5	3,372	0
mcf	6.9	21.5	639.4	0	92MB
pars	8.1	18.1	496.6	0	30MB
perl	17.9	32.1	311.7	8,192	0
twolf	742.6	234.5	420.3	0	0
vortex	6.4	3,798.5	8,157.4	0	0
vpr	23.9	35.8	416.5	0	0

Figure 2. Dynamic memory allocation activity for SPEC CINT2000 benchmarks.

has 28,438 calls to `malloc()` that request less than 64 bytes of space. The raw number of allocations varies significantly across the benchmarks and some benchmarks allocate very large single blocks of memory, e.g. gap, mcf, and parser.

Figure 2 also quantifies the total dynamic memory allocated according to allocation size as observed in each benchmark. The total allocated memory represents all memory space that is assigned from the heap through calls to the `malloc()` routine. For example gcc has 7,199.8KB of its dynamically-allocated memory allocated between 2KB and 256KB at a time. This data shows a drastic difference in memory allocation behavior across the SPEC CINT2000 benchmarks. Gap, mcf, and parser allocate the bulk of their dynamic memory through 1 very large allocation (100MB, 92MB, and 30MB respectively). Although small allocations dominate the call distribution, the larger less frequent allocations are responsible for the bulk of allocated memory simply because they are so large. In contrast, gcc, twolf, and vortex allocate most of their dynamic memory through a large number of `malloc()` calls that allocate less than 2KB of data at a time.

Even though these allocation patterns are significantly different, we will show in Section 6 that the initialization of these different allocation sizes demonstrate very similar locality. Most allocations are initialized soon after they are allocated, and they are often initialized by a sequential walk through the memory. Therefore a similar mechanism can be used to track small allocations just the same as very large allocations. This fundamental observation will be discussed more in Section 6.

5.2. Initialization of Allocated Memory

Since the cache block is the typical granularity of a bus transfer, memory initialization is tracked by cache block for all results. Once allocated, all blocks remain in the allocated-invalid state until they are initialized. A store is required to move the allocated-invalid blocks to the allocated-valid state. Figure 3 shows what percentage of dynamically allocated memory (at a cache block granularity) is initialized and if it is initialized by a store miss or a store hit. Eon, parser, twolf, and vpr use 40% or less of their allocated memory, while gap, mcf, perlbmk, and vortex initialize most allocated cache blocks. Interestingly, on average 88% of all blocks initialized (60% of all allocated blocks) are initialized by a store miss. As discussed in

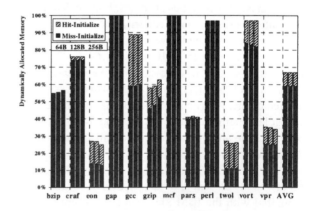

Figure 3. Initialization of dynamic memory
Initialization is shown for a 2MB 4-way set-associative cache with block sizes of 64, 128, and 256 bytes. On average, 60% of allocated cache blocks are initialized on a cache miss.

186

Section 2, these store misses are a source of invalid memory traffic. The miss rate of initializing stores gives insight into the reallocation of heap memory. If a memory block is initialized on a cache hit, and there is no prefetching, the block must have been brought into the cache on an earlier miss initialization from a previous allocation instance. The miss rates in Figure 3 are very high, so there is very little temporal reallocation of heap space. Section 5.3 will now discuss initialization misses and quantify how much of this cache miss traffic can be eliminated.

5.3. Invalid Cache Miss Traffic

Cache misses to the heap are references to memory allocated through `malloc()`, while non-heap misses are all other traffic, namely stack references and static variables. Store misses are distinguished as misses to either heap or non-heap memory space. Figure 4 illustrates all main memory accesses caused by stores initializing allocated-invalid memory (Initialize), stores that modify allocated-valid memory (Modify), and stores to non-heap memory (Non-Heap). Load misses represent the difference between the top of the accumulated store miss bars and 100% of cache misses. From Figure 4, 23% of all misses in a 2MB cache with 64 byte blocks initialize allocated-invalid memory space. All data fetches for these misses can be eliminated because they are invalid memory traffic that fetch invalid data just to initialize it when it eventually reaches the cache. Therefore nearly 1/4 of all incoming data traffic on the bus can be eliminated.

Figure 5 shows the sensitivity of the percentage of initializing stores to cache size and block size averaged across the SPEC CINT2000 benchmarks. One noticeable trend in this data is that the percentage of misses that initialize the heap (Initialize) increases with increasing cache

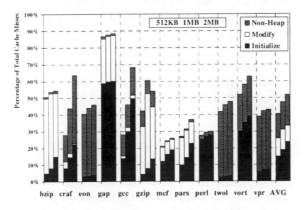

Figure 4. Cache miss breakdown
Misses are shown for cache sizes of 512KB, 1MB, and 2MB, all with associativity 4 and block size 64 bytes. Up to 60% and on average 23% of cache misses for 2MB of cache are initializing the heap.

capacity. However, initialization misses decrease with larger block sizes due to spatial locality prefetching from the larger blocks.

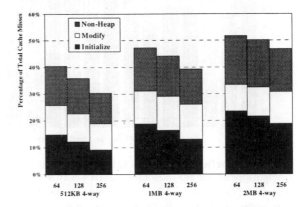

Figure 5. Initializing store miss percentage sensitivity to cache size and block size
The relative percentage of cache misses that initialize the heap (Initialize) increases with increasing cache capacity. However, initializing store ratios decrease as block size increases.

Reducing bus traffic by avoiding initialization misses can improve performance directly by reducing pressure on store queues and cache hierarchies. Indirectly, avoiding invalid memory traffic will decrease bus bandwidth requirements, enabling bandwidth-hungry performance optimizations such as prefetching and multi-threading to consume more bandwidth.

5.4. Compulsory Miss Initialization

Compulsory miss initializations occur when portions of the heap are initialized for the first time. Capacity miss initializations occur when data is evicted from cache and is subsequently re-allocated and re-initialized. Figure 6 demonstrates a semantic breakdown of all compulsory misses for a range of cache block sizes. Compulsory misses are categorized as initializing the heap (Initialize-Cold), non-heap stores (Non-Heap-Cold), or loads (Load-Cold). Note that compulsory misses, or *cold-start misses*, are caused by the first access to a block that has never been in the cache. Therefore the number of compulsory misses for any size cache is proportional only to block size. Figure 6 shows that for 2MB of cache, across all SPEC CINT2000 benchmarks approximately 50% of all cache misses are compulsory misses, and 35% of compulsory misses are initializing store misses. Thus 35% of compulsory misses are avoidable invalid memory traffic. Over 1/3 of all unique memory blocks cached are brought in as uninitialized heap data. As an extreme, mcf shows 95% of compulsory misses are initializing heap memory. The elimination of invalid compulsory miss traffic breaks the infinite cache

187

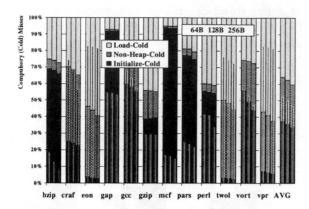

Figure 6. Cache compulsory miss breakdown
Compulsory misses are shown for a 2MB 4-way set-associative cache for 64, 128, and 256 byte blocks. The narrow bars inside each stacked bar represent the percentage of all cache misses that are compulsory for each program.

miss limit, where the number of compulsory misses of a finite-sized cache is equal and bound by that of an infinite-sized cache with the same block size [6]. Note that as block size increases, both the percentage of compulsory misses that initialize the heap (Initialize-Cold) and the percentage of all misses that are compulsory decrease. Larger block sizes perform spatial locality prefetches and reduce compulsory misses.

5.5. Initialization Throughout Execution

Figure 7 shows an accumulated distribution of all initializing stores identified in the first one billion instructions in the SPEC CINT2000 benchmarks. This data gives insight into the initialization of the heap throughout program execution. Here, largely as a design artifact of the SPEC benchmarks, most initializations of the heap occur in the first 500 million instructions. From Figure 2 gap, mcf, and parser are identified as having one very large dynamic memory allocation (100MB, 92MB, 30MB respectively). Figure 7 shows that these programs initialize their working set of dynamic memory rather quickly. Also from Figure 2 bzip2, gcc, gzip, twolf, and vortex are observed to allocate their memory in frequent, smaller chunks. Figure 7 shows these programs initialize their memory more steadily throughout the first one billion instructions of their execution. Note that although initializations are shown here for the first billion instructions (due to finite simulation time), dynamic memory allocation and initialization can occur steadily throughout program execution, depending on the application.

6. Identifying Initializing Stores

As discussed in Section 2, all initializing store misses in a write-allocate memory system cause invalid memory traffic (off-chip bus accesses) that can be eliminated. To eliminate this traffic we must be able to identify a cache miss as invalid before the cache miss handling procedure begins, i.e. before allocating entries in miss queues and arbitrating for the memory bus. A table structure that records allocation ranges used by the program can be used for this purpose. Each dynamic memory allocation creates a new range in the table. Table entries track the store (initialization) activity within the recorded allocation ranges using a base-bounds range summary technique. When a store miss to uninitialized heap memory is detected the cache block is automatically created in the cache hierarchy without a fetch to main memory (cache installation), effectively eliminating invalid memory traffic. In a cache coherent system, a processor can issue a cache installation (e.g. dcbz) as soon as write permission is granted for that block. Once granted, the block is installed in the cache with the value zero, thus realizing a zero-latency data prefetch for the uninitialized heap memory.

Before an implementation such as this can be feasible three main questions must be answered. (1) How can the hardware detect a dynamic memory allocation call? (2) Is the working set of allocation ranges small enough to cache in a finite table? (3) How can a single table entry track the behavior of potentially millions of cache blocks within a single allocation range?

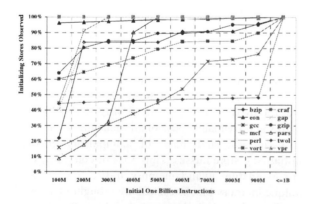

Figure 7. Initializing stores identified in the first one billion instructions

6.1. Identifying Allocations in Hardware

Again, this study is limited to programs written in C and C++, but could easily extend to all programs that utilize dynamic memory allocation, regardless of programming language. Identifying memory allocation through malloc() or any other construct can be accomplished with a new special instruction. A simple instruction that writes the address and size of the allocation into the base-bounds tracking table can be added to the memory allocation routine. In PowerPC a move to/from special register [11] can be used to implement these new operations, making identification of memory allocation quite straightforward.

6.2. Allocation Working Set

Figure 2 shows there are anywhere between 300 and 30,000 dynamic memory allocations during the first one billion instructions of the SPEC CINT2000 benchmarks. However, the working set of uninitialized allocations is much smaller. Figure 8 presents the number of allocations (tracked with a first-in-first-out FIFO policy) required to identify all initializing store misses to all allocations. This data shows that the initialization of the heap is not separated far from its allocation. For all benchmarks (except parser) it is necessary to track only the eight most recent dynamic memory allocations to capture over 95% of all initializing stores. Parser requires knowledge of the past 64 allocations. Even at 64 entries, a hardware allocation tracking table could feasibly be implemented to track this small subset of all allocations.

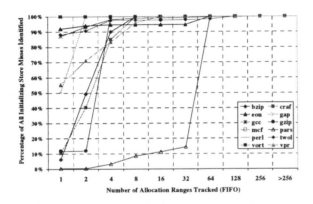

Figure 8. Memory allocation working set for FIFO initialization tracking table

6.3. Tracking Cache Block Initializations

The next question that must be addressed is how to efficiently represent large allocated memory spaces in a finite allocation cache. As discussed in Section 5.1., a cache block is the typical granularity of a bus transfer. Therefore memory initialization must be tracked by cache block or larger to identify invalid memory traffic. All cache blocks within an allocation range must be tracked in order to determine which pieces of the allocation space are valid and invalid. If all cache blocks can not be tracked then it is not possible to identify initializing stores at this granularity. The straightforward approach of maintaining a valid bit for each cache block in the allocated space is not feasible. The largest allocation in gap (100 MB) would require 1.56MB of valid bits in a single entry for 64 byte cache blocks. It

turns out the spatial and temporal locality of initializing stores lends nicely to implementation.

6.3.1. Initialization Distance From Allocation

The temporal distance (the number of memory references encountered between the time of allocation and the dynamic memory initialization) and the spatial distance (the distance from the beginning address of the allocation space to the dynamic memory initialization address) of initializing store instructions is presented in Figure 9.

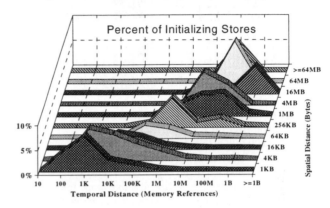

Figure 9. Average temporal and spatial distance of initializing stores from memory allocation
Dynamic instances of initializing stores are classified according to the distance away from the beginning of the allocation space (Spatial Distance) and the number of memory references after the allocation occurred (Temporal Distance).

This figure illuminates the locality pattern of initialization for all dynamic memory allocations, averaged across all SPEC CINT2000 benchmarks. A significant observation is that allocations tend to be initialized sequentially. Blocks at the beginning of an allocation range are initialized quickly and blocks toward the end of the range are initialized much later. This is shown by the diagonal bottom-left to top-right trend in Figure 9. The trend indicates that initializing stores that occur temporally early (to the left of the graph) also occur spatially near (towards the bottom of the graph) to the beginning of an allocation space. This observation coincides with Seidl and Zorn [18] who claim there may exist a sequential initialization bias of heap memory if large amounts of memory are allocated without subsequent deallocations. Figure 9 illustrates this sequential behavior is present across all allocation sizes.

6.3.2. Exploiting Initialization Patterns

Although an approximate sequential initialization pattern is shown in Figure 9, there are actually three main initialization patterns observed in the SPEC CINT2000 benchmarks: *sequential, alternating,* and *striding* as depicted in Figure 10. Three distinct heuristics for tracking these initialization patterns can be employed. *Forward*

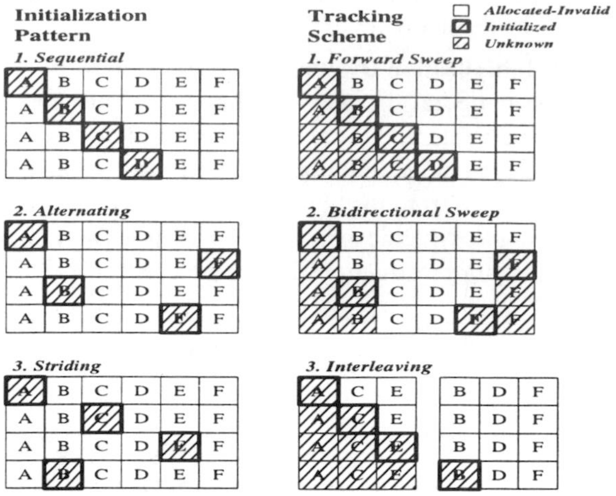

Initialization Pattern

Tracking Scheme

☐ *Allocated-Invalid*
☑ *Initialized*
☑ *Unknown*

1. Sequential

1. Forward Sweep

2. Alternating

2. Bidirectional Sweep

3. Striding

3. Interleaving

Figure 10. Tracking initialization patterns of dynamic memory allocations

Three main initialization patterns of dynamic memory ranges are observed in the SPEC CINT2000 benchmarks: *sequential, alternating,* and *striding.* Forward sweeping, bidirectional sweeping, and interleaving are effective range tracking schemes for capturing these unique initialization patterns.

sweep tracks the first and last address limits for each allocation, truncating the first address limit on initialization. *Bidirectional sweep* also tracks the two address limits per allocation, but truncates the first or last address limit depending on the location of the initialization. *Interleaving* maintains multiple address limit pairs for each allocation, splitting the range into multiple discontinuous segments. This scheme is extremely effective at capturing striding reference patterns. Writes are routed to an interleaved entry based on the write address, the interleaving granularity and the number of interleaves per range (address/granularity `modulo` interleaves). Forward or bidirectional sweeping is performed on each interleave entry. The idea is to route striding initializations to the *same* interleave entry so that each stride does not truncate the allocation range for all future store addresses; the range is only truncated for addresses that map to the same interleave entry. Thus future initializations to addresses *between* strides will route to a different interleave entry and can be correctly identified as initializing.

6.3.3. Allocation Range Cache

Figure 10 illustrates the tracking schemes that capture multiple initialization patterns in allocation ranges. The *base* and *bound* address limits representing the uninitialized portion of an allocation range are used to identify initialization activity into a single allocation. To identify writes to allocated-invalid memory in an allocation range, it is sufficient to determine if the write falls within the current address limits of the uninitialized portion of the range.

Figure 8 shows that the maximum working set of dynamic memory allocations for the SPEC CINT2000 benchmarks is typically 8 and at most 64 allocations. Tracking the 64 most recent allocations is sufficient to capture nearly all initializations. Therefore we propose a structure called the *Allocation Range Cache* to track the initialization of dynamic memory allocation ranges and identify initializing stores. Since the physical mapping for newly allocated space may not always exist, the Allocation Range Cache will track initializations by *virtual addresses.* To illustrate the operation of this structure we will walk through a simple allocation and initialization example. The example in Figure 11 shows an allocation of addresses *A* through *F* with initializing stores to addresses *A, C,* and *B.*

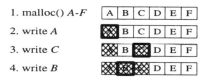

Figure 11. Initializing store example

We will now demonstrate how the Allocation Range Cache can track allocation *A-F* and identify the initializing stores to *A, C,* and *B.*

(1) To capture this activity the Allocation Range Cache represents the uninitialized allocation range *A-F* with two base-bound pairs as shown in Figure 12. This is two-way interleaving. The *Start-End* and *Base-Bound* values for both interleave entries are initialized to *A-F.*

(2) The write of address *A* occurs and a fully-associative search is performed on all *Start-End* pairs for a range that encompasses address *A.* When range *A-F* is found, address *A* is routed to interleave entry i=0 of this range. The *Base* and *Bound* values for this entry are referenced to determine if address *A* is to uninitialized memory. As this is the first write to this range, the *Base-Bound* pair still holds the initial value of *A-F.* Therefore, this write of address *A* is identified as an initializing store and the address is placed in the Initializing Store Table. The Initializing Store Table is simply a list of write addresses that have been identified as initializing stores by the Allocation Range Cache. To record this initialization, the Allocation Range Cache truncates the *Base* value of the referenced entry so that the *Base-Bound* values are now *B-F.* This is forward range sweeping.

(3) The write of address *C* is handled similarly to the previous write of address *A.* The write is identified as initializing by interleave entry i=0, address *C* is sent to the Initializing Store Table, and the *Base* value is truncated to address *D.*

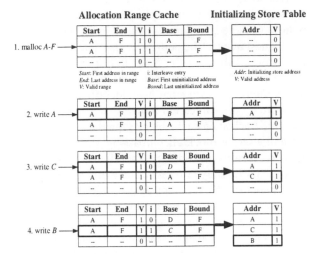

Figure 12. Allocation Range Cache

The Allocation Range Cache represents address range *A-F* with 2 base-bound pairs (2-way interleaving) as shown above. Assume that we interleave with a granularity such that addresses *A,C,* and *E* will be routed to interleave entry i=0, and addresses *B,D,* and *F* will be routed to entry i=1. The Initializing Store Table holds store addresses that have been identified as initializing stores by the Allocation Range Cache.

(4) The write of address *B* is routed to interleave entry i=1 for range *A-F*. Since this is the first reference to interleave i=1, the *Base-Bound* pair has the initial value *A-F*. Therefore this write of address *B* is identified as initializing, sent to the Initializing Store Table, and the *Base* value is truncated to address *C*. Note that if address *B* had been routed to interleave i=0, it would **not** have been identified as initializing because the previous write of address *C* truncated the *Base* value to address *D*. There would have been a lost opportunity to correctly identify an initializing store. This is an example of how range interleaving can track striding initialization patterns effectively.

The effectiveness of identifying initializing store misses dynamically with simple forward sweep and bidirectional sweep tracking policies is presented in Figure 13. Simple range sweeping, with one base-bound pair per allocation, captures nearly 100% of all initializations for ten benchmarks. Most benchmarks adhere strictly to sequential initializations. Perl exhibits alternating initialization; therefore a bidirectional policy is more effective than forward sweep.

Initializations in bzip2 and gzip are not captured well with forward or bidirectional range sweeping. These programs often initialize memory in strides of 128, 256, and 1024 bytes. Range interleaving as shown in Figure 10 is required to effectively capture striding initializations. Figure 14 shows that maintaining multiple base-bound pairs for

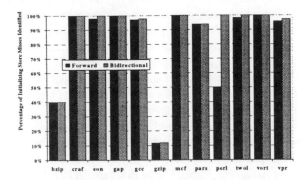

Figure 13. Identifying initializing stores with *forward* and *bidirectional* range sweeping

The percentage of all initializing stores that can be identified by range sweeping for a 1MB 4-way set-associative cache with 64 byte blocks is shown above.

each allocation can significantly improve the effectiveness of range sweeping at identifying initializing stores. Note that only 60% of all initializations in bzip2 can be captured by range sweeping. Bzip2 has one large allocation that is initialized at random locations at random times. Random initialization patterns are not captured with any range sweeping scheme proposed in Figure 10.

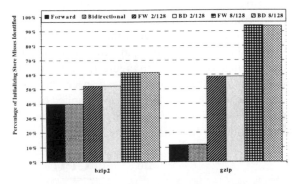

Figure 14. Improving identification of initializations with range sweeping by *interleaving* ranges

The percentage of all initializing stores that can be identified by range interleaving and sweeping, for a 1MB 4-way set-associative cache with 64 byte blocks, is shown above. Forward (FW) and bidirectional (BD) sweeping is performed at an interleave granularity of 128 bytes on two (2/128) and eight (8/128) interleaves per allocation.

7. Implementation and Performance

Initializing store misses cause *invalid memory traffic,* real data traffic between memory and caches that transfers invalid data from the heap. To avoid this traffic, store misses must be identified as invalid before the cache hierarchy initiates a bus request to fetch missed data from memory. The block written by the store can then be installed directly into the cache without fetching invalid data over the bus. This is *block-granular* cache installation. Initializing store miss identification can be done anytime after the store address is generated and before the store enters miss handling hardware. These relaxed timing constraints allow multiple cycles for an identification to resolve. Therefore the mechanism that identifies initializing stores, e.g. the Allocation Range Cache, is not latency sensitive and could be implemented as a small, fully-associative cache of base-bound pairs. This structure could effectively reduce bus bandwidth requirements at a minimal implementation cost. We now propose an integration of the Allocation Range Cache that can effectively identify and smash initializing store misses.

7.1. Smashing Invalid Memory Traffic

Figure 15 demonstrates a conceptual example of how an Allocation Range Cache and Initializing Store Table can be integrated into a typical cache hierarchy to smash invalid memory traffic. The identification of an initializing store in the Allocation Range Cache is accomplished using the *virtual address* of store instructions. When a store is presented to the cache hierarchy, the translation look-aside buffer (TLB) and Allocation Range Cache (ARC) are accessed in parallel. The TLB translates the store address tag from virtual to physical, sends the tag to the Level-1 cache for tag comparison, and also sends the physical tag to the ARC. Meanwhile the ARC uses the virtual store address to reference into its base-bound pairs to determine if the store is initializing, as described in Figure 12. If the store is identified as an initializing store to heap space, the Allocation Range Cache takes the physical tag (supplied by the TLB) and inserts the complete physical address of the store instruction into the Initializing Store Table.

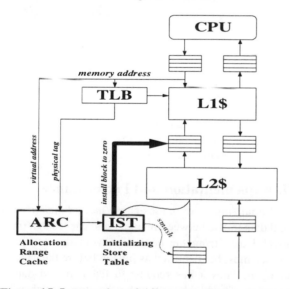

Figure 15. Integration of Allocation Range Cache

If a store address misses in the Level-1 and Level-2 caches, and at least one cache employs a write-allocate policy, a data fetch request is queued in the outgoing memory request queue. The address is also sent to the Initializing Store Table (IST). The IST performs a fully-associative search for a matching physical address. A match implies this store has been identified as an initializing store by the Allocation Range Cache. Since initializations are tracked on cache block granularity, we know that the entire cache block encompassing an initializing store address contains invalid data. Therefore we can install the entire block directly into cache and avoid fetching the data from memory. To accomplish this, the Initializing Store Table invalidates (smashes) the store address entry in the outgoing memory request queue and sends a response to the Level-1 cache queue, or whichever cache allocates on writes, to install the cache block with the value zero. Finally, the store address is removed from the Initializing Store Table. This demonstrates how the Allocation Range Cache can smash invalid memory traffic using cache installation.

7.2. Alternative Implementations

As discussed in Section 3, there are other methods for avoiding invalid memory traffic: sub-blocking and software-controlled cache installation. Sub-blocking has obvious limitations. First, sub-block valid bits cause significant storage overhead, especially in systems that allow un-aligned word writes or byte writes. In practice, fetch-on-write must be provided for un-aligned word writes. Second, sub-blocking requires that lower levels in the memory system support writes of partial cache lines. This can become a significant problem in a multi-processor environment with coherent caches, since the owner of a line may possess only a partially valid line, and cannot respond directly to the requestor.

Software-controlled cache installation (on a page granularity) can be accomplished by an operating system's page fault handler. When a mapping is created for a new page, the operating system can issue a cache installation (e.g. dcbz) for the entire page. This will install the entire page directly into cache, effectively prefetching all initialization misses to that page. However, this scheme can cause excessive cache pollution, e.g. given a 64 byte block size, 64 valid blocks could be evicted when a 4KB page is installed. This problem gets worse when the page size grows, as in the presence of superpages [13]. Given page sizes of 4MB or 16MB, directly installing an entire page into cache is not feasible. Page-granular installing is inefficient for large striding initialization patterns and this scheme cannot optimize capacity miss initializations to pages that have already been mapped. If heap space is reused, initializing store misses will occur if that heap space has fallen out of cache.

Tracking and eliminating initializing store miss data transfers at the cache block granularity can alleviate subblocking overhead and avoid excessive cache pollution from page-granular cache installation. We now evaluate the performance benefits of smashing invalid memory traffic via cache installation.

7.3. Performance Speedup via Cache Installation

Figure 16 presents performance results for smashing initializing store misses via cache installation by an Allocation Range Cache. This structure triggers cache block-granular installation instructions (dcbz) when an initializing store miss is identified. The entire cache block is installed directly into the Level-1 data cache, thus performing a zero-latency prefetch. The store instruction will now hit in cache. Note that coherence permission must be received before installing a cache block. The perfor-

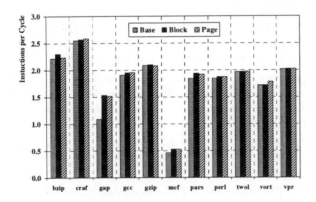

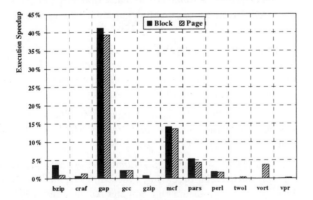

Figure 16. Performance speedup via block- and page-granular cache installation
Instructions per cycle (IPC) comparisons for page-granular (Page) and block-granular (Block) cache installation schemes using dcbz are shown on the top. Execution speedups are presented on the bottom graph. All programs were simulated for one billion instructions.

mance of a page-granular installation scheme (Page) as performed by the AIX page fault handler is compared against our block-granular scheme (Block). Results are reported relative to a baseline machine configuration (Base) as described in Section 4.1. The dcbz cache installation instruction is disabled in this baseline. For most programs, smashing invalid memory traffic results in a direct performance improvement. In bzip2, gap, mcf, parser, and perlbmk using the Allocation Range Cache to trigger block-granular cache installations outperforms the page-granular installation scheme. Figure 6 shows that mcf and gap have the largest percentage of compulsory misses that are initialization misses, 95% and 92% respectively. Figure 16 demonstrates that avoiding these compulsory misses can have significant performance benefits.

Bzip2 and gzip exhibits striding initialization patterns with observed strides of 1024 bytes as discussed in Section 6.3.2. With this large stride, a new 4KB page is encountered every fourth stride. From Figure 16, installing the entire 4KB page after the first initialization is causing significant cache pollution since block-granular installations provide larger performance gains. The Allocation Range Cache does not excessively pollute the cache with extraneous prefetching. Rather, blocks are installed on demand, eliminating cache pollution effects for striding initializations.

8. Conclusion

This paper introduces the concept of *invalid memory traffic* - real data traffic that transfers invalid data. Such traffic arises from fetching uninitialized heap data on cache misses. We find that initializing store misses are responsible for approximately 23% of all cache miss activity across the SPEC CINT2000 benchmarks for a 2MB cache. By smashing invalid memory traffic, 35% of compulsory misses and 23% of all cache miss data traffic on the bus can be avoided. This is an encouraging result, since compulsory misses, unlike capacity and conflict misses, cannot be eliminated by improvements in cache locality, replacement policy, size, or associativity. Eliminating invalid compulsory miss traffic breaks the infinite cache limit, where compulsory misses of a finite-sized cache are finite and bound by that of an infinite-sized cache [6].

We propose a hardware mechanism, the Allocation Range Cache, that tracks initialization of dynamic memory allocation regions on a cache block granularity. By maintaining multiple base-bound representations of an allocation range (interleaving), this structure can identify nearly 100% of all initializing store misses with minimal storage overhead. By directly allocating and initializing a block into cache (cache installing) when an initializing store miss is identified, it is possible to avoid transferring invalid memory over the bus. This is essentially a zero-latency prefetch of a cache miss. Reducing bus traffic via cache installation can directly improve performance by reducing pressure on store queues and cache hierarchies. We quantify a direct performance improvement from avoiding initialization misses to the heap. Speedups of up to 41% can be achieved by smashing invalid memory traffic with the Allocation Range Cache triggering cache block installations. Indirectly, smashing invalid memory traffic will decrease bus bandwidth requirements, enabling bandwidth-hungry performance optimizations such as prefetching and multi-threading to consume more bandwidth and improve performance even further.

9. Future Work

There are issues to be addressed for avoiding invalid memory traffic in a multi-processor environment, including coherence of the Allocation Range Cache. For correctness, all ARC entries must be coherent across multiple threads or processors. The ARC can be kept coherent among multiple threads in the same address space by architecting the cache entries as part of coherent physical memory. Thus updates to an ARC entry by one thread will be seen by other threads through the existing coherence mechanisms. Coherence is more challenging when virtual address aliasing to shared physical memory exists. These issues are subject of continued research.

10. References

[1] AIX Version 4.3 Base Operating System and Extensions Technical Reference, Volume 1, *http://www.unet.univie.ac.at/aix/libs/basetrf1/malloc.htm*

[2] Barrett David A., Zorn, Benjamin G. *Using lifetime predictors to improve memory allocation performance.* ACM SIGPLAN Notices, v.28 n.6, p.187-196, June 1993.

[3] Burger, D., Goodman, J.R., Kägi, A. *Memory Bandwidth Limitations of Future Microprocessors.* Proceeding of the 23rd Annual International Symposium on Computer Architecture, pages 78-89, PA, USA, May 1996.

[4] Chen, T.-J., Baer, J.-L. *Reducing Memory Latency via Non-blocking and Prefetching Caches.* Proceedings of the 5th International Conference on Architectural Support for Programming Languages and Operating Systems, pp. 51-61, Boston, MA, October, 1992.

[5] Chen, T.-J., Baer, J.-L. *A Performance Study of Software and Hardware Data Prefetching Schemes.* Proceedings of the 21st annual International Symposium on Computer Architecture, pp. 223 - 232 Chicago, IL, 1994.

[6] Cragon, H.G. Memory Systems and Pipelined Processors. Jones and Bartlett Publishers, Inc., Sudbury, ME, 1996.

[7] Diwan, A., Tarditi, D., Moss, E. *Memory System Performance of Programs with Intensive Heap Allocation.* ACM Transactions on Computer Systems, Vol13, No 3, pp. 244-273, August 1995.

[8] Dubois, M., Skeppstedt, J., Ricciulli, L., Ramamurthy, K., Stenström, P. *The Detection and Elimination of Useless Misses in Multiprocessors.* Proceedings of the 20th Annual International Symposium on Computer Architecture, pp. 88-97, May 1993.

[9] Gonzalez, J., Gonzales, A. *Speculative execution via address prediction and data prefetching.* Proceed-ings of the 11th International Conference on Supercomputing, pp. 196-203, June 1997. [10]

[10] Grunwald, D., Zorn, B., Henderson, R. *Improving the Cache Locality of Memory Allocation.* ACM SIGPLAN PLDI'93, pp. 177-186, Albuquerque, N.M., June 1993.

[11] IBM Microelectronics, Motorola Corporation. PowerPC Microprocessor Family: The Programming Environments. Motorola, Inc., 1994.

[12] Jouppi, Norman P. *Cache write policies and performance.* ACM SIGARCH Computer Architecture News, v.21 n.2, p.191-201, May 1993.

[13] Talluri, M., Hill, Mark D. *Surpassing the TLB performance of superpages with less operating system support.* ACM SIGPLAN Notices, v.29 n.11, p.171-182, Nov. 1994.

[14] Peng, C.J., Sohi, G. *Cache memory design considerations to support languages with dynamic heap allocation.* Technical Report 860, University of Wisconsin-Madison, Dept. of Computer Science, July 1989.

[15] Rosenblum, M., Herrod, S., Witchel, E., Gupta, A. *Complete Computer Simulation: The SimOS Approach.* IEEE Parallel and Distributed Technology, Fall 1995.

[16] Rosenblum, M., Bugnion, E., Devine, S., Herrod, S. *Using the SimOS Machine Simulator to Study Complex Computer Systems.* ACM Transactions on Modeling and Computer Simulation, vol. 7, no. 1, pp.78-103, January 1997.

[17] Saulsbury, A., Pong, F., Nowatzyk, A. *Missing the Memory Wall: The Case for Processor/Memory Integration.* Proceedings of the 23rd Annual International Symposium on Computer Architecture, pages 90-101, PA, USA, May 1996.

[18] Seidl, Matthew L., Zorn, Benjamin G. *Segregating heap objects by reference behavior and lifetime.* ACM SIGPLAN Notices, v.33 n.11, p.12-23, Nov. 1998.

[19] Tullsen, D.M., Eggers, S.J. *Limitation of cache prefetching on a bus-based multiprocessor.* Proceedings of the 20th Annual International Symposium on Computer Architecture, 1993.

[20] Wulf, Wm.A. and McKee, S.A. *Hitting the Memory Wall: Implications of the Obvious.* ACM Computer Architecture News. Vol. 23, No.1 March 1995.

Going the Distance for TLB Prefetching:
An Application-driven Study*

Gokul B. Kandiraju   Anand Sivasubramaniam
Dept. of Computer Science and Engineering
The Pennsylvania State University
University Park, PA 16802.
{kandiraj,anand}@cse.psu.edu

Abstract

The importance of the Translation Lookaside Buffer (TLB) on system performance is well known. There have been numerous prior efforts addressing TLB design issues for cutting down access times and lowering miss rates. However, it was only recently that the first exploration [26] on prefetching TLB entries ahead of their need was undertaken and a mechanism called Recency Prefetching was proposed. There is a large body of literature on prefetching for caches, and it is not clear how they can be adapted (or if the issues are different) for TLBs, how well suited they are for TLB prefetching, and how they compare with the recency prefetching mechanism.

This paper presents the first detailed comparison of different prefetching mechanisms (previously proposed for caches) - arbitrary stride prefetching, and markov prefetching - for TLB entries, and evaluates their pros and cons. In addition, this paper proposes a novel prefetching mechanism, called Distance Prefetching, that attempts to capture patterns in the reference behavior in a smaller space than earlier proposals. Using detailed simulations of a wide variety of applications (56 in all) from different benchmark suites and all the SPEC CPU2000 applications, this paper demonstrates the benefits of distance prefetching.

Keywords: Prefetching, Memory Hierarchy, Translation Lookaside Buffer, Simulation, Application-driven Study.

1. Introduction

Address translation using the Translation Lookaside Buffer (TLB) is one of the most critical operations in determining the delivered performance of most high performance CPUs. Several studies have quantified the importance of TLB performance on system execution and the necessity of speeding up the miss handling process [15, 9, 22, 3, 14, 25]. Anderson et al. [3] show that TLB miss handling is the most frequently executed kernel service

and has an important consequence on performance. TLB miss handling has been shown to constitute as much as 40% of execution time [14] and upto 90% of a kernel's computation [25]. Studies with specific applications [26] have also shown that the TLB miss rate can account for over 10% of their execution time even with an optimistic 30-50 cycle miss overhead.

There are several approaches to improve the delivered performance of TLBs. On the software side - at the application, compiler or operating system level - optimizations for improving locality can help lower the number of TLB entries needed to cover the working set of the execution at any instant. On the hardware side, TLB structure in terms of its size and associativity, as well as multilevel hierarchies, can have a significant impact on both the miss rates as well as on the access times [28, 7]. Another solution to boost TLB coverage is by the use of superpaging [28, 27]. Finally, on the miss handling side, a considerable amount of effort has been expended on tuning software miss handlers [25] or for performing the necessary actions in hardware.

However, it is only recently [26, 24, 4] that the issue of prefetching/preloading TLB entries to hide all or some of the miss costs has started drawing interest. Some of these [4, 24] consider prefetching TLB entries only for the cold starts, which in many long running programs (such as the SPEC 2000 suite) constitute a much smaller fraction of the misses. The first work on prefetching TLB entries for capacity related misses has been undertaken in [26]. Despite the voluminous literature on prefetching techniques available for other levels of the memory hierarchy, prefetching TLB entries has not gained much attention. This is, perhaps, due to the fear of slowing down the critical path of TLB accesses (which is usually much more important than the other levels of the memory hierarchy) and the possible cost/space of the additional real-estate (one could make a less strong argument about this with the ability to pack in millions of transistors on chip, though there is still the issue of power consumption and distribution that needs to be considered) that may need to be provisioned on-chip. However, we need to understand the benefits and ramifications of prefetching TLB entries inorder to be able to make these

---
*This research has been supported in part by several NSF grants including Career Award 9701475, 0103583, 0097998, 9988164, 9900701, 9818327 and 0130143.

trade-offs. In this paper, we specifically focus on the data TLB (d-TLB), which is usually much more of a problem than instruction TLB (i-TLB) in terms of miss rates [18].

Addressing the critical path issue, Saulsbury et al. [26] propose a new mechanism, called Recency-based Prefetching (RP), that maintains an LRU stack of page references and prefetches the pages adjacent to the one currently referenced (on either side of the stack). The associated logic is placed after the TLB, i.e. it has the privilege of examining only the misses from the TLB (and does not look at the actual reference stream). However, this mechanism can possibly increase memory traffic due to the need for manipulating LRU stack pointers kept in the page table.

A number of prefetching mechanisms have been proposed in the context of caches [29, 8, 16, 12, 17, 20] and I/O. To our knowledge, no prior study has investigated the suitability of these earlier proposals for TLB prefetching. It would be very interesting to see how these earlier proposals would work with the miss stream coming out of the TLB. While many of these schemes may require a little more logic/real-estate on-chip than RP, they usually do not impose as much storage and bandwidth requirements as RP.

It is well beyond the scope of this paper to cover a detailed survey/classification of prefetching mechanisms or to evaluate all of them (if one is interested, a survey of these can be found in [29]). Rather, we want to cover some representative points of the spectrum of mechanisms in the context of TLB prefetching. In a broad sense, prefetching mechanisms can be viewed in two classes: ones that capture strided reference patterns (using less history, such as sequential prefetching or arbitrary stride prefetching (ASP) [12, 8]), and those that base their decisions on a much longer history (such as markov prefetching (MP)[16] or even the recency based mechanism (RP) discussed above).

Reference behavior can also be viewed as following broadly one of these categories: (a) showing regular/strided accesses to several data items that are touched only once; (b) showing regular/strided accesses to several data items that are touched several times; (c) showing regular/strided accesses to several data items, but the stride itself can change over time for the same data item; (d) not having constant strided accesses (either keeps changing constantly or there is no regularity in the stride at all), but repeating the same irregularity from one access to another for the same data item over time; and (e) not having any regularity either in strides and not obeying previous history either. Usually stride based schemes are a better alternative than history based schemes for (a) (there is no history established here), while both categories can do well for (b). Some of the more intelligent/adaptive stride based schemes such as ASP can track (c) also fairly well, but the history based schemes are not as good for such behavior. On the other hand, history based schemes can do a much better job than stride based schemes for (d). In (e), it is very difficult for any prefetching scheme to be able to do a good job.

As we can observe, neither of the classes can do well across all of (a) through (d). Instead, we propose a new

prefetching mechanism called *Distance Prefetching (DP)*[1] in this paper that tries to get the better of both approaches. The idea is to approximate the behavior of stride based mechanisms whenever there are very regular strided accesses (and capture first time references as well which are not possible in a history based mechanism), and track the history of strides (that is indexed by the stride itself). The hope is that whenever the stride changes, the changes themselves form a historical pattern and we can refer to this history to make better predictions. We find that DP can do fairly well (approximating the better of the two classes) for all of (a) through (d). DP is a general prefetching technique, that can be used in several situations (for caches, I/O etc.). In this paper, apart from proposing this new general purpose technique, we specifically illustrate its design and use for tracking TLB misses (placed after the TLB) to make good predictions. It takes space that is comparable to that of some of the earlier history based mechanisms such as Markov (usually a 256 entry direct mapped table suffices), while making much more accurate predictions. It also incurs much less memory traffic compared to RP which is the only other prefetching technique proposed and evaluated specifically for TLBs. The benefits of DP are demonstrated using a wide range of diverse applications spanning several benchmark suites (26 applications from SPEC CPU2000 [11], 20 applications from MediaBench [21], 5 applications from the Etch traces [1], and 5 applications from the Pointer Intensive Benchmark suite [2]).

The rest of this paper is organized as follows. Section 2 discusses the prefetching mechanisms, together with some of the hardware that is required, Section 3 gives performance results with actual applications and Section 4 concludes with a summary of contributions.

2. Prefetching Mechanisms

Since we extensively refer and compare against previously proposed prefetching mechanisms (including those used for caches), we briefly go over these to refresh the reader and to point out the exact implementation that is used later on in the evaluations. We also present our new prefetching mechanism - DP - in this section. It is to be noted that for uniformity in this adaptation, all these mechanisms initiate prefetches only by looking at the miss stream from the TLB, that is done in the earlier proposed RP mechanism [26] for TLB prefetching. All these mechanisms bring the prefetched entry into a "prefetch buffer" that is concurrently looked up with the TLB, and the entry is moved over to the TLB only on an actual reference to that entry from the application. Prefetching can thus not increase the miss rates of the original TLB. There is, however, the issue of additional memory traffic that is induced

---

[1]Distance Prefetching also tracks strides to make predictions. In the interest of distinguishing this mechanism clearly from the earlier stride based mechanisms, we give it a different name using the term "distance". "Distance" and "stride" mean the same thing and refer to the spatial separation (could be positive or negative) between any two successive references.

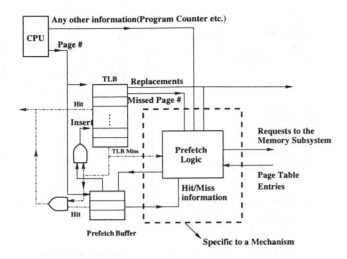

Figure 1. Schematic of Hardware for Prefetching in all the Considered Mechanisms

by prefetching, which can have a bearing on the execution time. In ASP, MP and DP, the prefetching engine uses a prediction table that has a given number of rows (r). MP and DP allow aggressive predictions, and each row of the table can have s slots. In ASP, each row contains only one slot as defined in [8] since this mechanism makes at most one prediction on a given reference. The indexing of the rows and what goes into each slot is specific to a scheme. The slots essentially determine what entries to prefetch, and thus s puts a bound on number of entries that can be prefetched on a given miss. The prefetch buffer size b is the same across all the mechanisms. A schematic of the overall prefetching hardware implementation is given in Figure 1.

2.1. Sequential Prefetching (SP)

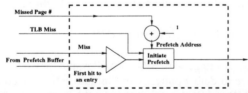

Figure 2. Schematic of Hardware for SP

This mechanism tries to exploit the sequentiality of references, and prefetches the next sequential unit (page table entry) based on the current reference. Several variations have been proposed, that are discussed by Vanderwiel and Lilja [29]. They point out that of all the schemes, *tagged* sequential prefetching - where a prefetch is initiated on every demand fetch and on every first hit to a prefetched unit, is very effective. Another variation proposed by Dahlgren and Stenstrom [12] dynamically varies the number of units to prefetch based on the success rate. However, simulations have shown only slight differences between these schemes

[29, 12]. Consequently, we limit ourselves to the tagged version of SP in this paper. On a TLB miss, if the translation also misses in the prefetch buffer, it is demand fetched and a prefetch is initiated for the next virtual page translation (stride = 1) from the page table. The CPU resumes as soon as the demand page translation arrives. In case of a prefetch buffer hit, CPU is given back the translation (and resumes), the entry is moved to the TLB, and a prefetch is initiated for the next translation in the background. A simplified hardware block diagram implementing SP is given in Figure 2.

2.2. Arbitrary Stride Prefetching (ASP)

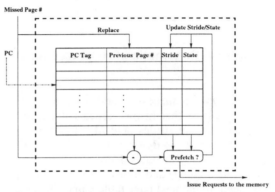

Figure 3. Schematic of Hardware for ASP

SP captures only spatial proximity, but there are several applications that have regular strided reference patterns. Prefetching mechanisms to address this have been proposed by Chen and Baer [8], Patel and Fu [13] and several others. It has been pointed out [29] that the scheme proposed by Chen and Baer is the most aggressive of these. We use this scheme, referred to as Arbitrary Stride Prefetching (ASP) in this paper, for comparisons. ASP uses the program counter (PC) to index a table (referred to in [8] as Reference Prediction Table (RPT)). Each row has one slot which stores a tuple containing (i) the address that was referenced the last time the PC came to this instruction, (ii) the corresponding stride, and (iii) a state (PC tag may also need to be maintained for indexing). The address field needs to be updated each time the PC comes to this instruction, and the prefetch is initiated only when there is no change in the stride for more than two references by that instruction (the state is used to keep track of this information). Such a safeguard tries to avoid spurious changes in strides. This is the mechanism that is evaluated in this paper, though there are several variations proposed [8]. A simplified hardware block diagram implementing ASP is given in Figure 3.

2.3. Markov Prefetching (MP)

The previous two are representative of schemes that attempt to detect regularity of accesses (by observing sequentiality or strides), and fail if there is no such regularity in the

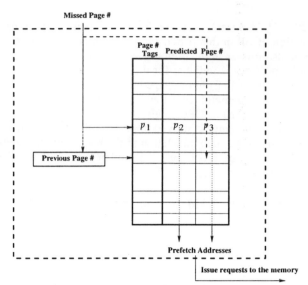

Figure 4. Schematic of Hardware for MP

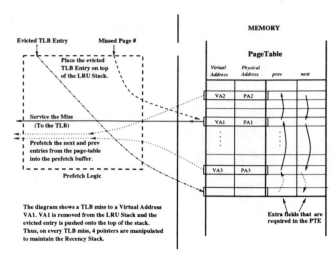

The diagram shows a TLB miss to a Virtual Address VA1. VA1 is removed from the LRU Stack and the evicted entry is pushed onto the top of the stack. Thus, on every TLB miss, 4 pointers are manipulated to maintain the Recency Stack.

Figure 5. Schematic of Hardware for RP

differences between successive address references. However, it is possible that history repeats itself, even without any regularity in strides, and MP tries to address that angle. MP attempts to dynamically build a Markov state transition diagram with states denoting the referenced unit (pages in this context) and transition arcs denoting probability of needing the next page table entry when the current page is accessed. The probabilities are tracked from prior references to that unit, and a table is used to approximate this state diagram. This scheme was initially proposed for caches [16], and we have extended this to work with TLBs as discussed below.

The prediction table for MP is indexed by the virtual page address that misses. Each row of the table has s slots, with each slot containing a virtual page address that is initially empty (they correspond to entries to be prefetched when this address misses the next time). On a miss, this table is indexed based on the address that misses. If not found, then this entry is added, and the s slots for this entry are kept empty. In addition, we also go to the entry of the previous page that missed, and add the current miss address into one of its s slots (whichever is free). If all the slots are occupied, then we evict one based on LRU policy. As a result, the s slots for each entry correspond to different virtual pages that also missed immediately after this page. If a missed address hits in the table, then a prefetch is initiated for the corresponding s slots of this address. Since the table has limited entries, an entry (row) could itself be replaced because of conflicts. A simplified hardware block diagram of MP with $s = 2$ is given in Figure 4.

2.4. Recency Based Prefetching (RP)

While all the previous mechanisms have been proposed for caches, Recency Prefetching is the first mechanism, to our knowledge, that has been proposed solely for TLBs.

This mechanism works on the principle that pages referenced at around the same time in the past will also be referenced at around the same time in the future. It builds an LRU stack of page table entries to achieve this. Specifically, when an entry is evicted from the TLB it is put on top of the stack, its next pointer is set to the previous entry that was evicted (whose previous pointer is set to this entry). As a result, each entry has two pointers, which are actually stored in the page table (this scheme requires considerably more space than the other schemes, and increases the page table size). When an entry is loaded on a miss, the prefetch mechanism fetches the entries corresponding to the next and previous pointers into the prefetch buffer in the hope that they will be needed as well (this is the mechanism that is implemented and evaluated here, though there is a variation in [26] with regard to prefetching some more entries). RP, thus, keeps its prediction information in the page table itself and does not have additional storage costs on-chip. This comes at the cost of an increase in page table size. Further details can be found in [26] and a hardware schematic of this mechanism is given in Figure 5.

2.5. Distance Prefetching (DP)

The advantage with SP and ASP is that they take very little space to detect patterns and initiate actions accordingly, while MP and RP can take considerably more space because they can detect more patterns than the restricted patterns that SP and ASP can detect. They also take a while to learn a pattern, since only repetitions in addresses can effect a prefetch for RP and MP (not first time references). Our DP mechanism can be viewed as trying to detect many of the patterns that RP or MP can accommodate (and maybe some that even they cannot), while benefiting from the regularity/strided behavior of an execution. In fact, if there is so much regularity that SP and ASP can do very well in a reference pattern, then DP should automatically take only as much space as these two. Remember that MP and RP need considerable space even to capture sequential scans while

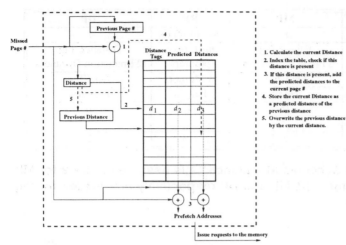

Figure 6. Schematic of Hardware for DP

Distance Tags — Predicted Distances

d_1 | d_2 | d_3

1. Calculate the current Distance
2. Index the table, check if this distance is present
3. If this distance is present, add the predicted distances to the current page #
4. Store the current Distance as a predicted distance of the previous distance
5. Overwrite the previous distance by the current distance.

SP and ASP can do this in little space.

DP works on the hypothesis that if we could keep track of differences between successive addresses (spatial separation or stride, which we call as *distance* for this mechanism) then we could make more predictions in a smaller space. For instance, let us say that the reference string is 1, 2, 4, 5, 7, and 8. Then, if we just keep track of the fact that a distance of "1" is followed by a (predicted) distance of "2" and vice versa, then we would need only a 2 entry table to make a prediction as opposed to the markov mechanism where an entry is needed for each page (6 entries in this example). This is exactly what our distance prefetching mechanism does. A reference string touching all pages sequentially (that SP optimizes) can be captured by DP using an entry saying distance of "1" is followed by a (predicted) distance of "1". The reader is referred to [19] for several such reference string examples that show how DP can provide better predictions than the other schemes.

The hardware implementation (Figure 6 shows the schematic with $s = 2$) for DP requires that the table be indexed by the current distance (difference of current address and previous address). Each entry has a certain number of slots (maintained in LRU order) corresponding to the next few distances that are likely to miss when the current distance is encountered (similar to how MP keeps the next few addresses based on the current address). Pages corresponding to the distances in these slots are prefetched when this virtual address misses. One could, perhaps, envision indexing this table using the PC value together with the distance, or using a set of consecutive distances. These are issues that could be investigated in future research, and are not discussed in this paper.

2.6. Review of Hardware Requirements

Table 1 gives a quick review of the above description by comparing the schemes in terms of the hardware requirements and functionality. ASP usually subsumes SP, and we do not show SP separately here or in the experimental re-

sults. For the ASP, MP and DP mechanisms, we uniformly use a parameter r to study its effect on the resulting performance as mentioned earlier. The previously proposed RP mechanism, keeps information (2 pointers) in each entry of the page table. Since the number of virtual pages is usually quite large, the space taken by RP considerably dominates over the much smaller r (32 to 1024 rows) that we consider for ASP, MP and DP. The only benefit for RP in this regard is that the storage is in main memory, while the other three require on-chip real-estate. These two pointers for RP refer to the previous and next pointers of the LRU stack. Both MP and RP, index the information based on the page number that misses in the TLB, and DP indexes using the current distance (stride). ASP, on the other hand, indexes using the PC value. In ASP, MP and DP, the corresponding tag information (of the indexing field) needs to be maintained to ensure the corresponding match since more than one entry can map on to a single row. There is, thus, not a significant difference in storage requirements across the schemes for a single row.

ASP, MP and DP, have all the necessary information to initiate a prefetch on-chip, and thus need not incur any additional memory references. On the other hand, removing the page table entry that is currently required and pushing the evicted entry on top of LRU stack requires manipulating four pointers in RP. This can become an issue in increasing memory traffic, thus interfering not only with other prefetch actions but also with normal data traffic.

The maximum number of prefetches that can be initiated on a miss for MP and DP depend on the chosen s values. This is, typically, quite small (around 2-4) that is not only shown to be a good operating point later in this paper, but has also been pointed out by [16] for MP. ASP, as defined in [8], prefetches the address incremented by the corresponding stride. RP prefetches entries on either side of the LRU stack upon a miss, and there is also a version discussed in [26] that prefetches three entries. It should be noted, that the number of prefetches that are initiated is not necessarily indicative of the performance of the scheme. Eventually, the prefetches are put in the (small) prefetch buffer, and a more aggressive scheme can end up evicting entries before they are used.

3 Performance Evaluation

3.1. Experimental Setup

We have conducted an extensive evaluation of the prefetching mechanisms for a wide variety of applications spanning several benchmark suites. Our evaluations use all 26 applications from SPEC CPU2000 [11], 20 applications from MediaBench [21], 5 applications (bcc, mpegply, msvc, perl4, and winword) from the Etch traces [1] and 5 applications (anagram, bc, ft, ks and yacr2) from the Pointer Intensive Benchmark suite [2]. In all, we have considered 56 applications that we hope are representative enough of realistic scenarios. The MediaBench ap-

	ASP	MP	RP	DP
How many rows?	r	r	No. of PTEs	r
What are the contents of a row ?	PC Tag, Page #, Stride and State	Page # Tag 2 Prediction Page #s	*next, prev* pointers	Distance Tag, 2 Prediction Distances
Where is the table?	On-Chip	On-Chip	In Memory	On-Chip
How is the table indexed?	PC	Page #	Page #	Distance
How many memory system operations per miss? (*excluding prefetching*)	0	0	4	0
How many prefetches can be initiated?	1	2	1-3	2

Table 1. Comparing the Hardware Issues of the Schemes at a glance. s **is assumed to be 2 for MP and DP. PC Tag, Page # Tag, and Distance Tag for ASP, MP and DP respectively are needed for tag comparison when indexing/looking up the table.**

plications are characteristic of those in embedded and media processing systems, and the Etch applications are characteristic of desktop/PC applications. The Pointer Intensive suite helps us evaluate the mechanisms for non-array based reference behavior, which can be more irregular. The SPEC 2000 applications are really long running codes and it is extremely difficult to simulate all of them completely, as has been pointed out by others [6, 23]. In this paper, we fast forward (skip) the first two billion instructions of their execution, and present results for the subsequent one billion instructions. The simulations have been conducted using SimpleScalar [5], using the default configuration parameters. Most of the simulations are conducted using sim-cache since we are mainly interested in the memory system references, and the prediction accuracies of the schemes. We also present one set of execution cycle results for one billion instructions with five of the applications with high TLB miss rates to compare DP and RP using sim-outorder (as can be imagined, these experiments take an excessively long time). The MediaBench, Etch and Pointer Intensive suite were simulated using Shade [10]. Though it is also important to consider the effect of the OS, the evaluations are only for application behavior in these results as in the earlier study [26].

We consider different TLB configurations - 64, 128 and 256 entries that are 2-way, 4-way and fully associative, and different values for prefetch buffer size (16, 32 and 64 entries). We have also varied the s and r values for the prediction table configurations of the mechanisms. We present representative results using 128 entry fully associative TLB and 16 entry prefetch buffer, with a page size of 4096 bytes. The reader is referred to [19] for a more detailed sensitivity analysis of different TLB configurations, prefetching parameters and page sizes.

3.2. Comparing the Schemes

In our first set of evaluations, we compare RP, MP, DP and ASP (compared qualitatively until now) with the 56 workloads in Figures 7 and 8. Since MP, DP and ASP predictions depend largely on the size of the prediction table

that is allowed, we have varied r (the number of entries) as 32, 64, 128, 256, 512 and 1024. Further, we have allowed the corresponding tables to be indexed as direct-mapped (D), set associative (2 and 4 way) and fully associative (F). Since the graph becomes very difficult to read, we show results for DP and ASP only with direct-mapped (D) configurations. We show F, 2 and 4 way associativity influence only for MP. We would like to point out that the indexing mechanism for the prediction table (F, 2 or 4 way) has very little influence on the prediction accuracy in most cases (as one would infer from the bars for MP, and in the bars for DP later in section 3.3). In these graphs, the left-most bar for each application is for RP, following which is a gap and then the bars for MP, a gap, bars for DP, a gap and finally the bars for ASP. In some cases, the bars are either completely or partially absent because the prediction accuracy is close to 0.

These mechanisms are compared in terms of their prediction accuracy, which has been the metric used in earlier research [26] to argue the capabilities and potential of TLB prefetching. Prediction accuracy is defined as the percentage of TLB misses that hit in the prefetch buffer at the time of the reference. Accuracy is an important concern since it has a direct bearing on the amount of stall time incurred by the CPU during a TLB miss. Uniformly, a prefetch buffer of size $b = 16$ entries is used in all these experiments. Remember, that *a mechanism which fetches more aggressively can evict entries from this buffer before they are actually used for the translation* (and will consequently have an effect on the prefetch accuracy). One can in fact observe this effect with ASP, when the prediction accuracy decreases for a more aggressive $r = 1024$ entry table (compared to smaller prediction table sizes) in some applications like apsi, ft and wupwise.

There are applications such as facerec, galgel, art, gap, and mesa where nearly all mechanisms give quite good prediction accuracies. In these applications, there are regular strided accesses that repeatedly go over the items already accessed in the same regular fashion. Consequently, both stride-based predictions (ASP) and history-based predictions (RP and MP) do a fairly good job of pre-

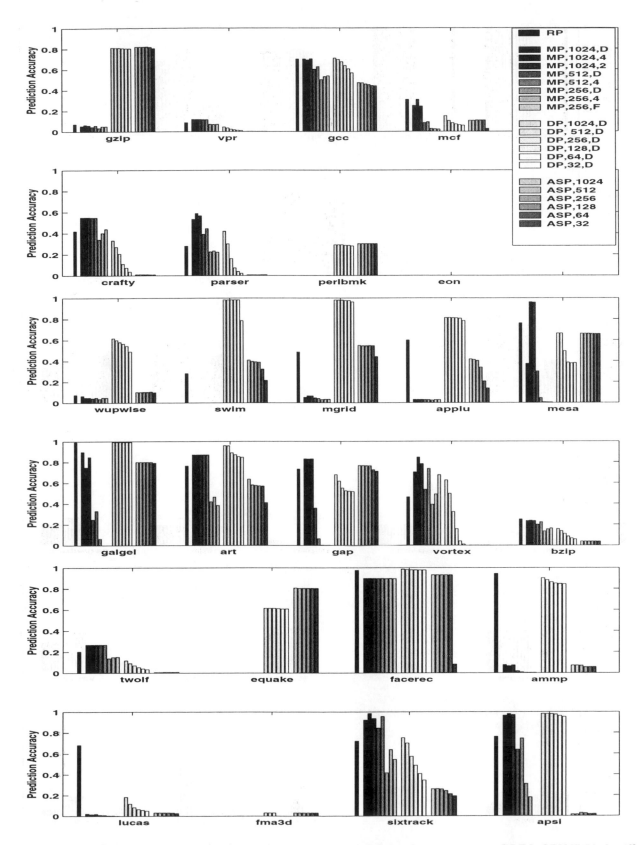

Figure 7. Prediction Accuracy of different Prefetching mechanisms for all the SPEC CPU2000 Applications

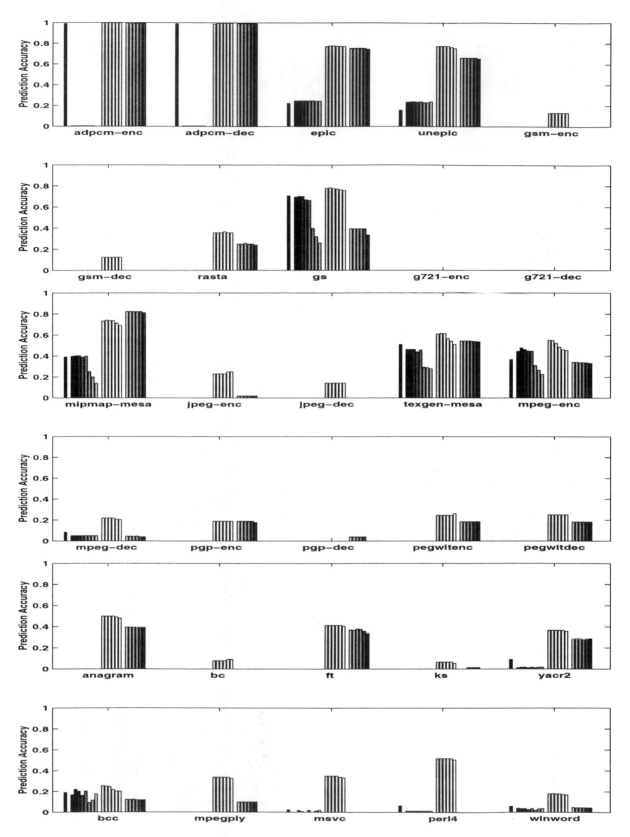

Figure 8. Prediction Accuracy of different Prefetching mechanisms for Mediabench, Etch and Pointer Intensive benchmark Suites. Legends are same as in Figure 7.

dicting the future. The only exception is that in some cases (such as galgel, art, mesa) MP performs poorly with small r. Since these are quite large datasets, keeping the history for all the references needs considerably more space, and small tables are not adequate for this purpose. RP, on the other hand, builds the history in memory and is not limited by on-chip storage as in MP. We find that our DP mechanism gives good prediction accuracies, being able to capture the strided patterns, without requiring the higher space requirements of MP to maintain history. Even a $r = 32$ predictor table for DP, gives very good predictions. In the following discussion, we go over each mechanism pointing out where it does the best and when it does not do as well.

Apart from the above five where all mechanisms give good performance, we find RP giving the best, or close to the best performance for applications such as gcc, crafty, ammp, lucas, sixtrack, apsi, adpcm-enc/dec, gs, and texgen. These applications have good repetition of history, i.e. the next reference after a given address is very likely to remain the same the next time we come to this address again.

MP gives the best or close to best performance for many of the applications that RP does very well. However, as was pointed out a little earlier, sometimes the history information that needs to be maintained can get quite long, and this can lead to poor predictions for small tables (such as $s = 32$). In some applications, where past history is a good indication of the future (i.e. RP does very well) such as in adpcm-enc/dec, MP performs very poorly for this very reason. RP is able to track history for all addresses since it keeps the information in memory, but MP does not have that luxury and may have to keep evicting its table entries from the on-chip storage. There are some applications such as parser and vortex where MP does better than even RP despite this downside. The possible reason is that RP can look at only what happened at this address the previous time the program came to it, while MP can possibly keep track of what happened the last few times (depending on the s value of its table). In these applications, it is possible that there is alternation (i.e. a sequence such as 1, 2, 3, 4, 1, 5, 2, 6, 3, 7, 4, 8, 1, 2, 3, 4, ... would do better with MP than RP for $s = 2$) in history that is leading to this behavior (this is also the reason ASP does not do well for these applications).

ASP does very well in many of the applications that are suited to RP and MP such as facerec, galgel, art, gap and mesa, and also in some where RP does better than MP (adpcm-enc/dec and texgen). The regularity in strides in these applications help this mechanism provide good accuracy. This regularity also helps ASP capture many of the first time reference predictions that history based mechanisms are not very well suited to, as in gzip, perlbmk, equake, epic/unepic, mipmap, pgp-enc/dec, anagram, and yacr2. The working sets are much smaller in some of the non-SPEC 2000 applications, and cold misses do become prominent for these. On the other hand, there are applications such as crafty and parser where the accesses are not strided enough for ASP

to perform well, but historical indications can give a much better perspective of future behavior for RP and MP.

Moving on to DP, we find that it gives very good prediction accuracies in several cases. DP comes very close to RP or MP in several applications where history-based predictions do the best such as gcc, mesa, galgel, gap, parser, and ammp. On the other hand, if history is not a good indication (or has not established) but strides are more determining (as in gzip, adpcm-enc/dec, mipmap, and perlbmk where ASP does very well), DP is able to deliver as good accuracies as ASP. Beyond coming close to the better of history or stride based schemes, there are several applications such as wupwise, swim, mgrid, applu, mpeg-dec, bc, mpegply, msvc, and perl4 where DP does much better than the others. In fact, for gsm-enc/dec, jpeg-enc/dec, ks, msvc and bc, DP is the only mechanism which makes any noticeable predictions (even if the accuracy does not exceed 20%).

We would like to point out, that there are a few applications such as eon, fma3d, g721-enc/dec and pgp-dec where none of the mechanisms are able to make any significant predictions. Many of these applications (eon, g721-enc/dec, pgp-dec, bc, ks) have so few TLB misses that a significant history does not build up nor does a strided pattern (and *TLB prefetching is not as important for them anyway*). In fma3d, the irregularity makes it very difficult for any mechanism to do well, and this motivates the need for further work on prefetching mechanism.

In summary, DP gives very good predictions for many of the applications. In fact, it provides the best or within 10% of the best prediction accuracy in 39 (and best in 36) of the 56 applications considered (the others are less than half this number). DP does well for regular and irregular applications, and applications that have strided and/or history-based access patterns. Another important point to note is that *DP can provide such good predictions with just a 32-256 entry prediction table*, compared to the others (MP and ASP) which may need many more entries, nor requiring the considerable storage and memory bandwidth taken by RP. Examining only the miss stream from the TLB, and not the actual reference stream (which to a certain extent can be viewed as a case in favor of RP because there is an implicit LRU tracking within the TLB) does not seem to penalize DP in any significant way.

DP also turns out to be the best in terms of the average prediction accuracy that was calculated over all the benchmarks($(\Sigma\ p_i)/n$) for each scheme. From the second column in Table 2, we can see that DP and RP take the first and second places respectively. One could argue, that *it is important to not just provide good accuracies for all applications, but to those where it really matters* (i.e. the higher TLB miss rate incurring applications). To capture this effect we present the weighted average ($\Sigma\ (m_i \times p_i)/(\Sigma\ m_i)$) of the prediction accuracy (i.e. the accuracy p_i for each benchmark is weighted by the corresponding TLB miss rate m_i) for the schemes in the third column of Table 2. As we can see, RP comes out a little in front (around 5% better) of DP in this case because a long history helps a select set of ap-

Prefetching Scheme	Average $(\Sigma\, p_i)/n(=56)$	Weighted Average $\Sigma\,(m_i \times p_i)/(\Sigma\, m_i)$
DP	0.43	0.82
RP	0.29	0.86
ASP	0.28	0.73
MP	0.11	0.04

Table 2. Table showing the average and weighted average of prediction accuracy for the prefetching schemes which was calculated using the miss rates(m_i) and prediction accuracies(p_i) over all the 56 applications. $s = 2$ and $r = 256$ for DP, MP and ASP.

plications with very high miss rates (even though DP does better in a majority of applications). However, this comes at a higher storage cost in memory, as well as higher memory traffic. Consequently, the rest of this subsection gets into greater detail comparing DP with RP, in terms of performance implications of these prediction accuracies, particularly for the applications with higher TLB miss rates.

Comparing DP with RP in greater Detail: Having compared the prediction capability of the mechanisms using all the applications and all the different configurations, we specifically focus on 8 applications (galgel, adpcm-encoder, ammp, mcf, vpr, twolf, lucas, apsi) which have the highest TLB miss rates (0.228, 0.192, 0.0113, 0.090, 0.016, 0.013, 0.016, and 0.018 respectively) for a 128 entry fully associative TLB amongst all these applications [18]. Of these 8 chosen applications, RP provides better accuracy than DP for 5 applications - vpr, mcf, twolf, ammp and lucas. Further, RP is the only other prefetching mechanism explored for TLBs, and we would like to show some of the trade-offs that DP provides over RP despite slightly lower prediction accuracies in these 5 applications (which is what tilted the balance in favor of RP in Table 2).

RP requires as many as 6 possible memory system references upon a TLB miss. While the CPU resumes computation as soon as the miss is serviced, there are other references needed to maintain the LRU stack. If the item was in the middle of the stack, then it needs to be removed (taking 2 references), and the evicted item needs to be put on top (taking 2 references). After this, the actual prefetching can proceed (since it prefetches on either side of the removed item, this takes 2 more references). On the other hand, DP references memory only to bring in the s (which is 2 here) predicted entries, i.e. DP does not need to update any state information in memory. It is conceivable, that some or all of these references in both these schemes can be serviced from the cache. However, in the following discussion we model these as actual memory references.

To study the impact of the additional memory traffic imposed by RP and DP, we conduct a simple experiment using

SimpleScalar, wherein we use its memory system model to account for the overheads associated with the prefetch operations. It should be noted that in this examination, the prefetch memory traffic does not contend with the normal data traffic, but only with other prefetch traffic (this in fact, *is a more biased model that favors RP over DP*). When the CPU incurs a TLB miss, and does not find the data in the prefetch buffer, but the prefetch for that entry has already been issued, it is made to stall until the entry arrives. Further, if a prefetch needs to be issued on a TLB miss, this memory loading operation will be impacted by any prior issued prefetch memory transactions (such as the pointer manipulations for RP, or the actual prefetching of entries for DP and RP). One other issue where we give the benefit of doubt for RP in its implementation is that, if there is a TLB miss soon after the previous one (and not for the same entry) and the prefetching initiated earlier is not complete, we only wait for the LRU stack to get updated and do not prefetch those items at that time (this is as though there was a wrong prediction, but we are not going to incur the corresponding memory traffic in fetching the nearby entries at that time). In this case, there would be only 4 memory transactions instead of 6. These applications are run using sim-outorder (with a 4 issue width) to account for actual CPU cycles. The prefetching and state maintenance (for RP) operations are treated as cache misses and need to be serviced from main memory with a cost of 50 cycles. A constant TLB miss penalty of 100 cycles is assumed.

We present the results from this experiment in terms of the cycles taken for execution of the programs (normalized with respect to no prefetching for the billion instructions considered) as shown in Table 3. The results are presented for the five benchmarks where RP has better accuracy over DP (as can be expected, for the rest, DP automatically provides better performance than RP).

	RP	DP
ammp	0.97	0.86
mcf	1.09	0.95
vpr	0.99	0.98
twolf	0.98	0.98
lucas	1.00	0.99

Table 3. Comparing DP with RP: Normalized execution cycles(w.r.t. no prefetching) for RP and DP for 1 billion instructions after the first 2 billion instructions. $s = 2$ and $r = 256$ for DP.

We find that despite the slightly higher prediction accuracy that RP provides for these applications, DP still comes out in front when considering execution cycles (one can also see the execution time savings, that is more significant in ammp, with prefetching compared to the execution without any prefetching in place). This is because RP generates much more memory traffic ranging from anywhere between 2-3 times that for DP [19]. As was pointed out, DP gives fairly good predictions even with $r = 32$ which incurs even lower traffic. It should be remembered that in this simulation, we are in fact more biased towards RP, since the prefetch traffic does not interfere with the normal data traffic, and consequently a more realistic model would favor DP further.

3.3. Sensitivity Analysis of DP

The impact of several parameters such as table configuration (r), table associativity (D, 2, 4, F), number of prediction entries (s), prefetch buffer size (b), TLB configurations and page size on the effectiveness of DP has also been studied. Some of these results are shown in Figure 9 and the reader is referred to [19] for further results/details. In general, we found that DP is fairly insensitive to many of these parameters, and even a small direct-mapped 32-256 entry table suffices to give very good predictions.

4   Concluding Remarks

There is a plethora of related literature [29] on prefetching mechanisms that try to examine patterns in reference behavior to predict references for the near future. Nearly all of them have been proposed to alleviate latencies in the memory hierarchy by prefetching blocks into the cache or for prefetching data from I/O devices. However, there has been only one prior study [26] that has proposed, evaluated and demonstrated the benefits of prefetching entries for the TLB. However, the suitability and associated benefits of the previously proposed prefetching mechanisms for caches has not been examined for prefetching TLB entries until now.

Prefetching mechanisms usually try to detect strided behavior or history-based behavior to make their predictions. With the former, one can make good predictions with very little space, whenever there are regular/strided reference patterns. However, they may not do a good job when there is no such regularity. History-based predictions can do better than stride-based predictors, albeit at a higher storage cost, when previous references can give a good indication of what to expect next (even when references are not strided).

In this paper, we have presented a new mechanism called *Distance Prefetching* (DP), that can automatically provide strided predictions when there is such behavior, and becomes more history-based when there is not. It exploits the fact that even if there is variability in strides, there is probably a pattern to this variability itself and the past information on such variability can help make future predictions. While DP is a fairly generic mechanism, that can possibly be used in the context of caches, I/O etc., in this paper we have specifically evaluated it for TLBs.

Considering representative examples from stride-based (Arbitrary Stride Prefetching) and history-based (Markov Prefetching) predictors, we have presented a qualitative and quantitative comparison of our DP mechanism for TLB prefetching with these earlier proposals. In addition, we have also evaluated our mechanism with the only other proposal - RP - for TLB prefetching which has been shown to improve TLB performance significantly. We find that DP gives better prediction accuracy than the others in many of the applications, and in fact, DP gives the best or close to the best prediction in 39 of the 56 considered applications. Even in the applications where we found RP to be a little better in terms of prediction accuracy, we demonstrated that DP comes out in front in terms of execution cycles.

DP can operate fairly well with a small direct-mapped prediction table of 32-256 entries, with most of the results quite insensitive to a wide spectrum of table and indexing parameters. Further, the prediction accuracies are quite good even with a 16 entry prefetch buffer. DP is able to make good predictions across different TLB configurations and page sizes as well.

The contributions of this paper are in: (a) the novel mechanism - Distance Prefetching - that can be used to predict application reference behavior using a relatively small space (which can possibly be used in the context of different levels of the storage hierarchy - TLBs, caches, I/O), (b) adaptation and qualitative comparison of this mechanism and others previously proposed for caches to the domain of TLB prefetching, (c) a detailed application-driven evaluation of all these mechanisms using a wide spectrum of public-domain benchmarks to show the benefits of distance prefetching, and (d) identifying the parameters for a distance prefetcher implementation, based on a sensitivity analysis. Our ongoing work is examining issues about using other information (PC, several previous distances, etc.) within the context of this new mechanism, and evaluating its benefits for other levels of the storage hierarchy (caches and I/O). We are also investigating prefetching issues in a multiprogrammed environment (flushing/switching the prefetch tables), the effect of the OS and the effect of superpaging.

References

[1] Etch traces.   http://memsys.cs.washington.edu/memsys/html/traces.html.

[2] Pointer-intensive benchmark suite. http://www.cs.wisc.edu/ austin/ptr-dist.html.

[3] T. E. Anderson, H. M. Levy, B. N. Bershad, and E. D. Lazowska.   The Interaction of Architecture and Operating System Design. In *Proceedings of the Fourth International Conference on Architectural Support for Programming Languages and Operating Systems*, pages 108–120, Santa Clara, California, April 1991.

[4] K. Bala, M. F. Kaashoek, and W. E. Weihl.   Software Prefetching and Caching for Translation Lookaside Buffers. In *Proceedings of the Usenix Symposium on Operating Systems Design and Implementation*, pages 243–253, 1994.

[5] D. Burger and T. Austin. The SimpleScalar Toolset, Version 3.0. http://www.simplescalar.org.

[6] J. F. Cantin and M. D. Hill.   Cache Performance for Selected SPEC CPU2000 Benchmarks.   October 2001. http://www.cs.wisc.edu/multifacet/misc/spec2000cache-data/.

[7] J. B. Chen, A. Borg, and N. P. Jouppi. A Simulation Based Study of TLB Performance.   In *Proceedings of the 19th*

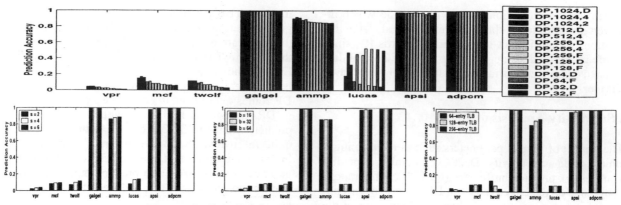

Figure 9. Sensitivity of DP to Hardware Parameters

Annual International Symposium on Computer Architecture, pages 114–123, 1992.

[8] T. Chen and J. Baer. Effective hardware based data prefetching for high-performance processors. *IEEE Transactions on Computers*, 44(5):609–623, May 1995.

[9] D. W. Clark and J. S. Emer. Performance of the VAX-11/780 Translation Buffers: Simulation and Measurement. *ACM Transactions on Computer Systems*, 3(1), 1985.

[10] B. Cmelik and D. Keppel. Shade: A fast instruction-set simulator for execution profiling. In *Proceedings of the 1994 ACM SIGMETRICS Conference on the Measurement and Modeling of Computer Systems*, pages 128–137, May 1994.

[11] S. P. E. Corporation. http://www.spec.org.

[12] F. Dahlgren, M. Dubois, and P. Stenstrom. Fixed and adaptive sequential prefetching in shared memory multiprocessors. *International Conference on Parallel Processing*, pages 56–63, August 1993.

[13] J. W. C. Fu and J. H. Patel. Stride directed prefetching in scalar processors. In *Proceedings of the 25th MICRO*, pages 102–110, 1992.

[14] J. Huck and J. Hays. Architectural support for translation table management in large address space machines. In *Proceedings of the 20th Annual International Symposium on Computer Architecture*, pages 39–50, May 1993.

[15] B. L. Jacob and T. N. Mudge. A look at several memory management units, TLB-refill mechanisms, and page table organizations. In *Proceedings of the Eigth International Conference on Architectural Support for Programming Languages and Operating System*, pages 295–306, 1998.

[16] D. Joseph and D. Grunwald. Prefetching Using Markov Predictors. *IEEE Transactions on Computer Systems*, 48(2):121–133, 1999.

[17] N. Jouppi. Improving direct-mapped cache performance by addition of a small fully associative cache and prefetch buffers. In *Proceedings of the 17th International Symposium on Computer Architecture*, Seattle, WA, 1990.

[18] G. B. Kandiraju and A. Sivasubramaniam. Characterizing the d-TLB Behavior of SPEC CPU2000 Benchmarks. In *Proceedings of the ACM SIGMETRICS Conference on Measurement and Modeling of Computer Systems*, June 2002.

[19] G. B. Kandiraju and A. Sivasubramaniam. Going the Distance for TLB Prefetching: An Application-driven Study.

Technical Report CSE-01-032, Dept. of Comp. Sci. & Eng., Penn State Univ., November, 2001.

[20] D. Koppelman. Neighborhood prefetching on multiprocessors using instruction history. In *Proceedings of the International Conference on Parallel Architectures and Compilation Techniques*, 2000.

[21] C. Lee, M. Potkonjak, and W. Magione-Smith. Mediabench: A tool for evaluating and synthesizing multimedia and communications systems. In *International Symposium on Microarchitecture*, pages 330–335, 1997. http://www.cs.ucla.edu/ leec/mediabench/.

[22] D. Nagle, R. Uhlig, T. Stanley, S. Sechrest, T. Mudge, and R. Brown. Design Tradeoffs for Software Managed TLBs. In *Proceedings of the 20th Annual International Symposium on Computer Architecture*, pages 27–38, 1993.

[23] A. K. Osowski, J. Flynn, N. Meares, and D. J. Lilja. *Adapting the SPEC2000 Benchmark Suite for Simulation-based Computer Architecture Research*. Kluwer-Academic Publishers, 2000. (papers from Workshop on Workload Characterization).

[24] J. S. Park and G. S. Ahn. A Software-controlled Prefetching Mechanism for Software-managed TLBs. *Microprocessors and Microprogramming*, 41(2):121–136, May 1995.

[25] M. Rosenblum, E. Bugnion, S. Devine, and S. Herrod. Using the SimOS Machine Simulator to Study Complex Computer Systems. *ACM Transactions on Modeling and Computer Simulation*, 7(1):78–103, January 1997.

[26] A. Saulsbury, F. Dahlgren, and P. Stenstrom. Recency-based TLB preloading. In *Proceedings of the 27th Annual International Symposium on Computer Architecture*, pages 117–127, June 2000.

[27] M. Swanson, L. Stoller, and J. Carter. Increasing TLB reach using Superpages backed by Shadow Memory. In *Proceedings of the 25th Annual International Symposium on Computer Architecture*, pages 204–213, 1998.

[28] M. Talluri. *Use of Superpages and Subblocking in the Address Translation Hierarchy*. PhD thesis, Dept. of CS, Univ. of Wisconsin at Madison, 1995.

[29] S. VanderWiel and D. Lilja. Data prefetch mechanisms. *ACM Computing Surveys*, 32(2):174–199, June 1999.

Session 6: Dynamic Optimization

Timekeeping in the Memory System:
Predicting and Optimizing Memory Behavior

Zhigang Hu[†]   Stefanos Kaxiras[‡]   Margaret Martonosi[†]

[†]Department of Electrical Engineering   [‡] Communication Systems and Software
Princeton University   Agere Systems
{hzg, mrm}@ee.princeton.edu   kaxiras@agere.com

Abstract

Techniques for analyzing and improving memory referencing behavior continue to be important for achieving good overall program performance due to the ever-increasing performance gap between processors and main memory. This paper offers a fresh perspective on the problem of predicting and optimizing memory behavior. Namely, we show quantitatively the extent to which detailed timing characteristics of past memory reference events are strongly predictive of future program reference behavior. We propose a family of time-keeping techniques that optimize behavior based on observations about particular cache time durations, such as the cache access interval or the cache dead time. Timekeeping techniques can be used to build small, simple, and high-accuracy (often 90% or more) predictors for identifying conflict misses, for predicting dead blocks, and even for estimating the time at which the next reference to a cache frame will occur and the address that will be accessed. Based on these predictors, we demonstrate two new and complementary time-based hardware structures: (1) a time-based victim cache that improves performance by only storing conflict miss lines with likely reuse, and (2) a time-based prefetching technique that hones in on the right address to prefetch, and the right time to schedule the prefetch. Our victim cache technique improves performance over previous proposals by better selections of what to place in the victim cache. Our prefetching technique outperforms similar prior hardware prefetching proposals, despite being orders of magnitude smaller. Overall, these techniques improve performance by more than 11% across the SPEC2000 benchmark suite.

1 Introduction

For several decades now, memory hierarchies have been a primary determinant of application performance. As the processor-memory performance gap has widened, increasingly aggressive techniques have been proposed for understanding and improving cache memory performance. These techniques have included prefetching, victim caches, and more [3, 7, 8, 12, 15, 16, 17, 18]. More recently, the static and dynamic power dissipation of cache structures has also been a vexing problem, and has led to another set of techniques for improving cache behavior from the power perspective [6, 9, 13, 19, 23].

For most of these cache power and performance optimizations, a key hurdle for their success lies in classifying behavior such that hardware and software can deduce which optimizations to apply and when. For example, classification schemes that identify conflict misses or that predict upcoming reuse may be useful in determining which items would be best to store in a victim cache.

Most prior work on caches has focused on time-independent reference activity. In these approaches, event ordering and interleaving are of prime importance. In contrast, the time durations between events play a lesser role. For example, Tam et al. propose managing multi-lateral caches using cache-line access information [20]. They take into account the number of times a cache line is accessed but not any timing information about the accesses themselves. Charney and Reeves were first to propose address correlation in hardware for data prefetching [2]. Likewise, Joseph and Grunwald propose a Markov-based predictor to guide prefetch, but they use a time-independent Markov model; it tracks the sequence of accesses but not the time durations between them [7].

In contrast, this paper shows quantitatively that the timing characteristics of reference events can be strongly predictive of program reference behavior. Time-based tracking of memory references in programs can be a powerful way of understanding and improving program memory referencing behavior. Just as one example, tracking the time duration between when a cached item is last successfully used and when it is evicted (i.e., the *dead time*) can be an accurate predictor of whether the cached data is involved in a mapping conflict for which a victim cache may be helpful.

Mendelson et al. proposed an analytical model for predicting the fraction of live and dead cache lines [14] of a process, as a function of the process' execution time and the behavior of other processes in a multitasking environment [11]. Wood et al. introduced one notion of time-based techniques as a way of improving the accuracy of cache sampling techniques in simulations [22]. They showed that one can deduce the miss rates of unprimed references at the beginning of reference trace samples by considering the proportion of cycles a cache line spends *dead* or waiting to be evicted. More recently, work on cache decay is another example of time-based methods for managing cached data [9]. Here each cache line has a 2-bit timer associated with it to track recency of accesses to it. That work used this tracking to propose that cache lines that have not been recently accessed be turned off, or "decayed", in order to save leakage energy.

Our work studies the predictive and classificatory role of timing statistics more broadly. In particular, this paper shows that time-based techniques are quite effective in deducing aspects of cache behavior that have previously been either hard to discern on-the-fly in a single program run, or hard to discern at all. For example, identification of conflict misses often uses multiple simulation runs [5] or elaborate hardware structures [3]. Our work here shows that conflict misses can be identified with good accuracy simply based on small cache line counters.

The paper makes contributions at three levels:

- First, we construct an expanded set of useful metrics regarding generational behavior in cache lines, and we provide quantitative characterizations of the SPEC2000 benchmarks for these metrics.

- Second, using these metrics, we introduce a fundamentally different approach for on-the-fly categorization of application reference patterns. We give reliable predictors of conflict misses, dead blocks and other key aspects of reference behavior.

- Third, based on our ability to discover these reference patterns on-the-fly, we propose hardware structures that exploit this knowledge to improve performance. In particular, we propose and evaluate mechanisms to manage victim caches and prefetching. Our victim cache technique improves over previous proposals by better selecting what to place in it. Our hardware prefetching technique also outperforms prior related proposals and is orders of magnitude smaller as well. These techniques improve performance by more than 11% across the SPEC2000 benchmark suite.

More broadly, we expect that these metrics and methods will offer researchers even more intuition for further hardware structures in the future.

The remainder of the paper is structured as follows. Section 2 presents the experimental methods used in the paper. Section 3 outlines terminology and gives overview statistics regarding the generational aspect of cache behavior which is fundamental to our approach. Then, in Section 4, we present a hardware-efficient method to improve victim cache performance using timekeeping techniques. Section 5 then discusses an even more aggressive application of timekeeping techniques: we propose a prefetching system based on (i) dead block prediction, (ii) reuse analysis, and (iii) reference timing, all mainly discerned from simple-to-implement timekeeping metrics. Finally, Section 6 discusses some remaining details and offers our conclusions.

2 Methodology and Modeling

2.1 Simulator

To evaluate our proposals, we use a modified version of Simplescalar 3.0 [1] to simulate an aggressive 8-issue out-of-order processor. The main processor and memory hierarchy parameters are shown in Table 1. Because contention can have important influence on performance, we have incorporated a simulator modification that accurately models contention at the L1/L2 and memory buses [10]. As in [10], the busses always give processor memory requests priority over hardware prefetch requests.

2.2 Benchmarks

We evaluate our results using the SPEC CPU2000 benchmark suite [21]. The benchmarks are compiled for the Alpha instruction set using the Compaq Alpha compiler with SPEC *peak* settings, which include aggressive software prefetching.

Processor Core	
Clock rate	2GHZ
Instruction Window	128-RUU, 128-LSQ
Issue width	8 instructions per cycle
Functional Units	8 IntALU,3 IntMult/Div, 6 FPALU,2 FPMult/Div, 4 Load/Store Units
Memory Hierarchy	
L1 Dcache Size	32KB, 1-way, 32B blocks 64 MSHRs
L1 Icache Size	32KB, 4-way, 32B blocks
L1/L2 bus	32-byte wide, 2GHZ
L2 I/D	each 1MB, 4-way LRU, 64B blocks,12-cycle latency
L2/Memory bus	64-byte wide, 400MHZ
Memory Latency	70 cycles
Prefetcher	
Prefetch MSHRs	32
Prefetch Request Queue	128 entries

Table 1: Configuration of Simulated Processor

In our simulation, we treat these software prefetches as normal memory reference instructions. In section 5, we also experiment with ignoring all the software prefetches to evaluate the effect of software prefetching on our timekeeping prefetching.

For each program, we skip the first 1 billion instructions to avoid unrepresentative behavior at the beginning of the program's execution. We then simulate 2 billion instructions using the reference input set. We include some overview statistics here for background. Figure 1 shows how much the performance (IPC) of each benchmark would improve if *all* conflict and capacity misses in L1 data cache could be eliminated. This is the target we aim for in our memory optimizations. The programs are sorted from left to right according to the amount they would speed up if conflict and capacity misses could be removed. Figure 2 breaks down the misses of these programs into three stacked bar segments denoting cold, conflict and capacity misses. An interesting observation here is that the programs that exhibit the biggest potential for improvement (RHS of Figure 2) also tend to have comparatively more capacity misses than conflict misses. Thus, we expect that eliminating capacity misses will result in larger benefit than eliminating conflict misses. This is confirmed in later sections. Although we focus mainly on those benchmarks that benefit the most from the elimination of conflict and capacity misses, we also present results for other benchmarks for completeness.

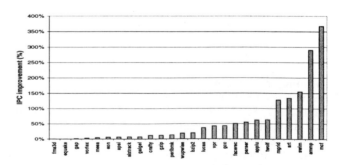

Figure 1: Potential IPC improvement if all conflict and capacity misses in L1 data cache could be eliminated for SPEC2000 benchmarks.

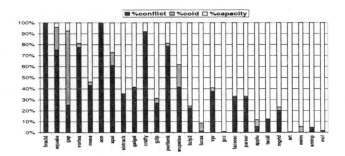

Figure 2: Breakdown of program L1 data cache misses into three categories: conflict, cold and capacity.

3 Generational Behavior of Cache Lines: Metrics and Motivation

The generational behavior of cache lines is a well-established phenomenon. As illustrated in Figure 3, each generation is defined as beginning with a cache miss that brings new data into this level of the memory hierarchy. A cache line generation ends when data leaves the cache because a miss to some other data causes its eviction. Each cache line generation is divided into two parts: the *live time* of the cache line, where the line is actively accessed by the processor and the *dead time*, awaiting eviction.

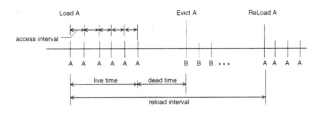

Figure 3: Timeline depicting a generation of the cache line with A resident, followed by A's eviction to begin a generation with B resident. Eventually, A is re-referenced to begin yet another generation.

The live time of a cache line starts with the miss that brings the data into the cache and ends with the last successful hit before the item is evicted. The dead time is defined as the time duration where the cached data will not be used again successfully *within this generation*. That is, the dead time is the time between the last hit and when the data is actually evicted. Many times we see only a single miss and then eviction. We consider these cases to have zero live time; therefore the generation time equals to the dead time. Such cases are important for classifying misses, as we will show in later sections.

There are further metrics that also turn out to be of practical interest. These include the access interval and reload interval. Access interval refers to the time intervals between successive accesses to the same cache line *within the live time of a generation*. In contrast, reload interval is used to denote the time duration between the beginnings of two generations that involve the same memory line. The reload interval in one level of the hierarchy (eg, L1) is actually the access interval in the next lower level of the hierarchy (eg, L2) assuming the data is resident there.

We examine four of the metrics illustrated in Figure 3 (live time, dead time, access interval and reload interval) and give an initial sense of their distributions and how they compare.

Ultimately, the goal of these data is the following. Imagine that execution is at some arbitrary point along the timeline depicted in Figure 3. We can know something about past history along that timeline, but we wish to predict what is likely to happen soon in the future. First, we wish to deduce *where we currently are*. That is, are we currently in live time or dead time? Dead time cannot be perfectly known until it is over, but if we can predict it accurately, we can build power and performance optimizations based on this dead block prediction. Second, we wish to deduce *what will happen next*: a re-reference of the current cached data? Or a reference to new data that begins a new generation? Accurately deducing what will be referenced next *and when* is a crux issue for building effective victim caches and prefetchers. This paper demonstrates quantitatively that our timekeeping techniques allow effective predictions and optimizations that address both of these questions.

Overview Distributions: Live Time, Dead Time, Access Interval and Reload Interval   Figure 4 illustrates a distribution for SPEC2000 benchmarks of *live times* and *dead times* within cache generations. Recall that Live time is defined as the time duration between when a memory line arrives in cache, and when it experiences its last successful use (last hit) before it is evicted to end the generation. Dead time is defined as the time duration between when an item in the cache is last used successfully as a cache hit, and when it is evicted from the cache. An effective prefetching technique might be based on deducing when a line will be dead, and then proactively prefetching the next line that will map there. We discuss such strategies in Section 5.

Dead times are in general much longer than average live times. For example, over all of the SPEC suite, 58% of live times are 100 cycles or less. In contrast, only 31% of dead times are less than 100 cycles. This is a useful observation because it hints that we can succeed in discerning dead versus live times a priori based on the durations observed.

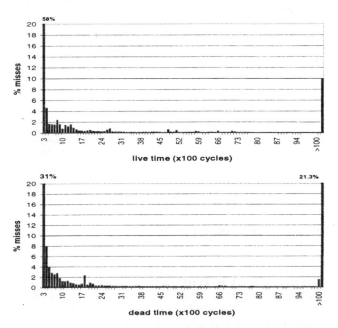

Figure 4: Distribution of live times and dead times for all generations of cache lines in the SPEC2000 simulations.

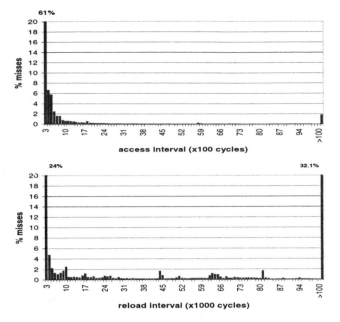

Figure 5: Distribution of access intervals and reload intervals for all generations of cache lines in the SPEC2000 simulations.

Two additional metrics: access interval and reload interval, also help to classify references. Access interval is the time duration between successive references (hits) within a cache live time. In contrast, reload interval is the time between the beginnings of two successive generations involving the same memory line. For data resident in L2 cache, a reload interval in the L1 cache corresponds to the access interval of the same data in the L2 cache, down one level in the hierarchy. Figure 5 illustrates access interval and reload interval distributions. Note that reload intervals are plotted with the x-axis 1000X space cycles rather than 100X as in the access interval graph. The distributions here are even more distinct. 91% of access intervals are less than 1000 cycles, while only 24% of reload intervals are in that range. In addition to the distributions of absolute values for these metrics, their variability over time is also of interest. We revisit this issue in Section 5.

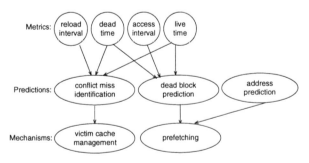

Figure 6: Timekeeping metrics, some resulting predictions based on them, and related hardware mechanisms.

From Statistics to Hardware   Figure 6 depicts the stages one goes through in using timekeeping metrics to build mechanisms for improving memory behavior. In the top layer are basic metrics, all of which appear in Figure 3. They include reload interval, dead time, access interval, and live time. As subsequent sections will show, these *metrics* can be used to

identify *predictions* about program behavior. These predictions might include identifying conflict misses or deducing dead cache blocks. Interestingly, sometimes more than one metric can be used as a predictor of the same behavior. For example, reload interval, dead time, and live time can each be turned into a conflict miss predictor (see Section 4), each with different tradeoffs in terms of predictive accuracy and coverage. Finally, these predictions can, in turn, be composed into *mechanisms* that actively respond and optimize based on the prediction. Tracking the timekeeping metrics requires little hardware; essentially just coarse-grained simple counters that are ticked periodically (but not necessarily every cycle) from the global cycle counter provided on most microprocessors. We discuss mechanisms and their implementations in the sections that follow.

4   Timekeeping Metrics to Identify and Avoid Conflict Misses

Canonically, cache misses are classified into 3 categories: cold miss, conflict miss and capacity miss [4]. Cold misses occur when a cache line is loaded into the cache the first time. Conflict misses are those misses which can be eliminated by a fully-associative cache. Capacity misses are those which will miss even with a fully-associative cache.

Interpreting Hill's definitions with generational behavior, a conflict miss occurs because its last generation was unexpectedly interrupted—something that would have not happened in a fully associative cache. Similarly, a capacity miss occurs because its last generation was ended because of lack of space—again, something that would not have happened in a larger cache. In this section we quantitatively correlate the miss types with timekeeping metrics. When we correlate metrics to a miss type we always refer to the timekeeping metrics of the last generation of the cache line that suffers the miss. In other words, what happens to the current generation of a cache line tells us something about its next miss.

4.1   Identifying Conflict Misses

By Reload Interval   While Figure 5 showed reload intervals over all generations, Figure 7 splits the reload interval distribution into two graphs for different miss types. These statistics show vividly different behavior for conflict and capacity misses. In particular, reload intervals for capacity misses are overwhelmingly in the tail of the distribution. In contrast, reload intervals for conflict misses tend to be fairly small: an average of roughly 8000 cycles. The average reload interval for a capacity miss is one to two orders of magnitude larger than that for a conflict miss! Large reload intervals for capacity misses make sense: for an access to an item to be classified a capacity miss, there must be at least 1024 (total number of blocks in the cache) unique accesses to drive the item out of a fully-associative cache after its last access. In a processor that typically issues 1-2 memory accesses per cycle, the time for 1024 accesses is on the order of a thousand cycles, and it may take much longer before 1024 *unique* lines have been accessed. On the contrary, a conflict miss has no more than 1024 unique cache accesses after their last access; this leads to their small reload intervals.

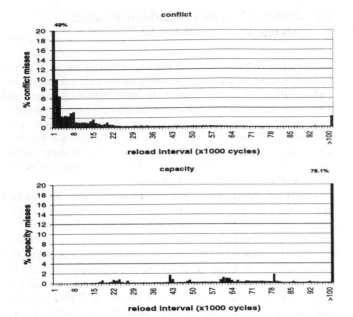

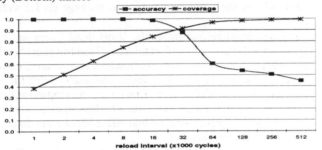

Figure 7: Distribution of reload interval for conflict (Top) and capacity (Bottom) misses

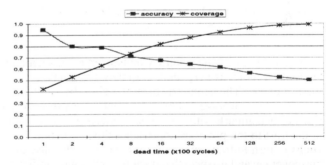

Figure 8: Accuracy and coverage for conflict miss predictions based on *reload interval*. Each data point indicates what the accuracy or coverage would be for predicting conflict misses to be all instances where the *reload interval* is less than the quantity on the x-axis.

Reload intervals make excellent predictors of conflict misses. Figure 8 shows accuracy and coverage when reload interval is used as predictor. For each point on the x-axis, one curve gives the accuracy of predicting that reload intervals less than that x-axis value denote conflict misses. The other curve gives the coverage of that predictor: i.e., how often it makes a prediction.

When conflict misses are defined as small reload intervals (about 1000 cycles or less) prediction accuracy is close to perfect. Coverage, the percent of conflict misses captured by the prediction, is low at that point, however, about 40%. The importance of reload interval, though, shows in the behavior of this predictor as we increase the threshold: up to 16K cycles, accuracy is stable and nearly perfect, while coverage increases to about 85%. This is appealing for selecting an operating point because it means we can walk out along the accuracy curve to 16K cycles before accuracy sees any substantive drop. The clear drop there makes that a natural breakpoint for setting up a conflict predictor based on reload intervals smaller than 16K.

By Dead Time Figure 9 shows the distribution of dead time divided by miss types. Again, we see trends similar

to reload interval distribution, though not as clear cut. That is, dead times are typically small for conflict misses, while much larger for capacity misses. These observations about dead times hint at a phenomenon one could exploit. Namely, one can deduce that an item has been "prematurely" evicted from the cache due to a conflict miss, if its dead time is quite short. Where dead times are quite large, it hints at the fact that the item probably left the cache at the end of its "natural lifetime"; that is, it was probably evicted as a capacity miss at the end of its usage.

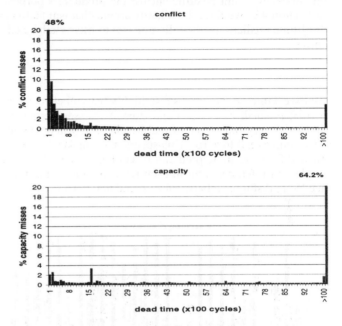

Figure 9: Distribution of dead time for conflict (Top) and capacity (Bottom) misses

Figure 10: Accuracy and coverage for conflict miss predictions based on *dead time*. Each data point indicates what the accuracy or coverage would be for predicting conflict misses to be all instances where the *dead time* is less than the quantity on the x-axis.

Figure 10 shows accuracy and coverage of a predictor that predicts an upcoming conflict miss based on the length of the dead time of the current generation. Namely, for a point on the x-axis, accuracy and coverage data indicate what the prediction outcome would be if one considered dead times less than that value as indicators of conflict misses. Coverage is essentially the fraction of conflict misses for which we make a prediction. Accuracy is the likelihood that our prediction is correct, for the instances where we do make a prediction.

As Figure 10 shows, predicting a conflict miss if the dead time of its last generation is smaller than a given threshold is very accurate (over 90%) for small thresholds (100 cycles or less). But coverage is only about 40% (attesting to the fact that most dead times are large). Increasing the dead-time threshold degrades accuracy but increases coverage. A likely method for choosing an appropriate operating point would be to walk down the accuracy curve (i.e., walk out towards larger dead times) until just before accuracy values drop to a point of insufficient accuracy. One can then check that the coverage at this operating point is sufficient for the predictor's purpose. In Section 4.2, we describe a hardware mechanism that uses dead-time predictions of conflict misses to filter victim cache entries.

By Live Time Live time is also highly biased between conflict (very small live times) and capacity misses (larger live times). A very important special case here is when we have a live time equal to zero. This special case makes for a simple and fairly accurate predictor of conflict misses. In fact, a single ("re-reference") bit in each L1 cache line is all that is needed to distinguish between zero and non-zero live times.

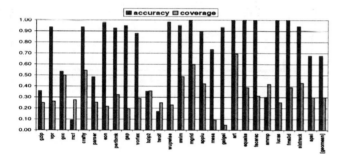

Figure 11: Accuracy and coverage of using "live time = 0" as a predictor of conflict misses.

Figure 11 shows the accuracy and coverage of such a prediction. Accuracy is very high: for many programs, accuracy is close to one. The geometric mean for all SPEC2000 is 68% accuracy, but coverage is low. Coverage varies from benchmark to benchmark with a geometric mean of roughly 30%. In contrast to the previous approaches this prediction has no knobs to turn to trade accuracy for coverage. Because of the low coverage and its specialized nature, live-time conflict prediction is likely to be useful in few situations. We include it here mainly to demonstrate how different metrics can classify or predict behavior.

Prediction Location Conflict predictors based on dead times (or live times) rely only on L1-centric information. In contrast, conflict predictors based on reload intervals would most likely be implemented by monitoring access intervals in the L2 cache. As a result, one's choice of how to predict conflict misses might depend on whether the structure using the predictor is more conveniently implemented near the L1 or L2 cache.

4.2 Utilizing Conflict Miss Identification: Managing a Victim cache

A victim cache is a small fully-associative cache that reduces L1 miss penalties by holding items evicted due to recent conflicts. Victim caches help with conflict misses, and in the previous subsection we discussed timekeeping metrics that can be used as reliable indicators of conflict misses, particularly dead time and reload interval.[1] Here, we propose using these conflict indicators to manage the victim cache. In particular, we want to avoid entering items into the victim cache that are unlikely to be reused soon.

Small reload intervals are highly correlated to conflict misses and they are an effective filter for a victim cache. The intuition that ties reload intervals to victim caches is the following: Since the size of victim cache is small, a victim block will stay only for a limited time before it is evicted out of the victim cache. In terms of generational behavior, this means that only victim blocks with small reload intervals are likely to hit in the victim cache. Blocks with large reload intervals will probably get evicted before their next access so it is wasteful to put them into the victim cache. Unfortunately, reload intervals are only available for counting in L2. This makes it difficult for their use as a means to manage an L1 victim cache.

Besides short reload intervals, short dead times are also very good indicators of conflict misses. Dead times are readily available in L1 at the point of eviction and as such are a natural choice for managing a victim cache associated with the L1. We use a policy in which the victim cache only captures those evicted blocks that have dead times of less than a *threshold* of 1K cycles. Figure 9 shows that these blocks are likely to result in conflict misses.

The hardware structure of the dead-time victim filter is shown in Figure 12. A single, coarse-grained counter per cache line measures dead time. The counter is reset with every access and advances with global ticks that occur every 512 cycles. Upon a miss the counter contains the time since the last access, i.e., the dead time. An evicted cache line is allowed into the victim cache if its counter value is less than or equal to 1 (giving a range for the dead time from 0 to 1023 cycles). Our experiments show that for a 32-entry victim cache managed in this way, the traffic into the victim cache is reduced by 87%. This reduction is achieved without sacrificing performance, as seen in Figure 13.[2]

Collins et al. [3] suggest filtering the victim cache traffic by selecting only victims of possible conflict misses. Their solution requires storing an extra tag for each cache line (remembering what was there before) to distinguish conflict misses from capacity misses. Comparing our approach with a Collins-style filter in Figure 13, we see similar traffic reduction, but our timekeeping based filter leads to higher IPC for most of the benchmarks. Note that as in Figure 1, in Figure 13 the potential for speedup increases to the right, but the ratio of conflict misses to total misses increases to the left. In Figure 13, the programs that experience the largest speedups

---

[1] We do not further examine the zero-live-time predictor because of its relatively low coverage and significant overlap with the technique based on dead time.

[2] The traffic reduction by our filter also implies power reduction but we have not examined this in depth since it is beyond the scope of this paper.

with our timekeeping victim filter are clustered in the middle of the graph. Programs to the far left have little room for improvement. Programs to the far right whose misses are overwhelmingly capacity misses are *negatively* affected with an *unfiltered* victim cache, but they retain their performance if a conflict filter (either Collins-style or timekeeping) is employed.

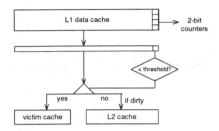

Figure 12: Implementation of a timekeeping victim cache filter

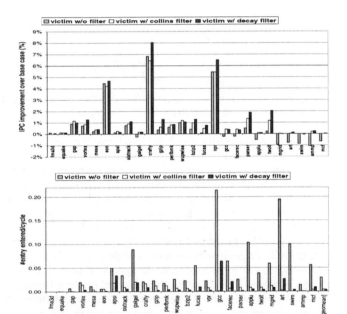

Figure 13: IPC improvement (Top) and fill traffic to victim cache (Bottom) for timekeeping victim cache filter compared to Collins filter.

The performance of our timekeeping victim filter indicates that the parameters (dead-time threshold, cache sizes, etc.) are well matched. This is not coincidental. What makes our timekeeping techniques invaluable is that they provide a sound framework to reason about such parameters rather than to revert to trial-and-error. We will informally "prove" that the optimal dead-time threshold actually stems from the size of the victim cache and the reuse characteristics of the program. It is essentially a form of Little's Law, from queueing theory. The reasoning is as follows:

1. We can think of a victim cache as providing associativity for some frames of the direct-mapped cache. Without any filtering, associativity is provided on a first-come, first-served basis: every block that is evicted gets an entry in the victim cache.

2. Our timekeeping filtering based on dead time results in a careful selection of the frames for which the victim cache is allowed to provide associativity. Timekeeping filtering culls out blocks with dead times greater than the threshold. In turn, the dead-time threshold controls the *number* of frames for which associativity is provided for.

3. Our filtering ensures that the victim cache will provide associativity *only* for the "active" blocks that are fairly-recently used at the time of their eviction.

4. Since the victim cache cannot provide associativity to more frames than its entries, the best size of the victim cache relates to the amount of cache in active use. A larger set of "active" blocks dilute the effectiveness of the victim cache associativity. In the data here, with a 1K cycle dead time threshold, only about 3% of cache blocks resident at any moment meet the threshold. Since 3% of 1024 total cache blocks is 30.72, a 32-entry victim cache is a good match.

The relation of the dead-time threshold and the size of the victim cache not only gives us a good policy to statically select an appropriate threshold, but also points to adaptive filtering techniques. Although beyond the scope of this paper, adaptive filtering adjusts the dead time threshold at run-time so the number of candidate blocks remains approximately equal to the number of the entries in the victim cache. With a modest amount of additional hardware an adaptive filter would perform even better than static filter shown above, which already outperforms previous proposals.

5 Timekeeping Metrics for Dead-Block Prediction and Prefetch

In addition to identifying conflict misses, timekeeping metrics are also of much broader use. We show them here used as a guide in coordinating data prefetches. Managing data prefetch can be thought of in terms of three sub-problems:

- Identifying dead blocks in cache, into which we should prefetch the next block to be referenced.
- Identifying which next block should be prefetched
- Identifying *when* the prefetch must occur, in order for it to be timely.

Timekeeping metrics can form the basis of building efficient hardware prefetch mechanisms. Predicting prefetch targets can be orthogonal to the timeliness of the prefetch, but as we will show in this section it can also be integrated well with time predictions.

5.1 Dead Block Prediction

Dead block prediction is important for prefetch, because prefetches that arrive into the cache before the resident block is dead will induce extra cache misses. Live time, dead time and access interval statistics are closely related to the liveness of a block. In this section, we explore these correlations to construct predictors for dead blocks. First, we discuss a simple predictor which simply differentiates among large dead times and short access intervals. We then propose a dead block predictor that is based on the regularity of live times.

5.1.1 By Dead Time

One method of identifying dead blocks is by measuring time between accesses [9]. If we measure an inordinately large time since the last access, and we have yet to encounter the next access then chances are that we are within dead time.

Both access intervals and dead times refer to time between consecutive accesses to the same cache frame. The difference is that during the dead time the current block in the frame turns out to be dead. A dead block predictor can be constructed by dynamically distinguishing dead times from access intervals. From Figure 5, we observe that most access intervals are very short and clustered around zero. On the other hand, a number of dead times are quite large and thus clearly distinguishable from access intervals. Based on this observation, a dead block predictor could be constructed as follows: if the idle time of a block exceeds some threshold, we predict that it is in its dead time. Figure 14 shows the accuracy and coverage of this predictor with different threshold values. To get high accuracy, the threshold must be more than 5120 cycles. At this point the coverage (the percent of the blocks for which we do make a prediction) is only about 50%.

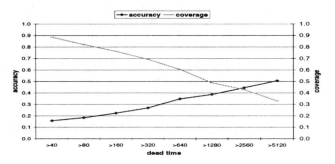

Figure 14: Dead block prediction based on dead time: Accuracy and coverage.

5.1.2 By Live Time

Dead block prediction based on dead time is very successful in reducing leakage energy in caches, because that application benefits from the many CPU cycles spent in the heavy tail of the dead time distribution. But for prefetching, dead-time prediction does not have enough coverage to be useful. Even more important, once one waits a long decay interval to make a decision about deadness, it could potentially be too late to do a timely prefetch. In this section, we will look at an alternate way of determining that a block is dead (and therefore ready for something to be prefetched on top of it.) If we can accurately predict how long a live time is, then we will know that prefetches arriving just after this live time ends should be timely. This paper is the first to show the degree to which live times can be predicted; we then use this to schedule timely prefetches.

As with other predictors, past history is our guide in predicting the next live time of a block. The simplest history-based predictor is to predict that the live time of a block will be the live time of its previous generation. To test this, we profiled variability of consecutive live times per block using counters with a resolution of 16 cycles. Figure 15 shows the profiling results for selected SPEC2000 programs (which have significant speedup potential and are discussed in detail

in section 5.2.3) and for the geometric mean for all SPEC2000 programs. A significant percentage (more than 20%) of the differences are less than 16 cycles.

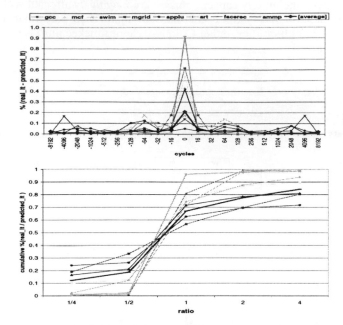

Figure 15: Distribution of absolute difference (Top) and cumulative distribution of relative ratio (Bottom) of consecutive live times.

Based on this regularity of the live times we can construct a predictor for dead blocks as follows: at the start of a block's generation we predict that its live time is going to be similar to its last live time. After its predicted live time is over, we wait a brief interval and then we predict the block to be dead. The question is: how long should we wait before predicting the block is dead? To account for some variability in the live time we could add a fixed number of cycles to the predicted live time. Because live times have a wide range in magnitude, however, we chose instead to scale the added time to the predicted live time. To choose an appropriate scaling factor, the second graph of Figure 15 shows the cumulative distribution of the ratio of the current live time divided by the previous live time. As we can see in this graph, on average, about 80% of the current live times are less than twice the previous live time.

Thus, a simple heuristic is to predict that a block is dead at a time twice its previous live time from the start of its current generation. Additional justification for this predictor comes from our observation in Section 2 that dead times are significantly larger than live times. Using this dead block predictor, Figure 16 shows the accuracy and coverage for the SPEC2000 programs. Coverage in this case refers to the percentage of blocks for which we do make a prediction. Blocks with a generation *shorter* than twice their predicted live time have already been evicted by the time of the prediction so they are not covered by our predictor. On average (for all SPEC2000), accuracy is around 75% and coverage about 70%, both better than those of the dead-time dead block predictor in the previous section. There is also a discernible trend for increased accuracy and coverage to the right of the graph towards the programs with significant percentage of capacity misses and significant potential for speedup.

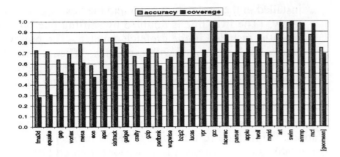

Figure 16: Accuracy and coverage of live time based dead block prediction

5.2 Timekeeping Prefetch

A full-fledged prefetching mechanism needs to establish both what to prefetch and when to prefetch it. Regarding what to prefetch, a history-based predictor can help to provide accurate address prediction, as discussed, for example, in [2], [7] and [10]. Regarding when to prefetch, a live-time dead-block prediction is an efficient mechanism to schedule prefetches but this also requires a predictor structure to predict live times.

In this section we show that the *same* structure that can predict addresses can also predict live-times (or vice-versa), unifying the two predictors into a single structure. We propose a compact, history-based, predictor for both addresses and live-times that outperforms previous proposals for most of the SPEC2000 benchmarks. Furthermore, it requires only a tiny fraction of the area compared to prior proposals: about two orders of magnitude smaller than [10].

5.2.1 Address and Live-Time Predictor

Our predictor is a correlation table not unlike the Dead Block Correlating Predictor (DBCP) table in [10]. In our case, the reference history used by our predictor is just the most recent miss address per frame, which is readily available in L1. In contrast, the DBCP approach also requires a PC trace which, in many cases, is complex to obtain from within the out-of-order core. We use miss address per cache frame, rather than the global miss trace of the cache. This means that a prediction that refers to a specific frame takes into account only the miss trace of this frame. The issue is complicated somewhat in set-associative caches where we use *per set* miss trace history but we still perform all timekeeping and accounting on a per frame basis. Per set miss trace history removes some of the conflict misses that are dispersed within the history of the capacity misses. This is an advantage for our prefetching mechanism since it caters mostly to capacity misses as we will show later in this section.

Each predictor entry stores both the prediction for the prefetch address and the predicted live time of the block to be replaced by the prefetch. We use a 1-miss history to get these predictions. For example, assume that block A occupies a cache frame. At the point when block B replaces A we access the predictor using the (per-frame) history (A,B). The predictor returns a prediction that block C should replace B *and* a prediction for the live time of B. Using the predicted live time of B, we apply our live-time-based dead-block prediction and we "declare" B to be dead at a time twice its predicted live time. At that point in time, we schedule the prefetch to C to

occur. (One could also estimate when C needs to arrive, and exploit any slack to save power or smooth out bus contention.)

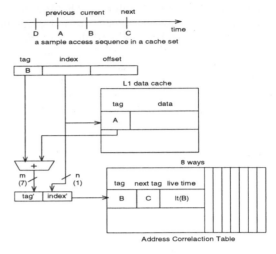

Figure 17: Structure of Timekeeping Address Correlation Table

5.2.2 Implementation Details

Figure 17 shows how we access the address correlation table and in particular the indexing mechanism we use. When block B replaces block A in a cache frame we add the *tags* of A and B (using truncated addition as per [10]). When combined with A and B's common index, the sum of the tags gives us a pointer to the correlation table. The pointer is constructed by taking m bits from the sum of the tags and n bits from the index. The correlation table is typically set-associative so the pointer selects a set in this table. We then select the correct entry in the set by matching the tag of the block B to the identification tag in the predictor entry. The selected predictor entry predicts the *tag* of the block to be prefetched. The index is implied and is the same as in A and B. The same entry also gives a prediction for the live time of B. This live-time prediction is at the crux of our ability to do timely prefetch.

We have tested several sizes of this table ranging from megabytes to just a few kilobytes. Even very small tables work surprisingly well. An interesting observation arises when we index this table using mainly tag information and only partial index information (n less than 10). In this case, histories from different cache frames (or sets) may map to the same entry. This results in *constructive* aliasing and allows our table to have much smaller size than the table in [10]. The intuition behind this constructive aliasing is that often multiple distinct data structures are traversed similarly. If accesses in one data structure imply accesses to another data structure, it does not matter what particular element is accessed in the one or the other. A contrived and simplistic example is to imagine a loop that adds elements of two arrays and stores them in a third array. Many triads of elements accessed can share a single entry in the correlation table as long as their tags remain the same! They all exhibit the same access pattern.

Within every cache line, we need the following timekeeping hardware for our prefetch: two counters, a register, and two extra tag fields, as shown in Figure 18. The two counters and the register are only 5 bits long each. The results we present in this paper are for an 8KB, 8-way set-associative correlation table. We index the table using seven bits from the sum of tags (*m*=7) and one bit from the cache index (*n*=1).

One counter (gt_counter) and one register (lt_register) are needed to track live time as follows. The gt_counter is initialized at the beginning of a generation and is continuously incremented by the global tick until the next miss. At this point the counter contains the generation time. At every intermediate hit the gt_counter is copied over to the lt_register so at any point in time the lt_register trails the gt_counter by one access. Thus, when a generation ends, the value of the lt_register is the time from the start of the generation to the last access, i.e., the live time. An additional counter (prefetch_counter) and a tag field (next_tag) are needed to schedule a prefetch while another tag (prev_tag) is needed for predictor update as discussed below.

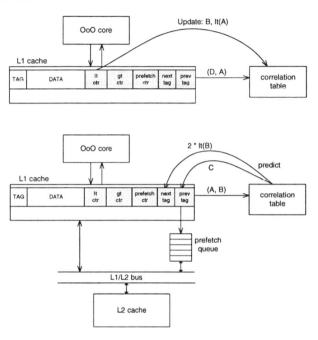

Figure 18: Update of a predictor entry (Top) and predictor access to make a prediction (Bottom)

Figure 18 shows the overall structure for timekeeping prefetch. The correlation table sits besides the L1 cache. Assume we have the following sequence of blocks in a cache frame: D,A,B,C, as shown in the top part of Figure 17. When a miss on address B attempts to replace block A, the lt_counter contains the live time of A, the prev_tag contains D, and the following actions occur:

1. A demand fetch is sent to the L2 for block B.

2. Predictor update (top diagram of Figure 18). An index is computed from A and its precursor D. The predictor table is accessed with history (D,A) and the entry corresponding to A is updated with B as the predicted next tag and lt(A) as the next prediction for the live time of A. Then A is installed in prev_tag.

3. Predictor access (bottom diagram of Figure 18). An index is computed from B and the currently evicted block A. The predictor is accessed with history (A,B) and an entry is selected that corresponds to B. Predictions for the live time of B and the next tag C are obtained and

installed in the prefetch_counter and the next_tag respectively. (The live time is doubled by shifting one bit before it is installed in the prefetch counter.) The prefetch counter is decremented with every tick. When it reaches zero the prefetch to C is put into an 128-entry prefetch queue (which is modeled as in other prefetching work).

5.2.3 Results

Figure 19 shows the IPC improvement over the base configuration. We include results for our 8KB timekeeping correlation table and we compare to the prior proposed DBCP table of 2MB size. Our timekeeping based prefetch achieves higher IPC improvement than DBCP in all SPEC2000 benchmarks except mcf and ammp. In addition, it improves performance for all but four of the SPEC2000 programs. Overall, our prefetch mechanism achieved 11% IPC improvement while DBCP only achieved about 7% improvement. Referring back to Figure 1, we see that our prefetching mechanism achieves significant speedups for many of the programs with a very large percentage of capacity misses (programs to the right of the graph in Figures 1 and 19) without harming those heavy on conflict misses (programs to the left of the graphs). The best performers are gcc, facerec, applu, mgrid, art, swim, ammp, and mcf. From the programs with the highest potential for speedup only two, twolf and parser, do not benefit from prefetch. These two programs exhibit very low accuracy in address prediction which results in a slight performance loss for twolf; the same programs are problematic even with a 2MB DBCP.

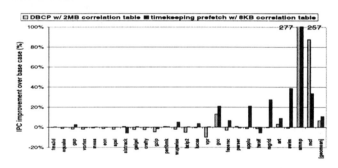

Figure 19: IPC improvement using timekeeping prefetch with an 8KB correlation table vs. DBCP prefetch with a 2MB correlation table

Considering only the eight best performers we see that, although the achieved speedups are significant, there is still room for improvement when compared to the ideal case. The differences are explained by close examination of the accuracy and coverage of our address prediction and the *timeliness* of our prefetches. Figure 20 shows the address accuracy and coverage for our 8KB address correlation table. Coverage in this case refers to the hit rate of the predictor; if we miss in the predictor we cannot make an address prediction. Figure 21 classifies the timeliness of the prefetches for the correct and wrong address predictions. Each bar (from bottom to top) shows prefetches that are:

- "early," arrived early and displaced the current *live* block
- "discarded," thrown out of the prefetch queue before been issued to the L2 to make space for new prefetches
- "timely," arrived within the dead time and before the next miss

- "started_but_not_timely," issued, but arrived late (after the next miss)

- "not_started," did not even issue before the next miss

From Figures 20 and 21 we can deduce the following. For two programs mgrid and facerec, while their address accuracy and coverage are fair, only 40% and 30% respectively of their correct prefetches are timely, while most of their other prefetches are late. This is because these two programs have short generation times and it is difficult to pinpoint their dead times. Two programs, art and to a lesser extent gcc, have a lot of discarded prefetches because of burstiness. This was also observed in DBCP prefetching. In addition art suffers from low address accuracy. The reason why mcf does not achieve its full potential is because of its low address accuracy. This program benefits from very large address correlation tables and this is the reason why it is doing well with a 2MB DBCP. We observed better performance for mcf with our timekeeping prefetch when we used a larger address correlation table of 2MB. Finally, ammp which speeds up by 257% — almost all of its potential — shows very good address accuracy and coverage and in addition shows very timely prefetches. As a general observation, the timeliness of our prefetches, especially with respect to earliness, correlates well with the accuracy of the address prediction: when we predict addresses well, we tend not to displace live blocks (Figure 21).

The results shown in this section are obtained using SPEC2000 binaries compiled with *peak* compiler settings, which aggressively employ software prefetching. We observed similar results when ignoring all compiler inserted prefetches. The interaction between compiler prefetch and timekeeping prefetch is out of the scope of this paper, but makes an interesting topic for future work.

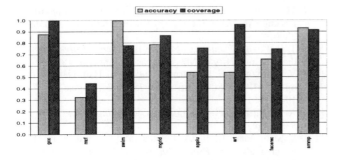

Figure 20: Address accuracy of the 8KB correlation table for the eight best performers

6 Conclusions

This paper demonstrates the predictive power of using time-based techniques to identify and optimize for various aspects of memory referencing behavior. We show that timing generational characteristics such as live times, dead times, access intervals, and reload intervals allows one to classify misses and deduce other characteristics of reference behavior with high accuracy. Only few, small counters per cache line are needed to obtain the time measurements we use for miss classification or prediction.

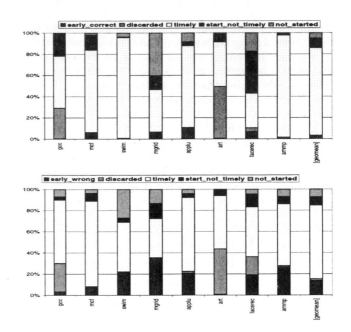

Figure 21: Timeliness of prefetches for correct (Top) and wrong (Bottom) address predictions

We first observe that our time-based metrics can be used to distinguish among conflict and capacity misses. Typically a block's generation is expected to exhibit a short live time followed by a long dead time, a characteristic exploited in cache decay. However, conflict misses are "catastrophic" to the typical generation of a block in that they cut its live time or dead time short. A generation resulting from a conflict exhibits either a zero live time or an inordinately short dead time. Furthermore, since the block is thrown out of the cache despite being alive, its reload interval (the access interval in the next lower level of the cache hierarchy) is also very short. These observations lead to three different run-time predictions of conflict misses. We explore the accuracy and the coverage of these predictions and we propose a mechanism to take advantage of such run-time prediction. Specifically, we propose filtering a victim cache so as to feed it only with blocks evicted as a result of a conflict. We demonstrate this filter using a dead time conflict predictor. Our victim cache filtering results in both IPC improvements and significant reduction in victim cache traffic. Our filter outperforms a previous proposal that predicts conflict misses remembering previous tags in the cache.

We then use our timekeeping techniques to tackle the problem of predicting when a block is dead and prefetch another block in anticipation of the next miss. With this technique we attempt to address the problem of capacity misses. Cache decay readily offers such a dead block prediction based on the time difference among access intervals and dead times. Unfortunately, the accuracy and coverage of decay, although fine for leakage control, are not ideally suited for prefetching. One of the contributions of this paper is the discovery that live times, when examined on a per cache-frame basis, exhibit regularity. Predicting the live time of the current block (based on its previous live times) allows us to schedule a prefetch to take place shortly after the block "dies." To implement a timekeeping prefetch we need both an address and a live time predictor. We propose a new history-based predictor that provides both predictions simultaneously. Our predictor is a correlation table accessed using the history of the previous and current miss in a frame. It predicts the live time of the current block, and the address to prefetch next. Because we index this predictor using mostly tag information we observe significant *constructive aliasing* both for addresses and live times. This allows us to outperform a 2MB DBCP predictor [10] using just 8KB of predictor state for all SPEC2000 with an average IPC improvement (over the base configuration) of 11%.

To summarize how our contributions affect the performance of the programs in the SPEC2000 suite we present an overview in the form of a Venn diagram in Figure 22. The diagram depicts three intersecting sets of programs:

1. programs with few memory stalls (negligible speedup is expected for these programs),

2. programs helped by timekeeping victim cache filter,

3. programs helped by timekeeping prefetch

Next to each program we indicate the IPC improvement (for programs in the intersections of the sets we indicate the maximum improvement). We note that, for the most part, our timekeeping victim cache filter helps with programs that suffer mostly from conflict misses while our timekeeping prefetch helps with programs suffering from capacity misses. Few programs benefit from both mechanisms. Overall, Figure 22 shows that our mechanisms are complementary in handling potential memory stalls.

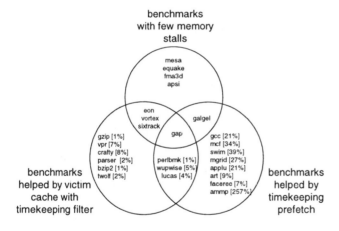

Figure 22: Effect of timekeeping victim cache and timekeeping prefetch on SPEC2000 benchmarks

Although our mechanisms cover many of the programs for which speedup can be expected, there is still some room for improvement. Timekeeping techniques can offer new perspective for predicting memory behavior and improving program memory performance. Using these techniques, we expect that researchers will be able to uncover other effective, hardware-efficient performance and power optimizations.

7   Acknowledgments

We would like to thank An-Chow Lai for insightful discussions and for providing us with detailed bus models for SimpleScalar. Our thanks to the anonymous referees for providing helpful comments as well. This work was supported in part by NSF ITR grant 0086031 and by donations from IBM and Intel.

References

[1] D. Burger and T. M. Austin. The SimpleScalar Tool Set, Version 2.0. *Computer Architecture News*, pages 13–25, June 1997.

[2] M. J. Charney and A. P. Reeves. Generalized correlation-based hardware prefetching. Technical Report EE-CEG-95-1, School of Electrical Engineering, Cornell University, 1995.

[3] J. Collins and D. Tullsen. Hardware identification of cache conflict misses. In *Proc. 32nd Intl. Symp. on Microarchitecture*, pages 126–135, 1999.

[4] M. Hill. *Aspects of Cache Memory and Instruction Buffer Performance*. PhD thesis, University of California at Berkeley, Nov. 1987.

[5] M. D. Hill and A. J. Smith. Evaluating associativity in CPU caches. *IEEE Transactions on Computers*, 38(12):1612–1630, 1989.

[6] M. G. Johnson Kin and W. H. Mangione-Smith. The filter cache: An energy efficient memory structure. In *Proc. Micro-30*, Nov. 1997.

[7] D. Joseph and D. Grunwald. Prefetching using markov predictors. In *24th Annual International Symposium on Computer Architecture*, June 1997.

[8] N. Jouppi. Improving Direct-Mapped Cache Performance by the Addition of a Small Fully-Associative Cache and Prefetch Buffers. In *Proc. ISCA-17*, May 1990.

[9] S. Kaxiras, Z. Hu, and M. Martonosi. Cache Decay: Exploiting Generational Behavior to Reduce Cache Leakage Power. In *Proc. 28th Annual Intl. Symp. on Computer Architecture*, 2001.

[10] A.-C. Lai, C. Fide, and B. Falsafi. Dead-Block Prediction and Dead-Block Correlating Prefetchers. In *Proc. 28th Annual Intl. Symp. on Computer Architecture*, 2001.

[11] A. Mendelson, D. Thiébaut, and D. K. Pradhan. Modeling live and dead lines in cache memory systems. *IEEE Transactions on Computers*, 42(1):1–16, Jan. 1993.

[12] T. C. Mowry, M. S. Lam, and A. Gupta. Design and evaluation of a compiler algorithm for prefetching. In *Proc. ASPLOS-V*, pages 62–73, Oct. 1992.

[13] M. D. Powell et al. Gated-Vdd: A Circuit Technique to Reduce Leakage in Deep-Submicron Cache Memories. In *ISLPED*, 2000.

[14] T. R. Puzak. *Analysis of cache replacement algorithms*. PhD thesis, University of Massachusetts, Amherst, 1985.

[15] V. Santhanam, E. H. Gornish, and W.-C. Hsu. Data prefetching on the HP PA-8000. In *Proc. ISCA-24*, pages 264–73, June 1997.

[16] A. J. Smith. Cache memories. *Computing Surveys*, 14(3):473–530, Sept. 1982.

[17] S. Srinivasan, R. Ju, A. Lebeck, and C. Wilkerson. Locality vs. criticality. In *Proc. 28th Annual Intl. Symp. on Computer Architecture*, 2001.

[18] S. T. Srinivasan and A. R. Lebeck. Load latency tolerance in dynamically scheduled processors. In *International Symposium on Microarchitecture*, pages 148–159, 1998.

[19] C. Su and A. Despain. Cache Designs for Energy Efficiency. In *Proceedings of the 28th Hawaii Int'l Conference on System Science*, 1995.

[20] E. S. Tam, J. A. Rivers, V. Srinivasan, G. S. Tyson, and E. D. Davidson. Active management of data caches by exploiting reuse information. *IEEE Transactions on Computers*, 48(11):1244–1259, 1999.

[21] The Standard Performance Evaluation Corporation. WWW Site. http://www.spec.org, Dec. 2000.

[22] D. A. Wood, M. D. Hill, and R. E. Kessler. A Model for Estimating Trace-Sample Miss Ratios. In *ACM SIGMETRICS*, pages 79–89, June 1991.

[23] H. Zhou, M. Toburen, E. Rotenberg, and T. Conte. Adaptive mode control: A static-power-efficient cache design. Sept. 2001.

Implementing Optimizations at Decode Time

Ilhyun Kim and Mikko H. Lipasti

Dept. of Electrical and Computer Engineering
University of Wisconsin–Madison
ikim@cae.wisc.edu, mikko@ece.wisc.edu

Abstract

The number of pipeline stages separating dynamic instruction scheduling from instruction execution has increased considerably in recent out-of-order microprocessor implementations, forcing the scheduler to allocate functional units and other execution resources several cycles before they are actually used. Unfortunately, several proposed microarchitectural optimizations become less desirable or even impossible in such an environment, since they require instantaneous or near-instantaneous changes in execution behavior and resource usage in response to dynamic events that occur during instruction execution. Since they are detected several cycles after scheduling decisions have already been made, such dynamic responses are infeasible. To overcome this limitation, we propose to implement optimizations by performing what we call speculative decode. *Speculative decode alters the mapping between user-visible instructions and the implemented core instructions based on observed runtime characteristics and generates speculative instruction sequences. In these sequences, optimizations are pre-scheduled in a manner compatible with realistic pipelines with multicycle scheduling latency. We present case studies on memory reference combining and silent store squashing, and demonstrate that speculative decode performs comparably or even better than impractical in-core implementations that require zero-cycle scheduling latency.*

1. Introduction

Program compilation and optimization consists of a sequence of semantic bindings that bridge the gap between high-level programming languages and the hardware primitives used to implement their semantics. These bindings can occur early, as in a static compiler (Figure 1a) that creates an optimized binary by exploiting high-level program knowledge and global analysis to remove redundant code, perform common subexpression elimination, assign variables to registers, and so on. Semantic binding can also occur later in the program's life-cycle, during program load time with a just-in-time (JIT) compiler (Figure 1b), or even as a set of peephole optimizations performed at near run-time on the program code residing in a processor's trace cache (Figure 1c) [2]. Finally, optimizing transformations that affect or determine which hardware primitives are employed to realize program semantics can even be applied within the processor's execution pipeline (Figure 1e). The degree and accuracy of dynamic information that is available to guide such optimization increases as the process of semantic binding is delayed until right before the hardware primitives are executed. It is these types of late run-time optimizations that interest us; ones that both require dynamic knowledge of program execution characteristics in order for them to be fruitful, and are difficult to implement earlier in the program's lifetime.

In this paper, we argue that technology and implementation trends make it impractical to delay the semantic bindings that implement such run-time optimizations any further than a processor's decode stage. In classic out-of-order processors based on Tomasulo's algorithm [21], dynamic events observed during instruction execution could be used as inputs into the scheduling process to affect scheduling decisions for the very next cycle. As shown in Figure 2, modern out-of-order processors like the Alpha 21264 [14] and Intel Pentium4 [16] implement deep execution pipelines that separate dynamic instruction scheduling from instruction execution by several stages. Unfortunately, the *scheduling latency* induced by these additional pipeline stages in modern designs prevents such instantaneous feedback, since the execution schedules have to be created several cycles in advance. As a result, such pipelines cannot feasibly implement run-time optimizations that derive benefit from the processor's ability to immediately react to observed events and reassign execution resources for the very next execution cycle.

Given these implementation trends, run-time optimization inside the dynamic execution window is no longer practical; in our view, the most feasible time for implementing run-time optimizations is in the decode stage (Figure 1d). In this paper, we propose implementing dynamic optimizations at decode time without perturbing the dynamic scheduling logic by performing what we call *speculative decode* (SD). SD alters the mapping between user-visible and implemented-core instructions based on observed runtime characteristics, and generates an instruction stream that directly expresses the run-time optimization.

SD exploits the translation layer that often exists to bridge the gap between the user-visible architected instruction set (*U-ISA*) and a realizable implementation instruction set (*I-ISA*). A number of working examples that perform translations between U-ISA and I-ISA exist, ranging from trap-based translators where unimplemented instructions are emulated in the operating system's invalid instruction exception handler (e.g. MicroVAX, PowerPC 604); to microcoded emulation routines stored in an on-

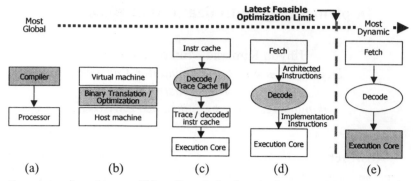

Figure 1. Optimizations in various layers. Although optimizations in the execution core may benefit from the most dynamic information, it becomes impractical with the introduction of speculative scheduling

chip lookup table (e.g. Intel Pentium Pro and it's derivatives and IBM Power4); to software-based binary translation approaches (e.g. Crusoe's Code Morpher).

This paper proposes and evaluates SD as a feasible mechanism for implementing late, run-time optimizations. Section 2 describes the difficulties in implementing in-core optimizations in a realistic processor pipeline, and introduces SD to overcome those difficulties. In Section 4, we present two case studies that address inefficiencies in the handling of memory instructions by performing speculative transformations. Section 5 provides a detailed performance evaluation of these case studies and shows that SD can reap many of the benefits and at times exceed the performance of impractical pure hardware implementations for a set of SPEC95 and SPEC2000 integer benchmarks.

2. Speculative decode

2.1. Speculative scheduling overview

Out-of-order processors are based on Tomasulo's algorithm [21], in which instructions that finish execution wake up their dependent instructions and the scheduling logic selects issue candidates from the pool of ready instructions. As shown in Figure 2a, this atomic wakeup/select process occurs in parallel with instruction execution. In recent designs, the number of pipeline stages between instruction issue and execution has increased to accommodate the latency needed for reading the register file and performing other book-keeping duties. As instruction issue and execution stages are further separated, a naive implementation would fail to achieve maximum ILP because back-to-back execution of dependent instructions is no longer possible. To address this problem, current-generation processor implementations [14][16] use *speculative scheduling* in which the scheduler speculatively wakes up and selects dependent instructions assuming the parent instruction has a fixed execution latency, as illustrated in Figure 2b. Since load latency is not deterministic, dependent instructions are scheduled assuming the common case cache hit latency for the parent load. If the load latency is mispredicted due to e.g. cache misses, load-dependent instructions that have issued within the *load shadow* [13] will get incorrect val-

ues, so they must be *replayed* [16] with correct inputs. Of course, structural hazards (e.g. cache ports and functional units) are also resolved speculatively, based on fixed latency and common-case resource needs. Once an instruction leaves the scheduler, all operations needed for its execution are performed in a lock-step fashion that prevents dynamic changes in instruction behavior and resource allocation.

2.2. Problems with in-core optimizations and speculative scheduling

Run-time optimizations are performed in the execution core based on observed dynamic behavior. Instructions that are control, data, or resource-dependent on the optimization target benefit since they are able to execute sooner. However, if the optimizations require run-time knowledge that is not available until the optimization target is in the execution window, it will be too late to benefit these dependent instructions. For example, consider an optimization like memory reference combining [9] that avoids using a cache port, thus making it available to a subsequent instruction. If the scheduler is unaware that the memory reference is going to be combined when it is constructing the execution schedule for the pipeline, it cannot reassign the cache port to another instruction. Hence, avoiding use of the port provides no direct performance benefit. Figure 3a illustrates such a scenario, in which none of the instructions issued in the cycles following the optimization target are able to benefit from the optimization since they have already been scheduled to behave as if the optimization had not been performed.

In general, in-core implementations of microarchitectural optimizations become undesirable or even impossible in a processor that implements speculative scheduling if they depend on any of following attributes:

- *Instant re-execution*: Any technique that assumes instant re-execution of dependent instructions becomes considerably less efficient. One example that assumes instant re-execution is the next-cycle selective reissue mechanism used in value prediction and other speculative techniques.

- *Variable execution latency*: If a technique implies vari-

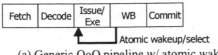

(a) Generic OoO pipeline w/ atomic wakeup / select

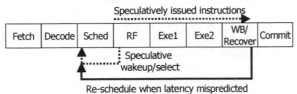

(b) 8-stage OoO pipeline w/ speculative scheduling

Figure 2. Speculative Scheduling.

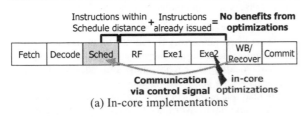

(a) In-core implementations

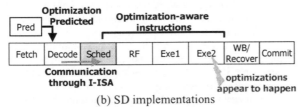

(b) SD implementations

Figure 3. Different approaches to optimizations.

able instruction latency, dependent instructions--which must be scheduled with fixed latency--cannot benefit. If the latency assumed is longer than the actual latency, there is no benefit from the reduced latency; if the actual latency is longer, recovery is required (similar to handling a load miss). One example of variable execution latency is a sequential-associative cache [15].

- *Instant resource allocation/deallocation*: It is impractical to dynamically re-allocate processor resources once they are scheduled. For instance, store/load forwarding or memory cloaking [17] does not reduce load port contention unless it is detected and scheduled beforehand because another load cannot fill the deallocated slot.

2.3. Enabling in-core optimizations via speculative decode

We propose using speculative transformations at decode-time to overcome the challenges of implementing run-time in-core optimizations in processors with realistic scheduling latency. The key idea for enabling such optimizations is to communicate them directly to the processor core via a different sequence of instructions that express the run-time optimization explicitly, as shown in Figure 3b. Of course, the dynamic events that guide such optimizations must be predicted, since the decision to optimize must be made before the instructions leave the scheduler.

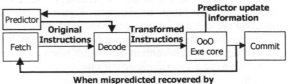

When mispredicted recovered by branch/exception handler (Squashing & Re-fetching)

Figure 4. SD integrated into a pipeline.

Figure 4 illustrates the basic concept of SD. The predictor is trained by signals from the core that record dynamic events pertinent to the optimization at hand. If an optimization condition is predicted based on observed runtime characteristics, the decode logic transforms the architected instruction into one or more implementation instructions that express the optimization explicitly. Misprediction is detected by verification code inserted into the transformed sequence and the correct architected state is recovered by draining the pipeline, fetching the original instructions, and executing them without any speculative transformations.

Increasing the complexity of the decode logic to support such translation may seem difficult to justify. However, since translation between U-ISA and I-ISA already occurs in many processors, we believe that the current and future generation decoders will be able to incorporate SD without significantly affecting processor cycle time. For example, in an experimental S/390 processor [12] that applies a table look-up approach for instruction translation, some instructions have more than one look-up entry mapped to different sequences depending on architectural states. Moreover, existing decoders such as those for IA-32 [16] and Power4 [18] already perform one-to-multiple instruction transformations similar to the transformations proposed here. However, if a processor does not have pre-existing translation stages, SD becomes less attractive since the added complexity in the decode stage may negatively affect overall performance by either increasing cycle time or requiring additional pipeline stages. We study sensitivity to pipeline depth in Section 5.4.

In summary, the potential benefits of SD are 1) it pre-schedules optimizations in a manner compatible with realistic pipelines with multicycle scheduling latency. It does not negatively affect instruction scheduling since the optimization is transparent to the scheduler. 2) It reuses existing data path and resources in the processor core if an optimization is implemented using existing I-ISA instructions. This helps to reduce the cost of processor core redesign for new optimizations. 3) It reduces resource and queue contention better than an in-core implementation since SD affects all stages from schedule to commit.

3. Simulation Environment

3.1. Base machine model

Our execution driven simulator is based on *SimpleScalar* [6]. We model a detailed 8-stage out-of-order processor with speculative scheduling, as shown in Figure 2b. The base machine configurations are shown in Table 1. For the translation layer in which SD is performed, we assume decode-time translation as shown in Figure 1d. We also modeled the degraded processing bandwidth due to SD by assuming that speculatively decoded instructions consume decode/dispatch/issue/commit bandwidth when an instruction is decoded into multiple operations.

3.2. Benchmark programs

We used eight benchmark programs from SPECINT95 and five from SPECINT2000 as presented in Table 2. All binaries are compiled by the gcc-pisa compiler with maximum optimizations (-O3).

4. Implementing Optimizations via SD

In this section, we discuss two possible optimizations via SD: memory reference combining [9] and silent store squashing [5]. Earlier proposals have described pure hardware implementations for these techniques. We describe how these techniques are implemented via SD, and also compare them with aggressive, even unrealistic, in-core implementations.

Table 1: Machine configuration.

Out-of-order Execution	8-stage, 4-wide fetch/issue/commit, 64-entry RUU, 32-entry load / 16-entry store schedulers, speculative scheduling, replays load-dependent instructions when load misses, fetch stops at first taken branch in a cycle
Branch Prediction	Combined bimodal (4k entries) / gshare (4k entries) with a selector (4k entries), 16 RAS, 1k-entry 4-way BTB, at least 8 cycles taken for misprediction recovery
Memory System (latency)	64KB 2-way 32B line IL1 (2), 64KB 4-way 16B line DL1 (2), 512KB 4-way 64B line unified L2 (8), main memory (50), 2 store buffers outside the OoO core
Functional Units (latency)	4 integer ALUs (1), 2 floating ALUs (2), 2 integer MULT/DIV (3/20), 2 floating MULT/DIV (4/12), 2 load ports, 1 store port, load/store ports are mutually exclusive

Table 2: Benchmark programs tested.

Benchmarks	Input sets	Instruction count
compress	compress.in	35.7M
gcc	genoutput.i	58.3M
go	go.in	85.6M
ijpeg	tinyrose.ppm	74.8M
li	queen6.lsp	41.7M
m88ksim	m88ksim.in	100M
perl	trainscrabbl.in	40.5M
vortex	vortex.in	65.1M
bzip	input.random	4.5B
gzip	input.compressed	1.3B
mcf	mdred.in	601M
parser	parsertest.in	3.1B
vpr	net.in, arch.in	1.5B

4.1. Memory reference combining

SD memory reference combining converts multiple narrow references into a single wider reference, resulting in a net reduction of accesses to the data cache. This technique is enabled by the presence of wide data paths in support of instruction set extensions that have now been added to many general-purpose instruction sets, as either a 64-bit execution mode or 128-bit media processing instructions. Despite these 64/128-bit extensions, it is expected that the vast majority of user-mode and even kernel code will continue to execute in 32-bit mode. SD memory reference combining enables existing binaries to benefit from wider memory datapaths without recompiling them. Furthermore, such an approach could logically be extended for wider reference combining up to the full cache line provided that wider data paths become available.

4.1.1. In-core implementations

There are numerous proposals to utilize a wide data path and achieve higher memory bandwidth by exploiting spatial locality in cache lines and satisfying multiple requests with a single cache access. Figure 5 shows a possible load queue modification that combines multiple loads to the same doubleword, similar to [9]. In this configuration, each load queue entry has a buffer to hold 64-bit data from memory until the entry is committed. When a load value is available from a previous entry, the value is forwarded from the buffer. 128-bit load combining can be implemented by widening the datapath from cache and increasing the buffer size. Store combining cannot be implemented this way since it could commit stores out of order. Instead, we perform store combining by allowing write merging in the store buffer [19].

Although this scheme appears to be effective in reducing cache port contention and improving load latency, there are real problems in implementing hardware load reference combining in a pipeline with multicycle scheduling latency. To obtain benefit in such a pipeline, the piggybacked (i.e. combinable) loads must be identified at schedule time so they can avoid allocating a cache port and hence their dependent instructions can be scheduled for reduced latency. However, since effective addresses are not available at schedule time, combinability cannot be determined, and all loads must allocate a cache port and schedule dependent instructions assuming the longer cache hit latency. As a result, reference combining that avoids using

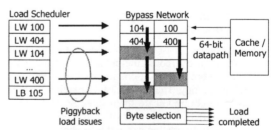

Figure 5. A possible in-core implementation for load combining.

Load Combining

```
lw      r1, 0(r10)
lw      r2, 4(r10)
lw      r3, 8(r10)
lw      r4,12(r10)
```

When r10 is predicted as doubleword-aligned:

load 64 bits from the memory	`dlw     r1, 0(r10)`
extract a higher word into r2	`exthi   r2, r1`
load 64 bits from the memory	`dlw     r3, 8(r10)`
extract a higher word into r4	`exthi   r4, r3`

- -

Store Combining

```
sw      r1, 0(r10)
sw      r2, 4(r10)
sw      r3, 8(r10)
sw      r4,12(r10)
```

When r10 is predicted as word-aligned only:

	`sw      r1, 0(r10)`
merge into one 64-bit register	`sethi   r2, r3`
store 64 bits to memory	`dsw     r2, 4(r10)`
	`sw      r4, 12(r10)`

Figure 6. Examples of double-word SD memory reference combining.

the allocated cache port provides no performance benefit, and its benefit is reduced strictly to reducing power consumption by eliminating accesses to the data cache.

4.1.2. Memory Reference Combining via SD

In memory reference combining via SD, loads and stores that access consecutive memory locations are explicitly merged into one wider memory instruction. The advantage of explicit conversion is 1) it reduces load/store scheduler contention since it dispatches fewer memory instructions, and 2) it moves combining decisions from the critical path outside the out-of-order execution window. For simplicity of presentation, we only describe double-word (64-bit) combining; quad-word (128-bit) combining is implemented in an analogous manner. Performance results for both are presented in Section 5.2.

Reference Combining Mechanism. Figure 6 shows examples of double-word combining. For load combining, two loads that access consecutive memory locations are merged into one double-word load operation. An extract instruction (`exthi`) is inserted after a double-word load (`dlw`) to put the higher word into the target register. The decoded sequence can vary depending on ISAs. For example, as long as the higher 32 bits loaded in the register are ignored when a 64-bit implementation of PowerPC architecture is running in 32-bit mode, the sequence shown in Figure 6 works as illustrated. In the MIPS architecture, a double-word load instruction puts a 64-bit value into two logically adjacent registers so the decoder logic could manipulate the rename table to put values into arbitrary target registers without any ALU operations to extract the high word value. In our simulations, we assume that one load and one ALU operation are needed. Store combining can be accomplished in an analogous manner. One ALU operation (`sethi` in the example) to merge two 32-bit values into a 64-bit register and one double-word store operation are needed for store combining. Wider reference combining may either utilize datapaths and storage that exist for media processing instructions (e.g. PowerPC

Table 3: History bit patterns and their corresponding predictions in double-word combining.

History bit pattern (rightmost is newest 1:aligned 0:unaligned)	Prediction	Description
1 1 1 1	Combine	Effective address is very likely to be doubleword-aligned
1 0 1 0	Combine	Base register value is changing by word-aligned amounts
Other patterns	Do not Combine	Cannot predict the alignment or unlikely to be doubleword-aligned

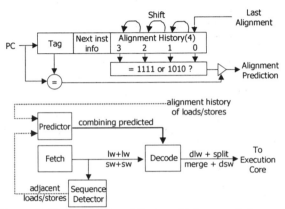

Figure 7. The structure of the combining predictor and the pipeline front-end.

Altivec extensions [20]) or, as in the case of hardware combining, require modifications to the load/store queue to hold wider values.

Detection / Prediction. Detecting combinable instructions that are not located near to each other in the dynamic instruction stream can be challenging. Furthermore, maintaining precise exceptions for store combining can be difficult in cases where an instruction between two combinable stores throws an exception. To simplify these issues, our mechanism is restricted to combining load sequences interrupted only by ALU instructions or uninterrupted store sequences. Finally, many architectures require naturally aligned memory accesses, and misaligned references can cause exceptions or soft traps. However, it is hard to statically decide whether the combined reference will be naturally aligned at decode time. We propose a structure called the *Combining Predictor* to predict the alignment of the combined references and direct the decoder to perform transformations. Its structure and the pipeline are illustrated in Figure 7. The sequence detector monitors the dynamic instruction stream and detects combinable references by examining offset fields that differ by 4 with the same base register and also ensuring the second load's base register is not overwritten by the first instruction. Although sub-word references (e.g. load-halfword and load-byte) could be combined into wider references, we did not consider such cases since they happen infrequently. The sequence detector can be easily implemented by using a

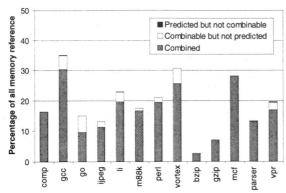

Figure 8. Percentage of combined memory instructions captured by a 1024-entry predictor.

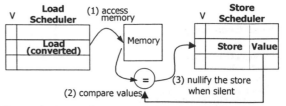

Figure 9. A possible in-core implementation for silent store squashing.

few narrow adders and gates to examine offset fields and base registers, as presented in [10]. Because the sequence detector only adds a new entry to the combining predictor and it is located outside the decode path, the processor's critical path will not be affected by the latency for detections. When a combinable group is identified, a new predictor entry is allocated in the predictor.

A predictor entry records the last 4 alignment outcomes under the assumption that two instructions are combined. After several instances, references are combined based on bit patterns stored in the history fields if the pattern indicates that the next reference is likely to be double-word aligned. Table 3 summarizes the bit patterns and corresponding predictions.

Misprediction Recovery. When a combined reference tries an unaligned access to memory due to a misprediction, it is detected by the existing exception handling mechanism. The pipeline is drained and the original instruction are fetched again, and instructions are decoded without any combining transformations after the recovery.

In Figure 8, we show the coverage and accuracy of a double-word combining predictor with 1k direct-mapped entries. The percentages of combined instructions range from 2.67% of all memory references in *bzip* to a maximum of 30.4% in *gcc*. Our predictor captures roughly 80% of combinable references in all cases except for *go*, in which only 64% are captured. On the other hand, the misprediction rate due to misaligned memory accesses is extremely low (0.1% of all memory references in most benchmarks). Performance improvements from double and quad-word memory reference combining are discussed in Section 5.2, compared with optimistic hardware schemes [9][19] discussed in the previous section.

4.2. Silent store squashing

A silent store is an instruction which writes a value that exactly matches the value already stored at the memory location that is being written [3][5][7]. Because silent stores do not change the machine state, eliminating them is safe and has several advantages: reducing the pressure on cache write ports, reducing the pressure on store queues or other microarchitectural structures used to track pending

writes, reducing the need for store forwarding to dependent loads, and reducing both address and data bus traffic to lower levels in the memory hierarchy [3][5].

4.2.1. In-core implementations

The initial approach for eliminating silent stores as originally proposed in [5] requires converting each store into three implicit operations; a load, a comparison, and a conditional store that is initiated when the memory value and the new value to be written do not match (illustrated in Figure 9). As pointed out in [4], this simple approach has drawbacks when it is applied to every single store; it can place additional pressure on cache ports and other execution resources since unnecessary load and compare operations are performed even for non-silent stores. The next section introduces silence prediction, which can be used to reduce the frequency of silent store verifies.

An additional complication for store verification arises from the fact that many processors [16][18] have separate scheduling queues for loads and stores. Separate load/store schedulers imply that a store instruction must occupy both queues: the load queue for the store verify, and the store queue for the conditional store. Naturally, this will increase contention. Furthermore, multicycle scheduling latency for store ports may negate much of the benefit of squashing silent stores, since a successful store verify must complete releasing and reallocating the port before the store issue.

Additional techniques for reducing the cost of store verifies are discussed in [4]; we do not consider them here since they entail significant changes to the processor's load/store queues and/or data cache hierarchy. Our approach is able to achieve comparable performance benefits.

4.2.2. Silent Store Squashing via SD

SD silent store squashing is implemented by removing the store from the decoded instruction stream. Instead, a store is decoded into a load and a compare that verify its silence to guarantee correctness. Since verify operations are explicitly injected into the processor core, implicit load verifies and conditional stores do not adversely affect the scheduling logic. However, transforming all stores incurs recovery overhead when they are not silent; therefore, we need a prediction mechanism that filters out many of the non-silent stores.

Silence Prediction. Training a silence predictor is difficult because silence outcomes become available only when store verifies are being performed. Once the predictor state machine reaches a terminal state and hence the predictor

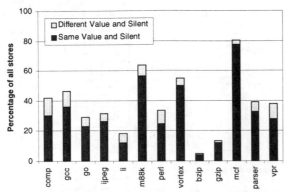

Figure 10. Percentage of silent stores categorized by the last store value.

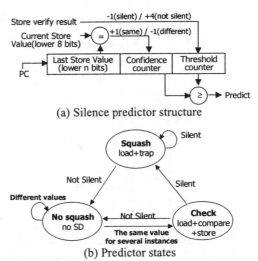

(a) Silence predictor structure

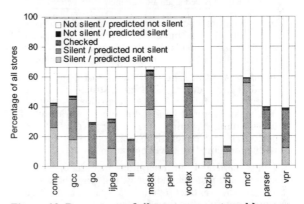

(b) Predictor states

Figure 11. The structure of a silence predictor and its state diagram.

determines that a store is not silent, no outcome history would be available to transition out of that state. Instead, our predictor mechanism exploits a silent store characteristic that was reported in [3]: static stores that consecutively write the same value are more likely to be silent than if they were storing different values. Figure 10 shows the likelihood of a store being silent as a function of whether a static store writes the same value as the last store value, regardless of effective memory addresses. We see that in most benchmarks over 70% of all silent stores can be captured by correlating with the last store value.

Our silence predictor is a PC-indexed direct-mapped table where each predictor entry has two saturating counters and a value history field as shown in Figure 11a. The value history field contains only lower 8 bits of the last store value since initial experiments determined that this was sufficient for providing reasonable prediction accuracy and significantly reduces the size of the predictor. Depending on whether the same value as the history is written, the confidence counter is increased or decreased. However, a store may not be silent even when the same value is stored repeatedly since the stores can be to a different address or intervening stores to the same location can alter the stored value. To reduce mispredictions due to such aliasing, our predictor mechanism has a dynamic threshold counter that changes according to the silence outcome history. We show the state diagram of the silence predictor in Figure 11b.

Silence Squashing Mechanism and Misprediction Recovery. After the same value is observed repeatedly by the predictor and the confidence reaches the threshold, the store is decoded into a store plus a load and a compare to check silence. If the store is silent, its threshold counter is decreased; otherwise the threshold is increased by a fixed penalty and the confidence counter is cleared, which makes it harder for the store to transition out of the 'No squash' state. When a store is predicted to be silent, only a load and a conditional trap are generated until a store verify fails. Figure 13 shows an example of SD silent store squashing. If a silence misprediction in 'Squash' state is detected by a trap operation, the mispredicted store is fetched and issued again without transformations after draining the pipeline.

In Figure 12, we show the performance of the silence

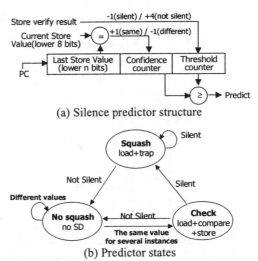

Figure 12. Percentage of silent stores captured by a predictor with 1k entries and 6-bit threshold counters.

predictor used in our simulations, with the configurations of 1024 direct-mapped entries, 8-bit last value fields, and 6-bit confidence and threshold counters (1k X (8+6+6 bits) = 2.5 kB). It correctly predicts (silent / predicted silent) 45.5% of all silent stores on average, which accounts for 5~55% of all dynamic stores. Compared with same-value-silent stores shown in Figure 10, some benchmarks such as *go*, show relatively low prediction rates since many non-silent stores also repeatedly write the same value and hence decrease the efficiency of our predictor. The misprediction rates (not silent / predicted silent) range from 0.02% in *li* to 1.7% in *m88ksim*. Performance via SD and in-core implementations will be discussed later in Section 5.3.

5. Microarchitectural Evaluations

5.1. Performance effects incurred by SD

Speculative decode can affect program executions in the following ways:

- *Replacement effect*: Original instructions are translated

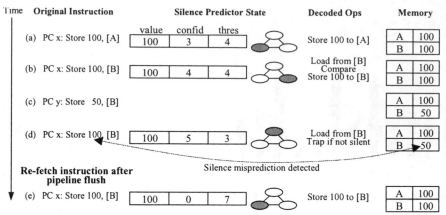

Figure 13. An example of silent store squashing via SD.

(a) The confidence counter is increased regardless of effective addresses if the store value matches the history in the predictor

(b) The confidence reaches the threshold and a load is issued to see if the store is silent. The threshold is decreased when it is silent.

(c) An intervening store changes the value of memory B.

(d) Only a load and a trap are issued when the confidence exceeds the threshold. The trap is triggered when values do not match.

(e) After the misprediction, the confidence counter is cleared and the threshold is increased by a penalty (4 in this example) and the store is fetched and issued again after draining the pipeline.

into semantics that interact differently with surrounding operations. For example, stores in silent store squashing are decoded as loads that do not create RAW or WAW memory dependences for subsequent instructions.

- *Bandwidth effect*: The total number of instructions executed changes due to SD. If an instruction expands into several operations, SD consumes more dispatch/issue/commit bandwidth, queue entries and functional units, which may negatively affect the performance. Conversely, SD may help to reduce bandwidth consumed by fewer operations.

- *Latency effect*: Extra operations in a depencence chain increase the instruction latency. E.g. piggyback loads get values after extract operations (exthi in Figure 6), which may increase their latency.

5.2. Evaluations of SD for memory reference combining

We evaluate SD double-word (SDC8) and quad-word (SDC16) combining, comparing with in-core implementations that perform double (HWC8) and quad-word (HWC16) combining together with store merging, similar to [9][19]. As discussed in Section 4.1.1, HWC is not easy to integrate into a pipeline with realistic scheduling latency. For purposes of comparison, we assume an optimistic oracle scheduler that identifies piggyback loads at schedule time before effective addresses are known.

Figure 14a shows normalized DL1 cache accesses reduced by HWC and SDC, with respect to the base machine. Since HWC is not restricted to adjacent instructions and combines across several references, it captures significantly more references and in turn reduces more cache accesses than SDC in all benchmarks (on average 19.3% (HWC8), 6.8% (SDC8), 27.5% (HWC16) and 10.4% (SDC16), respectively). Based on the cache accesses, one might expect that HWC would give much greater performance improvements than SDC. However,

the improvements come from different sources: fewer memory instructions reduce cache accesses in SDC while HW combining achieves the reduction by buffering them. SDC gets benefits from the positive *bandwidth* (fewer memory instructions) and *replacement* (fewer address generations) *effects* in load/store schedulers and ALUs. On the other hand, HWC still performs dispatch, issue and commit of all memory instructions and experiences the same amount of resource contention as in the base machine, except that the improved throughput helps to resolve some contention. Figure 14b shows that there is less load/store scheduler contention in SDC in all cases except for *bzip*, in which SDC achieves a very low rate of combining.

We show the speedups achieved by SDC and HWC in Figure 15. In general, SDC achieved comparable speedups although HWC captures many more memory references than SDC. In *gcc*, SDC shows even better improvements. In some benchmarks SDC8 shows better performance than SDC16 because quad-word alignments are harder to predict than double-word alignments and result in higher misprediction rates. It is interesting that the contention reduction in SDC does not always correlate to better performance improvements. Besides the differences in the numbers of combined references, this is mostly because SDC transfers the contention from the load/store schedulers to the RUU, whose contention becomes another bottleneck (RUU full rates of $0.14 \rightarrow 0.41$ and $0.24 \rightarrow 0.77$ in *vortex* and *mcf*, respectively). In *mcf*, frequent cache misses cause the RUU to be filled up, which prevents speculatively decoded extract instructions from being committed. Another reason SDC does not always improve performance is the *latency effect* of extract operations. When piggyback loads are on the program critical path, performance is degraded compared to the base case in which loads are issued in parallel. If SDC were applied selectively depending on memory port contention or criticality of load latency, we would expect greater speedups

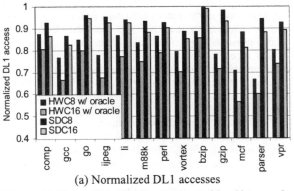

(a) Normalized DL1 accesses

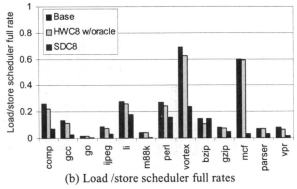

(b) Load /store scheduler full rates

Figure 14. Normalized DL1 accesses and load/store scheduler full rates in HW and SD memory reference combining.

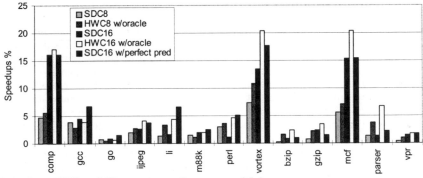

Figure 15. Speedups from HW and SD memory reference combining.

from it. The rightmost bars in Figure 15 are the potential SDC16 speedups from a perfect combining predictor and show that SDC with a perfect predictor outperforms HWC with the oracle scheduler in some benchmarks.

In summary, memory reference combining via SD provides comparable or even better performance than the impractical in-core implementation because SD pre-schedules this optimization and eliminates contention more effectively.

5.3. Evaluations of SD for silent store squashing

To evaluate SD for silent store squashing (SDSSS), it is compared with the predictor-based in-core silent store squashing (HWSSS), derived from [5]. A load verify is performed only on predicted stores in both cases. This HWSSS has several advantages over SDSSS. First, HWSSS does not need any recovery such as draining the pipeline in SD from mispredictions, since the store is conditional depending on the store verify. Second, it does not require the 'check' state of the silence predictor because the purpose of the state was to reduce the misprediction penalty. Third, the dedicated compare logic reduces contention in the ALUs. We discussed the details of HWSSS, and potential difficulties in Section 4.2.1. The silence predictor and SDSSS were described in Section 4.2.2.

Detecting silent stores may improve memory disambiguation, allowing later loads to bypass earlier stores with unresolved effective addresses [11]. Delaying the later

loads after unresolved silent stores to avoid memory dependence violations is unnecessary because silent stores do not change the values of the memory location. Improved memory disambiguation is achieved by the *replacement effect* of SDSSS since predicted silent stores are converted into loads that do not block subsequent memory accesses. On the other hand, HWSSS still dispatches silent stores and requires extra logic to obtain this benefit [11]. Figure 16 shows the average extra cycles needed for a load instruction to wait until earlier store addresses are resolved. We measure a 14% reduction in store-to-load block cycles in SDSSS compared to those of the base machine. It is expected that the potential performance improvements would be greater on register-starved ISAs such as Intel x86, on which the average performance improvement is reported as 4%, ranging from 0.2% to 14.7% according to the initial study by Yoaz et. al.[11].

Figure 17 reports the performance improvements from HWSSS and SDSSS when they use both a silence predictor previously discussed and a perfect silence predictor. Speedups are calculated based on the total execution time since SD changes the total number of committed instructions and IPC numbers are no longer comparable. Performance degrades in SDSSS marginally on half of the benchmarks where HWSSS also shows minor speedups or slowdowns. This is primarily because SDSSS suffers from silence mispredictions. Especially in *m88ksim* the performance is degraded noticeably due to a high misprediction

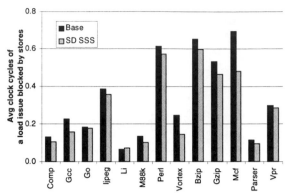

Figure 16. Improved memory disambiguation via SD silent store squashing.

rate. The negative *bandwidth effect* is another source of SDSSS slowdowns since extra silence verify operations in check and squash states consume ALU and cache port bandwidth.

On the other hand, significant performance improvements are observed in *compress, vortex* and *mcf* (up to 13.8%, 18.1% and 19.7%, respectively). The perfect predictor in *mcf* achieves lower speedup than our silence predictor due to a second-order LRU effect in the L2 cache: since silent store squashing avoids setting the dirty bit in the L1 cache, lines are evicted silently and do not update the L2 LRU, leading to additional L2 misses. In these benchmarks, SDSSS outperforms HWSSS with a perfect predictor because SDSSS benefits from improved memory disambiguation and HWSSS does not reduce contention in the store scheduler.

5.4. Performance sensitivity to pipeline depth

As discussed in Section 2.3, SD should be evaluated critically if the processor does not have a translation stage or SD requires extra decode latency. Figure 18 shows the performance sensitivity to the decode stage depth when both double-word memory reference combining (SDC8) and silent store squashing (SDSSS) are performed. In this graph, the execution time is normalized to the base machine with 1 decode stage. Although performance degrades in all cases as the decode stage pipeline gets

deeper, 8 benchmarks (*compress, gcc, ijpeg, vortex, bzip, gzip, mcf* and *parser*) still perform as well or better than the base machine with no extra stage even when SD requires 1 extra pipeline stage. All benchmarks except for *m88ksim* show speedups compared with each base case. To better understand the effect of pipeline depth on SD performance, we present detailed sensitivity results on three benchmarks that achieve significant speedups from our optimizations in both SD and HW.

In Figure 19a, we show performance sensitivity of base, HW and SD to the decode pipeline depth. The front-end pipeline depth affects overall performance by increasing the time spent on recovery from either branch or speculative optimization mispredictions (alignment and silence in our study). Although the penalty for a SD misprediction is significant and HW does not suffer from it, the relative performance degradation in SD is surprisingly slight, mainly because our SD predictors are highly accurate.

On the other hand, additional pipeline stages between schedule and writeback (EX pipeline) have greater impact on performance than additional front-end stages. Besides a longer misprediction penalty and more mis-scheduled instructions under load shadow [13], a longer EX pipeline increases contention in out-of-order execution queues due to increased occupancy. HW does not reduce or even increases contention while SD reduces queue occupancy in the memory schedulers and hence HW performance is noticeably more degraded than SD as the EX pipeline gets longer, as presented in Figure 19b. In summary, SD may provide benefits in an even longer pipeline where HW would fail to do so since SD is less sensitive than HW to this portion of the pipeline.

6. Related Work

Jacobson et. al. [1] and Friendly et. al. [8] suggested transforming instructions based on peephole optimizations during a trace cache construction to implement better instruction scheduling, constant propagation, instruction collapsing and etc. Chou and Shen [2] proposed the instruction path co-processor, which is a programmable internal processor that operates on instructions of the core processor to transform them into a more efficient stream, and showed the performance gain from similar optimiza-

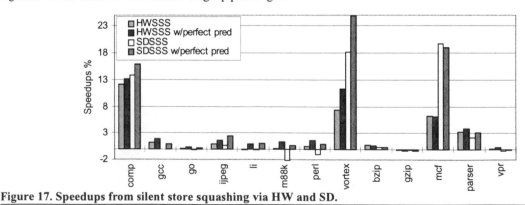

Figure 17. Speedups from silent store squashing via HW and SD.

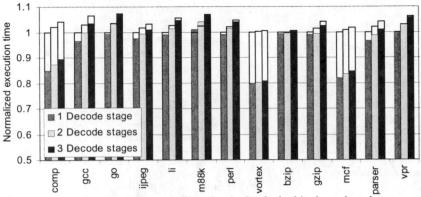

Figure 18. SD performance varying the decode pipeline depth. Stacked white bars show base execution time when no optimization is performed (slowdowns in *m88ksim* indicated as lines).

tions. Prior work has focused primarily on safe code optimizations in the presence of hardware mechanisms such as predication or trace cache. Rather, SD may be efficiently implemented through those transformation mechanisms. The most significant difference between our approach and these prior experiments is that we relax the *safety* constraint. That is, by employing speculative transformations that are not conservatively guaranteed to be safe with respect to program semantics, we expose greater opportunity for performance enhancement and simpler implementations in a manner compatible with speculative scheduling. Borch et. al. [13] studied the effect of critical architectural loops in speculative scheduling and proposed a hierarchical register file design to shorten the EX pipeline. On the other hand, SD reduces contentions in the EX pipeline by pre-scheduling optimizations and hence it is less sensitive to the longer EX pipeline than in-core implementations.

6.1. Memory reference combining

Wilson et. al. [9] proposed a comprehensive evaluation of several techniques that subsequent accesses to the same line are satisfied by a single memory access. This approach discusses on improving the effective memory bandwidth between the processor core and the data cache with a restricted number of cache ports. It assumes a generic out-of-order pipeline with atomic wakeup/select and does not consider the problems that may occur in speculative scheduling. Lopez et. al. suggested a hardware mechanism to compact two load/stores into a single wide reference with help of the compiler [10]. This work is conceptually similar to the approach via SD but the latency needed to detect references, memory alignment and merging and splitting values into/from a wider instruction were not discussed.

6.2. Silent store squashing

Molina et. al. [7] and Lepak and Lipasti [5] showed there is a significant amount of redundancies in store instructions. [7] proposed to put a simple comparator to reduce unnecessary cache accesses due to store instructions. The initial approach to eliminate silent stores in [5] is

converting all stores into store verify operations. [4] proposed several lower-cost store verify approaches: one is verifying stores using only idle load ports and the other is exploiting temporal and spatial locality in the load/store queue, issuing no extra load. Considering the scheduling distance and contentions in separate load/store schedulers, we demonstrated that SD is a better approach to implement this optimization. Yoaz et. al. [11] proposed the path information-based silence predictor. They also suggested other possible applications of detecting silent stores to exploit dead instructions and enhance memory disambiguation. Although their silence prediction shows very high coverage and accuracy, their work did not discuss the training cost incurred by verifying silence for every store.

7. Conclusions

We make five major contributions in this work. First, we describe the difficulties in implementing in-core optimizations in a realistic processor pipeline. Second, we introduce speculative decode as a feasible mechanism for implementing late, run-time optimizations. Third, we present two novel compact predictor designs: memory reference combining and silence predictors with very low implementation cost and high coverage and accuracy. Fourth, we demonstrate that memory reference combining and silent store squashing implemented via speculative decode can perform comparably or better than impractical in-core implementations. Fifth, we study the effect of pipeline depth on the overall performance and show that optimizations via speculative decode are less sensitive to a longer execution pipeline than in-core implementations.

8. Acknowledgements

This work was supported in part by the National Science Foundation with grants CCR-0073440, CCR-0083126, EIA-0103670 and CCR-0133437, and generous financial support and equipment donations from IBM and Intel. We would also like to thank the anonymous reviewers for their many helpful comments.

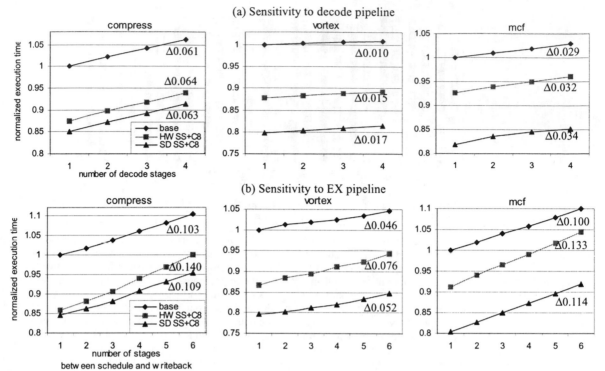

Figure 19. Performance sensitivity to the pipeline depth. The number denoted with Δ shows the normalized execution time difference on each case.

9. References

[1] Q. Jacobson and J. E. Smith, *Instruction Pre-Processing in Trace Processors*, in Proc. of 5th International Symposium on High Performance Computer Architecture, 1999.

[2] Y. Chou and J. P. Shen, *Instruction Path Coprocessors*, in Proc. of 27th International Symposium on Computer Architecture, June 2000.

[3] G. B. Bell, K. M. Lepak and M. H. Lipasti, *Characterization of Silent Stores*, in Proc. of International Conference on Parallel Architectures and Compilation Techniques, October 2000.

[4] K. M. Lepak and M. H. Lipasti, *Silent Stores for Free*, in Proc. of 33rd International Symposium on Microarchitecture, December 2000.

[5] K. M. Lepak and M. H. Lipasti, *On the Value Locality of Store Instructions*, in Proc. of 27th International Symposium on Computer Architecture, June 2000.

[6] D. C. Burger and T. M. Austin, *The Simplescalar Tool Set, Version 2.0*, Technical Report CS-TR-97-1342, University of Wisconsin, Madison, June 1997.

[7] C. Molina, A. Gonzalez and J. Tubella, *Reducing Memory Traffic Via Redundant Store Instructions*, in Proc. of Conference on High Performance Computing and Networking, 1999.

[8] D. Friendly, S. Patel and Y. Patt, *Putting the Fill Unit to Work: Dynamic Optimizations for Trace Cache Microprocessors*, in Proc. of 31st International Symposium on Microarchitecture, December 1998.

[9] K. M. Wilson, K. Olukotun and M. Rosenblum, *Increasing Cache Port Efficiency for Dynamic Superscalar Microprocessors*, in Proc. of 29th international symposium on Microarchitecture, 1996.

[10] D. Lopez, M. Valero, J. Llosa and E. Ayguade, *Increasing Memory Bandwidth with Wide Buses: Compiler, Hardware and Performance trade-offs*, in Proc. of International Conference on Supercomputing, 1997.

[11] A. Yoaz, R. Ronen, R. S. Chappell and Y. Almog, *Silence is Golden?*, in work-in-progress workshop of 7th High-Performance Computer Architecture, January 2001.

[12] R. Hilgendorp and W. Sauer, *Instruction Translation for an Experimental S/390 Processor*, in Workshop on Binary Translation in Parallel Architectures and Compilation Techniques, October 2000.

[13] E. Borch, E. Tune, S. Manne and J. Emer, *Loose Loops Sink Chips*, in Proc. of 8th International Symposium on High Performance Computer Architecture, 2002.

[14] Compaq Computer Corporation, *Alpha 21264 Microprocessor Hardware Reference Manual*, July 1999.

[15] B. Calder, D. Grunwald and J. Emer, *Predictive Sequential Associative Cache*, in Proc. of 2nd International Symposium on High Performance Computer Architecture, 1996.

[16] G. Hinton et. al., *The Microarchicture of the Pentium 4 Processor*, Intel Technology Journal Q1, 2001.

[17] A. Moshovos and G. S. Sohi, *Speculative Memory Cloaking and Bypassing*, in Proc. of 32nd International Symposium on Microarchitecture, December 1999.

[18] J. M. Tendler et. al., *POWER4 System Microarchitecture*, IBM technical white paper, October 2001.

[19] D. A. Patterson and J. L. Hennessy, *Computer Architecture: a Quantitative Approach*, 2nd ed., p. 382, Morgan Kaufmann, 1996.

[20] K. Diefendorff, P. Dubey, R. Hochsprung, and H. Scale, *AltiVec Extension to PowerPC Accelerates Media Processing*, IEEE Micro, vol. 20, no. 2, pp. 85-95, 2000.

[21] R. M. Tomasulo, *An Efficient Algorithm for Exploiting Multiple Arithmetic Units*, IBM Journal, Vol. 11, pp. 25-33, January 1967.

Managing Multi-Configuration Hardware via Dynamic Working Set Analysis

Ashutosh S. Dhodapkar and James E. Smith
Dept. of Electrical and Computer Engineering,
University of Wisconsin-Madison.
{dhodapka, jes}@ece.wisc.edu

Abstract

Microprocessors are designed to provide good average performance over a variety of workloads. This can lead to inefficiencies both in power and performance for individual programs and during individual phases within the same program. Microarchitectures with multi-configuration units (e.g. caches, predictors, instruction windows) are able to adapt dynamically to program behavior and enable/disable resources as needed. A key element of existing configuration algorithms is adjusting to program phase changes. This is typically done by "tuning" when a phase change is detected – i.e. sequencing through a series of trial configurations and selecting the best.

Algorithms that dynamically collect and analyze program working set information are studied. To make this practical, we propose working set signatures – highly compressed working set representations (e.g. 32-128 bytes total). Algorithms use working set signatures to 1) detect working set changes and trigger re-tuning; 2) identify recurring working sets and re-install saved optimal reconfigurations, thus avoiding the time-consuming tuning process; 3) estimate working set sizes to configure caches directly to the proper size, also avoiding the tuning process. Multi-configuration instruction caches are used to demonstrate the performance of the proposed algorithms. When applied to reconfigurable instruction caches, an algorithm that identifies recurring phases achieves power savings and performance similar to the best algorithm reported to date, but with orders-of-magnitude savings in the number of re-tunings.

1. Introduction

As microarchitecture and chip technology evolve, tradeoffs involving performance, power, and complexity become increasingly difficult, and optimization methods become increasingly sophisticated. One promising optimization method is to configure microarchitecture features dynamically to adapt to changing program characteristics [1-13]. As a program runs, it passes through phases of execution where its performance characteristics and, consequently, its hardware resource requirements may vary [14, 15]. Performance and/or power consumption can be optimized *on-the-fly* if significant phase changes can be detected and dynamic microarchitecture reconfiguration can be invoked in response to the phase changes.

In most proposed implementations, configurable units are designed to have a number of fixed configurations, e.g. four different cache sizes. Then, the runtime configuration algorithm selects from one of the multiple available configurations. Thus far, algorithms for determining the optimal hardware configuration have primarily been *ad hoc*, and consequently, there are about as many algorithms as there are proposals for multi-configuration units.

The research reported here is directed primarily toward development of configuration algorithms rather than developing new types of multi-configuration units. The goal is to find fundamental techniques that can be applied across a broad range of units. These algorithms will not only improve performance of individual multi-configuration units, but also permit unified control of several such units simultaneously. We envision these algorithms being implemented with co-designed virtual machine software [16], but that aspect is not essential to the research presented here; hardware or conventional software implementations could also be used.

As a basis for constructing reconfiguration algorithms, we are studying dynamic analysis of program working sets. There are three aspects of working sets that are of interest. Detection of a working set *change* indicates a program phase change, and can be used to trigger a search for an optimal configuration. Working set *size* can be used directly to choose the optimal configurations when performance is directly related to working set size (e.g. caches). Finally, the working set *identity* can be used to reduce re-optimization overhead: when a previously encountered working set can be identified, the optimal configuration for that working set can be stored and re-instated.

Working sets can be quite large, and it is likely impractical to work with full representations of working sets. Consequently, we propose a small hardware table (on the order of 32-128 bytes) to capture a working set "signature" that contains enough information to permit an estimation of the important working set characteristics. This working set information can be incorporated into a number of reconfiguration algorithms, and we demonstrate the use of working set signatures for multi-configuration instruction caches.

In the next three subsections, we summarize proposed methods for dynamically configuring hardware, describe reconfiguration algorithms, and discuss ways program working set behavior can be used in configuration algorithms.

1.1 Dynamically configurable hardware

A number of proposals have been made for adaptive/configurable hardware mechanisms targeted at performance and/or power optimization. A few important examples follow.

- *Configurable caches and TLBs* – line sizes and associativity are adjusted in response to program referencing behavior [2, 3, 5].
- *Allocation of memory hierarchy resources* – cache memory resources are divided among levels in the cache hierarchy [4] or configured for other uses, e.g. instruction reuse [6].
- *Allocation of memory buffer resources* – the same buffer resources are used for stream buffers or victim buffers, depending the current needs of the program [3].
- *Configurable branch predictors* – the length of the global history register [7] in a *gshare* (or related) predictor is varied.
- *Configurable instruction windows* – sections of the issue window are disabled when there is low instruction level parallelism [8, 9].
- *Configurable pipelines* – portions of clustered microarchitectures can be disabled [10], or a pipeline can vary between in order, out-of-order, and pipeline gating [11].

Of course, these various methods are not mutually exclusive, and in practice a combination of adaptive techniques will likely be used in the same processor. This leads to a fairly complex optimization problem, especially if the methods interact with one another. Huang et al. [12], describe a general framework and algorithms that are intended to deal with processors containing several configurable units.

1.2 Dynamic reconfiguration algorithms

Methods for controlling multi-configuration hardware generally involve a form of feedback where some performance characteristic (e.g. instructions per cycle (IPC) or miss rate) is measured and reconfiguration decisions are based on current and past measurements. The more sophisticated optimization schemes run for a fixed interval (also called a "window", "step", etc.) while monitoring some performance or program characteristic. This information is used to determine whether there has been a program phase change. If so, the configuration algorithm undertakes a *tuning* sequence, i.e. it systematically tries a number of configurations and measures the performance of each. It then selects the optimal one and continues, waiting for the next phase change.

The algorithm shown in Fig. 1 is proposed in [4]. This algorithm is both one of the better documented and the best performing we have found; henceforth, we use this algorithm for comparisons and refer to it as the *Rochester algorithm*. In [4], it is used to control a multi-configuration data cache hierarchy. That system repeatedly runs for a fixed number of instructions (100,000), and then makes a pass through the algorithm given in the figure. The system has two states: STABLE and UNSTABLE. As long as the configurable unit's performance, *unit_perf*, does not change more than *perf_noise* level and the number of branches does not change more than a *br_noise* level, the phase is STABLE and nothing is done. Otherwise, the phase is considered to be UNSTABLE, and the algorithm goes through a tuning sequence, looking for the best configuration. It begins with the smallest configuration and goes to the largest, unless the performance exceeds the *threshold*. Then, the algorithm selects the best performing configuration, makes the system state STABLE, and continues. If the tuning process selects the same configuration as in the previous phase, the noise levels are increased to prevent unnecessary tunings in the future. When stable, the noise thresholds are reduced until they reach a minimum level; in essence, the algorithm dynamically changes the threshold in order to detect major phase changes.

Reconfiguration algorithms have three basic properties that determine their applicability and effectiveness.

Detection efficiency – the ability of an algorithm to detect program phase changes. Low detection efficiency can lead to lost reconfiguration opportunities and non-optimal hardware configurations.

Reconfiguration overhead – the overhead associated with the transition from one configuration to another. The reconfiguration overhead depends on the amount of state contained in the structure. Flushing and/or re-learning the state can take 10's of cycles to 1000's of cycles (e.g. for reconfiguring a data cache).

Tuning overhead – the time spent searching for an optimal configuration. A high tuning overhead leads to higher number of reconfigurations and more time spent in the non-optimal configurations. This is a more serious problem in microarchitectures with several multi-configuration units. For example, three units with three configurations each, can lead to up to 27 combinations to explore (depending on the degree to which they interact). In a proposed method for resizing global branch history [7], up to 16 different configurations are explored.

```
Initially:
unit_perf_noise = base_perf_noise;
br_noise = base_br_noise;

After each sampling interval:
if (state == STABLE)
   if (|unit_perf - last_unit_perf| < perf_noise   AND
       |num_br - last_num_br| < br_noise)
       perf_noise = max (perf_noise – perf_dec, base_perf_noise);
       br_noise = max(br_noise - br_dec, base_br_noise);
       last_num_br = num_br;
       last_unit_perf = unit_perf;
   else
       last_unit_size = unit_size;
       unit_size = SMALLEST;
       state = UNSTABLE;

else if (state == UNSTABLE)
   record overall_perf;
   if (unit_perf < threshold   AND  unit_size != LARGEST)
       unit_size ++ ;
   else
       unit_size = select that with best overall_perf;
       state = STABLE;
       last_num_br = num_br;
       last_unit_perf = unit_perf;
       if (unit_size == last_unit_size)
           br_noise += br_inc;
           perf_noise += perf_inc;
```

Figure 1. An algorithm that detects a phase change and then searches for the best configuration [4].

It is important to differentiate between number of *tunings* and number of *reconfigurations*. Each tuning can possibly be composed of multiple reconfigurations. Hence, reducing the number of tunings leads to significantly fewer reconfigurations, less time spent in non-optimal configurations, and better performance/power efficiency.

1.3 Configuration algorithms using working set analysis

Because phase changes are manifestations of working set changes [17], we consider algorithms based on analysis of explicit working set information. In Section 2, we define a working set *signature*, a lossy-compressed representation of the true working set. By using working set signatures to detect phase changes, very accurate configuration algorithms can be developed. In Section 3, we apply the working set detection method to variations of the Rochester algorithm and show that similar average cache sizes and miss-rates can be achieved with fewer reconfigurations in some cases.

For some multi-configuration units, the optimal configuration is directly related to working set size. In Section 4, we show that the working set signature can be used for estimating size and develop a simple algorithm for finding an optimal cache configuration. This algorithm significantly reduces reconfigurations.

Finally, working sets can be used to identify recurring phases. Re-tuning is done only when a program phase change actually occurs. If the phase has occurred in the past, the optimum configuration is looked up in a table thereby eliminating the tuning overhead. As far as we know, none of the reconfiguration algorithms reported in literature exploit knowledge of recurring phases. In Section 5, we propose such an algorithm and show that reuse of configuration information can lead to a 95% reduction in number of tunings on average for integer benchmarks. Section 6 describes the implementation of hardware and software required to enable our reconfiguration scheme.

2. Working with working sets

For decades, operating system researchers have studied working set behavior to optimize memory hierarchy usage, and they have shown that working sets are the cause of phase behavior.

2.1 Basic definitions

Classically, a *working set* $W(t_i, \tau)$ for i=1,2..., is a set of distinct segments $\{s_1, s_2,.., s_\omega\}$ touched over the ith *window* of size τ [16]. The working set size is ω, the cardinality of the set. The segments are typically memory regions of some fixed size, such as a page.

Following some initial studies of working sets, researchers focused on more general models of program behavior and developed the *phase transition model* [17, 18]. Batson and Madison defined a *phase* as a maximal interval during which a given set of segments stay on top of the LRU stack [18]. In other words, a phase is defined as the maximum interval over which the working set remains more or less constant. The phase transition model states that programs follow a series of steady state phases with rather abrupt transitions in between. Phase transition studies have shown that programs have a marked phase behavior and bigger phases are composed of several smaller phases.

Most of the early working set research was directed at program paging behavior, but as one would expect, similar behavior occurs with smaller, cache line-size addressing units that are more in line with applications to configurable hardware. Also, early work tended to lump instructions and data together. We distinguish instruction and data working sets, and in this paper we focus on the instruction working set.

As defined, capturing a working set requires a *window*. The window size determines the finest granularity at which phases can be resolved. In this paper, we consider fine grain working sets containing cache line sized elements (32-256 bytes) because we primarily deal with multi-configuration units (e.g. caches and predictors) that work at this granularity. Also, for design simplicity, a series of non-overlapping windows is used, rather than a sliding window as is often used in paging studies.

The method of *sampling* information is another important parameter. In this paper, we assume that sampling occurs at every committed instruction. One could, however, resort to periodic sampling or random sampling to reduce sampling overhead. This will be an area of future research.

We are interested in identifying working sets, measuring sizes and detecting changes in working sets. In order to do this, we need a measure of similarity because the same phase may not always touch *exactly* the same segments in each working set window. There is some level of noise in the measurements partially due to mismatch in the phase and window boundaries and partially due to small differences in execution. We define the *relative working set distance*

$$\delta = \frac{\left| W(t_i, \tau) \cup W(t_j, \tau) \right| - \left| W(t_i, \tau) \cap W(t_j, \tau) \right|}{\left| W(t_i, \tau) \cup W(t_j, \tau) \right|}, \quad (1)$$

to compare two phases with working sets $W(t_i, \tau)$ and $W(t_j, \tau)$. A large δ value indicates a working set change whereas a small δ indicates no change. At the extreme ends, $\delta = 0$ when the sets are identical, and $\delta = 1$ when the working sets are totally different. We define a *threshold* δ_{th} and say there is a *working set change* if $\delta > \delta_{th}$.

2.2 Working set signatures

Representing and manipulating complete working sets is probably impractical for our application. Consequently, we propose a lossy-compressed working set representation that we call the *working set signature*.

The working set signature is an n-bit vector formed by mapping working set elements into n-buckets using a randomizing hash function (see Fig. 2). As mentioned before, the working set elements are of cache line granularity and hence the low-order b address bits are ignored when hashing. The size of the bit-vector is in the range of $32 - 128$ bytes. One could consider varying size dynamically to suit the application; this however, is a topic of future research. The bit-vector is cleared at the beginning of every interval (window) to remove stale working set information.

Working set signatures can be used to estimate the size, change, and identity attributes of the full working set. The *size* (number of ones) of the signature is probabilistically

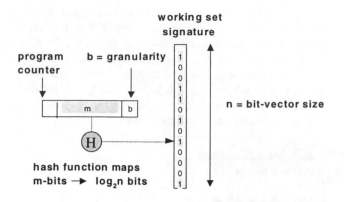

Figure 2. Mechanism for collecting working set signatures. *m* bits selected from the program counter are used to address a table containing *n* bits. The table is cleared at the beginning of each window, and a bit is set if the corresponding instruction block is touched.

related to the true working set size. When K random keys are hashed into n buckets, the fraction of buckets filled, f, is given by

$$f = 1 - (1 - \frac{1}{n})^K. \quad (2a)$$

Given the fraction of the signature filled, the working set size can be estimated using the relation

$$K = \log(1 - f) / \log(1 - \frac{1}{n}). \quad (2b)$$

Using this relation, we find that a 90% filled table corresponds to a working set size about 2.5 times larger than the number of filled entries. In Section 3 this relationship will be experimentally validated.

To detect working set changes and identities, we use a measure of similarity analogous to the one defined above for working sets. For two signatures S_1 and S_2, the *relative signature distance* is defined as

$$\Delta = \frac{\left| S_1 \oplus S_2 \right|}{\left| S_1 + S_2 \right|}, \quad (3)$$

i.e., (ones count of exclusive OR)/(ones count of inclusive OR). As with full signatures, we will use a threshold value Δ_{th} to detect phase changes.

3. Measuring working set changes

In this section we use instruction working set signatures to detect phase changes (working set changes) and then incorporate this mechanism in an example configuration algorithm.

3.1 Methodology

To evaluate the properties of working set signatures, we used a modified version of the SimpleScalar toolset [19] and a subset of benchmarks from the SPEC 2000 suite. The benchmarks were compiled using the base level optimizations. The choice of benchmarks was based on the presence of 1) long and short term phases with differing performance, 2) recurring phases, to test our working set identification scheme, and 3) different working sets in the same benchmark that led to similar behavior for certain cache/predictor configurations and completely different behavior for others – to show variable effectiveness of reconfiguration.

For collecting working set signatures, a window of 100K instructions is used (unless stated otherwise), and all benchmarks are run for 20,000 such intervals or 2 billion instructions. The signature bit vector size for most of the experiments is 1024 bits (128 bytes); in Section 6.3, we show that signatures as small as 32 bytes perform nearly as well. The hash function used during simulation is based on the C library functions `srand` and `rand`.

3.2 Signature accuracy

In order to evaluate the accuracy of working set signature distances (as compared with full working sets), we measured the relative distances between pairs of consecutive windows. Fig. 3a is a plot of the relative working set distance (y-axis) versus the relative distance for the corresponding signatures (x-axis). This particular graph is for *gzip*, but all the benchmarks display very similar behavior. That these distances are highly correlated is evident. There is some slight dispersion due to hash collisions when forming signatures. It is clear that using signatures for detecting phase changes will be nearly as accurate as using full working sets.

For comparison, the Rochester algorithm uses the dynamic count of conditional branches to measure working set changes. We define a relative distance metric for conditional branch counts in the same way as signature distances i.e.,

$$\Delta = \frac{BR\_CNT_i - BR\_CNT_{i-1}}{BR\_CNT_{i-1}}, \qquad (4)$$

where, BR_CNT_i is the conditional branch count for the ith window. A plot of full working set distances versus the branch count distances shows some correlation, but with a high level of dispersion (Fig. 3b). More importantly, there are several significant working set changes that are associated with very small relative branch distances.

In order to detect a phase change, we need to define the value of *threshold* – Δ_{th}. The threshold is defined empirically. Thresholds that are powers of two (0.125, 0.25, 0.5...) are used because the implied division for forming the relative distance becomes a matter of shifting and

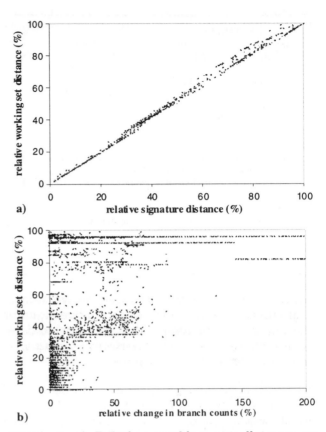

Figure 3. a) Relative working set distance vs. relative signature distance for benchmark *gzip* using a 32-byte signature. b) Relative working set distance vs. relative branch distance (Eq. 4).

comparing. Experiments showed that the ability to detect phase changes is relatively insensitive to the threshold, because, as was noted in [17], a phase change tends to be abrupt and very pronounced. Consequently, a threshold of 0.5 is used, which filters out most of the noise and detects only the significant phase changes.

3.3 Evaluation: managing configurable hardware

In this subsection, we use working set signatures for detecting phase changes, and incorporate phase change detection into a reconfiguration algorithm. To illustrate its performance, it is applied to a multi-configuration instruction cache.

The algorithm we propose is given in Fig. 4 and will be referred to as the *signature based* algorithm. The signature size is 128 bytes. This algorithm has three states: STABLE - when the program working set is stable and the configuration is optimal, UNSTABLE – when the working set is in transition and TUNING – when the working set is stable and different configurations are being explored.

At the end of each window (100K instructions), the relative signature distance with respect to the previous signature is computed. Assuming the system is initially

```
if (state == STABLE)
  if ( working_set # last_working_set > DELTAMAX )
    state = UNSTABLE;

else if (state == UNSTABLE)
  if ( working_set # last_working_set <= DELTAMAX )
    unit_size = SMALLEST;
    state = TUNING;

else if (state == TUNING)
  if ( working_set # last_working_set < DELTAMAX )
    record overall_performance;
    if (unit_perf > THRESHOLD  AND unit_size != LARGEST)
      unit_size ++ ;
    else
      unit_size = select best from among those tried;
      state = STABLE;
  else
    state = UNSTABLE;
```

Figure 4. Basic algorithm based on working set signatures. The algorithm uses relative signature distances (represented with # operator) to detect phase changes and then performs tuning when the phase transition completes.

STABLE, if the distance is greater than the threshold (0.5), the state becomes UNSTABLE and subsequent intervals wait for the distance to go below the threshold, indicating stability has been restored. When this happens,

the state transitions to TUNING, and the algorithm begins searching for the optimal configuration. Once the optimal configuration is found, the state transitions to STABLE. On the other hand, the state transitions back to UNSTABLE if the signature distance exceeds the threshold while TUNING is in progress.

The Rochester algorithm and the signature-based algorithm are similar in overall structure, but one difference is that the signature-based algorithm does not tune while the working set is in transition; it waits for the phase to stabilize.

To illustrate the algorithm's performance, we consider an instruction cache that can be reconfigured to 2KB, 8KB, 32KB or 128KB, depending on the requirements of the program. The goal is to save power by using the smallest cache that gives good performance. We use the cache miss rate as a measure of performance, the number of reconfigurations/tunings as a measure of overhead, and the average cache size as a measure of power consumption.

For comparison we use the Rochester algorithm given in Fig. 1, adapted to instruction cache configuration. As noted earlier, this algorithm detects phase changes using dynamic branch counts. The parameters used for the algorithm [4, 23] are $base\_br\_noise = 4500$, $br\_dec = 50$, $br\_inc = 1000$, $base\_perf\_noise = 450$, $perf\_dec = 5$, $perf\_inc = 100$ and $threshold = 2\%$.

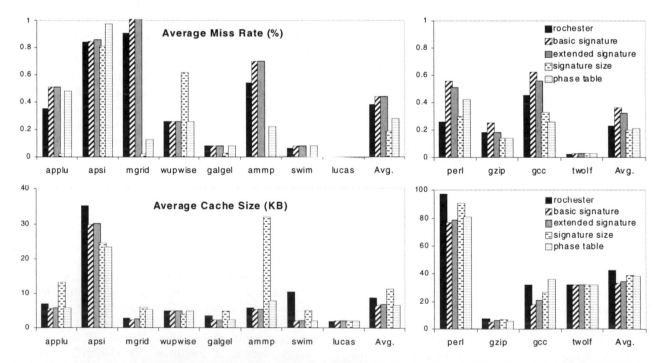

Figure 5. Average miss rates and cache sizes for SPEC2K floating-point (left) and integer (right) benchmarks. The last column in each graph shows the average over all the benchmarks in that graph. Results are shown for the Rochester algorithm, basic signature based and extended signature based algorithms (Sec. 3.3); signature size based algorithm (Sec. 4.2); phase table based algorithm (Sec. 5.1).

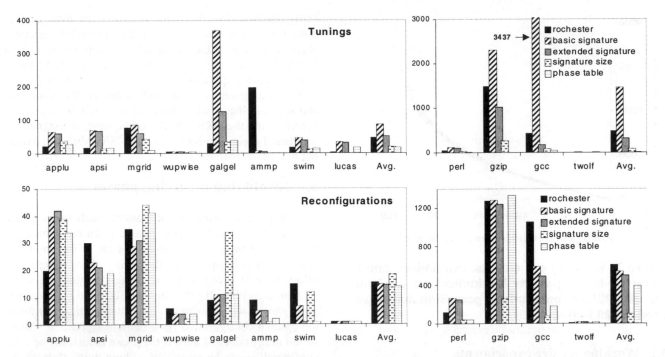

Figure 6. Number of tunings and reconfigurations for SPEC2K floating-point (left) and integer (right) benchmarks. The last column in each graph shows the average over all the benchmarks in that graph. Results are shown for the Rochester algorithm, basic signature based and extended signature based algorithms (Sec. 3.3); signature size based algorithm (Sec. 4.2); phase table based algorithm (Sec. 5.1).

Fig. 5 shows the average cache miss rate and average cache size for the Rochester and basic signature-based algorithms (first two bars; other bars will be described later). On average, all the algorithms perform very similarly in terms of miss rates and average cache sizes. A point to emphasize here is that any algorithm with a sufficient number of tunings will achieve near-optimal instruction cache sizes and miss rates, and in the remainder of the paper, we do not draw any real distinctions among algorithms on that basis. These results do show the advantage of the dynamic configuration approach, however. For example, compared to a configuration having 128KB instruction cache (0% miss rate on average, not shown in the figure), the signature-based algorithm reduces average cache size by 82% for an increased miss-rate of just 0.4%.

The number of tunings and reconfigurations (Fig. 6) are the key distinguishing features directly related to the algorithm's performance overhead, and we focus on these measures in comparing algorithms. Recall that a *tuning* occurs when the algorithm initiates a search for the optimal configuration; a *reconfiguration* occurs whenever the configuration changes.

The signature-based algorithm is comparable to the Rochester algorithm in number of reconfigurations; however, the Rochester algorithm has the advantage of performing far fewer tunings. This is mainly because the Rochester algorithm detects when unnecessary tunings occur and "backs off" by increasing the *noise* levels. This

feature is especially useful when there are frequent phase changes that do not require reconfiguration. On the other hand, the basic signature-based algorithm performs tunings every time a phase change is detected; there is no "back off".

To reduce unnecessary tunings, we extend the signature-based algorithm to wait for 4 stable intervals before tuning. Also, if the state is UNSTABLE for more than 10 intervals and performance is below threshold, the cache size is increased to the maximum. This acts as a backup strategy in cases where the working set does not stabilize, so tuning is never performed. With the extended algorithm, the number of tunings is reduced by 74% on average, compared to the basic algorithm (Fig. 6).

4. Measuring working set sizes

As mentioned earlier, the signature size (one's count of the signature) is closely related to the actual working set size. Thus, in those cases where performance is directly related to the working set size, for example instruction and data caches, the signature size can be used to determine the optimal configuration; there is no need for tuning.

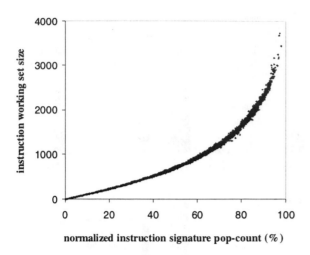

Figure 7. Working set size vs. normalized one's count of the signature for instruction working set of SPEC2K benchmark *gcc*. Signature size used is 128 bytes.

4.1 Working set size experiments

We collected the true working set and the working set signature for each window of 100K instructions. Then, the true size of the working set versus the signature size was plotted. Since a randomizing hash is used, the graphs for all the benchmarks are essentially identical (and fit Eq. 2b). A representative plot for the instruction working set is shown in Fig. 7.

As expected, for small working sets, the graph is close to linear with a slope of 1 and as the working set gets bigger, the graph becomes non-linear. Even in the non-linear section, the signature can give reasonably accurate working set size estimates 3-4x the maximum signature size. This means that a typical signature size we have been considering (32-128 bytes) with line-size granularities (32-128 bytes) can be used to estimate working set sizes of many tens to hundreds of Kbytes – adequate for reconfiguring L1 caches. By increasing the granularity (future research), we expect the reach to be extended to L2 cache sizes.

4.2 Evaluation: reconfiguration using signature size

The extended signature-based algorithm can be modified to use the signature size for selecting an optimal cache configuration – the smallest that holds the current working set (plus 10% to allow for some noise). To determine the appropriate size, equation 2 (Section 2) is used. This eliminates the need to tune, and it typically reduces the number of reconfigurations as well. The main advantage lies in the significantly smaller number of re-

configurations (Fig. 6: *signature size*) – on average, 75-80% fewer than the Rochester and extended signature algorithms. The effect is much more prominent in a benchmark like *gzip*. *Gzip* has lots of dynamic phases with a cache requirement of 8KB, separated by phases with a requirement of 2KB. When tuning, the Rochester and signature-based algorithms try the 2KB configuration before trying the 8KB. On the other hand, the signature-size based algorithm sets the size to 8KB directly, avoiding half of the reconfigurations.

5. Identifying recurring phases

As a program executes, it goes through many phase changes. However, the same phases often recur multiple times during program execution. As far as we know, no previous work has proposed the saving of recurring phase information to avoid rc-tuning. In this section, we study such an algorithm. Briefly, this will be done by maintaining a *phase table* in memory. After tuning has determined the optimal configuration for a particular phase, it will be stored in the table. Later, if the phase recurs, the optimal configuration can be reinstated without going through the tuning process.

5.1 Phase statistics

Table 1 shows some general characteristics of phases as identified in the simulations. The program execution consists of a sequence of stable 100K instruction intervals separated by unstable intervals. Each "run" of stable intervals is defined as one *dynamic phase*. If the relative signature distance between two different dynamic phases is within the 0.5 threshold, we say that they are the same *static phase*. The average phase lengths are computed by averaging the lengths of all the dynamic phases.

In general, the floating-point benchmarks have longer phases, typically 10's of millions of instructions – primarily due to the long loops of numerical code. The integer benchmarks on the other hand have much shorter phases; less than one million instructions for *gzip* and *gcc*. For many of the floating point benchmarks 99+% of the time is spent in stable phases. As the average phase length decreases there are more transitions, and hence the fraction of time in a stable region decreases (60-80% for *gzip* and *gcc*).

The presence of recurring phases is evident in all the benchmarks by comparing the number of dynamic phases with the number of static phases. However, the degree to which phases recur is reduced by the relatively short benchmark runtimes (2 billion instructions). Several benchmarks were run for 10 billion instructions and the number of dynamic phases was almost three orders of magnitude greater than the number of static phases. This

Table 1. Benchmark characteristics. Columns are benchmark name, number of dynamic and static phases, number of static phases that lead to 95% of stable time, average phase length in units of 100K instructions and the percentage of time spent in stable phases.

Bench-mark	#Dynamic Phases	# Static Phases	95% Stable Time	Avg. Phase Length	Stable Time (%)
applu	66	26	12	301	99.61
apsi	72	15	6	276	99.36
mgrid	86	9	4	230	99.01
wupwise	6	5	3	3331	99.95
galgel	371	39	12	51	95.14
ammp	7	1	1	2854	99.92
swim	45	14	10	442	99.66
lucas	33	18	13	604	99.69
perl	119	21	5	166	99.13
gzip	2301	10	4	7	81.79
gcc	3437	57	19	3	61.77
twolf	17	13	2	1174	99.84

indicates that the gains of reusing configuration information for recurring phases increase with time.

The "95% stable time" column of the table is the number of static phases that account for 95% of the dynamic phases. These numbers are quite low, fewer than 20 in every case. This indicates that a relatively small signature table will be sufficient for covering most recurring phases.

5.2 Evaluation: recurring working sets

The algorithm for exploiting recurring working sets is similar to the one given in Fig. 4. However, on detecting a phase change, the algorithm first performs a table lookup to see if configuration information for the phase exists in the table. If so, the optimal configuration is reinstated. If not, the algorithm goes into the TUNING state. At the end of tuning, the optimal configuration is committed to the signature table.

In addition to the configuration information, the table also keeps track of phase lengths. If, during its last execution, the length was fewer than four intervals (400,000 instructions), then tuning is not performed. This avoids tuning for insignificant phases. Four intervals are chosen because the tuning process takes a maximum of four intervals.

The results for the algorithm are shown in Figs. 5 and 6, labeled *phase table*. The important difference lies in the number of tunings performed by the phase table algorithm. The algorithm performs 67% fewer tunings for floating point benchmarks and 92% fewer tunings for the integer benchmarks compared with the extended signature

based algorithm. In situations where the tuning process is complex, this can lead to significant improvements in performance.

6. Implementation

To implement configuration algorithms, we propose a combination of hardware and software. Software performs higher-level configuration decisions, and hardware collects working set signatures, and, possibly, performs some of the lower level analysis.

6.1 VMM based configuration management

To perform working set analysis and manage configurable hardware of wide variety and complexity, we are developing a co-designed virtual machine monitor (VMM) [16] – a layer of software designed concurrently with the hardware implementation. This software is hidden from all conventional software and would typically be developed as part of the hardware design effort. The base technology is used in the Transmeta Crusoe [20] and the IBM Daisy/BOA projects [21] primarily to support whole-system binary translation. In this work, we are not interested in the binary translation aspect. In fact, for managing configurable hardware, there needs to be no changes made to existing binaries.

Of course, VMM software is not the only option for managing the optimization process. Low-level operating system software could also be used. This, however, requires the addition of implementation dependent code to the OS. One could also consider microcode in place of VMM software. The microcode can reside in ROM, but there must still be some hidden memory for maintaining data structures such as the phase table. A special purpose co-processor [22] is another good candidate for managing the hardware configuration. It has the advantage of saving optimization time overhead at the expense of additional hardware.

In the most straightforward implementation, working set signatures are collected by hardware, and then the raw signature data is read and analyzed by VMM software. The working set size/difference algorithms we propose can easily be performed in software. With the assumed window size, VMM software is invoked very 100K instructions. Because in most cases the relative signature distance will be very small, the VMM overhead will also be small – probably a few tens of instructions. If this overhead is still too high, a longer sampling interval can be used, or hardware can be used to perform some of the low level analysis. This is described in the next subsection.

A phase table lookup ostensibly requires a linear search of signatures, but it can be made more efficient by using techniques such as hashing based on the signature size, early exits when the phase is same as the previous one, etc. This will be a topic for future study as the VMM is implemented.

6.2 Hardware working set analysis

Besides collecting working set signatures, hardware can also be used for estimating working set size and/or to detect working set changes, thereby reducing software overhead. In particular, detecting working set changes in hardware avoids invoking the VMM between each interval; the VMM has to be invoked only when the working set actually changes. Furthermore, for very simple reconfigurations that are directly related to working set size (e.g. cache configurations), it may not be necessary to enter the VMM at all; hardware can determine the proper configuration based only on the size of the working set signature. It is important to emphasize that this hardware is not on the critical path and hence can be implemented with slow, low power transistors.

To measure size, there must be a hardware counter which increments whenever a bit in the signature changes from 0 to 1. This requires reading the signature entry before writing to it.

To measure the relative signature distance, a second signature register is required to hold the signature for the previous window. As defined in section 2.2, the relative signature distance is the ratio of the exclusive-OR to the inclusive-OR of the signatures – say X/N. X and N can be evaluated dynamically as follows.

Initially, X=N=count of ones in the previous signature. For each signature access, both the previous and current signature values are read. If previous=0 and current=0, both X and N are incremented. If previous=0 and current=1, nothing is done; if previous=1 and current=0, then the bit in the previous signature is cleared and X is decremented; the case previous=1 and current=1 should never happen. Then at the end of the interval, hardware can find the relative signature distance X/N (or approximate it by shifting and comparing, when the threshold is a power of two). The VMM can set up the hardware to trap to VMM software on values above the threshold.

6.3 Implementation cost

The primary cost is the working set signature. This consists of 128 bytes and can be placed off the critical path. Using smaller signatures can further reduce the hardware cost. Fig. 8 shows that a signature as small as 32 bytes can resolve most of the dynamic phases resolved by a 512-byte signature. Small signatures are unable to resolve certain phase changes for benchmarks with large working sets (*perl* and *gcc*) due to collisions in the signature table, which lead to smaller relative distances. Preliminary experiments have shown that using smaller

thresholds is a solution. Dynamically varying thresholds and/or signature sizes, to accommodate larger working sets is a topic of future research.

In the simple implementation (where the VMM performs the relative distance computation) the memory only has to be written in normal operation. Furthermore, it is not critical that every instance of an element of the working set be recorded. Only one occurrence of the element has to be recorded and most elements appear multiple times. Thus, if occasionally dropping an element simplifies hardware (for example, retiring instructions from different cache blocks in one cycle) little accuracy is lost. For the determining the relative signature distance in hardware, two copies of the signature memory are needed, and they are both read and written during the collection phase.

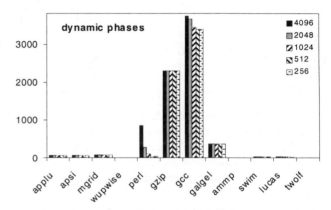

Figure 8. Number of dynamic phases resolved by signatures of sizes 256–4096 bits (32-512 bytes). The elements sampled are 32-byte blocks except for the 256-bit signature, where they are 128 bytes. This is done to increase the "reach" of the signature.

7. Related work

Previous work related to hardware reconfiguration was discussed in Sec. 1.1. In this section, we briefly discuss work related to working set analysis.

Sherwood et al. [24] proposed the use of program phase information to speed up simulation. They use basic block execution frequency information as a *fingerprint* for an interval of execution. The goal then, is to find a small set of intervals whose fingerprint matches that of the whole program. Detailed simulation over these intervals can give a fairly accurate estimate of the performance of the whole program.

Adaptive mode control (AMC) caches, proposed by Zhou et al. [25], keep track of the working set in order to enable/disable cache lines. The AMC cache keeps a counter for each of the tags to measure activity. If the cache line is not accessed for a particular interval, then it is put to sleep. However, the corresponding tag entry is not put to sleep, thereby allowing continuous monitoring of the working set and avoiding "just-in-case" periodic upsizing.

HP Dynamo [26], a run time dynamic optimization system, uses a measure of working set change to flush stale data translations from a cache. Dynamo optimizes traces of the program to generate fragments, which are stored in a fragment cache. At steady state, most of the instructions are fetched from the fragment cache. When the working set changes, the rate of fragment formation increases. This is used as a trigger to flush stale fragments from the cache, making room for the new ones.

Merten et al. [27] describe a framework for dynamic optimization, which profiles branches to detect working set *hot-spots*. This is mainly done using a branch behavior buffer, which collects frequently executed branches. The hot-spot information can be fed into a run-time optimizer such as Dynamo to achieve performance improvements.

8. Conclusions and future research

We introduced the concept of a working set signature, a lossy-compressed representation of the program working set. The signatures provide a robust mechanism for detecting working set changes. Also, unlike previously reported methods, the signatures can be used to identify specific working sets. This provides an opportunity for storing configuration information associated with recurring working sets. Algorithms using complex tuning mechanisms can benefit significantly from reuse of configuration information.

When applied to an instruction cache reconfiguration algorithm, the signatures detect most of the major working set changes. This algorithm achieves 27% fewer tunings and 18% fewer reconfigurations than the Rochester algorithm – probably the best published to date.

Working set size information can be derived from the signature and can be used to configure the instruction caches directly. An algorithm based on this achieves performance similar to the signature-based algorithm using 74% fewer reconfigurations.

Finally, an algorithm based on reuse of configuration information leads to 80% fewer reconfigurations compared to the Rochester algorithm. These results suggest that an algorithm based on reuse of configuration information can potentially perform much better than other algorithms when the tuning overhead is high.

We plan to continue the development of a VMM that implements these algorithms. This development will include

- Algorithms for tuning multiple interacting units in a way that optimizes performance and/or power efficiency. The work in [12] is an important first step in this direction.

- Study of the relationship between the signature size, the PC bits, sample interval and thresholds. It is likely that the VMM can adjust the PC bits and sample interval dynamically to adapt to working set size.
- Study of sampling schemes such as periodic sampling, to reduce sampling overhead.
- Study of algorithms for building and managing the signature table. In particular, it will be necessary to develop fast algorithms for searching the table to find recurring phases.

The ultimate goal is to define the overall VMM structure and to apply it to a highly configurable microarchitecture.

9. Acknowledgements

We would like to gratefully acknowledge Todd Bezenek and Timothy Heil for several valuable discussions. This work is being supported by SRC grants 2000-HJ-782 and 2001-HJ-902, NSF grants EIA-0071924 and CCR-9900610, Intel and IBM.

10. References

[1]   D. Albonesi, "Dynamic IPC/Clock Rate Optimization," *Proc. of the 25th Intl. Sym. on Computer Architecture*, July 1998, pp. 282-292.

[2]   S.-H. Yang, M. Powell, B. Falsafi, K. Roy and T. N. Vijaykumar, "An Integrated Circuit/Architecture Approach to Reducing Leakage in Deep Submicron High-Performance I-Caches," *Proc. of the 7th Intl. Sym. on High Performance Computer Architecture*, Jan. 2001.

[3]   A. Veidenbaum, W. Tang, R. Gupta, A. Nicolau and X. Ji, "Adapting Cache Line Size to Application Behavior," *Intl. Conf. on Supercomputing*, July 1999, pp. 145-154.

[4]   R. Balasubramonian, D. Albonesi, A. Buyuktosunoglu and S. Dwarkadas, "Memory Hierarchy Reconfiguration for Energy and Performance in General Purpose Architectures," *Proc. of 33rd Intl. Sym. on Microarchitecture*, Dec. 2000, pp. 245-257.

[5]   D. H. Albonesi, "Selective Cache Ways: On-demand Cache Resource Allocation," *Proc. of 32nd Intl. Sym. on Microarchitecture*, Dec. 1999, pp. 248-259.

[6]   P. Ranganathan, S. Adve and N. Jouppi, "Reconfigurable Caches and Their Application to Media Processing," *Proc. of the 27th Intl. Sym. on Computer Architecture*, June 2000, pp. 214-224.

[7]   T. Juan, S. Sanjeevan and J. Navarro, "Dynamic History-Length Fitting: A Third Level of Adaptivity for Branch Prediction," *Proc. of the 25th Intl. Sym. on Computer Architecture*, July 1998, pp. 155-166.

[8] A. Buyuktosunoglu, S. Schuster, D. Brooks, P. Bose, P. Cook and D. Albonesi, "An Adaptive Issue Queue for Reduced Power at High Performance," *Workshop on Power-Aware Computer Systems (PACS2000, held in conjunction with ASPLOS-IX)*, Nov. 2000.

[9] D. Folegnani and A. González, "Reducing Power Consumption of the Issue Logic," *Workshop on Complexity-Effective Design (WCED2000, held in conjunction with ISCA27)*, June 2000.

[10] R. Bahar and S. Manne, "Power and Energy Reduction via Pipeline Balancing," *Proc. of the 28th Intl. Sym. on Computer Architecture*, July 2001.

[11] S. Ghiasi, J. Casmira and D. Grunwald, "Using IPC Variations in Workloads with Externally Specified Rates to Reduce Power Consumption", *Workshop on Complexity Effective Design 2000 (WCED2000, held in conjunction with ISCA27)*, June 2000.

[12] M. Huang, J. Reneau, S.-M. Yoo and J. Torrellas, "A Framework for Dynamic Energy Efficiency and Temperature Management," *Proc. of the 33rd Intl. Sym. on Microarchitecture*, Dec. 2000, pp. 202-213.

[13] D. Brooks and M. Martonosi, "Adaptive Thermal Management for High-Performance Microprocessors," *Workshop on Complexity Effective Design 2000 (WCED2000, held in conjunction with ISCA27)*, June 2000.

[14] Timothy Sherwood and Brad Calder, "Time Varying Behavior of Programs," *UC San Diego Technical Report UCSD-CS99-630*, August 1999.

[15] Bingxiong Xu and D. H. Albonesi, "Runtime Reconfiguration Techniques for Efficient General-Purpose Computation," *IEEE Design and Test of Computers*, Vol. 17, Issue 1, Jan. – Mar. 2000, pp. 42-52.

[16] A. S. Dhodapkar and J. E. Smith, "Saving and Restoring Contexts via Co-Designed Virtual Machines," *Workshop on Complexity-Effective Design (held in conjunction with ISCA28)*, June 2001.

[17] P. Denning, "Working Sets Past and Present," *IEEE Transactions on Software Engineering*, Vol. SE-6, No. 1, Jan. 1980.

[18] A. Batson and W. Madison, "Measurements of major locality phases in symbolic reference strings," *Proc. of the Intl. Sym. Computer Performance and Modeling, Measurement and Evaluation*, ACM SIDMETRICS and IFIP WG7.3, Mar. 1976, pp. 75-84.

[19] D. Burger and T. Austin, "The SimpleScalar Tool Set, Version 2.0," *University of Wisconsin-Madison Computer Sciences Department Technical Report #1342*, June 1997.

[20] A. Klaiber, "The Technology Behind Crusoe Processors," Transmeta Technical Brief, *http://www.transmeta.com/dev*, Jan. 2000.

[21] K. Ebcioglu and E. Altman, "DAISY: Dynamic Compilation for 100% Architecture Compatibility, *Proc. of the 24th Intl. Sym. on Computer Architecture*, June 1997, pp. 26-37.

[22] Y. Chou and J. Shen, "Instruction Path Coprocessors," *Proc. of the 27th Intl. Sym. on Computer architecture*, 2000, pp. 270-281.

[23] Rajeev Balasubramonian, Sandhya Dwarkadas and David Albonesi, personal correspondence.

[24] T. Sherwood, E. Perelman, and B. Calder, "Basic Block Distribution Analysis to Find Periodic Behaviour and Simulation," *Proc. of the Intl. Conf. on Parallel Architectures and Compilation Techniques*, Sep. 2001, pp. 3-14.

[25] H. Zhou, M. Toburen, E. Rotenberg, and T. Conte, "Adaptive Mode Control: A Static-Power-Efficient Cache Design," *Proc. of the Intl. Conf. on Parallel Architectures and Compilation Techniques*, Sep. 2001, pp. 61-72.

[26] V. Bala, E. Duesterwald, S. Banerjia, "Dynamo: A Transparent Dynamic Optimization System," *Proc. of the Conf. on Prog. Language Design and Implementation*, ACM SIGPLAN, 2000, pp. 1-12.

[27] M. Merten, A. Trick, R. Barnes, E. Nystrom, C. George, J. Gyllenhaal, and W.-M. Hwu, "An Architectural Framework for Runtime Optimization," IEEE Transactions on Computers, June 2001, pp. 567-589.

Session 7: Data and Storage Networks

Queue Pair IP: A Hybrid Architecture for System Area Networks

Philip Buonadonna, David Culler

philipb@eecs.berkeley.edu, culler@eecs.berkeley.edu

Electrical Engineering and Computer Science Department   *Intel Research, Berkeley*
University of California, Berkeley   *Intel Corporation*

Abstract

We propose a SAN architecture called Queue Pair IP (QPIP) that combines the interface from industry proposals for low overhead, high bandwidth networks, e.g. Infiniband, with the well established inter-network protocol suite. We evaluate how effectively the queue pair abstraction enables inter-network protocol offload. We develop a prototype QPIP system that implements basic queue pair operations over a subset of TCP, UDP and IPv6 protocols using a programmable network adapter,. We assess this prototype in terms of basic application performance, underlying processing costs, and a network storage application. With modest hardware support, QPIP can perform as well as traditional inter-network protocol implementations at a fraction of the host CPU overhead. With hardware support equivalent to Infiniband, QPIP would achieve similar performance targets.

1. Introduction

I/O systems today are on the verge of an architectural revolution motivated by ever-increasing interconnectivity demands. Present system architectures form a bottleneck that limits performance. Processing units communicate with I/O devices using low latency load/store semantics or DMA across a shared bandwidth bus, such as the Peripheral Component Interconnect (PCI). The bus extends at most a few feet from the processor, and supports a limited number of devices and minimal fault-tolerance.

A proposed solution to this problem is to merge present I/O architectures and modern networks into a new paradigm of I/O based networks. Processor/Memory combinations and I/O devices (*e.g.* disks and WAN adapters) are connected directly to a switched interconnect fabric and communicate through network-oriented protocols. Communication can be processor-to-processor or processor-to-device. The switch-based design permits a large array of devices to be connected in

a manner that provides scalable throughput and the network protocols provide for a high degree of fault-tolerance. However, network latency must be comparable to the μsec latency of busses, with few instructions of host overhead. The class of networks that support this concept of networked I/O have been termed System Area Networks (SAN).

A key component to the success of SANs is developing a standardized architecture around which interoperable systems can be designed and built. At present, there are two prominent, and somewhat competing, efforts toward this goal. One of these is a cooperative industry standard called Infiniband [17]. At the other is a series of IETF groups looking to employ established inter-network protocols[1] in the SAN environment.

Infiniband is the merger of several industry projects in SAN architectures: the VI Architecture, Next Generation I/O and Future I/O. The core concept of Infiniband is to interconnect host processor/memory modules and I/O devices by a switched network fabric, effectively eliminating the traditional I/O bus. In order to meet performance targets of low latency, high bandwidth and low host overhead, Infiniband proposes extensive hardware support combined with a completely new communication stack. At the top, it defines a new communication abstraction called the Queue Pair (QP). It also specifies the management transport, network, link, and physical layers.

By comparison, Inter-network protocol proposals in this area define only the higher-layers of the network stack. There are separate specs for the management, transport and network layers, and there are no specific assumptions about the underlying link or physical layers. Historically, traditional operating system interfaces to simple network adapters have been successful. Additionally, as processors and links have become faster,

---

[1] This is paper, *inter-network protocols* refers to the suite of established IETF protocols that include TCP, UDP and IP. It can be used interchangeably with *IP protocols*.

these implementations have demonstrated increased bandwidth. However, the host-based nature of these implementations has caused debate on whether or not host overhead and latency can meet the performance demands of the SAN. Efforts to accelerate inter-network protocol stacks have met with limited success as discussed below. The majority of these sought to maintain the traditional communication abstraction (*i.e.* sockets) and host-based nature of the stack, while optimizing implementation internals either though software techniques or link layer assistance.

In this paper, we propose a SAN architecture called Queue Pair IP (QPIP) that combines modern industry proposals for high-performance networks with the well established inter-network protocol suite. Specifically, the architecture implements the Queue Pair (QP) communication abstraction proposed by industry efforts directly over standard inter-network protocols implemented in an intelligent network interface.

Our hypothesis is that the queue pair abstraction enables effective offload of inter-network protocols onto the network interface. Using a programmable network adapter, we have developed a prototype QPIP system that implements basic QP operations over a subset of TCP, UDP and IPv6 protocols. We assess this prototype in terms of basic performance, host overhead, network interface occupancy and network storage performance. Our results show that QPIP can perform equal to or better than traditional inter-network protocol implementations at a fraction of the host CPU overhead. Further, the QPIP model enables a straightforward design that does not require highly specialized or complex hardware to support this level of performance. Such simplification provides an opportunity for specialized hardware acceleration that would enable meeting the performance requirements of the SAN regime in an interoperable framework.

The rest of this paper is organized as follows. Section 2 presents a background of work in System Area Networks, Infiniband, and inter-network protocols. Section 3 describes the QPIP architecture. Section 4 details our QPIP prototype and presents an analysis of its performance. Section 5 discusses key lessons learned from the QPIP implementation. Section 6 presents our conclusions and future work.

2. Background and Related Work

2.1. System Area Networks & Infiniband

There have been several efforts aimed at high performance interfaces for system area networks [12, 23, 27, 30, 31, 33, 34]. These have explored a variety of concepts including usage abstractions and OS bypass mechanisms. The results demonstrate that changing the usage abstraction enables low overhead, high bandwidth communication.

Infiniband draws upon these previous research efforts and utilizes a memory-based user-level communication abstraction. The communication interface in Infiniband is the *Queue Pair* (QP), which is the logical endpoint of a communication link. The QP is a memory-based abstraction where communication is achieved through direct memory-to-memory transfers between applications and devices. It consists of a send and a receive queue of work requests (WR). Each WR contains the necessary meta-data for the message transaction including pointers into registered buffers to receive/transmit data to/from.

There are two classes of message transactions in the QP model: *send-receive* and *remote DMA* (RDMA). To conduct transfers, the user process constructs a WR and posts it to a QP. The posting method adds the WR to the appropriate queue and notifies the adapter of a pending operation. In the send-receive paradigm, the target pre-posts receive WRs that identify memory regions where incoming data will be placed. The source posts a send WR that identifies the data to send. Each send operation on the source consumes a receive WR on the target. In this scheme, each application manages its own buffer space and neither end of the message transaction has explicit information about the peer's registered buffers. In contrast, RDMA messages identify both the source and destination buffers. Data can be directly written to or read from a remote address space without involving the target process. However, both processes must exchange information regarding their registered buffers using some out-of-band mechanism such as a send-receive operation.

Closely coupled with the QP is the *completion queue* (CQ). When a QP is created, its individual send and receive channels are bound to one or separate CQs. A single CQ may have multiple QPs associated with it. When a WR completes, a token is added to the completion queue and can be detected by the application through polling or an event. The binding of multiple queues to a CQ permits applications to group related QPs into a single monitoring point.

The QP and CQ functionality is implemented in the Infiniband network interface or *channel adapter*. Channel adapters incorporate a high degree of hardware support to minimize host overhead and protocol processing occupancy in the interface itself.

Infiniband also defines the mechanisms beneath the communication abstraction. It includes specifications for the transport reliability levels, connection and connectionless communication, management, network routing, link layer formats and physical layer properties. With the exception of using the IPv6 addressing scheme for inter-subnet packets, it is largely divested from standard inter-network protocols. The architecture does export a raw link layer interface that can be used by traditional inter-network protocol implementations, but it does not provide the same performance guarantees. The QPIP architecture seeks to invert this strategy and make inter-network protocols the core transport underneath the QP model.

2.2. Inter-network Protocols

Standard inter-network protocols have seen a great deal of success in usage and throughput capacity. Their high-level, link-independent nature has permitted deployment on a wide variety of platforms and enjoyed a tremendous growth in bandwidth. Additionally, the open forum of development has permitted continued refinement and introduction of new application spaces. However, the general nature of these protocols has led to principally host-based software implementations that incur non-negligible overhead on the host processors that impact latency and other computation. Thus, it is frequently perceived that inter-network protocols are not suited for SAN environments.

Detailed analysis of inter-network protocols [3, 19-22, 28] have identified host overhead and bottlenecks for the TCP/IP protocol combination. There have been efforts to mitigate these problems through techniques such as Integrated Layer processing [1, 5], reducing caches misses and memory cycles [4, 25] and *fbufs*[10]. The thrust of all these efforts has been to focus on internal protocol mechanisms and buffer management without changing the application interface. Even so, significant host overhead remains. QPIP advocates an alternative memory-based interface that eliminates major sources of overhead and allows the complete offload and a simplified implementation of inter-network protocols.

Afterburner [8] explored providing hardware support for minimizing data movement in kernel based inter-network protocol implementations. Edwards [13, 14] used Afterburner in conjunction with Jetstream [35] for user-space inter-network protocol implementations. The core trait of these projects was to optimize mechanisms at the lower-level, thus only eliminating some of the overhead. The bulk of the inter-network stack remained on the host and used a traditional interface.

The OSIRIS network adapter [9, 11], U-Net [33], Arsenic [29], Trapeze [16], and Windows Sockets Direct Path [24] explored techniques for direct user-level access to network hardware with an inter-network protocol stack as an application library. This demonstrated some performance improvement, but the inter-network communication path was still significantly slower than the direct access path to the hardware and incurred host overhead associated with the user-level protocol library. QPIP seeks to make the inter-network stack *the* fast path and provide a light weight abstraction on top instead of underneath the stack.

Pushing inter-network protocol processing all the way to the interface has also been examined. However, many of the historical efforts are not well documented. The Nectar communications processor provided fully offloaded network functionality, including TCP/IP, under a user-level interface based on shared memory semantics[7]. Using this technique, Nectar demonstrated TCP throughput of 24 Mbit/sec vs. 6.4 Mbits/sec when employed as a simple link layer underneath a host-based stack. However, best performance was achieved by using a specialized protocol on the adapter. Moreover, the TCP/IP stack in Nectar was used primarily to show the flexibility of the complex runtime system. The complexity of the Nectar design led to a lengthy development cycle and prevented it from keeping pace with host-based stacks on faster host processors. QPIP builds on the Nectar approach by making the inter-network stack a core component of the runtime system. It employs a simple interface that can be implemented either on programmable NIs on a competitive growth curve or by specialized hardware design.

Recent industry efforts have sought to utilize special hardware to achieve inter-network protocol acceleration. Alacritech's SLIC [2] provides support for common TCP/IP data movement, including zero-copy, underneath existing socket abstractions. QPIP explores full protocol offload for all protocol functions underneath a lightweight memory based abstraction. The iReady Internet Tuner [18] provides a full inter-network protocol implementation in a chip, but is designed for embedded device applications using a serial interface. It only supports a small number of connections and does not have a high performance interface. The Emulex GN9000 [15] supports a VI Architecture abstraction over TCP/IP protocols, but adds an additional protocol layer between TCP and the application interface. QPIP seeks to implement the QP abstraction directly on top of the TCP/UDP transport layer without an intervening protocol layer.

3. The QPIP Architecture

The QPIP architecture is a hybrid approach that combines the QP communication model over inter-network protocols implemented in an intelligent adapter. Using inter-network protocols eliminates the need to re-engineer the transport, network and link layer components and brings the wealth of understanding and services of these protocols to the SAN space.

At the top of the network stack, the QP replaces the socket as the communication abstraction. Communication is achieved by sending and receiving messages on a QP as opposed to a series of read() and write() calls to a socket. Beneath this, the transport (UDP/TCP), network (IP) and link layers are processed within the network interface. These can be simplified because of the application interface and the intimacy with the network.

A key design point of the QPIP architecture is that it uses established protocol formats for inter-network protocols and does not add any additional protocol formats. This provides a straightforward means to bridge the SAN to external networks using conventional means such as a firewall or router. Communication can occur between QPIP applications or QPIP and traditional (socket) systems. QP to QP is the high performance mode for communication within the SAN. In the latter mode, the remote end sees a conventional IP sockets, but the QP end is aware of the remote limitations and may have to re-assemble incoming data into a complete unit. This reassembly could be done by an optional library or perhaps with assistance from the interface.

For best effort datagrams using UDP, a QP is created that is bound to a particular UDP port. The WRs in a UDP QP identify the target or source address/port for sent or received messages respectively. Data is encapsulated directly in the UDP datagrams without an additional protocol layer. As soon as a UDP message is sent, the associated send WR is marked as complete. Incoming UDP datagrams, from either another QP or a socket, consume a WR in the destination QP.

For reliable communication using TCP, a connection is established between two QPs using the same rendezvous model as sockets, avoiding the need to define a new connect protocol (sec. 12 of [17]). The server application instructs the interface to monitor a TCP port for incoming connections. The client creates a QP, binds it to a TCP port, and initiates a connection to the server that mates the connection to an idle QP in the server application. Connection establishment uses standard SYN-ACK state processing of TCP. However, the handshake is handled in the interface with the host only being notified when the connection is established. When a send WR is posted, the message data is encapsulated into TCP segments for delivery to the target QP. This WR completes when all the data for that message is acknowledged by the destination.

Identifying message boundaries in the TCP byte stream for QP-to-QP communication can be accomplished in a variety of ways and we explore one method in section 4. For QP-to-socket connections, there is no framing information available, thus the application may have to reassemble individual segments into a complete message.

The CQ mechanism in QPIP performs the same functionality as the select() system call for traditional interfaces. However, the CQ is the primary mechanism for detecting completions and is not optional.

3.1. Organization

The QPIP network interface provides the core functionality of the QPIP architecture. Its operation can be broken down into four logical finite state machines (FSMs) as shown in Figure 1. A common data structure is used to maintain the state of the individual QPs and includes the inter-network protocol specific information, namely the TCP transmission control block (TCB). The doorbell FSM, a key concept from the VI Architecture and implicit in Infiniband, continuously monitors the QP notification mechanisms and updates the state table with the number of outstanding WRs in the queue. The management FSM processes privileged commands from the host operating system. These include QP/CQ creation and removal, establishment of registered memory bindings and QP connection management.

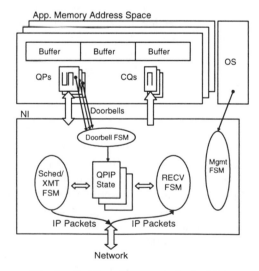

Figure 1. The QPIP organization.

250

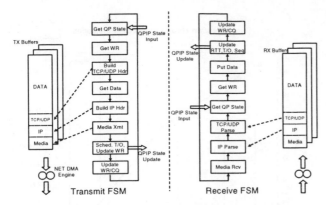

Figure 2. QPIP transmit and receive state machines and data structures.

The other two state machines form the communication core, as illustrated in detail in Figure 2. The transmit finite state machine serves as the scheduler and transmit control path. The state machine polls all active communication endpoints for outstanding data that needs to be sent. In the case of TCP, it additionally monitors for timeout/retransmit events pending on a QP. If a transmit or retransmit operation needs to occur, the state machine services the endpoint. It obtains and parses the appropriate work request from the QP, identifies the data to send, and then builds the necessary TCP/UDP and IP headers. Once a packet is formatted, it is encapsulated in a link layer header and pushed into the network. For TCP, the state machine sets the necessary timeout events and updates the TCB state in the QPIP state table. Finally, any status updates are posted back to the WR and the associated QP. Unless there is an error, TCP based communication will not post completion updates at this stage, as this will be done when a packet is acknowledged.

The receive state machine operates in the reverse fashion. It is invoked whenever a packet arrives from the network. Of note, a pure TCP acknowledgement is simply a special case of a regular data receive operation, except that no data is delivered to the application. Instead, the WR that *sent* the data being acknowledged is updated with a completion status and an appropriate token entered into its completion queue.

4. QPIP Prototype

We have implemented a functioning QPIP prototype on a PCI based system with a widely used SAN. On this prototype, we have conducted basic performance benchmarks and compared them to existing network implementations. We also evaluated performance in the context of the Network Block Device storage application.

4.1. Design

The prototype uses the Myrinet SAN with the LANai 9 programmable network interface as the QPIP intelligent NIC. The interface has a 133 MHz general purpose RISC processor, 2 megabytes of on-board SRAM, two PCI DMA engines and 2 network transfer engines (send and receive). The network itself is switched and uses source-based, oblivious cut-through routing. Individual links operate at 2.0 Gbs (full-duplex) and support arbitrary sized MTUs. The DMA controller hardware includes support for computing IP checksums and has a specialized doorbell mechanism where writes to a region of PCI address space are stored in a FIFO in the interface SRAM. The programmable nature of this interface permitted quick prototyping and could be instrumented to provide performance details.

The implementation consists of three major software components: a kernel driver, an application software library and the network interface firmware. The kernel driver provides basic hardware initialization and mechanisms for mapping address space and translating virtual to physical addresses for registered buffers. It also provides a lightweight interrupt service routine to process events. The library provides the basic communication methods - PostSend(), PostRecv(), Poll() and Wait() - as well as communication management functions. Internal details of the QP and CQ structures are hidden from the application by the library. These structures are resident in host memory and are accessed by the NIC through DMA. The library methods can be used both in the kernel and directly at user level. The network interface firmware provides the core functionality of the QPIP architecture. It implements the four state machines and data structures as outlined in the previous section and provides a functional subset of the QP operations and inter-network protocols. It supports the send-receive class of QP messaging in both unreliable (UDP) and reliable (TCP) delivery modes. It also includes a facility for translating virtual addresses in WRs to physical addresses for use in DMA transactions.

Underneath the QP abstraction, the firmware implements a subset of the TCP, UDP and IPv6 standard protocols. The implementations are based on existing inter-network protocol stacks to shorten development time and ensure correctness. The protocol subsets are sufficient to provide meaningful comparisons with existing implementations under common-case network conditions in the SAN environment. Specifically, we assume the network to be robust and packet loss or reordering seldom occurs. The common-cases are specifically those that meet the header prediction requirements as presented in [32].

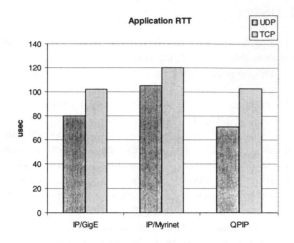

Figure 3. Application-to-Application round trip time.

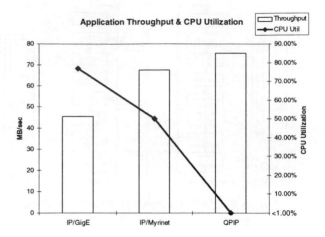

Figure 4. Application-to-application throughput and CPU utilization.

The IPv6 protocol layer is based on the FreeBSD v4.x distribution and provides support for basic connectivity. Address resolution is provided by a static table that maps IPv6 addresses to switch routes. We chose the IPv6 protocol as we believe it reflects the next generation of network systems. Although we don't explore fragmentation issues, the IPv6 standard supports only end-to-end fragmentation which is better suited to hardware based protocol implementations.

The UDP and TCP implementations are based on those found in [6, 32]. The UDP protocol is fully functional. Unreliable QP messages are encapsulated directly in UDP datagrams for transmission over the network. The TCP stack implements RTT estimation, window management, and congestion and flow control mechanisms. It also includes RFC 1323 time-stamp and window scaling performance enhancements. Support for out-of-order reassembly or urgent data was not included. For this prototype, we chose to map QP messages one-for-one onto TCP segments (i.e. a segment *is* a message). This mapping is fairly straightforward to implement and does not require additional information to be included in the packets. The tradeoff being that the TCP segments are arbitrarily sized and performance could suffer if subsequent IP fragments are lost. However, in the SAN environment, loss is expected to be minimal and the benefits of this simple mapping can be exploited.

4.2. Performance

Analysis of the QPIP prototype was conducted using Dell Poweredge 6350 servers (4x550MHz Pentium-III processors, 1GB of physical RAM and a 64-bit/33MHz PCI bus) running Linux version 2.4. Installed on the I/O bus were the Myrinet LANai 9 NIC and an Intel Pro1000 Gigabit Server Adapter.

4.2.1. Basic communication benchmarks. The basic communication benchmarks included application to application round-trip time (RTT) and throughput. The round-trip time refers to the latency of a single 1 byte message to travel from one application to another and back. Throughput is the maximum sustainable bandwidth between two applications. We compare the QPIP results with the Linux host-based IPv4 stack running over Gigabit Ethernet (1500 Byte MTU) and the Myrinet adapter running Myricom's GM v.1.4 software (9000 Byte MTU). Due to an artifact of the Myrinet hardware, the QPIP prototype cannot exploit hardware assisted IP checksums on the receive side. As we are interested in a high-level comparison of the architecture, the results in the figures were obtained using an emulated hardware IP checksum on the receive-side. For completeness, we also report the results obtained using firmware based checksumming.

Figure 3 presents the RTT comparison for the three implementations for both TCP and UDP protocols. Using a firmware checksum, the QPIP latency is 73µsec (UDP) and 113 µsec (TCP). We perform a closer analysis of the RTT later in this section.

Throughput results were derived from the *ttcp* (v1.4) benchmark. The tests involved a 10MB transfer in 16KB chunks with the TCP_NODELAY option set. Figure 4 presents the throughput and CPU utilization results for the three implementations using native MTUs (16KB in the case of QPIP). Using a firmware based checksum on the QPIP prototype, the throughput is 26.4 MB/sec (<1% utilization). For the native MTU case the QPIP prototype outperforms the other implementations at 75.6 MB/sec with <1% CPU utilization when the other inter-network implementations consume half to ¾ of a host processor. For the smaller MTUs, the limited CPU capacity of the interface becomes apparent and performs 22% less than the gigabit Ethernet in the 1500 Byte MTU case at 35.4 MB/sec. For the 9000 Byte MTU, QPIP outperforms the IP over Myrinet case at 70.1 MB/sec. In both cases the CPU utilization in the QPIP prototype is <1% thus exhibiting the lightweight nature of the interface.

4.2.2. Overhead analysis. Table 1 presents the send and receive host overhead for a 1 byte message using TCP for the host-based and QPIP implementations The overhead for the host-based inter-network stack was determined by measuring RTT through the loopback interface on an individual host. These results are a lower bound on overhead for a message sent through the host-based network stack because they do not include instructions executed by a particular interface driver. The QPIP overhead measurements were determined by directly timing the associated communication methods from user-space.

Table 1. Host overhead for transmit and receive paths.

	Time (µsec)	Cycles
Host-based IP	29.9	16445
QPIP	2.5	1386

One of the potential bottlenecks of offloading inter-network protocols is how much time is occupied in the network interface for protocol processing. Tables 2 & 3 present an occupancy breakdown for the transmit and receive side TCP processing, respectively, for the QPIP prototype. The measurements were made using the LANai 9 cycle counter and assume a hardware assisted IP checksum on the receive side as described above. There are different processing costs depending on whether the message is data or an acknowledgement (ACK). On the transmit side, an ACK is simply a special case of a data send. On the receive side, an ACK causes RTT estimators and other state to be updated which invokes other processing costs.

For the receive side ACK processing, parsing the TCP header induces a high processing cost because of a series of multiply operations for the RTT estimators. The LANai 9 processor has no hardware multiply, thus these operations are implemented in software. A more specialized interface design would dramatically reduce these costs.

4.2.3. Network storage application. The Network Block Device (NBD) is a client-server application where client block I/O requests are forwarded to a server that emulates a network attached disk (Figure 5). NBD is distributed as

Table 2. Transmit side network interface processing costs.

Stage	Data Send Time (µsec)	ACK Send Time (µsec)
Doorbell Process	1	1
Schedule	2	2
Get WR	5.5	-
Get Data	4.5	-
Build TCP Hdr	5	5
Build IP Hdr	1	1
Send	1	1
Update	1.5	1.5

Table 3. Receive side network interface processing costs.

Stage	Data Recv Time (µsec)	ACK Recv Time (µsec)
Doorbell Process	1	1
Media Rcv	1	1
IP Parse	1.5	1.5
TCP Parse	7	14
Get WR	5.5	-
Put Data	4.5	-
Update	1.5	9 (WR and QP State)

part of the Linux kernel and includes a client-side driver and user-level server application. We modified both to use QPIP (Figure 6) and compared client performance to the sockets-based implementation. The benchmark was a 409 MB sequential read and write over an ext2 file system. Writes were flushed to disk using 'sync' and the device was un-mounted between reads to invalidate the client buffer cache. For the QPIP implementation a 9000 Byte MTU was used. Figure 7 presents the results for throughput and CPU efficiency (in MBytes transferred per CPU-second). The QPIP based NBD provides a 40% to 137% throughput performance improvement at up to 133% better CPU effectiveness. Note, for all three implementations, the raw CPU utilization during the benchmark is at least 26% for filesystem processing. For QPIP, none of this is associated with the TCP/IP stack as this is entirely within the adapter.

Integrating the QP interface into NBD was straightforward and proved simpler than the socket implementation by eliminating multiple socket calls and OS specific wrappers to enable kernel-level socket operation.

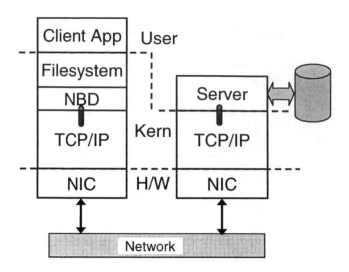

Figure 5: Socket based NBD. Dashed lines represent the user, kernel and hardware boundaries

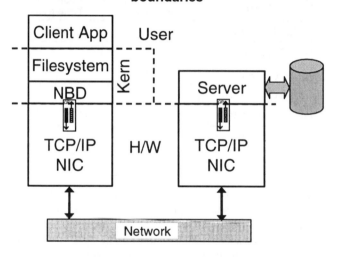

Figure 6: QPIP based NBD.

5. Analysis

The QPIP prototype demonstrates the feasibility of achieving a low-overhead interface to IP based networks using the QP abstraction. In this section we present the lessons learned and the implications they have for both inter-network protocols and industry proposed SAN standards such as Infiniband.

5.1. Implications for inter-network protocols

Employing the QP abstraction as the communication interface to inter-network protocols has distinct advantages. First, it provides a virtualized, protected channel from the application to the network that enables tighter integration with the host platform [26]. It also provides the ability to exploit cache coherency

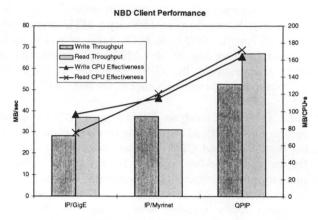

Figure 7. NBD client throughput and CPU effectiveness.

mechanisms. For example, applications polling a CQ can spin in the processor cache, as opposed to un-cached accesses across the memory bus. The QP interface directly extends to kernel based applications, as well, without complex software wrappers.

Second, using the QP communication abstraction greatly simplifies the buffer management schemes of the protocol implementation. In traditional systems, the protocol stack in conjunction with the operating system uses mechanisms, such as *mbufs* or *fbufs*, to reduce buffer size and management overhead. The QP model eliminates these complex schemes through straightforward direct data placement. Also, the QP model provides a transparent method of dynamically tuning the receiver window: the more receive buffer space posted, the larger the TCP receive window the sender can utilize. With sockets, adjusting these parameters requires system calls and/or setting OS specific variables.

Third, QPIP also simplifies the mechanisms for scheduling transmit and receive operations. Host based inter-network stacks are dependent on the use of the operating system scheduler. Operating system schedulers must support several types of services which tend to introduce complexity. By placing the inter-network stack beneath the QP in an intelligent interface, the scheduling mechanism can be tailored to meet the needs of the network; effectively an inter-network runtime system. This is indicated in Table 2 by the short scheduling overhead relative to other processing components on the NI.

Finally, QPIP demonstrates that employing an alternative interface to inter-networks enables significant gains for network based I/O. The QP interface provides a simple bridge between common I/O abstractions and network protocols. It is able to take advantage of zero-copy mechanisms and offloaded processing without the constraints of using a sockets interface.

5.2. Implications for System Area Networks

In terms of SAN standards, the QPIP architecture demonstrates a practical means of merging established protocols with a modern SAN usage abstraction to achieve low latency, low overhead and high bandwidth. In our prototype, most of the latency is due to high network interface occupancy as a result of modest hardware support. Even so, it is capable of producing performance comparable if not better than established host based stacks. SAN proposals, such as Infiniband, engineer a high degree of specialized hardware support in the interface. This includes special protocol engines and direct attachment to the host memory subsystem. Functionally, the processing required from native Infiniband protocols would be little different than that in TCP/UDP or IP. Thus, if the same degree of hardware support were to be applied to QPIP then an equivalent performance could be reached. From our prototype results, key areas for hardware support include lightweight doorbell mechanisms, IP checksums, UDP/TCP connection de-multiplexing and advanced mathematical functions.

With respect to Infiniband in particular, QPIP introduces some benefits over the existing specification. First it employs a simple set of packet formats for communication. There is no distinction between packet formats for inter and intra subnet packets. This simplifies protocol processing and enables a straightforward method to bridge the SAN to external networks as described in section 3. It also brings the collection of well-understood transport mechanisms and behaviors to the SAN that do not exist in the present specification. These mechanisms could either be end-to-end or could include network-based mechanisms such as RED or ECN. Inter-network protocols do not bar the use of intelligence in the SAN fabric that can improve performance.

6. Conclusions and Future Work

The integration of the network as a first-class citizen in system architectures presents unique challenges for SAN design. The network must be capable of meeting the demands of low latency, low overhead and high bandwidth. Inter-network architectures, which have been very successful because of their flexibility and open development, are perceived to be unable to meet such demands. Thus, efforts to develop a new standard SAN architecture, such as Infiniband, have focused on completely re-engineering network stacks including the abstraction, transport layer and network layer. The QPIP

architecture is based on the premise that standard inter-networks *are* capable of performing in the SAN. By adopting the lightweight queue pair interface of the Infiniband specification and using this as the interface to IP networks, host overhead is significantly reduced while simultaneously enabling efficient offload of the protocol stack. Results from our prototype demonstrate that, with modest hardware, latency and bandwidth equivalent to modern inter-network implementations on powerful processors can be achieved at a fraction of the overhead. Further, our results suggest that applying the degree of hardware support expected for Infiniband to QPIP, similar performance targets of latency and throughput can be achieved. While tailored hardware can deliver performance, we also note that a programmable aspect to the interface is also important for higher level operations. It allows for changes as inter-network protocols continually evolve and introduce new functionality and permits for a degree of flexibility in terms of scheduling and monitoring.

7. Acknowledgements

The authors thank Alan Mainwaring and Kevin Fall for their support and guidance. This work was supported by Intel Corporation, Compaq Corporation, Microsoft Corporation, DARPA contract no. N66001-99-2-8913, LLNL Memorandum Agreement no. B504962 under DOE contract No. W-7405-ENG-48, NSF Infrastructure Grant no. EIA-9802069 and by NASA contract no. NAGII-1210. The information presented here does not necessarily reflect the position of the Government and no official endorsement should be inferred.

8. References

[1] M. B. Abbott and L. L. Peterson, "Increasing network throughput by integrating protocol layers," *IEEE/ACM Transactions on Networking*, vol. 1, pp. 600-10, 1993.
[2] Alacritech Inc., "Alacritech, Inc.," http://www.alacritech.com, 2001.
[3] P. Barford and M. Crovella, "Critical path analysis of TCP transactions," *IEEE/ACM Transactions on Networking*, vol. 9, pp. 238-48, 2001.
[4] T. Blackwell, "Speeding up protocols for small messages," *Proceedings of ACM SIGCOMM '96*, ACM, Stanford, CA, USA, 1996.
[5] T. Braun and C. Diot, "Protocol implementation using integrated layer processing," *Proceedings of ACM SIGCOMM '95*, ACM, Cambridge, MA, USA, 1995.
[6] D. Comer and D. L. Stevens, *Internetworking with TCP/IP*, 2nd ed. Englewood Cliffs, N.J.: Prentice Hall, 1991.
[7] E. C. Cooper, P. A. Steenkiste, R. D. Sansom, and B. D. Zill, "Protocol implementation on the Nectar communication processor," *Proceedings of ACM SIGCOMM '90*, ACM, Philadelphia, PA, USA, 1990.

[8] C. Dalton, G. Watson, D. Banks, C. Calamvokis, A. Edwards, and J. Lumley, "Afterburner (network-independent card for protocols)," *IEEE Network*, vol. 7, pp. 36-43, 1993.

[9] B. S. Davie, "A host-network interface architecture for ATM," *Proceedings of ACM SIGCOMM '91*,ACM, Zurich, Switzerland, 1991.

[10] P. Druschel and L. L. Peterson, "Fbufs: a high-bandwidth cross-domain transfer facility," *Proceedings of 14th ACM Symposium on Operating Systems Principles*,ACM, Ashville, NC, USA, 1993.

[11] P. Druschel, L. L. Peterson, and B. S. Davie, "Experiences with a high-speed network adaptor: A software perspective," *Proceedings of ACM SIGCOMM '94*,ACM, London, UK, 1994.

[12] C. Dubnicki, L. Iftode, E. W. Felten, and L. Kai, "Software support for virtual memory-mapped communication," *Proceedings of IPPS '96.*,IEEE Comput. Soc. Press, Honolulu, HI, USA, 1996.

[13] A. Edwards and S. Muir, "Experiences implementing a high performance TCP in user-space," *Proceedings of ACM SIGCOMM '95*,ACM, Cambridge, MA, USA, 1995.

[14] A. Edwards, G. Watson, J. Lumley, D. Banks, C. Calamvokis, and C. Dalton, "User-space protocols deliver high performance to applications on a low-cost Gb/s LAN," *Proceedings of ACM SIGCOMM '94*,ACM, London, UK, 1994.

[15] Emulex Corporation, "Emulex Corporation," http://www.emulex.com, 2001.

[16] A. Gallatin, J. Chase, and K. Yocum, "Trapeze/IP: TCP/IP at near-gigabit speeds," *Proceedings of the FREENIX Track. 1999 USENIX Annual Technical Conference Proceedings of the FREENIX Track. 1999 USENIX Annual Technical Conference*,USENIX Assoc., Monterey, CA, USA, 1999.

[17] Infiniband Trade Assoc, "Infiniband Architecture Specification, Release 1.0," vol. Vol 1: Infiniband Trade Assoc. (http://www.infinibandta.org), 2000.

[18] iReady Corporation, "iReady Corporation," http://www.iready.com, 2001.

[19] V. Jacobson, R. Braden, and D. Borman, "TCP Extensions for High Performance," *RFC 1323*, 1992.

[20] J. Kay and J. Pasquale, "The importance of non-data touching processing overheads in TCP/IP," *Proceedings of ACM SIGCOMM '93*,ACM, San Francisco, CA, USA, 1993.

[21] J. Kay and J. Pasquale, "Profiling and reducing processing overheads in TCP/IP," *IEEE/ACM Transactions on Networking*, vol. 4, pp. 817-28, 1996.

[22] J. Kay and J. Pasquale, "A summary of TCP/IP networking software performance for the DECstation 5000," *Proceedings of 1993 ACM Sigmetrics Conference on Measurement and Modeling of Computer Systems*,ACM, Santa Clara, CA, USA, 1993.

[23] A. M. Mainwaring and D. E. Culler, "Design challenges of virtual networks: fast, general-purpose communication," *Proceedings of Seventh ACM SIGPLAN Symposium on Principles and Practice of Parallel Programming*,ACM, Atlanta, GA, USA, 1999.

[24] Microsoft Corporation, "Winsock Direct Path," Microsoft Corporation (http://www.microsoft.com), 2000.

[25] D. Mosberger, L. L. Peterson, P. G. Bridges, and S. O'Malley, "Analysis of techniques to improve protocol processing latency," *Proceedings of ACM SIGCOMM '96*,ACM, Stanford, CA, USA, 1996.

[26] S. S. Mukherjee and M. D. Hill, "Making network interfaces less peripheral," *Computer*, vol. 31, pp. 70-6, 1998.

[27] S. Pakin, M. Lauria, and A. Chien, "High performance messaging on workstations: Illinois fast messages (FM) for Myrinet," *Proceedings of SC '95*,ACM, San Diego, CA, USA, 1995.

[28] D. Perkovic and P. J. Keleher, "Responsiveness without interrupts," *Proceedings of the 13th Association for Computer Machinery International Conference on Supercomputing*,ACM, Rhodes, Greece, 1999.

[29] I. Pratt and K. Fraser, "Arsenic: a user-accessible gigabit Ethernet interface," *Proceedings IEEE INFOCOM 2001. Conference on Computer Communications.*,IEEE, Anchorage, AK, USA, 2001.

[30] L. Prylli and B. Tourancheau, "BIP: a new protocol designed for high-performance networking on Myrinet," *Proceedings IPPS/SPDP '98*,Springer-Verlag, Orlando, FL, USA, 1998.

[31] E. Salo and J. Pinkerton, "Scheduled Transfers OS Bypass API," in *Proceedings of the November '98 HIPPI Ad Hoc Working Meeting*. Mountain View, CA: http://www.hippi.org/cSTAPI.html, 1998.

[32] W. R. Stevens and G. R. Wright, *TCP/IP illustrated*. Reading, Mass.: Addison-Wesley Pub. Co., 1994.

[33] T. von Eicken, A. Basu, V. Buch, and W. Vogels, "U-Net: a user-level network interface for parallel and distributed computing," *Proceedings of Fifteenth AC Symposium on Operating Systems Principles*,ACM, Copper Mountain Resort, CO, USA, 1995.

[34] T. von Eicken, D. E. Culler, S. C. Goldstein, and K. E. Schauser, "Active messages: a mechanism for integrated communication and computation," *Proceedings of ISCA '92. 19th Annual International Symposium on Computer Architecture*,ACM, Gold Coast, Qld., Australia, 1992.

[35] G. Watson, D. Banks, C. Calamvokis, C. Dalton, A. Edwards, and J. Lumley, "AAL5 at a gigabit for a kilobuck," *Journal of High Speed Networks*, vol. 3, pp. 127-45, 1994.

Experiences with VI Communication for Database Storage

Yuanyuan Zhou[1], Angelos Bilas[2], Suresh Jagannathan[1], Cezary Dubnicki[1], James F. Philbin[1], and Kai Li[3]

[1]Emphora Inc.,
4 Independence Way,
Princeton, NJ–08540, USA

[2]Department of Electrical and
Computer Engineering,
10 King's College Road,
University of Toronto, Toronto,
Ontario M5S3G4, Canada

[3]Department of Computer Science,
35 Olden Street,
Princeton University,
Princeton, NJ–08544, USA

ABSTRACT

This paper examines how VI–based interconnects can be used to improve I/O path performance between a database server and the storage subsystem. We design and implement a software layer, DSA, that is layered between the application and VI. DSA takes advantage of specific VI features and deals with many of its shortcomings. We provide and evaluate one kernel–level and two user–level implementations of DSA. These implementations trade transparency and generality for performance at different degrees, and unlike research prototypes are designed to be suitable for real–world deployment. We present detailed measurements using a commercial database management system with both micro-benchmarks and industrial database workloads on a mid–size, 4 CPU, and a large, 32 CPU, database server.

Our results show that VI–based interconnects and user–level communication can improve all aspects of the I/O path between the database system and the storage back-end. We also find that to make effective use of VI in I/O intensive environments we need to provide substantial additional functionality than what is currently provided by VI. Finally, new storage APIs that help minimize kernel involvement in the I/O path are needed to fully exploit the benefits of VI–based communication.

1 INTRODUCTION

User–level communication architectures have been the subject of recent interest because of their potential to reduce communication related overheads. Because they allow direct access to the network interface without going through the operating system, they offer applications the ability to use customized, user–level I/O protocols. Moreover, user–level communication architectures allow data to be transferred between local and remote memory buffers without operating system and processor intervention, by means of DMA engines. These features have been used with success in improving the performance and scalability of parallel scientific applications. The Virtual Interface (VI) architecture [10] is a well–known, industry–wide standard for system area networks based on these principles that has spawned a

number of initiatives, such as the Direct Access File Systems (DAFS) [11], that target other important domains.

In this paper, we study the feasibility of leveraging VI–based communication to improve I/O performance and scalability for storage–centric applications and in particular database applications executing real–world online transaction processing loads. An important issue in database systems is the overhead of processing I/O operations. For realistic on–line transaction processing (OLTP) database loads, I/O can account for a significant percentage of total execution time [26]. Achieving high transaction rates, however, can only be realized by reducing I/O overheads on the host CPU and providing more CPU cycles for transaction processing. For this reason, storage architectures strive to reduce costs in the I/O path between the database system and the disk subsystem.

In this work we are primarily interested in examining the effect of user–level communication on block I/O performance for database applications. We focus on improving the I/O path from the database server to storage by using VI–based interconnects. High–performance database systems typically use specialized storage area networks (SANs), such as Fibre Channel (FC), for the same purpose. We propose an alternative storage architecture called VI–attached Volume Vault (V3) that consists of a storage cluster which communicate with one or more database servers using VI. Each V3 storage node in our cluster is a commodity PC consisting of a collection of low–cost disks, large memory, a VI–enabled network interface, and one or more processors. V3 is designed for real–world deployment in next generation database storage systems, and as such addresses issues dealing with reliability, fault-tolerance, and scalability that would not necessarily be considered in a research prototype. V3 has also been deployed and tested in customer sites.

Because VI does not deal with a number of issues that are important for storage applications, we design a new block-level I/O module, DSA (Direct Storage Access), that is layered between the application and VI (Figure 1). DSA uses a custom protocol to communicate with the actual storage server, the details of which are beyond the scope of this paper. DSA takes advantage of specific VI features and addresses many of its shortcomings with respect to I/O–

intensive applications and in particular databases. DSA exploits RDMA capabilities and incurs low overheads for initiating I/O operations and accessing the network interface. More importantly, DSA deals with issues not addressed by VI. For example, VI does not provide flow control, is not suited for applications with large numbers of communication buffers or large numbers of asynchronous events, and most existing VI implementations do not provide strong reliability guarantees. In addition, although certain VI features such as RDMA can benefit even kernel–level, legacy APIs, the current VI specification is not well–suited for this purpose.

We evaluate three different implementations of DSA, one kernel–level implementation and two user-level that trade transparency and generality for performance at different degrees. We present detailed measurements using a commercial database management system, Microsoft *SQL Server 2000*, with both micro-benchmarks and industrial database workloads (*TPC–C*) on a mid size (4 CPU) and a large (32 CPU) database server with up to 12 TB of disk storage.

Our results show that:

1. Effective use of VI in I/O intensive environments requires substantial modifications and enhancements to flow control, reconnection, interrupt handling, memory registration, and lock synchronization.

2. VI–based interconnects and user–level communication can improve all aspects of the I/O path between the database system and the storage back-end and result in transaction rate improvements of up to 18% for large database configurations.

3. New storage APIs that help minimize kernel involvement in the I/O path are needed to fully exploit the benefits of VI–based communication.

The rest of the paper is organized as follows. Section 2 presents the V3 architecture and the various DSA implementations. Section 3 presents our performance optimizations for DSA. Section 4 presents our experimental platforms and Sections 5 and 6 discuss our results. Finally, we present related work in Section 7 and draw our conclusions in Section 8.

2 SYSTEM ARCHITECTURE

To study feasibility and design issues in using user–level communication for database storage, we define a new storage architecture that allows us to attach a storage back-end to database systems through a VI interconnect. This section provides a brief overview of the VI-attached Volume Vault (V3) architecture and then focuses on DSA and its implementations.

2.1 V3 Architecture

Figure 1 shows the overall V3 architecture. A V3 system consists of database servers (V3 clients) and storage nodes

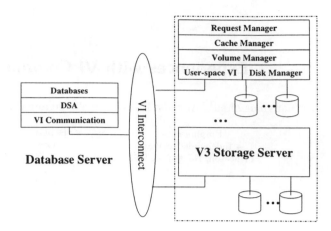

Figure 1: V3 Architecture overview.

(V3 servers). Client configurations can vary from small–scale uniprocessor and SMP systems to large–scale multiprocessor servers. Clients connect to V3 storage nodes through the VI interconnect.

Each V3 server provides a virtualized view of a disk (V3 volume). To support industrial workloads and to avoid single points of failure, each V3 server node has redundant components (power supplies, system disks, network interfaces, etc.). Each V3 volume consists of one or more physical disks attached to V3 storage nodes. V3 volumes can span multiple V3 nodes using combinations of RAID, such as concatenation and other disk organizations. With current disk technologies, a single V3 volume can provide more than 2 TB of storage. Since existing VI networks support a large number of nodes (up to 128), a multi–node V3 back-end can provide more than 250 TB of storage. V3 uses large main memories as disk buffer caches to help reduce disk latencies [31].

While the V3 back-end can provide storage to any application, it is designed specifically with database applications in mind. A V3 server is structured differently from a typical disk subsystem. It is controlled by custom software (Figure 1) that includes several modules: a request manager, a cache manager, a volume manager, and a disk manager. The server employs a lightweight pipeline structure for the I/O path that avoids synchronization overheads and allows large numbers of I/O requests to be serviced concurrently. The V3 server code runs at user level and communicates with clients with user–level, VI primitives. Because the focus of this work is on the feasibility of using VI for database storage, we do not elaborate further on V3's internal structure, although we refer to its properties when appropriate.

2.2 DSA Implementations

Direct Storage Access (DSA) is a client-side, block-level I/O module specification that is layered between the application and VI. DSA deals with issues not supported in VI but are necessary for supporting storage I/O intensive applications and takes advantage of VI-specific features.

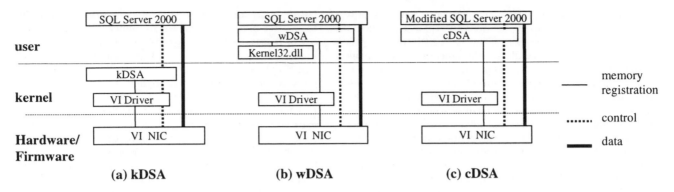

Figure 2: The I/O path in each of our three DSA implementations.

The new features provided by DSA include flow control, retransmission and reconnection that are critical for industrial–strength systems, and performance optimizations for alleviating high-cost operations in VI. DSA's flow control mechanism allows for large numbers of outstanding requests and manages client and server buffers appropriately to avoid overflow errors. DSA includes optimizations for memory registration and deregistration, interrupt handling, and lock synchronization issues to minimize their performance impact. These issues are discussed in greater detail in Section 3.

DSA takes advantage of a number of VI features. It uses direct access to remote memory (RDMA) to reduce overheads in transferring both data and control information. I/O blocks are transferred between the server cache and application (database) buffers without copying. Issuing I/O operations can be done with a few instructions directly from the application without kernel involvement. Moreover, I/O request completion can happen directly from the V3 server with RDMA. Finally, DSA takes advantage of the low packet processing overhead in the NIC and allows for large numbers of overlapping requests to maximize I/O throughput even at small block sizes.

We discuss one kernel and two user–level implementations of DSA. Our kernel–level implementation is necessary to support storage applications on top of VI-based interconnects by using existing operating system APIs. Our user–level implementations allow storage applications to take advantage of user–level communication. Figure 2 shows the I/O path for each DSA implementation. The I/O path includes three basic steps: (i) register memory, (ii) post read or write request, and (iii) transfer data. Next, we briefly discuss each implementation.

Kernel–level Implementation: To leverage the benefits of VI in kernel–level storage APIs we provide a kernel–level implementation of DSA (*kDSA*). *kDSA* is implemented on top of a preliminary kernel–level version of the VI specification [10] provided by Giganet [17]. The API exported by *kDSA* is the standard I/O interface defined by Windows for kernel storage drivers. Thus, our kernel–level implementation for DSA can support any existing user–level or kernel–level application without any modification. *kDSA* is built

as a thin monolithic driver to reduce the overhead of going through multiple layers of software. Alternative implementations, where performance is not the primary concern, can layer existing kernel modules, such as SCSI miniport drivers, on top of *kDSA* to take advantage of VI–based interconnects. In our work, we optimize the kernel VI layer for use with DSA. Our experience indicates that a number of issues, especially event completions are different from user–level implementations. In particular, we find that although kernel–level VI implementations can provide optimized paths for I/O completions, the user–level specification of the VI API [10] does not facilitate this approach.

User–level Implementations: To take advantage of the potential provided by user–level communication we also provide two implementations of DSA at user level. These implementations differ mainly in the API they export to applications.

wDSA is a user–level implementation of DSA that provides the Win32 API and replaces the Windows standard system library, `kernel32.dll`. *wDSA* filters and handles all I/O calls to V3 storage and forwards other calls to the native `kernel32.dll` library. *wDSA* supports the standard Windows I/O interface and therefore can work with applications that adhere to this standard API without modifications.

wDSA communicates with the V3 server at user–level and it eliminates kernel involvement for issuing I/O requests. Requests are directly initiated from application threads with standard I/O calls. *wDSA* still requires kernel involvement for I/O completion due to the semantics of `kernel32.dll` I/O calls. Since *wDSA* is unaware of application I/O semantics, it must trigger an application–specific event or schedule an application–specific callback function to notify the application thread for completions of I/O requests. Interrupts are used to receive notifications from VI for V3 server responses. Upon receiving an interrupt, *wDSA* completes the corresponding I/O request and notifies the application. Support for these mechanisms may involve extra system calls, eliminating many of the benefits of initiating I/O operations directly from user–level. Moreover, we find that implementing `kernel32.dll` semantics is non–trivial and makes *wDSA* prone to portability issues across different versions of Windows.

cDSA is a user–level implementation of DSA that provides a new I/O API to applications to exploit the benefits of VI–based communication. The new API consists primarily of 15 calls to handle synchronous or asynchronous read/write operations, I/O completions, and scatter/gather I/Os. Similarly to any customized approach, this implementation trades off transparency for performance. The new *cDSA* API avoids the overhead of satisfying the standard Win32 I/O semantics and hence is able to minimize the amount of kernel involvement, context switches, and interrupts. However, this approach requires cognizance of the database application's I/O semantics, and, in some cases, modification of the application to adhere to this new API.

The main feature of *cDSA* relevant to this work is an application–controlled I/O completion mode. Using the *cDSA* interface, applications choose either polling or interrupts as the completion mode for I/O requests. In polling mode, an I/O completion does not trigger any event or callback function, and the application explicitly polls the I/O request completion flag. *cDSA* updates the flag using RDMA directly from the storage node. By doing this, it can effectively reduce the number of system calls, context switches, and interrupts associated with I/O completions. An application can switch from polling to interrupt mode before going to sleep, causing I/O completions to be handled similarly to *wDSA*.

To evaluate *cDSA* we use a slightly modified version of Microsoft *SQL Server 2000*. This version of *SQL Server 2000* replaces the Win32 API with the new API provided by *cDSA*. Since the completion flags in the *cDSA* API are also part of the Win32 API, the modifications to *SQL Server 2000* are minor. We note that *cDSA* also supports more advanced features, such as caching and prefetching hints for the storage server. These features are not used in our experiments and are beyond the scope of this paper.

3 SYSTEM OPTIMIZATIONS

In general, our experience shows that VI can be instrumental in reducing overheads in the I/O path. However, we have also encountered a number of challenging issues in using VI–based interconnects for database storage systems including memory registration and deregistration overhead, interrupt handling, and lock synchronization. To deal with these issues, we explore various optimizations for DSA and quantify their impact on performance in Section 6. Because *wDSA* must precisely implement the semantics defined by the Win32 API, opportunities for optimizations are severely limited and not all optimizations are possible. For this reason, we focus mostly on optimizations for *kDSA* and *cDSA*.

3.1 VI Registration and Deregistration

Memory registration and deregistration are expensive operations that impact performance dramatically when performed dynamically. I/O buffers in VI need to remain pinned until a transfer finishes. Current VI–enabled NICs have a limitation on how much memory they can register. For instance, the Giganet cLan card [17] we use allows 1

GB of outstanding registered buffers and takes about $10\mu s$ to register and deregister an 8K buffer. When the number of registered buffers exceeds this limit, the application needs to deregister memory and free resources on the NIC. The simple solution of pre–registering all I/O buffers at application startup cannot be applied in database systems, since they use large caches and require large numbers of I/O buffers. Given that we need to dynamically manage registered memory, previous work for user–level communication [8, 4] has shown how the NIC can collaborate with host–level software (either kernel or user–level) to manage large amounts of host memory. These solutions have been evaluated in cases where the working set of registered memory is small. However, database systems use practically all available I/O cache for issuing I/O operations so the expected hit ratio on the NIC translation table would be low. Moreover, in *SQL Server 2000* virtual to physical mappings can be changed by the application, providing no simple way to invalidate cached registrations without access to source code or interception of system calls.

In our work, we first optimize the existing VI code and we eliminate pinning and unpinning from the registration and deregistration paths. In *kDSA* the Windows I/O Manager performs these operations and passes pinned buffers to *kDSA*. In *cDSA* we use the Address Windowing Extensions (AWE) [22] to allocate the database server cache on physical memory. AWE is a feature of Windows for IA32 (x86) systems with large amounts of physical memory. The AWE extensions provide a simple API that applications can use to allocate physical memory and map it to their virtual address space. Applications can then access large amounts of physical memory by manually mapping the regions of interest to virtual addresses with low-overhead calls. Application memory allocated as AWE memory is always pinned.

Finally, we use a new optimization, called *batched deregistration* to reduce the average cost of deregistering memory. VI–enabled NICs usually register consecutive I/O buffers in successive locations in a NIC table. DSA uses extensions to the VI layer (kernel or user–level) to divide this NIC table into small regions of one thousand consecutive entries (4 MB worth of host memory). Instead of deregistering each I/O buffer when the I/O completes, we postpone buffer deregistration for a short period of time and deregister full regions with one operation when all buffers in the region have been completed. Thus, we perform one deregistration every one thousand I/O operations, practically eliminating the overhead of deregistration when I/O buffers are short-lived. Note that if a single buffer in a region is not used then the whole region will not be deregistered, consuming resources on the NIC. Finally, registration of I/O buffers cannot be avoided, unless we delay issuing the related I/O operation. For this reason, we register I/O buffers dynamically on every I/O.

3.2 Interrupts

Interrupts are used to notify the database host when an asynchronous I/O request completes. To improve performance, database systems issue large numbers of asynchronous I/O requests. In V3, when the database server receives a response from a V3 storage node, the DSA layer needs to notify the database application with a completion event. DSA uses interrupts to receive notifications for I/O responses from the NIC. As in most operating systems, interrupt cost is high on Windows, in the order of 5–10μs on our platforms. When there is a large number of outstanding I/Os, the total interrupt cost can be prohibitively high, in excess of 20–30% of the total I/O overhead on the host CPU. In this work, we use interrupt batching to reduce this cost as described next.

kDSA uses a novel scheme to batch interrupts. It observes the number of outstanding I/O requests in the I/O path and if this number exceeds a specified threshold it disables explicit interrupts for server responses. Thus, instead of using interrupts, *kDSA* checks synchronously for completed I/Os during issuing new I/O operations. Interrupts are re–enabled if the number of outstanding requests falls below a minimum threshold; this strategy avoids unnecessarily delaying the completion of I/O requests when there is a small number of outstanding I/Os. This method works extremely well in benchmarks where there is a large number of outstanding I/O operations, as is the case with most large–scale database workloads.

cDSA takes advantage of features in its API to reduce the number of interrupts required to complete I/O requests. Upon I/O completion, the storage server sets via RDMA a completion flag associated with each outstanding I/O operation. The database server polls these flags for a fixed interval. If the flag is not set within the polling interval, *cDSA* switches to waiting for an interrupt upon I/O completion and signals the database appropriately. Under heavy database workloads this scheme almost eliminate the number of interrupts for I/O completions.

3.3 Lock Synchronization

Using run–time profiling we find that a significant percentage of the database CPU is spent on lock synchronization in the I/O path. To reduce lock synchronization time we optimize the I/O request path to reduce the number of lock/unlock operations, henceforth called synchronization pairs. In *kDSA* we perform a single synchronization pair in the send path and a single synchronization pair in the receive path. However, besides *kDSA*, the Windows I/O Manager uses at least two more synchronization pairs in both the send and receive paths and VI uses two more, one for registration/deregistration and one for queuing/dequeuing. Thus, there is a total of about 8–10 synchronization pairs involved in the path of processing a single I/O request.

cDSA has a clear advantage with respect to locking, since it has control over the full path between the database server and the actual storage. The only synchronization pairs that are not in our control are the four in the VI layer. In *cDSA* we also lay out data structures carefully to minimize processor cache misses. Although it is possible to reduce the number of synchronization pairs in VI by replacing multiple fine–grain locks with fewer, coarser–grain locks, preliminary measurements show, that the benefits are not significant.

The main reason is that VI synchronization pairs are private to a single VI connection. Since DSA uses multiple VI connections to connect to V3 storage nodes, in realistic experiments this minimizes the induced contention.

4 EXPERIMENTAL PLATFORM

To cover a representative mix of configurations we use two types of platforms in our evaluation: a mid-size, 4–way and an aggressive, 32–way Intel–based SMP as our database servers. Tables 1 and 2 summarize the hardware and software configurations for the two platforms. The database system we use is Microsoft *SQL Server 2000*. Our mid-size database server configuration uses a system with four 700MHz Pentium II Xeon processors. Our large database server configuration uses an aggressive, 32–way SMP server with 800MHz Pentium II Xeon processors. The server is organized in eight nodes, each with four processors and 32 MB of third–level cache (total of 256 MB). The server has a total of 32 GB of memory organized in four memory modules. The four memory modules are organized in a uniform memory access architecture. Every pair of nodes and all memory modules are connected with a crossbar interconnect with a total of four crossbar interconnects for the four pairs of nodes.

Component	Mid–size	Large
CPU	4 x 700 MHz PII	32 x 800 MHz PII
Cache/CPU		
L1 (I/D)	8KB/8KB	8KB/8KB
L2 (Unified)	1MB	2MB
L3 (Unified)	N/A	32MB/Node
Memory	4 GB	32 GB
# PCI slots (66MHz, 64bit)	2	96
NICs	4 cLan	8 cLan
# Local Disks	176	640
Windows Version	2000 AS	XP
DBase Server	*SQL Server 2000*	*SQL Server 2000*
Database Size	1 TB	10 TB
# Warehouses	1,625	10,000

Table 1: Database host configuration summary for the mid–size and large database setups.

Each V3 storage server in our experimental setup contains two, 700 MHz Pentium II Xeon processors and 2–3 GB of memory. Each database server connects to a number of V3 nodes as specified in each experiment. In all our experiments, the same disks are either connected directly to the database server (in the local case), or to V3 storage nodes. Both the mid-size and the large configurations use a Giganet network [17] with one or more network interface cards (NICs) that plug in PCI–bus slots. The user–level communication system we use is an implementation of the VI Specification [13] provided by Giganet [17]. For communicating in the kernel, we use a kernel level implementation of a subset of the VI specification that was initially provided by Giganet and which we optimize for our system. In

Component	Mid–size	Large
# V3 Nodes	4	8
CPU	2 x 700 MHz PII	2 x 700 MHz PII
Cache/CPU L1 (I/D) L2 (Unified)	 8KB/8KB 1MB	 8KB/8KB 1MB
Memory/Node	2GB	3GB
V3 Cache/Node	1.6GB	2.4GB
Disk Type	SCSI, 18GB 10K RPM	FC, 18GB 15K RPM
Disk Controller	UltraSCSI 320	Mylex eXtreme RAID 3000 [23]
Total # Disks	60	640
Total Disk Space	1 TB	11.5 TB
Windows Version	2000 Workstation	2000 Workstation

Table 2: V3 server configuration summary for the mid–size and large database setups.

our setups, the maximum end-to-end user-level bandwidth of Giganet is about 110 MB/s and the one-way latency for a 64–bytes message is about 7 μs.

5 MICRO–BENCHMARK RESULTS

We use various workloads to investigate the base performance of V3 and the different DSA implementations. We first examine the overhead introduced by DSA compared to raw VI. Then we examine the performance of V3–based I/O when data is cached and finally we compare the performance of V3 against a configuration with local disks.

In our experiments, the V3 configuration uses two nodes, a single application client that runs our micro-benchmark and a single storage node that presents a virtual disk to the application client. The disk appears to the client as a local disk. The local case uses a locally-attached disk, without any V3 software. We use kDSA as representative of the DSA implementations, and comment on the others where appropriate. All configurations use the same server implementation.

We mainly present three types of statistics for various I/O request sizes: response times, throughput, and execution time breakdowns. The I/O request size is usually fixed in a given database configuration but may vary across database configurations. We use request sizes between 512 and 128K bytes, which cover all realistic I/O request sizes in databases. For these measurements, the cache block size is always set to 8 KB.

5.1 DSA Overhead

We first examine the overhead introduced by DSA compared to the raw VI layer (Figure 3). The raw VI latency test includes several steps: (1) the client registers a receive buffer; (2) the client sends a 64 bytes request to the server; (3) the server receives the request; (4) the server sends the data of requested sizes from a preregistered send buffer to the client using RDMA; (5) the client receives an interrupt

on the VI completion queue; (6) the client deregisters the receive buffer, and repeats. All these steps are necessary to use VI in the I/O path for database storage. In this experiment, we always use polling for incoming messages on the server and interrupts on the client. The reason is that, in general, polling at this level will occupy too much CPU time on the client (the database server) and can only be used in collaboration with the application. Therefore, besides the typical message packaging overhead and wire latency, the VI numbers shown in Figure 3 also include registration/deregistration cost (5-10 microseconds each) and interrupt cost on the client (5-10 microseconds).

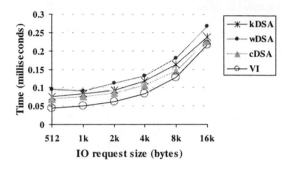

Figure 3: Latency of raw VI and DSA for various request sizes.

The V3 latency tests are measured by reading a data block from the storage server using each of the three DSA implementations. We see that V3 adds about 15–50 μs overhead on top of VI. This additional overhead varies among the different client implementations. cDSA has the least overhead, up to 15% better than kDSA, and up to 30% than wDSA because it incurs no kernel overhead in the I/O path. wDSA has up to 20% higher latency than kDSA. Since there is only one outstanding request in the latency test, optimizations like batching of deregistrations and interrupts are not helpful here.

To better understand the effect of using VI–based interconnects on database performance, we next examine the source of overhead in the different implementations. Figure 4 provides a breakdown of the DSA overhead as measured on the client side. This is the round–trip delay (response time) for a single, uncontended read I/O request as measured in the application. We instrument our code to provide a breakdown of the round–trip delay to the following components:

- CPU overhead is the overhead spent by the CPU to initiate and complete I/O operations. This overhead is incurred in full on the host CPU and is one of the most important factors in determining overall database system performance. Since database servers tend to issue a large number of I/O operations, high CPU overheads reduce the number of cycles available to handle client requests and degrade overall performance.

- Node–to–node latency includes the processing overhead

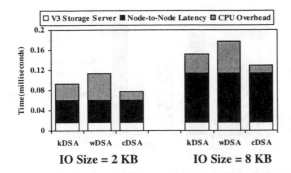

Figure 4: Response time breakdown for a read I/O request.

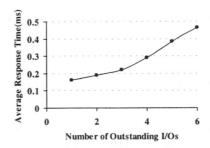

Figure 5: V3 read response time for cached blocks (8 KB requests).

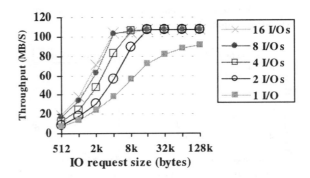

Figure 6: V3 read throughput for cached blocks.

at the NIC, the data transfers from memory over the PCI bus to the NIC at the sender the transfer over the network link, and the transfer from the NIC to memory at the receiver.

- *V3 server overhead* includes all processing related to caching, disk I/O, and communication overhead on the V3 server.

For smaller I/O sizes (2 KB), the cost of I/O processing on the storage server is about 20% of the total cost. For larger I/O sizes, e.g. 8 KB, where communication latency becomes more pronounced, storage server overheads as a percentage of the total cost decreases to about 9%. *cDSA* has the lowest CPU overhead among the three, with *wDSA* incurring nearly three times more overhead than *cDSA*. The primary reason is that *cDSA* does not have the requirement of satisfying the standard Windows I/O semantics and hence is able to minimize the amount of kernel involvement, context switches, and interrupts.

5.2 V3 Cached–block Performance

Next we examine the overhead of V3–based I/O with caching turned on. Since the local case does not have as much cache as a V3 system, we only present numbers for the V3 setup. Furthermore, since in database systems writes have to commit to disk we only examine cached read I/O performance.

Figure 5 shows the average response time for reading an 8 KB block from the V3 cache. When the number of outstanding requests is less than four the average response time increases slowly. Above this threshold, the average response time increases linearly and is a function of network queuing.

Figure 6 shows the V3 *read* throughput for different numbers of outstanding requests. With one outstanding request, the throughput reaches a maximum of about 90 MB/s with 128 KB requests. However, with more outstanding requests, the peak VI throughput of about 110 MB/s is reached at smaller request sizes. With four outstanding read requests, the VI interconnect is saturated even with 8 KB requests.

5.3 V3 vs. Local Case

Finally, we compare the performance of a V3–based I/O subsystem to the local case. For these experiments the V3 server cache size is set to zero and all V3 I/O requests are serviced from disks in the V3 server. In each workload all I/O operations are random.

Figure 7 shows that the V3 setup has similar random read response time as the local case when the read size is less than 64 KB. The extra overhead introduced by V3 is less than 3%. For larger I/O request sizes, however, V3 introduces higher overheads, which are proportional to the request size. For example, V3 has around 10% overhead for 128 KB reads because of increased data transfer time. In addition, the packet size in the cLan VI implementation is $64K - 64$ bytes. Therefore, to transfer 128 KB requires breaking the data to three VI RDMAs. Write response time behaves similarly, For request sizes up to 32 KB, V3 has response times similar to the local case. For larger request sizes, V3 is up to 10% slower due to network transfer time.

Figure 8 presents throughput results for 100% read and write workloads with two outstanding I/O operations. As mentioned above, with one outstanding request V3 adds 3-10% overhead compared to the local case. However, when the number of outstanding I/O requests increases, the throughput difference between a V3 volume and a local disk decreases due to pipelining (Figure 8). V3 can achieve the same *read* throughput as a local disk with two outstanding requests and the same *write* throughput with eight out-

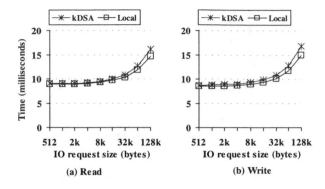

(a) Read **(b) Write**

Figure 7: V3 and local read and write response time (one outstanding request).

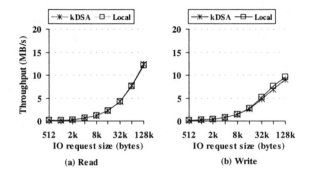

(a) Read **(b) Write**

Figure 8: V3 and local read and write throughput (two outstanding requests).

standing requests. Since databases always generate more than one outstanding requests to tolerate I/O latency, V3 can provide the same throughput as local disks even with a 0% cache hit ratio for realistic database loads.

6 OLTP RESULTS

Differences in simple latency and throughput tests cannot directly be translated to differences in database transaction rates since most commercial databases are designed to issue multiple concurrent I/Os and to tolerate high I/O response times and low–throughput disks. To investigate the impact of VI-attached storage on realistic applications we use *TPC–C*, a well known on-line transaction processing (OLTP) benchmark [28]. *TPC–C* simulates a complete computing environment where a population of users executes transactions against a database. The benchmark is centered around the principal activities of an order–entry environment. *TPC–C* involves a mix of concurrent transactions of different types and complexity, either executed on-line or queued for deferred execution. The I/O requests generated by *TPC–C* are random and they have a 70% read–30% write distribution. The performance of *TPC–C* is measured in transactions per minute (tpmC). Due to re-

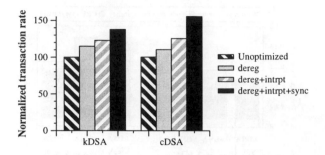

Figure 9: Effect of optimizations on tpmC for the large configuration. Results are normalized to the unoptimized case.

strictions imposed by the TPC council, we present relative tpmC numbers, normalized to the local case.

6.1 Large Database Configuration

To evaluate the impact of our approach on absolute performance and scalability of databases, we run *TPC–C* on an aggressive, state-of-the-art 32–processor database server. To keep up with CPU capacity we also use large database sizes and numbers of disks as shown in Table 2. The database working set size is around 1 TB, much larger than the aggregate cache size (about 52 GB) of the database server and the V3 storage server. In our experiments, there are 8 Giganet cLan NICs on the server, each connected to a single V3 storage node. Each V3 storage node has 80 physical disks locally attached, for a total of 640 disks (11.2 TB).

We first consider the impact of various optimizations on the *TPC–C* transaction rates for the large configuration for *kDSA* and *cDSA*. Figure 9 shows that these optimizations result in significant improvements on performance. Batched deregistration increases the transaction rate by about 15% for *kDSA* and 10% for *cDSA*. These benefits are mainly due to the fact that deregistration requires locking pages, which becomes more expensive at larger processor counts. Batching interrupts improves system performance by about 7% for *kDSA* and 14% for *cDSA*. The improvement for *cDSA* is larger because *SQL Server 2000* mostly uses polling for I/O completions under *cDSA*. Finally, reducing lock synchronization shows an improvement of about 12% for *kDSA* and about 24% for *cDSA*. Reducing lock synchronization has the largest performance impact in *cDSA* because *cDSA* can optimize the full I/O path from the database to the communication layer.

We next consider absolute database performance. Figure 10 shows the normalized *TPC–C* transaction rate for V3 and a Fibre Channel (FC) storage system; the results for V3 reflect optimizations in the *kDSA* and *cDSA* implementations. The FC device driver used in the local case is a highly optimized version provided by the disk controller vendor. We find that *kDSA* has competitive performance to the local case. *cDSA* performs 18% better than the local case. *wDSA* performs the worst, with a 22% lower transaction rate than *kDSA*. Figure 11 shows the execution time

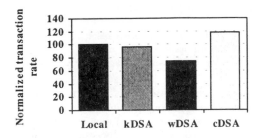

Figure 10: Normalized *TPC-C* transaction rates for the large configuration.

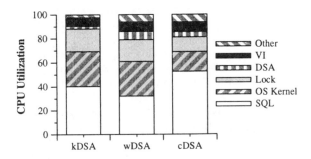

Figure 11: CPU utilization breakdown for *TPC-C* for the large configuration.

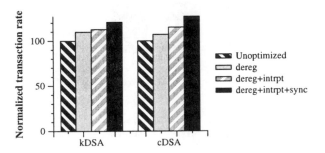

Figure 12: Effect of optimizations on tpmC for the mid-size configuration.

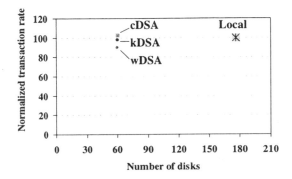

Figure 13: Normalized *TPC-C* transaction rate for the mid-size configuration.

breakdown on the database host for the three client implementations. We do not present the exact breakdown for the local case because it was measured by the hardware vendor and we are limited in the information we can divulge by licensing agreements. However, *kDSA* is representative of the local case. CPU utilization is divided into six categories: (1) *SQL Server 2000*, (2) OS kernel processing, (3) locking overhead, (4) DSA, (5) VI overhead (library and drivers), and (6) other overhead including time spent inside the socket library and other standard system libraries. The lock time is a component of either *kDSA* and the OS kernel, *wDSA*, or *cDSA* that we single out and present separately, due to its importance. Lock synchronization and kernel times include overheads introduced by *SQL Server 2000*, such as context switching, that are not necessarily related to I/O activity. First, we see that *cDSA* spends the least amount of time in the OS and lock synchronization. This leaves more cycles for transaction processing and leads to higher tpmC rates. We also note that *kDSA* spends the least amount of time in the DSA layer, since most I/O functionality is handled by the OS kernel. *wDSA* spends the highest time in the kernel and the DSA layer due to the complex `kernel32.dll` semantics. Finally, VI overhead remains relative constant across all implementations. Second, we notice that the portion of the CPU time not devoted to transaction processing is high even in *cDSA*. For *kDSA* and *wDSA*, the time spent executing database instructions is below 40%, whereas in *cDSA* this percentage increases to about 50%. This difference is the primary reason for the higher transaction rates in *cDSA*. In this configuration, locking and kernel overheads account

for about 30% of the CPU time. About 15% is in the DSA layer (excluding locking) and about 5% is unaccounted. Our results indicate that the largest part of the 30% is due to non-I/O related activity caused by *SQL Server 2000*. We believe further improvements would require restructuring of *SQL Server 2000* and Windows XP code.

6.2 Mid-size Database Configuration

In contrast to the large configuration which aims at absolute performance, the mid-size configuration is representative of systems that aim to reduce the cost–performance ratio.

We first consider the impact of each optimization on tpmC rates. Figure 12 shows that batched deregistration results in a 10% improvement in *kDSA* and 7% in *cDSA*. Batching interrupts increases the transaction rate by an additional 2% in *kDSA* and 8% in *cDSA*. The reason for the small effect of batching interrupts, especially in *kDSA* is that under heavy I/O loads, many replies from the storage nodes tend to arrive at the same time. These replies can be handled with a single interrupt, resulting in implicit interrupt batching. Finally, as in our large configuration, lock synchronization shows the highest additional improvement, about 7% in *kDSA* and 10% in *cDSA*.

Next, we look at how V3 performs compared to local SCSI disks. Figure 13 shows the tpmC rates for the local and different V3 configurations. We see that *kDSA*, *cDSA*, and the local case are comparable in the total tpmC achieved.

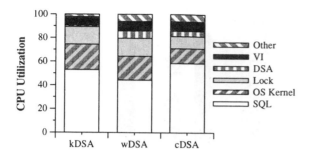

Figure 14: CPU utilization breakdown for *TPC-C* for the mid-size configuration.

.

kDSA is about 2% worse than the local case and *cDSA* is about 3% better than the local case. Finally, *wDSA* is 10% slower compared to the local case.

Note that the different DSA implementations are competitive with the local case, but use only one third of the total number of disks (60 as opposed to 176), with the addition of 8GB of memory (6.4GB used for caching) on the V3 server. Although it is not straight forward to calculate system prices, preliminary calculations of cost components show that the V3 based system has a lower price leading to a better $/tpmC ratio. The reduction in the total number of disks is possible due to the following reasons: VI-based communication reduces host CPU overhead. VI has very low latency and requires no memory copying. This allows more I/O operations to be issued by the database server. Also, VI's low latency magnifies the effect of V3 server caching, which has 40-45% hit ratio for reads in this experiment. With 1,625 warehouses, the database working set size is 100 GB, greater than the aggregate cache size on the V3 server.

Figure 14 shows the execution time breakdown for the different implementations. The breakdowns are similar to the large configuration. However, we note that the kernel and lock overheads for *kDSA* and *wDSA* are much less pronounced on the mid-size than the large size configuration, and the maximum CPU utilization (in *cDSA*) is about 60%, compared to 50% in the large configuration.

6.3 Summary

We find that VI-attached storage incurs very low overheads, especially for requests smaller than 64 KB. In comparing the three different approaches of using VI to connect to database storage, we see that *cDSA* has the best performance because it incurs the least kernel and lock synchronization overhead. The differences among our client implementations become more apparent under large configurations due to increased kernel and synchronization contention. However, our CPU utilization breakdowns indicate that the I/O subsystem overhead is still high even with *cDSA*. Reducing this overhead requires effort at almost every software layer including the database server, the communication layer, and the operating system.

7   RELATED WORK

Our work bears similarity with research in the areas of (i) user-level communication, (ii) using VI in databases, and (iii) storage protocols and storage area networks.

User-level communication: Our work draws heavily on previous research on system area networks and user-level communication systems. Previous work has examined issues related to communication processing in parallel applications and the use of commodity interconnects to provide low-latency and high-bandwidth communication at low-cost. Besides VI, specific examples of user-level communication systems include Active Messages [9], BDM [19], Fast Messages [25], PM [27], U-Net [3], and VMMC [12]. Previous work in user-level communication has also addressed the issue of dynamic memory registration and deregistration [8, 4]. These solutions target applications with small working sets for registered memory and require modifications either in the NIC firmware or the OS kernel.

Using VI for databases: VI-based interconnects have been used previously by database systems for purposes other than improving storage I/O performance. Traditionally, clients in a LAN connect to database servers through IP-based networks. Using VI-based communication between the server and the clients reduces CPU cycles needed to handle client requests by reducing TCP/IP stack processing on the server, which can improve application transaction rates by up to 15% [24, 5, 16]. VI-based networks have also been used to enable parallel database execution on top of clusters of commodity workstations, e.g. in [5, 24], as opposed to tightly integrated database servers.

Storage protocols and storage area networks: The Direct Access File System (DAFS) [11] collaborative defines a file access and management protocol designed for local file sharing on clustered environments connected using VI-based interconnects. Similar to our work, DAFS provides a custom protocol between clients and servers in a storage system over VI. An important difference between DAFS and the communication protocol used in *DSA* is that DAFS operates at the file system level, while our focus has been on block level I/O.

Traditionally storage area networks are mostly implemented with SCSI or FC interconnects. Recent efforts in the area have concentrated on optimizing these networks for database applications. For instance, SCSI controllers and drivers are optimized to reduce the number of interrupts on the receive path, and to impose very little overhead on the send path [23]. This requires offloading storage related processing to customized hardware on the storage controller. However, this approach still requires going through the kernel and incurs relatively high CPU overheads. One can view the use of VI-based interconnects as an alternative approach to providing scalable, cost-effective storage area networks. Recent, industry-sponsored efforts try to unify storage area networks with traditional, IP-based LANs. Examples include SCSI over IP (iSCSI), FC over IP (FC/IP), or VI over IP (VI/IP). Since most of these protocols are in the prototyping stage, their performance characteristics have not yet been studied.

Our work is directly applicable to systems that attempt to use Infiniband as a storage area network. Infiniband [20] is a new interconnection network technology that targets the scalability and performance issues in connecting devices, including storage devices, to host CPUs. It aims at addressing scalability issues by using switched technologies and the performance problems by reducing host CPU overhead and providing Gbit–level bandwidth using ideas from past research in user–level communication systems and RDMA support.

There has also been a lot of work in the broader area of databases and storage systems. For instance, Compaq's TruCluster systems [6] provide unified access to remote disks in a cluster, through a memory channel interconnect [18], which bears many similarities with VI interconnects. Recent work has also examined the use of VI in other storage applications, such as clustered web servers [7]. The authors in [26, 21, 1] study the interaction of OLTP workloads and various architectural features, focusing mostly on smaller workloads than ours. Also, work in disk I/O [30, 15, 14, 29, 2] has explored many directions in the general area of adding intelligence to the storage devices and providing enhanced features. Although our work shares similarities with these efforts, it differs in significant ways, both in terms of goals and techniques used.

8 CONCLUSIONS

In this work, we study how VI–based interconnects can be used to reduce overheads in the I/O path between a database system and a storage back-end. We design a block–level storage architecture (V3) that takes advantage of features found in VI–based communication systems. In addition, we provide and evaluate three different client-side implementations of a block-level I/O module (DSA) that sits between an application and VI. These different implementations trade transparency and generality for performance at different degrees. We perform detailed measurements using Microsoft *SQL Server 2000* with both micro-benchmarks and real–world database workloads on a mid-size (4–CPU) and a large (32–CPU) database server.

Our work shows that new storage APIs that help minimize kernel involvement in the I/O path are needed to fully exploit the benefits of user–level communication. We find that on large database configurations *cDSA* provides a 18% transaction rate improvement over a well–tuned, Fibre Channel implementation. On mid–size configurations, all three DSA implementations are competitive with optimized Fibre Channel implementations, but provide substantial potential for better price–performance ratios. Our results show that the CPU I/O overhead in the database system is still high (about 40–50% of CPU cycles) even in our best implementation. Reducing this overhead requires efforts, not only at the interconnect level, but at almost every software layer including the database server, the communication layer, and the operating system, and especially on the interfaces among these components. More aggressive

strategies than *cDSA* are also possible. Storage protocols can provide new, even database–specific, I/O APIs, that take full advantage of user–level communication and allow applications to provide hints and directives to the I/O system. Such protocols and APIs are facilitated by the availability of low–cost CPU cycles on the storage side as found in the V3 architecture.

Our experience shows that VI–based interconnects have a number of advantages compared to more traditional storage area and IP–based networks. (i) RDMA operations available in VI help avoid copying in I/O write operations and to transfer I/O buffers directly from application memory to the V3 server cache. Also, RDMA can be used to set flags in application memory and directly notify the application upon completion of I/O requests without any application processor intervention. Even though the application still needs to poll these flags, their value is updated without the application losing the CPU. (ii) The low overhead in initiating I/O operations can reduce application CPU utilization to a bear minimum. (iii) VI interconnects can reach their peak throughput at relatively small message sizes (smaller than the size of I/O buffers). This allows for one NIC to service heavy I/O rates, reducing overall system cost and complexity. However, VI–based interconnects also pose a number of challenges to higher layers, especially in I/O–intensive environments, such as database system. In particular, dealing with flow control, memory registration and deregistration, synchronization, interrupts, and reducing kernel involvement are significant challenges for storage systems.

Finally, there is currently a number of efforts to incorporate VI–type features in other interconnects as well. Most notably, Infiniband and iSCSI address many of the issues related to storage area networks and include (or there is discussion about including) features such as RDMA capabilities. Our work is directly applicable to systems with Infiniband interconnects and relevant for systems with future iSCSI interconnects.

9 ACKNOWLEDGMENTS

We thankfully acknowledge the technical and administrative support of all our colleagues at Emphora, Inc. We are also indebted to Microsoft, Unisys, and NEC Research Institute for their help with various aspects of this work. Finally, we would also like to thank the anonymous reviewers for their useful comments and suggestions.

REFERENCES

[1] A. Ailamaki, D. J. DeWitt, M. D. Hill, and D. A. Wood. DBMSs on a modern processor: Where does time go? In M. P. Atkinson, M. E. Orlowska, P. Valduriez, S. B. Zdonik, and M. L. Brodie, editors, *Proceedings of the Twenty-fifth International Conference on Very Large Databases*, 1999.

[2] D. C. Anderson, J. S. Chase, S. Gadde, A. J. Gallatin, K. G. Yocum, and M. J. Feeley. Cheating the I/O bottleneck: Network storage with Trapeze/Myrinet. In *Proceedings of the USENIX 1998 Annual Technical Conference*, 1998.

[3] A. Basu, V. Buch, W. Vogels, and T. von Eicken. U-net: A user-level network interface for parallel and distributed computing. *Proceedings of the 15th ACM Symposium on Operating Systems Principles (SOSP), Copper Mountain, Colorado*, December 1995.

[4] A. Basu, M. Welsh, and T. von Eicken. Incorporating memory management into user-level network interfaces. http://www2.cs.cornell.edu/U-Net/papers/unetmm.pdf, 1996.

[5] B. C. Bialek. Leading vendors validate power of clustering architecture, detail of the tpc-c audited benchmark. http://wwwip.emulex.com/ip/pdfs/performance/IBM_TPC-C_Benchmark.pdf, Jul. 2000.

[6] W. M. Cardoza, F. S. Glover, and W. E. Snaman, Jr. Design of the TruCluster multicomputer system for the Digital UNIX environment. *Digital Technical Journal of Digital Equipment Corporation*, 8(1):5–17, 1996.

[7] E. V. Carrera, S. Rao, L. Iftode, and R. Bianchini. User-level communication in cluster-based servers. In *Proceedings of the 8th IEEE International Symposium on High-Performance Computer Architecture (HPCA 8)*, 2002.

[8] Y. Chen, A. Bilas, S. N. Damianakis, C. Dubnicki, and K. Li. UTLB: A mechanism for address translation on network interfaces. In *Proceedings of the Eighth International Conference Architectural Support for Programming Languages and Operating Systems ASPLOS*, pages 193–203, San Jose, CA, Oct. 1998.

[9] B. N. Chun, A. M. Mainwaring, and D. E. Culler. Virtual network transport protocols for myrinet. In *Hot Interconnects Symposium V*, Stanford, CA, August 1997.

[10] Compaq/Intel/Microsoft. *Virtual Interface Architecture Specification, Version 1.0*, Dec. 1997.

[11] DAFS Collaborative. *DAFS: Direct Access File System Protocol Version: 1.00*, Sept. 2001.

[12] C. Dubnicki, A. Bilas, Y. Chen, S. Damianakis, and K. Li. VMMC-2: efficient support for reliable, connection-oriented communication. In *Proceedings of Hot Interconnects*, Aug. 1997.

[13] D. Dunning and G. Regnier. The Virtual Interface Architecture. In *Proceedings of Hot Interconnects V Symposium*, Stanford, Aug. 1997.

[14] G. A. Gibson, D. F. Nagle, K. Amiri, J. Butler, F. W. Chang, H. Gobioff, C. Hardin, E. Riedel, D. Rochberg, and J. Zelenka. A cost-effective, high-bandwidth storage architecture. In *Proceedings of the Eighth International Conference on Architectural Support for Programming Languages and Operating Systems*, 1998.

[15] G. A. Gibson, D. F. Nagle, K. Amiri, F. W. Chang, E. M. Feinberg, H. Gobioff, C. Lee, B. Ozceri, E. Riedel, D. Rochberg, and J. Zelenka. File server scaling with network-attached secure disks. In *Proceedings of the 1997 ACM SIGMETRICS International Conference on Measurement and Modeling of Computer Systems*, 1997.

[16] Giganet. Giganet whitepaper: Accelerating and scaling data networks microsoft sql server 2000 and giganet clan. http://wwwip.emulex.com/ip/pdfs/performance/-sql2000andclan.pdf, Sept. 2000.

[17] Giganet. Giganet cLAN family of products. http://www.emulex.com/products.html, 2001.

[18] R. Gillett, M. Collins, and D. Pimm. Overview of network memory channel for PCI. In *Proceedings of the IEEE Spring COMPCON '96*, Feb. 1996.

[19] H. Gregory, J. Thomas, P. McMahon, A. Skjellum, and N. Doss. Design of the BDM family of myrinet control programs, 1998.

[20] InfiniBand Trade Association. Infiniband architecture specification, version 1.0. http://www.infinibandta.org, Oct. 2000.

[21] K. Keeton, D. Patterson, Y. He, R. Raphael, and W. Baker. Performance characterization of a Quad Pentium Pro SMP using OLTP Workloads. In *Proceedings of the 25th Annual International Symposium on Computer Architecture (ISCA-98)*, 1998.

[22] Microsoft. Address windowing extensions and microsoft windows 2000 datacenter server. Windows Hardware Engineering Conference: Advancing the Platform. Also available at: http://msdn.microsoft.com/library/default.asp?url=/library/en-us/dnw2k/html/awewindata.asp, March 30 1999.

[23] Mylex. eXtremeRAID 3000 High Performance 1Gb Fibre RAID Controller. http://www.mylex.com.

[24] ORACLE. Oracle net vi protocol support, a technical white paper. http://www.vidf.org/Documents/whitepapers/Oracle_VI.pdf, February 2001.

[25] S. Pakin, V. Karamcheti, and A. A. Chien. Fast Messages: Efficient, portable communication for workstation clusters and massively parallel processors (MPP). *IEEE Concurrency*, 5(2):60–73, April-June 1997. University of Illinois.

[26] M. Rosenblum, E. Bugnion, S. A. Herrod, E. Witchel, and A. Gupta. The impact of architectural trends on operating system performance. In *Symposium on Operating Systems Principles*, pages 285–298, 1995.

[27] H. Tezuka, A. Hori, and Y. Ishikawa. PM: A high-performance communication library for multi-user parallel environments. Technical Report TR-96015, Real World Computing Partnership, Nov. 1996.

[28] Transaction Processing Performance Council. *TPC Benchmark C*. Shanley Public Relations, 777 N. First Street, Suite 600, San Jose, CA 95112-6311, May 1991.

[29] M. Uysal, A. Acharya, and J. Saltz. Evaluation of active disks for decision support databases. In *Proceedings of the Sixth International Symposium on High-Performance Computer Architecture*, pages 337–348, Toulouse, France, Jan. 8–12, 2000. IEEE Computer Society TCCA.

[30] J. Wilkes, R. Golding, C. Staelin, and T. Sullivan. The HP AutoRAID hierarchical storage system. *ACM Transactions on Computer Systems*, 14(1):108–136, Feb. 1996.

[31] Y. Zhou, J. F. Philbin, and K. Li. The multi-queue replacement algorithm for second level buffer caches. In *USENIX Annual Technical Conference*, pages 91–104, June 2001.

Session 8: Vector Architectures

Speculative Dynamic Vectorization

Alex Pajuelo, Antonio González and Mateo Valero
Departament d'Arquitectura de Computadors
Universitat Politècnica de Catalunya
Barcelona – Spain
{mpajuelo, antonio, mateo}@ac.upc.es

Abstract

Traditional vector architectures have shown to be very effective for regular codes where the compiler can detect data-level parallelism. However, this SIMD parallelism is also present in irregular or pointer-rich codes, for which the compiler is quite limited to discover it. In this paper we propose a microarchitecture extension in order to exploit SIMD parallelism in a speculative way. The idea is to predict when certain operations are likely to be vectorizable, based on some previous history information. In this case, these scalar instructions are executed in a vector mode. These vector instructions operate on several elements (vector operands) that are anticipated to be their input operands and produce a number of outputs that are stored on a vector register in order to be used by further instructions. Verification of the correctness of the applied vectorization eventually changes the status of a given vector element from speculative to non-speculative, or alternatively, generates a recovery action in case of misspeculation.

The proposed microarchitecture extension applied to a 4-way issue superscalar processor with one wide bus is 19% faster than the same processor with 4 scalar buses to L1 data cache. This speed up is due basically to 1) the reduction in number of memory accesses, 15% for SpecInt and 20% for SpecFP, 2) the transformation of scalar arithmetic instructions into their vector counterpart, 28% for SpecInt and 23% for SpecFP, and 3) the exploitation of control independence for mispredicted branches.

1. Introduction

Vector processors [2, 6, 10, 16] are very effective to exploit SIMD parallelism, which is present in numerical and multimedia applications. Vector instructions' efficiency comes from streamed memory accesses and streamed arithmetic operations. Traditionally, the burden to exploit this type of parallelism has been put on the compiler and/or the programmer [1, 24].

The average programmer can deal with codes whose vectorization is relatively straightforward. The compiler has a partial knowledge of the program (i.e. it has a limited knowledge of the values of the variables). Because of that, it generates code that is safe for any possible scenario according to its knowledge, and thus, it may loose significant opportunities to exploit SIMD parallelism. On top of that, we have the problem of legacy codes that have been compiled for former versions of the ISA with no SIMD extensions and therefore are not able to exploit new SIMD extensions incorporated in newer ISA versions.

In this paper we present a mechanism for dynamically generating SIMD instructions (also referred to as vector instructions). These SIMD instructions speculatively fetch and precompute data using the vector units of the processor. This vectorization scheme works even for codes in which a typical vectorizing compiler would fail to find SIMD parallelism. The vectorization process begins when the processor identifies a load operation that is likely to have a constant stride (based on its past history). Any instruction whose operands have been vectorized is also vectorized. In this way, the 'vectorizable' attribute is propagated down the dependence graph. The scalar unit has to verify the correctness of the vectorization. For this purpose, the corresponding scalar instructions are converted into 'check' operations that basically validate that the operands used by the vector instructions are correct. This is very similar in concept to other checker proposed in the past for other purposes such as fault tolerance [3, 13]. In case of a vectorization misspeculation, the current instances of the vector instructions are executed in scalar mode.

The proposed mechanism also allows the processor to exploit control-flow independence. When a branch is mispredicted, the scalar pipeline is flushed but the vector operations are not squashed. The new scalar instructions corresponding to the correct path will check whether the operations performed by the vector instructions are still correct and if this is the case, their results will be committed. Otherwise, a vectorization misspeculation will be fired, which will discard the vector results.

With the dynamic vectorization mechanism the number of memory requests decreases by 15% for SpecInt and 20% for SpecFP, and the number of executed arithmetic instructions is 25% lower for SpecInt in a 4-way superscalar processor with one wide bus. This reduction in memory requests and executed instructions results in significant speedups. For instance, a 4-way superscalar processor with dynamic vectorization and one wide data cache bus is 19% faster than a 4-way superscalar processor with 4 scalar buses and no dynamic vectorization.

The rest of the paper is organized as follows. Section 2 motivates this work by presenting some statistics about strided memory accesses. Section 3 presents the hardware implementation of the dynamic vectorization mechanism. Performance statistics are discussed in section 4. Section 5 outlines the related work. We conclude in section 6.

2. Motivation

Strided memory loads [7,8] are the instructions that fire the proposed speculative dynamic vectorization mechanism. To identify a strided load, at least three dynamic instances of the static load are needed. The first dynamic instance sets the first memory address that is accessed. The second dynamic instance computes the initial stride, subtracting the memory address of the first dynamic instance from the current address. The third dynamic instance checks if the stride is repeated computing the current stride and comparing it with the first computed stride.

Figure 1 shows the stride distribution for SpecInt95 and SpecFP95 (for this figure, the stride is computed dividing the difference of memory addresses by the size of the accessed data). Details of the evaluation framework can be found in section 4.1.

As shown in Figure 1, the most frequent stride for SpecInt95 and SpecFP95 is 0. This means that dynamic instances of the same static load access the same memory address. For SpecInt this stride is due, mainly, to the accesses of local variables and memory addresses referenced through pointers. For SpecFP the stride 0 is mainly due to spill code.

Usually, for SpecFP, the most frequent stride is stride 1 because these applications execute the same operations over every element of some array structures. However, due to the code optimizations [4,9] included by the scalar compiler, such as loop unrolling, some stride 1 accesses become stride 2, 4 or 8. The bottom line of this statistics is that strided accesses are quite common both in integer and FP applications.

The results in Figure 1 also suggest that a wide bus to the L1 data cache can be very effective at reducing the number of memory requests. For instance, if the cache line size is 4 elements, multiple accesses with stride lower than 4 can be served with a single request if the bus width is

equal to the line size. These types of strides represent 97,9% and 81,3% of the total strided loads for SpecInt95 and SpecFP95 respectively.

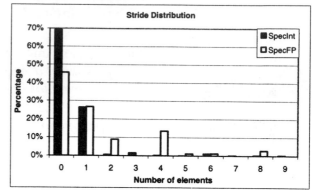

Figure 1. Stride distribution for SpecInt95 and SpecFP95.

3. Dynamic vectorization

The microarchitecture proposed in this work is a superscalar core extended with a vector register file and some vector functional units. Figure 2 shows the block diagram of the processor where black boxes are the additional vector resources and related structures not usually found in a superscalar processor, and grey boxes are the modified structures to implement the speculative dynamic vectorization mechanism.

3.1. Overview

Speculative dynamic vectorization begins when a strided load is detected. When this happens, a vectorized instance of the instruction is created and it is executed in a vector functional unit storing the results in a vector register. Next instances of the same static instruction are not executed but they just validate if the corresponding speculatively loaded element is valid. This basically consists in checking that the predicted address is correct and the loaded element has not been invalidated by a succeeding store. Every new instance of the scalar load instruction validates one element of the corresponding destination vector register.

Arithmetic instructions are vectorized when any of the source operands is a vector register. Succeeding dynamic instances of this instruction just check that the corresponding source operands are still valid vector elements (details on how the state of each element is kept is later explained).

When a validation fails, the current and following instances of the corresponding instruction are executed in scalar mode, until the vectorizing engine detects again a new vectorizable pattern. With this dynamic vectorization mechanism, as shown in Figure 3, with unbounded resources, 47% of the SpecInt95 instructions and 51% of the SpecFP95 instructions can be vectorized.

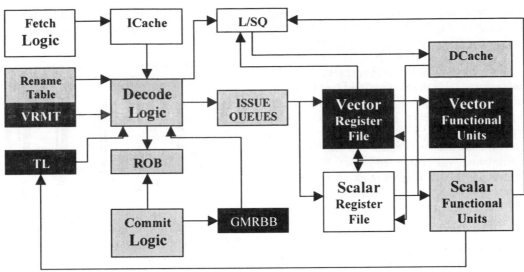

Figure 2.Block diagram of a superscalar processor with the speculative dynamic vectorization mechanism. Black blocks are structures or resources added and gray blocks are structures modified.

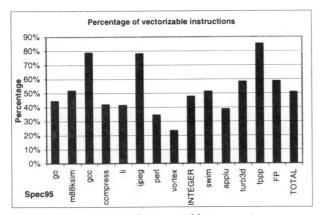

Figure 3: Percentage of vectorizable instructions.

3.2. Instruction vectorization

The first step to create vector instances of an instruction is detecting a strided load [7,8]. To do this, it is necessary to know the recent history of memory accesses for every load instruction. To store this history the processor includes a Table of Loads (TL in Figure 2) where, for every load, the PC, the current address, the stride and a confidence counter are stored as shown in Figure 4.

PC	Last Address	Stride	Confidence Counter

Figure 4.Table of Loads.

When a load instruction is decoded, it looks for its PC in the TL. If the PC is not in this table, the last address field is initialized with the current address of the load and the stride and confidence counter fields are set to 0.

Next dynamic instances compute the new stride and compare the result with the stride stored in the table, increasing the confidence counter when both strides are equal or resetting it to 0 otherwise. When the confidence counter is 2 or higher, a new vectorized instance of the instruction is generated. The last address field is always modified with the current memory address of the dynamic instance.

When a vectorized instance of an instruction is generated, the processor allocates a vector register to store its result. The processor maintains the associations of vector registers and vector instructions in the Vector Register Map Table (VRMT in Figure 2). This table contains, for every vector register the PC of the associated instruction, the vector element (offset) corresponding to the last fetched scalar instruction that will validate (or has validated) an element of this vector, the source operands of the associated instruction, and, if the instruction is vectorized with one scalar operand and one vector operand, the value of the scalar register is also stored, as shown in Figure 5.

PC	Offset	Source Operand 1	Source Operand 2	Value

Figure 5.Contents of each entry of the Vector Register Map Table.

Every time a scalar instruction is fetched, this table is checked and if its PC is found the instruction is turned into a validation operation. In this case, the offset field determines which vector element must be validated and then, the offset is incremented. In the case that the offset is equal to the vector register length, another vectorized version of the instruction is generated and a free vector register is allocated to it. The VRMT table entry corresponding to this new vector register is initialized with the content of the entry corresponding to the previous instance, excepting the field offset, which is set to 0.

The register rename table is also modified (see Figure 6) to reflect the two kind of physical registers (scalar and vector). Every logical register is mapped to either a physical scalar register or a physical vector register, depending on whether the last instruction that used this register as destination was vectorized or not. Every entry of the table contains a V/S flag to mark if the physical register is a scalar or a vector register and the field offset indicates the latest element for which a validation has entered in the pipeline.

Physical Register	V/S	Offset

Figure 6.Entry of the modified Rename Table.

When every instruction is decoded the V/S flags (vector/scalar) of their source operands are read and if any of the two is set to V, the instruction is vectorized. In parallel, the VRMT table is accessed to check if the instruction was already vectorized in a previous dynamic instance. If so, the instruction is turned into a validation operation. Validation is performed by checking if the source operands in the VRMT table and those in the rename table are the same. If they differ, a new vectorized version of the instruction is generated. Otherwise, the current element pointed by offset is validated and this validation is dispatched to the reorder buffer in order to be later committed (see next section for further explanation). Besides, if the validated element is the last one of the vector, a new instance of the vectorized instruction is dispatched to the vector data-path.

An arithmetic instruction that has been vectorized with one vector source operand and one scalar register operand, waits in the decode stage, blocking the next instructions, until the value of the physical register associated to the scalar source operand is available. Then, it checks if the value of the register matches the value found in the VRMT and if so, a validation is dispatched to the reorder buffer. Otherwise, a new vectorized instance of the instruction is created. This stalls do not impact much performance since the number of vectorized instructions with one scalar operand that is not ready at decode is low. Figure 7 shows the differents IPC's obtained blocking these instructions (black bar) and the ideal case (white bar) where no one of these instructions are blocked.

Note that the cost of a context switch is not increased since only the scalar state of the processor needs to be saved. The additional structures for vectorization are just invalidated on a context switch. When the process restarts again the vectorization of the code starts from scratch at the point where the process was interrupted.

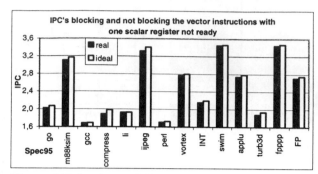

Figure 7.IPCs obtained blocking (real) and not blocking (ideal) the vector instructions with one scalar register not ready for a 4-way processor with 1 port and 128 vector registers.

3.3. Vector registers

Vector register is one of the most critical resources in the processor because they determine the number of scalar instructions that can be vectorized. Vector registers can be regarded as a set of scalar registers grouped with the same name.

A vector register is assigned to an instruction in the decode stage when this instruction is vectorized. If no free vector register is available, the instruction is not vectorized, and continues executing in a scalar mode.

To manage the allocation/deallocation of vector registers, each register contains a global tag and each element includes a set of flags of bits as shown in Figure 8.

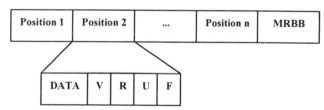

Figure 8.(Top) Vector register structure for dynamic vectorization.

The V (Valid) flag indicates whether the element holds committed data. This bit is set to 1 when the validation associated to the corresponding scalar instruction commits.

The R (Ready) flag indicates whether the element has been computed. Depending on the kind of instruction the data will be ready when is brought from memory or computed by a vector functional unit.

When a validation of an element has been dispatched but not committed yet, the U (Used) flag is set to 1. This prevents the freeing of the physical register until the validation is committed (details on the conditions to free a vector register are described below).

The F (Free) flag indicates whether the element is not longer needed. This flag is set to 1 when the next scalar instruction having the same logical destination register or its corresponding validation commits.

A vector register will be release when all its computed elements have been freed (i.e. are not needed any more). Besides, a register is also released if all validated elements are freed and no more elements need to be produced. In order to estimate when no more elements will be computed, we assume that this will happen when the current loop is terminated. For this purpose, the processor includes a register that is referred to as GMRBB (Global Most Recent Backward Branch) that holds the PC of the last backward branch that has been committed [19]. Each vector register stores in the MRBB (Most Recent Backward Branch) tag the PC of the most recently committed backward branch when the vector register was allocated. This backward branch, usually, coincides with the last branch of a loop, associating a vector register to an instruction during some iterations.

A vector register is freed when one of the following two conditions holds:

1) All vector elements have the flags R and F set to 1. This means that all elements have been computed and freed by scalar instructions.

2) Every element with the flags V set, has the flag F set, and all the elements have the flag R set and flag U cleared, and the content of the tag MRBB is different of the register GMRBB. This means that all the validated elements have been freed. Furthermore, all elements have been computed and no element is in use by a validation instruction. It is very likely that the loop where the vector operation that allocated the register was, has been terminated.

3.4. Vector data path

Vector instructions wait in the vector instruction queues until their operands are ready and a vector functional unit is available (i.e. instruction are issued out-of-order). Vector functional units are pipelined and hence can begin the computation of a new vector element every cycle. Every time an element is calculated, the vector functional unit sets to 1 the flag R associated to that position, allowing others functional units to use it.

Vector functional units can compute operations having one vector operand and one scalar operand. To do this, the functional units must have access to the scalar register file and the vector register file. In the case of the scalar register, the element is read just once.

Note that some vector instruction can be executed having a different initial offset for their source vector operands. This can happen, for example, when two load

instructions begin vectorization in different iterations and their destination vector registers are source operands of an arithmetic instruction. To deal with these cases, vector functional units compare these offsets to obtain the greatest. The difference between this offset and the vector register length determines the number of elements to compute. Fortunately, the percentage of the vector instructions whose source operands' offsets are different from 0 is very low, as shown in Figure 9.

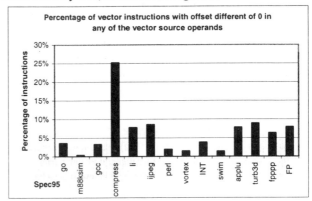

Figure 9.Percentage of vector instructions with offset different of 0 in any of the vector source operands for an 8-way processor with 128 vector registers.

3.5. Branch mispredictions and control-flow independence

When a branch misprediction is detected, a superscalar processor recovers the state of the machine by restoring the register map table and squashing the instructions after the branch.

In the proposed microarchitecture, the scalar core works in the same way as a conventional processor, i.e. a precise state is recovered, but vector resources are not modified: vector registers are not freed, and no vector functional unit aborts the execution because they can be computing data that can be used in the future. The objective is to exploit control-flow independence [14, 15, 18]. When the new path enters again in the scalar pipeline, the source operands of each instruction will be checked again, and if it happens that the vector operands are still valid, the instruction does not need to be executed. Figure 10 shows the percentage of instructions in the 100 instructions (100 is a size arbitrarily chosen) that follow a mispredicted branch that do not need to be executed since they were executed in vector mode and continue to have the same source operands after the misprediction.

Note that when a scalar instruction in a wrongly predicted speculative path is vectorized, the vector register may remain allocated until the end of the loop to which the instruction belongs. This wastes vector registers but fortunately only happens for less than 1% of the vector instructions in our benchmarks.

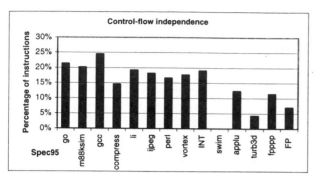

Figure 10: *Percentage of scalar instructions that are reused after a branch misprediction (limited to the 100 instructions that follow each mispredicted branch).*

3.6. Memory coherence

To ensure memory coherence, stores are critical instructions because these instructions make changes in memory that the processor cannot recover. For this reason, a store instruction modifies the memory hierarchy only when it commits.

A vectorized load copies memory values into a register. However, there may be intervening stores before the scalar load operation that would have made the access in a non-vectorized implementation. Thus, stores must check the data in vector registers to maintain coherence.

For this purpose, every vector register has two fields, the first and the last address of the corresponding memory elements (used only if the associated vector instruction is a load) to indicate the range of memory positions accessed. Stores check whether the addresses that are going to modify are inside the range of addresses of any vector register. If so, the VRMT entry associated to this vector register is invalidated. Then, when the corresponding scalar instruction is decoded, it will not find its PC in the VRMT and another vector instance of this instruction will be created. Besides, all the instructions following the store are squashed.

Fortunately, the percentage of the stores whose memory address is inside the range of addresses of any vector register is low (4,5% for SpecInt and 2,5% for SpecFP).

Due to the complexity of the logic associated to store instructions, only two store instructions can commit in the same cycle.

3.7. Wide bus

To exploit spatial locality a wide bus of 4 words has been implemented. This bus is able to bring a whole cache line every time the cache is accessed. In parallel, the range of addresses held in this cache line are compared with the addresses of pending loads, and all loads that access to the same line are served from the single access (in our approach, only 4 pending loads can be served at the same

cycle). This organization has been previously proposed elsewhere [11, 12, 22, 23].

Wide buses are especially attractive in the presence of vectorized loads, since multiple elements can be retrieved by a single access if the stride is small, as it is in most cases.

4. Performance evaluation

4.1. Experimental framework

For the performance evaluation we have extended the SimpleScalar v3.0a [5], which is a cycle-level simulator of a dynamically scheduled superscalar processor, to include the microarchitectural extensions described above.

To evaluate the mechanism we use 2 superscalar configurations with different issue width: 4-way and 8-way. To evaluate the memory impact of the wide bus and the dynamic vectorization mechanism we will use configurations with 1, 2 and 4 L1 data cache ports (scalar or wide). Other parameters of the microarchitecture are shown in Table 1.

Parameter	4-way	8-way
Fetch width	4 instructions (up to 1 taken branch)	8 instructions (up to 1 taken branch)
I-cache	64Kb, 2-way set associative, 64 byte lines, 1 cycle hit, 6 cycle miss time	64Kb, 2-way set associative, 64 byte lines, 1 cycle hit, 6 cycle miss time
Branch Predictor	Gshare with 64K entries	Gshare with 64K entries
Inst. window size	128 entries	256 entries
Scalar functional units (latency in brackets)	3 simple int(1); 2 int mul/div (2 for mult and 12 for div); 2 simple FP(2); 1 FP mul/div (4 for mult and 14 for div); 1 to 4 loads/stores	6 simple int(1); 3 int mul/div (2 for mult and 12 for div); 4 simple FP(2); 2 FP mul/div (4 for mult and 14 for div); 1 to 4 loads/stores
Load/Store queue	32 entries with store-load forwarding	64 entries with store-load forwarding
Issue mechanism	4-way out of order issue loads may execute when prior store addresses are known	8-way out of order issue loads may execute when prior store addresses are known
D-cache	64KB, 2-way set associative, 32 byte lines, 1 cycle hit time, write-back, 6 cycle miss time up to 16 outstanding miss	64KB, 2-way set associative, 32 byte lines, 1 cycle hit time, write-back, 6 cycle miss time up to 16 outstanding miss
L2 cache	256Kb,4-way set associative, 32 byte lines, 6 cycles hit time, 18 cycle miss time	256Kb,4-way set associative, 32 byte lines, 6 cycles hit time, 18 cycle miss time
Commit width	4 instructions	8 instructions
Vector registers	128 registers of 4 64-bit elements each	128 registers of 4 64-bit elements each
Vector functional units (latency in brackets)	Pipelined; 3 simple int(1); 2 int mul/div (2 mult, 12 div); 2 simple FP(2); 1 FP mul/div (4 mult and 14 div); 1 to 4 loads	Pipelined; 6 simple int(1); 3 int mul/div (2 mult, 12 div); 4 simple FP(2); 2 FP mul/div (4 mult and 14 div); 1 to 4 loads
TL	4-way set assoc. with 512 sets	4-way set assoc. with 512 sets
VRMT	4-way set assoc. with 64 sets	4-way set assoc. with 64 sets

Table 1. *Processor microarchitectural parameters.*

276

For the experiments we use the complete SpecInt95 benchmark suite and four SpecFP95 benchmarks (swim, applu, turb3d and fpppp). Programs were compiled with the Compaq/Alpha compiler using –O5 –ifo –non_shared optimization flags. Each program was simulated for 100 million instructions after skipping the initialization part.

We have chosen vector registers with 4 elements because the average vector length for our benchmarks is relatively small: 8,84 for SpecInt and 7,37 for SpecFP applications.

For both configurations, the size of the required additional resources is the same:

- The vector register file requires 4 kilobytes (4 element per vector register * 8 bytes per element * 128 vector registers).
- The VRMT requires 4608 bytes (4 ways * 64 elements per way * 18 bytes per element).
- The TL requires 49152 bytes (4 ways * 512 elements per way * 24 bytes per element).

This results in a total of 56Kbytes of extra storage. Although this is not negligible this is certainly affordable in current designs.

4.3. Performance results

Figure 11 shows the performance for the 8-way and 4-way processors depending on the number of ports to L1 data cache. Each figure compares the performance of a superscalar processor (xpnoIM), a superscalar processor with a wide bus (xpIM) and a superscalar processor with a wide bus and dynamic vectorization (xpV) for a different number (x) of L1 data cache ports.

As shown in Figure 11, in most cases the configurations with wide buses increase clearly the performance of the configurations with scalar buses. The main reason is the bottlenecks due to the memory systems in configurations like an 8-way superscalar processor with 1 scalar bus. For this configuration the average IPC increased from 1,77 to 2,16 when a wide bus substitutes the scalar bus. The benefits for the configurations with 2 or 4 scalar buses are smaller since they already have a significant memory bandwidth.

Speculative dynamic vectorization reduces the pressure on the memory ports as shown in Figure 12. This Figure shows the memory port occupancy for the different processor configurations.

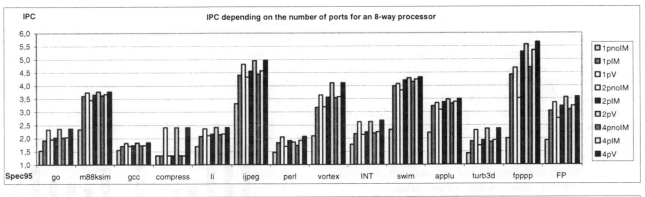

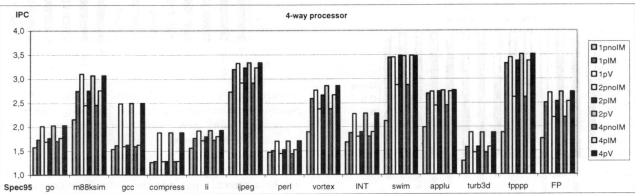

Figure 11. IPC for the baseline configuration (xpnoIM), wide buses (xpIM), wide buses plus dynamic vectorization (xpV), for different number (x) of L1 data cache ports for an 8-way and a 4-way processor.

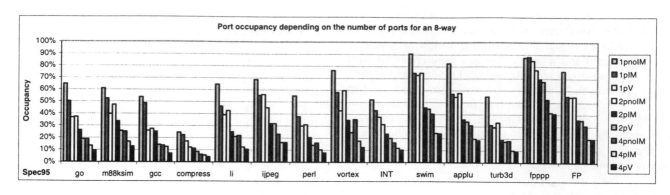

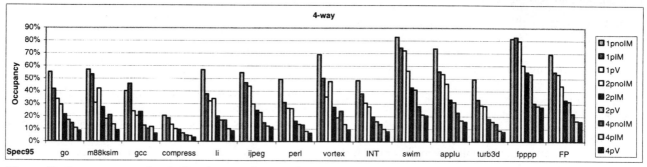

Figure 12. *Bus occupancy for the baseline configuration (xpnoIM), wide buses (xpIM), wide buses plus dynamic vectorization (xpV), for different number (x) of L1 data cache ports.*

Speculative dynamic vectorization increases the memory elements that need to be read/written due to misspeculations. However, this is shadowed by the increase in the effectiveness of the wide ports, since most vector instructions have a small stride and thus, multiple elements can be read in a single access.

Figure 13 shows the percentage of memory lines read from cache that contribute with 1, 2, 3 or 4 useful words, and the percentage of speculative (unused) accesses. It can be observed that a significant percentage of memory accesses serve multiple words and the number of useless accesses is relatively small except for compress.

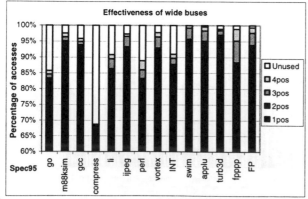

Figure 13. *Percentage of read lines that contribute with 1,2,3 or 4 useful words for a 4-way processor with 1 memory port.*

Figure 14 shows the percentage of scalar instructions that are turned into a validation operation for an 8-way superscalar processor with one wide bus. These instructions represent 28% and 23% of the total instructions for the integer and FP benchmarks respectively.

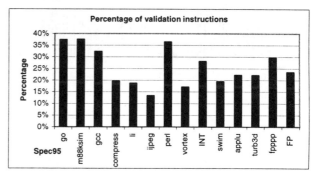

Figure 14. *Percentage of instructions that validate a position in a vector register for an 8-way superscalar processor with one wide bus and the dynamic vectorization mechanism.*

Figure 15 shows the average number of vector elements that have been computed by the vector functional units and validated (comp. used), have been computed but not validated (comp. not used) and have not been computed (not comp) for an 8-way processor with 128 vector registers.

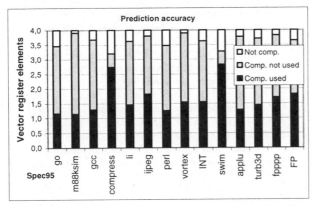

Figure 15. *Average number of vector elements that have been computed and used (comp. used), computed but not used (comp. not used) and not computed (not comp.) for an 8-way processor with 128 vector registers with 4 elements per register.*

On average only 1,75 elements are validated out of the 3,75 computed elements. This means that more than half of the speculative work is useless due to mispredictions. Although these misspeculations have a minor impact on performance, there may be an issue for power consumption. Reducing the number of misspeculations is an area that is left for future work.

As described in section 3.6, the recovery mechanism does not squash vector instructions after branch mispredictions. Due to this, the control-flow independence instructions can reuse the data computed in vector registers. As shown in Figure 10, among the first 100 instructions following a mispredicted branch (this suppose the 10,53% of total executed instructions for SpecInt95 on a 4-way superscalar processor with 1 bus and a gshare branch predictor with 64K entries), 17% of them can reuse the data stored in vector registers.

To summarize, speculative dynamic vectorization results in significant speedups that are mainly due to: a) the exploitation of SIMD parallelism, b) the ability to exploit control-flow independence, and c) the increase in the effectiveness of wide buses.

5. Related work

Vajapeyam [21] presents a dynamic vectorization mechanism based on trace processors. The mechanism executes in parallel some iterations of a loop. This mechanism tries to enlarge the instruction window capturing in vector form the body of the loops. The whole loop body is vectorized provided that all iterations of the loop follow the same control flow. The mechanism proposed in this paper is more flexible/general in the sense that it can vectorize just parts of the loop body and may allow different control flows in some parts of the loop.

The CONDEL architecture [20] proposed by Uht captures a single copy of complex loops in a static instruction window. It uses state bits per iteration to determine the control paths taken by different loop iterations and to correctly enforce dependences.

The use of wide buses has been previously considered to improve the efficiency of the memory system for different microarchitectures [12, 22, 23].

Rotenberg et al. present a mechanism to exploit control flow independence in superscalar [14] and trace [15] processors. Their approach is based on identifying control independent points dynamically, and a hardware organization of the instruction window that allows the processor to insert the instructions after a branch misprediction between instructions previously dispatched, i.e., after the mispredicted branch and before the control independent point.

Lopez et al. [11] propose and evaluate aggressive wide VLIW architectures oriented to numerical applications. The main idea is to take advantage on the existence of stride one in numerical and multimedia loops. The compiler detects load instructions to consecutive addresses and combines them into a single wide load instruction that can be efficiently executed in VLIW architectures with wide buses. The same concept is applied to groups of instructions that make computations. In some cases, these wide architectures achieve similar performance, compared to architectures where the buses and functional units are replicated, but at reduced cost.

6. Conclusions

In this paper we have proposed a speculative dynamic vectorization scheme as an extension to superscalar processors. This scheme allows the processor to prefetch data into vector registers and to speculatively manipulate these data through vector arithmetic instructions. The main benefits of this microarchitecture are a) the use of SIMD parallelism, even in irregular codes; b) the exploitation of control-flow independence; and c) the increase in the effectiveness of wide memory buses.

We have shown that these benefits result in significant speedups for a broad range of microarchitectural configurations. For instance, a 4-way superscalar processor with one wide port and speculative dynamic vectorization is 3% faster than an 8-way superscalar processor with 4 scalar ports. Speculative dynamic vectorization increases the IPC of a 4-way superscalar processor with one wide bus by 21,2% for SpecInt and 8,1% for SpecFP.

Acknowledgments

This work has been supported by the Ministry of Science and Technology of Spain and the European Union

(FEDER funds) under contract TIC2001-0995-C02-01 and by a research grant from Intel Corporation. We also acknowledge the European Center for Parallelism of Barcelona (CEPBA) for supplying the computing resources for our experiments.

References

[1] J. R. Allen and K. Kennedy, "Automatic Translation of Fortran Programs to Vector Forms", *in ACM Transactions on Programming Languages and Systems, Vol. 9, no. 4,* October 1987, pp. 491-452.

[2] K. Asanovic. "Vector Microprocessors". *Phd Thesis. University of California, Berkeley,* Spring 1998.

[3] T. M. Austin, "DIVA: A Reliable Substrate for Deep Submicron Microarchitecture Design", *in Proceedings of the 32nd Symposium on Microarchitecture,* Nov. 1999.

[4] D. F. Bacon, S. L. Graham and O. J. Sharp, "Compiler Transformations for High Performance Computing", *Technical Report No. UCB/CSD-93-781, University of California-Berkeley,* 1993.

[5] D. Burger and T. Austin, "The SimpleScalar Tool Set, Version 2.0", *Technical Report No. CS-TR-97-1342, University of Wisconsin-Madison,* Jun. 1997.

[6] R. Espasa. "Advanced Vector Architectures", *PhD Thesis. Universitat Politècnica de Catalunya, Barcelona,* February 1997.

[7] J. González, "Speculative Execution Through Value Prediction", *PhD Thesis, Universitat Politècnica de Catalunya,* January 2000.

[8] J. González and A. González. "Memory Address Prediction for Data Speculation", *in Proceedings of Europar97, Passau(Germany), August 1997.*

[9] K. Kennedy, "A Survey of Compiler Optimization Techniques," *Le Point sur la Compilation,* (M. Amirchahy and N. Neel, editors), INRIA, Le Chesnay, France, (1978), pages 115-161.

[10] Corinna G. Lee and Derek J. DeVries. "Initial Results on the Performance and Cost of Vector Microprocessors", *in Proceedings of the 13th Annual IEEE/ACM International Symposium on Microarchitecture, Research Triangle Pk United States.* December 1 - 3, 1997.

[11] D. López, J. Llosa, M. Valero and E. Ayguadé, "Widening Resources: A Cost-Effective Technique for Aggressive ILP Architectures", *in Proceedings of the 31st International Symposium on Microarchitecture, pp 237-246,* Nov-Dec 1998.

[12] J. A. Rivers, G. S. Tyson, E. S. Davidson and T. M. Austin, "On High-Bandwidth Data Cache Design for Multi-Issue Processors", *in Proceedings of the 30th Symposium on Microarchitecture,* 1997.

[13] E. Rotenberg, "AR-SMT: A Microarchitectural Approach to Fault Tolerance in Microprocessors", *in 29th Fault-Tolerant Computing Symposium,* June 1999.

[14] E. Rotenberg, Q. Jacobson and J. Smith, "A Study of Control Independence in Superscalar Processors", *in Proceedings of the 5th International Symposium on High Performance Computing Architecture,* January 1999.

[15] E. Rotenberg and J. Smith, "Control Independence in Trace Processors", *in Proceedings of 32nd Symposium on Microarchitecture,* January 1999.

[16] R. M. Russell, "The Cray-1 Computer System", *in Communications of the ACM, 21(1) pp 63-72,* January 1978.

[17] J. E. Smith, G. Faanes and R. Sugumar, "Vector Instructions Set Support for Conditional Operations", *in Proceedings of the 27th Symposium on Computer Architecture,* 2000.

[18] A. Sodani and G. S. Sohi, "Dynamic Instruction Reuse", *in Proceedings of the 24th International Symposium on Computer Architecture,* 1997.

[19] J. Tubella and A. González, "Control Speculation in Multithread Processors through Dynamic Loop Detection", *in Proceedings of the 4th International Symposium on High-Performance Computer Architecture, Las Vegas (USA),* February, 1998.

[20] A. K. Uht, "Concurrency Extraction via Hardware Methods Executing the Static Instruction Stream", *IEEE Transactions on Computers, vol. 41,* July 1992.

[21] S. Vajapeyam, J.P. Joseph and T. Mitra, "Dynamic Vectorization: A Mechanism for Exploiting Far-Flung ILP in Ordinary Programs", *in Proceedings of the 26th International Symposium on Computer Architecture,* May 1999.

[22] S. W. White and S. Dhawan, "Power2", *in IBM Journal of Research and Development, v.38, n. 5, pp 493-502,* Sept 1994.

[23] K. M. Wilson and K. Olukotun, "High Bandwidth On-Chip Cache Design", *IEEE Transactions on Computers, vol. 50, no. 4,* April 2001.

[24] H. P. Zima and B. Chapman, "Supercompilers for Parallel and Vector Processors", *in ACM Press Frontier Series/Addison-Wesley,* 1990.

Tarantula: A Vector Extension to the Alpha Architecture

Roger Espasa, Federico Ardanaz, Joel Emer[‡], Stephen Felix[‡], Julio Gago, Roger Gramunt,
Isaac Hernandez, Toni Juan, Geoff Lowney[‡], Matthew Mattina[‡], André Seznec[‡*]

Compaq–UPC Microprocessor Lab
Universitat Politècnica Catalunya
Barcelona, Spain

[‡]Alpha Development Group
Compaq Computer Corporation
Shrewsbury, MA

Abstract

Tarantula is an aggressive floating point machine targeted at technical, scientific and bioinformatics workloads, originally planned as a follow-on candidate to the EV8 processor [6, 5]. Tarantula adds to the EV8 core a vector unit capable of 32 double-precision flops per cycle. The vector unit fetches data directly from a 16 MByte second level cache with a peak bandwidth of sixty four 64-bit values per cycle. The whole chip is backed by a memory controller capable of delivering over 64 GBytes/s of raw bandwidth. Tarantula extends the Alpha ISA with new vector instructions that operate on new architectural state. Salient features of the architecture and implementation are: (1) it fully integrates into a virtual-memory cache-coherent system without changes to its coherency protocol, (2) provides high bandwidth for non-unit stride memory accesses, (3) supports gather/scatter instructions efficiently, (4) fully integrates with the EV8 core with a narrow, streamlined interface, rather than acting as a co-processor, (5) can achieve a peak of 104 operations per cycle, and (6) achieves excellent "real-computation" per transistor and per watt ratios. Our detailed simulations show that Tarantula achieves an average speedup of 5X over EV8, out of a peak speedup in terms of flops of 8X. Furthermore, performance on gather/scatter intensive benchmarks such as Radix Sort is also remarkable: a speedup of almost 3X over EV8 and 15 sustained operations per cycle. Several benchmarks exceed 20 operations per cycle.

1. Introduction

As CMOS technology progresses, we are able to integrate an ever-growing number of transistors on chip and the interconnect within the die can be used to achieve massive amounts of bandwidth from on-chip caches. The challenge architects face is governing effectively this large amount of computation resources that CMOS makes available.

If a large number of resources such as functional units, memory ports, etc. are to be controlled individually, the amount of real estate devoted to control structures grows non-linearly. The lack of control aggregation results in long, slow global wires that limit overall performance and hinder scalability. Both wide superscalar and VLIW architectures suffer from this problem, due to the small granularity of their instructions. Scalar instructions typically only encode one, sometimes two, operations to be performed by the processor (an add, an add and a memory access, a multiply-add, etc.). Yet, the number of control structures required to execute each instruction is growing with processor complexity and frequency.

In contrast, vector ISAs provide an efficient organization for controlling a large amount of computation resources. Vector instructions offer a good aggregation of control by localizing the expression of parallelism. Furthermore, vector ISAs emphasize local communication and provide excellent computation/transistor ratios. These properties translate in regular VLSI structures that require very simple, distributed control. Combining the parallel execution capabilities of vector instructions with the effectiveness of on-chip caches, good speedups over a conventional superscalar processor can be obtained with a main memory bandwidth on the order of 1 byte per flop. Since increasing memory bandwidth is one of the most expensive pieces of a system's overall cost, maximizing the computation capabilities attached to a given memory bandwidth seems the right path to follow. In particular, a large L2 cache can provide tremendous bandwidth to a vector engine. Such an L2 will naturally have a long latency. Nonetheless, the latency-tolerant properties of vector instructions offsets this downside while taking advantage of the bandwidth offered. The

---

*While on sabbatical from INRIA

281

main difficulties in this mixture of vectors and caches are non-unit strides and gather/scatter operations.

Tarantula is an aggressive floating point machine targeted at technical, scientific and bioinformatics workloads, originally planned as a follow-on candidate to the *EV8* processor [5, 6]. Tarantula adds to the *EV8* core a vector unit capable of 32 double-precision flops per cycle. The vector unit fetches data directly from a 16 MByte second level cache with a peak bandwidth of sixty four 64-bit values per cycle. The whole chip is backed by a memory controller capable of delivering over 64 GBytes/s of raw bandwidth.

Tarantula's architecture and implementation have a number of features worth highlighting. The vector unit can be tightly integrated into an aggressive out-of-order wide-issue superscalar core with a narrow, streamlined interface that consists of: instruction delivery, kill signals, scalar data and a handshaking protocol for cooperative retirement of instructions. The new vector memory instructions fully integrate into the Alpha virtual-memory cache-coherent system without changes to its coherency protocol. Our design shows that the vector unit can be easily integrated into the existing *EV8* physical L2 design simply by duplicating some control structures and changing the pipeline flow slightly. An address reordering scheme has been devised to allow conflict-free vector requests to the L2. This technique provides very good bandwidth on both unit and non-unit strides. *Tarantula* also provides high bandwidth for gather and scatter instructions and smoothly integrates them into the aggressive out-of-order memory pipeline. The vector execution engine uses register renaming and out-of-order execution and supports the SMT paradigm [18, 19] to easily integrate with the *EV8* core.

Finally, the question of commercial viability must also be addressed from two points of view: first, the cost of converting the installed customer base to a vector ISA and second, the market demand for a chip such as *Tarantula*.

Despite all its advantages, a vector ISA extension doesn't come without a cost. The major investment comes from software compatibility: new vector instructions require application recompilation and tuning to effectively use the on-chip vector unit. Compiler support to integrate tiling techniques with vectorization techniques is needed to extract maximum performance from the memory hierarchy. Also, our experience coding benchmarks for *Tarantula* shows that proper data prefetching is of paramount importance to achieve good performance.

Concerning market demand, we note the scientific computing segment still represents a multi-billion dollar market segment. Many of the applications in this domain exhibit a large degree of vector (data) parallelism and manipulate large volumes of data. This vector parallelism is not correctly accommodated by the small first level caches of current off-the-shelf microprocessors: poor cache behavior

ruins performance. We believe performance of chip multiprocessors on vector codes will suffer from the same difficulty: processors will compete for the L2 and contention will lead to poor performance. So, although the rapidly growing workstation and PC market segment has oriented the whole computer industry (including the server industry) towards using standard off-the-shelf microprocessors, we believe the time is ready again for architecture specialization to better match application needs.

2. Instruction Set Extension

Tarantula adds to the Alpha ISA new architectural state in the form of 32 vector registers (v0..v31) and their associated control registers: vector length (vl), vector stride (vs), and vector mask (vm). Each vector register holds 128 64-bit values. The vl register is an 8-bit register that controls the length of each vector operation. The vs register is a 64-bit register that controls the stride between memory locations accessed by vector memory operations. The vm register is a 128-bit register used in instructions that operate under mask.

To operate on this new architectural state, 45 new instructions (not counting data-type variations) are added to the instruction set. The new instructions can be broadly grouped into five categories: vector-vector operate (VV), vector-scalar operate (VS), strided memory access (SM), random memory access (RM), and vector control (VC). Figure 1 presents the semantics of a representative instruction of the first four groups. The instructions semantics are straightforward extensions of the existing scalar Alpha instructions to allow operating on the vector registers.

A novel feature of the ISA is the approach to vector mask computation. To avoid long latency data transfers back and forth between the *Vbox* ALUs and the *EV8* scalar register file (a 20-cycle round-trip delay), vector comparisons store the resulting boolean vector in a full vector register. This allows coding complex if-statements without vector-scalar communication. For example, the translation of A(i).ne.0.and.B(i).gt.2 would be:

```
vloadq      A(i)       --> v0
vloadq      B(i)       --> v1
vcmpne      v0, #0     --> v6
vcmpgt      v1, #2     --> v7
vand        v6, v7     --> v8
setvm       v8         --> vm
```

The final *setvm* instruction indicates that the v8 register is to be copied into the vm register. Subsequent instructions that use the "under-mask" specifier will use this vm value. Since the vm register is renamed in the *Vbox*, the next mask value can be pre-computed while using the current one and

Group	Example	Semantics

VV	VVADDQ Va, Vb, Vc	`for (i = 0; i < vl; i++) {`
		`  Vc[i] = Va[i] + Vb[i]`
		`}`
		`for (i = vl; i < 128; i++) {`
		`  Vc[i] = <UNPREDICTABLE>`
		`}`

VS	VSMULQ Va, Fb, Vc	`for (i = 0; i < vl; i++) {`
		`  Vc[i] = Va[i] * Fb`
		`}`
		`for (i = vl; i < 128; i++) {`
		`  Vc[i] = <UNPREDICTABLE>`
		`}`

SM	VLOADQ Vc, off(Rb)	`S = GEN_RANDOM_PERMUT(0,VL-1)`
		`foreach i in S {`
		`  ea = Rb + off + (i * vs)`
		`  Vc[i] = MEM[ea]`
		`}`
		`for (i = vl; i < 128; i++) {`
		`  Vc[i] = <UNPREDICTABLE>`
		`}`

RM	VSCATQ Va, Rb, Vc	`S = GEN_RANDOM_PERMUT(0,VL-1)`
		`foreach i in S {`
		`  ea = Va[i] + Rb`
		`  MEM[ea] = Vc[i]`
		`}`

Figure 1. The four major instruction groups in *Tarantula*. For each group, a representative instruction is shown and its semantics presented.

compilers can interleave instructions from two separate if-then-else statements in a loop body.

Following the Alpha tradition, register v31 is hardwired to zero. Therefore, vector prefetches, including gather and scatter prefetches, can be trivially crafted by using v31 as the destination register. As in most Alpha implementations, page faults and TLB misses caused by vector prefetches are simply ignored.

Tarantula provides a precise exception model at the instruction level granularity. If a vector instruction causes a trap (TLB miss, divide-by-0, etc.), the system software will be provided with the PC of the faulting instruction, but no extra information on which element (or elements) within the vector caused the fault.

3. Tarantula Architecture

3.1. Block Diagram

Figure 2 shows a high-level block diagram of the *Tarantula* processor. The *EV8* core is extended with a vector unit (*Vbox*) that handles the execution of all new vector instructions. The *EV8* core performs all scalar computations and is also responsible for fetching, renaming and retiring vector instructions on behalf of the *Vbox*. Furthermore, *EV8* also notifies the *Vbox* whenever instructions must be killed due to mispredicts or faults. *Vbox* and the *EV8* core also cooperate for retiring vector memory writes.

Tarantula reuses the memory controller (*Zbox*) and the inter-processor router (*Rbox*) from the *EV8* design. We do however assume that in the 2006 time frame we should be

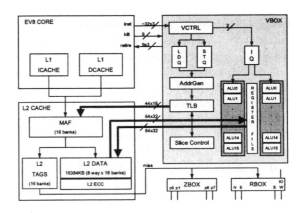

Figure 2. Block diagram of the *Tarantula* processor

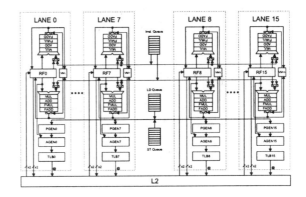

Figure 3. *Vbox* Lanes.

able to roughly quadruple main memory bandwidth from the current 12.8 GBytes/s to over 50 GBytes/s. While the exact memory technology to be employed is not currently known, for the purposes of this study we assumed the *Zbox* would control 32 RAMBUS channels, grouped as eight ports (roughly 64 GBytes/s raw bandwidth assuming 1066 Mhz parts).

3.2. Vector Execution Engine

The vector execution engine is organized as 16 lanes (see Figure 3). Each lane has a slice of the vector register file, a slice of the vector mask file, two functional units, an address generator and a private TLB. Notice the regularity of the overall engine: all lanes are identical and the instruction queues are located in the middle. There is no communication across lanes, except for gather/scatters (see below).

Regularity and design simplicity are not the only advantages that lanes give us. The schedulers that govern the allocation of this large number of functional units are very simple too. To them, the 32 functional units appear only as just two resources: the north and south issue ports. When an instruction is launched onto one of the two ports, the sixteen associated functional units work fully synchronously on the instruction. Thus, the port is marked busy for $\lceil vl/16 \rceil$ cycles (typically, 8 cycles). To put it in another way: a simple dual-issue window is able to fully utilize 32 functional units.

The fact that the full register file is sliced into sixteen pieces is yet another advantage of the vector instruction paradigm. The bandwidth between the vector register file and the functional units is 64+32 operands per cycle. A unified register file would be totally out of the question. In contrast, the sliced register file enables that each lane only needs 4R+2W for the functional units[1]. Note that, as opposed to clustering techniques [11], writes into one register file lane do not need to be made visible to other lanes.

Finally, the vector mask register file is also sliced across the 16 lanes. The mask file is very small compared to the vector register file (256 bits per lane, including all rename copies per thread) and only requires three 1-bit read ports and two 1-bit write ports.

3.3. *Vbox*-Core Interface

Another positive aspect of the vector extension is that the *Vbox* can be integrated with the core with a relatively small interface (see Figure 2). In *Tarantula*, a 3-instruction bus carries renamed instructions from the *EV8* renaming unit (*Pbox*) to the *Vbox*. Routing space was scarce and, hence, a larger bus seemed impractical to use. When instructions complete in the *Vbox*, the vector completion unit (VCU) sends back to the *EV8* core their instruction identifiers (3x9 bits). Final instruction retirement is performed by the *EV8* core, which is responsible for reporting to the system software any exceptions occurred in the vector instruction flow. The other major interface is a double bus to carry two 64-bit values from the *EV8* register file to the *Vbox*. We note that all vector instructions except those of the VV group require a scalar operand as a source operand. These two buses are used to supply this data. Finally, the *EV8* core must also provide a kill signal, so that the vector unit can squash misspeculated instructions. Of course, tightly coupling to *EV8* also imposed some constraints: for example, to avoid excessive burden onto the operating system, the *Vbox* was also multithreaded. This decision forced using a much larger register file.

3.4. Vector Memory System

The *Tarantula* processor was targeted as a replacement for *EV8* in Compaq's mid-to-high end range servers and had to be a board-compatible replacement for *EV8*. Consequently, *Tarantula* had to integrate seamlessly into the Alpha virtual memory and the cache coherency architecture

of *EV8*. Of course, these requirements completely ruled out exotic packaging technologies from vector supercomputers that provide more than 10,000 pins per cpu. Vector memory accesses had to be satisfied from the on-chip caches. We faced several important challenges to meet these requirements.

First, load/store bandwidth into the vector register file had to be an adequate match to the 32 flops of the vector engine. In *Tarantula*, we set our design goal to a 1:1 ratio between flops and bandwidth to the cache for unit stride cache accesses (i.e., a 64-bit datum for every flop). Attaching the vector engine to the L1 cache did not seem a very promising avenue. Typical L1 sizes are too small to hold the working sets of common engineering, scientific and bioinformatics applications. Moreover, re-designing *EV8*'s L1 cache to provide sixteen independent ports to support non-unit strides was out of the question. We were left with the obvious choice of having the *Vbox* communicate directly to the L2 cache (as already proposed in [15]).

Second, dealing with non-unit strides was a central problem in the design. Despite unit-strides being very common, they only account for around 80% of all vector memory accesses. Large non-unit strides account roughly for another 10%, while stride-2, the next most common case, accounts for a 4% [20, 14]. Cache lines and non-unit strides clearly don't blend together very well. Previous research on the topic either focused on providing good bandwidth only for unit stride vector accesses [15, 8] or simply went for a classical cache-less design [1, 22]. The Cray SV1 system sidestepped the problem by using single-word cache lines [4]. In *Tarantula*, we developed an address reordering scheme, described below, that enabled a 1:2 ratio between flops and cache accesses for non-unit stride instructions (i.e., sixteen independent 64-bit words per cycle from the cache).

Third, we had to integrate gather/scatter instructions smoothly into the pipeline. Gather/scatter instructions contain random addressing patterns to which the reordering scheme can not be applied. *Tarantula* employs a conflict-resolution unit, also described below, that sorts gather/scatter addresses into bank conflict-free buckets. Then, these sorted addresses can be sent as normal vector requests to the L2 cache.

Reusing *EV8*'s L2 design

Analyzing *EV8*'s L2 physical design we realized it already contained an enormous number of independent banks each with its own address decoder: *EV8*'s 4 Mbyte cache was physically laid out as 128 independent banks (8 ways times 16 banks per way). In addition, the design called for cycling eight banks in parallel on an L2 access, and then selecting the correct way.

---

[1]There are also 2R+2W ports to support stores and loads.

Thus, both from a structural and a power perspective, *EV8*'s L2 could easily accommodate reading 16 independent cache lines and then selecting one quadword[2] from each cache line provided each cache line was located on a different physical bank. The problem of delivering high bandwidth to non-unit stride requests reduced then to generating groups of 16 addresses that were cache-bank conflict-free. This is a variation of an old problem in vector memory design for supercomputers [20, 21], and next section describes the particular solution employed in *Tarantula*.

Conflict-free Address Generation

As discussed in the previous section, the key to high performance is the ability to read in parallel sixteen cache lines from the sixteen L2 cache banks. Two conditions must hold to allow this parallel read: first, the addresses must be tag-bank and data-bank conflict free (since both arrays are equally banked, these two conditions are equivalent). Second, once the sixteen data items have been read from the L2, they must be written into the sixteen lanes of the vector register file without conflicts. That is, each lane can only accept one quadword from the memory system per cycle.

We proved that, for any 128 consecutive elements of any vector with stride $S = \sigma \times 2^s$ with σ odd and $s \leq 4$, there exists a requesting order that can group these 128 elements into 8 groups (each with 16 addresses) which are both L2-bank conflict free and register-lane conflict-free. This order can be implemented using a ROM distributed across the lanes that contains 2.1 Kbytes of information and a specialized 64-by-7 multiplier in each lane that uses the ROM contents to compute the starting address for each address generator.

The downside of our algorithm is that, as elements in the vectors are accessed out-of-order, we must wait for the full 128 elements to come back from the L2 before chaining a dependent operation. Consequently, vector instructions with vector length below 128 still pay the full eight cycles to generate all their addresses. The detailed address reordering algorithm is further described and analyzed in [16].

A group of 16 conflict-free addresses is called a "slice". Note that a slice need not be fully populated. Some of the addresses in it may have the valid bit clear (due to `vl` being less than 128 or due to a masked memory operation). All the vector memory pipeline is built around the concept of slices. Each slice is tagged with a slice identifier when it is created in the address generators and this tag is used throughout the memory pipeline to track it.

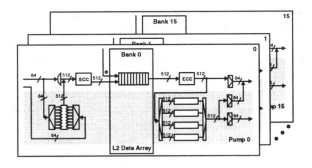

Figure 4. Pump structure used to accelerate stride-1 reads and writes.

Stride-1 Double Bandwidth Mode

Stride-1 instructions are treated specially to take advantage of their spatial locality. If properly aligned, the 128 quadwords requested by a stride-1 instruction are contained in exactly 16 cache lines (17 if the base address is not aligned to a cache line boundary). Rather than generating 8 slices, each with 16 addresses, we changed the address generation control to produce the *starting* address of each of the sixteen cache lines required instead. We then set the "pump" bit on the resulting slice[3].

The PUMP, shown in Figure 4, is a new structure located at the output of each bank in the L2 data array dedicated to accelerate both read and write stride-1 requests. Strides marked with the "pump" bit read out 16 cache lines from the data array just like any other slice does. But, as opposed to normal slices, the sixteen *full* cache lines are latched into one of the four registers (16x512 bits each) of the PUMP structure. From there, a sequencer in each bank reads *two* quadwords per cycle and sends them to the *Vbox*. The write path works similarly: the *Vbox* sends 32 quadwords worth of data every cycle, which get written into the accumulator register (to the left on Figure 4). When all 128 quadwords have been received (i.e., four cycles later), the PUMP will ECC the full register and write it in a single cycle into the data array. We note that using the PUMP, we can sustain a bandwidth of 64 qw/cycle (32 from a stride-1 read and 32 from a stride-1 write).

Gather/Scatters and Self-Conflicting Strides

Gather and scatter instructions do not use a stride value to generate their addresses. Rather, the programmer supplies a vector register that contains arbitrary addresses. Consequently, addresses do not form an arithmetic series and our reordering algorithm does not apply. However, in order

---

[2]A quadword (abbrv. "qw") is defined in the Alpha Architecture Reference Manual to be a 64-bit object.

[3]For misaligned stride-1 cases, the address generators will be forced to generate two slices, both with the pump bit set.

to integrate them into the memory pipeline, we must pack these random addresses into slices.

Our solution is to take the 128 addresses of a gather/scatter and feed them to a piece of logic, the conflict resolution box (CR), whose goal is to sort the addresses into buckets corresponding to the sixteen cache banks. As a group of sixteen addresses comes out of the address generators, their bank identifiers (bits <9:6> of each address) are sent to the CR box. The CR box compares all sixteen bank identifiers with each other and selects the largest subset that are conflict-free. The resulting subset is packed into a slice and sent down the memory pipe for further processing. As new addresses (rather, bank identifiers) become available, the CR box will run again a selection tournament across whatever addresses where left from the previous round and as many new bank identifiers up to a limit of sixteen. By repeating this tournament procedure, eventually all addresses of the gather/scatter instruction will be packed into slices (worst case, when all addresses map to the same bank, an instruction may generate 128 different slices).

Self-conflicting strides are those strides that cause all addresses to map to only a handful of banks. More formally, strides $S = \sigma \times 2^s$ with σ odd and $s > 4$ are considered self-conflicting. Any instruction with such a stride is treated exactly like a gather/scatter and run through the CR box (instead of applying the reordering algorithm).

Virtual Memory

To keep the large number of functional units in the *Vbox* busy, it is important to avoid TLB misses. Piggy-backing on other work developed at Compaq to support large pages, the *Tarantula* architecture adopted a 512 Mbyte virtual memory page size [2, 3, 9].

The vector TLB is a parallel array of sixteen 32-entry fully associative TLBs, one TLB per lane. Each TLB is devoted to mapping the addresses generated by the address generator in its lane. Whenever a slice experiences a TLB miss, control is transferred to system software to initiate a TLB refill. System software may follow two strategies to refill the missing mappings: (1) it may simply look at the missing translations and refill those lanes where the miss has occurred, or (2) PALcode may peek at the vs value and refill the TLBs with all the mappings that might be needed by the offending instruction.

While we would rather use sixteen direct-mapped TLBs from a cost and power perspective, we note that a complication appears with some very large strides: a programmer could easily craft a stride that referenced 128 different pages which mapped onto the same TLB index (even with 512 Mbyte pages). Consequently, each TLB must be at least 8-way set-associative to guarantee that forward progress is

possible on instructions with such strides. Given this restriction, a CAM-based implementation seemed more effective and we compensated the extra power consumption by choosing a small TLB per lane (32 entries only).

Servicing Vector Misses

Another interesting challenge appears when a vector memory instruction experiences a cache miss: The *Vbox* has sent a read slice to the L2 cache and several of its sixteen addresses miss in the lookup stage. How do we deal with this vector miss?

Our solution was to treat the slice as an atomic entity. If one of the addresses in a slice experiences one or more misses, the slice waits in the L2 cache (in the Miss Address File, MAF) until the corresponding system requests are made and all the missing cache lines are received from their home nodes. The slice is "put to sleep" in the MAF and a "waiting" bit is set for each of its sixteen addresses that missed. As each individual cache line arrives to the L2 from the system, it searches the MAF for matching addresses. For each matching address, its "waiting" bit is cleared. When all "waiting" bits are clear, the slice wakes up and goes to the Retry Queue (a structure within the L2 cache itself). From there, the slice will retry, walk down the L2 pipe again and lookup the tag array a second time. The hope is this second time the slice will succeed in reading/writing its data. To avoid the potential livelock we introduced a replay threshold value. If a slice replays more times than the threshold, the MAF enters "panic mode" and starts NACKing all L1, *Vbox* and interprocessor requests that may prevent forward progress for that slice. Only when the slice is finally serviced, the MAF resumes normal operation.

Scalar-Vector Coherency

Coherency problems appear in *Tarantula* because the *EV8* core is reading and writing from the L1 cache and the *Vbox* is reading/writing into the L2 cache behind its back. We must ensure that the data read/written both by *EV8* and the *Vbox* are the same as if both where writing sequentially into the same memory space.

The protocol used to achieve the desired scalar-vector coherency is based on the ideas presented in [15]. Each tag in the L2 cache is extended with a "presence" bit (P-bit). The presence bit indicates whether the cache line was loaded into the L2 due to a request from the *EV8* core or not. In essence, the P-bit is like a soft-ownership bit and is set whenever the *EV8* core touches a cache line. The P-bit is used whenever the *Vbox* is checking the L2 tags to know whether there is the danger that the cache lines being read/written might also be in the L1 cache. If the P-bit is set, then invalidate commands must be sent to the L1 to synchronize the state of both caches. The invalidate commands

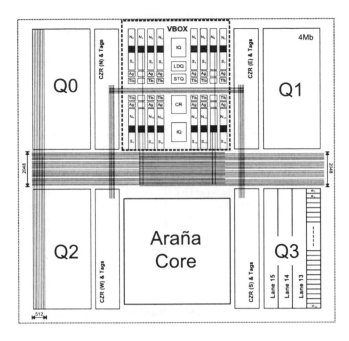

Figure 5. *Tarantula* **floorplan.**

Circuitry	CMP-*EV8* Area (%)	CMP-*EV8* Power (W)	*Tarantula* Area (%)	*Tarantula* Power (W)
Core	42	54,3	15	22,2
IO Drivers		26,5		26,5
IO logic	14	6,6	8	4,3
L2 cache	33	5,1	43	7,6
R/Z Box	5	6,3	7	10,1
Vbox	–	–	15	30,9
Other	6	7,9	12	18,2
Total (+20%)		128,0		143,7
Die Area	250 mm^2		286 mm^2	
Peak Gflops	20		80	
Gflops/Watt	0,16		0,55	

Table 1. Power and area estimates for a CMP-*EV8* processor and for *Tarantula*. The "Total" line includes a 20% extra power attributed to leakage.

either remove the line from the L1 if it is clean, or force a write-through of the line to L2 if it's dirty. Also, when a line is evicted from the L2, if it's P-bit is set, it will also cause an Invalidate command to be sent to the *EV8* core.

The P-bit solves most of the coherency problems that arise due to the out-of-order execution of vector and scalar read/write instructions. However, one case is not covered and requires programmer intervention: a scalar write followed by a vector read[4]. In *EV8*, a scalar store sits in the store queue, potentially with its associated data, until it retires. At that time, it moves from the store queue into the write buffer *without informing* either the L1 cache or the L2 cache. A younger vector read going out to the L2 has no visibility into either the write buffer or the store queue. It may well be that no P-bit is set in the L2. Therefore, the vector load has no way of knowing it's reading stale data. The programmer/compiler must insert a special memory barrier called *DrainM* to solve this problem. When *DrainM* is about to retire, it sends a purge command to the write buffer. This purge forces all previous stores out of the store queue and into the cache hierarchy, and also updates their associated L2 P-bits. When the purge is complete, the *DrainM* retires and causes a *replay trap* on the following instruction. Thus, all instructions younger than the *DrainM* are killed and re-fetched, ensuring correct behavior.

---

[4]A scalar write followed by a vector write is correctly handled by having all scalar writes write-through to the L2 before actually letting the vector write proceed. This behavior is only forced for those threads that have vector instructions.

4. Floorplan

The current *Tarantula* floorplan is shown in Figure 5. As it can be seen, the floorplan is highly symmetric. The cache is located at the outer corners of the die. The cache holds a total of 16 MBytes and is split into four quadrants, indexed by bits <7:6> of the address. Each quadrant holds 4 cache lanes, selected by bits <9:8>, for a total of 16 lanes. Each cache lane holds 48 stacked banks, over which run 512 wires to read/write the cache line data. The wiring uses a coarse-level metal because the distance to the central bus area is rather large.

The central bus area implements the crossbar between the cache lanes and the *Vbox* lanes. As already discussed, a quadword from any of the cache lanes may have to go to any of the *Vbox* lanes. We take advantage of the fact that bits flowing from the quadrants have to "take two turns" on their path to the *Vbox*. This means that the point were the north-south wires have to be connected to the east-west wires is an ideal place to put the different crossbar connections. The central bus itself carries 4096 bits, but is folded onto itself by using alternate East-West metal layers, so that it uses an area equivalent to a 2048-bit bus.

The floorplan also illustrates how the different *Vbox* lanes are organized in four groups of four lanes. Each lane shows a shaded area in the middle, the register file, and a north and south functional unit. The instruction queue is replicated and located in between the lanes to minimize wiring delays. In each lane, one can see an address generator. The alignment of the address generators with the lanes is fundamental to ease the wiring for the scatter/gather addresses. Again, the load and store queues are located at the center of the address generators to equalize delays. The CR box is also located at the center of all address generators.

Benchmark	Description	Inputs	Comments	Pref?	DrainM?	Vect. %
MicroKernels						
STREAMS [12]	Copy, Scale, Add, Triadd Kernels	Reference	Padding=65856 bytes			99.5
RndCopy	B(i) = A(index(i))	A,B=4096000 elements	Prefetched into L2	yes		99.9
RndMemScale	B(index(i)) = B(index(i)) + 1	B=512000 elements	All data from memory	yes		99.9
SpecFP2000						
swim	Shallow Water Model	Reference	Tiled following [17]			
art	Image Recognition/Neural Networks	Reference			yes	99.3
sixtrack	High Energy Nuclear Physics	Reference				93.7
Algebra						
dgemm	Dense, Tiled, Matrix Multiply	640x640		yes		99.0
dtrmm	Triangular matrix multiply	519x603	Dense, Tiled	yes		98.9
Sparse MxV	Sparse matrix-vector product	24696x24696	887937 non-zeroes	yes		99.3
fft	Radix-4 Fast Fourier Transform	5120 FFTs	1024 elements per FFT	yes		98.7
lu	Lower-Upper Matrix decomposition	519x603	Tiled Version		yes	98.6
Linpack100	Dense Linear Equation Solver	100x100	No code reorganization		yes	85.5
LinpackTPP	Dense Linear Equation Solver	1000x1000	Tiled		yes	96.5
Bioinformatics						
moldyn	Molecular Dynamics	500 molecule system				99.5
Integer						
ccradix	Tiled Integer Sort	2000000 elements	From [10]			98.0

Table 2. Benchmark descriptions. Columns "Prefetch" and "DrainM" indicate whether the benchamrk uses those features.

The CR box needs the bank information from each address generator to sort the addresses into conflict-free slices.

5. Power Estimates

We estimated the power of the *Tarantula* processor by scaling *EV7*'s power and area estimates down to 65 nm technology. Table 1 presents a breakdown of power and area estimates assuming a voltage slightly under 1V and a clock frequency of 2.5 Ghz. The table presents estimates for two different architectures: a CMP-style processor based on two *EV8* cores[5] and the *Tarantula* processor described so far. Both processors use the same L2 cache and memory subsystem. The power consumption of the *Vbox* is extrapolated using the power-density of the floating point units of *EV7*, and thus should be considered a lower bound, since the TLBs and address generation logic are not properly accounted for.

Our estimates show that *Tarantula* is 3.4X better in terms of Gflops/Watt than a CMP solution based on replicating two *EV8* cores. We note that adding floating point multiply-accumulate units (FMAC) to *Tarantula*, this rate could be doubled with very little extra complexity and power. In contrast, adding FMAC instructions that require an extra third operand to *EV8* would require an expensive rework of *EV8*'s instruction queue and renaming units.

[5]Notice that in the *Tarantula* floorplan, a *Vbox* or an *EV8* core could be used interchangeably, and yet keep the same memory system.

6. Performance Evaluation

Evaluation Methodology

The *Tarantula* processor is targeted at scientific, engineering and bioinformatics applications. Consequently, we selected a number of applications and program kernels from these areas to use them as our workload. Unfortunately, no vectorizing compiler that could generate the new *Tarantula* instructions was available. Hence, we used profiling to determine the hot routines of each benchmark and, then, these were coded in vector assembly by hand. All programs were compiled using either Compaq's C or Fortran, versions 5.9 and 5.2 respectively. The benchmarks chosen are described in Table 2.

For our simulations, we used the ASIM infrastructure [7] developed by Compaq's VSSAD group. Included in the ASIM framework is a cycle-accurate *EV8* simulator, that is validated against the *EV8* RTL description. We modified this base code to derive the *Tarantula* simulator, by hooking up the *Vbox* to it and modifying the *Cbox* model to accept vector requests. No changes were made to the internals of the *Zbox* or *Rbox* (except, of course, adding more ports). All our simulations run in single-thread, single-processor mode.

The *Tarantula* architecture's main parameters are shown in Table 3. The other architectures under study are also included: *EV8* is the baseline against which we compare the *Tarantula* processor. *EV8+* is an *EV8* processor equipped with *Tarantula*'s memory system. Finally, we include also *Tarantula4*, an aggressively clocked *Tarantula* processor.

Symbol	EV8	EV8+	T	T4
Core Speed (Ghz)	2.13	2.13	2.13	4.8
Ops per Cycle:				
Core Issue	8	8	8	8
Vbox Issue	–	–	3	3
Peak Int/FP	8/4	8/4	32	32
Peak Ld+St	2+2	2+2	32+32	32+32
EV8-Vbox latency	–	–	10	10
L1 assoc	2	2	2	2
L1 line (bytes)	64	64	64	64
L2 size (x2^{20})	4	16	16	16
L2 assoc	8	8	8	8
L2 line (bytes)	64	64	64	64
L2 BW (GB/s)	273	273	1091	2457
L2 Load-to-use lat.				
Scalar Req	12	12	28	28
Vector Stride-1	–	–	34	34
Vector Odd stride	–	–	38	38
RAMBUS:				
Ports	2	8	8	8
Speed (Mhz)	1066	1066	1066	1200
BW (GB/s)	16.6	66.6	66.6	75.0

Table 3. Characteristics of the four architectures under study. Note that the L2 BW refers to maximum sustainable bandwidth: for *EV8*, both a line read and a line write can proceed in parallel. For *Tarantula*, in stride-1 mode, 16 lines can be read every 4 cycles and, in parallel, 16 lines can be written every 4 cycles. Latencies are given in cycles.

The frequency for each processor is derived from the corresponding RAMBUS frequency by using either a 1:2 ratio or a 1:4 ratio.

Memory System Microbenchmarks

Table 4 presents the performance of the three microbenchmarks targeted at measuring memory system behavior running on *Tarantula*.

To understand the copy loop bandwidth, note that out of a peak raw bandwidth of 66.625 GB/s (8 channels at 1066 Mhz), 1/3 is consumed by directory updates. The loop kernel is composed of a memory read, a *wh64* instruction that generates a directory transition from Invalid to Dirty (i.e., a read from RAMBUS), and the store that eventually causes a memory write. Thus, 2/3 are "useful" bandwidth. Out of this peak, read-to-write transitions on the RAMBUS bus limit our achieved bandwidth to 90%, or 40.3 GB/s. As a reference, the top STREAMS copy bandwidth for a single cpu, as of Oct 31st, 2001 [12], corresponds to the NEC SX/5 [13] with a value of 42.5 GB/s. The best single-cpu non-vector result is a Pentium4 1.5 Ghz system manufactured by Fujitsu with a copy bandwidth close to 2.4 GB/s.

The RndCopy microkernel tests our gather/scatter band-

STREAMS	Streams BW	Raw BW
Copy	42983	64475
Scale	41689	62492
Add	43097	57463
Triadd	47970	63960
RndCopy	73456	NA
RndMemScale	7512	50106

Table 4. Sustained bandwidth in MBytes/s on *Tarantula* for several microkernels. The "Raw" column includes all memory transactions performed at the RAMBUS controller, including those necessary to update the directory information. The "Streams" column reports useful read/write bandwidth using the STREAMS method without accounting for directory traffic.

width from L2 cache (no TLB misses and no L2 cache misses). Here, the limitation are the bank conflicts encountered by the CR box when dealing with a random address stream. The bandwidth delivered corresponds to an address generation bandwidth of around 4.3 addresses/cycle.

The RndMemScale microkernel tests the random bandwidth achievable from RAMBUS. Here, the limitation is not only the address generation, but the fact that randomly touching RAMBUS "pages" causes an extra amount of "opening" and "closing" of memory pages: compared to STREAMS Copy, RndMemScale performs 2.5X more row activates and 2X more row precharges per memory request.

Benchmark Performance

We turn now to the performance of the remaining benchmarks. The results of our simulations are shown in Figure 6. For each benchmark, we present the number of sustained "operations per cycle" (OPC) broken into three categories: flops per cycle (FPC), memory operations per cycle (MPC) and other (including integer arithmetic and scalar instructions).

The results show that for most benchmarks, *Tarantula* sustains over 10 operations per cycle, and it's not uncommon to exceed 20 operations per cycle. The benchmarks with less parallelism are, not surprisingly, those where gather/scatter operations dominate: the sparse matrix-vector multiply and the two versions of radix sort. Also note how short vector length also impacts performance: linpack100 is significantly slower than the TPP counterpart.

As opposed to a conventional cache-less vector machine, *Tarantula*, like any conventional superscalar or CMP design, must pay careful attention to exploiting data reuse at

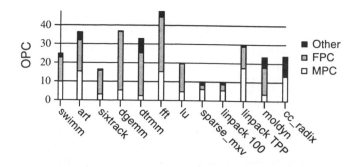

Figure 6. Operations per cycle sustained in *Tarantula*. **Each bar is broken down into Flops per cycle (FPC), Memory Operations per Cycle (MPC) and Other (which includes integer and scalar operations).**

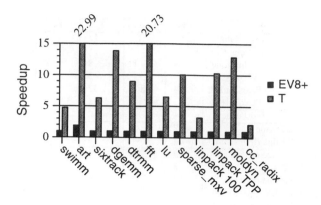

Figure 7. Speedup of *EV8+* **and** *Tarantula* **over** *EV8*.

the memory hierarchy level. Consequently, all our benchmarks are either cache-friendly or have been turned into cache-friendly codes by using standard tiling techniques. To stress the importance of tiling for the memory hierarchy in *Tarantula*, we also run a "naive" non-tiled versions of swim (not shown in the graph). The slowdown was significant: the non-tiled version was almost 2X slower. Also, benchmarks LU and LinpackTPP perform very similar tasks, yet LinpackTPP shows 50% more operations per cycle. The reason is that we performed register tiling for LU but not for LinpackTPP, thus reducing LU's memory demands.

Figure 7 presents the speedup of the *Tarantula* processor over *EV8*. As a reference, the speedup of *EV8+* is also included. The speedup results show that, typically, *Tarantula* achieves a speedup of at least 5X over *EV8*. Given that these are floating point applications, the nominal speedup based on raw floating point bandwidth is 8X. Thus, *Tarantula* delivers a very good fraction of its promised peak performance. Furthermore, as the *EV8+* results show, this performance advantage can not be attributed to the bigger cache and better memory system alone: it's the use of vector instructions that enables squeezing maximum performance from this improved memory system.

Interestingly, six applications exceed this 8X speedup factor. There are a number of reasons for this: First, *Tarantula* has a better flop:mem ratio than *EV8* (32:64 versus 4:4) for those programs that use mostly stride 1. Second, *Tarantula* has many more registers available, which turns into more data reuse and less memory operations when tiling the iteration space. Third, all these programs have been hand vectorized and hand tuned. To be fair to *EV8*, the same care should be applied optimizing the scalar inner loops. Moreover, the *EV8* versions are compiled using an EV6 scheduler because no EV8 scheduler was yet available. This

is specially significant in dgemm where *EV8* only reaches 2.5 flops/cycle. Scheduling specifically targeted to EV8 would most likely increase the flop rate to the peak and, consequently, reduce *Tarantula*'s speedup. Fourth, vectorization provides advantages because it reduces the impact of branches and pointer-maintenance instructions. For programs like fft, where lots of ILP are available, if *EV8* used all issue slots to execute 4 flops and 4 memory operations, none would be left to execute loop-related control instructions. Vector masks are also a significant source of speedup in moldyn: by executing under mask, *Tarantula* avoids hard-to-predict branches and obtains some extra speedup. Finally, the *Tarantula* versions use aggressive prefetching techniques: note that a single vector load with a stride of 64 bytes can preload a total of 128 cache lines, or 8 KB worth of data. In comparison, *EV8* needs a separate prefetch instruction for every cache line it wants to preload. A similar argument explains the speedup of sparsemxv: Driving an eight-channel RAMBUS memory controller is quite difficult for a superscalar machine that can generate at most 64 misses before stalling. In contrast, a handful of gather instructions can easily generate 1024 distinct cache line misses, and, consequently, drive the RAMBUS array to full usage.

Scalability

We also explored how well performance scales as frequency increases. Figure 8 presents the results. The main consequence of increasing frequency is that the processor-to-Rambus ratio grows very fast. Hence, memory operations take substantially longer to complete and performance will only scale if (a) the program is working mostly from cache or (b) there's enough parallelism and prefetching capabilities to cover up for the increased latency.

Our simulations show that, as expected, those programs

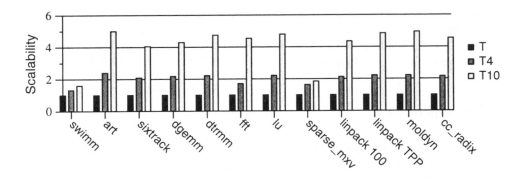

Figure 8. Performance Scaling when Frequency is increased to 4.8Ghz (T4) and to 10.6Ghz (T10). The latter frequency results from a 1:8 ratio to a RAMBUS chip running at 1333Mhz.

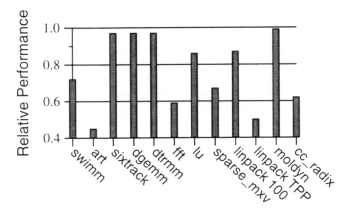

Figure 9. Slowdown due to disabling the stride-1 double-bandwidth mode.

that mostly access the L2 cache scale very well. In contrast, sparsemxv barely reaches speedups of 1.6 and 1.8 when scaling the frequency by 2.2X and 5X respectively. The results are encouraging, as they show that a *Tarantula* core could have a very long life by shrinking and, thus, the design cost could be amortized over multiple technology generations.

Stride-1 Double Bandwidth mode

The final experiment we present is a set of simulations that measure the effect of using the PUMP structure to accelerate stride-1 requests. The simulation results are shown in Figure 9.

Naturally, the programs that did not have their iteration space tiled suffer the most when stride-1 bandwidth is dropped from thirty-two 64-bit words per cycle down to sixteen. A second effect that must be taken into account is that the pressure on the MAF grows by a factor of 8X, since, without the pump, each stride-1 request now con-

sumes eight MAF slots for its eight slices as opposed to a single slot with the PUMP scheme. Note the performance of sparsemxv drops significantly without the pump. This may appear surprising, but the algorithm we tested makes good use of stride-1 performance. Also, one would expect ccradix to be dominated by gather/scatters, but stride-1 performance is important here as well.

7. Conclusions

There still exist a wide number of applications where a vector processor is the most efficient way of achieving high performance. In this paper we have presented *Tarantula*, a vector extension to the Alpha architecture that can achieve up to 104 operations per cycle (96 vector operations; 32 integer or floating point arithmetic operations, 32 loads and 32 stores; and 8 scalar instructions). *Tarantula* is the proof that the vector paradigm can be fully exploited in a real microprocessor environment.

The huge bandwidth required to feed the 32 functional units of *Tarantula* can only be provided from a large L2 cache. Given the restrictions of a microprocessor design, the main challenges that had to be solved to achieve the target performance are: (1) integration into the existing Alpha virtual-memory cache-coherent system, (2) good performance for non-unit strides, (3) support for gather and scatter instructions, and (4) reuse as much as possible the *EV8* core to reduce design and development time.

Our performance studies are very promising. The sustained number of operations per cycle ranges from 10 to almost 50. This performance translates into speedups from 2 to 20 over *EV8* (an aggressive high performance superscalar microprocessor that could execute up to 8 instructions per cycle). Also, when coupling our performance results with the initial power estimates, we believe the performance-per-watt would hardly be achievable by any other kind of architecture.

Generating the right code for *Tarantula* is fundamental to fully benefit from the L2 cache bandwidth. Our experience in hand coding the benchmarks studied indicates that both tiling and aggressive prefetching are fundamental to achieve the performance levels achieved.

Credits and Acknowledgments

G. Lowney and J. Emer have pushed this project forward from its creation up to the moment the Alpha team was transferred to Intel. Without their encouragement and technical insights, the project would have not been possible.

The core *Tarantula* team is: R. Espasa: Lead Architect. F. Ardanaz: *CR box*, benchmarking. S. Felix: floorplan, wireplan and power estimates. J. Gago: *Cbox*, benchmarking. R. Gramunt: *Vbox*, masks, benchmarking. I. Hernandez: *Zbox*, benchmarking. T. Juan: floorplan, quad-cache proposal. M. Mattina: *Cbox*. A. Seznec: memory accessing scheme, memory coherency.

We would like to give very special thanks to the ASIM team, for a terrific modeling environment that made this project so much easier: J. Emer, P. Ahuja, N. Binkert, E. Borch, R. Espasa, T. Juan, A. Klauser, C.K. Luk, S. Manne, S. Mukherjee, H. Patil, and Steven Wallace. Also, thanks to M. Jiménez for tiling most of our benchmarks and J. Corbal for the Rambus model.

Finally we would also like to thank the following individuals for their valuable input: T. Fossum, P. Bannon, S. Root, J. Leonard, B.J. Jung, R. Foster, G. Chrysos, S. Samudrala, R. Weiss, B. Noyce, J. Piper, B. Hanek, and the GEM compiler team.

References

[1] K. Asanovic, J. Beck, B. Irissou, B. Kingsbury, N. Morgan, and J. Wawrzynek. The T0 Vector Microprocessor. In *Hot Chips VII*, pages 187–196, August 1995.

[2] P. Bannon. Alpha 21364: A Scalable Single-chip SMP. In *Microprocessor Forum*, October 1998.

[3] P. Bannon. EV7. In *Microprocessor Forum*, October 2001.

[4] Cray, Inc. Cray SV1. In *http://www.cray.com/products/systems/sv1/*, 2001.

[5] K. Diefendorff. Compaq Chooses SMT for Alpha. *Microprocessor Report*, 13(16):5–11, December 1999.

[6] J. Emer. Simultaneous multithreading: Multiplying alpha's performance. In *Microprocessor Forum*, October 1999.

[7] J. Emer, P. Ahuja, N. Binkert, E. Borch, R. Espasa, T. Juan, A. Klauser, C.-K. Luk, S. Manne, S. S. Mukherjee, H. Patil, and S. Wallace. Asim: A Performance Model Framework. *IEEE Computer*, 35(2):68–76, February 2002.

[8] R. Espasa and M. Valero. Exploiting Instruction- and Data-Level Parallelism. *IEEE Micro*, pages 20–27, September/October 1997.

[9] L. Gwennap. Alpha 21364 to Ease Memory Bottlenck. *Microprocessor Report*, 12(16):12–15, October 1998.

[10] D. Jimenez-Gonzalez, J. J. Navarro, and J. Larriba-Pey. The effect of local sort on parallel sorting algorithms. In *10th Euromicro Workshop on Parallel, Distributed and Network-based Processing*, January 2002.

[11] J. Keller. The 21264: A Superscalar Alpha Processor with Out-of-Order Execution. In *Microprocessor Forum*, October 1996.

[12] J. D. McCalpin. Memory Bandwidth and Machine Balance in Current High Performance Computers. *IEEE TCCA Newsletter, see also http://www.cs.virginia.edu/stream*, December 1995.

[13] NEC, Inc. NEC SX5, Vector Technology. In *http://www.nec.com.au/hpcsd/vector.htm*, 2001.

[14] F. Quintana. *Vector Accelerators for Superscalar Processors*. PhD thesis, Universidad de las Palmas de Gran Canaria, 2001.

[15] F. Quintana, J. Corbal, R. Espasa, and M. Valero. Adding a Vector Unit to a Superscalar Processor. In *International Conference on Supercomputing (ICS)*. ACM Computer Society Press, 1999.

[16] A. Seznec and R. Espasa. Conflict free accesses to strided vectors on a banked cache. *In Preparation*.

[17] Y. Song and Z. Li. New tiling techniques to improve cache temporal locality. In *SIGPLAN Conference on Programming Language Design and Implementation*, pages 215–228, 1999.

[18] D. M. Tullsen, S. J. Eggers, J. S. Emer, H. M. Levy, J. L. Lo, and R. L. Stamm. Exploiting choice: Instruction fetch and issue on an implementable simultaneous multithreading processor. In *ISCA*, pages 392–403, 1995.

[19] D. M. Tullsen, S. J. Eggers, and H. M. Levy. Simultaneous multithreading: Maximizing on-chip parallelism. In *ISCA*, pages 191–202. ACM Press, May 1996.

[20] M. Valero, T. Lang, J. Llaberia, M. Peiron, and J. Navarro. Increasing the number of strides for conflict-free vector access. *International Symposium on Computer Architecture*, pages 372–381, 1992.

[21] M. Valero, T. Lang, M. Peiron, and E. Ayguadé. Conflict-Free Access for Streams in Multimodule Memories. *IEEE Transactions on Computers*, 44(5):634–646, May 1995.

[22] J. Wawrzynek, K. Asanovic, B. Kingsbury, D. Johnson, J. Beck, and N. Morgan. Spert-II: A vector microprocessor system. *Computer*, 29(3):79–86, 1996.

Session 9: Supporting Deep Speculation

Design Tradeoffs for the Alpha EV8 Conditional Branch Predictor*

André Seznec
IRISA/INRIA
Campus de Beaulieu
35042 Rennes
France
seznec@irisa.fr

Stephen Felix
Intel
334 South Street
Shrewsbury, MA 01545
USA
Stephen.Felix@intel.com

Venkata Krishnan
StarGen, Inc.
225 Cedar Hill Street
Marlborough, MA 01752
USA
krishnan@stargen.com

Yiannakis Sazeides
Dept of Computer Science
University of Cyprus
CY-1678 Nicosia
Cyprus
yanos@cs.ucy.ac.cy

Abstract

This paper presents the Alpha EV8 conditional branch predictor. The Alpha EV8 microprocessor project, canceled in June 2001 in a late phase of development, envisioned an aggressive 8-wide issue out-of-order superscalar microarchitecture featuring a very deep pipeline and simultaneous multithreading. Performance of such a processor is highly dependent on the accuracy of its branch predictor and consequently a very large silicon area was devoted to branch prediction on EV8. The Alpha EV8 branch predictor relies on global history and features a total of 352 Kbits.

The focus of this paper is on the different trade-offs performed to overcome various implementation constraints for the EV8 branch predictor. One such instance is the pipelining of the predictor on two cycles to facilitate the prediction of up to 16 branches per cycle from any two dynamically successive, 8 instruction fetch blocks. This resulted in the use of three fetch-block old compressed branch history information for accesing the predictor. Implementation constraints also restricted the composition of the index functions for the predictor and forced the usage of only single-ported memory cells.

Nevertheless, we show that the Alpha EV8 branch predictor achieves prediction accuracy in the same range as the state-of-the-art academic global history branch predictors that do not consider implementation constraints in great detail.

1 Introduction

The Alpha EV8 microprocessor [2] features a 8-wide superscalar deeply pipelined microarchitecture. With minimum branch misprediction penalty of 14 cycles, the performance of this microprocessor is very dependent on the branch prediction accuracy. The architecture and technology of the Alpha EV8 are very aggressive and new challenges were confronted in the design of the branch predictor. This paper presents the Alpha EV8 branch predictor in great detail. The paper expounds on different constraints that were

faced during the definition of the predictor, and on various trade-offs performed that lead to the final design. In particular, we elucidate on the following: (a) use of a global history branch prediction scheme, (b) choice of the prediction scheme derived from the hybrid skewed branch predictor *2Bc-gskew*[19], (c) redefinition of the information vector used for indexing the predictor that combines compressed branch history and path history, (d) different prediction and hysteresis table sizes: prediction tables and hysteresis tables are accessed at different pipeline stages, and hence can be implemented as physically distinct tables, (e) variable history lengths: the four logical tables in the EV8 predictor are accessed using four different history lengths, (f) guaranteeing conflict free access to the bank-interleaved predictor with single-ported memory cells for up to 16 branch predictions from any two 8-instruction dynamically succesive fetch blocks, and (g) careful definition of index functions for the predictor tables.

This work demonstrates that in spite of all the hardware and implementation constraints that were encountered, the Alpha EV8 branch predictor accuracy was not compromised and stands the comparison with virtually all equivalent in size, global history branch predictors that have been proposed so far.

The overall EV8 architecture was optimized for single process performance. Extra performance obtained by simultaneous multithreading was considered as a bonus. Therefore, the parameters of the conditional branch predictor were tuned with single process performance as the primary objective. However, the EV8 branch predictor was found to perform well in the presence of a multithreaded workload.

The remainder of the paper is organized as follows. Section 2 briefly presents the instruction fetch pipeline of the Alpha EV8. Section 3 explains why a global history branch predictor scheme was preferred over a local. In Section 4, we present the prediction scheme implemented in the Alpha EV8, *2Bc-gskew*. This section also presents the design space of *2Bc-gskew*. The various design dimensions were

---

*This work was done while the authors were with Compaq during 1999

295

harnessed to fit the EV8 predictor in 352 Kbits memory budget. Section 5 presents and justifies the history and path information used to index the branch predictor. On the Alpha EV8, the branch predictor tables must support two independent reads of 8 predictions per cycle. Section 6 presents the scheme used to guarantee two conflict-free accesses per cycle on a bank-interleaved predictor. Section 7 presents the hardware constraints for composing index functions for the prediction tables and describes the functions that were eventually used. Section 8 presents a step by step performance evaluation of the EV8 branch predictor as constraints are added and turn-around solutions are adopted. Finally, we provide concluding remarks in Section 9.

2 Alpha EV8 front-end pipeline

To sustain high performance, the Alpha EV8 fetches up to two, 8-instruction blocks per cycle from the instruction cache. An instruction fetch block consists of all consecutive valid instructions fetched from the I-cache: an instruction fetch block ends either at the end of an aligned 8-instruction block or on a **taken** control flow instruction. **Not taken** conditional branches do not end a fetch block, thus up to 16 conditional branches may be fetched and predicted in every cycle.

On every cycle, the addresses of the next two fetch blocks must be generated. Since this must be achieved in a single cycle, it can only involve very fast hardware. On the Alpha EV8, a *line predictor* [1] is used for this purpose. The line predictor consists of three tables indexed with the address of the most recent fetch block and a very limited hashing logic. A consequence of simple indexing logic is relatively low line prediction accuracy.

To avoid huge performance loss, due to fairly poor line predictor accuracy and long branch resolution latency (on the EV8 pipeline, the outcome of a branch is known the earliest in cycle 14 and more often around cycle 20 or 25), the line predictor is backed up with a powerful program counter (PC) address generator. This includes a conditional branch predictor, a jump predictor, a return address stack predictor, conditional branch target address computation (from instructions flowing out of the instruction cache) and final-address selection. PC-address-generation is pipelined in two cycles as illustrated in Fig. 1: up to four dynamically succesive fetch blocks A, B, C and D are simultaneously in flight in the PC-address-generator. In case of a mismatch between line prediction and PC-address-generation, the instruction fetch is resumed with the PC-address-generation result.

3 Global vs Local history

The previous generation Alpha microprocessor [7] incorporated a hybrid predictor using both global and local branch history information. On Alpha EV8, up to 16 branch outcomes (8 for each fetch block) have to be predicted per

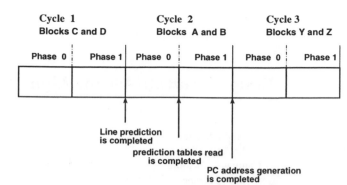

Figure 1. PC address generation pipeline

cycle. Implementing a hybrid branch predictor for EV8 based on local history or including a component using local history would have been a challenge.

Local branch prediction requires for each prediction a read of the local history table and then a read of the prediction table. Performing the 16 local history reads in parallel requires a dual-ported history table. One port for each fetch block is sufficient since one can read in parallel the histories for sequential instructions on sequential table entries. But performing the 16 prediction table reads would require a 16-ported prediction table.

Whenever an occurrence of a branch is inflight, the speculative history associated with the younger inflight occurrence of the branch should be used [8]. Maintaining and using speculative local history is already quite complex on a processor fetching and predicting a single branch per cycle[20]. On Alpha EV8, the number of inflight branches is possibly equal to the maximum number of inflight instructions (that is more than 256). Moreover, in EV8 when indexing the branch predictor there are up to three fetch blocks for which the (speculative) branch outcomes have not been determined (see Fig. 1). These three blocks may contain up to three previous occurrences of every branch in the fetch block. In contrast, single speculative global history (per thread) is simpler to build and as shown in Section 8 the accuracy of the EV8 global history prediction scheme is virtually insensitive to the effects of three fetch blocks old global history.

Finally, the Alpha EV8 is a simultaneous multithreaded processor [25, 26]. When independent threads are running, they compete for predictor table entries. Such interference on a local history based scheme can be disastrous, because it pollutes both the local history and prediction tables. What is more, when several parallel threads are spawned by a single application, the pollution is exacerbated unless the local history table is indexed using PC **and** thread number. In comparison, for global history schemes a global history register must be maintained per thread, and parallel threads - from the same application - benefit from constructive aliasing [10].

4 The branch prediction scheme

Global branch history branch predictor tables lead to a phenomenon known as *aliasing* or *interference* [28, 24], in which multiple branch information vectors share the same entry in the predictor table, causing the predictions for two or more branch substreams to intermingle. "De-aliased" global history branch predictors have been recently introduced: the enhanced skewed branch predictor *e-gskew* [15], the agree predictor [22], the bimode predictor [13] and the YAGS predictor [4]. These predictors have been shown to achieve higher prediction accuracy at equivalent hardware complexity than larger "aliased" global history branch predictors such as *gshare* [14] or *GAs* [27]. However, hybrid predictors combining a global history predictor and a typical bimodal predictor only indexed with the PC [21] may deliver higher prediction accuracy than a conventional single branch predictor [14]. Therefore, "de-aliased" branch predictors should be included in hybrid predictors to build efficient branch predictors.

The EV8 branch predictor is derived from the hybrid skewed branch predictor *2Bc-gskew* presented in [19]. In this section, the structure of the hybrid skewed branch predictor is first recalled. Then we outline the update policy used on the EV8 branch predictor. The three degrees of freedom available in the design space of the *2Bc-gskew* predictor are described: different history lengths for the predictor components, size of the different predictor components and using smaller hysteresis tables than prediction tables. These degrees of freedom were leveraged to design the "best" possible branch predictor fitting in the EV8 hardware budget constraints.

4.1 General structure of the hybrid skewed predictor 2Bc-gskew

The enhanced skewed branch predictor *e-gskew* is a very efficient single component branch predictor [15, 13] and therefore a natural candidate as a component for a hybrid predictor. The hybrid predictor *2Bc-gskew* illustrated in Fig. 2 combines *e-gskew* and a bimodal predictor. *2Bc-gskew* consists of four 2-bit counters banks. Bank **BIM** is the bimodal predictor, but is also part of the *e-gskew* predictor. Banks **G0** and **G1** are the two other banks of the *e-gskew* predictor. Bank **Meta** is the meta-predictor. Depending on **Meta**, the prediction is either the prediction coming out from **BIM** or the majority vote on the predictions coming out from **G0**, **G1** and **BIM**

4.2 Partial update policy

In a multiple table branch predictor, the update policy can have a bearing on the prediction accuracy [15]. Partial update policy was shown to result in higher prediction accuracy than total update policy for *e-gskew*.

Applying partial update policy on *2Bc-gskew* also results in better prediction accuracy. The bimodal component ac-

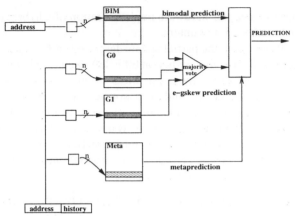

Figure 2. The *2Bc-gskew* **predictor**

curately predicts strongly biased static branches. Therefore, once the metapredictor has recognized this situation, the other tables are not updated and do not suffer from aliasing associated with easy-to-predict branches.

The partial update policy implemented on the Alpha EV8 consists of the following:

- **on a correct prediction**:
  when all predictors were agreeing do not update (see Rationale 1)
  otherwise: strengthen **Meta** if the two predictions were different, and strengthen the correct prediction on all participating tables **G0**, **G1** and **BIM** as follows:
  -strengthen **BIM** if the bimodal prediction was used
  -strengthen all the banks that gave the correct prediction if the majority vote was used
- **on a misprediction**:
  when the two predictions were different, first update the chooser (see Rationale 2), then recompute the overall prediction according to the new value of the chooser:
  -correct prediction: strengthens all participating tables
  -misprediction: update all banks

Rationale 1 The goal is to limit the number of strengthened counters on a correct prediction. When a counter is strengthened, it is harder for another (address,history) pair to "steal" it. But, when the three predictors **BIM**, **G0** and **G1** are agreeing, one counter entry can be stolen by another (address, history) pair without destroying the majority prediction. By not strengthening the counters when the three predictors agree, such a stealing is made easier.

Rationale 2 The goal is to limit the number of counters written on a wrong prediction: there is no need to steal a table entry from another (address, history) pair when it can be avoided.

4.3 Using distinct prediction and hysteresis arrays

Partial update leads to better prediction accuracy than total update policy due to better space utilization. It also allows a simpler hardware implementation of a hybrid predictor with 2-bit counters.

When using the partial update described earlier, on a correct prediction, the prediction bit is left unchanged (and not written), while the hysteresis bit is strengthened on participating components (and need not be read). Therefore, a correct prediction requires only one read of the prediction array (at fetch time) and (at most) one write of the hysteresis array (at commit time). A misprediction leads to a read of the hysteresis array followed by possible updates of the prediction and hysteresis arrays.

4.4 Sharing a hysteresis bit between several counters

Using partial update naturally leads to a *physical* implementation of the branch predictor as two different memory arrays, a prediction array and a hysteresis array.

For the Alpha EV8, silicon area and chip layout constraints allowed less space for the hysteresis memory array than the prediction memory array. Instead of reducing the size of the prediction array, it was decided to use half size hysteresis tables for components **G1** and **Meta**. As a result, two prediction entries share a single hysteresis entry: the prediction table and the hysteresis table are indexed using the same index function, except the most significant bit.

Consequently, the hysteresis table suffers from more aliasing than the prediction table. For instance, the following scenario may occur. Prediction entries A and B share the same hysteresis entry. Both (address, history) pairs associated with the entries are strongly biased, but B remains always wrong due to continuous resetting of the hysteresis bit by (address, history) pair associated with A. While such a scenario certainly occurs, it is very rare: any two consecutive accesses to B without intermediate access to A will allow B to reach the correct state. Moreover, the partial update policy implemented on the EV8 branch predictor limits the number of writes on the hysteresis tables and therefore decreases the impact of aliasing on the hysteresis tables.

4.5 History lengths

Previous studies of the skewed branch predictor [15] and the hybrid skewed branch predictor [19] assumed that tables **G0** and **G1** were indexed using different hashing function on the (address, history) pair but with the same history length used for all the tables. Using different history lengths for the two tables allows slightly better behavior. Moreover as pointed out by Juan et al. [12], the optimal history length for a predictor varies depending on the application. This phenomenon is less important on a hybrid predictor featuring a bimodal table as a component. Its significance is further reduced on *2Bc-gskew* if two different history lengths are used for tables **G0** and **G1**. A medium history length can be used for **G0** while a longer history length is used for **G1**.

	BIM	G0	G1	Meta
prediction table	16K	64K	64K	64K
hysteresis table	16K	32K	64K	32K
history length	4	13	21	15

Table 1. Characteristics of Alpha EV8 branch predictor

4.6 Different prediction table sizes

In most academic studies of multiple table predictors [15, 13, 14, 19], the sizes of the predictor tables are considered equal. This is convenient for comparing different prediction schemes. However, for the design of a real predictor in hardware, the overall design space has to be explored. Equal table sizes in the *2Bc-gskew* branch predictor is a good trade-off for small size predictors (for instance 4*4K entries). However, for very large branch predictors (i.e 4 * 64K entries), the bimodal table **BIM** is used very sparsely since each branch instruction maps onto a single entry.

Consequently, the large branch predictor used in EV8 implements a **BIM** table smaller than the other three components.

4.7 The EV8 branch predictor configuration

The Alpha EV8 implements a very large *2Bc-gskew* predictor. It features a total of 352 Kbits of memory, consisting of 208 Kbits for prediction and 144 Kbits for hysteresis. Design space exploration lead to the table sizes indexed with different history lengths as listed in Table 1. It may be remarked that the table BIM (originally the bimodal table) is indexed using a 4-bit history length. This will be justified when implementation constraints are discussed in Section 7.

5 Path and branch outcome information

The accuracy of a branch predictor depends both on the prediction scheme and predictor table sizes as well as on the information vector used to index it. This section describes how pipeline constraints lead to the effective information vector used for indexing the EV8 Alpha branch predictor. This information vector combines the PC address, a compressed form of the three fetch blocks old *branch and path* history and path information form the three last blocks.

5.1 Three fetch blocks old block compressed history

Three fetch blocks old history Information used to read the predictor tables must be available at indexing time. On the Alpha EV8, the branch predictor has a latency of two cycles and two blocks are fetched every cycle. Fig. 1 shows that the branch history information used to predict a branch outcome in block D can not include any (speculative) branch outcome from conditional branches in block D itself, and also from blocks C, B and A. Thus the EV8 branch predictor can only be indexed using a three fetch blocks old branch history (i.e updated with history information from Z) for predicting branches in block D.

Block compressed history lghist When a single branch is predicted per cycle, at most one history bit has to be shifted in the global history register on every cycle. When up to 16 branches are predicted per cycle, up to 16 history bits have to be shifted in the history on every cycle. Such an update requires complex circuitry. On the Alpha EV8, this complex history-register update would have stressed critical paths to the extent that even older history would have had to be used (five or even seven-blocks old).

Instead, just a single history bit is inserted per fetch block [5]. The inserted bit combines the last branch outcome with path information. It is computed as follows: whenever at least one conditional branch is present in the fetch block, the outcome of the last conditional branch in the fetch block (1 for taken, 0 for not-taken) is exclusive-ORed with bit 4 in the PC address of this last branch. The rationale for exclusive-OR by a PC bit the branch outcome is to get a more uniform distribution of history patterns for an application. Highly optimized codes tend to exhibit less taken branches than not-taken branches. Therefore, the distribution of "pure" branch history outcomes in those applications is non-uniform.

While using a single history bit was originally thought of as a compromising design trade-off - since it is possible to compress up to 8 history bits into 1 - Section 8 shows that it does not have significant effect on the accuracy of the branch predictor.

Notation The block compressed history defined above will be referred to as *lghist*.

5.2 Path information from the three last fetch blocks

Due to EV8 pipeline constraints (Section 2), three fetch-blocks old *lghist* is used for the predictor. Although, no branch history information from these three blocks can be used, their addresses are available for indexing the branch predictor. The addresses of the three previous fetch blocks are used in the index functions of the predictor tables.

5.3 Using very long history

The Alpha EV8 features a very large branch predictor compared to those implemented in previous generation microprocessors. Most academic studies on global history branch predictors have assumed that the length of the global history is smaller or equal to log_2 of the number of entries of the branch predictor table. For the size of predictor used in Alpha EV8, this is far from optimal even when using

lghist. For example, when considering "not compressed" branch history for a 4*64K 2-bit entries *2Bc-gskew* predictor, using equal history length for **G0**, **G1** and **Meta**, history length 24 was found to be a good design point. When considering different history lengths, using 17 for **G0**, 20 for **Meta** and 27 for **G1** was found to be a good trade-off.

For the same predictor configuration with three fetch blocks old *lghist*, slightly shorter length was found to be the best performing. However, the optimal history length is still longer than log_2 of the size of the branch predictor table: for the EV8 branch predictor 21 bits of *lghist* history are used to index table G1 with 64K entries.

In Section 8, we show empirically that for large predictors, branch history longer than log_2 of the predictor table size is almost always beneficial.

6 Conflict free bank interleaved branch predictor

Up to 16 branch predictions from two fetch blocks must be computed in parallel on the Alpha EV8. Normally, since the addresses of the two fetch blocks are independent, each of the branch predictor tables would have had to support two independent reads per cycle. Therefore the predictor tables would have had to be multi-ported, dual-pumped or bank-interleaved. This section presents a scheme that allowed the implementation of the EV8 branch predictor as 4-way bank interleaved using only single-ported memory cells. Bank conflicts are avoided **by construction**: the predictions associated with two dynamically successive fetch blocks are assured to lie in two distinct banks in the predictors.

6.1 Parallel access to predictions associated with a single block

Parallel access to all the predictions associated with a single fetch block is straightforward. The prediction tables in the Alpha EV8 branch predictor are indexed based on a hashing function of address, three fetch blocks old *lghist* branch and path history, and the three last fetch block addresses. For all the elements of a single fetch block, the same vector of information (except bits 2, 3 and 4 of the PC address) is used. Therefore, the indexing functions used guarantee that eight predictions lie in a single 8-bit word in the tables.

6.2 Guaranteeing two successive non-conflicting accesses

The Alpha EV8 branch predictor must be capable of delivering predictions associated with two fetch blocks per clock cycle. This typically means the branch predictor must be multi-ported, dual-pumped or bank interleaved.

On the Alpha EV8 branch predictor, this difficulty is circumvented through a bank number computation. The bank number computation described below guarantees **by construction** that any two dynamically successive fetch

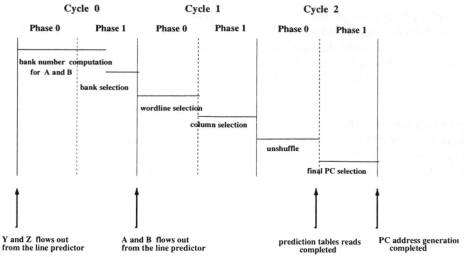

Figure 3. Flow of the branch predictor tables read access

blocks will generate accesses to two distinct predictor banks. Therefore, bank conflicts never occur. Moreover, the bank number is computed on the same cycle as the address of the fetch block is generated by the line predictor, thus no extra delay is added to access the branch predictor tables (Fig. 3). The implementation of the bank number computation is defined below:

let B_A be the bank number for instruction fetch block A, let Y, Z be the addresses of the two previous access slots, let B_Z be the number of the bank accessed by instruction fetch block Z, let (y52,y51,..,y6,y5,y4,y3,y2,0,0) be the binary representation of address Y, then B_A is computed as follows:
if $((y6,y5)==B_Z)$ then $B_A=(y6,y5\oplus 1)$ else $B_A= (y6,y5)$

This computation guarantees the prediction for a fetch block will be read from a different bank than that of the previous fetch block. The only information bits needed to compute the bank numbers for the two next fetch blocks A and B are bits *(y6,y5)*, *(z6,z5)* and B_Z: that is two-block ahead [18] bank number computation. These information bits are available one cycle before the effective access on the branch predictor is performed and the required computations are very simple. Therefore, no delay is introduced on the branch predictor by the bank number computation. In fact, bank selection can be performed at the end of Phase 1 of the cycle preceding the read of the branch predictor tables.

7 Indexing the branch predictor

As previously mentioned, the Alpha EV8 branch predictor is 4-way interleaved and the prediction and hysteresis tables are separate. Since the logical organization of the predictor contains the four *2Bc-gskew* components, this should translate to an implementation with 32 memory tables. However, the Alpha EV8 branch predictor only implements eight memory arrays: for each of the four banks there is an array for prediction and an array for hysteresis. Each word line in the arrays is made up of the four *logical* predictor components.

This section, presents the physical implementation of the branch predictor arrays and the constraints they impose on the composition of the indexing functions. The section also includes detailed definition of the hashing functions that were selected for indexing the different logical components in the Alpha EV8 branch predictor.

7.1 Physical implementation and constraints

Each of the four banks in the Alpha EV8 branch predictor is implemented as two physical memory arrays: the prediction memory array and the hysteresis memory array. Each word line in the arrays is made up of the four *logical* predictor components.

Each bank features 64 word lines. Each word line contains 32 8-bit prediction words from **G0**, **G1** and **Meta**, and 8 8-bit prediction words from **BIM**. A single 8-bit prediction word is selected from the word line from each predictor table **G0**, **G1**, **Meta** and **BIM**. A prediction read spans over 3 half cycle phases (5 phases including bank number computation and bank selection). This is illustrated in Fig. 3 and 4. A detailed description is given below.

1.**Wordline selection:** one of the 64 wordlines of the accessed bank is selected. The four predictor components share the 6 address bits needed for wordline selection. Furthermore, these 6 address bits can not be hashed since the wordline decode and array access constitute a critical path for reading the branch prediction array and consequently - inputs to decoder must be available at the very beginning of the cycle.

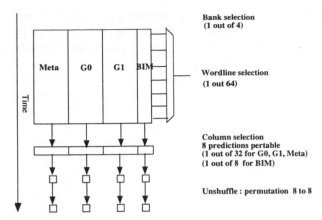

Bank selection
(1 out of 4)

Wordline selection
(1 out 64)

Column selection
8 predictions pertable
(1 out of 32 for G0, G1, Meta)
(1 out of 8 for BIM)

Unshuffle : permutation 8 to 8

Figure 4. Reading the branch prediction tables

2. **Column selection:** each wordline consists of multiple 8-bit prediction entries of the four logical predictor tables. One 8-bit prediction word is selected for each of the logical predictor tables. As only one cycle phase is available to compute the index in the column, only a single 2-entry XOR gate is allowed to compute each of these column bits.

3. **Unshuffle:** 8-bit prediction words are systematicaly read. This word is further rearranged through a XOR permutation (that is bit at position i is moved at position $i \oplus f$). This final permutation ensures a larger dispersion of the predictions over the array (only entries corresponding to a branch instruction are finally useful). It allows also to discriminate between longer history for the same branch PC, since the computation of the parameter f for the XOR permutation can span over a complete cycle: each bit of f can be computed by a large tree of XOR gates.

Notations The three fetch-blocks old *lghist* history will be noted H= (h20, .., h0). A= (a52,..,a2,0,0) is the address of the fetch block. Z and Y are the two previous fetch blocks. I = (i15,..,i0) is the index function of a table, (i1,i0) being the bank number, (i4,i3,i2) being the offset in the word, (i10,i9,i8,i7,i6,i5) being the line number, and the highest order bits being the column number.

7.2 General philosophy for the design of indexing functions

When defining the indexing functions, we tried to apply two general principles while respecting the hardware implementation constraints. First, we tried to limit aliasing as much as possible on each individual table by picking individual indexing function that would spread the accesses over the predictor table as uniformly as possible. For each individual function, this normally can be obtained by mixing a large number of bits from the history and from the address to compute each individual bit in the function. However, general constraints for computing the indexing functions only allowed such complex computations for the unshuffle bits. For the other indexing bits, we favored the use

of *lghist* bits instead of the address bits. Due to the inclusion of path information in *lghist*, *lghist* vectors were more uniformly distributed than PC addresses. In [17], it was pointed out that the indexing functions in a skewed cache should be chosen to minimize the number of block pairs that will conflict on two or more ways. The same applies for the *2Bc-gskew* branch predictor.

7.3 Shared bits

The indexing functions for the four prediction tables share a total of 8 bits, the bank number (2 bits) and the wordline number (i10, .., i5). The bank number computation was described in Section 6.

The wordline number must be immediately available at the very beginning of the branch predictor access. Therefore, it can either be derived from information already available earlier, such as the bank number, or directly extracted from information available at the end of the previous cycle such as the three fetch blocks old *lghist* and the fetch block address.

The fetch block address is the most natural choice, since it allows the use of an effective bimodal table for component **BIM** in the predictor. However, simulations showed that the distribution of the accesses over the **BIM** table entries were unbalanced. Some regions in the predictor tables were used infrequently and others were congested.

Using a mix of *lghist* history bits and fetch block address bits leads to a more uniform use of the different word lines in the predictor, thus allowing overall better predictor performance. As a consequence, component **BIM** in the branch predictor uses 4 bits of history in its indexing function.

The wordline number used is given by $(i10,i9,i8,i7,i6,i5) = (h3,h2,h1,h0,a8,a7)$.

7.4 Indexing BIM

The indexing function for **BIM** is already using 4 history bits, that are three fetched blocks old, and some path information from two fetched block ahead (for bank number computation). Therefore path information from the last instruction fetch block (that is Z) is used. The extra bits for indexing **BIM** are $(i13,i12,i11,i4,i3,i2) = (a11, a9 \oplus a5, a10 \oplus a6, a4, a3 \oplus z6, a2 \oplus z5)$.

7.5 Engineering the indexing functions for G0, G1 and Meta

The following methodology was used to define the indexing functions for **G0**, **G1** and **Meta**. First, the best history length combination was determined using standard skewing functions from [17]. Then, the column indices and the XOR functions for the three predictors were manually defined applying the following principles as best as we could:
1.favor a uniform distribution of column numbers for the choice of wordline index.

Column index bits must be computed using only one two-entry XOR gate. Since history vectors are more uniformly distributed than address numbers, to favor an overall good distribution of column numbers, history bits were generally preferred to address bits.

2. if, for the same instruction fetch block address A, two histories differ by only one or two bits then the two occurrences should not map onto the same predictor entry in any table : to guarantee this, whenever an information bit is X-ORed with another information bit for computing a column bit, at least one of them will appear alone for the computation of one bit of the unshuffle parameter.

3. if a conflict occurs in a table, then try to avoid it on the two other tables: to approximate this, different pairs of history bits are XORed for computing the column bits for the three tables.

This methodology lead to the design of the indexing functions defined below:

Indexing G0   *To simplify the implementation of column selectors,* **G0** *and* **Meta** *share* $i15$ *and* $i14$. Column selection is given by
$(i15, i14, i13, i12, i11) = (h7 \oplus h11, h8 \oplus h12, h4 \oplus h5, a9 \oplus h9, h10 \oplus h6)$.
Unshufling is defined by $(i4, i3, i2) = (a4 \oplus a9 \oplus a13 \oplus a12 \oplus h5 \oplus h11 \oplus h8 \oplus z5, a3 \oplus a11 \oplus h9 \oplus h10 \oplus h12 \oplus z6 \oplus a5, a2 \oplus a14 \oplus a10 \oplus h6 \oplus h4 \oplus h7 \oplus a6)$.

Indexing G1   Column selection is given by
$(i15, \quad i14, \quad i13, \quad i12, \quad i11) = (h19 \oplus h12, h18 \oplus h11, h17 \oplus h10, h16 \oplus h4, h15 \oplus h20)$.
Unshuffling is defined by $(i4, i3, i2) = (a4 \oplus a11 \oplus a14 \oplus a6 \oplus h4 \oplus h6 \oplus h9 \oplus h14 \oplus h15 \oplus h16 \oplus z6, a3 \oplus a10 \oplus a13 \oplus h5 \oplus h11 \oplus h13 \oplus h18 \oplus h19 \oplus h20 \oplus z5, a2 \oplus a5 \oplus a9 \oplus h4 \oplus h8 \oplus h7 \oplus h10 \oplus h12 \oplus h13 \oplus h14 \oplus h17)$

Indexing Meta   Column selection is given by
$(i15, \quad i14, \quad i13, \quad i12, \quad i11) = (h7 \oplus h11, h8 \oplus h12, h5 \oplus h13, h4 \oplus h9, a9 \oplus h6)$.
Unshuffling is defined by $(i4, i3, i2) = (a4 \oplus a10 \oplus a5 \oplus h7 \oplus h10 \oplus h14 \oplus h13 \oplus z5, \quad a3 \oplus a12 \oplus a14 \oplus a6 \oplus h4 \oplus h6 \oplus h8 \oplus h14, a2 \oplus a9 \oplus a11 \oplus a13 \oplus h5 \oplus h9 \oplus h11 \oplus h12 \oplus z6)$

8   Evaluation

In this section, we evaluate the different design decisions that were made in the Alpha EV8 predictor design. We first justify the choice of the hybrid skewed predictor *2Bc-gskew* against other schemes relying on global history. Then step by step, we analyze benefits or detriments brought by design decisions and implementation constraints.

8.1   Methodology

8.1.1   Simulation
Trace driven branch simulations with immediate update were used to explore the design space for the Alpha EV8

branch predictor, since this methodology is about three orders of magnitude faster than the complete Alpha EV8 processor simulation. We checked that for branch predictors using (very) long global history as those considered in this study, the relative error in number of branch mispredictions between a trace driven simulation, assuming immediate update, and the complete simulation of the Alpha EV8, assuming predictor update at commit time, is insignificant.

The metric used to report the results is mispredictions per 1000 instructions (misp/KI). To experiment with history length wider than log_2 of table sizes, indexing functions from the family presented in [17, 15] were used for all predictors, except in Section 8.5. The initial state of all entries in the prediction tables was set to weakly not taken.

8.1.2   Benchmark set
Displayed simulation results were obtained using traces collected with Atom[23]. The benchmark suite was SPECINT95. Binaries were highly optimized for the Alpha 21264 using profile information from the *train* input. The traces were recorded using the *ref* inputs. One hundred million instructions were traced after skipping 400 million instructions except for *compress* (2 billion instructions were skipped). Table 2 details the characteristics of the benchmark traces.

8.2   2Bc-gskew vs other global history based predictors

We first validated the choice of the *2BC-gskew* prediction scheme against other global prediction schemes. Fig. 5 shows simulation results for predictors with memorization size in the same range as the Alpha EV8 predictor. Displayed results assume *conventional branch history*. For all the predictors, the best history length results are presented. Fig. 6 shows the number of additional mispredictions for the same configurations as in Fig. 5 but using log_2 of the table size, instead of the best history length.

The illustrated configurations are:

- a 4*32K entries (i.e. 256 Kbits) *2Bc-gskew* using history lengths 0, 13, 16 and 23 respectively for **BIM**, **G0**, **Meta** and **G1**, and a 4*64K entries (i.e. 512Kbits) *2Bc-gskew* using history lengths 0, 17, 20 and 27. For limited(log_2) history length, the lengths are equal for all tables and are 15 for the 256Kbit configuration and 16 for the 512Kbit.

- a bimode predictor [13] consisting of two 128K entries tables for respectively biased taken and not taken branches and a 16 Kentries bimodal table, for a total of 544 Kbits of memorization[1]. The optimum history

---

[1]The original proposition for the bimode predictor assumes equal sizes for the three tables. For large size predictors, using a smaller bimodal table is more cost-effective. On our benchmark set, using more than 16K entries in the bimodal table did not add any benefit.

Benchmark	compress	gcc	go	ijpeg	li	m88ksim	perl	vortex
dyn. cond. branches (x1000)	12044	16035	11285	8894	16254	9706	13263	12757
static cond. branches	46	12086	3710	904	251	409	273	2239

Table 2. Benchmark characteristics

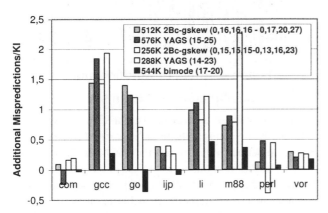

Figure 5. Branch prediction accuracy for various global history schemes

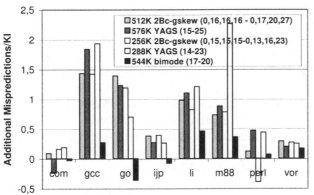

Figure 6. Additional Mispredictions when using log_2 table size history

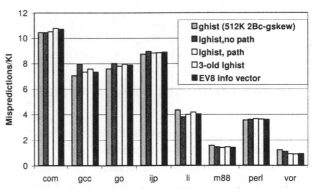

Figure 7. Impact of the information vector on branch prediction accuracy

First, our simulation results confirm that, at equivalent memorization budget *2Bc-gskew* outperforms the other global history branch predictors except *YAGS*. There is no clear winner between the *YAGS* predictor and *2Bc-gskew*. However, the *YAGS* predictor uses (partially) tagged arrays. Reading and checking 16 of these tags in only one and half cycle would have been difficult to implement. Second, the data support that, predictors featuring a large number of entries need very long history length and log_2 table size history is suboptimal.

8.3 Quality of the information vector

The discussion below examines the impact of successive modifications of the information vector on branch prediction accuracy assuming a 4*64K entries *2Bc-gskew* predictor. For each configuration the accuracies for the best history lengths are reported in Fig. 7. *ghist* represents the conventional branch history. *lghist,no path* assumes that *lghist* does not include path information. *lghist+path* includes path information. *3-old lghist* is the same as before, but considering three fetch blocks old history. *EV8 info vector* represents the information vector used on Alpha EV8, that is three fetch blocks old *lghist* history including path information plus path information on the three last blocks.

lghist As expected the optimal *lghist* history length is shorter than the optimal real branch history: (15, 17, 23) instead of (17, 20, 27) respectively for tables **G0**, **Meta** and **G1**. Quite surprisingly (see Fig. 7), *lghist* has same performance as conventional branch history. Depending on the application, there is either a small loss or a small benefit in accuracy. Embedding path information in *lghist* is gener-

length (for our benchmark set) was 20. For log_2 history length 17 bits were used.
- a 1M entries (2M bits) *gshare*. The optimum history length (on our benchmark set) was 20 (i.e log_2 of the predictor table size).
- a 288 Kbits and 576 Kbits YAGS predictor [4] (respective best history length 23 and 25) the small configuration consists of a 16K entry bimodal and two 16K partially tagged tables called direction caches, tags are 6 bits wide. When the bimodal table predicts taken (resp. not-taken), the *not-taken* (resp. *taken*) direction cache is searched. On a miss in the searched direction cache, the bimodal table provides the prediction. On a hit, the direction cache provides the prediction. For log_2 history length 14 bits (resp 15 bits) were used. 1

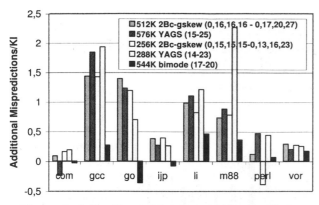

Figure 8. Adjusting table sizes in the predictor

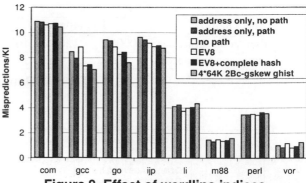

Figure 9. Effect of wordline indices

ally beneficial: we determined that is more often useful to de-alias otherwise aliased history paths.

The loss of information from branches in the same fetch block in *lghist* is balanced by the use of history from more branches (eventhough represented by a shorter information vector): for instance, for *vortex* the 23 *lghist* bits represent on average 36 branches. Table 3 represents the average number of conditional branches represented by one bit in *lghist* for the different benchmarks.

Three fetch blocks old history   Using three fetch blocks old history slightly degrades the accuracy of the predictor, but the impact is limited. Moreover, using path information from the three fetch blocks missing in the history consistently recovers most of this loss.

EV8 information vector   In summary, despite the fact that the vector of information used for indexing the Alpha EV8 branch predictor was largely dictated by implementation constraints, on our benchmark set this vector of information achieves approximately the same levels of accuracy as without any constraints.

8.4   Reducing some table sizes

Fig. 8 shows the effect of reducing table sizes. The base configuration is a 4*64K entries *2Bc-gskew* predictor (512Kbits). The data denoted by *small BIM* shows the performance when the **BIM** size is reduced from 64K to 16K 2-bit counters. The performance with a small BIM and half the size for **GO** and **Meta** hysteresis tables is denoted by *EV8 Size*. The latter fits the 352Kbits budget of the Alpha EV8 predictor. The information vector used for indexing the predictor is the information vector used on Alpha EV8.

Reducing the size of the **BIM** table has no impact at all on our benchmark set. Except for *go*, the effect of using half size hysteresis tables for **G0** and **Meta** is barely noticeable. *go* presents a very large footprint and consequently is the most sensitive to size reduction.

8.5   Indexing function constraints

Simulations results presented so far did not take into account hardware constraints on the indexing functions. 8 bits of index must be shared and can not be hashed, and computation of the column bits can only use one 2-entry XOR gate Intuitively, these constraints should lead to some loss of efficiency, since it restricts the possible choices for indexing functions.

However, it was remarked in [16] that (for caches) partial skewing is almost as efficient as complete skewing. The same applies for branch predictors: sharing 8 bits in the indices does not hurt the prediction accuracy as long as the shared index is uniformly distributed.

The constraint of using unhashed bits for the wordline number turned out to be more critical, since it restricted the distribution of the shared index. Ideally for the EV8 branch predictor, one would desire to get the distribution of this shared 8 bit index as uniform as possible to spread accesses on **G0**, **G1** and **Meta** over the entire table.

Fig. 9 illustrates the effects of the various choices made for selecting the wordline number. *address only, no path* assumes that only PC address bits are used in the shared index **and** that no path information is used in *lghist*. *address only, path* assumes that only PC address bits are used in the shared index, but path information is embedded in *lghist*. *no path* assumes 4 history bits and 2 PC bits as wordline number, but that no path information is used in *lghist*. *EV8* illustrates the accuracy of the Alpha EV8 branch predictor where 4 history bits are used in the wordline number index **and** path information is embedded in the history. Finally *complete hash* recalls the results assuming hashing on all the information bits and *4*64K 2Bc-gskew ghist* represents the simulation results assuming a 512Kbits predictor with no constraint on index functions and conventional branch history.

Previously was noted that incorporating path information in *lghist* has only a small impact on a *2Bc-gskew* predictor indexed using hashing functions with no hardware constraints. However, adding the path information in the history for the Alpha EV8 predictor makes the distribution of *lghist* more uniform, allows its use in the shared index

	compress	gcc	go	ijpeg	li	m88ksim	perl	vortex
lghist/ghist	1.24	1.57	1.12	1.20	1.55	1.53	1.32	1.59

Table 3. Ratio lghist/ghist

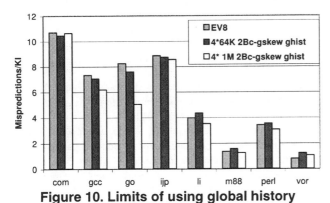

Figure 10. Limits of using global history

and therefore can increase prediction accuracy.

The constraint on the column bits computation indirectly achieved a positive impact by forcing us to very carefully design the column indexing and the unshuffle functions. The (nearly) total freedom for computing the unshuffle was fully exploited: 11 bits are XORed in the unshuffling function on table *G1*. The indexing functions used in the final design outperform the standard hashing functions considered in the rest of the paper: these functions (originally defined for skewed associative caches [17])exhibit good interbank dispersion, but were not manually tuned to enforce the three criteria described in Section 7.5.

To summarize, the 352 Kbits Alpha EV8 branch predictor stands the comparison against a 512 Kbits *2Bc-gskew* predictor using conventional branch history.

9   Conclusion

The branch predictor on Alpha EV8 was defined at the beginning of 1999. It features 352 Kbits of memory and delivers up to 16 branch predictions per cycle for two dynamically succesive instruction fetch blocks. Therefore, a global history prediction scheme had to be used. In 1999, the hybrid skewed branch predictor *2Bc-gskew* prediction scheme [19] represented state-of-the-art for global history prediction schemes. The Alpha EV8 branch predictor implements a *2Bc-gskew* predictor scheme enhanced with an optimized update policy and the use of different history lengths on the different tables.

Some degrees of freedom in the definition of *2Bc-gskew* were tuned to adapt the predictor parameters to silicon area and chip layout constraints: the bimodal component is smaller than the other components and the hysteresis tables of two of the other components are only half-size of the predictor tables.

Implementation constraints imposed a three fetch blocks

old compressed form of branch history, *lghist*, instead of the effective branch history. However, the information vector used to index the Alpha EV8 branch predictor stands the comparison with complete branch history. It achieves that by combining path information with the branch outcome to build *lghist* and using path information from the three fetch blocks that have to be ignored in *lghist*.

The Alpha EV8 is four-way interleaved and each bank is single ported. On each cycle, the branch predictor supports requests from two dynamically succesive instruction fetch blocks but does not require any hardware conflict resolution, since bank number computation guarantees **by construction** that any two dynamically succesive fetch blocks will access two distinct predictors banks.

The Alpha EV8 branch predictor features four logical components, but is implemented as only two memory arrays, the prediction array and the hysteresis array. Therefore, the definition of index functions for the four (logical) predictor tables is strongly constrained: 8 bits must be shared among the four indices. Furthermore, timing constraints restrict the complexity of hashing that can be applied for indices computation. However, efficient index functions turning around these constraints were designed.

Despite implementation and size constraints, the Alpha EV8 branch predictor delivers accuracy equivalent to a 4*64K entries *2Bc-gskew* predictor using conventional branch history for which no constraint on the indexing functions was imposed.

In future generation microprocessors, branch prediction accuracy will remain a major issue. Even larger predictors than the predictor implemented in the Alpha EV8 may be considered. However, this brute force approach would have limited return except for applications with a very large number of branches. This is exemplified on our benchmark set in Fig. 10 that shows simulation results for a 4*1M 2-bit entries *2Bc-gskew* predictor. Adding back-up predictor components [3] relying on different information vector types (local history, value prediction [9, 6], or new prediction concepts (e.g., perceptron [11]) to tackle hard-to-predict branches seems more promising. Since such a predictor will face timing constraints issues, one may consider further extending the hierarchy of predictors with increased accuracies and delays: line predictor, global history branch prediction, backup branch predictor. The backup branch predictor would deliver its prediction later than the global history branch predictor.

References

[1] B. Calder and D. Grunwald. Next cache line and set prediction. In *Proceedings of the 22nd Annual International Symposium on Computer Architecture*, 1995.

[2] K. Diefendorff. Compaq Chooses SMT for Alpha. *Microprocessor Report*, December 1999.

[3] K. Driesen and U. Holzle. The cascaded predictor: Economical and adaptive branch target prediction. In *Proceeding of the 30th Symposium on Microarchitecture*, Dec. 1998.

[4] A. N. Eden and T. Mudge. The YAGS branch predictor. In *Proceedings of the 31st Annual International Symposium on Microarchitecture*, Dec 1998.

[5] G. Giacalone and J. Edmonson. Method and apparatus for predicting multiple conditional branches. In *US Patent No 6,272,624*, August 2001.

[6] J. Gonzalez and A. Gonzalez. Control-flow speculation through value prediction for superscalar processors. In *Proceedings of International Conference on Parallel Architectures and Compilation Techniques (PACT)*, 1999.

[7] L. Gwennap. Digital 21264 sets new standard. *Microprocessor Report*, October 1996.

[8] E. Hao, P.-Y. Chang, and Y. N. Patt. The effect of speculatively updating branch history on branch prediction accuracy, revisited. In *Proceedings of the 27th Annual International Symposium on Microarchitecture*, San Jose, California, 1994.

[9] T. Heil, Z. Smith, and J. E. Smith. Improving branch predictors by correlating on data values. In *32nd Int. Symp. on Microarchitecture*, Nov. 1999.

[10] S. Hily and A. Seznec. Branch prediction and simultaneous multithreading. In *Proceedings of the 1996 Conference on Parallel Architectures and Compilation Techniques (PACT '96)*, Oct. 1996.

[11] D. Jimenez and C. Lin. Dynamic branch prediction with perceptrons. In *Proceedings of the Seventh International Symposium on High Performance Computer Architecture*, January 2001.

[12] T. Juan, S. Sanjeevan, and J. Navarro. Dynamic history-length fitting: A third level of adaptivity for branch prediction. In *Proceedings of the 25th Annual International Symposium on Computer Architecture (ISCA-98)*, volume 26,3 of *ACM Computer Architecture News*, pages 155–166, New York, June 27–July 1 1998. ACM Press.

[13] C.-C. Lee, I.-C. Chen, and T. Mudge. The bi-mode branch predictor. In *Proceedings of the 30th Annual International Symposium on Microarchitecture*, Dec 1997.

[14] S. McFarling. Combining branch predictors. Technical report, DEC, 1993.

[15] P. Michaud, A. Seznec, and R. Uhlig. Trading conflict and capacity aliasing in conditional branch predictors. In *Proceedings of the 24th Annual International Symposium on Computer Architecture (ISCA-97)*, June 1997.

[16] A. Seznec. A case for two-way skewed-associative caches. In *Proceedings of the 20th Annual International Symposium on Computer Architecture*, May 1993.

[17] A. Seznec and F. Bodin. Skewed associative caches. In *Proceedings of PARLE' 93*, May 1993.

[18] A. Seznec, S. Jourdan, P. Sainrat, and P. Michaud. Multiple-block ahead branch predictors. In *Architectural Support for Programming Languages and Operating Systems (ASPLOS-VII)*, pages 116–127, 1996.

[19] A. Seznec and P. Michaud. De-aliased hybrid branch predictors. Technical Report RR-3618, Inria, Feb 1999.

[20] K. Skadron, M. Martonosi, and D. Clark. Speculative updates of local and global branch history: A quantitative analysis. *Journal of Instruction-Level Parallelism, vol. 2, Jan. 2000*, January 2000.

[21] J. Smith. A study of branch prediction strategies. In *Proceedings of the 8th Annual International Symposium on Computer Architecture*, May 1981.

[22] E. Sprangle, R. S. Chappell, M. Alsup, and Y. Patt. The agree predictor: A mechanism for reducing negative branch history interference. In *Proceedings of the 24th Annual International Symposium on Computer Architecture (ISCA-97)*, pages 284–291, June 1997.

[23] A. Srivastava and A. Eustace. ATOM: A system for building customized program analysis tools. *ACM SIGPLAN Notices*, 29(6):196–205, 1994.

[24] A. Talcott, M. Nemirovsky, and R. Wood. The influence of branch prediction table interference on branch prediction scheme performance. In *Proceedings of the 3rd Annual International Conference on Parallel Architectures and Compilation Techniques*, 1995.

[25] D. M. Tullsen, S. Eggers, and H. M. Levy. Simultaneous multithreading: Maximizing on-chip parallelism. In *Proceedings of the 22th Annual International Symposium on Computer Architecture*, June 1995.

[26] D. M. Tullsen, S. J. Eggers, J. S. Emer, H. M. Levy, J. L. Lo, and R. L. Stamm. Exploiting choice : Instruction fetch and issue on an implementable simultaneous MultiThreading processor. In *Proceedings of the 23rd Annual International Symposium on Computer Architecure*, May 1996.

[27] T.-Y. Yeh and Y. Patt. Alternative implementations of two-level adaptive branch prediction. In *Proceedings of the 19th Annual International Symposium on Computer Architecture*, May 1992.

[28] C. Young, N. Gloy, and M. Smith. A comparative analysis of schemes for correlated branch prediction. In *Proceedings of the 22nd Annual International Symposium on Computer Architecture*, June 1995.

Acknowledgement

The authors would like to recognise the work of all those who contributed to the architecture, circuit implementation and verification of the EV8 Branch Predictor. They include Ta-chung Chang, George Chrysos, John Edmondson, Joel Emer, Tryggve Fossum, Glenn Giacalone, Balakrishnan Iyer, Manickavelu Balasubramanian, Harish Patil, George Tien and James Vash.

Difficult-Path Branch Prediction
Using Subordinate Microthreads

Robert S. Chappell†   Francis Tseng‡   Adi Yoaz#   Yale N. Patt‡

†EECS Department
The University of Michigan
Ann Arbor, Michigan 48109-2122
robc@eecs.umich.edu

‡ECE Department
The University of Texas at Austin
Austin, Texas 78712-1084
{tsengf, patt}@ece.utexas.edu

Texas Development Center
Intel Corporation
Austin, TX 78746
adi.yoaz@intel.com

Abstract

Branch misprediction penalties continue to increase as microprocessor cores become wider and deeper. Thus, improving branch prediction accuracy remains an important challenge. Simultaneous Subordinate Microthreading (SSMT) provides a means to improve branch prediction accuracy. SSMT machines run multiple, concurrent microthreads in support of the primary thread. We propose to dynamically construct microthreads that can speculatively and accurately pre-compute branch outcomes along frequently mispredicted paths. The mechanism is intended to be implemented entirely in hardware. We present the details for doing so. We show how to select the right paths, how to generate accurate predictions, and how to get this information in a timely way. We achieve an average gain of 8.4% (42% maximum) over a very aggressive baseline machine on the SPECint95 and SPECint2000 benchmark suites.

1. Introduction

Branch mispredictions continue to be a major limitation on microprocessor performance, and will be for the foreseeable future [9]. Though modern prediction mechanisms can achieve impressive accuracies, the penalty incurred by mispredictions continues to increase with wider and deeper machines. For example, a futuristic 16-wide, deeply-pipelined machine with 95% branch prediction accuracy can achieve a twofold improvement in performance solely by eliminating the remaining mispredictions[1].

Simultaneous Subordinate Microthreading [2] has the potential to improve branch prediction accuracy. In this approach, the machine "spawns" subordinate *microthreads* to

generate some of the predictions, which are used in place of the hardware predictions. Because microthreads are not limited by hardware implementation and can target very specific behavior, they can generate very accurate predictions. Examples have been shown in previous research [2, 18].

However, effective use of microthreads for branch prediction is challenging. Microthreads compete with the primary thread for resources, potentially decreasing performance. Because of this drawback, subordinate microthreading is not a good general solution—it must be targeted such that mispredictions are removed without incurring so much overhead that the performance gains are overshadowed. To maximize gains, it is important to have the following goals:

- **Spawn only useful threads**. A microthread incurs useless overhead if it generates a prediction for a correctly predicted branch, or if a microthread is spawned but the prediction is never used. Additionally, if the branch is correctly predicted, there is a risk of introducing additional mispredictions with microthreads.

- **Generate accurate microthread predictions**. A microthread is useless if it does not generate a correct prediction. In fact, it can be harmful if the hardware prediction is correct and the microthread prediction is not.

- **Complete microthreads in time to be useful**. A microthread is useless if it does not complete before the target branch is resolved—at that point, the machine has already computed the actual outcome of the branch. Microthreads should complete as early as possible to eliminate or reduce misprediction penalties.

We propose using a set of *difficult-paths* to guide microthread branch prediction with the above goals in mind. Path-based confidence mechanisms [10] have demonstrated

---

[1] Averages over SPECint95 and SPECint2000. See Section 5 for experimental setup.

that the predictability of a branch is correlated to the control-flow path leading up to it. We extend this notion by classifying the predictability of branches by control-flow path, rather than as an aggregate of all paths to a branch. In this manner, we identify *difficult paths* that frequently lead to mispredictions. These are the mispredictions we attack with specially-constructed microthreads.

The remainder of this paper describes our difficult-path classification method and how to construct microthreads that will remove a significant number of hardware mispredictions, while keeping microthread overhead in check. In addition, our mechanism can be implemented entirely in hardware, unlike previous schemes that rely on profile-based, compile-time analysis. We present the details of this hardware implementation in Section 4.

This paper is organized as follows. Section 2 discusses prior research relevant to this paper. Section 3 describes our new approach of using difficult paths to guide microthreaded branch prediction. Section 4 describes the algorithms and hardware necessary to implement our difficult-path branch prediction scheme. Section 5 provides experimental results and analysis. Section 6 provides conclusions.

2. Related Work

Branch prediction using subordinate microthreads was first proposed by Chappell *et al.* as an application of the Simultaneous Subordinate Microthreading (SSMT) paradigm [2]. SSMT was proposed as a general method for leveraging spare execution capacity to benefit the primary thread. Subsequent authors have referred to subordinate microthreads as "helper threads." The original microthread branch prediction mechanism used a hand-generated microthread to exploit local correlation of difficult branches identified through profiling. Many concepts from this previous work carry over to this paper, such as the basic microthreading hardware and the means by which to communicate branch predictions to the primary thread. In this paper, we attack a larger set of branch mispredictions with an automated, run-time mechanism that constructs more accurate microthreads.

Zilles and Sohi [18] proposed using *speculative slices* to pre-compute branch conditions and prefetching addresses. Their method used profiling data to hand-construct backward slices of computation for instructions responsible for many branch mispredictions or cache misses. The processor executed these speculative slices as helper threads to generate branch predictions and prefetches. Backward slices could contain control-flow, and several speculative optimizations were suggested to improve slice performance. Hardware mechanisms were proposed to coordinate dynamic branch prediction instances with the front-end and to squash useless threads on incorrect control-flow paths. Our

work differs in the following ways: we target mispredictions using difficult paths, our hardware-based mechanism does not rely on profiling and hand analysis to generate microthreads, we leverage run-time information to create more timely microthreads, and we present simpler mechanisms for aborting useless microthreads and communicating microthread predictions to the front-end.

Roth and Sohi [16] proposed a processor capable of using *data-driven threads* (DDT) to perform critical computations—chains of instructions that lead to a mispredicted branch or cache miss. The DDT threads were non-speculative and the values produced were capable of being integrated into the primary thread via register integration [15]. The construction of the threads was performed automatically at compile-time using profiling data to estimate when DDT construction would be useful. This scheme did not convey branch predictions to the front-end, but instead pre-computed the results of branches so that they could be integrated back into the primary thread at rename time, thus shrinking misprediction penalties but not removing them. Our mechanism targets mispredictions with difficult paths, does not rely on the compiler, and is not constrained by the non-speculative nature of the threads.

Farcy *et al.* proposed a mechanism to target highly mispredicted branches within *local loops* [6]. The computations leading up to applicable branches were duplicated at decode time and used to pre-compute the conditions of the branches several loop iterations ahead of the current iteration. In order to get ahead, their scheme used stride value prediction for live-input values. This paper also proposed a mechanism by which to communicate predictions to the appropriate later iterations of the local loop. Though clever, the applicability of their overall mechanism was limited only to local loop branches based on predictable live-input values.

Roth *et al.* also proposed hardware pre-computation mechanisms to predict virtual function call targets [13] and to prefetch linked data structures [14]. In these mechanisms, the machine detected specific instruction sequences leading to virtual function call targets or linked-list jump pointers. These mechanisms did not use separate threads to perform the computations, but instead mimicked them on a separate execution engine.

Several papers have recently investigated the use of pre-computation threads for prefetching. Collins, *et al.* proposed speculative pre-computation [4] and then dynamic speculative pre-computation [3]. The former used a profiling-based, compile-time mechanism to build simple address computations for load instructions that caused many cache misses. The follow-on paper proposed a hardware mechanism for dynamically capturing the computations. Luk proposed a mechanism for doing compiler-controlled prefetching using separate threads [12]. In this mechanism, the machine would fork multiple speculative copies of the primary thread in order to prefetch irregular address patterns. Annavaram *et al.* proposed using a separate pre-computation engine to execute threads generated on-the-fly at fetch time [1]. This mechanism essentially prioritized computations for loads accounting for many cache misses.

Assisted Execution [5], proposed by Dubois and Song, is a multithreading paradigm that uses compiler-generated *nanothreads* in support of the primary thread. This previous work proposed a nanothread prefetching scheme and suggested other general ways which nanothreads could be used to improve single-threaded performance. This paper did not address branch prediction and suggested nanothreads as a means for the compiler to interact with a running program.

3. Difficult-Path Classification and Branch Prediction

In this paper, we refer to a *path* as a particular sequence of control-flow changes that lead to either a conditional or indirect *terminating branch*. We use the addresses of the n taken branches prior to the terminating branch to specify the path. These n addresses are combined in a shift-XOR hash to yield a path identifier, or $Path\_Id$.

Figure 1 shows all paths with $n \leq 2$ to terminating branch A (paths leading away from A are not shown). When $n = 1$, there are 2 paths: BA and EA. For $n = 2$, there are 5 paths: CBA, DBA, FEA, GEA, and HEA. The $Path\_Id$ for each would be computed using a shift-XOR hash of the n branch address. For example, the $Path\_Id$ of path GEA would use the addresses of branches G and E.

A *difficult path* has a terminating branch that is poorly predicted *when on that path*. More formally, given a threshold T, a path is difficult if its terminating branch has a misprediction rate greater than T when on that path. Note that it is entirely possible (and desirable) that many other paths to the same terminating branch are not difficult.

An important concept related to control-flow paths is *scope*. We define the scope of a path to be the sequence of instructions that comprise the n control-flow blocks of that path[2]. Figure 1 shows the scope of path GEA in the shaded blocks. This set of instructions is guaranteed to execute each time path GEA is taken to branch A. Note that the block containing branch G is not part of the scope, since it could have multiple entry points that alter the sequence of instructions executed before the branch instruction G.

---

[2]This is similar to the idea of an instruction's "neighborhood" as defined in [6]. A branch's neighborhood was used as the set of instructions to be analyzed for detecting local loops.

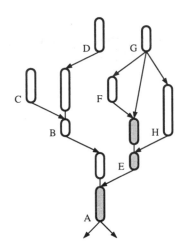

Figure 1. Paths are identified by a terminating branch (A) and the last n control-flow changes. Ovals indicate blocks adjacent along fall-through paths. Letters indicate taken branches. The scope of path GEA is the set of instructions in the shaded blocks.

3.1. Measuring Path Characteristics

We characterized the behavior of our chosen benchmarks in terms of paths and average scope as described in the previous section. The results are shown in Table 1 for several values of n.

As one would expect, the number of unique paths escalates quickly as n increases. A larger value of n results in the differentiation of several unique paths that would be considered a single path with a smaller value of n. Adjusting the value of n adjusts the resolution at which paths are differentiated.

The average scope among unique paths also tends to increase with n. Paths get longer as more control-flow blocks are added. It is interesting to note that, with relatively small values of n, it is possible to produce paths with scopes in excess of 100 instructions.

The number of difficult paths does not change markedly as T is varied between .05 and .15, especially with higher values of n. This is interesting, since it implies there is a fairly stable set of difficult paths that really are difficult.

3.2. Using Difficult Paths

Our goal is to improve machine performance via higher branch prediction accuracy. Previous research has demonstrated that more accurate branch predictions can be produced using subordinate microthreads. For these mechanisms to be successful, microthreads must target hardware mispredictions, compute accurate predictions, and complete

309

Table 1. Unique paths, average scope size (in # of instructions), and number of difficult paths for different values of n and T.

Bench	n = 4					n = 10					n = 16				
	path	scope	T=.05	T=.10	T=.15	path	scope	T=.05	T=.10	T=.15	path	scope	T=.05	T=.10	T=.15
comp	1332	49.38	349	329	315	3320	123.77	723	682	646	8205	195.64	1307	1228	1145
gcc	131967	37.14	51259	41776	34942	428613	89.18	148513	129331	113982	886147	137.82	254463	229376	208212
go	113825	51.16	61526	54830	48127	681239	113.49	295722	273068	250213	1697537	171.80	589034	555140	519209
ijpeg	7679	62.98	1567	1263	1083	30624	153.64	7837	6873	6146	94023	228.17	21174	19401	17716
li	4095	36.16	576	491	457	8933	88.13	1401	1204	1093	16602	142.26	2615	2304	2084
m88ksim	5342	41.20	1266	1072	928	12397	99.60	2819	2486	2198	23460	164.51	4851	4445	4043
perl	11003	39.75	3109	3027	2926	26572	91.98	8116	7948	7717	47152	137.67	12311	12130	11929
vortex	36951	48.12	6231	4973	4415	76350	114.28	11929	9766	8672	119339	178.32	15672	13193	11779
bzip2_2k	23585	216.94	8861	6884	5685	836082	551.77	195652	180377	162349	4455846	541.59	935579	913986	882787
crafty_2k	59559	83.76	23225	18980	15806	361879	214.84	96830	86047	76964	942334	351.84	175022	159997	146174
eon_2k	15986	44.77	2584	2340	2147	32789	102.88	5021	4565	4182	48633	160.16	6540	5980	5493
gap_2k	28760	52.17	6883	5799	4966	84630	131.52	17855	15506	13455	165838	217.80	28742	25333	22332
gcc_2k	203334	55.63	75697	63754	54165	671250	132.41	185210	167533	151113	1191885	205.37	262718	244412	226077
gzip_2k	21942	100.94	9311	8091	7111	472396	267.46	118583	112095	105213	1973159	412.21	340683	332439	322094
mcf_2k	7707	46.05	2834	2387	2090	65498	118.08	17960	16357	15010	232125	165.48	45391	42793	40289
parser_2k	22174	49.65	8567	7851	7296	105758	119.59	29265	27014	25026	374747	181.99	74828	69928	65378
perlbmk_2k	12608	47.38	5145	5083	4996	22337	112.44	8108	8020	7920	28475	175.75	9207	9109	9011
twolf_2k	24280	62.46	7894	7097	6403	91321	162.95	23630	21395	19457	240853	251.63	48833	44970	41313
vortex_2k	57718	65.13	9285	8103	7384	130800	148.84	18813	16991	15820	208697	229.24	24619	22534	21086
vpr_2k	34589	111.11	10977	9586	8579	1330809	348.34	247932	240666	230405	4895234	550.59	616776	613795	608067
Average	41222	65.09	14857	12686	10991	273680	164.26	72096	66396	60879	882515	239.99	173518	166125	158311

in a timely manner. This section describes how, using difficult paths, we can construct microthreads to accomplish these goals.

3.2.1. Targeting Mispredictions.

We wish to use microthreads only for branch instances likely to be mispredicted. As described in Section 1, any microthread spawned for a correctly predicted branch incurs useless overhead (note that such overhead is not *always* useless, if significant prefetching occurs). Any microthread spawned for a correctly predicted branch also risks introduction of a misprediction.

In practice, targeting mispredictions is somewhat complicated. Predictability must be considered at the time microthreads are constructed. Previous studies have targeted mispredictions simply by concentrating on static branches that exhibit poor predictability. We propose to use difficult paths instead.

A correlation exists between dynamic control-flow information and branch predictability [10]. Given this, it follows that a set of difficult paths can achieve greater "misprediction resolution" than a set of difficult branches. This also makes sense intuitively: difficult branches often have many easy paths, and easy branches often have a few difficult paths. By considering only the set of difficult paths, we eliminate a great number of branch instances.

Table 2 shows the misprediction and execution coverages for the SPECint95 and SPECint2000 benchmark suites for different values of n and T. The same definition of "difficult" ($mispr\_rate > T$) applies to both branches and paths. The table shows that, generally, classifying by paths increases coverage of mispredictions, while lowering execution coverage.

3.2.2. Accurate Microthreads.

The importance of accurate microthread predictions should be clear: if a microthread generates an incorrect prediction, it causes a misprediction recovery and lowers performance.

Previous research has shown that pre-computation threads can very accurately pre-compute branch conditions [6, 16, 18] (see Section 2). However, these mechanisms require hand-analysis or complex profiling to generate microthreads. Hand-analysis methods clearly have limited applicability. Previous profiling methods require analysis to consider and reconcile all possible paths to each difficult branch. The storage and complexity both scale with the control-flow depth considered.

We propose to construct a pre-computation microthread to predict the terminating branch of each difficult path. Because microthreads *pre-compute* the outcome of the branch, the predictions are very accurate. Because each microthread need predict the terminating branch for a single difficult path, the construction process is very simple.

To construct a microthread, we consider the *scope* of the difficult path (the set of instructions guaranteed to execute each time the path is encountered). By observing the data-flow within the scope, we can easily extract a subset of instructions that will pre-compute the branch condition and target address. This subset of instructions becomes the prediction microthread for the given difficult path. The construction process is simple enough to implement in hardware. Details are presented in Section 4.

3.2.3. Timely Microthreads.

Microthread predictions must arrive in time to be useful. Ideally, every microthread would complete before the fetch of the corresponding branch. However, late predictions are still useful to ini-

Table 2. Misprediction and execution coverages for difficult branches (Branch) and difficult paths ($n = \{4, 10, 16\}$). Each percentage represents the fraction of total mispredictions or dynamic branch executions covered by the set of difficult branches or paths.

Bench	$T = .05$ Branch mis%	exe%	$n=4$ mis%	exe%	$n=10$ mis%	exe%	$n=16$ mis%	exe%	$T = .10$ Branch mis%	exe%	$n=4$ mis%	exe%	$n=10$ mis%	exe%	$n=16$ mis%	exe%	$T = .15$ Branch mis%	exe%	$n=4$ mis%	exe%	$n=10$ mis%	exe%	$n=16$ mis%	exe%
comp	98.2	18.3	98.2	17.5	98.2	15.8	97.9	15.1	94.6	16.5	94.2	15.5	95.3	13.8	94.9	13.2	94.6	16.5	88.5	13.1	91.0	12.1	92.1	12.0
gcc	83.3	31.6	85.3	26.0	88.4	22.8	90.2	20.6	63.6	17.6	72.1	16.4	78.1	15.3	81.4	14.1	47.2	10.6	60.4	11.4	68.5	11.3	73.5	10.8
go	96.3	66.2	94.9	57.8	95.2	47.9	96.1	40.9	85.2	49.0	84.6	41.4	87.5	35.7	90.0	31.3	68.3	34.2	73.8	31.6	79.0	27.9	83.3	25.2
ijpeg	90.6	25.8	90.1	21.0	91.6	17.5	93.1	16.8	85.5	21.8	83.7	14.6	88.7	15.0	91.6	15.4	65.7	10.9	81.8	13.6	86.3	13.8	88.6	13.8
li	89.6	18.3	92.1	15.5	95.8	14.8	94.8	12.2	79.6	13.9	83.1	11.2	91.2	12.1	92.8	11.2	64.6	10.0	80.9	10.5	87.3	11.0	86.3	9.5
m88ksim	58.7	4.0	64.9	3.8	69.3	3.2	87.9	6.3	48.4	2.6	57.7	2.8	62.8	2.3	67.8	2.5	41.2	2.0	47.0	1.8	56.4	1.8	60.7	1.8
perl	68.4	6.1	90.7	7.7	95.7	5.2	97.0	4.3	58.2	4.2	71.6	3.7	91.0	4.1	94.1	3.7	38.5	1.8	63.5	2.8	86.8	3.6	90.7	3.3
vortex	75.8	4.0	81.2	3.0	87.6	2.9	90.8	2.7	61.2	2.7	72.7	2.2	78.5	2.1	83.6	2.1	34.4	1.1	59.3	1.4	68.3	1.5	73.1	1.5
bzip2_2k	96.8	38.5	96.0	33.2	96.0	29.2	97.0	23.5	91.7	32.5	91.7	28.1	90.5	23.1	93.4	19.1	81.4	25.5	84.6	23.3	85.5	19.6	90.2	17.0
crafty_2k	80.6	26.6	86.2	22.4	90.3	18.3	92.4	15.9	56.9	12.8	70.7	13.2	79.4	11.8	84.0	10.9	35.6	5.7	56.2	8.2	69.5	8.4	75.9	8.1
eon_2k	78.6	6.5	81.9	5.7	88.1	5.6	90.6	5.5	65.4	4.0	67.5	3.3	75.1	3.5	78.3	3.5	36.4	1.2	55.2	2.1	62.0	2.3	67.7	2.5
gap_2k	78.6	6.9	86.1	5.6	90.0	5.0	92.4	4.4	56.4	3.5	75.7	4.0	79.7	3.4	86.2	3.5	48.2	2.7	63.3	2.9	69.0	2.4	74.4	2.4
gcc_2k	84.0	31.7	88.9	26.4	91.1	20.7	93.5	19.0	66.7	18.7	76.7	16.7	83.4	14.8	86.5	13.5	49.1	11.0	65.6	11.9	75.1	11.1	79.8	10.5
gzip_2k	91.4	38.0	87.1	24.3	91.8	21.0	93.9	18.0	78.9	27.1	79.0	17.2	85.8	15.9	89.0	13.8	43.5	9.3	72.2	14.0	80.6	13.4	84.6	11.7
mcf_2k	73.5	21.6	84.6	21.2	83.9	15.3	85.1	13.1	47.7	9.8	62.2	10.6	66.1	7.3	73.6	7.2	40.6	7.9	34.5	3.5	59.0	5.5	68.0	5.7
parser_2k	85.7	21.0	94.1	22.2	94.0	17.6	95.4	16.6	78.9	16.9	84.2	15.8	88.9	14.2	90.2	13.1	67.7	12.7	69.4	10.0	79.0	10.6	83.8	10.8
perlbmk_2k	86.6	0.11	90.5	0.08	93.5	0.07	94.5	0.07	83.4	0.09	88.7	0.07	92.3	0.07	93.2	0.06	80.6	0.08	87.0	0.07	89.7	0.06	91.2	0.05
twolf_2k	91.7	22.9	95.8	21.2	96.5	18.0	97.0	16.6	87.8	20.0	91.1	17.5	92.9	15.1	93.8	14.0	79.4	16.3	84.5	14.3	88.8	13.1	90.6	12.5
vortex_2k	82.5	3.9	87.8	2.5	90.7	2.3	91.5	2.1	54.9	1.8	80.1	1.8	83.5	1.7	85.9	1.7	35.5	0.8	69.7	1.3	76.3	1.4	77.6	1.3
vpr_2k	90.9	28.9	96.5	30.7	98.4	23.5	99.2	14.2	87.5	24.4	91.6	25.0	96.3	21.1	98.4	13.3	85.0	22.8	85.4	20.8	92.5	18.6	96.8	12.2
Average	84.1	21.1	88.6	18.4	91.3	15.3	93.5	13.4	71.6	15.0	79.0	13.0	84.3	11.6	87.4	10.4	56.9	10.1	69.1	9.9	77.5	9.5	81.4	8.6

tiate early recoveries (we assume that microthread predictions will always be more accurate).

Timeliness requires two components: early spawns and quick microthread execution. Unfortunately, these two factors tend to work against each other—earlier spawns tend to require longer, and slower, microthread computations to pre-generate the branch outcome.

We can obtain earlier spawn points by increasing the scope of the difficult paths (by increasing n). This allows the microthread to be launched further "ahead" of the branch, while maintaining the important microthread characteristics described in the previous sections. There are downsides to doing this, such as increasing the number of unique paths and the number of extraneous spawns. These problems are adequately handled in our mechanism.

We propose to shorten microthread computations using a technique called *pruning*, which is applied at the time microthreads are constructed. Value and address predictability are known to exist in applications [11, 17]. We intend to prune sub-trees of computation by exploiting this predictability[3]. An example of pruning is shown in Figure 2.

Pruning requires two capabilities. First, the machine must identify predictable values and addresses at the time microthreads are being constructed. If this is done at compile-time, profiling information could be used. If this is done at run-time, this information must be tracked by the construction hardware.

[3]González and González proposed to use value speculation for the inputs to branch comparisons [8]. It was done at prediction time by a hardware mechanism. This is similar to pruning in that it shortcuts the branch predicate calculation.

Second, the machine must be able to dynamically generate value and address predictions for use in pruned microthread computations. To accomplish this, we add two new micro-instructions, Vp_Inst and Ap_Inst. Either of these instructions is used to replace each pruned sub-tree of computation. The machine executes these new instructions by querying special-purpose value and address predictors.

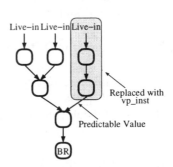

Figure 2. An example of pruning.

4. Building and Using Difficult-Path Microthreads

This section presents a hardware implementation of our mechanism. It includes structures to identify difficult paths, construct and optimize microthreads, and communicate microthread predictions to the primary thread. Compile-time implementations, which we have also investigated, are outside the scope of this paper.

4.1. Identifying Difficult Paths: The Path Cache

Our hardware mechanism for identifying difficult paths is straightforward. We assume that the front-end can trivially generate our $Path\_Id$ hash and associate the current value to each branch instruction as it is fetched. A back-end structure, called the *Path Cache*, maintains state to identify difficult paths.

The Path Cache is updated as follows. As each branch retires from the machine, its $Path\_Id$ is used to index the Path Cache and update the corresponding entry. Each Path Cache entry contains two counters: one for the number of occurrences of the path, and another for associated number of hardware mispredictions of the terminating branch.

We define a number of occurrences, called the *training interval*, over which to measure a path's difficulty. At the end of a training interval, the hardware misprediction rate represented by the counters is compared to the difficulty threshold T. A *Difficult* bit stored in each Path Cache entry is set to represent the current difficulty of the path, as determined during the last training interval. After the *Difficult* bit is updated, the occurrence and misprediction counters are reset to zero.

Allocation and replacement in the Path Cache is tuned to favor *difficult* paths. We allocate a new entry only if the current terminating branch was mispredicted by the hardware predictor. Because of this, roughly 45% of the possible allocations can be ignored for an 8K-entry Path Cache, leaving more space to track difficult paths. When a Path Cache entry must be replaced, we use a modified LRU scheme that favors entries without the *Difficult* bit set.

4.2. Building Microthreads for Difficult Paths

Our mechanism uses microthreads to predict the terminating branches of difficult paths. The Path Cache, described above, identifies difficult paths at run-time. Now we must build microthreads to predict them.

4.2.1. Promotion and Demotion.
We refer to the decision to predict a difficult path with a microthread as *path promotion*. The opposite decision is called *path demotion*.

In the simplest case, promotion and demotion events should correspond to changes in a Path Cache entry's *Difficult* bit. When the *Difficult* bit transitions from 0 to 1, we promote the path. When the *Difficult* bit transitions from 1 to 0, we wish to demote the path. To keep track of which paths are promoted, we add a *Promoted* bit to each Path Cache entry.

The *promotion logic* is responsible for generating promotion requests. Each time a Path Cache entry is updated (ie. when a branch retires), the entry's *Difficult* and *Promoted* bits are examined. In the case that the *Difficult* bit is

set, but the *Promoted* bit is not set, a request is sent to the *Microthread Builder* to begin construction. If the builder can satisfy the request, the *Promoted* bit is then set.

4.2.2. The Basics of Building Microthreads.
We refer to the the hardware associated with generating microthreads as the *Microthread Builder*. Figure 3 shows a high-level diagram of the various components.

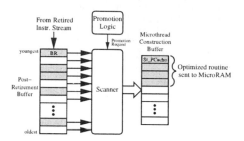

Figure 3. The Microthread Builder

The *Post-Retirement Buffer* (PRB) is used to store the last i instructions to retire from the primary thread (we assume $i = 512$ in our implementation). Instructions enter the PRB after they retire and are pushed out as younger instructions are added. Dependency information, computed during instruction execution, is also stored in each PRB entry.

When a promotion request is received, the Microthread Builder extracts the data-flow tree needed to compute the branch outcome. The PRB is frozen and scanned from youngest to oldest (the branch will always be the youngest instruction, as it just retired). Instructions making up the data-flow tree are identified and extracted into the *Microthread Construction Buffer (MCB)*. The identification is not difficult, as the dependency information is already stored in the PRB. The basic extraction of the data-flow tree in this manner is similar to the mechanism in [3].

Termination of the data-flow tree occurs when any of the following conditions are satisfied: 1) the MCB fills up, 2) the next instruction being examined is outside the path's scope, or 3) a memory dependency is encountered (the store is not included). At this point, the MCB can be examined to turn the extracted data-flow tree into a microthread.

To create a functional microthread, we convert the terminating branch into a special $Store\_PCache$ microinstruction. When executed, the $Store\_PCache$ communicates the branch outcome generated by the microthread to the front-end of the machine. The communication takes place via the Prediction Cache (see Section 4.3.3).

The last step in in microthread construction is to select a *spawn point*. This is the point in the primary thread's execution that we wish the microthread to be injected into the machine—logically, a single program instruction. Choosing an effective spawn point is a difficult problem. In the current mechanism, we assume only that we wish to launch the microthread as early as possible. As such, we choose the earliest instruction possible that is both within the path's scope and satisfies all of the microthread's live-in register and memory dependencies.

Our current design assumes there is only one Microthread Builder, and that it can construct only one thread at a time. Our experiments have shown that the microthread build latency, unless extreme, does not significantly influence performance.

4.2.3. Basic Microthread Optimizations.

Move elimination and constant propagation are simple code optimizations we employ in the MCB to further improve the timeliness of our microthreads. We find that microthreads frequently span many control-flow levels in the program. As such, they tend contain many un-optimized sequences of code, many resulting from stack pointer manipulations or loop-carried variables. Hardware implementations of both of these optimizations have been previously proposed in fill-unit research [7]. Similar functionality could be installed in a hardware MCB.

4.2.4. Memory Dependencies.

Memory dependencies also provide an opportunity for optimization. We terminate data-flow tree construction upon a memory dependency. The spawn point is chosen such that this memory dependency will be satisfied architecturally when the microthread is spawned. This assumes, pessimistically, that memory dependencies seen at construction time will always exist. The opposite case also occurs—if the memory dependency did not exist at construction time, it results in an optimistic speculation that there will never be a dependency in the future.

Our hardware mechanism naturally incorporates memory dependency speculation into the microthreads. The decision to speculate is simply based on the data-flow tree at construction time. We prevent over-speculation by rebuilding the microthread if a dependence violation occurs during microthread execution. When the microthread is rebuilt, the current mis-speculated dependency will be seen and incorporated into the new microthread.

A more advanced rebuilding approach might correct only speculations that cause *repeated* violations. We find that our simpler approach approximates this fairly well and requires almost no additional complexity.

4.2.5. Pruning.

Pruning, introduced in Section 3.2.3, is an advanced optimization applied in the MCB that uses value and address predictability to eliminate sub-trees of computation within a microthread. When pruning is successful, the resulting microthread is smaller, has shorter dependency chains, and has fewer live-in dependencies.

To implement pruning, the machine must support the Vp_Inst and Ap_Inst micro-instructions. To provide this

functionality, we add separate value and address predictors to the back-end of the processor. These predictors are trained on the primary thread's retirement stream just before the instructions enter the PRB. Since these predictors will not be integrated into the core, they can be kept apart from the critical sections of the chip.

The decision to prune is straightforward. We assume our value and address predictors have an integrated confidence mechanism. We access the current confidence and store it with each retired instruction in the PRB. When a microthread is constructed, instructions marked as confident represent pruning opportunities.

Pruning actually occurs in the MCB. Value-pruned instructions are removed from the MCB, along with the sub-trees of data-flow leading up to them. In place of the removed data-flow, a Vp_Inst microinstruction is inserted to provide the output register value. Address-pruned instructions are treated similarly, except that the prunable load itself is not removed from the routine, and the Ap_Inst provides the address base register value.

When the microthread is spawned, the Vp_Inst and Ap_Inst microinstructions must contain all the information necessary to access the value and address predictors to receive a prediction. This process seems to be complicated by the fact that predictions must be made in advance of the progress of the primary thread (recall that the predictors are trained on retiring primary thread instructions). The distance between the spawn point and the instruction being predicted must be reconciled. This is actually simple to accomplish, since every microthread is tied to the scope of a particular path. At construction time, we need only compute the number of predictions that the Vp_Inst/Ap_Inst is ahead. At execution time, this information is passed to the value or address predictor, which generates a prediction for the correct instance. Adapting the predictor design to support this operation is trivial, if we restrict our predictors to handle only constant and stride-based predictions. We assume this in our mechanism.

4.3. General SSMT Hardware

This section provides a brief overview of the general mechanism for spawning and simultaneously executing microthreads on an SSMT core. A more detailed description is not possible due to space limitations. We assume the general capabilities described in [2]. A high-level diagram of the core is shown in Figure 4.

4.3.1. General Microthread Operation.

A microthread is invoked when its spawn point is fetched by the primary thread. If resources are available, the machine allocates a microcontext[4] for the newly spawned microthread. A spawn request is sent to the MicroRAM—the structure that stores

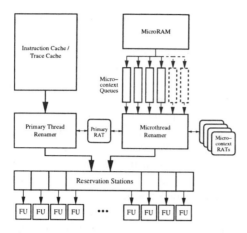

Figure 4. Basic SSMT Processor Core

SSMT routines. The MicroRAM delivers instructions from the specified routine into a microcontext queue. Each cycle, active microcontext queues are processed to build a packet of microthread instructions. These instructions are renamed and eventually issued to the reservations stations, where they execute out-of-order simultaneously with the primary thread. A microcontext is de-allocated when all instructions have drained from its issue queue.

4.3.2. Abort Mechanism. Our SSMT machine contains a mechanism to detect and abort useless microthreads. Microthreads are often spawned to predict branches on control-flow paths that the machine doesn't take. Our mechanism uses a concatenated path hash, called *Path_History*, to detect when the machine deviates from the path predicted by an active microthread. When this occurs, these microthreads are aborted and the microcontext is reclaimed. We assume microthread instructions already in the out-of-order window cannot be aborted.

The abort mechanism is very important. Our machine is very wide and deep, which means spawns must be launched very early to stay ahead of the primary thread. Many useless spawns occur, but the abort mechanism is able to keep the overhead in check. On average, 67% of the attempted spawns are aborted before allocating a microcontext. 66% of successful spawns are aborted sometime before the microthread has completed.

4.3.3. The Prediction Cache. The Prediction Cache, originally proposed by Chappell *et al.* in [2], is the structure responsible for communicating branch predictions between microthreads and the primary thread. We have modified the Prediction Cache slightly from its original incarnation to support our path-based prediction scheme. Its operation within the front-end is summarized in Figure 5.

---

[4] A *microcontext*, proposed in [2], is the set of state associated with an active microthread.

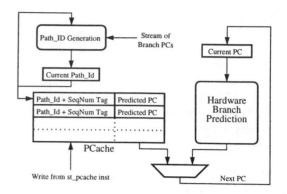

Figure 5. Prediction Cache Operation

A microthread writes the Prediction Cache using the *Path_Id* hash and the instruction sequence number, *Seq_Num*[5], of the branch instance being predicted. The microthread computes the target branch *Seq_Num* by adding the predetermined instruction separation to the *Seq_Num* of the spawn. Because each (*Path_Id*, *Seq_Num*) pair specifies a particular instance of a branch on a particular path, our Prediction Cache naturally matches up microthread predictions written by *Store_PCache* instructions and the branches intended to consume them. Because both *Path_Id* and *Seq_Num* are used, aliasing is almost non-existent.

The (*Path_Id*, *Seq_Num*) pair is also used to match late microthread predictions with branch instances currently in-flight. If a late microthread prediction does not match the hardware prediction used for that branch, it is assumed that the microthread prediction is more accurate, and an early recovery is initiated. Because of the width and depth of our baseline machine, late predictions occur rather frequently.

The Prediction Cache does not need to maintain many concurrently active entries. Stale entries are easily de-allocated from the Prediction Cache by comparing the (*Path_Id*, *Seq_Num*) pair to the current position of the front-end. Because entries can be quickly de-allocated, the space can be more efficiently used. Our Prediction Cache can be made quite small (128 entries) with little impact on performance.

5. Performance Analysis

5.1. Machine Model

Our baseline configuration for these experiments modeled an aggressive wide-issue superscalar machine. The machine parameters are summarized in Table 3. All experiments were performed using the SPECint95 and

---

[5] An instruction sequence number, or *Seq_Num*, is assigned to each instruction to represent its order within the dynamic instruction stream. Many machines already use sequence numbers for normal processing.

Table 3. Baseline Machine Model

Fetch, Decode, Rename	64KB, 4-way associative, instruction cache with 3 cycle latency capable of processing 3 accesses per cycle; 16-wide decoder with 1 cycle latency; 16-wide renamer with 4 cycle latency
Branch Predictors	128K-entry gshare/PAs hybrid with 64K-entry hybrid selector; 4K-entry branch target buffer; 32-entry call/return stack; 64K-entry target cache (for indirect branches); all predictors capable of generating 3 predictions per cycle; total misprediction penalty is 20 cycles
Execution Core	512-entry out-of-order window; physical register file has 4 cycle latency; 16 all-purpose functional units, fully-pipelined except for FP divide; full forwarding network; memory accesses scheduled using a perfect dependency predictor
Data Caches	64KB, 2-way assoc L1 data cache with 3 cycle latency; 4 L1 cache read ports, 1 L2 write port, 8 L1 cache banks; 32-entry store/write-combining buffer; stores are sent directly to the L2 and invalidated in the L1; 64B-wide, full-speed L1/L2 bus; 1MB, 8-way associative L2 data cache with 6 cycle latency once access starts, 2 L2 read ports, 1 L2 write port, 8 L2 banks; caches use LRU replacement; all intermediate queues and traffic are modeled
Busses and Memory	memory controller on chip; 16 outstanding misses to memory; 32B-wide core to memory bus at 2:1 bus ratio; split address/data busses; 1 cycle bus arbitration; 100 cycle DRAM part access latency once access starts, 32 DRAM banks; all intermediate queues modeled

SPECint2000 benchmark suites compiled for the Alpha EV6 ISA with -fast optimizations and profiling feedback enabled.

It is important to note that our experiments focused on improving an *aggressive* baseline. When using our approach, it is more difficult to improve performance when the primary thread already achieves high performance. Spawns must occur very early for microthreads to "stay ahead." This fact necessitates longer microthreads and causes many more useless spawns. This results in more overhead contention with the primary thread, despite the fact that our wide machine generally has more resources to spare.

Our machine also used an idealized front-end, also to avoid biasing our results. Microthreads take advantage of resources unused by the primary thread. A fetch bottleneck would unfairly under-utilize execution resources and leave more for the microthreads to consume. Our front-end can handle three branch predictions and three accesses to the instruction cache per cycle. In a sense, we are modeling a very efficient trace cache.

5.2. Potential of Difficult-Path Branch Prediction

Figure 6 shows the potential speed-up (in IPC) gained by perfectly predicting the terminating branches of difficult paths. Difficult paths were identified using $T = .10$ and $n = \{4, 10, 16\}$. We tracked difficult paths dynamically using an 8K-entry Path Cache and a training interval of 32. The MicroRAM size, which determines the number of concurrent promoted paths, was also set to 8K. We simulated many other configurations that we cannot report due to space limitations.

It is interesting that our potential speed-up was not closer to perfect branch prediction, since Table 2 suggests difficult paths have large misprediction coverage. However, Table 1 shows that benchmarks often have tens to hundreds of thousands of difficult paths. Our simple, realistic Path Cache simply could not track the sheer number of difficult paths well enough at run-time. Improving difficult path identification, both with the Path Cache and using the compiler, is an area of future work.

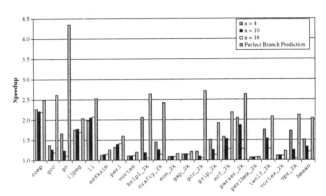

Figure 6. Potential speed-up from perfect prediction (8K-entry Path Cache, $T = .10$).

5.3. Realistic Performance

Figure 7 shows realistic machine speed-up when using our full mechanism. Speed-up is shown with and without the pruning optimization. Also shown is the speed-up when including microthread overhead, but not the microthread predictions. Parameters for difficult path identification were set as in the previous experiment. Microthread build latency was set to a fixed 100 cycles.

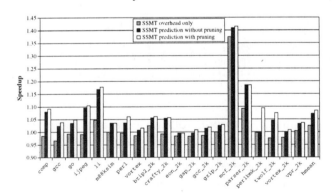

Figure 7. Realistic speed-up ($n = 10$, $T = .10$).

Our mechanism was successful at increasing performance in all benchmarks except eon_2k, which saw a slight loss. eon_2k and some other benchmarks are relatively well-behaved and do not have much tolerance for microthread overhead. Microthreads have a difficult time trying to "get ahead" of the front-end and compete more heavily for execution resources. We are experimenting with feedback mechanisms to throttle microthread usage to address these problems.

Figure 7 also demonstrates the effectiveness of pruning. Pruning succeeded at increasing performance over our baseline microthread mechanism. We examine the reasons for this in the next section.

The remaining bar of Figure 7 shows speed-up due to microthread overhead alone. This measures the impact of overhead on the primary thread, without the positive effect of increased prediction accuracy. Pruning was disabled for this run. The majority of benchmarks saw a slight loss, which is to be expected. A couple benchmarks, notably mcf_2k, saw a significant gain. This can be attributed to prefetching effects from the microthread routines—a very pleasant side-effect.

5.4. Timeliness of Predictions

The pruning optimization increases performance by enabling smaller and faster microthread routines. This not only results in more timely microthread predictions, but also a smaller impact on the primary thread.

Figure 8 shows the average routine size and average longest dependency chain length of all routines generated with and without pruning. In general, pruning succeeded both at shortening microthread routines and reducing the critical dependency chains.

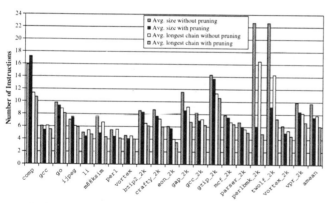

Figure 8. Average routine size and average longest dependency chain length (in # insts).

In a few interesting cases, such as compress, pruning increased the average routine length. This is because many live-in address base registers (typically global) were replaced by an *Ap_Inst* instruction, eliminating the live-in dependency but also lengthening the routine by one instruction. Even so, pruning was still successful at reducing the average longest dependency chain.

Microthread predictions can arrive before the branch is fetched (early), after the branch is fetched but before it is resolved (late), or after the branch is resolved (useless). Fig-

ure 9 shows the breakdown of prediction arrival times for our realistic configurations. Use of pruning resulted in an increased number of early predictions and useful (early + late) predictions. Use of pruning also slightly increased the overall number of predictions generated. This is because smaller microthreads free microcontexts more quickly, allowing more spawns to be processed.

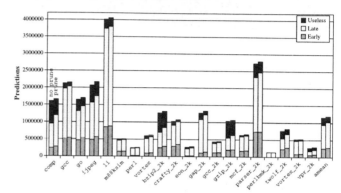

Figure 9. Prediction timeliness broken down into early, late, and useless. The left and right bars represent no pruning and pruning, respectively. *Useless* **does not include predictions for branches never reached.**

It is interesting to note from Figure 9 that, even with pruning, the majority of predictions still arrive after the branch is fetched. This is due, to some extent, to our idealistic fetch engine and rapid processing of the primary thread. However, it also indicates that there is still potential performance to be gained by further improving microthread timeliness.

6. Conclusions

Achieving accurate branch prediction remains a key challenge in future microprocessor designs. Previous research has proposed the use of subordinate microthreads to predict branches that are not handled effectively by known hardware schemes. Though microthread mechanisms have great potential for improving accuracy, past mechanisms have been limited by applicability and microthread overhead.

This paper proposes using difficult paths to improve prediction accuracy. We have shown how to build microthreads that better target hardware mispredictions, accurately predict branches, and compute predictions in time to remove some or all of the misprediction penalty. To demonstrate our approach, we have presented a hardware-only implementation of our scheme. We propose to identify difficult paths using the Path Cache, construct and optimize microthreads using the Microthread Builder, and communicate predictions to the primary thread using a modified Prediction Cache.

Because our mechanism can be implemented in hardware, we are not limited by compile-time assumptions. We do not depend on profiling data to construct our threads, and our mechanism can adapt during the run of a program. We have shown how our implementation can exploit runtime information to dynamically perform microthread optimizations. These optimizations include memory dependency speculation and pruning, a novel method of improving microthread latency based on value and address prediction.

Although this paper has shown our initial mechanism to be successful, there are many ways in which it could be improved. In particular, our future work includes ways to better track the often vast numbers of paths, further limit useless spawns, and further improve microthread timeliness.

7. Acknowledgments

Robert Chappell is a Michigan PhD student on an extended visit at The University of Texas at Austin. We gratefully acknowledge the Cockrell Foundation and Intel Corporation for his support. Francis Tseng's stipend is provided by an Intel fellowship. We also thank Intel for their continuing financial support and for providing most of the computing resources we enjoy at Texas. Finally, we are constantly mindful of the importance of our regular interaction with the other members of the HPS group and our associated research scientists, including Jared Stark and Stephen Melvin.

References

[1] M. Annavaram, J. Patel, and E. Davidson. Data prefetching by dependence graph precomputation. In *Proceedings of the 28th Annual International Symposium on Computer Architecture*, pages 52 – 61, 2001.

[2] R. Chappell, J. Stark, S. Kim, S. Reinhardt, and Y. Patt. Simultaneous subordinate microthreading (ssmt). In *Proceedings of the 26th Annual International Symposium on Computer Architecture*, pages 186 – 195, 1999.

[3] J. Collins, D. M. Tullsen, H. Wang, and J. Shen. Dynamic speculative precomputation. In *Proceedings of the 34th Annual ACM/IEEE International Symposium on Microarchitecture*, 2001.

[4] J. Collins, H. Wang, D. M. Tullsen, C. Hughes, Y.-F. Lee, D. Lavery, and J. Shen. Speculative precomputation: Long-range prefetching of delinquent loads. In *Proceedings of the 28th Annual International Symposium on Computer Architecture*, 2001.

[5] M. Dubois and Y. Song. Assited execution. In *CENG Technical Report 98-25*, 1998.

[6] A. Farcy, O. Temam, R. Espasa, and T. Juan. Dataflow analysis of branch mispredictions and its application to early resolution of branch outcomes. In *Proceedings of the 31th Annual ACM/IEEE International Symposium on Microarchitecture*, pages 69–68, 1998.

[7] D. H. Friendly, S. J. Patel, and Y. N. Patt. Putting the fill unit to work: Dynamic optimizations for trace cache microprocessors. In *Proceedings of the 31th Annual ACM/IEEE International Symposium on Microarchitecture*, 1998.

[8] J. González and A. González. Control-flow speculation through value prediction for superscalar processors. In *Proceedings of the 1999 ACM/IEEE Conference on Parallel Architectures and Compilation Techniques*, 1999.

[9] G. Hinton. Computer Architecture Seminar, The University of Texas at Austin, Nov. 2000.

[10] E. Jacobsen, E. Rotenberg, and J. E. Smith. Assigning confidence to conditional branch predictions. In *Proceedings of the 29th Annual ACM/IEEE International Symposium on Microarchitecture*, pages 142–152, 1996.

[11] M. H. Lipasti, C. Wilkerson, and J. P. Shen. Value locality and load value prediction. In *Proceedings of the 7th International Conference on Architectural Support for Programming Languages and Operating Systems*, pages 226–237, 1996.

[12] C.-K. Luk. Tolerating memory latency through software-controlled pre-execution in simultaneous multithreading processors. In *Proceedings of the 28th Annual International Symposium on Computer Architecture*, pages 40 – 50, 2001.

[13] A. Roth, A. Moshovos, and G. Sohi. Improving virtual function call target prediction via dependence-based precomputation. In *Proceedings of the 1999 International Conference on Supercomputing*, 1999.

[14] A. Roth and G. Sohi. Effective jump pointer prefetching for linked data structures. In *Proceedings of the 26th Annual International Symposium on Computer Architecture*, 1999.

[15] A. Roth and G. Sohi. Register integration: A simple and efficient implementation of squash reuse. In *Proceedings of the 33th Annual ACM/IEEE International Symposium on Microarchitecture*, 2000.

[16] A. Roth and G. Sohi. Speculative data-driven multithreading. In *Proceedings of the Seventh IEEE International Symposium on High Performance Computer Architecture*, 2001.

[17] Y. Sazeides and J. E. Smith. The predictability of data values. In *Proceedings of the 30th Annual ACM/IEEE International Symposium on Microarchitecture*, pages 248–257, 1997.

[18] C. Zilles and G. S. Sohi. Execution-based prediction using speculative slices. In *Proceedings of the 28th Annual International Symposium on Computer Architecture*, 2001.

A Scalable Instruction Queue Design Using Dependence Chains

Steven E. Raasch, Nathan L. Binkert, and Steven K. Reinhardt

Electrical Engineering and Computer Science Dept.
University of Michigan
1301 Beal Ave.
Ann Arbor, MI 48109-2122
{sraasch,binkertn,stever}@eecs.umich.edu

Abstract

Increasing the number of instruction queue (IQ) entries in a dynamically scheduled processor exposes more instruction-level parallelism, leading to higher performance. However, increasing a conventional IQ's physical size leads to larger latencies and slower clock speeds. We introduce a new IQ design that divides a large queue into small segments, which can be clocked at high frequencies. We use dynamic dependence-based scheduling to promote instructions from segment to segment until they reach a small issue buffer. Our segmented IQ is designed specifically to accommodate variable-latency instructions such as loads. Despite its roughly similar circuit complexity, simulation results indicate that our segmented instruction queue with 512 entries and 128 chains improves performance by up to 69% over a 32-entry conventional instruction queue for SpecINT 2000 benchmarks, and up to 398% for SpecFP 2000 benchmarks. The segmented IQ achieves from 55% to 98% of the performance of a monolithic 512-entry queue while providing the potential for much higher clock speeds.

1 Introduction

To stay on the microprocessor industry's historical performance growth curve, future generations of processors must schedule and issue larger numbers of instructions per cycle, selected from ever larger windows of program execution [18]. In a conventional dynamically scheduled microarchitecture, the execution window size is determined primarily by the capacity of the processor's instruction queue (IQ), which holds decoded instructions until their operands and an appropriate function unit are available. Unfortunately, processor cycle time constrains the size of this physical structure severely. The latency of wakeup logic—which marks queued instructions as ready to execute when their input dependences are satisfied—increases quadratically with both issue width and instruction queue size [17]. Both wakeup and the following selection phase—which chooses a subset of the ready instructions for execution—generally occur within a single cycle, forming a critical path. Advances in semiconductor technology will not provide a solution: although the number of available transistors will continue to increase exponentially, the number of gates reachable in a single cycle will at best stay constant, and possibly decrease [22, 1, 12].

The poor scalability of conventional wakeup logic results from its broadcast nature. To identify the instructions that become ready as a result of newly available values, the identities of these values (i.e., register tags) are broadcast to all queued instructions. The quadratic dependence of latency on IQ size is a direct result of the wire delay involved in driving these tags across the entire queue [17]. However, only a small fraction of the queued instructions become ready in any given cycle; in fact, a significant number of queued instructions cannot possibly become ready, as they depend on other instructions that have not yet been issued.

Dependence-based instruction queue designs [17, 5, 15, 6] seek to address this inefficiency. These modified queues order buffered instructions based on dependence information, with the goal that an instruction is not considered for issue (and thus need not be searched by wakeup or selection logic) until after the instructions on which it depends have issued. However, designs proposed to date have the potential to introduce dispatch or issue dependences that do not reflect actual data dependences (We use dispatch to refer to the process of sending decoded instructions to the instruction queue, and issue to refer to the process of sending instructions from the instruction queue to function units). These artificial dependences limit the ability of the dynamic scheduling mechanism to tolerate unpredictable, long-latency operations such as cache misses.

This paper presents a novel dependence-based instruction queue design that uses only true dependences to constrain instruction flow, allowing flexible dynamic scheduling in the face of unpredictable latencies. We break the IQ into segments, forming a pipeline. Instructions are issued to function units from only the final segment. The flow of instructions from segment to segment is governed by a combination of data dependences and predicted operation latencies. Ideally, instructions reach the final segment only when their inputs are, or will soon be, available.

Our design dynamically constructs subtrees of the data dependence graph as instructions are inserted into the IQ. These subtrees, referred to as *chains*, typically begin with a variable-latency instruction. The edges of the graph are annotated with the expected latency of the value-producing operation from the time it issues; these edge weights are used to schedule instruction issue within a chain.

Because instruction wakeup and selection logic operate independently on each queue segment, the latency of this critical path is determined by the size of each segment, not the overall queue size. Our design can be scaled across varying window sizes and clock frequencies by varying the number of segments and the number of instruction slots per segment.

Our simulations of this design with thirty-two–instruction segments show that our design can achieve from 55% to 98% of the performance of an idealized, monolithic instruction queue. Average performance is 85% of an ideal queue for a 256-element queue, and 81% of an ideal queue for a 512-element queue.

The remainder of this paper begins with a discussion of related work. Sections 3 and 4 describe our basic design and a set of critical enhancements, respectively. Sections 5 and 6 describe our experimental methodology and results. Section 7 discusses future directions for this research, and Section 8 concludes.

2 Related work

Palacharla et al. [17] performed the initial analysis of complexity-induced circuit delay on superscalar processor clock rates, identified the wakeup/select path as a critical bottleneck, and proposed the first dependence-based instruction queue organization. Their design uses a set of FIFOs for the instruction queue. Only the FIFO heads are considered for issue, meaning that the wakeup/select latency scales with the number of FIFOs rather than the number of instruction slots. Dispatch logic attempts to place each instruction in a FIFO immediately behind a preceding instruction that produces one of its operands. If an instruction's operands are available, or if the single FIFO position that immediately succeeds the producer is occupied, the instruction is placed at the head of an empty FIFO. If there are no empty FIFOs, dispatch stalls until one becomes available.

A second form of dependence-based IQ design was proposed independently by Canal and González [5, 6] and by Michaud and Seznec [15]. The common idea among these schemes is to use predicted operation latencies to build what we term a "quasi-static" schedule at dispatch time. The IQ contains a *scheduling array*, a two-dimensional array of instruction slots. The rows of the array correspond to future issue cycles; the instructions within a given row are predicted to become ready in the same cycle, after instructions in preceding rows and before instructions in later rows. Because the schedule is determined at dispatch time, it is more dynamic and adaptive than a static, compiler-generated schedule. However, operand availability is not perfectly predictable even at dispatch time due to cache misses and resource conflicts. The various proposals deal with these unpredictable latencies by augmenting the static scheduling array with a small fully associative buffer similar to a conventional IQ, though they differ in how this buffer is used.

Canal and González's initial "distance" scheme [5] places the fully associative buffer before the scheduling array. Instructions whose ready time cannot be accurately predicted (e.g., due to dependence on an outstanding load) are held in this buffer until their ready time is known. Instructions are thus guaranteed to be ready when they reach the oldest row of scheduling array.

Michaud and Seznec's "prescheduling" approach [15] and Canal and González's "deterministic latency" scheme [6] place the fully associative buffer after the scheduling array. In Michaud and Seznec's model, the fully associative "issue buffer" is located between the scheduling array and the issue stage; instructions from the oldest row of the scheduling array are written into the issue buffer, and instructions are issued out of the issue buffer only. Canal and González's scheme differs only in that instructions may be issued directly from the oldest row of the scheduling array, and are copied to their equivalent of the "issue buffer" only if a mispredicted latency causes them to reach the oldest row before becoming ready.

There are several complementary approaches to decoupling IQ size from latency which could be used in conjunction with a dependence-based IQ design. Most clustered architectures [13, 14, 17, 19, 8] divide the instruction queue among execution clusters, effectively dividing the IQ into "vertical" slices along the width of the machine, rather than the "horizontal" slices provided by our segmented design. Stark et al. [21] propose speculative wakeup based on the availability of "grandparent" values (i.e., the operands of an instruction's producers) to allow pipelining of the wakeup/select operation over two cycles. Brown et al. [3] propose a technique which moves selection logic off the critical path, allowing the wakeup logic to consume a full cycle. Multiscalar architectures [20] expand the instruction window by fetching from multiple points within a logically single-threaded program.

Limiting the number of instructions that can wake up when a single value becomes available allows the use of direct-mapped or low-associativity queue structures [24, 16, 5, 6]. Goshima et al. [10] discuss an alternative wakeup circuit which avoids associative search for small windows.

3 The segmented instruction queue

The goal of our design is to exploit dependence information and predictable execution latencies—as do the dependence-based schedulers discussed in Section 2—while maintaining scheduling flexibility to deal with the unpredictable effects of cache misses and resource contention.

As in [15], our scheme issues instructions only from a small "issue buffer", structured like a conventional IQ, and

Instruction	Latency	Delay Value
i_0: add *,* -> r1	1	0
i_1: mul *,* -> r2	2	0
i_2: add r2,* -> r4	1	2
i_3: mul r4,* -> r6	2	3
i_4: mul r6,* -> r8	2	5
i_5: add r1,* -> r3	1	1
i_6: add r3,* -> r5	1	2
i_7: add r5,* -> r7	1	3
i_8: add r6,r7 -> r9	1	5

(a)

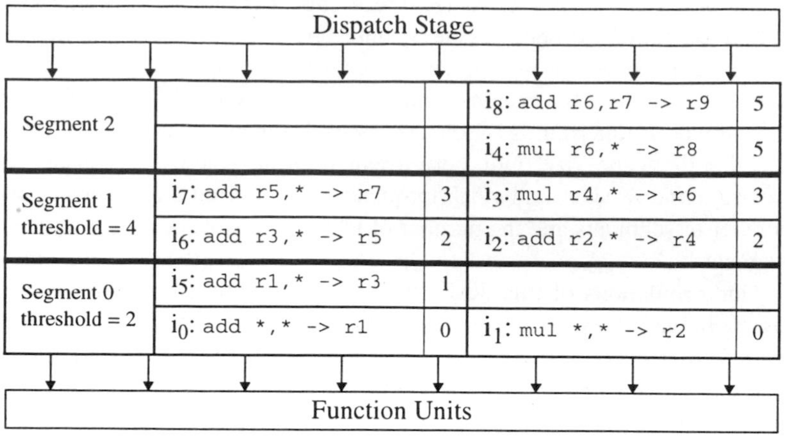

Dispatch Stage				
Segment 2			i_8: add r6,r7 -> r9	5
			i_4: mul r6,* -> r8	5
Segment 1 threshold = 4	i_7: add r5,* -> r7	3	i_3: mul r4,* -> r6	3
	i_6: add r3,* -> r5	2	i_2: add r2,* -> r4	2
Segment 0 threshold = 2	i_5: add r1,* -> r3	1		
	i_0: add *,* -> r1	0	i_1: mul *,* -> r2	0
Function Units				

(b)

Figure 1. (a) Example code sequence with delay values. Operands denoted by '*' are available. (b) Desired position of instructions within instruction queue after all instructions are dispatched. Numbers to the right of instructions in (b) are the delay values from (a). The column layout shown in part (b) is for illustrative purposes only.

attempts to maximize the efficiency of this small buffer by inserting instructions only when they are expected to be ready to issue. The remainder of the IQ structure is dedicated to staging instructions in such a way that they are available to be inserted in the issue buffer at the time they are predicted to be ready.

The novel aspect of our design is that this staging area is also scheduled dynamically, allowing the IQ to tolerate latencies that are not predictable at dispatch time. Of course, using a large, monolithic, conventional IQ structure as a staging area does not address wakeup/select complexity in a scalable fashion. Instead, we construct the staging area from a pipeline of small, identical queue structures. Each of these structures, or *segments*, is managed using logic similar to the wakeup and select logic of a conventional IQ. However, the individual segments can be sized to meet cycle-time requirements. The overall IQ size—and thus the size of the machine's window for extracting ILP— is determined by the product of the individual segment size and the number of segments. Because each segment is a random-access element, the structure of our segmented IQ does not create inherent scheduling dependences, in contrast to previously proposed FIFO structures.

For the sake of discussion, we present our segmented IQ as a vertical pipeline, with dispatch at the top and issue at the bottom. Instructions are dispatched into the *top segment* and are *promoted* downward from segment to segment until they reach the *bottom segment*, which is the same as the "issue buffer" discussed above. For convenience, we occasionally refer to segments numerically, with segment 0 being the bottom segment and segment $n-1$ the top in an n-segment IQ. Our design controls the promotion process such that instructions are distributed among the segments according to when they are likely to become ready, with ready instructions in the bottom segment and those furthest from being ready in the upper segments.

Section 3.1 describes our basic scheduling model. Section 3.2 describes how we use dependence chains to efficiently maintain an adaptive schedule. Sections 3.3 and 3.4 provide further details on IQ implementation issues and the chain creation policy.

3.1 Scheduling model

To distribute instructions across the queue segments, we assign each instruction a delay value, which indicates the expected number of cycles until it is ready to issue. We then allow an instruction to promote only when its delay value is less than the *segment threshold* of the destination segment. Initial delay values are assigned by the dispatch stage based on predicted ready times; our process for updating these values as the execution progresses is described in the following sections.

Instructions with a zero delay value are expected to be ready to issue, and are allowed into the bottom segment. To enable back-to-back issue of single-cycle dependent instructions, we also allow instructions with a delay value of one into the bottom segment. We set the threshold of the bottom segment at two, excluding all other instructions, to avoid clogging this segment with instructions which will not soon be ready to issue.

We set the thresholds for subsequent segments using uniform increments of two cycles (resulting in thresholds of 4, 6, 8, etc.) to simplify the promotion logic described in the following section. Instructions may be dispatched into the top segment regardless of their delay value. As a result, a long chain of dependent instructions may fill the top segment; Section 4.1 describes an enhancement which mitigates this behavior.

Figure 1 presents a short example, including a code sequence, a snapshot of the delay values at a particular point in execution, and the desired positions of the instructions in a three-segment queue at that point. For this example, we assume function unit latencies of one cycle for ADD and two cycles for MUL instructions. Instructions i_0 and i_1 are ready to issue, and so are placed in the bottom segment. Instruction i_5 resides there also, so that it can be issued immediately after i_0. The remaining instructions are further from being ready to issue, and so are placed in higher segments.

Once the delay value of an instruction in segment k becomes smaller than the threshold of segment $k-1$, the instruction becomes eligible for promotion. The instruction queue entry signals its eligibility to the segment promotion logic, which selects some or all of the eligible instructions for promotion in the following cycle, in a manner very similar to the select logic of a conventional IQ. The number of instructions promoted is limited by the inter-segment bandwidth and by the number of available entries in the destination segment. In this paper, we assume the inter-segment bandwidth matches the issue width of the machine. The number of available instruction slots cannot be calculated and propagated through the entire instruction queue in a single cycle, so we assume that each segment's selection logic promotes based on the number of destination slots available in the previous cycle.

After an instruction reaches the bottom segment, it is scheduled for issue based on the actual readiness of its operands, as in a conventional IQ. Thus the delay values of instructions in the bottom segment need not be maintained.

3.2 Updating delay values using instruction chains

The key to providing flexible scheduling in our segmented IQ lies in maintaining appropriate delay values for each instruction. Simply decrementing each delay value on every cycle does not allow deviation from the predicted latency calculated at dispatch, and would be equivalent to the quasi-static schemes of Section 2. Instead, we would like the delay values to adapt dynamically to post-dispatch variations in the execution schedule.

Ideally, the delay value for each instruction should be continuously recalculated based on the latest delay values of the instructions which produce its operands. To achieve this effect, an instruction must communicate with its dependents every time its delay value is updated. Because every instruction in the IQ could update its delay value in any given cycle, and because the update must be broadcast to any IQ entry that may hold a dependent instruction, the cost of such communication is prohibitive.

We avoid this cost by managing instructions in groups called *chains*. A chain is made up of a *head* instruction and other instructions which depend directly or indirectly on the head, i.e., a subtree of the data dependence graph rooted at the head. Each instruction maintains its delay value as a fixed latency behind its chain head. This latency is computed at dispatch as the sum of the predicted latencies along the execution path from the head to the target instruction.

Each chain-head instruction is itself a non-head member of another chain, and calculates its delay value based on the predicted latency from its respective chain head.

Delay values are thus maintained by broadcasting status-change updates for chain-head instructions only. In our design, a chain head signals the other chain members only when it is promoted between segments. Because each segment corresponds to a two-cycle latency increment, chain members decrement their delay values by two when notified that their head has promoted.

Once a chain head reaches the bottom segment and issues to an execution unit, the remaining instructions in the chain enter *self-timed mode*, in which each instruction decrements its delay value on each clock cycle. In effect, the instructions do not see the head promote beyond the bottom segment, but their notion of their appropriate distance behind the head is reduced cycle by cycle until they reach the bottom segment themselves.

Figure 1(b) divides the example instructions into two columns to illustrate one possible assignment of these instructions to two chains: Instruction i_0 is a chain head and i_5, i_6, and i_7 belong to its chain. Similarly, i_1 is a chain head and i_2, i_3, i_4, and i_8 belong to this chain. If instruction i_0 issues, then i_5, i_6, and i_7 will enter self-timed mode, gradually promote into segment 0, and then issue. Meanwhile, if i_1 does not issue, then i_2, i_3, i_4, and i_8 will remain in place.

Within a chain, then, instructions are scheduled quasi-statically, much like in previous dependence-based IQ designs [15, 6]. However, *between* chains, our segmented IQ provides fully dynamic scheduling. When a chain head reaches the bottom segment, the entire chain will cease advancing until the head issues. If the head is delayed, the remainder of the chain will not promote into the bottom segment, and valuable issue slots will not be consumed prematurely by these instructions.

Note that some instructions, such as i_8 in the example, may depend indirectly on multiple chain heads. Our most general model allows such instructions to belong to two chains, one for each operand. In this case, the instruction maintains two separate delay values, and dynamically chooses the larger value (indicating the later-arriving operand) to control its segment promotion. Section 4.3 describes the use of operand prediction to choose only one chain for such instructions, as illustrated in Figure 1(b).

3.3 Implementation details

In our proposed design, chain-head promotion and issue information is propagated on a set of *chain wires* using a one-hot encoding (i.e., one wire per chain). When a chain head is selected for promotion or issue, it asserts the wire assigned to its chain. The non-head instructions in the chain monitor this wire to decrement their delay values. Because chain members cannot pass the chain head, promotion signals need to propagate only unidirectionally from the chain head location toward the top of the queue. To minimize wire delay, the chain wires are pipelined from segment to segment. That is, the chain wires asserted in segment k in a given cycle are the union of the set of wires asserted by chain heads promoting from k to $k-1$ in that cycle and the set of wires asserted in segment $k-1$ in the previous cycle.

A *register information table* in the dispatch stage is used to assign chains and delay values to instructions as they are dispatched. This table is indexed by architected register number and contains four fields: the chain ID of the instruction which will produce the register value, the expected latency of this register value relative to when the chain head will issue, the chain head location (segment number), and a flag to indicate if this chain's instructions are currently in self-timed mode. The status of an instruction's source operands in this table determines the chain or chains to which the instruction is assigned and the initial delay value(s). Once the instruction's chain assignment is complete, the table entry for the destination register is updated.

The register information table monitors the chain wires to keep its entries up to date, much as the instruction queue slots do. When the table notes that a chain head has issued and the chain has entered self-timed mode, the latency field decrements once each cycle to indicate more accurately the number of cycles until the register value is ready. Once the delay value reaches zero, we assume that the value is available for scheduling purposes.

Each instruction queue entry maintains four fields for each chain to which the instruction belongs: the chain ID, the delay value, the chain head location (segment number), and the self-timed mode flag. The delay value is initialized in dispatch to $2 \times S_H + D_H$, where S_H is the chain-head segment number and D_H is the relative delay of this instruction from the chain head. Whenever the entry observes a chain-wire assertion for the specified chain, the delay value is decremented by two and the chain-head location is decremented by one. When a chain-wire assertion occurs and the chain-head location is zero, the instruction enters self-timed mode on that chain. The IQ entry also carries a flag to indicate whether the instruction is a chain head, and the ID of the chain it heads (if any).

3.4 Chain creation

Determining which instructions should become the heads of new chains is a key policy issue in our design. Creating too few chains reduces the IQ's dynamic scheduling ability, increasing the impact of dispatch-stage latency mispredictions on performance. However, chain wires are a critical resource, as will be seen in Section 6. If no free chain wires are available for a new chain head, the dispatch stage must stall; these stalls will be aggravated by an overly aggressive chain creation policy.

In this paper, we focus on latency variations induced by cache misses, so our base design creates a new chain on each load instruction. Section 4.4 describes the use of a hit/miss predictor to further conserve chain resources by starting chains only on loads that are likely to be cache misses.

For the most general variant of our design, which allows an instruction to belong to two chains, all such two-chain instructions must themselves be chain heads. Marking each two-chain instruction as a chain head prevents later instructions from needing to follow more than two chains to capture their operand data dependences.

For the design described thus far, it is most appropriate to mark as a chain head every instruction that depends on a variable-latency instruction. The chain heads will reach the bottom segment according to the producer's predicted latency, but their dependents will not advance until the producer completes and the chain heads issue. Unfortunately, this strategy requires the creation of multiple chains to tolerate a single variable-latency instruction, consuming many chains when the fan-out is large. Instead, we make the variable-latency instruction itself the head of a chain. When this instruction issues, the chain members begin to self-time. However, when it becomes apparent that the chain head will not complete within the predicted latency—e.g., when a cache miss is detected for a load—an additional signal is sent up the chain wire, causing the chain members to suspend self-timing. Once the chain head completes, a final chain-wire signal resumes self-timed mode.

4 Design enhancements

The description in the previous section provides a nearly complete picture of a functional segmented IQ with chain-based promotion. This section details a number of design enhancements which improve the performance and/or feasibility of the basic design.

4.1 Improving utilization via instruction pushdown

A potential problem with static thresholds is that they are unlikely to result in uniform segment utilization. In particular, instructions at the end of long dependence chains may reside in the top segment for many cycles before they are eligible for promotion. The top segment then fills up and stalls the dispatch stage, even when many lower segments are empty. Adaptive thresholds could improve utilization, but would be complex to implement.

Instead, we address this problem by allowing a full segment to "push down" otherwise ineligible instructions into the next lower segment if entries are available. Specifically, if a segment has less than IW free entries (where IW is the issue width) and the segment below it has more than $1.5 \times IW$ free entries, the upper segment will consider up to IW of its oldest non-eligible instructions as eligible for promotion. In situations where many instructions have large delay values, this policy forces some instructions down into the lower segments to make room for more newly dispatched instructions. The pushdown mechanism is designed to augment the promotion mechanism: an instruction made eligible by pushdown will never take the place of an instruction promoting as a result of the normal chain-promotion process.

4.2 Reducing pipeline depth penalties via segment bypassing

A key shortcoming of an n-segment IQ as described thus far is that it adds at least $n-1$ stages to the pipeline before execution, increasing the branch misprediction penalty by $n-1$ or more cycles. With this penalty, a large segmented IQ has a severe negative impact on a number of integer benchmarks (e.g., gcc). To alleviate these effects of the extended pipeline, we allow instructions to *bypass* empty queue segments at dispatch time. We observed the best performance when the dispatch stage bypasses all empty queue segments, regardless of segment thresholds and the delay values of the dispatched instructions.

The bypass wires that allow the dispatch stage to direct newly dispatched instructions into any segment are the only wires in our IQ design that span more than one segment. For this reason, we designed the bypass scheme carefully to minimize its impact on cycle time. The bypass wires are driven unidirectionally from the dispatch stage, so large drivers and repeaters can be used to optimize signal propagation. The number of loads on these wires is equal to the number of segments, not the number of IQ entries, so the load grows slowly with IQ size. Finally, because only the first sequence of empty segments is bypassed, a segment will receive instructions on a given cycle either from the dispatch stage (if it is the highest non-empty segment) or from the segment above it (if any higher segments are non-empty)—never some from each—resulting in a simple two-input mux structure at each segment whose select signal should be available well in advance of the instruction data.

4.3 Reducing IQ complexity and chain count via operand prediction

The design we have describes thus far assumes that each instruction may belong to one or two chains. Our baseline design reveals that about 35% of all instructions have two unmet dependencies produced in different chains. Dynamically following two chains provides the best scheduling, guaranteeing that an instruction does not occupy a precious slot in segment 0 before both its operands are expected to be ready. Unfortunately, providing logic in every IQ entry to track two chains, and to decide dynamically which chain should be used to determine the appropriate segment, is a potentially significant overhead. Additionally, each instruction following two chains requires the allocation of a new chain, as described in Section 3.4.

If we can accurately predict which of the two operands will be available later, we can assign the instruction to that chain alone, and simplify the IQ design by having at most one chain per processor. In Section 6, we study the impact of using a table of two-bit counters, indexed by program counter, to predict which operand ("left" or "right") will be the critical path. A similar predictor was previously proposed by Stark et al. [21]. In addition to simplifying the IQ design, our left/right predictor reduces demand for chain wires. We will see in Section 6 that reducing the number of chains created is critical for maximizing performance with a fixed number of chain wires.

4.4 Reducing chain count using hit/miss prediction

Load instructions exhibit highly variable latencies depending on the level in the memory hierarchy that they access. Due to this variability, loads are prime candidates for chain heads; in fact, they are the primary source of chain heads considered in this paper, and account for an average of 65% of the chains in our base design. In most programs, however, most loads are cache hits, and can be scheduled with a known latency. We explore the use of a dynamic cache hit/miss predictor (HMP) [14, 25] to reduce the number of chains. We use the HMP to identify loads which have a high probability of hitting in the primary cache, and use this information to not start chains for these instructions.

In our scheme, predicting a hit reference as a miss incurs the small cost of an unnecessary chain head. On the other hand, predicting a miss reference as a hit, and not creating a new chain, will cause a potentially large number of instructions dependent on the load value to flood segment 0 well in advance of becoming ready. If segment 0 fills with non-ready instructions, performance degrades severely. As a result, we would like to predict a hit only when we have very high confidence in our prediction. We use a table of four-bit saturating counters, indexed by program counter. We increment a counter on a hit, clear it to zero on a miss, and predict a hit only if the counter is greater than 13. We show in Section 6 that this predictor achieves over 98% accuracy for hit predictions while achieving very good coverage of hits on most benchmarks.

Dependence-based prescheduling schemes that rely on accurate prediction of latencies could also benefit from a hit/miss predictor. Predicted hits that miss will have dire consequences similar to our scheme, but predicted misses that hit may still effectively suffer most or all of the miss latency if the scheduling of their dependents is delayed accordingly. Thus these schemes require high accuracy for *all* predictions, both hit and miss. In addition, these schemes must predict a specific latency—i.e., they must predict at which level in the memory hierarchy an access will hit, and cannot directly tolerate variable timing due to memory-system contention.

4.5 Deadlock recovery

The explicit scheduling dependences introduced by our segmented IQ reflect true data dependences, and thus cannot lead to scheduler deadlock. However, the resource dependence between segments—i.e., the fact that an instruction can be promoted only if the next segment has available entries—can, in rare circumstances, lead to a deadlock situation. This possibility arises because chains reflect only a subset of the dependence-graph edges. If the dispatch stage assigns a two-input instruction to the "wrong" chain—that is, the chain of the operand that becomes available earlier—then that instruction may be promoted beyond the instruction that produces its other operand. Additional instructions that depend on the incorrectly assigned instruction and are assigned to the same chain may also pass this producer; if a sufficient number do so, they may occupy all the entries of a segment below the producer. At this point the producer cannot be promoted, and deadlock occurs.

This situation is extremely rare, occurring during only 0.05% of the cycles that we simulate in Section 6. Fortunately, it is also straightforward to detect and resolve. We detect IQ deadlock when the IQ is not empty and no progress is being made; i.e., no instructions are issued or promoted from any segment, and no instructions are in execution. In this situation, we are guaranteed two things. First, there is at least one ready instruction (the oldest) that is eligible to promote to the bottom segment. Second, that instruction is not being promoted because of a lower segment that is full of instructions, none of which are eligible for promotion.

Our recovery scheme is very simple: for one cycle, we force every full segment to choose one of its ineligible instructions and promote it. This step guarantees a free entry in every segment to receive a promoted instruction. Segments with eligible instructions will promote one of those candidates. If the bottom segment is full of non-ready instructions, we recycle an instruction back to the top segment. After this cycle, we are guaranteed to have at least one eligible instruction closer to the bottom segment. Usually a single such cycle is sufficient to clear the deadlock condition; if not, the detection/recovery cycle will remain active until the deadlock is cleared. As long as eligible instructions are always promoted in preference to ineligible instructions, the oldest ready instruction is guaranteed to reach the bottom segment and issue eventually, generating forward progress.

5 Evaluation methodology

We evaluated our scheme by developing an execution-driven simulator based on the SimpleScalar toolkit [4]. Although our simulator was derived originally from SimpleScalar's *sim-outorder*, it has been largely rewritten to model a simultaneous multithreaded processor with sepa-rate instruction queue, reorder buffer, and physical register resources; a realistic pipeline depth; and a detailed event-driven memory hierarchy. The simulator executes Compaq Alpha binaries.

As in *sim-outorder*, memory reference instructions are split into an effective-address calculation, which is routed to the IQ, and a memory access, which is stored in a separate load/store queue (LSQ). The IQ schedules the effective-address calculation as an ordinary integer operation. On completion, its result is forwarded to the LSQ. The LSQ marks a memory access eligible for issue when its effective address is available and is known not to conflict with any pending memory access that precedes it in program order. Although the IQ designs modeled in this paper rely on the LSQ to enforce memory dependences, Michaud and Seznec [15] illustrate how a similar scheme can be augmented to enforce predicted memory dependences using store sets [7].

Processor parameters are listed in Table 1. Because we focus in this paper on the execution variability introduced by caches, we use a generous supply of function units to reduce variability due to resource constraints. For the same reason, we configure the ROB to be three times the size of the IQ. To account for added complexity, we add an extra cycle to the dispatch stage for both the segmented and pre-scheduling IQs.

Table 1: Processor parameters

Parameter	Value
Front-end pipeline depth	10 cycles fetch-to-decode, 5 cycles decode-to-dispatch
Fetch bandwidth	Up to 8 instructions per cycle; max 3 branches per cycle
Branch predictor	Hybrid local/global (a la 21264); global: 13-bit history reg, 8K-entry PHT local: 2K 11-bit history regs, 2K-entry PHT choice: 13-bit global history reg, 8K-entry PHT
Branch target buffer	4K entries, 4-way set associative
Dispatch/issue/ commit bandwidth	Up to 8 instructions per cycle
Function units	8 each: integer ALU, integer mul, FP add/sub, FP mul/div/sqrt, data-cache rd/wr port
Latencies	integer: mul 3, div 20, all others 1 FP: add/sub 2, mul 4, div 12, sqrt 24 all operations fully pipelined except divide & sqrt
L1 split I/D caches	Both: 64 KB, 2-way set associative, 64-byte lines Inst: 1-cycle latency (to simplify fetch unit) Data: 3-cycle latency, up to 32 outstanding misses
L2 unified cache	1 MB, 4-way set associative, 64-byte lines, 10-cycle latency, up to 32 outstanding misses, 64 bytes/cycle bandwidth to/from L1 caches
Main memory	100-cycle latency, 8 bytes/CPU cycle bandwidth

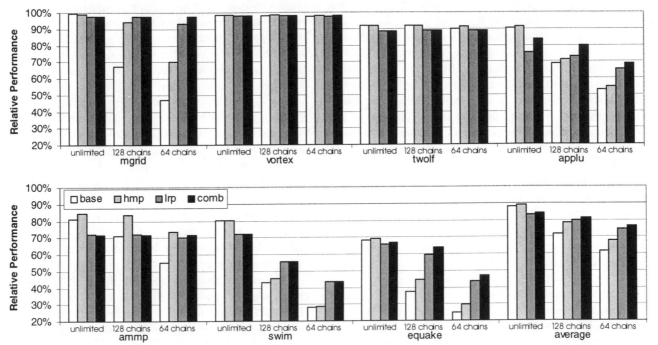

Figure 2. Performance of 512-entry segmented IQ configurations relative to ideal 512-entry IQ. Labels below the bars indicate the maximum number of chains available. "Comb" indicates a configuration using both the hit/miss predictor (HMP) and left/right predictor (LRP).

We use a subset of the SPEC CPU2000 benchmarks for our study. In all our studies, we start from a checkpoint 20 billion instructions into the benchmark's execution and simulate a sample of 100 million instructions. We compiled all of the CPU2000 benchmarks using Compaq's GEM compiler with full optimizations and simulated them using a range of IQ sizes. We then selected the two integer benchmarks (twolf and vortex) and five floating point benchmarks (ammp, applu, equake, mgrid, and swim) that show the greatest performance improvement as IQ size is increased. The FP benchmarks show the largest speedups: L2 cache misses limit their performance, and a large IQ (coupled with high branch-prediction accuracies) allows them to overlap large numbers of main-memory accesses. We also simulate gcc, which does not benefit from a larger IQ, to calibrate the impact of our design on applications with a high misspeculation rate and low ILP. The behavior of other benchmarks that do not benefit from a large instruction queue is similar to that of gcc.

6 Experimental results

We begin by comparing the performance of a 512-entry segmented IQ composed of sixteen 32-entry segments with that of an ideal, monolithic, single-cycle 512-entry conventional IQ. Section 6.1 discusses the segmented IQ's performance using an unlimited number of chains, and examines the impact of adding a hit/miss predictor (HMP) and a left/right operand predictor (LRP) on performance and chain

count. Section 6.2 repeats this analysis using realistic segmented IQs with finite chain resources. Finally, Section 6.3 examines the performance of realistic segmented IQs across a variety of IQ sizes, and compares their performance with our implementation of Michaud and Seznec's prescheduling scheme [15].

6.1 Segmented IQ with unlimited chains

Figure 2 plots the performance of several benchmarks using a 512-entry segmented IQ relative to their performance with an ideal single-cycle IQ of the same size. For space reasons, we omit gcc, whose behavior in this portion of the study is uninteresting (much like vortex). In this section, we focus on the first cluster of four bars for each benchmark, which indicate performance assuming an unlimited number of chain wires. The bars within the group correspond to four configurations. The first, labeled *base*, creates a new chain on every load and on every instruction with two outstanding input operands. The latter instructions are dynamically associated with two chains.

Examining the average results for the base configuration, we see that the segmented IQ's performance is within 16% of the ideal IQ. This performance gap is due to the segmented IQ's additional pipeline stages and its inability to issue instructions from all slots in the queue. Mgrid achieves the best relative performance, at 99.4% of the ideal. Our chain-based scheduling is very effective for mgrid: on average, the 32 entries in segment zero hold 16 ready instructions, representing more than 25% of all the ready instructions in the entire IQ.

Vortex and twolf also perform well because they actively use only a small fraction of the queue (no more than 136 out of 512 entries). The bypass mechanism moves the majority of their instructions past the top 8 queue segments, drastically reducing the impact of the pipeline delay. The lower IQ occupancy also means that a smaller fraction of all instructions wait in the upper queue segments; for both benchmarks, more than 33% of ready instructions reside in segment zero.

Unfortunately, most benchmarks require an excessive number of chains to achieve this performance. The first two columns of Table 2 show the measured average and peak chain counts for this unlimited-chains model. The peak chain usage numbers can be larger than the IQ size because we do not deallocate chains until the chain head instruction has written its result back to the register file.

For the segmented queue to be viable, we must reduce the required number of chains significantly. A hit/miss-predictor (HMP) avoids creating new chains for loads which are predicted to be L1 cache hits, as discussed in Section 4.4. A left/right operand predictor (LRP), discussed in Section 4.3, avoids creating chains on instructions with two outsting operands, and also simplifies the IQ by restricting each instruction to a maximum of one chain.

The second bar for each benchmark in Figure 2 shows the relative performance of the segmented IQ with the hit/miss predictor (HMP). Our predictor has a prediction accuracy of over 98%, predicting over 83% of all cache hits. Referring to Table 2, we see that the HMP reduces the average number of chains by 33%. The maximum savings is limited by the cache hit rate; swim sees only a negligible decrease in chains because over 90% of its loads miss in the L1 cache. (Only 20% of these misses cause L2 accesses; the remainder are "delayed hits", where a load references a block which is in the process of being fetched.) Figure 2 shows that the HMP actually improves performance

slightly. We believe this effect occurs because the delay counter values assigned by the dispatch stage do not compensate for the latencies of pipelining the chain promotion wires; thus giving a chain a small head start by using the hit latency for a delayed-hit access may allow some dependent instructions to issue sooner.

The LRP eliminates all multiple-chain instructions, reducing the number of chains and simplifying the IQ implementation. As with the HMP, however, an LRP misprediction will cause the mispredicted instruction, and its dependents on the same chain, to enter segment zero before all its operands are ready. In fact, an instruction may enter segment zero before the producer of its second operand, leading to potential deadlock as discussed in Section 4.5. Even if deadlock does not occur, the additional unissuable instructions in segment zero can block ready instructions from entering. Again referring to Table 2, we see that use of the LRP reduces the average number of chains required by 58%. Figure 2 shows that, unlike the HMP, LRP mispredictions do cause noticeable performance losses in several benchmarks, particularly ammp and applu.

Since the HMP and LRP address different sources of chain creation, their combination produces an even greater reduction in chain count: an average of 67% fewer than the base configuration. The performance effects are also mostly additive; performance with both predictors is at or slightly above the performance of LRP alone.

6.2 Evaluation of realistic queues

Of course, a real-world segmented IQ must be constructed using a finite number of chains. An eight-wide processor with a conventional 512-entry IQ using CAM-based wakeup logic would require $8 \times \log_2 512 = 72$ tag lines. To keep the wiring area comparable, we constrain the number of chain wires in our segmented IQ to a similar range. Specifically, we examine configurations of 64 and 128 chain wires. In these configurations, the dispatch stage will stall when it tries to dispatch a chain-head instruction but no

Table 2: Chain usage for 512-entry segmented IQ with unlimited chains

Benchmark	Baseline		HMP		LRP		Combined	
	Average	Peak	Average	Peak	Average	Peak	Average	Peak
AMMP	143	453	82	352	64	221	49	214
APPLU	294	661	202	646	119	360	99	358
EQUAKE	414	620	313	568	177	342	129	329
GCC	22	379	20	367	18	253	17	248
MGRID	389	577	139	577	102	246	52	246
SWIM	305	522	292	526	150	268	148	272
TWOLF	47	357	37	327	33	279	27	276
VORTEX	64	293	36	262	47	212	33	150
Average	210	483	140	453	89	273	69	261

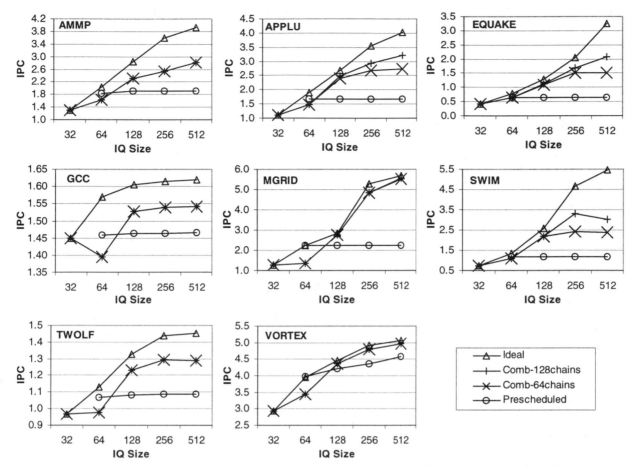

Figure 3. Performance of all benchmarks for varying queue sizes and configurations. The datapoints for the Prescheduled curves represent queue structures totaling 128, 320, 704, and 1472 instructions.

free chains are available. Table 2 indicates that these values should cover the average, though not the peak, chain demand when both an HMP and an LRP are used.

The second and third groups of bars in Figure 2 indicate the performance of a segmented IQ as the number of chains is fixed at 128 and 64, respectively. The first bar in each group, representing the performance without HMP or LRP, shows the importance of having a sufficient number of chains. On average, the 128-chain queues posted an additional 17% performance reduction over the unlimited-chains queue model (29% lower performance than the ideal queue), and the 64-chain queues posted a 27% reduction compared to the unlimited-chains model (39% lower than the ideal queue). Among the benchmarks, those requiring the fewest chains (vortex and twolf) suffered less than those requiring more chains (mgrid, equake and swim).

Adding the HMP reduces the chains required for loads, providing a significant performance improvement: an average 9% for 128 chains and 10% for 64 chains. As in the previous section, benchmarks with large cache miss rates (e.g., swim) do not benefit much from the HMP. Those with low chain usage (vortex and twolf) do not often run out of chains thus do not benefit much either. Mgrid and ammp,

which have fairly high chain usage and queue occupancy rates, but low cache-miss rates, benefit the most.

Using the LRP to reduce chain usage generally works well also. With the exception of ammp and twolf, the performance decreases seen in the unlimited-chains configuration are more than compensated for by the reduction in dispatch stalls due to lower chain usage.

As in the previous section, using the HMP and the LRP together generally provides additive benefits. The key exceptions are ammp and twolf, where HMP cannot address the performance loss due to LRP mispredictions.

6.3 Performance across multiple IQ sizes

In this section, we examine the benefits of our segmented IQ structure across a range of IQ sizes. Figure 3 presents performance results for IQs with 32 to 512 entries. The top line in each graph shows the performance of an ideal, single-cycle instruction queue at that size. We also plot the performance of our segmented IQ using both the HMP and LRP with 64 and 128 chains, assuming 32-entry segments. At an IQ size of 32 entries, our scheme degenerates to a single segment, and is thus equivalent to the conventional IQ. As IQ size increases, all three IQs show improved performance. The benefit tapers off quickly for gcc, and to some extent for twolf, due to branch mispredictions. The remaining benchmarks exhibit significant performance gains out to 512 entries.

Although the segmented queues generally show continued performance improvements for larger queues, the rate of improvement is less than that of the ideal queue. Gcc shows a 0.05 IPC drop in performance between 32 and 64 entries, due largely to the benchmark's sensitivity to pipeline depth and the fact that very little useful scheduling can be done in just two queue segments. Both swim and twolf show some reduction in performance when going from 256 to 512 entries. Neither of these benchmarks can make much use out of the additional queue slots, yet they suffer from the increased pipeline depth and reduced predictor accuracies that result. Equake, swim, and applu also suffer at larger queue sizes from the limited number of chains in the 64-chain IQ.

However, since the cycle time of our segmented IQ design is determined by the complexity of the individual 32-entry segments, we expect cycle times to be fairly constant across the range of sizes. In contrast, the cycle time of the ideal queue would be expected to grow quadratically with its size [17]. In fact, the complexity of a 32-entry segment zero is similar to that of a 32-entry conventional IQ; thus the performance gains of the segmented IQ over the ideal 32-entry queue can be viewed as the improvement made possible by adding queue segments.

We also compare our segmented queue design to Michaud and Seznec's prescheduling scheme [15]. Michaud and Seznec indicate that their prescheduling scheme outperforms Palacharla et al.'s FIFOs [15], while Canal and González indicate that their deterministic-latency scheme outperforms their distance scheme [6]. We believe that the performance of the prescheduling and distance schemes would be similar due to their structural similarity.

We implemented a similar prescheduling IQ in our simulator framework to provide a direct comparison with our segmented IQ. Unlike Michaud and Seznec's design, we continue to use a separate LSQ to manage memory dependences. Our prescheduling IQ is configured as suggested by the authors for best performance. It uses a 32-entry issue buffer (similar to our segment zero) and twelve instructions per line in the prescheduling array. Because the entries in the prescheduling array are much simpler than our IQ segment entries, we allot roughly three prescheduling-array entries for each additional segmented IQ entry; thus the four data points for the prescheduling scheme correspond to a 32-entry issue buffer plus 8, 24, 56, or 120 lines of 12 instructions (totaling 128, 320, 704, or 1472 total instruction slots).

For all benchmarks, the 128-entry prescheduling scheme performs better than the 64-entry segmented IQ. However, vortex is the only benchmark which shows any appreciable improvement as the size of the prescheduling array is increased. Our 128-entry segmented IQ outperforms any prescheduling-array size for every other benchmark. For vortex, our 256-entry IQ outperforms all prescheduling configurations. In general, the performance gap widens as IQ size is increased.

7 Future work

Power consumption is a significant concern in modern architectures; instruction-queue power consumption is particularly significant, as it already constitutes a sizable fraction of the power budget in high-performance processors [11]. Copying an instruction from segment to segment consumes more dynamic power than keeping the instruction in a single storage location between dispatch and issue; whether the performance benefit of the segmented IQ justifies this power consumption will depend on the detailed design and the target market. In any case, the segmented structure lends itself naturally to dynamic resizing by gating clocks and/or power on a segment granularity, based on power constraints or power/performance trade-offs [2, 9]. Individual segments are also amenable to power optimizations proposed for conventional IQ structures [9].

Another area of future work involves investigating the performance of segmented IQs under simultaneous multithreading (SMT) [23]. By scheduling across multiple threads, an SMT processor may obtain even larger benefits out of increased IQ sizes. Unlike other prescheduling schemes, the dynamic inter-chain scheduling of our segmented IQ should allow chains from independent threads to exploit thread-level parallelism effectively.

Finally, as mentioned in Section 2, we believe that future large IQs will employ both vertical segmentation, as we have proposed, and horizontal clustering, as in the Alpha 21264 [14]. There may be exploitable synergies between our chain-based scheme and a clustered approach. For example, chains seem to form a natural unit for assignment to function-unit clusters, and such an assignment may allow a more distributed our hierarchical broadcast of chain head promotion signals.

8 Conclusions

Two key paths to higher performance—larger instruction windows and lower cycle times—conflict directly in conventional instruction-queue designs. An associative search of a large structure to identify issuable instructions results in an inherently large cycle time. Previous work has shown that this trade-off may be overcome by constraining the search for issuable instructions to a likely subset of the instruction window, identified using data dependence information. Unfortunately, opportunities for instruction-level parallelism can easily be lost in the process of constraining this search. In particular, the use of predicted latencies for data-dependence scheduling can hamper the processor's ability to tolerate unpredictable latencies—one of the key benefits of dynamic scheduling.

This paper presents a novel instruction queue design that provides both quasi-static data-dependence scheduling to limit the scope of wakeup logic and flexible dynamic scheduling in the face of unpredictable latencies. We accomplish this combination by grouping instructions into *chains* representing subtrees of the dynamic data dependence graph. Instructions within a chain are scheduled quasi-statically based on predicted latencies; however, scheduling across chains is fully dynamic and can tolerate unpredictable latencies. We use these chains to manage the flow of instructions in a *segmented* instruction queue, effectively a pipeline of small structures similar to a conventional IQ. The cycle time of the segmented IQ is determined by the size of each segment, not the overall queue size. Our design can be scaled across varying window sizes and clock frequencies by varying the number of segments and the number of instruction slots per segment.

We also identify and evaluate a number of enhancements to the segmented IQ design, including a bypassing mechanism to reduce the pipeline depth penalty, and hit/miss and left/right operand predictors to reduce the number of chain wires needed and the complexity of IQ entries.

Despite its roughly similar circuit complexity, simulation results indicate that our segmented instruction queue with 512 entries and 128 chains improves performance by up to 69% over a 32-entry conventional instruction queue for SpecINT 2000 benchmarks, and up to 398% for SpecFP 2000 benchmarks. The segmented IQ achieves from 55% to 98% of the performance of a monolithic 512-entry queue while providing the potential for much higher clock speeds.

References

[1] Vikas Agarwal, M. S. Hrishikesh, Stephen W. Keckler, and Doug Burger. Clock rate vs. IPC: The end of the road for conventional microarchitectures. In *Proc. 27th Int'l Symp. on Computer Architecture*, pp. 248–259, June 2000.

[2] David H. Albonesi. Dynamic IPC/clock rate optimization. In *Proc. 25th Int'l Symp. on Computer Architecture*, pp. 282–292, June 1998.

[3] Mary D. Brown, Jared Stark, and Yale N. Patt. Select-free instruction logic. In *34th Int'l Symp. on Microarchitecture*, pp. 204–213, December 2001.

[4] Doug Burger, Todd M. Austin, and Steve Bennett. Evaluating future microprocessors: the SimpleScalar tool set. Technical Report 1308, Computer Sciences Department, University of Wisconsin–Madison, July 1996.

[5] Ramon Canal and Antonio González. A low-complexity issue logic. In *Proc. 2000 Int'l Conf. on Supercomputing*, pp. 327–335, May 2000.

[6] Ramon Canal and Antonio González. Reducing the complexity of the issue logic. In *Proc. 2001 Int'l Conf. on Supercomputing*, June 2001.

[7] George Z. Chrysos and Joel S. Emer. Memory dependence prediction using store sets. In *Proc. 25th Int'l Symp. on Computer Architecture*, pp. 142–153, June 1998.

[8] Keith I. Farkas, Paul Chow, Norman P. Jouppi, and Zvonko Vranesic. The multicluster architecture: Reducing cycle time through partitioning. In *30th Int'l Symp. on Microarchitecture*, pp. 149–159, December 1997.

[9] Daniele Folegnani and Antonio González. Energy-effective issue logic. In *Proc. 28th Int'l Symp. on Computer Architecture*, July 2001.

[10] M. Goshima, K. Nishino, Y. Nakashima, S. Mori, T. Kitamura, and S. Tomita. A high-speed dynamic instruction scheduling scheme for superscalar processors. In *34th Int'l Symp. on Microarchitecture*, pp. 225–236, December 2001.

[11] Michael K. Gowan, Larry L. Biro, and Daniel B. Jackson. Power considerations in the design of the alpha 21264 microprocessor. In *Proc. 35th Design Automation Conf.*, pp. 726–731, June 1998.

[12] Ron Ho, Kenneth W. Mai, and Mark A. Horowitz. The future of wires. *Proc. IEEE*, 89(4):490–504, April 2001.

[13] Gregory A. Kemp and Manoj Franklin. PEWs: A decentralized dynamic scheduler for ILP processing. In *Proc. 1996 Int'l Conf. on Parallel Processing (Vol. I)*, pp. 239–246, 1996.

[14] R. E. Kessler. The Alpha 21264 microprocesor. *IEEE Micro*, 19(2):24–36, March/April 1999.

[15] Pierre Michaud and André Seznec. Data-flow prescheduling for large instruction windows in out-of-order processors. In *Proc. 7th Int'l Symp. on High-Performance Computer Architecture (HPCA)*, pp. 27–36, January 2001.

[16] Soner Önder and Rajiv Gupta. Superscalar execution with dynamic data forwarding. In *Proc. 1998 Conf. on Parallel Architectures and Compilation Techniques*, pp. 130–135, October 1998.

[17] Subbarao Palacharla, Norman P. Jouppi, and J. E. Smith. Complexity-effective superscalar processors. In *Proc. 24th Int'l Symp. on Computer Architecture*, pp. 206–218, June 1997.

[18] Yale N. Patt, Sanjay J. Patel, Marius Evers, Daniel H. Friendly, and Jared Stark. One billion transistors, one uniprocessor, one chip. *IEEE Computer*, 30(9):51–57, September 1997.

[19] Eric Rotenberg, Quinn Jacobson, Yiannakis Sazeides, and Jim Smith. Trace processors. In *30th Int'l Symp. on Microarchitecture*, pp. 138–148, December 1997.

[20] Gurindar S. Sohi, Scott E. Breach, and T. N. Vijaykumar. Multiscalar processors. In *Proc. 22nd Int'l Symp. on Computer Architecture*, pp. 414–425, June 1995.

[21] Jared Stark, Mary D. Brown, and Yale N. Patt. On pipelining dynamic instruction scheduling logic. In *33rd Int'l Symp. on Microarchitecture*, pp. 57–66, December 2000.

[22] Dennis Sylvester and Kurt Keutzer. Rethinking deep-submicron circuit design. *IEEE Computer*, 32(11):25–33, November 1999.

[23] Dean M. Tullsen, Susan J. Eggers, and Henry M. Levy. Simultaneous multithreading: Maximizing on-chip parallelism. In *Proc. 22nd Int'l Symp. on Computer Architecture*, pp. 392–403, June 1995.

[24] Shlomo Weiss and James E. Smith. Instruction issue logic in pipelined supercomputers. *IEEE Trans. Computers*, C-33(11):1013–1022, November 1984.

[25] Adi Yoaz, Mattan Erez, Ronny Ronen, and Stephan Jourdan. Speculation techniques for improving load related scheduling. In *Proc. 26th Int'l Symp. on Computer Architecture*, pp. 42–53, May 1999.

Author Index

IEEE Computer Society Publications

The world-renowned IEEE Computer Society publishes, promotes, and distributes a wide variety of authoritative computer science and engineering texts. These books are available from most retail outlets. Visit the CS Store at *http://computer.org* for a list of products.

IEEE Computer Society Proceedings

The IEEE Computer Society also produces and actively promotes the proceedings of more than 160 acclaimed international conferences each year in multimedia formats that include hard and softcover books, CD-ROMs, videos, and on-line publications.

For information on the IEEE Computer Society proceedings, please e-mail to csbooks@computer.org or write to Proceedings, IEEE Computer Society, P.O. Box 3014, 10662 Los Vaqueros Circle, Los Alamitos, CA 90720-1314. Telephone +1-714-821-8380. Fax +1-714-761-1784.

Additional information regarding the Computer Society, conferences and proceedings, CD-ROMs, videos, and books can also be accessed from our web site at *http://computer.org/cspress*

Revised November 7, 2001